Hymns
of
Light and Love

"Whoso offereth praise glorifieth Me."
PSALM 50:23

CHRISTIAN YEAR PUBLICATIONS
BATH

Copyright © Christian Year Publications 1996

This book, or any part thereof, may not be reproduced in any form whatsoever without prior permission from the publisher.

ISBN 0 946214 05 0

Printed by Bookcraft (Bath) Ltd.
Midsomer Norton, Somerset

ARRANGEMENT OF HYMNS

FIRST PART

	No.		No.
To call to remembrance	1–23	Conflict	391–401
The Gathering Name	24–31	Pilgrimage	402–426
Entrance into the Holiest	32–39	Home Songs	427–441
The Sufferings of Christ	40–55	Prayer Meetings	442–464
The Mighty Victor	56–60	Seeking Blessing for	
"Thou art worthy"	61–75	Children	465–471
The Great High Priest	76–80	Scripture Reading	472–483
Praise to the Father, Son,		Service in the Gospel in	
and Holy Ghost	81–91	all lands	484–504
The Lord's Supper	92–140	Parting Hymns	505–522
The Father's Love	141–147	Farewell Meetings	523–532
Christ's Exaltation	148–155	Brief Words of Praise	533–547
His path on Earth	156–163	Brief Petitions	548–552
The path of His people	164–174	Baptism	553–558
The Lord's Coming	175–206	Marriage	559–566
Thanksgiving	207–247	Morning and Evening	567–571
A Living Sacrifice	248–272	New Year, Harvest, etc.	572–579
Communion	273–281	Thanksgiving for Meals	580–586
Experience	282–390	Burial	587–600

SECOND PART

Gospel Testimony	601–716	The Gospel Experienced	786–866
Invitations and Appeals	717–768	For Reviving and Blessing	867–877
Warning Messages	769–785	Children's Hymns	878–898

SUPPLEMENT

Tunes only   899–938

PREFACE

Hymns of Light and Love was first published in 1900 and quickly found favour in many parts of the world. Despite the proliferation of new hymn books in recent years it has been in continuing demand and many editions have been produced.

Hitherto a complete tune book has never been issued. Users have had to rely on a locally made selection of tunes and on a variety of tune books issued from time to time helped by a tune book to Part II only, issued jointly by Pickering and Inglis Limited and Echoes of Service.

It is in response to many requests that this first words-and-music edition has been produced.

The Compilers hope that the size adopted will be sufficiently small for general congregational use. The arrangement of hymns necessarily follows that in the words-only edition, being in two Parts. The first Part contains hymns predominantly suitable for Worship and the second Part mainly those suitable for Gospel outreach.

The index of first lines is preceded by alphabetical and metrical indexes of tunes. Most hymns have a selected tune with a named alternative. Some additional tunes appear at the end.

Acknowledgments
The Compilers gratefully acknowledge their indebtedness to several friends; also to many Authors, or their representatives, for permission to use hymns to which the Authors' names are appended.

They also tender their thanks to the following Publishers for permission to reprint hymns: Messrs. Nisbet & Company for Dr. Bonar's and Miss Havergal's; Pickering and Inglis Limited for many by Mr. R.C. Chapman from 'Choice Hymns and Meditations', also for some of Mr. D. Russell's; the Religious Tract Society for Miss Elliott's; Messrs. Broom & Rouse for Mr. J.G. Deck's; Marshall Morgan & Scott Limited and Messrs. Biglow & Main for those from *Sacred Songs and Solos*, *New Hymns and Solos* and *The Christian Choir* respectively. In addition we gratefully acknowledge the help of Marshall Morgan & Scott Limited, The Methodist Publishing

Company, The Scripture Union Publishing, the BBC Publishing Department and Inter-Varsity Press for permission to reproduce by photolithography some tunes used in hymn books published by them. For this reason the format of the music may vary. In particular, we thank the following for permission to reproduce the tunes indicated:

    Ladywell   The Royal School of Music
    St. Botolph   Oxford University Press
    Marching   J. Curwen & Sons Limited, London
    Finlandia   Breitkopf and Härtel, Wiesbaden

We are indebted to Mr. L. Raymond of Bath and Dr. Stephen S. Short of Weston-super-Mare for their invaluable help in the selection of suitable tunes.

Should any rights of Authors or Publishers have been unwittingly infringed—though much care has been exercised to avoid this—the Compilers trust that their apology will be accepted.

Profits from the sale of this Hymn Book will be used for the benefit of Widows (especially the aged ones) and young Fatherless Children of Servants of Christ who have laboured in other lands without salary or provision for their families.

HYMNS OF LIGHT AND LOVE

1 Hereford New 6.10.10.6

Horatius Bonar M.K.W. 1865

BLESSÈD be God, our God,
  Who gave for us His well-beloved Son,
His Gift of gifts, all other gifts in one—
  Blessèd be God, our God!

What will He not bestow,
  Who freely gave this mighty Gift unbought,
Unmerited, unheeded, and unsought—
  What will He not bestow?

He sparèd not His Son!
  'Tis this that silences each rising fear,
'Tis this that bids the hard thought disappear—
  He sparèd not His Son!

Who shall condemn us now,
  Since Christ has died, and risen, and gone above,
For us to plead at the right hand of Love—
  Who shall condemn us now?

'Tis God that justifies!
  Who shall recall the pardon or the grace,
Or who the broken chain of guilt replace?
  'Tis God that justifies!

The victory is ours!
  For us in might came forth the Mighty One;
For us He fought the fight, the triumph won—
  The victory is ours

2   Abney C.M.

Isaac Watts   (Belmont 26)   Asa Hull

1. ALAS! and did my Saviour bleed?
   And did my Sovereign die?
   Would He devote that sacred head
   For such a worm as I?

2. Was it for crimes that I had done,
   He groaned upon the tree?
   Amazing pity! grace unknown!
   And love beyond degree!

3. Well might the sun in darkness hide
   And shut his glories in,
   When the Incarnate Maker died
   For man His creature's sin.

4. Thus might I hide my blushing face
   While His dear cross appears;
   Dissolve, my heart, in thankfulness,
   And melt, mine eyes, to tears!

5. But drops of grief can ne'er repay
   The debt of love I owe;
   Here would I give myself away—
   'Tis all that I can do.

3   Augustine S.M.

Philip Doddridge   (St. Michael 309)   J.S. Bach

BEHOLD the amazing sight,
  The Saviour lifted high;
The Son of God, His soul's delight,
  Expires in agony!

For whom, for whom, my heart,
  Were all those sorrows borne?
Why did He feel that piercing smart,
  And wear that crown of thorn?

For love of us He bled,
  And all in torture died;
'Twas love that bowed His fainting head,
  And oped His gushing side.

We see, and we adore
  Thy deep, Thy dying love;
We feel its strong attractive power
  To lift our souls above.

In Thee our hearts unite,
  Nor share Thy grief alone,
But from Thy cross pursue our flight
  To Thy triumphant throne.

4   **Rest C.M.**
Anon   (St. Peter 24)   Handley C.G. Moule

BEHOLD! A spotless Victim dies,
  My Surety on the tree;
The Lamb of God the sacrifice—
  He gave Himself for me!

Whatever curse was mine, He bore,
  The wormwood and the gall;
There, in that lone mysterious hour;
  My cup—He drained it all!

Lord Jesus! Thou and none beside
  Its bitterness could know,
Nor other tell Thy joy's full tide
  That from that cup shall flow.

Thine is the joy, but yet 'tis mine—
  'Tis ours as one with Thee;
My joy flows from that grief of Thine,
  Thy death brings life to me!

And while the ages roll along,
  This shall my glory be;
And this the new and endless song,
  Thy love to us—to me!

5 St. Bernard C.M.
Horatius Bonar (Dalehurst 345) J. Richardson

ALL that we *were*—our sins, our guilt,
  Our death—was all our own:
All that we *are*, we owe to Thee,
  Thou GOD of grace alone.

Thy mercy found us in our sins,
  And gave us to believe;
Then, in believing, peace we found,
  And in Thy CHRIST we live.

All that we are, as saints on earth,
  All that we hope to be
When JESUS comes and glory dawns—
  We owe it all to Thee.

*For ever be the glory given
  To Thee, O Lamb of GOD!
Our every joy on earth, in heaven,
  We owe it to Thy blood.*

6 Rhodes S.M.
Mary Bowley (St. George 145) C. Warwick Jordan

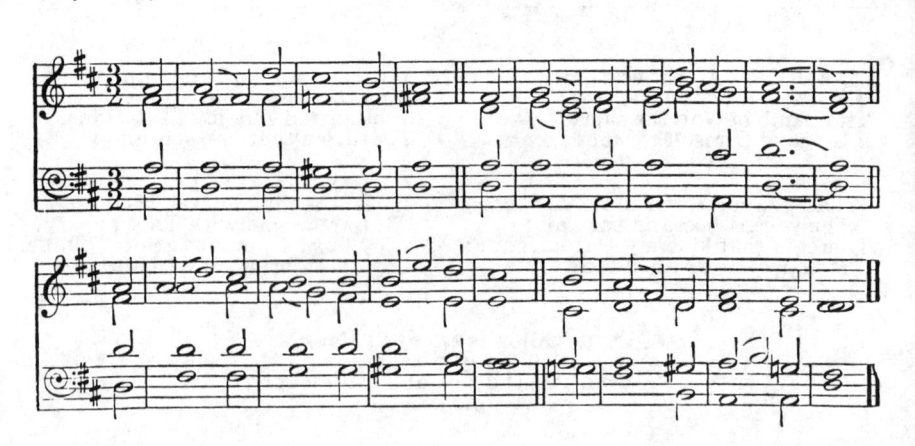

L ET earthly themes now cease,
   And joyful let us dwell
On our high theme of heavenly peace,
   Whose sweetness none can tell—

Peace with our holy GOD;
Peace from the fear of death—
Peace, O our SAVIOUR, through Thy
   blood!
True peace, the fruit of faith.

We worship at Thy feet,
We wonder and adore;
The coming glory still more sweet,
Yet sweet the peace before.

7   **Mount Calvary 7.7.7.7**
R.C. Chapman   (Redhead No. 47-100)   R.C. Chapman

O MY SAVIOUR, crucified!
   Near Thy cross would I abide,
There to look, with steadfast eye,
On Thy dying agony!

JESUS, bruised and put to shame,
Tells me all JEHOVAH'S name;
"GOD is Love," I surely know
By the Saviour's depths of woe.

In His spotless soul's distress
I perceive my guiltiness;
Oh how vile my low estate,
Since my ransom was so great!

Dwelling on mount Calvary,
Contrite shall my spirit be;
Rest and holiness shall find,
Fashioned like my Saviour's mind.

8
Lloyd C.M.
S. Stennett (St. Stephen 212) C. Howard

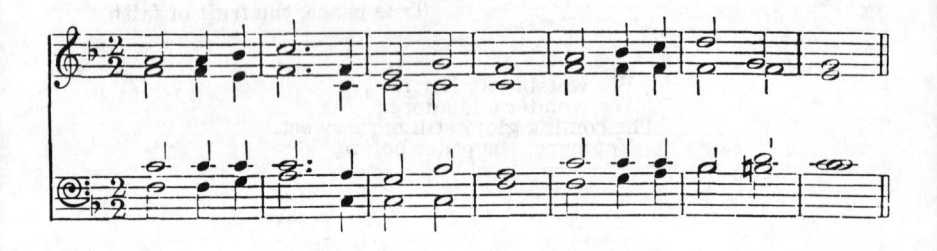

TO CHRIST the Lord let every tongue
　　Its noblest tribute bring;
Himself the subject of our song,
　　What joy it is to sing!

Behold the beauties of His face,
　　And on His glories dwell;
Think of the wonders of His grace,
　　And all His triumphs tell.

Majestic sweetness sits enthroned
　　Upon the Saviour's brow;
His head with radiant glories crowned,
　　His lips with grace o'erflow.

He saw me plunged in deep distress,
　　He flew to my relief;
For me He bore the shameful cross,
　　And carried all my grief.

To Him I owe my life and breath,
　　And all the joys I have;
He takes away the sting of death,
　　Gives victory o'er the grave.

To heaven, the place of His abode,
　　He'll bring my weary feet,
Display the glories of my GOD,
　　And make my joy complete.

9
Thos. Kelly

St. John 6.6.6.6.8.8
(Millennium 634)

J. Baptiste Calkin

THE atoning work is done,
　The Victim's blood is shed;
And JESUS now is gone
　His people's cause to plead:
He lives in heaven, their great High
　　Priest,　　　　　　　　[breast.
And bears their names upon His

He sprinkled with His blood
　The mercy-seat above,
For Justice had withstood
　The purposes of Love;
But Justice now withstands no more,
And Mercy yields her boundless store.

No temple made with hands
　His place of service is;
In heaven itself He stands,
　A heavenly priesthood His:
In Him the shadows of the law
Are all fulfilled, and now withdraw.

And though awhile He be
　Hid from the eyes of men,
His people look to see
　Their great High Priest again:
In brightest glory He will come,
And take His waiting people home.

10
Gopsal 6.6.6.6.8.8
(St. John (Calkin) 9)

Horatius Bonar G.F. Handel

DONE is the work that saves,
　Once and for ever done;
Finished the righteousness
　That clothes the unrighteous one:
The love that blesses us below
Is flowing freely to us now.

The sacrifice is o'er,
　The veil is rent in twain;
The mercy-seat proclaims
　The spotless Victim slain:
Now none need stand without, in fear,
The blood of CHRIST invites us near.

The gate is open wide;
　The new and living way
Is clear, and free, and bright,
　With love, and peace, and day:
Into the holiest now we come,
Our present and our endless home.

Enthroned in majesty
　The High Priest sits within;
His precious blood, once shed,
　Has made and keeps us clean:
With boldness let us now draw near;
That blood has banished every fear.

Then to the Lamb once slain
　Be glory, praise, and power—
Who died, and lives again,
　Who lives for evermore— [blood,
Who loved us, cleansed us by His
And made us kings and priests to GOD!

11   **Silchester S.M.**
Augustus Toplady   (Rhodes 6)   C. Malan

NOT to ourselves we owe
　That we, O GOD, are Thine!
JESUS, the Sun, our night broke
　through,
And gave us light divine.

The FATHER'S grace and love
　This blessèd mercy gave,
And JESUS left the throne above
　His wandering sheep to save.

No more the heirs of wrath,
　Thy smile of peace we see;
And, FATHER, in confiding faith,
　We cast ourselves on Thee!

With all the ransomed throng
　Soon shall we see Thy face,
And own with joy, in endless song,
　The riches of Thy grace!

Adoration 6.6.6.6.8.8

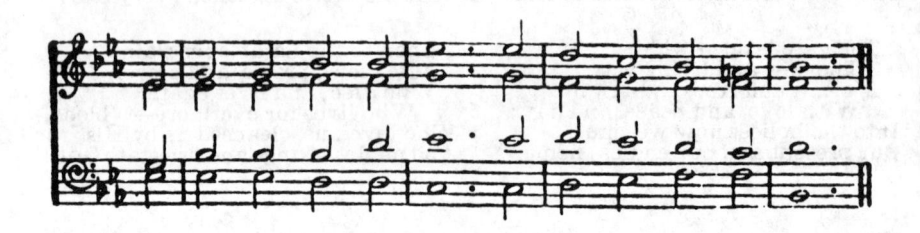

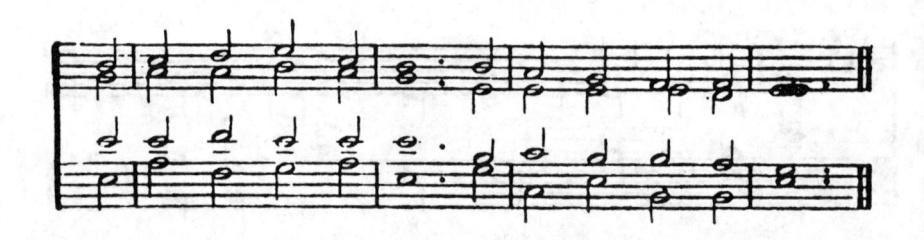

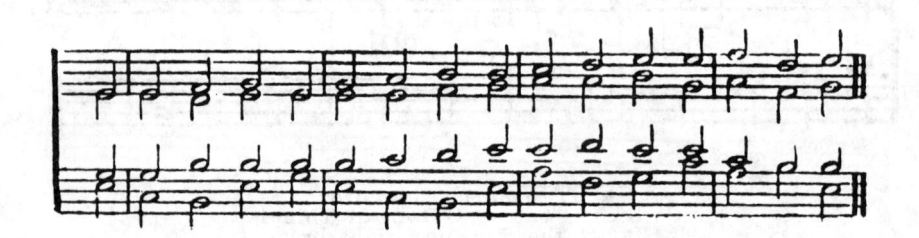

12
Ann Gilbert (Samuel 334) W.H. Havergal

WHAT was it, O our God,
　Led Thee to give Thy Son,
To yield Thy Well-beloved
　For us by sin undone?
'Twas love unbounded led Thee thus
To give Thy Well-beloved for us.

What led the Son of God
　To leave His throne on high,
To shed His precious blood,
　To suffer and to die?
'Twas love, unbounded love to us,
Led Him to die and suffer thus.

What moved Thee to impart
　　Thy SPIRIT from above,
That He might fill our heart
　　With heavenly peace and love?
'Twas love, unbounded love to us,
Moved Thee to give Thy SPIRIT thus.

What love to Thee we owe,
　　Our GOD, for all Thy grace!
Our hearts may well o'erflow
　　In everlasting praise:
Help us, O LORD, to praise Thee thus
For all thy boundless love to us.

13
R.C. Chapman

Jazer C.M.
(Dublin 30)

A.E. Tozer

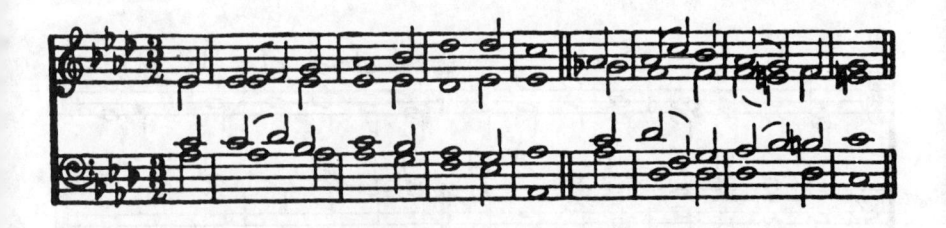

THE FATHER gave His only SON
　　For us upon the tree;
His death is our eternal life,
　　Our glorious liberty.

Love moved JEHOVAH's hand to smite,
　　Love moved the SON to bear;
How sweet on Calvary to stand—
　　The GOD of love is there!

14   **Triumph 8.7.8.7.8.7**
Thos. Kelly   (Dismissal 505)   H.J. Gauntlett

PRAISE the LORD, who died to save us,
  Praise His name for ever dear!
'Twas by Him the FATHER gave us
  Eyes to see, and ears to hear:
    Praise the Saviour!
  'Tis His love has banished fear.

Grace it was, yea, grace abounding,
  Brought Him down to save the lost;
Ye above, the throne surrounding,
  Praise Him, praise Him, all His host!
    Saints, adore Him,
  We are they who owe Him most.

Praise His name, who died to save us!
  'Tis by Him alone we live;
And in Him the FATHER gave us
  All that boundless love could give:
    Life eternal
  In our Saviour we receive!

15   **Benediction 8.7.8.7.8.7**
Thos. Kelly   (Regent Square 202)   S. Webbe

GLORY, glory everlasting,
    Be to Him who bore the cross;
Who redeemed our souls by tasting
    Death, the death deserved by us!
      Spread His glory
Who redeemed His people thus.

His is love, 'tis love unbounded,
    Without measure, without end;
Human thought is here confounded,
    'Tis too vast to comprehend;
      Praise the Saviour,
Magnify the sinner's Friend!

Dwelling on the wondrous story
    Of the Saviour's cross and shame,
Sing we, 'Everlasting glory
    Be to GOD and to the LAMB!'
      Saints and angels,
Give ye glory to His name!

16 Lymington 7.6.7.6.D

Mary Peters (Bentley 18) Robt. Jackson

BY Thee, O GOD, invited,
  We look unto Thy SON,
In whom Thy soul delighted,
  Who all Thy will hath done;
And by the one chief treasure
  Thy bosom freely gave,
Thine own pure love we measure,
  Thy willing mind to save.

O GOD, our gracious FATHER,
  Our one unchanging claim,
Our brightest hopes we gather
  From Christ's most precious name:
While ever sounding sweetly
  In Thine unwearied ear,
It frees our souls completely
  From every sinful fear.

The trembling sinner feareth
  GOD will not *all* forget;
But one full payment cleareth
  His memory of our debt;
When nought beside could ease us
  Or set our souls at large,
Thy holy name, LORD JESUS,
  Secured a full discharge.

No wrath GOD's heart retaineth
  To us-ward who believe;
No fear in ours remaineth
  When we His love receive;
Returning sons He kisses,
  And with His robe invests;
His perfect love dismisses
  All terror from our breasts.

17
Spohr 8.6.8.6.8.6

Anne R. Cousin   (Sheltered Dale 274)   Adapted from L. Spohr

O CHRIST, what burdens bowed
  Thy head!
Our load was laid on Thee;
Thou stoodest in the sinner's stead,
  To bear all ill for me:
A Victim led, Thy blood was shed—
  Now there's no load for me.

Death and the curse were in our cup;
  O CHRIST, 'twas full for Thee!
But Thou hast drained the last dark
    drop;
  'Tis empty now for me:
That bitter cup, Love drank it up—
  Now blessing's draught for me.

JEHOVAH lifted up His rod;
  O CHRIST, it fell on Thee!
Thou wast sore stricken of Thy GOD—
  There's not one stroke for me:
Thy tears, Thy blood beneath it flowed;
  Thy bruising healeth me.

The tempest's awful voice was heard;
  O CHRIST, it broke on Thee!
Thine open bosom was my ward;
  It braved the storm for me:
Thy form was scarred, Thy visage
    marred—
  Now cloudless peace for me.

For me, LORD JESUS, Thou hast died,
  And I have died in Thee;
Thou'rt risen; my bands are all untied,
  And now Thou liv'st in me:
The FATHER'S face of radiant grace
  Shines now in light on me.

18
Bentley 7.6.7.6.D
(Rutherford 137)

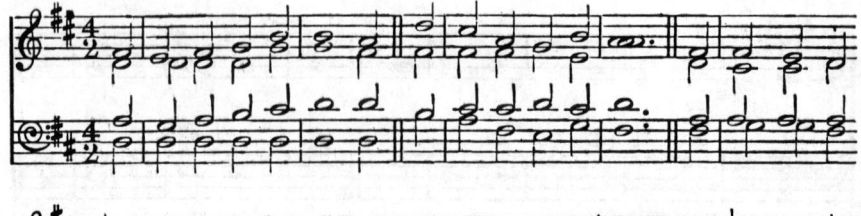

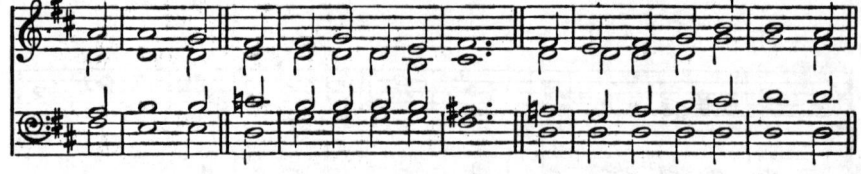

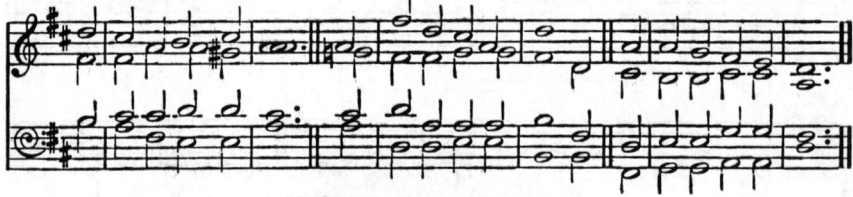

R.C. Chapman
J. Hullah

AUTHOR of our salvation,
  Once offered on the tree,
Our strength in all temptation,
  LORD, we remember Thee!
We, by Thy SPIRIT guided,
  To Golgotha repair;
The Lamb that GOD provided
  Was slaughtered for us there.

The sword of GOD was bidden
  His HOLY ONE to smite;
JEHOVAH'S face was hidden
  In terrors from Thy sight:
His tokens had declared Thee
  His SON that pleased Him well;
He pierced Thy soul, nor spared Thee
  When bruised by earth and hell.

Justice, our guilt to cover,
  Awoke the wrathful storm,
Dismay seized friend and lover;
  Thou saidst, "I am a worm":
Thou wast of GOD forsaken,
  As one by GOD abhorred;
The sinner's place was taken
  By Thee, our glorious LORD!

We on to ruin hurried—
  To misery's abyss;
But, dead with Thee, and buried,
  And raised to share Thy bliss,
We sing, with hearts united,
  Thy cross for evermore;
Once, like the world, benighted,
  Thy name we now adore.

19 Adoration 6.6.6.6.8.8

Isaac Watts (Darwall's 148th—246) W.H. Havergal

JOIN all the glorious names
  Of wisdom, love, and power,
That mortals ever knew,
  That angels ever bore;
All are too mean to speak Thy worth,
Too mean to set Thee, Saviour, forth.

Great Prophet of our GOD!
  Our tongue would bless Thy name;
By Thee the joyful news
  Of our salvation came—
The joyful news of sin forgiven,
Of hell subdued, of peace with heaven.

Be Thou our Counsellor,
  Our Pattern, and our Guide,
And through this desert land
  Still keep us near Thy side;
Oh, let our feet ne'er run astray,
Nor rove, nor seek the crooked way!

We love our Shepherd's voice:
  Thy watchful eye shall keep
Our wandering souls among
  The thousands of Thy sheep;
Still feed Thy flock and call our names,
And gently bear the tender lambs!

20 Nelson 6.6.8.6.8.8

J.G. Deck (Pisgah 141) Harmonised by G.F. Knowles

JESUS! I rest in Thee,
　Myself in Thee I hide;
Laden with guilt and misery,
　Where could I rest beside?
'Tis on Thy meek and lowly breast
My weary soul alone can rest.

Thou HOLY ONE of GOD!
　The FATHER rests in Thee,
And in the savour of that blood
　Which speaks to Him for me:
The curse is gone; through Thee I'm
　blest:
GOD rests in Thee; in Thee I rest!

The slave of sin and fear,
　Thy truth my bondage broke;
My happy spirit loves to wear
　Thy light and easy yoke; [breast,
Thy love, which fills my grateful
Makes duty joy, and labour rest.

Soon the bright, glorious day,
　The rest of GOD, shall come;
Sorrow and sin shall pass away,
　And I shall reach my home:
Then, of the promised land possest,
My soul shall know eternal rest.

21 St. Agnes, Durham C.M.

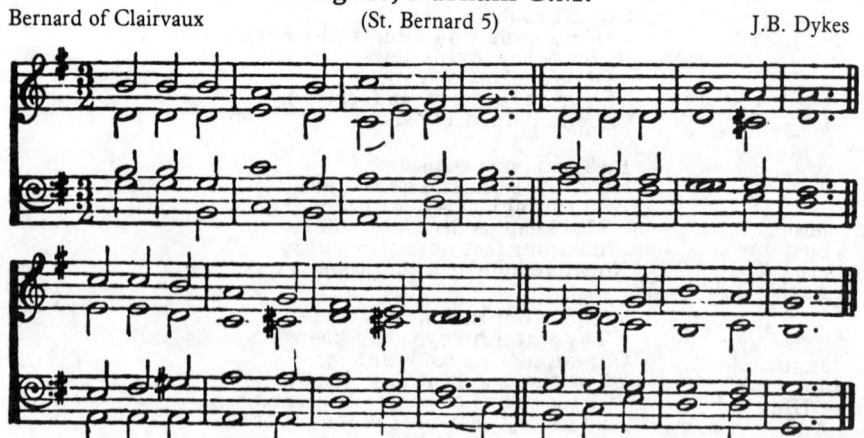

Bernard of Clairvaux (St. Bernard 5) J.B. Dykes

JESUS! the very thought of Thee
  With fragrance fills my breast;
But better far Thy face to see,
  And in Thy presence rest.

Nor voice can sing, nor heart can
  Nor can the memory find   [frame,
A sweeter sound than Thy blest name,
  O Saviour of mankind!

O hope of every contrite heart,
  O joy of all the meek!
To those who fall, how kind Thou art,
  How good to those who seek!

But what to those who find? ah! this
  Nor tongue nor pen can show—
The love of JESUS, what it is,
  None but His loved ones know!

    JESUS! our only strength be Thou,
      As Thou our crown wilt be;
    JESUS! be Thou our glory now,
      And through eternity!

22   **Sharon 8.7.8.7**
Denham Smith   (Stuttgart 217)   W. Boyce

RISE, my soul, behold 'tis JESUS!
  JESUS fills thy wondering eyes;
See him now, in glory seated,
  Where thy sins no more can rise.

There, in righteousness transcendent.
  Lo! He doth in heaven appear,
Shows the blood of His atonement
  As thy title to be there.

All thy sins were laid upon Him,
  JESUS bore them on the tree;
GOD, who knew them, laid them on Him,
  And, believing, thou art free.

GOD now brings thee to His dwelling,
  Spreads for thee His feast divine,
Bids thee welcome, ever telling
  What a portion there is thine.

In that circle of GOD's favour,
  Circle of the FATHER's love,
All is rest, and rest for ever—
  All is perfectness above.

Blessed, glorious word, "for ever"—
  Yea, "for ever" is the word!
Nothing can the ransomed sever,
  Nought divide them from the LORD.

23 Mainzer L.M.
Archibald Rutherford (Arizona 834) J. Mainzer

THE countless multitude on high,
  Who tune their songs to JESU'S
All merit of their own deny, [name,
  And JESU'S worth alone proclaim.

Firm on the ground of sovereign grace,
  They stand before Jehovah's throne;
The only song in that blest place
  Is—'Thou art worthy! Thou alone!

'Salvation's glory all be paid
  To Him who sits upon the throne,
And to the Lamb whose blood was
    shed— [alone!
  Thou, Thou art worthy! Thou

'For Thou wast slain, and in Thy
    blood [pure;
  These robes were washed so spotless
Thou mad'st us kings and priests to
    GOD—
  For ever let Thy praise endure!'

Let us with joy adopt the strain
  We hope to sing for ever there—
'Worthy's the Lamb for sinners slain,
  Worthy alone the crown to wear!'

Without one thought that's good to
    plead, [despair
Oh, what could shield us from
But this, though we are vile indeed,
  The LORD our righteousness is there!

24 St. Peter C.M.
John Newton (Lloyd 8) A.R. Reinagle

HOW sweet the name of JESUS
    In a believer's ear!   [sounds
It soothes his sorrows, heals his
    And drives away his fear. [wounds,
It makes the wounded spirit whole,
    And calms the troubled breast ;
'Tis manna to the hungry soul,
    And to the weary rest.
Dear name! the rock on which we
    Our shield and hiding-place ; [build,
Our never failing treasury filled
    With boundless stores of grace.

JESUS, our Shepherd, Saviour, Friend,
    Our Prophet, Priest, and King,
Our Lord, our Life, our Way, our
    Accept the praise we bring! [End—
Weak is the effort of our heart,
    And cold our warmest thought ;
But when we see Thee as Thou art,
    We'll praise Thee as we ought.
Till then we would Thy love proclaim
    With every fleeting breath,
And triumph in Thy blessèd name,
    Which quells the power of death.

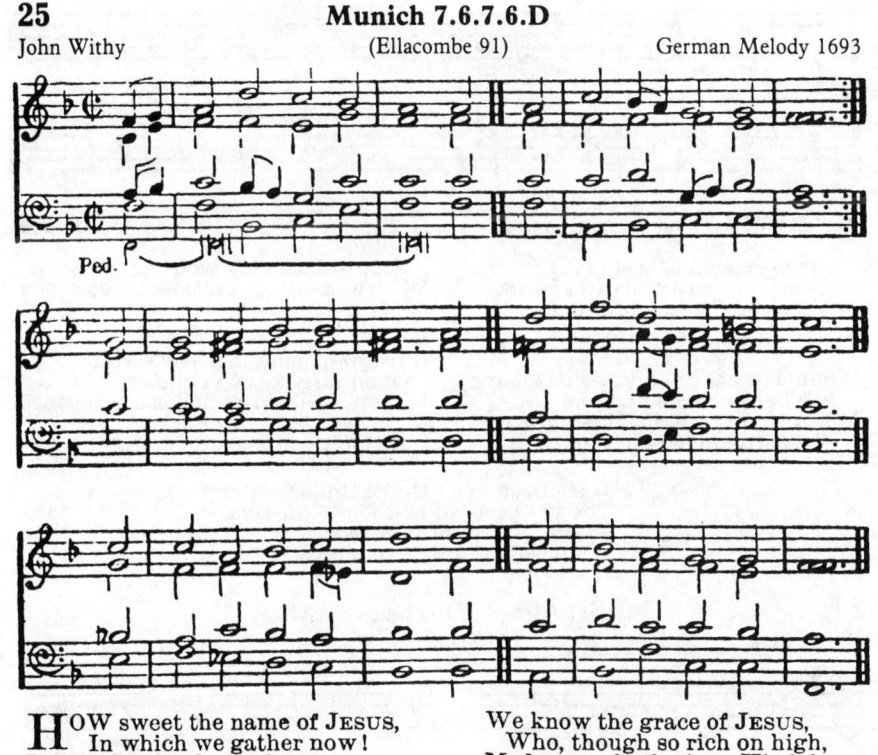

25 Munich 7.6.7.6.D
John Withy   (Ellacombe 91)   German Melody 1693

HOW sweet the name of JESUS,
    In which we gather now!
It lifts the cloud of sadness
    From off the careworn brow ;
Herein, for all the needy,
    A fulness is revealed ;
And fragrance round it sheddeth,
    Like odours sweet unsealed.

We know the grace of JESUS,
    Who, though so rich on high,
Made poor, hath given His fulness,
    Our poverty's supply ;
This well of rich salvation
    Springs all the desert way ;
Eternal love provided
    For us this staff and stay.

This name, our rock and refuge,
    And our foundation strong,
Is our sure pledge of blessing,
    Our sweetest joy and song ;
The name of JESUS ever
    Our watchword true shall stand—
The light to guide and cheer us
    On to our fatherland !

26 Belmont C.M.
(Albano 118)

S. Webbe

O SAVING name! O name of
   power!
The very soul of rest!
Our claim upon JEHOVAH's heart—
We plead Thee, and are blest!

O name of peace—mysterious name!
  In Thee doth conflict end;
Mercy and truth, in Thee agreed,
  Eternally do blend.

O name of balm! where conscience
   finds
A cure for every woe;
Where healing ointments aye are
   found,
And cleansing waters flow.

O fragrant name! for ever full
  Of odours rare and choice,
Where GOD doth find such incense
   sweet
As makes His heart rejoice.

Name of renown! the psalm of
  The very soul of rest!   [heaven
JESUS! Thy name adoringly
  We plead, and we are blest.

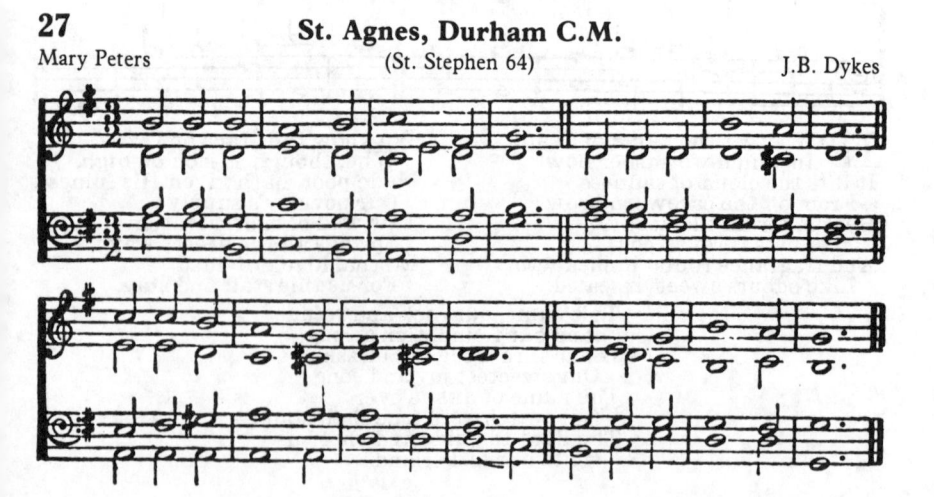

27 St. Agnes, Durham C.M.
(St. Stephen 64)

Mary Peters

J.B. Dykes

JESUS! how much Thy name unfolds
  To every opened ear!
The pardoned sinner's memory holds
  None other half so dear.

JESUS! it speaks a life of love,
  And sorrows meekly borne;
It tells of sympathy above,
  Whatever makes us mourn.

It speaks of righteousness complete,
  Of holiness to GOD;
And to our ears no tale so sweet
  As Thine atoning blood.

JESUS!—the One who knew no sin,
  Made sin to make us just—
Worthy art Thou our love to win,
  And worthy all our trust.

The mention of Thy name shall bow
  Our hearts to worship Thee;
The chicfest of ten thousand *THOU*,
  The chief of sinners *we*.

28   Ombersley L.M.

John Withy   (Whitburn 34)   W.H. Gladstone

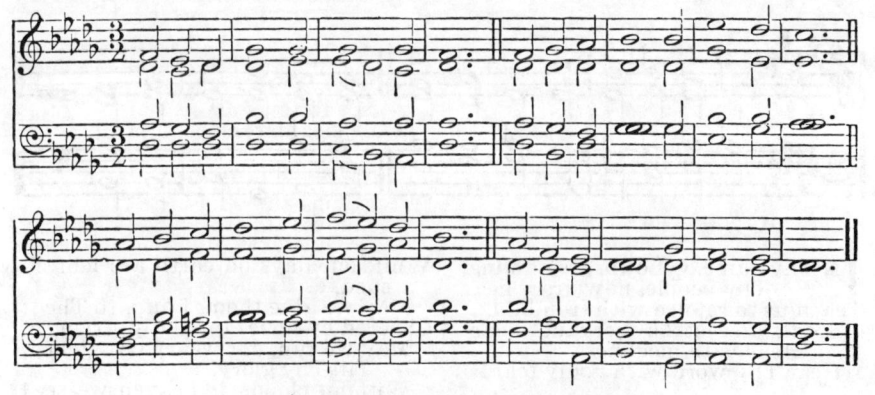

LORD JESUS, in Thy name alone
    Assembled, we Thy promise
      plead;
Thy presence in our midst be known,
  Our prayer and praise Thy SPIRIT
    lead!

EMMANUEL, God with us, Thou art,
  This is Thy dear, Thy chosen name;
Its savour fills the loving heart,
  To-day, and evermore, the same.

Thou art the Light, our feet to guide,
  Our Sun, to cheer the desert way;
The Rock, beneath whose shade we
    hide,
  Whose waters flow and never stay.

Blest in Thy fellowship divine,
  The heart has found a perfect rest;
In joy or tears we still recline
  For safety on Thy sheltering breast.

Here let our hearts for ever dwell,
  Live on Thy fulness, LORD, and be
Thy living witnesses, to tell
    The glories that are found in Thee!

29

Mannheim 8.7.8.7.8.7

Thos. Kelly   (Dismissal 505)   German

IN Thy name, O LORD, assembling,
  We, Thy people, now draw near;
Teach us to rejoice with trembling,
  Speak, and let Thy servants hear—
    Hear with meekness,
  Hear Thy word with godly fear!

While our days on earth are lengthened,
  May we give them, LORD, to Thee;
Cheered by hope, and daily strengthened,
  May we run, nor weary be,
    Till Thy glory,
  Without clouds, in heaven we see!

Then in worship purer, sweeter,
  Thee Thy people shall adore,
Tasting of enjoyment greater
  Far than thought conceived before—
    Full enjoyment,
  Full, unmixed, and evermore.

30

Dublin C.M.

Macleod Wylie   (Abridge 151)   J. Stevenson

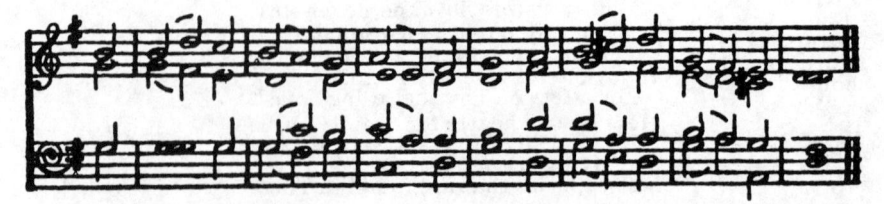

Once more, our God, with hallow-
　　ed joy,
　Thy willing people meet,
And plead the name of Thy dear Son
　Before the mercy-seat.

Thine eyes behold Him, gracious God!
　May we now see Him too!
The mystery of His grace reveal
　To faith's adoring view.

Thus feed, and teach, and lift us up,
　While from the world apart;
The memory of this sacred hour
　Engrave upon each heart.

May we, led on with heavenly joy,
　Long more for that bright scene
Where we in glory shall appear,
　Without a cloud between!

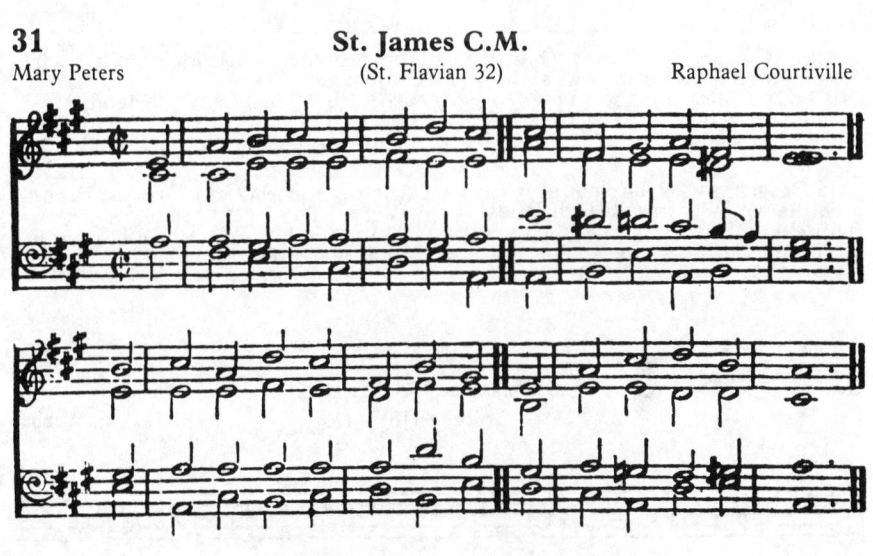

31 St. James C.M.
Mary Peters　　(St. Flavian 32)　　Raphael Courtville

O LORD, we know it matters nought
　　How sweet the sound may be,
No hearts but by Thy SPIRIT taught
　Make melody to Thee.

Then teach Thy gathered saints, O
　　LORD,
　To worship in Thy fear,
And dread lest any idle word
　Should reach Thy holy ear.

Thy blood hath made poor sinners
　　meet,
　Like saints in light, to come
And worship at the mercy-seat,
　Before the FATHER'S throne.

Thy precious name is all we show,
　Our only passport, LORD!
And now our FATHER'S love we know,
　Though we are self-abhorred.

　　Oh, largely give—'tis all Thine own—
　　　The SPIRIT'S goodly fruit;
　　Praise, issuing forth in life, alone
　　　Our living LORD can suit.

32 St. Flavian C.M.
R.C. Chapman (St. James 31) Day's Psalter 1562

OUR GOD, soon as Thy SON had died,
  Soon as the Lamb was slain—
His body lifeless on the tree—
  The veil was rent in twain.

Our FATHER, now Thy countenance
  Shines on Thy great High Priest—
Thine only SON, Thy Well-beloved,
  Thine everlasting rest.

Him crowned with glory, filled with joy.
  Thy First-born from the dead,
Our faith beholds; we share Thy love,
  The members with the Head!

Our GOD and FATHER, we are Thine;
  We, by Thy SPIRIT sealed,
All kings and priests, adore Thy name,
  In JESU'S cross revealed!

33 Belmont C.M.
J.G. Deck (Albano 118) S. Webbe

THE veil is rent—lo! JESUS stands
    Before the throne of grace,
And clouds of incense from His hands
    Fill all that glorious place.

His precious blood is sprinkled there,
    Before and on the throne;
And His own wounds in heaven declare
    His work on earth is done.

" 'Tis finished!" on the cross He said,
    In agonies and blood;
" 'Tis finished!" now He lives to plead
    Before the face of GOD.

" 'Tis finished!" here our souls can rest,
    His work can never fail;
By Him, our Sacrifice and Priest,
    We enter through the veil.

    Within the holiest of all,
      Cleansed by His precious blood,
    Before Thy throne Thy children fall,
      And worship Thee, our GOD!

34   Whitburn L.M.

Alex. Stewart   (Samson 568(2))   H. Baker

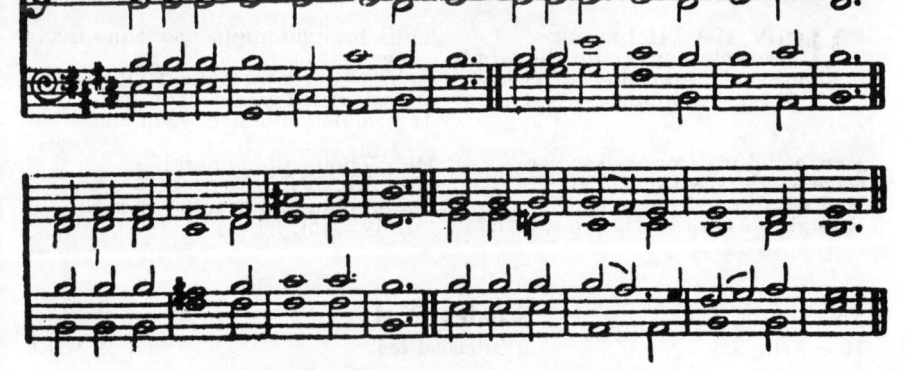

LORD JESUS CHRIST, we seek Thy face,
    Within the veil we bow the knee;
Oh, let Thy glory fill the place,
    And bless us while we wait on Thee!

We thank Thee for the precious blood
    That purged our sins and brought us nigh,
All cleansed and sanctified, to GOD,
    Thy holy name to magnify.

Shut in with Thee, far, far above
    The restless world that wars below,
We seek to learn and prove Thy love—
    Thy wisdom and Thy grace to know.

The brow that once with thorns was bound,
    Thy hands, Thy side, we fain would see;
Draw near, Lord Jesus, glory-crowned,
    And bless us while we wait on Thee!

35
F.W. Pitt **Weber 7.7.7.7** From Weber
(Buckland 159)

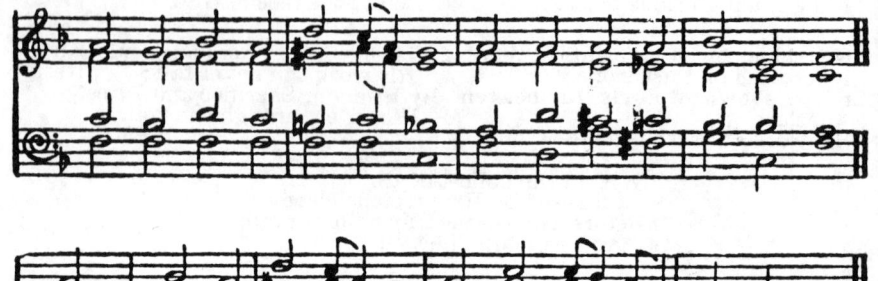

"HOLY, Holy, Holy LORD!"
  Seraphim proclaim the word,
And our souls, from sin set free,
"Holy!" now would cry to Thee.

How could we approach so near,
Gaze on glory without fear,
Had not JESUS by His blood
Brought us nigh to Thee, our GOD?

Thus brought nigh, and thus made
  meet,
In Thy courts we stand complete;
Thou Thyself canst see no spot,
JESU's blood removes each blot.

Holy Thou! all holiness!
Holy we, by JESU's grace,
Made so fit, and brought so nigh,
"Holy! Holy! Holy!" cry.

36
Thos. Kelly **Sawley C.M.** J. Walch
(Richmond 186)

NOW may the SPIRIT from above
  Impart His holy fire,
And cause our hearts to glow with
    love
  And vehement desire—

The sweet desire of holy things,
  That finds its element
In converse with the King of kings,
  With nought but this content—

    The pledge of sacred joys to come,
      Anticipation blest
    Of heaven, our everlasting home,
      Of heaven, our place of rest!

37   Rimington L.M.

Thos. Kelly   (Mainzer 23)   F. Duckworth

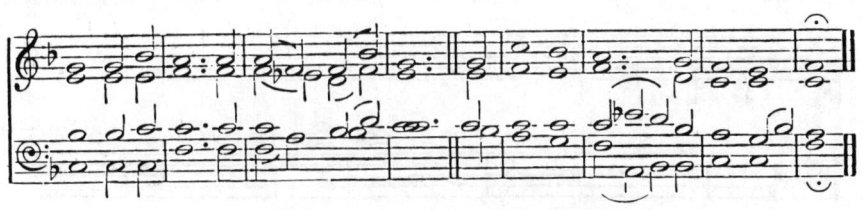

HOW pleasant is the sound of
    praise!
  It well becomes the saints of GOD;
Should we refuse our songs to raise,
  The stones might tell our shame
    abroad.

For Him who cleansed us with His
    blood,
  Let us our loudest songs prepare;
He sought us wandering far from GOD,
  And now preserves us by His care.

Though angels may with rapture see
  How mercy flows in JESU'S blood,
It is not theirs to prove, as we,
  The cleansing virtue of this flood.

What ceaseless cause of praise, both
    here
  And when we reach our home above,
That we, who lost and ruined were,
  Should be the objects of such love!

38 Abney C.M.
R.C. Chapman — (St. Fulbert 126) — Asa Hull
Slow.

THE contrite heart is incense sweet,
  Our gracious GOD, to Thee;
It worships at Thy mercy-seat
  In perfect liberty.

That gift which Thou wilt not despise
  Do Thou to us impart,
And then accept our sacrifice—
  A broken, contrite heart!

39 Adoration 6.6.6.6.8.8
Isaac Watts — (Darwall's 148th–246) — W.H. Havergal

LORD of the worlds above!
  How pleasant and how fair
The dwellings of Thy love,
  The heavenly mansions are
    To Thine abode
    Our hearts aspire,
    With warm desire
    To see our GOD.

There is the throne of grace,
  And there the sprinkled blood;
There lives, before Thy face,
  Our great High Priest, O God!
    His name our plea,
      We now draw near
    In holy fear
      To worship Thee!

We go from strength to strength
  Through this dark vale of tears,
Till each arrives at length,
  And safe in heaven appears:
    Oh, glorious seat,
      Where God the King
    Shall shortly bring
      Our willing feet!

40   **Mackinlay L.M.D.**   Alexander Lee
Isaac Watts   (Llef 306)   (Harmonised by G.F. Knowles)

Slow and with expression.

WHEN I survey the wondrous cross,
  On which the King of glory died,
My richest gain I count but loss,
  And pour contempt on all my pride.

Forbid it, Lord, that I should boast
  Save in the cross of Christ, my God;
All the vain things that charm me most,
  I sacrifice them to His blood.

See from His head, His hands, His feet,
  Sorrow and love flow mingled down!
Did e'er such love and sorrow meet,
  Or thorns compose so rich a crown?

Were the whole realm of nature mine,
  That were an offering far too small;
Love so amazing, so divine,
  Demands my soul, my life, my all.

41 Love Divine 8.7.8.7

Allen & Shirley (Sharon 22) J. Stainer

SWEET the moments, rich in blessing,
Which before the cross we spend,
Life, and health, and peace possessing,
From the sinner's dying Friend.

Here we rest, in wonder viewing
All our sins on JESUS laid,
And a full redemption flowing
From the sacrifice He made.

Here we find the dawn of heaven,
While upon the cross we gaze,
See our trespasses forgiven,
And our songs of triumph raise.

Oh that, near the cross abiding,
We may to the Saviour cleave,
Nought with Him our hearts dividing,
All for Him content to leave!

42 Celeste 8.8.8.8

Thos. Kelly (Trewen 315)

WE'LL sing of the Shepherd that died,
That died for the sake of the flock;
His love to the utmost was tried,
Yet firmly endured as a rock.

When blood from a victim must flow,
This Shepherd by pity was led
To stand between us and the foe,
And willingly die in our stead.

Our song then for ever shall be
Of the Shepherd who gave Himself thus;
No subject so glorious as He,
No theme so affecting to us.

We'll sing of such subjects alone,
None other our tongue shall employ,
Till better His love becomes known
In yonder bright regions of joy.

43
C. Wesley

St. Catherine 8.8.8.8.8.8
(Pater Omnium 44)

J.G. Walton

O LOVE divine, what hast Thou done!
The SON of GOD His blood hath shed!
The FATHER'S co-eternal SON
Had all our sins upon Him laid!
The SON of GOD for us hath died,
Our LORD, our Life, was crucified;

Was crucified for us in shame,
To bring us, rebels, back to GOD;
And now we glory in His name,
And know we're cleansèd by His blood—
Pardon and life flowed from His side
When He, our LORD, was crucified.

Then let us glory in the cross—
Make it our boast, our constant theme,
All things for CHRIST account but loss,
And now for Him despise the shame:
Let nought with Him our hearts divide,
Since He for us was crucified.

44   **Pater Omnium 8.8.8.8.8.8**

Tersteegen   (St. Catherine 43)   H.J.E. Holmes

THE Lamb was slain! let us adore,
   And all His gracious mercy own,
And prostrate now and evermore
   Before His piercèd feet fall down;
Serve without dread, with reverence
   love
The LORD, whose boundless grace we
   prove.

Through Him alone we live, for He
   Hath drownèd our transgressions all
In love's unfathomable sea:
   Oh, love unknown, unsearchable!
The holy Lamb for sin was slain,
That sinners endless life might gain.

As ground, when parched with summer's heat,
   Gladly drinks in the welcome shower,
So would we, listening at His feet,
   Receive His words, and feel His power:
May nothing in our hearts remain
Like this great truth—'The Lamb was slain!'

45   **Tallis' Canon L.M.**

       (Ombersley 28)   T. Tallis

FORSAKEN once e'en of Thy GOD,
  O LORD, our sins on Thee were
    laid ;
But now Thou art enthroned on high—
  The proof for us that peace is made.

The kingdom, power, and glory now
  Are Thine, LORD JESUS, by Thy
    blood—
The blood by which our peace is made,
By which our souls draw nigh to GOD.

The glory of Thy holy throne,
  Thy matchless name, Thy majesty,
All teach our souls to value more
  That blood once shed on Calvary.

We bow our hearts and bless Thy name
  Our grateful song to Thee we raise ;
We own Thee LORD, and worship Thee:
  Accept our worship and our praise !

46   **St. James C.M.**
R.C. Chapman   (Farrant 157)   R. Courtiville

THE Lamb of GOD to slaughter led,
  The King of glory see!
The crown of thorns upon His head,
  They nail Him to the tree!

The FATHER gives His only SON ;
  The LORD of glory dies
For us, the guilty and undone,
  A spotless sacrifice !

Thy name is holy, O our GOD,
  Before Thy throne we bow !
Thy bosom is Thy saints' abode,
  We call Thee FATHER now !

Enthroned with Thee now sits the
    LORD,
  And in Thy bosom dwells ;
Justice, that smote Him with the
    sword,
  Our perfect pardon seals.

    Eternal death was once our doom ;
      Now death has lost its sting ;
    We rose with JESUS from the tomb,
      JEHOVAH'S love to sing.

47   **Claremont C.M.**
E. Denny   (Dublin 30)   J. Foster

1.
TO Calvary, LORD, in spirit now
   Our weary souls repair,
To dwell upon Thy dying love,
   And taste its sweetness there.

2.
Sweet resting-place of every heart
   That feels the plague of sin,
Yet knows that deep mysterious joy—
   The peace of GOD within.

3.
There, through Thine hour of deepest woe,
   Thy suffering spirit passed;
Grace there its wondrous victory gained,
   And love endured its last.

4.
Dear suffering Lamb! Thy bleeding wounds,
   With cords of love divine,
Have drawn our willing hearts to Thee
   And linked our life with Thine.

5.
Thy sympathies and hopes are ours;
   O LORD, we wait to see
Creation all—below, above,
   Redeemed and blest by Thee.

6.
Our longing eyes would fain behold
   That bright and blessèd brow,
Once wrung with bitterest anguish, wear
   Its crown of glory now.

48   Deerhurst 8.7.8.7.D

J.G. Deck   (Hyfrydol 49)   J. Langran

LAMB of GOD! our souls adore Thee
  While upon Thy face we gaze;
There the FATHER'S love and glory
  Shine in all their brightest rays:
Thine almighty power and wisdom
  All creation's works proclaim;
Heaven and earth alike confess Thee
  As the ever great "I AM."

Lamb of GOD! Thy FATHER'S bosom
  Ever was Thy dwelling-place;
His delight, in Him rejoicing,
  One with Him in power and grace:
Oh, what wondrous love and mercy—
  Thou didst lay Thy glory by,
And for us didst come from heaven,
  As the Lamb of GOD, to die!

Lamb of GOD! when we behold Thee
  Lowly in the manger laid,
Wandering as a homeless stranger
  In the world Thy hands had made;
When we see Thee in the garden,
  In Thine agony of blood,
At Thy grace we are confounded,
  Holy, spotless Lamb of GOD!

When we see Thee, as the Victim,
  Bound for us upon the tree,
For our guilt and folly stricken,
  All our judgment borne by Thee—
LORD, we own, with hearts adoring.
  Thou hast loved us unto blood:
Glory, glory everlasting,
  Be to Thee, Thou Lamb of GOD!

49
J.G. Deck **Hyfrydol 8.7.8.7.D** R.H. Pritchard
(Deerhurst 48)

LAMB of GOD! Thou now art seated
  High upon Thy FATHER's throne;
All Thy gracious work completed,
  All Thy mighty victory won:
Every knee in heaven is bending
  To the Lamb for sinners slain;
Every voice with praise is swelling—
  'Worthy is the Lamb to reign.'

LORD, in all Thy power and glory,
  Still Thy thoughts and eyes are here.
Watching o'er Thy ransomed people,
  To Thy gracious heart so dear:
Thou for us art interceding,
  (Everlasting is Thy love,)
And a blessèd rest preparing
  In our FATHER's house above.

Lamb of GOD! Thou soon in glory
  Wilt to this sad earth return;
All Thy foes shall quake before Thee,
  All that now despise Thee mourn:
Then Thy saints appearing with Thee,
  With Thee in Thy kingdom reign;
Thine the praise, and Thine the glory,
  Lamb of GOD, for sinners slain!

50
Dr. Rossier **Farrant C.M.** R. Farrant
(Jazer 13)

LORD, e'en to death Thy love could
  go—
  A death of shame and loss;
To vanquish for us every foe,
  Thou didst endure the cross!

Oh, what a load was Thine to bear,
  Alone in that dark hour—
Our sins, in all their terror there,
  GOD's wrath, and Satan's power!

The storm that bowed Thy blessèd
  head
Is hushed for ever now,
And rest divine is ours instead,
  Whilst glory crowns Thy brow.

Within the FATHER's house on high,
  We soon shall sing Thy praise,
But here, where Thou didst bleed and
  die,
We learn that song to raise,

51 Luther's Chant L.M.
Denham Smith   (Mainzer 23)   H.C. Zeuner

JESUS, Thy dying love I own—
  A love unfathomed and unknown!
All other love can measured be,
But not Thy dying love to me.

Oh, wonder to myself I am,
Thou loving, bleeding, suffering Lamb,
That I can scan the mystery o'er
And not be moved to love Thee more!

'Tis well, my LORD, that 'twas *Thy* love,
Not *mine*, that brought Thee from
  above;
And well that 'twas Thy bitter grief,
Not mine, that gave my soul relief.

Loved now, and ever on Thy throne
Adored and loved, Thou timeless One!
Thou wilt, through one eternal day,
The height and depth of love display!

52   Eden L.M.

E. Denny   (Deep Harmony 224)   T.B. Mason

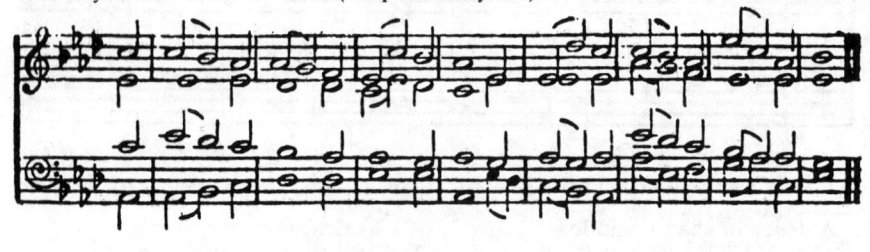

OH, wondrous hour, when, JESUS, Thou,
  Co-equal with the eternal GOD,
Beneath our sin didst deign to bow,
  And in our stead didst bear the rod!

On Thee, the FATHER'S blessèd SON,
  JEHOVAH'S utmost anger fell:
That all was borne, that all was done,
  Thine agony, Thy cross can tell.

When most in Satan's awful power,
  O LORD, Thy suffering spirit seemed,
Then, in that dark and fearful hour,
  Our souls were by Thy blood redeemed

'Tis in Thy cross, LORD, that we learn
  What Thou, in all Thy fulness, art;
There, through the darkening cloud, discern
  The love of Thy devoted heart.

'Twas mighty love's constraining power
  That made Thee, blessèd Saviour, die;
'Twas love, in that tremendous hour,
  That triumphed in Thy parting sigh.

'Twas all for us—our life we owe,
  Our hope, our crown of joy, to Thee;
Thy sufferings, in that hour of woe,
  Thy victory, LORD, have made us free!

53
Christopher Batty

Pembroke 8.8.6.8.8.6
(Meribah 153)

J. Foster

O JESUS, everlasting GOD!
  Who didst for sinners shed Thy
      blood
  Upon the shameful tree,
Didst finish there redemption's toil,
And win for us the happy spoil—
  All praise we give to Thee!

Fain would we think upon Thy pain,
Would find therein our life and gain,
  And firmly fix our heart
Upon Thy grief and dying love,
Nor evermore from Thee remove
  Though from all else we part.

The more, through grace, ourselves
      we know,
The more rejoiced we are to bow
  In faith beneath Thy cross;
To trust in Thine atoning blood,
To look to Thee for every good,
  And count all else but loss.

54 Eden L.M.
Zinzendorf (Abends 571) T.B. Mason

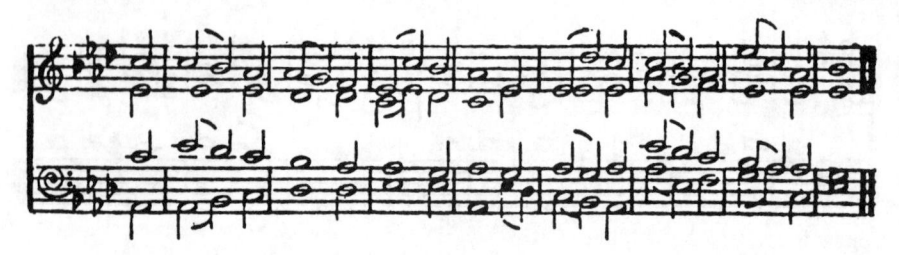

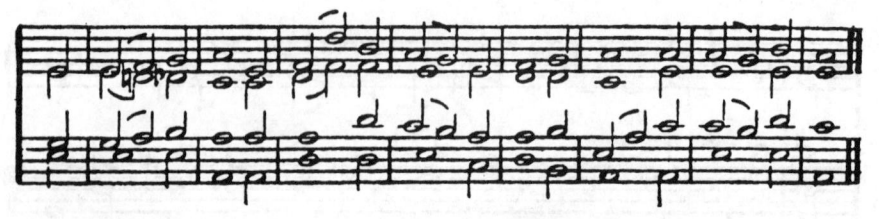

O COME, Thou stricken Lamb of God!
Who shed'st for us Thine own life-blood,
And teach us all Thy love; then pain
Were light, and life or death were gain.

Take Thou our hearts, and let them be
For ever closed to all but Thee;
Thy willing servants, may we wear
The seal of love for ever there.

How blest are they who still abide
Close sheltered by Thy watchful side;
Who life and strength from Thee receive,
And with Thee move, and in Thee live!

Ah! LORD, enlarge our scanty thought
To know the wonders Thou hast wrought;
Unloose our stammering tongues to tell
Thy love, immense, unsearchable.

First-born of many brethren Thou,
To whom both heaven and earth must bow—
Heirs of Thy shame, and of Thy throne,
We bear the cross, and seek the crown.

55 Whitburn L.M.
R.C. Chapman (Maryton 61) H. Baker

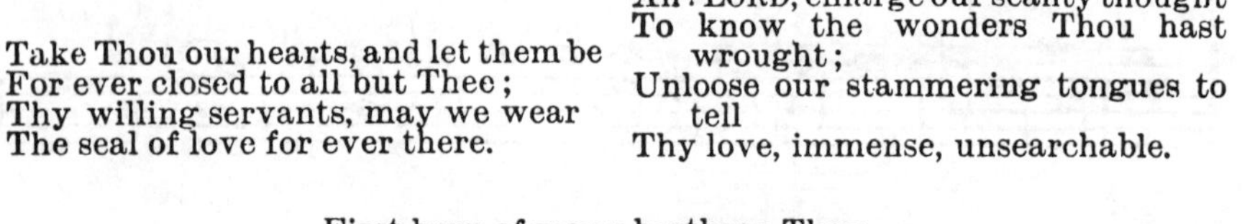

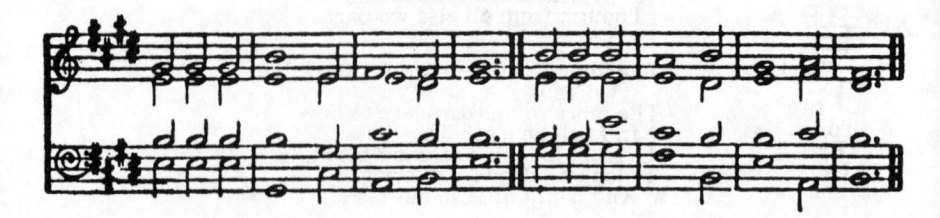

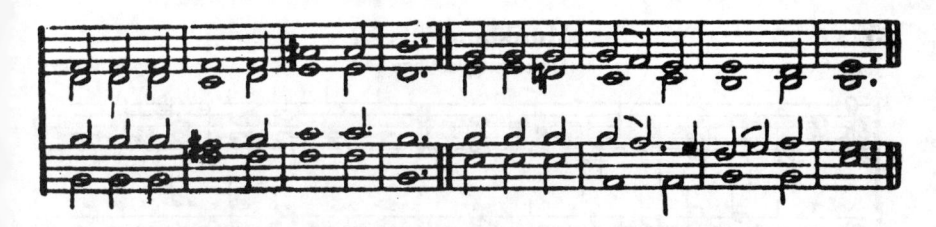

SHEW me Thy wounds, exalted Lord!
Thou hast the power and skill divine,
Since Justice smote Thee with the sword,
To make my heart resemble Thine.

Oh, grant me ever to behold,
With heavenly wisdom's piercing eye,
Thy pains of death, for they unfold
Thy name, Thou SON of GOD, Most High!

Shew me Thy wounds, and by Thy skill
May I, my Saviour, be refined,
To do, like Thee, the FATHER'S will,
And serve Him with a perfect mind.

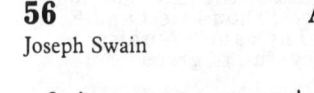

56 Adoration 6.6.6.6.8.8

Joseph Swain (Darwall's 148th–246) W.H. Havergal

ON earth the song begins,
In heaven more sweet and loud—
'To Him that cleansed our sins
By His atoning blood—
To Him,' we sing in joyful strain,
'Be honour, praise, and power. Amen.'

Alone He bore the cross,
Alone its grief sustained;
His was the shame and loss,
And He the victory gained:
The mighty work was all His own,
But we by grace shall share His throne.

57 Monkland 7.7.7.7
John Cennick (University College 149) J.B. Wilkes

BRETHREN, let us join to bless
  CHRIST, the LORD our righteousness;
Let our praise to Him be given,
High at GOD'S right hand in heaven.

SON of GOD, to Thee we bow!
Thou art LORD, and only Thou;
Thou the blessèd virgin's Seed,
Glory of the Church, and Head.

With Thy praise the heavens ring;
Thee we bless, Thou Priest and King;
Worthy is Thy name of praise,
Full of glory, full of grace.

Thou hast the glad tidings brought
Of salvation by Thee wrought,
Wrought to set Thy people free,
Wrought to bring our souls to Thee.

Thee, our Saviour, we adore,
And would serve Thee more and more
Till with joy Thy face we see,
And for ever dwell with Thee.

58 St. John 6.6.6.6.8.8
T. Haweis (Darwall's 148th–246) J. Baptiste Calkin

THE happy morn is come;
  Triumphant o'er the grave,
The Saviour leaves the tomb,
  Almighty now to save—
*Captivity is captive led,
Since JESUS liveth who was dead.*

Who now accuseth them
  For whom the Surety died?
Or who shall those condemn
  Whom GOD hath justified?—

CHRIST hath the ransom paid;
  The glorious work is done:
On Him our help was laid;
  The victory is won—

Hail! O triumphant LORD!
  The Resurrection Thou:
Hail! O incarnate Word!
  Before the throne we bow—

59 Hull 8.8.6.8.8.6
Thos. Kelly   (Meribah 153)   Old melody

OH, joyful day, oh, glorious hour,
  When JESUS, by almighty power,
    Revived and left the grave!
In all His works behold Him great—
Before, Almighty to create,
  Almighty now to save!

The First-begotten from the dead,
And risen now, His people's Head,
  He makes our life secure;
And if like Him we yield our breath,
Like Him we'll burst the bonds of
  Our resurrection sure.   [death,

Let not His people then be sad,
None have such reason to be glad
  As those redeemed to GOD:
JESUS, the mighty Saviour, lives;
To us eternal life He gives,
  The purchase of His blood.

Then let our gladsome praise resound,
And let us in His work abound
  Whose blessèd name is Love:
Our labour cannot be in vain,
And we with Him ere long shall
  With JESUS dwell above!   [reign,

60   Lynton C.M.
(Richmond 186)   A.J. Jamouneau

WE love to sing with one accord
   The riches of Thy grace;
We love to come before Thee, LORD—
   On earth no happier place.

We love to lean upon Thy breast
   In the repose of faith,
And find our soul's enduring rest
   In what Thy SPIRIT saith.

In songs of praise we would record
   Thy mercy while we live;
Soon in Thy presence shall we, LORD,
   Far sweeter praises give.

61   Maryton L.M.
R.C. Chapman   (Eden 54)   H. Percy Smith

OUR GOD, whose justice did awake
   The sword against Thy Well-
     beloved,
Thou didst Thine own dear SON
     forsake,
To mercy by His cries unmoved!

Thy perfect image, Thy delight,
   He ever had beheld Thy face;
Thy bosom was, of native right,
   His proper, secret dwelling-place.

Yet was the LORD made flesh, and
    nailed
By men, His creatures, to the tree;
By all the powers of hell assailed,
    And bruised and pierced, and slain
        by Thee!

In His own majesty arrayed,
    He spake and built the universe;
Yet to redeem us He was made
    A dying outcast and a curse!

    His depths unsearchable of woe
        Alone our utmost guilt proclaim;
    Through JESU'S cross make us to know
        The utmost glories of Thy name!

62   Moscow 6.6.4.6.6.6.4
(Olivet 680)   F. Giardini

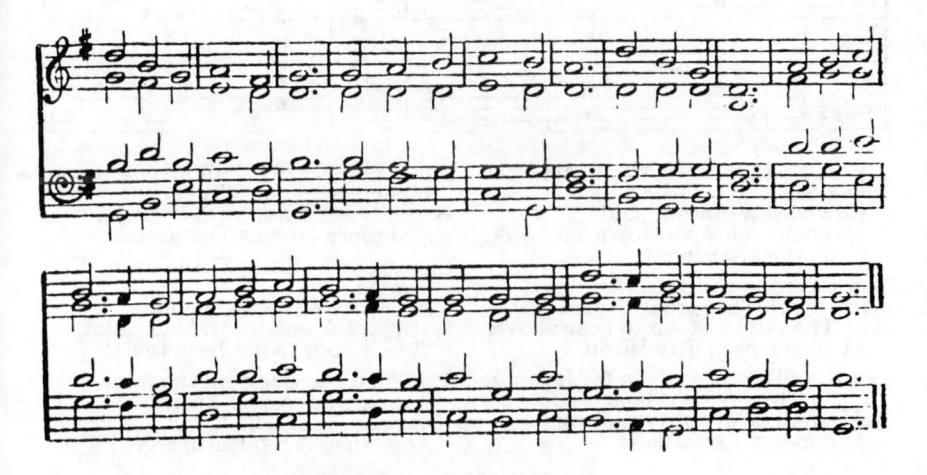

IN Thine own presence, LORD,
    We join with one accord
        To worship Thee;
With heart and voice we raise
Our gladsome hymn of praise,
And sing the boundless grace
        That made us free.

To give us peace with GOD
Through Thy most precious blood,
        The cross was Thine!
And now we humbly bring
A free-will offering
Of grateful praise, and sing
        Thy love Divine.

Soon Thou, our LORD, wilt come
And take us to our home,
        To sup with Thee;
Then shall our songs abound,
Then shall our praise resound,
And every note be found
        In harmony.

63 Tiverton C.M.
Mary Peters   (St. Stephen 64)   J. Grigg

O BLESSÈD LORD, what hast Thou done!
  How vast a ransom paid!
Who could conceive GOD'S only SON
  Upon the altar laid?

Thy FATHER, in His perfect love,
  Did spare Thee from His side;
And Thou didst stoop to bear above,
  At such a cost, Thy Bride.

LORD, while our souls in faith repose
  Upon Thy precious blood,
Peace like an even river flows,
  And mercy like a flood.

But boundless joy shall fill our hearts
  When, gazing on Thy face,
We fully see what faith imparts,
  And glory crowns Thy grace.

Unseen, we love Thee—dear Thy name
  But when our eyes behold,
With joyful wonder we'll exclaim,
  'The half hath not been told!'

For Thou exceedest all the fame
  Our ears have ever heard:
Happy are they who know Thy name,
  And trust Thy faithful word!

64 St. Stephen C.M.
(Richmond 186)   W. Jones

O BLESSED LORD, we praise Thee now
For all that Thou hast done—
Thy rich unfathomed ways of love,
The victory Thou hast won.

We praise Thee for the bitter cross,
The judgment Thou didst bear,
When, suffering in the sinner's stead,
GOD's love Thou didst declare.

We praise Thee, for Thou art our LORD,
Whose ever-gracious ways
Transport our souls, and teach our hearts
To yield Thee fervent praise.

65 **Deerhurst 8.7.8.7.D**
S.P. Tregelles (Hyfrydol 49) J. Langran

SON of GOD! with joy we praise Thee,
On the FATHER'S throne above;
All Thy wondrous work displays Thee,
Full of grace, and full of love:
LORD, accept our adoration—
For our sins Thou once wast slain;
Through Thy blood we have salvation,
And with Thee we soon shall reign.

GOD, in Thee His love unfolding,
Shows how rich has been His grace;
We are blest, with joy beholding
All His glory in Thy face:
In His counsel, ere creation,
All the Church He chose in Thee;
And our Surety for salvation
Thou wast then ordained to be.

When it seemed that sin must sever
All the chosen heirs from GOD,
Thou, with love which faileth never,
Didst redeem us by Thy blood:
Oh, the mercy which hath blest us,
Purposed thus ere time began—
Mercy which in Thee hath kept us,
Mercy vast, like heaven's span!

66 Goshen 7.7.8.7.D
S.P. Tregelles (Bishopsgarth 67)

THY name we bless, LORD JESUS!
  That name all names excelling:
How great Thy love, all praise above,
  Should every tongue be telling:
The FATHER'S loving-kindness
  In giving Thee was shewn us;
Now by Thy blood redeemed to GOD,
  As children He doth own us.

From that eternal glory
  Thou hadst with GOD the FATHER,
He sent His SON, that He in one
  His children all might gather:
Our sins were all laid on Thee,
  GOD'S wrath Thou hast endurèd;
It was for us Thou sufferedst thus,
  And hast our peace securèd.

Thou from the dead wast raisèd,
  And from all condemnation
The Church is free, as risen in Thee,
  Head of the new creation!
On high Thou hast ascended
  To GOD'S right hand in heaven;
The Lamb once slain, alive again—
  To Thee all power is given.

Thou hast bestowed the earnest
  Of that we shall inherit:
Till Thou shalt come to take us home,
  We're sealed by GOD the SPIRIT:
We wait for Thine appearing,
  When we shall know more fully
The Priest and King whose praise we sing,
  Thou Lamb of GOD most holy!

67   **Bishopsgarth 7.7.8.7.D**
W. Yerbury   (Goshen 66)   Arthur S. Sullivan

Stately.

1
THY name we love, LORD JESUS!
  And lowly bow before Thee;
And while we live, to Thee would give
  All blessing, worship, glory:
We sing aloud Thy praises,
  Our hearts and voices blending;
'Tis Thou alone we worthy own,
Thy worth is all transcending.

2
Thy name we love, LORD JESUS!
  It tells GOD'S love unbounded
To ruined man, ere time began,
  Or heaven and earth were founded;
Thine is a love eternal,
  That found in us its pleasure,
That brought Thee low, to bear our
    woe,
And make us Thine own treasure.

3
Thy name we love, LORD JESUS!
  It tells Thy birth so lowly,
Thy patience, grace, Thy gentleness
  Thy lonely path, so holy;
Thou wast the "Man of sorrows;"
  Our grief, too, Thou didst bear it;
Our bitter cup, Thou drankest up;
The thorny crown—didst wear it.

4
Thy name we love, LORD JESUS!
  GOD'S Lamb Thou wast ordainèd,
To bear our sin, Thyself all clean,
  And hast our guilt sustainèd;
We see Thee crowned with glory,
  Above the heavens now seated,
The victory won, Thy work well done.
Our righteousness completed.

68   Martyrdom C.M.
T.E. Purdom   (St. Bernard 5)   Hugh Wilson

LORD JESUS CHRIST, our Saviour Thou,
  With joy we worship Thee,
We know Thou hast redeemèd us,
  By dying on the tree!

We know the love that brought Thee down,
  Down from that bliss on high,
To meet our ruined souls' deep need—
  On Calvary's cross to die.

Our Saviour and our LORD Thou art,
  Eternal is Thy love;
Eternal, too, shall be our praise
  When with Thee, LORD, above.

E'en now we praise Thy grace divine,
  The love that shines in Thee;
The rich One Thou, for us made poor,
  By death didst set us free.

We praise, we worship, we adore,
  As round Thyself we meet;
Thy beauties, LORD, transport our souls
  While bowing at Thy feet.

O LORD, our theme of praise art Thou,
  Thy cross, Thy work, Thy word:
Oh, who can fathom all Thy love,
  Thou living blessèd LORD!

69   Luther's Chant L.M.
Jas. Montgomery   (Angelus 114)   H.C. Zeuner

COME, let us sing the song of songs,
   And yield in joyful heavenly
     strain
The homage which to CHRIST belongs:
   'Worthy the Lamb, for He was slain!'

Slain to redeem us by His blood,
   To cleanse from every sinful stain,
And make us kings and priests to GOD:
   'Worthy the Lamb, for He was slain!'

To Him who suffered on the tree,
   Our souls, at His soul's price, to gain,
Blessing, and praise, and glory be:
   'Worthy the Lamb, for He was slain!'

To Him, enthroned by filial right,
   All power in heaven and earth
     proclaim,
Honour, and majesty, and might:
   'Worthy the Lamb, for He was slain!'

   Long as we live, and should we die,
     And while in heaven with Him we
       reign,
   This song our song of songs shall be:
     'Worthy the Lamb, for He was slain!'

70   Dublin C.M.
J.G. Deck   (St. Stephen 212)   J. Stevenson

LORD JESUS, are we one with Thee?
   Oh height, oh depth of love!
Once slain for us upon the tree,
   We're one with Thee above.

Such was Thy grace, that for our sake
   Thou didst from heaven come down;
With us of flesh and blood partake,
   In all our sorrow one.

Our sins, our guilt, in love divine
   Confessed and borne by Thee,
The gall, the curse, the wrath were
     Thine,
   To set Thy members free.

Ascended now in glory bright,
   LORD, one with us Thou art!
Nor life, nor death, nor depth, nor
     height,
   Thy saints from Thee can part!

Oh, teach us, LORD, to know and own
   This wondrous mystery,
That Thou with us art truly one,
   And we are one with Thee!

Soon, soon shall come that glorious
     day,
   When, seated on Thy throne, [play
Thou shalt to wondering worlds dis-
   That we with Thee are one!

71 Winchester New L.M.
Denham Smith (Ombersley 28) B. Crasselius

JUST as *THOU art*—how wondrous fair,
Lord Jesus, all Thy members are!
A life divine to them is given—
A long inheritance in heaven.

Just as *I was* I came to Thee,
An heir of wrath and misery:
Just as *Thou art* before the throne,
I stand in righteousness Thine own.

Just as Thou art—how wondrous free
Loosed by the sorrows of the tree:
Jesus! the curse, the wrath were Thine,
To give Thy saints this life divine.

Just as Thou art, Thou Lamb Divine!
Life, light, and holiness are Thine;
Thyself their endless source I see,
And they, the life of God, in me.

Oh, teach me, Lord, this grace to own,
That self and sin no more are known:
That love—*Thy* love—in wondrous right,
Hath placed me in its spotless light!

Soon, soon, 'mid joys on joys untold,
Thou wilt this grace and love unfold,
Till worlds on worlds adoring see
The part Thy members have in Thee.

72   **Palmyra 8.6.8.6.8.8**
Josiah Conder   (Supremacy 74)   J. Summers

THOU art the everlasting Word,
  The FATHER'S only SON,
GOD manifestly seen and heard,
  And Heaven's belovèd One:
    Worthy, O Lamb of GOD, art Thou,
    That every knee to Thee should bow!

In Thee, most perfectly expressed,
  The FATHER'S glories shine,
Of the full Deity possessed,
  Eternally Divine—

True image of the Infinite,
  Whose essence is concealed;
Brightness of uncreated light,
  The heart of GOD revealed—

But the high mysteries of Thy name
  An angel's grasp transcend;
The FATHER only (glorious claim!)
  The SON can comprehend—

Yet loving Thee, on whom His love
  Ineffable doth rest,
Thy members all, in Thee above,
  As one with Thee are blest—

Throughout the universe of bliss
  (The centre Thou, and Sun!)
The eternal theme of praise is this,
  To Heaven's belovèd One—

73 Redemption 9.8.9.8.9.8 and Chorus

P. Billhorn

CHORUS

rit.

THOU life of my life, blessed Saviour,
  Thy death was the death that
    was mine,
For me was Thy cross and Thine
    anguish,
  Thy love and Thy sorrow divine;
Thou hast suffered the cross and the
    judgment,
  That I might for ever go free—
    *A thousand, a thousand thanks-
      givings
    I bring, my LORD JESUS, to Thee!*

For me hast Thou borne the re-
    proaches,
  The mockery, hate, and disdain,
The blows and the spitting of sinners,
  The scourging, the shame, and the
    pain;   [ment,
To save me from bondage and judg-
  Thou gladly hast suffered for me—

O LORD, from my heart do I thank
    Thee
  For all Thou hast borne in my room,
Thine agony, dying unsolaced,
  Alone in the darkness and gloom,
That I in the glory of heaven
  For ever and ever might be—

74   Supremacy 8.6.8.6.8.8
(Palmyra 72)

Norman Tomblin

ETERNAL WORD, eternal SON!
   The FATHER'S constant joy, [art
What Thou hast done and what Thou
   Shall all our tongues employ:
Our Life, our LORD, we Thee adore,
Worthy art Thou for evermore!

The SON, in whom all fulness dwells,
   Through whom all glories flow,
Thou didst the human form assume
   That we our GOD might know;
Our Life, our Head, we Thee adore,
Worthy art Thou for evermore!

   Declarer of the FATHER'S name,
     Expression of His grace,
   The Word of life, the Light of men,
     The LORD with unveiled face--
   Our Joy, our Hope, we Thee adore,
   Worthy art Thou for evermore!

75 Luther's Hymn 8.7.8.7.8.8.7

R.C. Chapman   M. Luther

THE LORD of glory! who is He?
  Who is the King of glory?
Only the SON of GOD can be
  The CHRIST, the King of glory:
Consider all His wounds, and see
How JESU'S death upon the tree
  Proclaims Him King of glory.

Above all heavens, at GOD'S
    right hand,
  Now sits the King of glory;
The angels by His favour stand
  Before the throne of glory;
Swiftly they fly at His command,
To guard His own of every land,
  To keep the heirs of glory.

Death and the grave confess the Lamb
  To be the King of glory;
The powers of darkness dread His
    name,
  All creatures show His glory:
He said, "Ere Abraham was I AM";
JESUS is evermore the same,
  The Almighty King of glory.

Thrice happy who in Him believe,
  They soon will share His glory;
Born of His SPIRIT, they receive
  His secret pledge of glory; [grieve,
Taught by His cross, for sin they
He calls them brethren, and they
    cleave
  To Him, their hope of glory.

76 Mainzer L.M.
(Arizona 834)

J. Mainzer

JESUS! in whom all glories meet,
  Whose praise through earth and
    heaven shall ring,
Thy name, than all beside more sweet,
  With hearts adoring would we sing.

Thou as our Paschal Lamb wast slain,
  Thy blood has met the avenger's
    eye;
Beneath that shelter we remain,
  And keep the feast, nor fear, nor die.

A Priest for ever, Thou art there
  For us, the holiest within;
Our names upon Thy breast to bear,
  Absolved from every charge of sin.

There, in the FATHER's love we dwell,
  Called by His grace His sons to be,
And now in songs adoring tell.
  We owe it all, O LORD, to Thee!

77   **Sharon 8.7.8.7**
R.C. Chapman   (Stuttgart 217)   Wm. Boyce

JESUS, in His heavenly temple,
  Sits with GOD upon the throne;
Now no more to be forsaken,
  His humiliation gone.

Never more shall GOD the FATHER
  Smite the Shepherd with the sword;
Ne'er again shall cruel scorners
  Set at nought our glorious LORD.

Dwelling in eternal sunshine
  Of the countenance of GOD,
JESUS fills all heaven with incense
  Of His reconciling blood.

On His heart our names are graven;
  On His shoulders we are borne;
Of our GOD beloved in JESUS,
  We now love Him in return.

78 Beatitudo C.M.
Isaac Watts (St. Bernard 5) John B. Dykes

JESUS! in Thee our eyes behold
  A thousand glories more
Than the rich gems and polished gold
  The sons of Aaron wore.

They first their own sin-offering brought,
  To purge themselves from sin;
Thy life was pure, without a spot,
  And all Thy nature clean.

Fresh blood, as constant as the day,
  Was on their altars spilt;
But Thy *one* offering took away
  For ever all our guilt.

Their priesthood ran through several hands,
  For mortal was their race;
Thy never-changing office stands
  Eternal as Thy days.

Their range was earth, nor higher soared;
  The heaven of heavens is Thine:
Thy majesty and priesthood, LORD,
  Through endless ages shine.

79 Goshen 7.7.8.7. D
W. Yerbury (Bishopsqarth 67)

THY love we own, LORD JESUS!
　In service unremitting,
Within the veil Thou dost prevail,
　Each soul for worship fitting:
Encompassed here with failure,
　Each earthly refuge fails us;
Without, within, beset with sin,
　Thy name alone avails us.

Thy love we own, LORD JESUS;
　For, though Thy toils are ended,
Thy tender heart doth take its part
　With those Thy grace befriended:
Thy sympathy, how precious!
　Thou succourest in sorrow,
And bid'st us cheer, while pilgrims here,
　And haste the hopeful morrow.

Thy love we own, LORD JESUS!
　Thy way is traced before Thee;
Thou wilt descend and we ascend,
　To meet in heavenly glory:
Soon shall the blissful morning
　Call forth Thy saints to meet Thee;
Our only LORD, by all adored,
　With gladness then we'll greet Thee.

Thy love we own, LORD JESUS!
　We wait to see Thy glory,
To know as known, and fully own
　Thy perfect grace before Thee:
We plead Thy parting promise,
　"Come quickly" to release us;
Then endless praise our lips shall raise,
　For love like Thine, LORD JESUS.

80 Penlan 7.6.7.6. D

Mary Peters   (Ewing 439)   D. Jenkins

UNWORTHY our thanksgiving,
  All service stained with sin,
Except as Thou art living,
  Our Priest, to bear it in ;
In every act of worship,
  In every loving deed,
Our thoughts around Thee centre,
  As meeting all our need.

A bond that nought can sever
  Has fixed us to the Rock—
Sin put away for ever
  For all the Shepherd's flock ;
And, LORD, Thy perfect fitness
  To do a Kinsman's part,
The HOLY GHOST doth witness
  To each believer's heart.

As dews that fall on Hermon
  Refresh the plains below,
The SPIRIT's holy unction
  Through Thee to us doth flow :
Ah, then, how good and pleasant
  As one to live in love,
And rise o'er all things present,
  In hope of joys above!

81 **Christchurch 6.6.6.6.8.8**
Isaac Watts   (Millennium 634)   C. Steggall

1 WE give eternal praise
   To GOD the FATHER'S love,
 For all our blessings here,
   And better hopes above:
 He sent His own belovèd SON
 To die for sins that man had done.

2 To GOD the SON belongs
   Eternal glory too,
 Who saved us by His blood
   From everlasting woe:
 And now He lives, and soon will reign,
 To see the fruit of all His pain.

3 To GOD the SPIRIT'S name,
   Eternal thanks we give,
 Whose new-creating power
   Made us, dead sinners, live.
 His work completes the great design,
 And fills our souls with joy divine.

82 Hold Thou My Hand 11.10.11.10

Margaret C. Campbell   (O Perfect Love 934)   H.P. Main

PRAISE ye JEHOVAH! Praise the
  LORD most holy,
Who cheers the contrite, girds with
  strength the weak;
Praise Him who will with glory crown
  the lowly,   [meek,
And with salvation beautify the

Praise ye the LORD for all His loving-
  kindness,
And all the tender mercies He has
  shewn;
Praise Him who pardons all our sin
  and blindness,
And calls us sons, and seals us for
  His own.

Praise ye JEHOVAH—Source of all our
  blessing
Before His gifts earth's richest boons
  wax dim;
Resting in Him, His peace and joy
  possessing,
All things are ours, for we have all
  in Him.

Praise ye the FATHER, GOD the LORD,
  who gave us,
With full and perfect love, His only
  SON!
Praise ye the SON, who died Himself
  to save us!
  Praise ye the SPIRIT! Praise the
  THREE in ONE!

83   Crüger 7.6.7.6. D
(Ellacombe 91)   J. Crüger

OUR FATHER, we would worship
   In JESU's holy name,
For He, whate'er our changes,
   For ever is the same;
Through Him Thy children's praises
   As incense sweet will be;
The songs Thy SPIRIT raises
   Can ne'er want melody.

The fire Thy love hath kindled
   Shall never be put out;
Thy SPIRIT keeps it burning,
   Though dimmed by sin and doubt:
Oh, make it burn more brightly,
   By faith more freely shine,
That we may value rightly
   The grace that made us Thine!

84 — St. Catherine 8.8.8.8.8.8
J.G. Deck (Pater Omnium 44) J.G. Walton

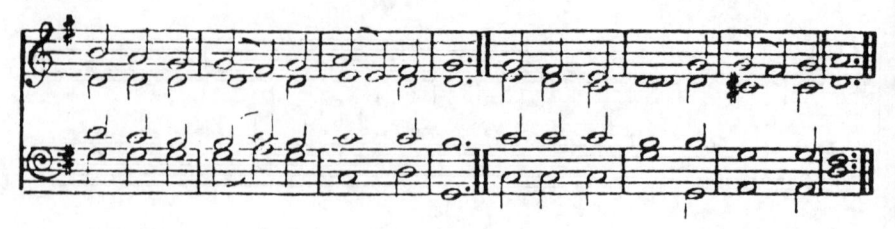

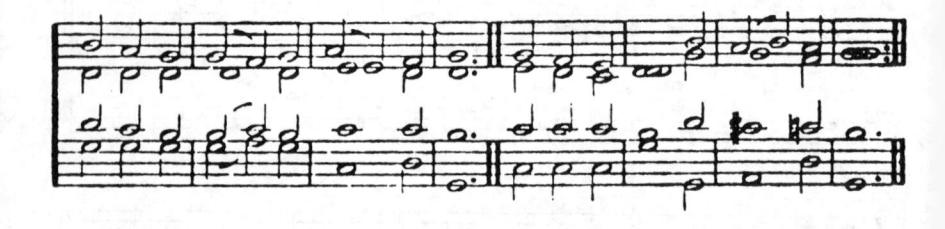

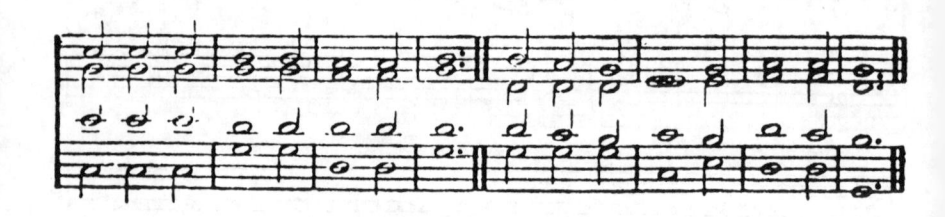

O GOD, Thou now hast glorified
 Thy holy, Thine eternal SON!
The Nazarene, the Crucified,
 Now sits exalted on Thy throne:
To Him, in faith, we cry aloud,
'Worthy art Thou, O Lamb of GOD!'

FATHER, Thy holy name we bless,
 And gladly hail Thy just decree,
That every tongue shall yet confess
 JESUS the LORD of all to be;
But Thy rich grace has taught *us* now
To Him as LORD the knee to bow.

Him as *our* LORD we gladly own,
 To Him alone we now would live;
We bow our hearts before Thy throne,
 And in His name our praises give;
Our willing voices cry aloud,
'Worthy art Thou, O Lamb of GOD!'

Nelson 6.6.8.6.8.8
(Pisgah 141)   Harmonised by G.F. Knowles

WE praise Thee, blessèd GOD,
   Thou everlasting King!
The joyful sound our ears have heard,
   Thy wealth of grace we sing:
We who were guilty, lost, undone,
Are saved by Thy belovèd SON.

Thou art our FATHER now,
   And we, Thy children dear,
Adoring, in Thy presence bow,
   With holy, filial fear:
We love to own a FATHER'S claim,
We glory in a SAVIOUR'S name.

Soon shall we sing Thy praise
   In fuller, richer strain,
And bid farewell to exile days,
   Nor grieve Thee e'er again:
'Twill need a whole eternity,
O GOD, our GOD, for praising Thee!

86 Calon Lan 8.7.8.7.D
(Excelling 87)

J.G. Deck   John Hughes (Glandwr)

"ABBA, FATHER!" we approach Thee
In our Saviour's precious name;
We, Thy children, here assembled,
Now Thy promised blessing claim:
From our sins His blood hath washed us,
'Tis through Him our souls draw nigh,
And Thy SPIRIT too hath taught us
"ABBA, FATHER," thus to cry.

Once as prodigals we wandered
In our folly far from Thee;
But Thy grace, o'er sin abounding,
Rescued us from misery:
Thou Thy prodigals hast pardoned,
Kissed us with a FATHER'S love,
Spread the festive board, and called us
E'er to dwell with Thee above.

Clothed in garments of salvation,
At Thy table is our place;
We rejoice, and Thou rejoicest,
In the riches of Thy grace:
'It is meet,' we hear Thee saying,
'We should merry be and glad;
I have found My once lost children,
Now they live who once were dead.'

"ABBA, FATHER!" all adore Thee,
All rejoice in heaven above,
While in *us* they learn the wonders
Of Thy wisdom, grace, and love:
Soon before Thy throne assembled,
All Thy children shall proclaim,
'Glory, everlasting glory,
Be to GOD and to the LAMB!

87   Excelling 8.7.8.7. D
Robt. Hawker   (Austria 89)   John Zundel

"ABBA, FATHER!" now we call Thee,
  Praise Thy name from day to day:
'Tis Thy children's right to know Thee,
  None but children "FATHER" say:
This high glory we inherit,
  Thy free gift, through JESU's blood:
GOD the SPIRIT with our spirit
  Witnesseth we're sons of GOD.

Thine own purpose gave us being,
  When, in CHRIST, in that vast plan,
Thou didst choose the Church in JESUS,
  Long before the world began:
Oh, what love the FATHER bore us,
  Oh, how precious is His sight,
When He gave His Church to JESUS—
  JESUS, His whole soul's delight!

Though our nature's fall in Adam
  Seemed to shut us out from GOD,
Thus it was His counsel brought us
  Nearer still, through JESU's blood;
For in Him we found redemption,
  Grace and glory in the SON—
Oh, the height and depth of mercy,
  CHRIST and we, thro' grace, are one!

Hence, through all the changing seasons—
  Trouble, sorrow, sickness, woe—
Nothing changeth GOD's affection,
  ABBA's love shall bring us through;
Soon shall all Thy blood-bought children
  Round the throne their anthems raise,
And, in songs of rich salvation,
  Sing to GOD's eternal praise.

88
Requiem 8.7.8.7.7.7.
(Gounod 213)

Mary Peters

W. Schulthes

Org.

HOLY FATHER, we address Thee,
   Loved in Thy belovèd SON:
Holy SON of GOD, we bless Thee—
   Boundless grace hath made us one;
May the SPIRIT aid our songs—
This glad work to Him belongs.

Wondrous was Thy love, our FATHER!
   Wondrous Thine, O SON of GOD!
Vast the love that bruised and wounded!
   Vast the love that bore the rod!
May the SPIRIT still reveal
How those stripes alone could heal.

Gracious FATHER, Thy good pleasure
   Is to love us as Thy SON,
Meting out the self-same measure,
   Since Thou seest us as one:
By Thee, SAVIOUR, loved are we,
As the FATHER loveth Thee!

Hallelujah! we are hasting
   To our FATHER'S house above;
By the way our souls are tasting
   Rich and everlasting love:
In JEHOVAH is our boast—
FATHER, SON and HOLY GHOST!

89 Austria 8.7.8.7.D
(Hyfrydol 49)

H. Maull F.J. Haydn

HOLY FATHER! we would praise Thee
For Thy love, exceeding great,
And give thanks, as we remember
All our helpless, lost estate:
Born in sin, from youth transgressing
Without hope, afar from GOD,
Thy rich mercy brought salvation,
Making peace through JESU's blood!

No more aliens, no more strangers,
But Thy sons and heirs, our GOD;
First-fruits of Thy new creation,
Made anew in CHRIST the LORD;
Quickened and together raisèd
By Thine own almighty power,
Now we sit in heavenly places,
Fall before Thee, and adore!

FATHER, we would likewise than' Thee
For the HOLY SPIRIT given,
Earnest of a full redemption
When the LORD descends from heaven:
Then shall we be changed and fashioned
Like unto Thy glorious SON,
Sound Thy praise through endless ages,
Telling what Thy grace hath done!

90 Ewing 7.6.7.6.D
H. Maull   (Lymington 16)   A. Ewing

WE bless Thee, O our FATHER,
  For Thine electing grace;
Before the world's foundation
  Thy purposes we trace—
That Thou wouldst have a people
  Redeemed by precious blood,
To dwell with Thee in glory,
  Beloved as sons of GOD.

We loved not Thee, our FATHER,
  But Thou didst first love us;
Didst send Thy SON as Saviour
  To bear our guilt and curse;
In whom Thy saints were chosen
  To stand in Him complete,
Awaiting that glad moment
  When we our LORD shall meet.

We come to Thee with singing,
  Our FATHER and our GOD,
Our grateful praises bringing
  Through JESUS CHRIST our LORD:
Thy SPIRIT, who hath sealed us,
  In grace doth lead us on,
Till we inherit glory,
  And bow before Thy throne.

91   **Ellacombe C.M.D.**
John Withy   (St. Matthew 116)   German

IN songs of praise, our GOD, to Thee
   We lift our voices high,
For each unfolded mystery
   Of grace to us brought nigh:
Wondrous the love that first began
   In counsel deep to lay
Foundation sure for ruined man,
   Thy glory to display.

We praise Thee for that gift divine—
   The SON, from off Thy throne,
Whose ways of truth and mercy shine
   In perfectness Thine own:
We praise Thee for the HOLY GHOST,
   Sent forth to win a Bride
From out the lost—a ransomed host—
   For JESUS glorified.

Father of mercies, Thee we praise!
   The glory Thine alone!
Thy SON, Thy SPIRIT, sent to raise
   Lost sinners to a throne!
And this throughout the hosts above
   The joy and song shall be—
The FATHER'S wondrous work of love,
   Redemption's mystery!

Whitburn L.M.

J.G. Deck   (Festus 332)   H. Baker

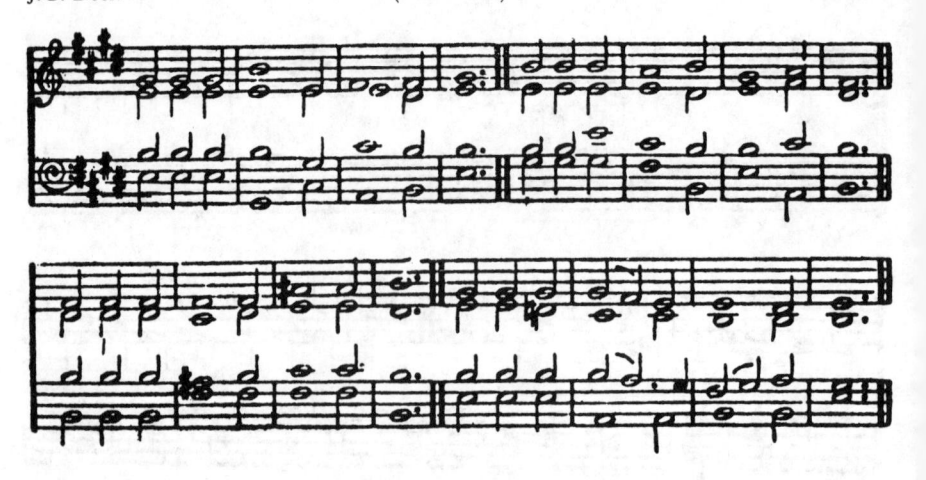

OFT we, alas! forget the love
  Of Him who bought us with His blood,
And now, as our High Priest above,
  Stands as our Advocate with GOD.

Oft we forget the woe, the pain,
  The sweat of blood, the accursèd tree,
The wrath His soul did once sustain,
  From sin and death to set us free.

Oft we forget that, strangers here,
  This world is not our rest or home;
That, waiting till our LORD appear,
  Our hearts should cry, 'Come, Saviour, come!'

Oft we forget that we are *one*
  With every saint that loves His name—
To Him united on the throne,
  Our life, our hope, our LORD the same.

Oh, then what love is here displayed,
  That JESUS did this feast provide
The very night He was betrayed,
  The very night before He died!

Here, in the broken bread and wine,
  We hear Him say, 'Remember Me:
I gave My life to ransom thine;
  I bore thy curse to set thee free!'

Lord, we are Thine, we praise Thy love;
  One with Thy saints, all one in Thee:
We would, until we meet above,
  In all our ways *remember Thee.*

93   Munich 7.6.7.6.D
Christian Gregor   (Crüger 83)   German melody

BEHOLD, my soul, the Saviour
  Pours out His life and blood,
Thee to restore to favour,
  And reconcile to GOD!
His death thy guilt erases,
  His stripes give thee relief;
Rise, then, and sing His praises
  Who turns to joy thy grief.

I see Him in the garden,
  In sorrow and in tears;
In prospect of sin's burden,
  I hear His earnest prayers!
I see Him faint and languish,
  As prostrate there He lay,
Till through His pores in anguish,
  The blood-sweat forced its way.

I fully am assurèd
  My Saviour loveth me,
By all He hath endurèd
  In His great agony;
His back ploughed o'er with furrows,
  His side pierced with a spear,
And unexampled sorrows,
  His boundless love declare.

My blessèd theme is JESUS;
  All else I count but loss;
No other subject pleases·
  I glory in His cross!
With inward spirit's ardour
  I praise Him for His grace;
O LORD, increase this fervour
  Till I shall see Thy face!

94 Cross of Jesus 7.6.7.6.D

Paul Gerhardt (Passion Chorale 115) Ira D. Sankey

O HEAD, so full of bruises,
  So full of pain and scorn;
'Midst other sore abuses,
  Mocked with a crown of thorn!
O Head, ere now surrounded
  With brightest majesty,
In death once bowed and wounded,
  Accursèd on the tree!

Thou Countenance transcendent,
  Thou life-creating Sun
To worlds on Thee dependent,
  Yet bruised and spit upon!
O LORD, what Thee tormented
  Was our sins' heavy load;
We had the debt augmented
  Which Thou didst pay in blood!

And oh, what consolation
  Doth in our hearts take place
When we Thy toil and passion
  Can gratefully retrace!
Ah! should we, while thus musing
  On our Redeemer's cross,
E'en life itself be losing,
  Great gain would be that loss!

We give Thee thanks unfeignèd.
  O JESUS, Friend in need,
For what Thy soul sustainèd
  When Thou for us didst bleed:
Grant us to lean unshaken
  Upon Thy faithfulness,
Until from hence we're taken
  To see Thee face to face!

95   **St. James C.M.**
S. Trevor Francis   (St. Flavian 32)   Raphael Courtiville

WE would remember, LORD, Thy
    cross,
  The tempest and the flood,
Thy soul for sin an offering,
  Thy precious, out-poured blood.

Thine opened side, Thy piercèd hands,
  Are tokens of Thy woe,
Unfolding that deep shoreless love
  Our hearts so feebly know.

O GOD, we worship, we adore!
  Thy love our theme must be;
And ever, as the ages roll,
  Shall praise ascend to Thee!

96   Bullinger 8.5.8.3
(Stephanos 658)   E.W. Bullinger

L ORD and Saviour, we remember,
  In Thine hour of shame,
Thou to GOD *Thyself* didst render—
  Praise Thy name!

Blessèd Saviour, we remember
  Thou didst meet our foe,
When the darkness gathered round
    Thee,
  And the woe.

Holy Saviour, we remember
  Bitter was Thy cry,
When, for sin by GOD forsaken,
  Wrath was nigh.

Glorious Saviour, we remember
  Thou didst overcome;
Through Thy victory we, once captive,
  Are brought home.

LORD and Saviour, we remember
  And would prize Thy love;
All its fulness do Thou teach us
  From above!

97   Hart's 7.7.7.7
(University College 149)   B. Milgrove

PRAISE thy Saviour, O my soul!
　　He has drunk the bitter gall,
Paid thy ransom, set thee free—
Praise Him, praise Him cheerfully.

Oh, the wonders of His love!
See Him coming from above
To atone, and die for thee—
Praise Him, praise Him cheerfully.

See the waves and billows roll
O'er His sinless, spotless soul;
O my soul, it was for thee!
Praise Him, praise Him cheerfully.

Yes, we seek to praise Him now,
Till with saints above we bow,
And to all eternity
Praise Him—praise Him cheerfully.

98   Abridge C.M.
Macleod Wylie   (Dalehurst 345)   Isaac Smith

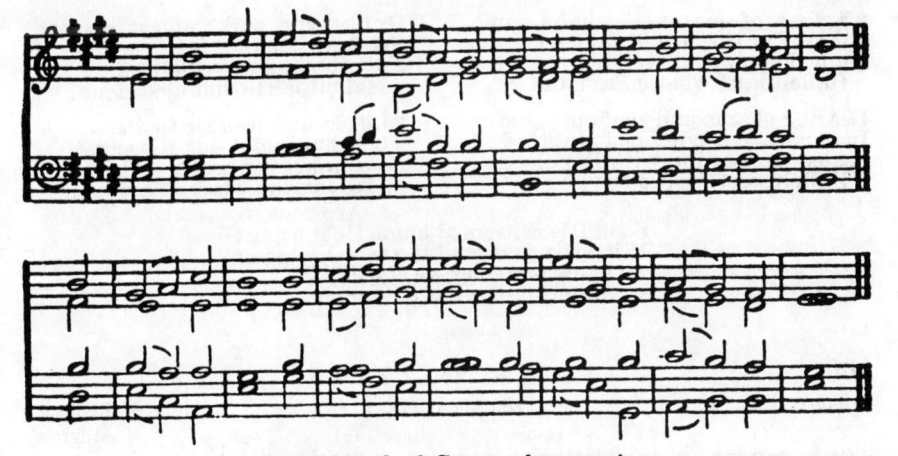

THE blood of CHRIST has precious
　　been;
'Tis precious now to me;
Through it alone my soul has rest,
　From fear and doubt set free.

Not all my well-remembered sins
　Can startle or dismay;
That precious blood atoned for all,
　And swept my guilt away.

Perhaps this feeble frame of mine
　Will soon in sickness lie;
But, resting on that precious blood,
　I peacefully can die!

Oh, wondrous is the crimson tide
　Which from my Saviour flowed!
In heaven above my song shall be—
　The precious, precious blood!

99   Man of Sorrows 7.7.7.8
P.P. Bliss   P.P. Bliss

"MAN of sorrows!" what a name
   For the SON of GOD, who came
Ruined sinners to reclaim!
   Hallelujah! what a Saviour!

Bearing shame and scoffing rude,
In our place condemned He stood;
Sealed our pardon with His blood:
   Hallelujah! what a Saviour!

Guilty, vile, and helpless, we;
Spotless Lamb of GOD was He:
Full atonement—can it be
   Hallelujah! what a Saviour!

"Lifted up" was He to die,
"It is finished," was His cry;
Now in heaven exalted high:
   Hallelujah! what a Saviour!

Soon His ransomed home He'll bring;
With His praise all heaven shall ring
As anew our song we sing:
   'Hallelujah! what a Saviour!'

100   Redhead No.47 7.7.7.6
S. Trevor Francis   (Buckland 159)   R. Redhead

JESUS, we remember Thee,
　Thy deep woe and agony,
All Thy suffering on the tree—
　　　JESUS, we adore Thee!

Calvary, O Calvary!
　Mercy's vast, unfathomed sea,
Love, eternal love to me—
　　　JESUS, we adore Thee!

Darkness hung around Thy head
　When for sin Thy blood was shed,
Victim in the sinner's stead—
　　　JESUS, we adore Thee!

JESUS, hail! Thou now art risen;
　Thou hast all our sins forgiven;
Haste we to our home in heaven—
　　　JESUS, we adore Thee!

　　Soon, with joyful, glad surprise,
　　　We shall hear Thy word—Arise!
　　Mounting upward to the skies,
　　　　With Thee, glory, glory!

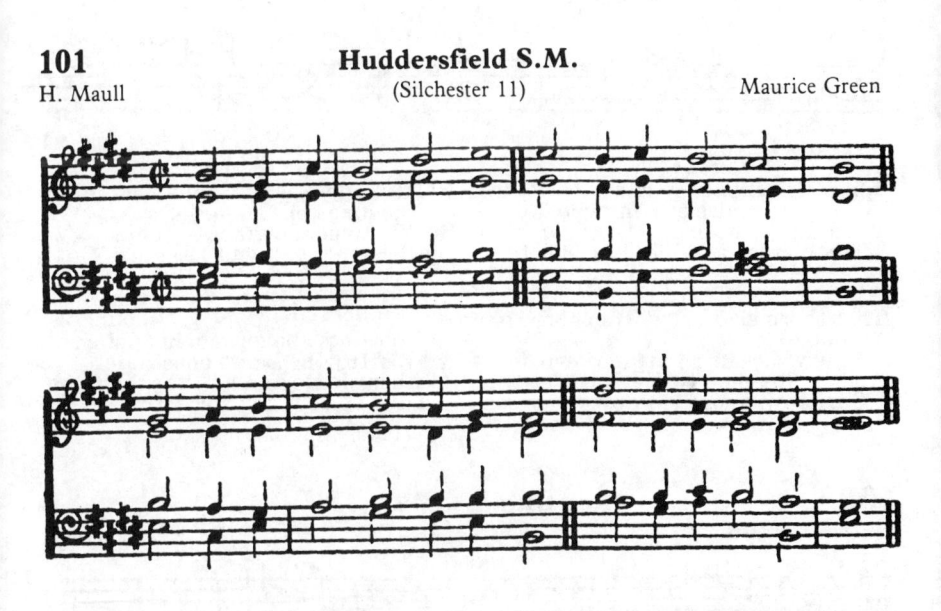

101　　　　　　**Huddersfield S.M.**
H. Maull　　　　　　(Silchester 11)　　　　　　Maurice Green

SAVIOUR, we worship Thee,
　We praise Thee for Thy grace;
Thy precious blood hath set us free
　To take the children's place.

Now, from vain idols turned,
　We serve the living GOD;
Delivered from the wrath to come,
　We wait to see Thee, LORD.

Soon, with a quickening word,
　Thou wilt from heaven come down;
The Archangel's voice, the trump of
　　GOD,
　Shall make Thy presence known.

The sleeping saints will rise,
　And we, with them, shall be
Changed in a moment, and our eyes
　Thy glory then shall see.

　　Till Thou shalt come, O LORD,
　　　We thus remember Thee;
　　Thy piercèd body, Thy shed blood,
　　　In symbol here we see.

102 Jazer C.M.
Mary M. Davis   (St. Peter 24)   A.E. Tozer

WITH contrite spirits now we sing
  The praise of Him who died;
With tender hearts, O LORD, we view
  Thy pierced and bleeding side!

Oh, may those hands, which cruel nails
  Transfixed on Calvary's cross,
Supply to us the grace to count
  All earthly gain but loss!

That thorn-clad brow which bore our
    curse
  Now wears its rightful crown,
And at Thy piercèd feet we'll cast
  Our crowns for ever down!

With saints above we join to sing,
  'Worthy the Lamb once slain!'
With girded loins we "keep the feast"
  Till Thou shalt come again.

103 Dublin C.M.
Douglas Russell   (Jazer 102)   J. Stevenson

AS, gathered to Thy precious name,
 Thy table we surround,
Thy death, LORD JESUS, to proclaim,
 Oh, may our praise abound!

We give what from Thee we receive,
 For all we have is Thine—
Oh, may each heart with joy believe,
 And echo 'Thine is mine!'

Grace, grace it was that brought Thee down;
 Love shone in all Thy ways;
Through death Thine is the Victor's crown,
 And Thine the endless praise.

We, or in silence, or in song,
 Together worship Thee;
Before our GOD we shall ere long
 Give praise eternally.

LORD JESUS CHRIST, Thou comest soon—
 To-day Thy death we show:
In light eclipsing sun at noon
 Its mystery we shall know.

104   Manoah C.M.
Gerard Noel   (Albano 118)   Rossini

IF human kindness meets return,
 And owns the grateful tie;
If tender thoughts within us burn,
 To feel a friend is nigh;

Oh! shall not warmer accents tell
 The gratitude we owe
To Him who died our fears to quell,
 By bearing all our woe?

While yet Thine anguished soul surveyed
 Those pangs Thou wouldst not flee:
What love Thy latest words displayed,
 'In this remember Me!'

Remember Thee—Thy death, Thy shame,
 Our wayward hearts to share;
O JESUS! be Thy holy name
 Deeply engraven there!

105 St. Magnus C.M.
Mary Peters   (Dublin 30)   J. Clark

AROUND Thy table, Holy Lord,
  In fellowship we meet,
Obedient to Thy gracious word,
  This feast of love to eat.

However poor, despised, or few,
  We know Thy changeless love
Is not one whit less warm and true,
  Now on the throne above.

Here every one who loves Thy name,
  Our willing hearts embrace—
Our life, our hope, our joy the same,
  The same Thy love and grace.

Commune with each at this blest
  hour,
And, when we hence depart,
May deeds of love and words of power
  Engage each faithful heart.

106 Munich 7.6.7.6.D
(Missionary 288)   German Melody

WE come, our gracious FATHER,
  With many hearts as one,
And here we only gather
  In memory of Thy SON:
We prize each happy token
  Of peace with Thee, our GOD,
The bread—His body broken;
  The wine—His precious blood.

Oh, give us grace to ponder,
  LORD JESUS, on Thy love,
And see, with silent wonder,
  What drew Thee from above!
Complete in Thy completeness,
  The Church, Thy favoured Bride,
Possesses all the meetness
  Thy perfect love supplied.

107   **Augustine S.M.**
R.C. Chapman   (Boylston 800)   J.S. Bach

WITH JESUS in our midst,
  We gather round the board;
Though many, we are one in CHRIST,
  One body in the LORD.

Our sins were laid on Him,
  When bruised on Calvary;
With CHRIST we died and rose again,
  And sit with Him on high.

Faith eats the bread of life,
  And drinks the living wine;
Thus we, in love together knit,
  On JESU'S breast recline.

Soon shall the night be gone,
  And we with JESUS reign;
The marriage supper of the Lamb
  Shall banish all our pain.

108 **Bullinger 8.5.8.3**

Douglas Russell (Stephanos 658) E.W. Bullinger

1. GATHERED, LORD, around Thy table,
   We now seek Thy face;
   Let us know Thy presence with us,
   LORD of grace!

2. Love divine first drew us to Thee,
   In our sin and need;
   For our sin, in deep compassion,
   Thou didst bleed.

3. Risen LORD, in glory seated,
   We are one with Thee;
   Thou hast snapt the chains that bound us,
   We are free.

4. Gratefully we Thee remember
   As we break the bread—
   Symbol of Thy body broken
   In our stead.

5. Drink we, too, "the cup of blessing"
   Which Thy love has filled;
   Through Thy blood we have redemption,
   Fears are stilled.

6. Backward look we, drawn to Calvary,
   Musing while we sing:
   Forward haste we to Thy coming,
   LORD and KING!

109   St. Alphege 7.6.7.6
(Barton 392)

H.J. Gauntlett

O LORD, by Thee invited,
   We gather in Thy name,
Each willing guest delighted
   Thy presence here to claim.

In time of deepest sadness,
   LORD JESUS, Thou didst prove
Thy heart could still find gladness
   In pouring forth its love.

Oh, depth of Thy compassion!
   The night Thou wast betrayed,
The emblems of Thy passion
   By Thee a feast were made!

The feast is Thine, O Saviour,
   The bread, the cup, are Thine;
Thy name the precious savour
   Of ointment all divine!

Thy body, LORD, was broken,
   That we might eat and live;
We drink the cup, the token
   That Thou Thy life didst give.

We show Thy death, confessing
   We wait for Thee to come;
And safe beneath Thy blessing
   We onward journey home!

110
Boethia Thompson

Banquet 8.7.8.7.D
(Calon Lan 86)

JESUS, LORD, we know Thee present
　At Thy table freshly spread,
Seated at Thy priceless banquet,
　With Thy banner overhead:
Precious moments at Thy table,
　From all fear and doubt set free;
Here to rest we now are able,
　Occupied alone with Thee.

Here, rejoicing in Thy nearness,
　Gladly by the SPIRIT led,
Calmly in the blest remembrance
　Of Thy precious blood once shed,
LORD, we take each simple token
　In fond memory of Thee;
Muse upon Thy body broken,
　And Thy blood which made us free,

Oh, what joy it is to see Thee,
  In these chosen emblems here;
  In the bread and wine of blessing—
    Bread to strengthen, wine to cheer!
Lord, behold us met together,
  One in Thee, our risen Head,
Thus we take the cup of blessing,
  Thus we share the broken bread.

Lord, we know how true Thy promise
  To be with us where we meet,
When in Thy loved name we gather
    To enjoy communion sweet;
Dearer still that looked-for promise,
  To each waiting, yearning heart,
That with Thee we soon shall be,
  Lord,
    Yea, "for ever" where Thou art.

111   Almsgiving 8.8.8.4

Geo. Rawson   (In Memoriam 363(2))   J.B. Dykes

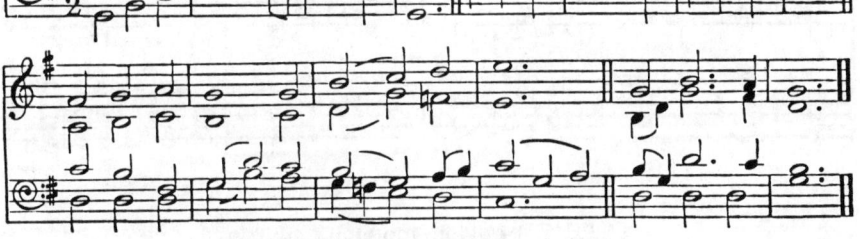

By Christ redeemed, in Christ restored,
We keep the memory adored,
And show the death of our dear Lord,
    Until He come.

His body broken in our stead
Is seen in this memorial bread,
And thus our feeble love is fed,
    Until He come.

The drops of His dread agony,
His life-blood shed for us, we see—
This wine doth tell the mystery,
    Until He come;

Until the trump of God be heard,
Until the ancient graves be stirred,
And with His great commanding word
    The Lord shall come.

Oh, blessèd hope! with this elate,
Let not our hearts be desolate,
But, strong in faith, in patience wait
    Until He come.

112   Pembroke 8.8.6.8.8.6

Mrs. Strong   (Meribah 153)   J. Foster

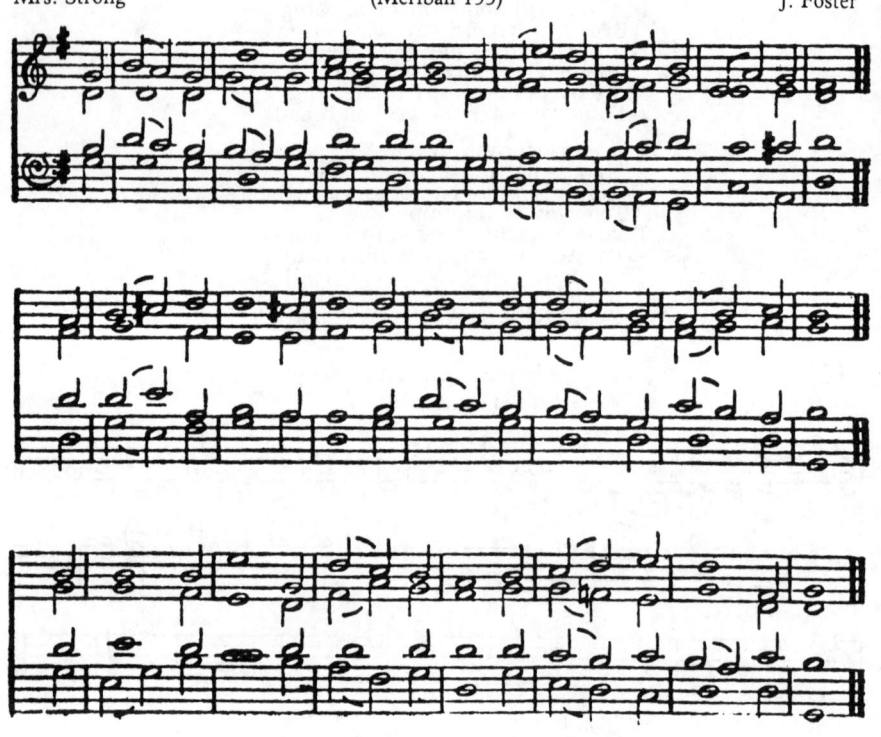

WHILE golden moments swiftly
    glide,
We would together, side by side,
    Shew forth Thy death, O Lord,
In unison Thy praises sing,
Thanksgivings unto Thee would
    bring,
    According to Thy word.

For this one brief yet precious hour
Transport us by Thy Spirit's power,
    Like him of Patmos isle,
To scenes in which earth has no place,
To living founts of love and grace—
    Our joy and peace Thy smile.

Faith backward turns her piercing
Once more to view Gethsemane, [eye
    And weep beneath the cross;
Remembering in the bread and wine
Thy love unspeakable, divine,
    We count all else but dross.

Hope points us forward to the day
When we, together caught away,
  Shall meet Thee in the air;
What joy shall fill our souls when we
Thy face in righteousness shall see,
  And Thine own image bear!

Love, like a mighty ocean tide—
Thy love, O GOD, so vast and wide,
  The same from age to age—
Has won our hearts and sealed us
  Thine;
Now may it brightly in us shine,
And all our thoughts engage.

113   Dennis S.M.
J.G. Deck   (Rhodes 6)   H.G. Nageli (Arr.)

WE bless our Saviour's name,
  Our sins are all forgiven;
To suffer, once to earth He came;
He now is crowned in heaven!

His precious blood was shed,
His body bruised for sin;
Remembering this we break the bread,
And joyful drink the wine.

LORD, we would ne'er forget
Thy rich, Thy precious love,
Our theme of joy and wonder here,
Our endless song above!

Oh, let Thy love constrain
Our souls to cleave to Thee,
And ever in our hearts remain
That word, '*Remember Me.*'

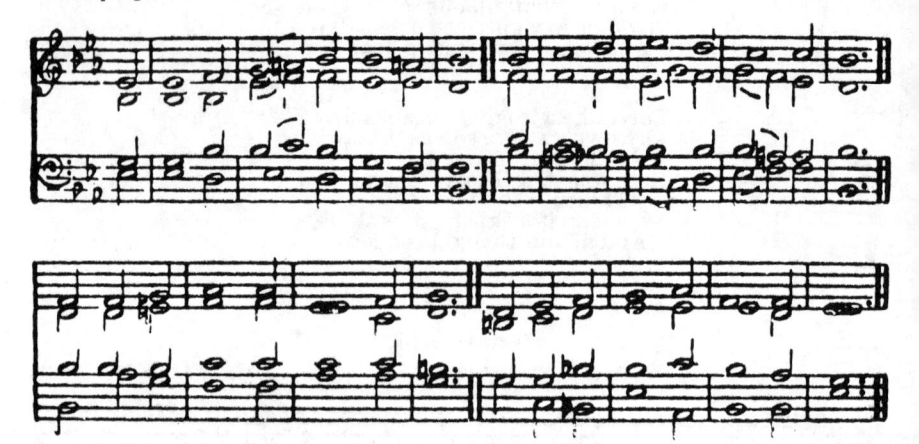

114 Angelus L.M.
C.H. Spurgeon — (Whitburn 34) — J. Scheffler

AMIDST us our Belovèd stands,
And bids us view His piercèd hands,
Points to His wounded feet and side—
Blest emblems of the Crucified.

What food luxurious loads the board,
When at His table sits the LORD!
The wine how rich, the bread how sweet,
When Jesus deigns the guests to meet!

If now, with eyes defiled and dim,
We see the signs but see not Him,
Oh, may His love the scales displace,
And bid us see Him face to face!

Thou glorious Bridegroom of our hearts,
Thy present smile a heaven imparts;
Oh, lift the veil, if veil there be,
Let every saint Thy beauties see!

115 Passion Chorale 7.6.7.6.D
R.C. Chapman — (Rutherford 137) — H.L. Hassler

NO bone of Thee was broken,
  Thou spotless, paschal LAMB!
Of life and peace a token
  To us who know Thy name;
The Head, for all the members,
  The curse, the vengeance bore,
And GOD, our GOD, remembers
  His people's sins no more.

We, Thy redeemed, are reaping
  What Thou didst sow in tears;
This feast which we are keeping
  Thy name to us endears:
It tells of Justice hiding
  The face of GOD from Thee,
Proud men around deriding
  Thy sorrows on the tree.

Thy death of shame and sorrow
  Was like unto Thy birth,
Which would no glory borrow,
  No majesty from earth:
Thy pilgrims, we are hasting
  To our eternal home,
Its joy already tasting
  Of victory o'er the tomb.

Thy life and death reviewing,
  We tread the narrow way;
Our homeward path pursuing,
  We watch the dawn of day:
We eat and drink with gladness
  The living bread and wine,
And sing with sweetest sadness
  Our song of love divine.

116   **St. Matthew C.M.D.**
Boethia Thompson   (Castle Rising 525)   W. Croft

HERE, LORD, we come Thyself to meet,
  As to this feast we come;
Like Mary, resting at Thy feet,
  To learn of Thee alone:
Our hearts recall what Thou hast said,
  "This do," remembering Me;
So thus we take the wine, the bread,
  In memory of Thee.

From *Thee*, O LORD, the bread we take,
  From Thy pierced hand the wine;
At rest, accepted for Thy sake,
  Our meetness, LORD, is Thine!
We praise Thee for this quiet hour,
  Spent with Thyself alone,
We thank Thee for the SPIRIT'S power,
  And His blest teachings own.

O LORD, we know that Thou art here;
  Enrich each memory!
Thy faithful promise brings Thee near,
  And gathers us to Thee:
Thy body broken, poured-out blood—
  Blest memories, ever dear!
Thou Son of Man! Thou Lamb of GOD!
  Thy voice our hearts would hear!

117
Ed. Denny

Zurich S.M.
(St. Michael 309)

Johann G. Nageli

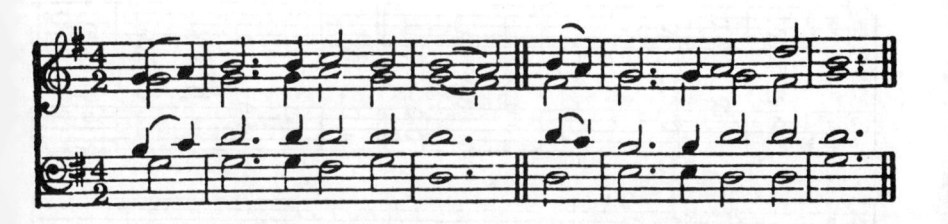

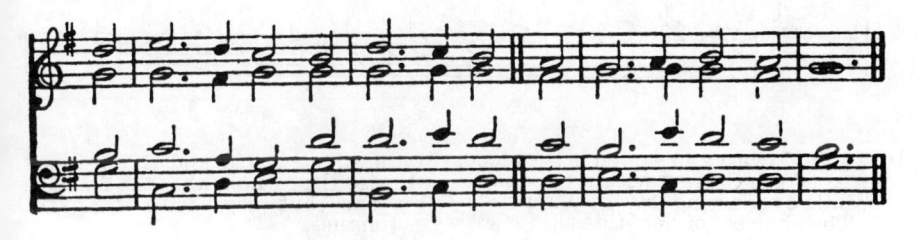

1. SWEET feast of love divine!
'Tis grace that makes us free
To feed upon this bread and wine,
In memory, LORD, of Thee.

2. Here every welcome guest
Waits, LORD, from Thee to learn
The secrets of Thy FATHER'S breast,
And all Thy grace discern.

3. Here conscience ends its strife,
And faith delights to prove
The sweetness of the bread of life,
The fulness of Thy love.

4. Thy blood that flowed for sin,
In symbol here we see,
And feel the blessèd pledge within,
That we are loved of Thee.

5. But if this glimpse of love
Is so divinely sweet,
What will it be, O LORD, above,
Thy gladdening smile to meet—

6. To see Thee face to face,
Thy perfect likeness wear,
And all Thy ways of wondrous grace
Through endless years declare!

118 Albano C.M.
Isaac Watts (St. Bernard 5) V. Novello

HOW sweet and sacred is the place,
  With CHRIST within the doors,
While everlasting love displays
  The choicest of her stores!

While all our hearts and all our songs
  Praise Him who makes the feast,
We can but cry, with thankful
    tongues,
  'LORD, why am *I* a guest?'

'Twas the same love that spread the
    feast
  That sweetly forced us in;
Else we had still refused to taste,
  And perished in our sin.

119 Augustine S.M.
Elizabeth R-Charles (Boylston 800) J.S. Bach

NO gospel like this feast,
　　Spread for Thy Church by Thee;
Nor prophets, nor evangelists
Preach the glad news more free :

All our redemption cost,
　All Thy redemption won ;
All it has won for us, the lost,
　All it cost Thee, the SON.

Thine was the bitter price,
　Ours is the free gift given ;
Thine was the blood of sacrifice,
　Ours is the wine of heaven.

Here we would rest midway,
　As on a sacred height—
That darkest and that brightest day
　Meeting before our sight.

From that dark depth of woes
　Thy love for us has trod,
We soar to heights of blest repose
　Thy love prepares with GOD.

Thus from self's chains released,
　One sight alone we see—
Still at the cross, while at this feast,
　We see Thee, *only Thee !*

120   St. Fulbert C.M.

W. Cowper   (St. Magnus 169)   Hy. J. Gauntlett

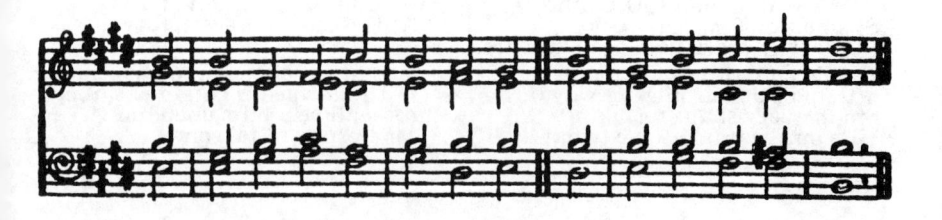

THIS is the feast of heavenly wine,
　And GOD invites to sup ;
The juices of the living Vine
　Were pressed to fill the cup.

We bless the Saviour as we eat,
　With royal dainties fed ;
Not heaven affords a costlier treat,
　For JESUS is the bread.

*For ever be the glory given
　To Thee, O Lamb of GOD !
Our every joy on earth, in heaven,
　We owe it to Thy blood.*

121 Love Divine 8.7.8.7
J.R. Macduff (Stuttgart 217) J. Stainer

BLESSÈD feast! Most gracious token
  Of Thy dying love, O LORD!
Symbols of Thy body broken,
  And Thy precious blood outpoured.

In this holy rite partaking,
  Help us on our pilgrim way;
Sin in every shape forsaking,
  Be our heart's resolve to-day.

Sacred pledge that nought can sever,
  Blessèd Saviour, from Thy love;
Sealed to be Thy guests for ever,
  At the ceaseless feast above.

There, in sweet communion blending,
  With the vast, ingathered throng,
Ours shall be a bliss unending,
  An eternal, festal song!

122 St. Bernard C.M.
Jas. Montgomery (St. Fulbert 120) J. Richardson

ACCORDING to Thy gracious word,
In meek humility,
This will I do, my dying LORD,
I will remember Thee.

Thy body, broken for my sake,
My bread from heaven shall be;
The cup of blessing I will take,
And thus remember Thee.

Gethsemane can I forget,
Or there Thy conflict see,
Thy agony and bloody sweat,
And not remember Thee?

When to the cross I turn mine eyes,
And rest on Calvary,
O Lamb of GOD, my sacrifice!
I must remember Thee;

Remember Thee, and all Thy pains,
And all Thy love to me—
Yea, while a breath, a pulse remains
Would I remember Thee.

And when, O LORD, Thou com'st again,
And I Thy glory see,
For ever, as the Lamb once slain,
Shall I remember Thee!

123   Wells 7.7.7.7.7.7

E.H. Bickersteth   (Maidstone 917)   Dmitri Bortnianski

"TILL He come!" Oh, let the words
Linger on the trembling chords;
Let the "little while" between
In their golden light be seen;
Let us think how heaven and home
Lie beyond that "Till He come."

When the weary ones we love
Enter on their rest above,
When their words of love and cheer
Fall no longer on our ear,
Hush! be every murmur dumb;
It is only ".Till He come."

Clouds and darkness round us press;
Would we have one sorrow less?
All the sharpness of the cross,
All that tells the world is loss,
Death, and darkness, and the tomb,
Pain us only "Till He come."

See, the feast of love is spread;
Drink the wine and eat the bread—
Sweet memorials, till the LORD
Call us round His heavenly board,
Some from earth, from glory some,
Severed only "*Till He come!*"

124   **Troyte's Chant 7.7.7.6**   A.H.D. Troyte
H. Bonar   (Thanksgiving 928)

FOR the bread and for the wine,
  For the pledge that seals Him mine,
For the words of love divine,
  We give Thee thanks, O LORD!

Only bread and only wine,
Yet to faith the solemn sign
Of the heavenly and divine—
  We give Thee thanks, O LORD!

For the words that turn our eye
To the cross of Calvary,
Bidding us in faith draw nigh,
  We give Thee thanks, O LORD!

For the words that tell of home,
Pointing us beyond the tomb—
'Do ye this until I come,'
  We give Thee thanks, O LORD!

"Till He come" we take the bread,
Type of Him on whom we feed,
Him who liveth and was dead!
  We give Thee thanks, O LORD!

"Till He come" we take the cup;
As we at His table sup,
Eye and heart are lifted up—
  We give Thee thanks, O LORD!

For that coming, here foreshown,
For that day to man unknown,
For the glory and the throne,
  We give Thee thanks, O LORD!

---

125   **St. John's, Hoxton 6.6.8.4**   E.H.G. Sargent
                           (Angeli 923)

LORD JESUS, in Thy name
  We round Thy table now
Remember thus Thy death of shame,
  Thy thorn-crowned brow.

Master! from Thy blest hand
  This broken bread we take,
Responsive to Thine own command,
  For Thy name's sake.

We in this wine would see
 The measure of Thy love,
That love which bids us joy in Thee,
 Enthroned above.

Here would we rest, O LORD,
 Here banish doubt and fear,
Here feast on Thee, Thou Living Word,
 And know Thee near.

Keep us Thine own, we pray,
 Our Saviour! so may we
In thought, in word, in deed, alway
 Remember Thee.

126   **St. Fulbert C.M.**
(St. Bernard 5)   H.J. Gauntlett

O LORD, how infinite Thy love!
 It spans all time and space,
Enwraps Thy loved ones to the end
 In its encircling grace.

We shew Thy death till Thy return—
 Thou for *our* sins didst die!
'Remember Me,' Thy parting word;
 'Amen,' our hearts reply.

In life and glory one with Thee,
 We own no place below
Save that which links us with **Thy**
  death,
 Whence life and glory flow.

With Thee, apart from all things here,
 We worship, we adore;
While pleasures at our GOD'S right
  hand
 Await us evermore.

127   **Excelling 8.7.8.7.D**
A.S.W.   (Bethany 242)   John Zundel

O THOU tender, gracious Shepherd,
   Shedding for us Thy life's blood,
Unto shame and death delivered,
   All to bring us nigh to GOD!
Now our willing hearts adore Thee;
   Now we praise Thy changeless love,
While by faith we come before Thee,
   Faith which lifts our souls above.

As our Surety we behold Thee,
   Ransoming our souls from death;
As the willing Victim view Thee,
   Yielding up to GOD Thy breath:
In this broken bread we own Thee,
   Bruised for us and put to shame;
And this cup, O LORD, we thank Thee,
   Speaks our pardon thro' Thy name.

Blessèd supper of thanksgiving,
   Feast of more than angels' food!
Bread of life and cup of blessing—
   This is fellowship with GOD!
Feeble praise we now are bringing;
   But when, LORD, we see Thy face,
Better songs of triumph singing,
   We shall own Thy matchless grace.

128   **Calon Lan 8.7.8.7.D**
Ed. Denny   (Excelling 127)   John Hughes (Glandwr)

WHILE in sweet communion feed-
    ing
  On this earthly bread and wine,
Saviour, may we see Thee bleeding
  On the cross to make us Thine!
Thus our eyes for ever closing
  To this fleeting world below,
On Thy gentle breast reposing,
  Teach us, LORD, Thy grace to know.

Though unseen, be ever near us,
  With the still, small voice of love,
Whispering words of peace to cheer
    us—
  Every doubt and fear remove;
Bring before us all the story
  Of Thy life and death of woe,
And with hopes of endless glory
  Wean our hearts from all below.

129
G.W. Frazer

Munich 7.6.7.6.D
(Missionary 288)

German Melody

ON that same night, LORD JESUS,
  In which Thou wast betrayed,
When without cause man's hatred
  Against Thee was displayed,
We hear Thy gracious accents—
  'This do; remember Me:'
With joyful hearts responding,
  We would remember Thee.

We think of all the darkness
  Which round Thy spirit pressed;
Of all those waves and billows
  Which rolled across Thy breast;
'Tis there Thy grace unbounded,
  And perfect love we see;
With joy and yet with sorrow
  We do remember Thee.

We know Thee now as risen,
  "The First-born from the dead;"
We see Thee now ascended,
  The Church's glorious Head:
In Thee by grace accepted,
  With heart and mind set free,
We think of all Thy sorrow,
  And thus remember Thee.

Till Thou shalt come in glory
  And call us hence away,
To share with Thee the brightness
  Of that unclouded day,
We show Thy death, LORD JESUS,
  And here would seek to be
More to that death conformèd,
  Whilst we remember Thee.

130
Mary Peters

Stuttgart 8.7.8.7
(Cross of Jesus, Stainer 142)

German

O H, how blessèd to be bidden
   To the marriage of the LAMB!
There the saints, now scattered, hidden,
  All will meet in JESU's name.

None shall thither come in weakness,
None without the power to taste,
None remain away through sickness,
None the rich provision waste.

Faith in our *eternal* union
  With each other and the LORD,
Makes these seasons of communion
  Rich, unfailing joy afford.

Are such broken portions pleasant?
  What must be the gathered whole?
What the bliss with Thee, LORD, present,
  As the joy of *every* soul?

Thou dost give this way-side earnest
  Of our gathering at the end,
And we wait till Thou returnest,
  Evermore our mighty Friend!

131   **Fingal C.M.**
         (Lloyd 8)
                                J.S. Anderson

J ESUS, Thou true and living Vine,
   Whose precious clusters press'd,
Yield us the new and cheering wine,
  We drink, and we are bless'd.

O LORD, we take from Thy pierced hand
  The cup—salvation free;
It tells that all our souls demand,
  In grace flows forth from Thee.

And soon the marriage feast will come,
  When Thou with us wilt share
The new wine in the FATHER's home,
  With joy for ever there.

The Bride, with Thee in glory crowned,
  The song of grace shall sing;
While to creation's utmost bound
  Thy name and praise shall ring.

132 St. Agnes 10.10.10.10

H. Bonar (Ellers 690) J. Langran

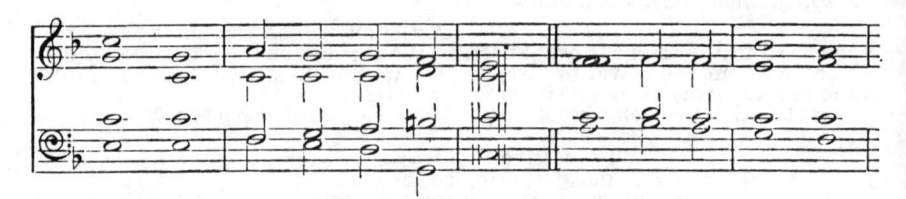

HERE, O my LORD, I see Thee face to face;
Here faith can touch and handle things unseen;
Here would I grasp with firmer hand Thy grace,
And all my weariness upon Thee [lean.

I have no help but Thine; nor do I need
Another arm save Thine to lean upon;
It is enough, my LORD, enough, indeed;
My strength is in Thy might, Thy might alone.

Here would I feed upon the bread of GOD;
Here drink with Thee the royal wine of heaven;
Here would I lay aside each earthly load;
Here taste afresh the calm of sin forgiven.

Too soon we rise, the symbols disappear;
The feast, though not the love, is past and gone;
The bread and wine remove, but Thou art here—
Nearer than ever—still my shield and sun.

Mine, mine the sin, but Thine the righteousness;
Mine, mine the guilt, but Thine the cleansing blood;
Here is my robe, my refuge, and my peace—
Thy blood, Thy righteousness, O LORD, my GOD!

Feast after feast thus comes and passes by,
Yet, passing, points to the glad feast above,
And gives sweet foretastes of the festal joy,
The LAMB'S great bridal feast of bliss and love.

133
Ed. Denny

Farrant C.M.
(Abridge 151)

R. Farrant

1. 'TIS past, the dark and dreary night,
   And, LORD, we hail Thee now
 Our Morning Star, without a cloud
   Of sadness on Thy brow.

2. Thy path on earth, the cross, the grave,
   Thy sorrows all are o'er;
 And oh, sweet thought, Thine eye shall weep,
   Thy heart shall break no more!

3. Deep were those sorrows—deeper still
   The love that brought Thee low;
 That bade the streams of life from Thee,
   A lifeless Victim, flow

4. The soldier, as he pierced Thee, proved
   Man's hatred, LORD, to Thee;
 While in the blood that stained the spear,
   Love, only love, we see.

5. Drawn from Thy pierced and bleeding side,
   That pure and cleansing flood
 Speaks peace to every heart that knows
   The virtue of Thy blood.

6. Yet 'tis not that we know the joy
   Of cancelled sin alone,
 But, happier far, Thy saints are called
   To share Thy glorious throne.

7. So closely are we linked in love,
   So wholly one with Thee,
 That all Thy bliss and glory then
   Thy gift to us shall be.

134 Agnus Dei 8.8.8.6

Mary J.D. Walker   Wm. Blow

THE wanderer no more will roam,
  The lost one to the fold hath come,
The prodigal is welcomed home,
    O Lamb of GOD, in Thee!

Though clad in rags, by sin defiled,
The FATHER hath embraced His child;
And I am pardoned, reconciled,
    O Lamb of GOD, in Thee!

It is the FATHER'S joy to bless,
His love has found for me a dress—
A robe of spotless righteousness,
    O Lamb of GOD, in Thee!

And now my famished soul is fed,
A feast of love for me is spread,
I feed upon the children's bread,
    O Lamb of GOD, in Thee!

Yea, in the fulness of His grace,
He puts me in the children's place,
Where I may gaze upon His face.
    O Lamb of GOD, in Thee!

And when I in Thy likeness shine,
The glory and the praise be Thine,
That everlasting joy is mine.
    O Lamb of GOD, in Thee!

135 Morcambe 10.10.10.10

W.P. Mackay   (St. Agnes, Langran 132)   F.C. Atkinson

THE LORD is risen; the Red Sea's
judgment flood
Is passed in Him who bought us with
His blood:
The LORD is risen; we stand beyond
the doom
Of all our sin, through JESU'S empty
tomb.

The LORD is risen; with Him we also
rose,
And in His grave see all our vanquished foes:
The LORD is risen; beyond the judgment land,
In Him, in resurrection-life, we stand.

The LORD is risen; shut in are we
with GOD,
To tread the desert which His feet
have trod:
The LORD is risen; the holiest is our
place;
Where now we dwell before the
FATHER'S face.

The LORD is risen; the LORD is gone
before;
We long to see Him, and to sin no
more:
The LORD is risen, our triumph-shout
shall be;
Thou hast prevailed! Thy people,
LORD, are free!

136   Wiltshire C.M.
(Westminster 551)   G. Smart

MY tongue shall spread the
Saviour's fame,
Whose grace I daily prove;
For since my soul has known His
name,
His banner has been—LOVE.

When walking in the paths of sin
I far from Him would rove;
By sweet constraint He drew me in,
And waved His banner—LOVE.

He spread the banquet, made me eat,
Bid all my fears remove;
My soul was filled with joy and peace
To see His banner—LOVE.

In every conflict I sustain,
My enemies shall prove,
Through Him the victory I obtain,
Beneath His banner—LOVE.

And when He calls me home at length,
To feast with Him above,
Through all eternity I'll sing
His never-changing LOVE.

137 Rutherford 7.6.7.6.7.6.7.5

Anne R. Cousins C. D'Urhan

THE sands of time are sinking,
　　The dawn of heaven breaks,
The summer morn I've sighed for,
　　The fair, sweet morn awakes;
Dark, dark hath been the midnight,
　　But dayspring is at hand,
And glory, glory dwelleth
　　In IMMANUEL'S land.

Oh, CHRIST, He is the fountain,
　　The deep, sweet well of love!
The streams on earth I've tasted,
　　More deep I'll drink above;
There, to an ocean fulness,
　　His mercy doth expand,
And glory, glory dwelleth
　　In IMMANUEL'S land.

Oh, I am my Belovèd's,
　　And my Belovèd's mine!
He brings a poor, vile sinner
　　Into His "house of wine;"
I stand upon His merit,
　　I know no other stand,
Not e'en where glory dwelleth
　　In IMMANUEL'S land.

With mercy and with judgment
　　My web of time He wove,
And aye the dews of sorrow
　　Were lustred with His love;
I'll bless the hand that guided,
　　I'll bless the heart that planned,
When throned where glory dwelleth
　　In IMMANUEL'S land.

The bride eyes not her garment,
　　But her dear bridegroom's face;
I will not gaze at glory,
　　But on my King of grace;
Not at the crown He giveth,
　　But on His piercèd hand;
The LAMB is all the glory
　　Of IMMANUEL'S land.

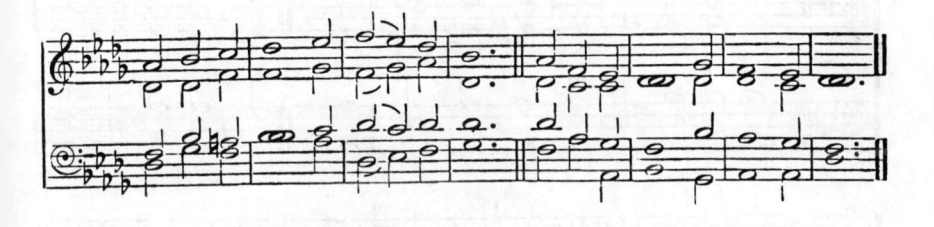

138 Ombersley L.M.
Bernard of Clairvaux   (Whitburn 34)   W.H. Gladstone

JESUS, Thou joy of loving hearts!
   Thou Fount of life! Thou light of
      men!
From the best bliss that earth imparts,
   We turn, unfilled, to Thee again.

Thy truth unchanged hath ever stood;
   Thou savest those that on Thee call;
To them that seek Thee, Thou art
      good,
   To them that find Thee, All in all!

We taste Thee, O Thou living Bread,
   And long to feast upon Thee still:
We drink of Thee, the Fountain-head,
   And thirst, our souls from Thee to
      fill.

Our restless spirits yearn for Thee
   Where'er our changeful lot is cast;
Glad when Thy gracious smile we see,
   Blest when our faith can hold Thee
      fast.

LORD JESUS, ever with us stay!
   Make all our moments calm and
      bright;
Chase the dark night of sin away,
   Shed o'er the world Thy holy light.

139   Kelso P.M.
H. Bonar   Anon.

NO blood, no altar now;
   The sacrifice is o'er;
No flame, no smoke ascends on high,
   The lamb is slain no more:
But richer blood has flowed from nobler veins,
To purge the soul from guilt, and cleanse the reddest stains.

We thank Thee for the *blood*,
   The blood of CHRIST, Thy SON;
The blood by which our peace is made,
   Our victory is won:
Great victory o'er hell and sin and woe,
That needs no second fight, and leaves no second foe.

We thank Thee for the *grace*,
   Descending from above,
That overflows our widest guilt—
   The eternal FATHER'S love,
Love of the FATHER'S everlasting SON,
Love of the HOLY GHOST—JEHOVAH, Three in One.

We thank Thee for the *hope*,
   So glad, and sure, and clear;
It holds the drooping spirit up
   Till the long dawn appear:
Fair hope! with what a sunshine does it cheer
Our roughest path on earth, our dreariest desert here!

We thank Thee for the *crown*
   Of glory and of life;
'Tis no poor, withering wreath of earth,
   Man's prize in mortal strife:
'Tis incorruptible as is the throne,
The kingdom of our GOD and His Incarnate SON.

140
Elizabeth Dark

Southgate 8.4.8.4.8.8.8.4
(Main 855)

T.B. Southgate

THROUGH Thy precious body
 broken—
  Inside the veil;
Oh, what words to sinners spoken—
  Inside the veil!
Precious, as the blood that bought us;
Perfect, as the love that sought us;
Holy, as the Lamb that brought us
  Inside the veil.

Lamb of GOD, through Thee we enter
  Inside the veil;
Cleansed by Thee, we boldly venture
  Inside the veil;
Not a stain—a new creation;
Ours is such a full salvation!
Low we bow in adoration
  Inside the veil.

When we see Thy love unshaken,
  Outside the camp;
Scorned of man, by GOD forsaken,
  Outside the camp;
Thine own love alone can charm us;
Shame doth now no more alarm us;
Glad we follow, nought can harm us
  Outside the camp.

Unto Thee, the homeless Stranger,
  Outside the camp,
Forth we hasten, fear no danger,
  Outside the camp;
Thy reproach far richer treasure
Than all Egypt's boasted pleasure;
Drawn by love that knows no measure.
  Outside the camp.

Soon Thy saints shall all be gathered
  Inside the veil;
All at Home, no more be scattered—
  Inside the veil:
Nought from Thee our heart shall
  sever; [never;
We shall see Thee—grieve Thee
Praise the LAMB! shall sound for ever
  Inside the veil.

141   Pisgah 6.6.8.6.8.8

Hannah K. Burlingham   (Nelson 20)   Anon.

O GOD of matchless grace,
  We sing unto Thy name;
We stand accepted in the place
  That none but CHRIST could claim;
Our willing hearts have heard Thy voice,
And in Thy mercy we rejoice.

'Tis meet that Thy delight
  Should centre in Thy SON;
That Thou shouldst place us in Thy sight
  In Him, Thy HOLY ONE:
Thy perfect love has cast out fear;
Thy favour shines upon us here.

Eternal is our rest,
  O CHRIST of GOD, in Thee!
Now of Thy peace, Thy joy possest,
  We wait Thy face to see:
Now to the FATHER'S heart received,
We know in whom we have believed.

A sacrifice to GOD,
  In life or death to be—
Oh keep us ever, blessèd LORD,
  Thus set apart to Thee:
Bought with a price, we're not our own;
We died, to live to GOD alone.

142 Cross of Jesus 8.7.8.7

R.C. Chapman (Sharon 22) John Stainer

HEAVENLY FATHER! in Thy
  wisdom
Thou art giving day by day
What is best for us as pilgrims,
  Best to speed us on our way.

In this present world as strangers,
  We the path of life pursue,
Waiting for Thy SON from heaven:
  Send Him, LORD, in season due!

With His bread and wine He makes us
  Strong in Him to run our race;
Crucified with Him and risen—
  Oh the mysteries of Thy grace!

From His hand our crown receiving,
  We shall cast it at His feet,
And adore Him with the myriads
  Made like Him, in Him complete.

143 Stuttgart 8.7.8.7

R.C. Chapman (Love Divine 121) German

HEAVENLY FATHER! joy and
  gladness
Fill the heart that rests in Thee;
By Thy SPIRIT, when in sadness,
  CHRIST, the "Lord of Peace," we see.

Power and Justice joined to bruise
  Him,
And to raise Him from the dead;
Now Thy HOLY SPIRIT shows Him
  Throned on high, our living Head.

Let not Satan's craft beguile us;
  Keep us walking in Thy light;
Let not unbelief defile us,
  Strong in our Redeemer's might.

FATHER, at Thy word we tremble;
  Pleasing Thee be our employ,
For our LORD will soon assemble
  All Thy saints to share His joy.

144 Beatitudo C.M.
J.N. Darby (St. Stephen 212) J.B. Dykes

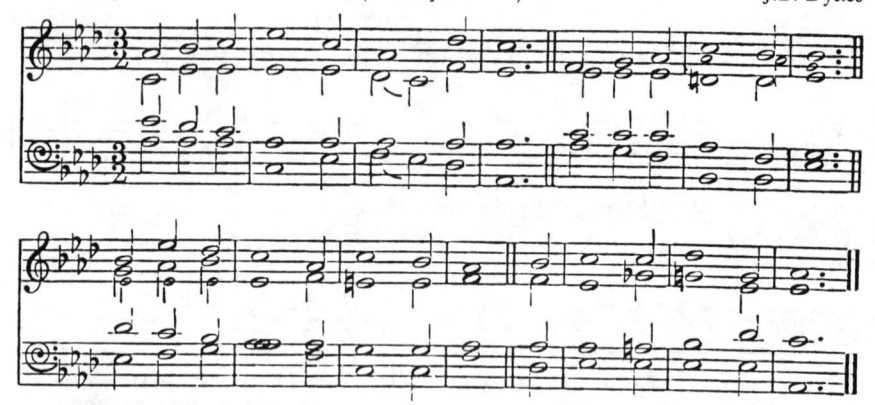

1. Father, Thy name our souls
     would bless,
   As children taught by grace;
   We lift our hearts in righteousness
     And joy before Thy face.

2. In the high purpose of Thy love
     Our place is now prepared,
   As sons with Him who sits above,
     Who all our sorrows shared.

3. Eternal ages shall declare
     The riches of Thy grace
   To those who with Thy Son shall share
     A son's eternal place.

4. Absent as yet, we rest in hope,
     Treading the desert path,
   Waiting for Him to take us up
     Beyond the power of death.

5. We joy in Thee; Thy holy love
     In Him our portion is—
   Like Thine own Son, *with* Him above,
     To share in heavenly bliss.

6. O Holy Father, keep us here
     In Thy blest name of Love,
   Walking before Thee without fear,
     Till joy be ours above.

145 St. George S.M.
R.C. Chapman (Rhodes 6) H.J. Gauntlett

FATHER, I praise Thy name,
  My GOD, I joy in Thee,
Who didst provide the spotless
    Lamb,
  Thine only SON, for me.

Thy SON is Thy delight,
  Thy First-born from the dead—
By faith I walk, and not by sight,
  With hidden manna fed.

His pilgrim track be mine,
  With His obedient ear;
Let JESU'S cross my soul refine,
  Thy holy name to fear.

Oh, keep me undefiled,
  Skilful to sing Thy praise,   [child
My GOD and FATHER'S pleasant
  In all my thoughts and ways

146 Wiltshire C.M.
H. Maull   (St. Bernard 5)   G. Smart

HOW great, our FATHER, was Thy
    love,
  How wonderful Thy grace,
In sending forth Thy Well-beloved
  To save our ruined race!

As being in the form of GOD,
  Eternally the same,
With Thee, the FATHER, He, the SON,
  Equality could claim.

But, Thy blest counsels to fulfil,
  He left His glorious throne;
And made Himself of no repute,
  A servant's form to own.

Thus found in fashion as a man,
  All blameless, spotless, pure,
He was obedient unto death,
  Sin's judgment to endure.

To Him, above all heavens, dost Thou
  His rightful place accord,
That every knee to Him should bow,
  Each tongue confess Him LORD.

Soon, thro' those open'd heavens again
  The Saviour will appear;
With Him in highest glory then,
  Our praises Thou wilt hear.

147
Rhuddlan 8.7.8.7.8.7

J.G. Deck (Praise my soul 155) Welsh Trad. Melody

'TWAS Thy love, O GOD, that knew us,
Earth's foundation long before;
That same love to JESUS drew us
By its sweet, constraining power.
And will keep us
Safely now, and evermore.

GOD of love, our souls adore Thee!
We would still Thy grace proclaim,
Till we cast our crowns before Thee.
And in glory praise Thy name;
Praise and blessing
Be to GOD and to the LAMB!

148
Hull 8.8.6. D

J.G. Deck (Meribah 153) Old Melody

O BLESSÈD Saviour, Son of God,
 Who hast redeemed us with Thy
   blood
From guilt, and death, and shame,
With joy and praise Thy people see
The crown of glory worn by Thee,
 And worthy Thee proclaim.

Exalted by the Father's love,
 All thrones, and powers, and names
   above,
 At His right hand in heaven,
Wisdom and riches, power divine,
Blessing and honour, Lord, are Thine—
 All things to Thee are given.

Head of the Church, Thou sittest
   there,
Thy members all Thy blessing share—
 Thy glory, Lord, is ours:
Our life Thou art; Thy grace sustains,
Thy strength in us each victory gains
 O'er sin and Satan's powers.

Soon shall the day of glory come,
 Thy Bride shall reach her destined
   home,
 And all Thy beauty see:
How great our joy to see Thee shine,
To hear Thee own us, Lord, as Thine,
 And ever dwell with Thee!

149　　　　　University College 7.7.7.7
John Withy　　　　(Buckland 159)　　　　H.J. Gauntlett

Son of God, exalted now,
 Highest honours crown Thy brow;
On the Father's throne divine,
All the Conqueror's triumphs Thine.

Here Thy cup was grief and shame,
Here, despised Thy lowly name;
Hour of darkness, power of hell,
On Thy spotless soul then fell.

Now Thy travail all is o'er,
Thou shalt humbled be no more;
Joy to Thee shall ever flow
From Thy toil and shame below.

Son of God, exalted now,
Thee we worship, bending low;
This the Father claims for Thee—
Reverent lip and bowèd knee.

Gather now full many a gem,
Saviour, for Thy diadem—
Trophies of Thy toil and love,
Meet to shine in courts above.

Speed the bright, millennial day,
Call Thy Bride to come away;
Through the earth let joy and song
Thy glad triumph roll along!

150 Adeste Fideles P.M.

Mary Peters   (Ems 535)   J. Reading

O LORD, we adore Thee,
  For Thou art the slain One
That livest for ever,
Enthronèd in heaven!
O LORD, we adore Thee,
For Thou hast redeemed us
Our title to glory
We read in Thy blood!

O GOD, we acknowledge
The depth of Thy riches;
For of Thee, and through Thee,
And to Thee are all things—
How rich is Thy mercy!
How great Thy salvation!
We bless Thee, we praise Thee:
Amen, and Amen!

151 Abridge C.M.

Thos. Kelly   Richmond 186)   Isaac Smith

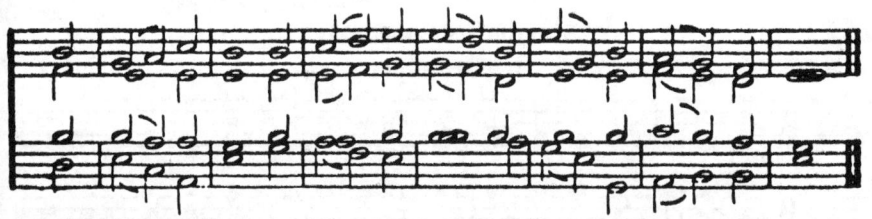

BEHOLD the Lamb with glory
   crowned!
To Him all power is given;
No place too high for Him is found,
No place too high in heaven.

He fills the throne—the throne above,
   He fills it without wrong;
The object of His Father's love,
The theme of heaven's song.

Though high, yet He accepts the praise
   His people offer here:
The faintest, feeblest cry they raise
Will reach the Saviour's ear.

This song be ours, and this alone,
   That celebrates the name
Of Him who sits upon the throne,
And that exalts the Lamb.

To Him whom men despise and slight,
   To Him be glory given!
The crown is His, and His by right
The highest place in heaven.

152   St. Oswald 8.7.8.7

J.N. Darby   (Mariners 921)   J.B. Dykes

HARK! ten thousand voices crying,
   'Lamb of God!' with one accord;
Thousand, thousand saints replying,
Wake at once the echoing chord.

'Praise the Lamb!' the chorus waking,
   All in heaven together throng;
Loud and far, each tongue partaking,
Rolls around the endless song.

Grateful incense this, ascending
   Ever to the Father's throne;
Every knee to Jesus bending,
All the mind in heaven is one

All the Father's counsels claiming
   Equal honours to the Son;
All the Son's effulgence beaming
Makes the Father's glory known.

By the Spirit all pervading,
   Hosts unnumbered round the Lamb,
Crowned with light and joy unfading,
Hail Him as the great "I AM."

Joyful now the new creation
   Rests in undisturbed repose,
Blest in Jesu's full salvation,
Sorrow now nor thraldom knows.

Hark! the heavenly notes again!
   Louder swells the song of praise,
Through creation's vault, "Amen!"
"Amen!" responsive joy doth raise.

153 Meribah 8.8.6.8.8.6
J.G. Deck (Pembroke 53) Lowell Mason

O JESUS, LORD, 'tis joy to know
　Thy path is o'er of shame and woe,
　　For us so meekly trod:
All finished is Thy work of toil,
Thou reapest now the fruit and spoil,
　　Exalted by our GOD!

Thy holy head, once bound with
　　thorns,
The crown of glory now adorns;
　　Thy seat the FATHER'S throne:
O LORD, e'en now we sing Thy praise,
And soon the eternal song shall raise—
　　Worthy the LORD alone!

　　As Head for us Thou sittest there;
　　Thy members here the blessing share
　　　　Of all Thou dost receive:
　　Thy wisdom riches, honours, powers—
　　Thy boundless love has made all ours
　　　　Who in Thy name believe.

154 Evan C.M.
(Dalehurst 345) W.H. Havergal

I FAIN would give Thee deepest thanks,
O LORD, who mad'st me Thine;
For into this lone heart have come
Thy light and love divine.

I thank Thee that the awful cross,
The bitterness and woe,
The wrath of GOD, Thou didst endure,
That I no wrath might know.

I thank Thee for the SPIRIT'S love,
Who caused mine eyes to see
The hollowness of earthly things,
And gave me peace in Thee.

155   Praise My Soul 8.7.8.7.8.7

S.P. Tregelles   (Regent Square 202)   John Goss

HOLY SAVIOUR! we adore Thee,
Seated on the throne of GOD,
While the heavenly hosts before Thee
Gladly sound Thy praise abroad—
Thou art worthy!
We are ransomed by Thy blood.

SAVIOUR! though the world despised Thee,
Though Thou here wast crucified,
High the FATHER'S glory raised Thee,
LORD of all creation wide—
Thou art worthy!
We now live, for Thou hast died.

Haste the day of Thy returning
With Thy ransomed Church to reign;
Then shall end our days of mourning,
We shall sing with rapture then—
Thou art worthy!
Come, LORD JESUS, come! Amen.

156 Maryton L.M.
F.W. Pitt (Festus 332) H. Percy Smith

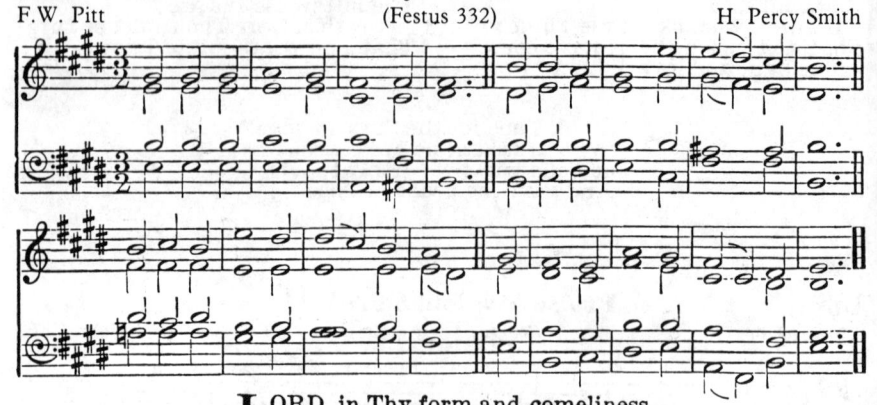

LORD, in Thy form and comeliness
  The FATHER'S brightest glories shine,
Displaying perfect holiness,
  Revealing all His love divine.

The world despised, rejected Thee:
  We bow in worship, and confess
That all Thy sufferings on the tree
  Proclaim our sin and guiltiness.

Though our transgressions wounded Thee,
  Thy precious blood our pardon sealed;
And, bruised for our iniquity,
  Thy stripes our sinful hearts have healed.

Ours was the guilt that kept us far
  From heaven, from happiness, from Thee;
Thine was the blood that brought us near,
  That cancelled sin, and set us free.

Thine was the blood, the precious blood,
  That cleansed each stain and made us meet
To worship in the courts of GOD,
  Redeemed and made in Thee complete.

157 Farrant C.M.
J.G. Deck (Dublin 30) R. Farrant

O LORD, we would the path retrace
  Which Thou on earth hast trod—
To man Thy wondrous love and grace,
  Thy faithfulness to GOD.

Thy love, by man so sorely tried,
  Proved stronger than the grave;
The very spear that pierced Thy side
  Drew forth the blood to save.

Faithful amidst unfaithfulness,
  'Midst darkness only light,
Thou didst Thy FATHER'S name confess,
  And in His will delight.

Unmoved by Satan's subtle wiles,
  Or suffering, shame, and loss,
Thy path, uncheered by earthly smiles,
  Led only to the cross!

O LORD, with sorrow and with shame,
  We meekly would confess
How little we, who bear Thy name,
  Thy mind, Thy ways express.

Give us Thy meek, Thy lowly mind;
  We would obedient be,
And all our rest and pleasure find
  In fellowship with Thee.

158   Lloyd C.M.
J.G. Deck   (Beatitudo 78)   C. Howard

O LORD, 'tis joy to look above
  And see Thee on the throne;
To search the heights and depths of love
  Which Thou to us hast shown;

To look beyond the long, dark night,
  And hail the coming day,
When Thou to all Thy saints in light
  Thy glories wilt display.

And, oh, 'tis joy the path to trace
  By Thee so meekly trod,
Learning of Thee to walk in grace,
  And fellowship with GOD;

Joy to confess Thy blessèd name,
  The virtues of Thy blood,
And to the wearied heart proclaim,
  "Behold the Lamb of GOD!"

159 Buckland 7.7.7.7
Archibald Rutherford   (Harts 97)   L.G. Hayne

GLORY unto JESUS be!
  From the curse He set us free;
All our guilt on Him was laid,
He the ransom fully paid.

All His blessèd work is done;
GOD's well pleasèd in His SON;
He has raised Him from the dead,
Set Him over all as Head.

All should sing His work and worth,
All above, and all on earth,
As they sing around the throne,
'Thou art worthy, Thou alone.'

Ye who love Him, cease to mourn,
He will certainly return;
All His saints with Him shall reign—
'Come, LORD JESUS, come! Amen.'

160 Westminster C.M.
Edward Denny   (Evan 178)   Jas. Turle

WHAT grace, O LORD, and beauty shone
  Around Thy steps below!
What patient love was seen in all
Thy life and death of woe!

For ever on Thy burdened heart
A weight of sorrow hung;
Yet no ungentle, murmuring word
Escaped Thy silent tongue.

Thy foes might hate, despise, revile,
Thy friends unfaithful prove;
Unwearied in forgiveness still,
Thy heart could only love.

Oh, give us hearts to love like Thee,
Like Thee, O LORD, to grieve
Far more for others' sins, than all
The wrongs that we receive.

One with Thyself, may every eye
In us, Thy brethren, see
That gentleness and grace which spring
From union, LORD, with Thee!

161 St. Fulbert C.M.
Macleod Wylie   (St. Bernard 163)   H.J. Gauntlett

A PERFECT path of purest grace,
  Unblemished and complete,
Was Thine, Thou spotless Nazarite,
  Pure, even to the feet!

Thy stainless life, Thy lovely walk,
  In every aspect true,
From the defilement all around
  No taint of evil drew.

No broken service, LORD, was Thine,
  No change was in Thy way;
Unsullied in Thy holiness,
  Thy strength knew no decay.

The vow was on Thee—Thou didst come
  To yield Thyself to death;
And consecration marked Thy path,
  And spoke in every breath.

Morning by morning Thou didst wake
  Amidst this poisoned air;
Yet no contagion touched Thy soul,
  No sin disturbed Thy prayer.

Thus, LORD, we love to trace Thy course,
  To mark where Thou hast trod,
And follow Thee with loving eye
  Up to the throne of GOD.

162   **Sharon 8.7.8.7**

J.A. Trench   (Cross of Jesus, Stainer 142)   Wm. Boyce

ALL the path the saints are treading,
  He once trod—the Son of God;
All the sorrows we are feeling,
  He has felt upon the road.

He is able thus to succour
  Those who tread the desert sand,
Pressing on to that bright glory
  Where He sits at God's right hand.

Now He praises in the assembly,
  Now His sorrow all is past;
His the earnest of our portion,
  We shall reach the goal at last.

Join the singing that He leadeth,
  Loud to God our voices raise
For each step that we have trodden,
  And each triumph of His grace.

Taken up in resurrection,
  We shall sing with Him above,
Tell the power of God's salvation,
  And His never-failing love.

163   **St. Bernard C.M.**

James Hutton   (St. Fulbert 161)   J. Richardson

OH, teach us more of Thy blest
  ways,
 Thou holy Lamb of GOD!
And fix and root us in Thy grace,
 As those redeemed by blood.

Oh, tell us often of Thy love,
 Of all Thy grief and pain;
And may our hearts with joy confess,
 From thence comes all our gain.

For this, oh, may we freely count
 Whate'er we have but loss,
The dearest object of our love,
 Compared with Thee, but dross!

Engrave this deeply on our hearts
 With an eternal pen,
That we may, in some small degree,
 Return Thy love again.

164   Weber 7.7.7.7

J.G. Deck   (St. Bees 352)   From Weber

JESUS, spotless Lamb of GOD,
  Thou hast bought us with Thy
   blood;
We would value nought beside
 JESUS—JESUS crucified!

We are Thine, and Thine alone;
 This we gladly, fully own,
And in all our works and ways,
 Now would only seek Thy praise.

Help us to confess Thy name,
 Bear with joy the cross and shame;
Only seek to follow Thee,
 Though reproach our portion be.

When Thou shalt in glory come,
And we reach our heavenly home,
Louder still each lip shall own,
We are Thine, and Thine alone!

165   **Doane 7.6.7.6.D**

J.G. Deck   (Lymington 174)   W.H. Doane

O LAMB of GOD, still keep us
  Near to Thy wounded side;
'Tis only there in safety
  And peace we can abide!
What foes and snares surround us!
  What lusts and fears within!
The grace that sought and found us
  Alone can keep us clean.

'Tis only in Thee hiding,
  We feel our life secure;
Only in Thee abiding,
  The conflict can endure:
Thine arm the victory gaineth
  O'er every hateful foe:
Thy love each heart sustaineth
  In all its cares and woe.

Soon shall our eyes behold Thee,
  With rapture, face to face;
One half hath not been told us
  Of all Thy power and grace!
Thy beauty, LORD, and glory,
  The wonders of Thy love,
Shall be the endless story
  Of all Thy saints above!

166
James Hutton

Day of Rest 7.6.7.6.D
(Crüger 83)

J.W. Elliott

1. O GRACIOUS Shepherd, bind us
   With cords of love to Thee,
   And evermore remind us
   How mercy set us free!
   Oh, may Thy HOLY SPIRIT
   Keep this before our eyes,
   That we Thy death and merit
   Above all else may prize!

2. We are of GOD's salvation
   Assurèd through Thy love,
   And, oh, in each temptation
   Thy succour may we prove!
   Thou hast our sins forgiven;
   Then, leaving all behind,
   We would press on to heaven,
   And bear the prize in mind.

3. Grant us henceforth, blest Saviour,
   While in this vale of tears,
   To look to Thee, and never
   Give way to anxious fears:
   Thou, LORD, wilt not forsake us,
   Though we are oft to blame;
   Oh, let Thy love then make us
   Hold fast Thy faith and name!

167   **Goodwin 7.6.7.6.D**
J.G. Deck   (Lymington 174)   G.J. Webb

O LORD, who now art seated
  Above the heavens on high—
The gracious work completed
  For which Thou cam'st to die—
To Thee our hearts are lifted,
  While pilgrims wandering here,
For Thou art truly gifted
  Our every weight to bear.

We know that Thou hast bought us,
  And cleansed us by Thy blood;
We know Thy grace has brought us
  As kings and priests to GOD;
We know that soon the morning,
  Long looked for, hasteneth near,
When we, at Thy returning,
  In glory shall appear.

O Lord, Thy love's unbounded,
 So full, so vast, so free!
Our thoughts are all confounded
 Whene'er we think of Thee!
For us Thou cam'st from heaven,
 For us to bleed and die,
That, purchased and forgiven,
 We might ascend on high.

Oh, let this love constrain us
 To yield ourselves to Thee;
Let nothing henceforth pain us
 But that which paineth Thee;
Our joy, our one endeavour,
 Through suffering, conflict, shame,
To serve Thee, gracious Saviour,
 And magnify Thy name!

168 University College 7.7.7.7
Thos. Kelly   (Buckland 159)   H.J. Gauntlett

LORD, accept our feeble song;
 Power and praise to Thee belong;
We would all Thy grace record,
Holy, Holy, Holy Lord!

Rich in glory, Thou didst stoop—
Thence is all Thy people's hope;
Thou wast poor, that we might be
Rich in glory, Lord, with Thee.

When we think of love like this,
Joy and shame our hearts possess—
Joy, that Thou couldst pity thus,
Shame for such returns from us.

Yet we wait the day to see,
When we shall from sin be free;
When, to Thee in glory brought,
We shall serve Thee as we ought.

169 St. Magnus C.M.
Thos. Kelly J. Clark

THE Head that once was crowned
    with thorns
  Is crowned with glory now;
A royal diadem adorns
  The mighty Victor's brow!

The joy of all who dwell above,
  The joy of saints below,
To us still manifest Thy love,
  That we its depths may know.

To us Thy cross, with all its shame,
  With all its grace be given!
Though earth disowns Thy lowly
    name,
  All worship it in heaven.

Who suffer with Thee, LORD, below,
  Will reign with Thee above,
Their glory and their joy to know
  The mystery of Thy love.

To us Thy cross is life and health,
  Though shame and death to Thee—
Our glory, peace, and boundless wealth.
  Throughout eternity.

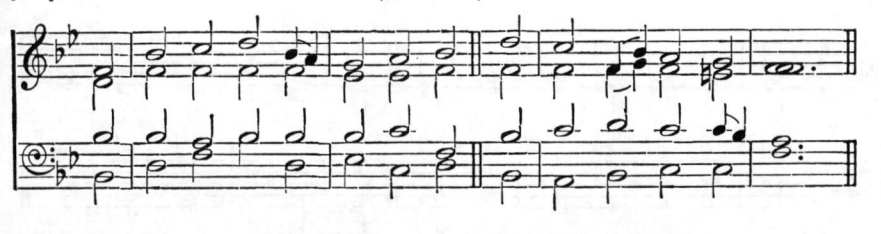

170   **Tiverton C.M.**
Joseph Stennett   (Dublin 30)   J. Grigg

O BLESSÈD Saviour, is Thy love
  So great, so full, so free?
Fain would we give our hearts, our minds,
  Our lives, our all, to Thee.

We love Thee for the glorious worth
  Which in Thyself we see;
We love Thee for the shameful cross
  Endured so patiently.

No man of greater love can boast
  Than for his friend to die;
Thou for Thine enemies wast slain!
  What love with Thine can vie?

Though in the very form of GOD,
  With heavenly glory crowned,
Thou, LORD, didst take the servant's form,
  Beset with sorrows round.

Thou wouldst like sinful man be made
  In everything but sin,
That we as like Thee might become
  As we unlike have been—

Like Thee in faith, in meekness, love,
  In every heavenly grace,
From glory unto glory changed.
  Till we behold Thy face.

O LORD, we treasure in our souls
  The memory of Thy love;
And ever may Thy name to us
  A grateful odour prove!

171   **Aurelia 7.6.7.6.D**
Paul Gerhardt   (Lymington 174)   S.S. Wesley

WE go to meet Thee, Saviour,
   Thy glorious face to see;
Oh, may our whole behaviour
   With this bright hope agree!
Love caused Thine incarnation,
   Love brought Thee from on high!
'Twas thirst for our salvation
   That made Thee come to die.

Not sinful man's endeavour,
   Nor any mortal's care,
Drew out Thy sovereign favour
   To sinners in despair:
Uncalled, Thou cam'st with gladness,
   From death our souls to raise,
And change our grief and sadness
   To songs of joy and praise.

172   **Bishopsgarth 7.7.8.7.D**
C. Wesley   (Goshen 66)   Arthur S. Sullivan

HEAD of the Church triumphant!
  We joyfully adore Thee:
Till Thou appear, Thy members here
Would sing like those in glory:
We lift our hearts and voices
  In blest anticipation,
And cry aloud, and give to GOD
The praise of our salvation.

While in affliction's furnace,
  And passing through the fire,
Thy love we praise, which tries our ways,
And ever brings us nigher:
We lift our hearts, exulting
  In Thine almighty favour;
Thy love divine, which makes us Thine,
Shall keep us Thine for ever.

Thou dost conduct Thy people
  Through torrents of temptation;
Nor will we fear, since Thou art near,
The fire of tribulation:
The world and sin and Satan
  Display their strength before us;
By Thee we shall break through them all,
And join the heavenly chorus.

173   **Dublin C.M.**
A. Midlane   (Abridge 151)   J. Stevenson

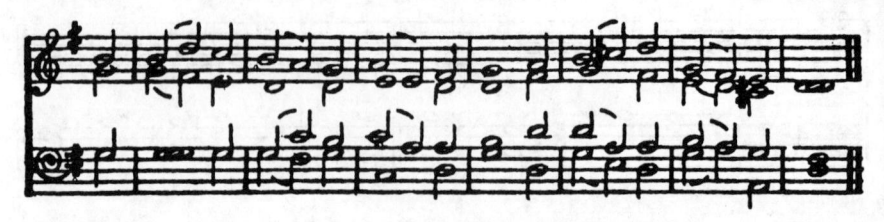

O PRECIOUS Saviour, deep Thy
   pain
When forth the life-blood flowed,
That washed our souls from every
   That paid the debt we owed! [stain,

Cleansed from our sins, renewed by
   grace,
Thy royal throne above,
Blest Saviour, is our destined place,
   Our portion there, Thy love.

Thine eye, in that bright, cloudless day,
   Shall, with supreme delight,
Thy fair and glorious Bride survey,
   Unblemished in Thy sight.

For ever be the glory given
   To Thee, O Lamb of GOD!
Our every joy on earth, in heaven,
   We owe it to Thy blood.

174   **Lymington 7.6.7.6.D**
W. Pennefather   (Ewing 90)   Robt. Jackson

O SAVIOUR! we adore Thee,
  We bless Thy precious name,
That Thou abidest faithful,
  That Thou art still the same;
We cried to Thee for succour,
  We looked for light to Thee;
Thy smile our souls has gladdened
  With holy radiancy!

We've sat beside the river,
  And tasted of Thy grace;
We long to reach the fountain,
  And see Thee face to face:
Meanwhile, with quickened footsteps,
  We'll run our heavenly way,
Until the shadows vanish—
  Until the break of day!

E'en now we blend our voices
  With yonder choirs above,
And swell the mighty anthem
  Which tells that "GOD is Love:"
Soon shall each fainting warrior,
  Soon shall the pilgrim band,
Have fought the last great battle—
  Have reached the promised land!

175   **St. Denio 11.11.11.11**
E. Grimley   (Montgomery 326)   Welsh Hymn Melody

1. OH, what shall we feel in Thy presence when first
The visions of glory upon us shall burst!
Our souls now are longing and thirsting for Thee,
Oh, when, blessèd Saviour, Thy face shall we see?

2. That face, once so marred, we shall gaze on at length,
And fearless behold, as the sun in its strength;
Those eyes, flames of fire, that so searching we prove,
Shall beam on us then inexpressible love.

3. Thy voice, like great waters—how calmly our soul
Shall hear in the glory its deep waters roll;
Though now it rebuke us, and humble our pride,
It shall speak only love to Thy glorified Bride.

4. O Thou who this world as a lone pilgrim trod,
Thy FATHER'S our FATHER, Thy GOD is our GOD;
To Thee we behold the bright seraphim bow;
LORD JESUS, what glory doth rest on Thee now!

Thy SPIRIT hath shewn GOD'S deep purpose to be
To empty, then fill us with glory, like Thee:
And now Thou dost wait Thy full joy to impart,
In that day of espousals—the joy of Thy heart.

Now moment by moment, to answer our needs,
Thy blood, holy Saviour, in righteousness pleads;
And sheltered by that, how serene and how calm,
Our souls on Thy bosom are shielded from harm!

    We see Thee, LORD JESUS, with great glory crowned,
    And waiting Thy coming, in peace would be found;
    The visions of glory turn all here to dross—
    For Thee give us grace to count all things but loss.

176   Veni Domine 10.8.8.4
Dent

LORD JESUS, come, crowned with Thy many crowns—
The Crucified, the Lamb once slain
To wash away sin's crimson stain—
    Come, Saviour, come!

LORD JESUS, come, and take Thy FATHER'S gift,
The people by Thy cross made Thine,
The trophy of Thy love divine—
    Come, Saviour, come!

LORD JESUS, come, and let Thy glory shine,
That quickly these changed bodies may
Each one reflect a living ray—
    Come, Saviour, come!

LORD JESUS, come, that lost in Thee our souls
May bow, and worship, and adore,
In Thy blest presence evermore—
    Come, Saviour, come!

LORD JESUS, come, and take Thy rightful place,
As Son of Man, Thou Risen One!
Come, LORD of all, to reign alone—
    Come, Saviour, come!

LORD JESUS, come! Let every knee bow down,
And every tongue to Thee confess;
As LORD of all, come forth to bless—
    Come, Saviour, come!

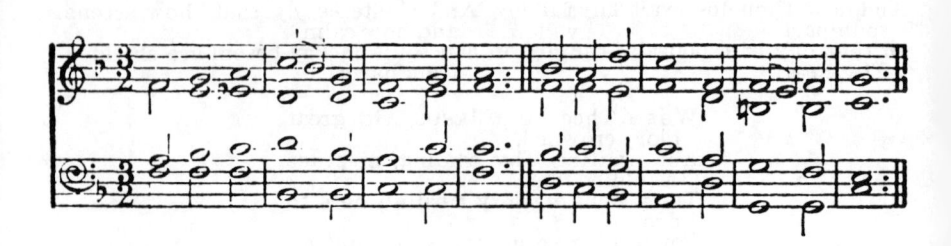

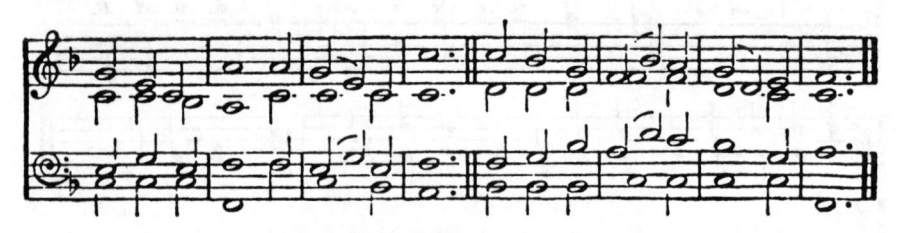

177 Pater Omnium 8.8.8.8.8.8
J.G. Deck   (Melita 351)   H.J.E. Holmes

1 " A LITTLE while!" our LORD shall come,
And we shall wander here no more;
He'll take us to our FATHER'S home,
Where He for us has gone before,
To dwell with Him, to see His face,
And sing the glories of His grace.

2 "A little while!" He'll come again!
Let us the precious hours redeem;
Our only grief to give Him pain,
Our joy to serve and follow Him;
Watching and ready may we be,
As those who long their LORD to see.

3 "A little while!" 'twill soon be past:
Why should we shun the shame and cross?
Oh, let us in His footsteps haste,
Counting for Him all else but loss;
Oh, how will recompense His smile
The sufferings of this "little while!"

"A little while!" Come, Saviour,
  come!
For Thee Thy Bride has tarried long;
Take us Thy waiting pilgrims home,
  To sing the new eternal song,
  To see Thy glory, and to be
In everything conformed to Thee!

178   Evan C.M.   W.H. Havergal
Carter   (St. Fulbert 120)

COME, let us of our blessèd hope,
  As saints of JESUS, sing,
While in anticipation now
  Our upward way we wing.

"A little while" of suffering,
  Of pain and weakness here;
"A little while" of patience yet,
  And JESUS will appear.

"A little while," and we no more
  A feeble few shall meet;
But there a mighty army stand
  Before His throne complete.

Sweet is the song of victory
  That ends the battle's roar;
And sweet the weary warrior's rest
  When all his toil is o'er.

Sweeter, beyond the "little while,"
  The dawn of morn to view,
The morning of a brighter day
  Than ever Eden knew.

Yet sweeter still to hear His voice,
  And see His glorious face,
Whilst heaven's ten thousand
    echoes wake,
  As we sound forth His grace.

179 Tranquillity (Jesus! I am resting) 8.7.8.5.D

S. Trevor Francis
Jas. Mountain

1 SAVIOUR, Thou art waiting, wait-
　　ing,
　Waiting for Thy blood-bought Bride,
　Waiting for Thy heart's deep longing
　　To be satisfied;
　Waiting for the joyous moment,
　　Watching us with tender care,
　Till at Thy command upspringing,
　　We Thy glory share.

2 Saviour, we are waiting, waiting,
　　Waiting, blessèd LORD, for Thee,
　Waiting for the calling upward,
　　With our LORD to be:
　Long and lone hath been the pathway,
　　Oft our hearts have failed with fear;
　But the guiding star of morning
　　Heralds Thee as near.

They are waiting, waiting, waiting,
 Loved ones who have gone before—
Waiting for the sweet home-bringing,
 Parting nevermore.
Oh, the joy, the bliss, the rapture—
 All our tears and sorrows past,
Singing, with triumphant praises,
 'Safely home at last!'

Keep us, blessèd JESUS, waiting,
 Clinging to Thy precious word;
Every footstep of the journey,
 Waiting for our LORD;
Waiting till within the mansions
 We behold Thy glorious face,
Singing all the wondrous story
 Of Thy matchless grace.

180   Huddersfield S.M.
J.G. Deck   (Swabia 615)   Maurice Green

SOON shall our Master come,
 Our toil and sorrow cease;
He'll call His waiting servants home
 To endless joy and peace.

Now may we do His will,
 In all His footsteps tread;
And, in a world of evil, still
 To grieve Him only dread.

May we His name confess
 'Midst suffering, shame, and loss;
Stand forth His faithful witnesses,
 And glory in the cross.

Watchful may we be found,
 Our loins well girded be;
In works of faith and love abound,
 Till we our Master see.

Then shall we soar above,
 Nor cease our sweet employ,
And hear Him say, with tenderest
  love,
 '*Enter thy Master's joy.*'

181
J.G. Deck
Yorkshire 10.10.10.10.10.10
(Unde et Memores 931)
J. Wainwright

SOON will the Master come—soon pass away
Our times of conflict, grief and suffering here;
Our night of weeping end in cloudless [day,
And sorrow's moment like a dream appear:
Eternity with JESUS, in the skies—
How soon that Sun of righteousness may rise!

We shall behold Him whom unseen we love,
We shall be with Him whom we long to see;
We shall be like Him, fit for realms above—
With Him, and like Him, for eternity:
If now to sit at JESU'S feet our choice,
How will fruition then our souls rejoice!

182
A. Midlane
Dennis S.M.
(Huddersfield 180)
H.G. Nageli (arr.)

'WITHOUT a cloud between;'
    To see Him face to face;
Not struck with dire amazement
    dumb,
But triumphing in grace.

'Without a cloud between;'
    To see Him "as He is:"
Oh, who can tell the height of joy—
The full, transporting bliss?

'Without a cloud between;'
    My longing spirit waits [soul
For that sweet hour, from which my
    Its highest glory dates.

'Without a cloud between;'
    How changed will all appear!
How different from the earthly path—
Our soul's experience here!

'Without a cloud between;'
    Lord Jesus, haste the day—
The morning bright, without a cloud—
And chase our tears away.

183 Nothing Between P.M.
E.H.H.

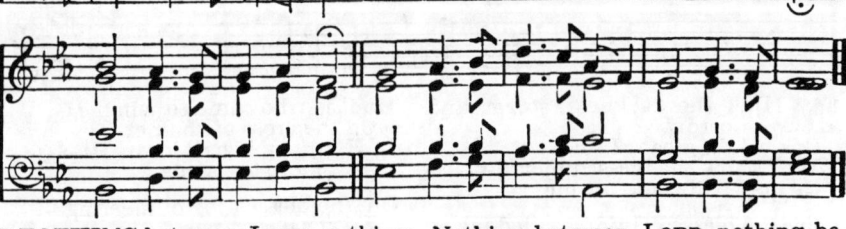

NOTHING between, Lord, nothing
    between;
Let me Thy glory see,
Draw my soul close to Thee,
Then speak in love to me—
    Nothing between.

Nothing between, Lord, nothing be-
    tween;
Let not earth's din and noise
Stifle Thy still, small voice;
In Thee let me rejoice—
    Nothing between.

Nothing between, Lord. nothing be-
    tween;
Nothing of earthly care,
Nothing of tear or prayer,
No robe that self may wear—
    Nothing between.

Nothing between, Lord, nothing be-
    tween;
Shine with unclouded ray,
Chasing each mist away;
O'er my whole heart bear sway—
    Nothing between.

Nothing between, Lord, nothing be-
    tween;
Thus may I walk with Thee,
Thee only may I see,
Thine only let me be—
    Nothing between.

Nothing between, Lord, nothing be-
    tween;
Till Thine eternal light,
Rising on earth's dark night,
Bursts on my open sight—
    Nothing between.

184 Pater Meus 8.5.8.5.D

Gerhardt Tersteegen (The Pleading Voice 920) J.H. Burke

1 'MIDST the darkness, storm, and sorrow,
   One bright gleam I see;
  Well I know the blessèd morrow—
   CHRIST will come for me!

2 Long the blessèd Guide has led me
   By the desert road;
  Now I see the golden towers—
   City of my GOD.

3 There, amidst the love and glory,
   He is waiting yet;
  On His hands a name is graven
   He can ne'er forget.

4 There made ready are the mansions,
   Glorious, bright, and fair;
  But the Bride the FATHER gave Him
   Still is wanting there.

5 Who is this who comes to meet me
   On the desert way,
  As the Morning Star foretelling
   GOD's unclouded day?

6 He it is who came to win me,
   On the cross of shame;
  In His glory I shall know Him
   Evermore the same.

7 Oh, the blessèd joy of meeting—
   All the desert past!
  Oh, the wondrous words of greeting
   He shall speak at last!

8 Meet companion then for JESUS,
   From Him, for Him made;
  Glory of GOD's grace for ever
   There in me displayed!

9 He, who in His hour of sorrow
   Bore the curse alone;
  I, who through the lonely desert
   Trod where He had gone—

10 He and I in that bright glory
    One deep joy shall share;
   Mine, to be for ever with Him;
    His, that I am there.

185   **Nyland 7.6.7.6.D**
J.G. Deck   (Bentley 18)   Finnish Melody

H OW long, O LORD, our Saviour,
   Wilt Thou remain away?
The careless world is mocking
   At Thy so long delay:
Oh, when shall come the moment,
   When, brighter far than morn,
The sunshine of Thy glory
   Shall on Thy people dawn?

How long, O gracious Master,
   Wilt Thou Thy household leave?
So long hast Thou now tarried,
   Few Thy return believe;
Thy very Bride her portion
   And calling hath forgot,
And seeks for ease and glory
   Where Thou, her LORD, art not.

Oh, wake Thy slumb'ring virgins,
   Send forth the solemn cry;
Let all Thy saints repeat it—
   'The Bridegroom draweth nigh!'
May all our lamps be burning,
   Our loins well girded be,
Each longing heart preparing
   With joy Thy face to see.

186 Richmond C.M.
S.P. Tregelles (Abridge 151) T. Haweis

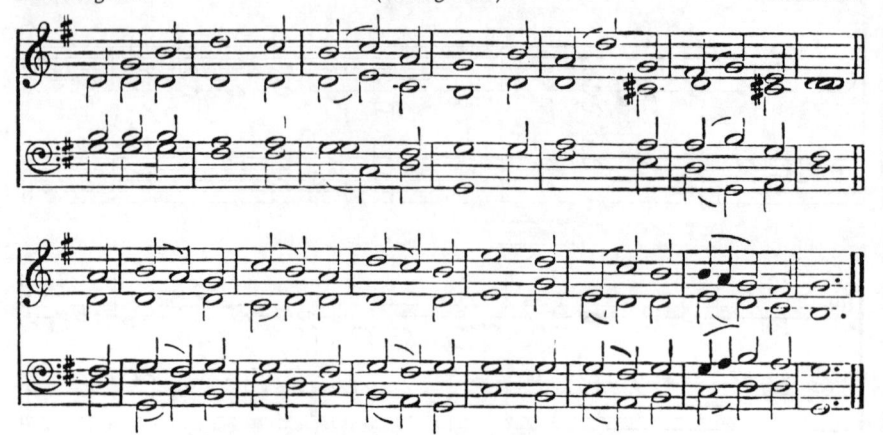

1 THE gloomy night will soon be past,
    The morning will appear;
  The day of glorious light at last
    Each waiting one will cheer.

2 Ah! yes, LORD JESUS, Thou whose heart
    Still for Thy saints doth care,
  We shall behold Thee as Thou art,
    And Thy full image bear.

3 Thy love sustains us on our way,
    While pilgrims here below;
  Thou dost, O Saviour, day by day,
    Thy suited grace bestow.

4 But, oh, the more we learn of Thee,
    And Thy rich mercy prove,
  The more we long Thy face to see,
    And fully know Thy love.

5 Then shine, Thou Bright and Morning Star,
    Dispel the dreary gloom;
  Oh, take from sin and grief afar
    Thy blood-bought people home!

187 Montgomery P.M.
Thos. Kelly J. Stanley

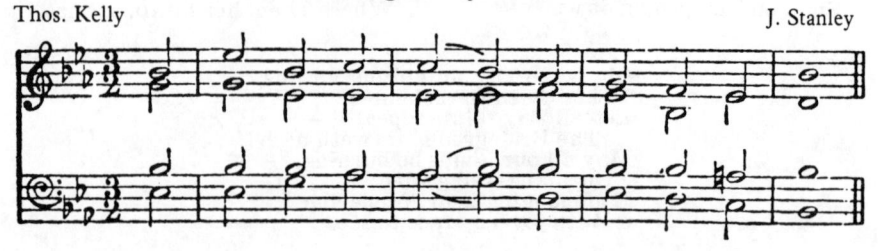

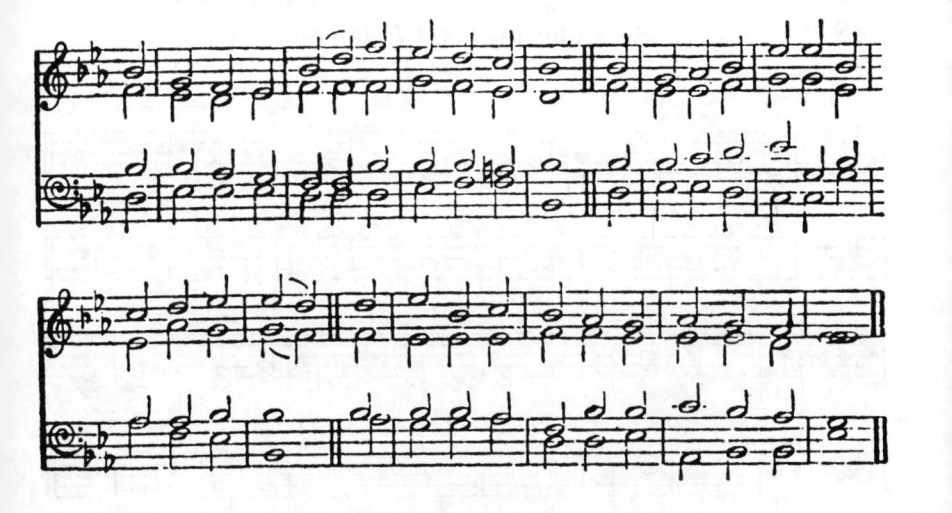

THE night is far spent, the day is
        at hand;
    Already the dawn may be seen in
        the sky;
Rejoice, then, ye saints, 'tis your
        LORD'S own command,
    Rejoice, for the coming of JESUS
        draws nigh.

What a day that will be, when the
        Saviour appears!
    How welcome to those who have
        shared in His cross!
A crown incorruptible then will be
        theirs,
    A rich compensation for suffering
        and loss.

Oh, pardon us, LORD, that our love to
        Thy name
    Is so faint, with so much our affec-
        tion to move!
Our coldness should fill us with grief
        and with shame—
    So much to be loved and so little to
        love!

Oh, kindle within us a holy desire,
    Like that which was found in Thy
        people of old,
Who tasted Thy love, and whose
        hearts were on fire,
    While waiting in patience Thy face
        to behold.

188

St. Columba 8.7.8.7 (Iambic)
(Dominus Regit Me 801)

Hoare
Trad. Irish Melody

THE night is wearing fast away,
   The glorious day is dawning,
When CHRIST shall all His grace display—
   The fair Millennial morning.

Gloomy and dark the night has been,
   And long the way, and dreary,
And sad each faithful saint is seen,
   And faint, and worn, and weary.

Lift up your heads—behold from far
   A flood of splendour streaming;
It is the Bright and Morning Star,
   In living lustre beaming.

He comes! the Bridegroom promised long;
   Go forth with joy to meet Him,
And raise the new and nuptial song,
   In cheerful strains to greet Him.

189

Lymington 7.6.7.6.D
(Goodwin 167)

Robt. Jackson

THE night shall soon be over,
　　The morning soon shall dawn;
The twilight and the darkness
　　Alike shall soon be gone:
Soon, soon shall come the day-spring.
　　When we from earth shall rise
To bright, celestial glories,
　　Far, far beyond the skies.

There joy in all its fulness
　　And pleasures evermore
Shall fill the heart with raptures
　　That ne'er were known before;
For we shall see our Saviour,
　　Our own Belovèd there,
The Chief among ten thousand,
　　The Altogether Fair!

Oh, may the love of JESUS
　　Constrain us here below
To cast aside earth's pleasures,
　　Its vain pursuits forego!
May none but "JESUS only"
　　Our praises here employ—
To serve Him and Him only,
　　Our highest aim and joy!

190   Bentley 7.6.7.6.D
(Ewing 90)

J. Hullah

1. MAN'S day is fast receding,
    The day of GOD will come,
And lingering feet are needing
    Oft to be speeded home ;
We need to stir affection,
    Dull conscience to awake,
Faith's shield for our protection
    With firmer grasp to take.

2. The world hath many a wonder,
    And many a witching snare ;
But see the glory yonder—
    What can with that compare ?
The LORD a crown is keeping
    For all who faithful stand,
Who, midst a world that's sleeping,
    Watch for the day at hand.

3. Our labour and our pleasure
    Be this—to do His will;
To fill our little measure
    With loving service still :
The cup of water given
    For Him, will find reward,
Both now and soon in heaven,
    Remembered by the LORD.

Lord, may Thy love constrain us
  Through all the "little while,"
Nor fear of man restrain us,
  Nor love of praise beguile;
Then, at Thy glorious coming,
  Enough, O Lord, if we
Shall hear Thy voice approving
  Aught we have done for Thee.

191
Edward Denny
　　　　　　　　Evan C.M.
　　　　　　(St. Stephen 212)
　　　　　　　　　　　　　　W.H. Havergal

Hope of our hearts, O Lord, appear,
  Thou glorious Star of day!
Shine forth, and chase the dreary night,
  With all our tears, away!

No resting-place have we on earth,
  No loveliness would see;
Our eye is on the royal crown
  Prepared for us by Thee.

But, blessèd Lord, however bright
  That crown of joy above,
What is it to the brighter hope
  Of dwelling in Thy love?

What to the joy, the deeper joy,
  Unmingled, pure, and free,
Of union with our living Head,
  Of fellowship with Thee?

This joy e'en now on earth is ours;
  But only, Lord, above,
Our hearts, without a pang, shall know
  The fulness of Thy love.

There, near Thy heart, upon the throne
  Thy ransomed Bride shall see
What grace was in the bleeding Lamb,
  Who died to make her free!

192   There's a Light 8.7.8.7.D
S. Trevor Francis   (Hyfrydol 49)   M.L. Wostenholm

1 I AM waiting for the dawning
    Of that bright and blessèd day,
  When the darksome night of sorrow
    Shall have vanished far away;
  When for ever with the Saviour,
    Far beyond this vale of tears,
  I shall swell the song of worship
    Through the everlasting years.

2 I am looking at the brightness
    (See, it shineth from afar)
  Of the clear and joyous beaming
    Of the Bright and Morning Star;
  Through the dark, grey mist of morn-
    Do I see its glorious light;   [ing
  Then away with every shadow
    Of this sad and weary night.

3 I am waiting for the coming
    Of the LORD who died for me;
  Oh, His words have thrilled my spirit,
    'I will come again for thee:'
  Faith can almost hear His footfall
    On the threshold of the door,
  And my heart, my heart is longing
    To be with Him evermore.

193   **St. Aidan 8.8.8**
(Delhi 927)   F.R. Grey

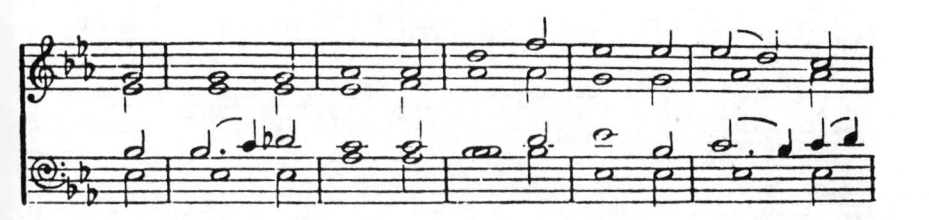

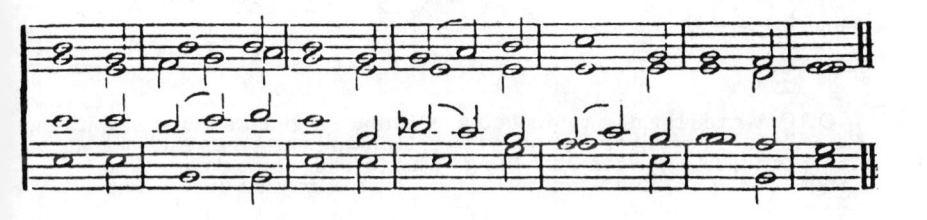

From far we see the glorious day
When He who bore our sins away
Will all His majesty display.

A Man of sorrows once below,
His visage marred by grief and woe,
His steps were watched by many a foe.

He groaned beneath sin's awful load,
For in the sinner's place He stood,
And died to bring us nigh to God.

But now He reigns, with glory crowned,
While angel hosts His throne surround,
And aye His lofty praise resound.

And soon the glorious day will come
When He will take His people home.
And seat them with Him on the throne.

Lord, may Thy love, Thy cross, still be
Our theme, as witnesses for Thee,
Till we Thy glorious face shall see!

Come, Lord, come quickly from above,
That we may see Thee, and may prove,
The depths of everlasting love!

194   **Sussex 8.7.8.7**
Mary Peters   (Stuttgart 217)   English Trad. Melody

LORD, we see the day approaching
  When Thou wilt again appear;
Sinners still, Thy garments touching,
  Stay Thee in Thy coming here.

Day by day Thy hand is dealing
  Full salvation where Thou wilt;
By delay Thy grace is healing
  Souls oppressed with fear and guilt.

Coming judgments round us darken,
  Human hearts may fail for fear;
But to Thee alone we hearken—
  Our redemption draweth near.

Thou, our LORD, art coming hither—
  Light in darkness, joy in grief;
Hope deferred would quickly wither
  Hearts that had not this relief.

  Make us patient and obedient,
    Stay each anxious heart on this:
  If Thy going were expedient,
    Surely Thy return is bliss.

195   **Regent Square 8.7.8.7.8.7**
Wm. Reid   (Cwm Rhondda 200)   H. Smart

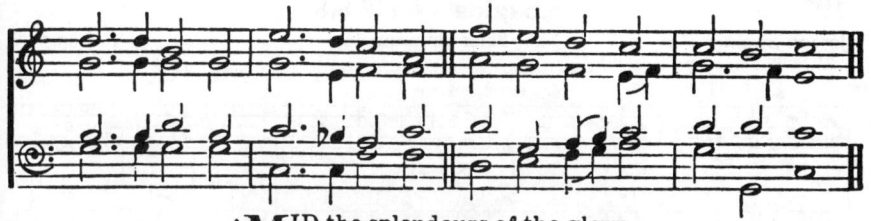

'MID the splendours of the glory,
  Which we hope ere long to share,
Christ our Head, and we His members,
  Shall appear divinely fair:
    Oh, how glorious,
  When we meet Him in the air!

Oh, what gifts shall then be granted—
  Palms, and crowns, and robes of white—
When the hope for which we've panted
  Bursts upon our gladdened sight,
    And our Saviour
  Makes us glorious through His might!

Bright the prospect soon that greets us
  Of that longed-for nuptial day,
When our heavenly Bridegroom meets us
  On His kingly, conquering way:
    In the glory,
  Bride and Bridegroom reign for aye!

196   Wimborne 8.7.8.7

H. Bonar   (St. Oswald 152)   J. Whitaker

THIS is not our place of resting,
  Ours a city yet to come;
Onward to it we are hasting,
  On to our eternal home:

In it all is light and glory,
  O'er it shines a nightless day;
Every trace of sin's sad story,
  All the curse, has passed away.

There the Lamb, our Shepherd, leads us
  By the streams of life along;
On the freshest pasture feeds us,
  Turns our sighing into song.

Soon we pass this desert dreary,
  Soon we bid farewell to pain;
Nevermore be sad or weary,
  Never, never sin again!

197
Joseph Swain

Sagina 8.8.8.8.8.8
(Pater Omnium 44)

T. Campbell

WHAT will it be to dwell above,
    And with the Lord of glory reign,
Since the sweet earnest of His love
    So brightens all this dreary plain?
No heart can think or tongue can tell
What joy 'twill be with CHRIST to
    dwell.

When sin no more obstructs our sight,
    When sorrow pains the heart no
    more,
When we shall see the Prince of light,
    And all His works of grace explore—
What heights and depths of love
    divine
Will then through endless ages shine!

And GOD has fixed the happy day
  When the last tear shall dim our
    eyes,
When He will wipe all tears away,
  And fill our hearts with glad surprise
To hear His voice, and see His face,
  And learn the riches of His grace.

This is the joy we seek to know,
  For this with patience we would
    wait
Till, called from earth and all below,
  We rise our glorious LORD to meet,
Our harps to strike, our crowns to
    wear,
And praise the love that brought us
    there!

198   **Trentham S.M.**

G.V. Wigram   (Swabia 615)   R. Jackson

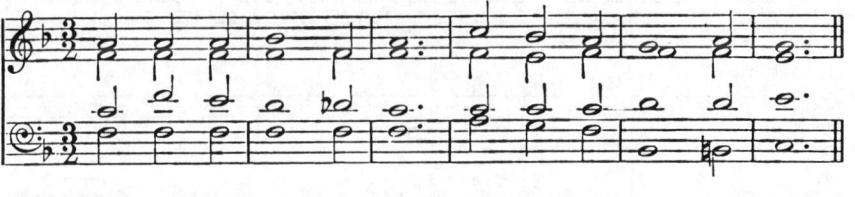

WHAT raised the wondrous
    thought,
  Or who did it suggest,   [brought,
That blood-bought saints to glory
  Should with the SON be blest?

FATHER, the thought was Thine,
  And only Thine could be—
Fruit of the wisdom, love divine
  Peculiar unto Thee.

And JESUS joys to own
  His chosen Bride as His—
Flesh of His flesh, bone of His bone—
  To share His weight of bliss.

The FATHER and the SON,
  And HOLY SPIRIT too,   [shewn
In counsel deep, and power have
  What wonders love can do.

Now, Saviour, Thy delight
  Is to prepare Thy Bride,
Till in the glory, clothed in white,
  She's seated at Thy side.

199
Penlan 7.6.7.6.D

J. Ryland – J.D. Deck (Ellacombe 91) D. Jenkins

THE day of glory bearing
  Its brightness far and near,
The day of CHRIST'S appearing,
  We now no longer fear;
For we shall rise to meet Him,
  Triumphant in the sky,
And every heart shall greet Him
  With songs of victory.

He once, a spotless Victim,
  For us, on Calvary bled;
JEHOVAH did afflict Him,
  And bruise Him in our stead:
To Him by grace united,
  We joy in Him alone,
And now, by faith, delighted,
  Behold Him on the throne.

There He is interceding
  For all who on Him rest;
And grace from Him proceeding
  Tells how in Him we're blest:
Soon, to His place in glory,
  His waiting saints He'll raise,
To chant their joyful story
  In songs of loudest praise!

200
J.R. Macduff — Cwm Rhondda 8.7.8.7.8.7 (Triumph 14) — J. Hughes

CHRIST *is coming!* Let creation
  From her groans and travail cease;
Let the glorious proclamation
  Hope restore, and faith increase:
    CHRIST *is coming!*
  Come, Thou blessèd Prince of Peace!

Earth can now but tell the story
  Of Thy bitter cross and pain;
She shall yet behold Thy glory
  When Thou comest back to reign:
    CHRIST *is coming!*
  Let each heart repeat the strain.

Long Thine exiles have been pining,
  Far from rest, and home, and Thee
Soon, in heavenly glory shining,
  Their Redeemer they shall see;
    CHRIST *is coming!*
  Haste the joyful jubilee.

With that blessèd hope before us,
  Let no harp remain unstrung;
Let the mighty advent chorus
  Onward roll on every tongue:
    CHRIST *is coming!*
  Come, LORD JESUS, quickly come!

201   **Helmsley** 8.7.8.7.8.7
J. Cennick-C. Wesley   (Cwm Rhondda 200)   M. Madan

LO! He comes, with clouds descending,
Once for favoured sinners slain;
Thousand thousand saints attending
Swell the triumph of His train:
Hallelujah!
JESUS comes, and comes to reign!

Every eye shall now behold Him,
Robed in glorious majesty:
Those who set at nought and sold Him,
Pierced and nailed Him to the tree,
Deeply wailing,
Shall the true Messiah see.

Lo! the tokens of His passion
Still His glorious body bears;
Cause of endless exultation
To His ransomed worshippers:
Hallelujah!
Now the day of CHRIST appears.

Yea, Amen! let all adore Thee,
High on Thine eternal throne;
Saviour, take the power and glory,
Claim the kingdoms for Thine own:
Oh, come quickly!
Hallelujah! come, LORD, come!

Regent Square 8.7.8.7.8.7
(Crown Him 923)

Thos. Kelly   H. Smart

LOOK, ye saints, the sight is glorious—
See the "Man of sorrows" now,
From the fight returned victorious;
Every knee to Him shall bow:
Crown Him! crown Him!
Crowns become the Victor's brow.

Crown the Saviour! angels own Him!
Rich the trophies JESUS brings;
In each ransomed heart enthrone Him,
While the vault of heaven rings:
Crown Him! crown Him!
Crown the Saviour "KING of kings."

Sinners in derision crowned Him,
Mocking thus the Saviour's claim:
Saints and angels crowd around Him,
Own His title, praise His name:
Crown Him! crown Him!
Spread abroad the Victor's fame.

Hark, those bursts of acclamation!
Hark, those loud, triumphant chords!
JESUS takes the highest station—
Oh, what joy the sight affords!
Crown Him! crown Him!
"KING of kings, and LORD of lords!"

203 Rimington L.M.
Isaac Watts   (Arizona 834)   F. Duckworth

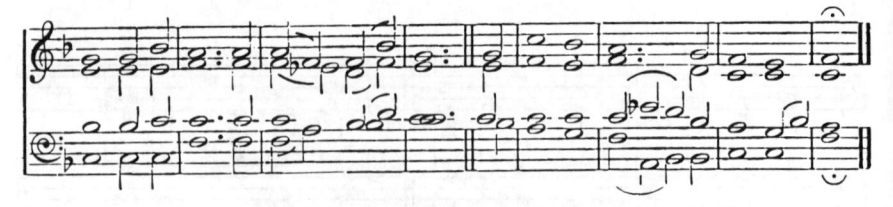

JESUS shall reign where'er the sun
  Does its successive journeys run;
His kingdom stretch from shore to
  shore,
Till moons shall wax and wane no
  more.

People and realms of every tongue
Dwell on His love with sweetest song;
And infant voices, too, proclaim
Their early blessings on His name.

Blessings abound where'er He reigns:
The prisoner leaps to lose his chains,
The weary find eternal rest,
And all the sons of want are blest.

Where He displays His healing power,
Death and the curse are known no
  more;
In Him the sons of Adam boast
More blessings than their father lost.

Soon shall the whole creation sing
The praises of its GOD and King,
Angels resound with praise again,
And earth repeat the loud "Amen!"

204 Crüger 7.6.7.6.D
J. Montgomery   (Lymington 16)   J. Crüger

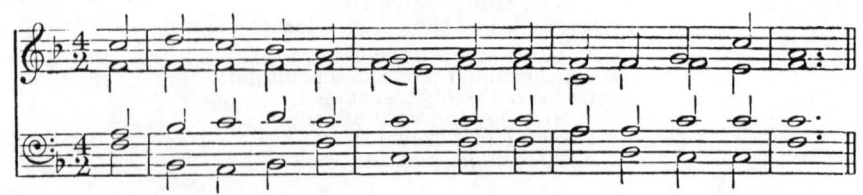

HAIL to the LORD'S Anointed,
  Great David's greater Son,
Who, in the time appointed,
  His reign on earth begun:
He came to break oppression,
  To set the captive free;
To take away transgression,
  And rule in equity.

He shall come down, like showers,
  Upon the fruitful earth;
Love, joy and hope, like flowers,
  Spring in His path to birth;
Before Him on the mountains
  Shall peace, the herald, go;
And righteousness, as fountains,
  From hill to valley flow.

Kings shall fall down before Him,
  And gold and incense bring;
All nations shall adore Him,
  His praise all people sing;
For He shall have dominion
  O'er river, sea, and shore,
Far as the eagle's pinion
  Or dove's light wing can soar.

O'er every foe victorious,
  He on His throne shall rest;
From age to age more glorious,
  All blessing and all blest:
The tide of time shall never
  His covenant remove;
His name shall stand for ever;
  That name to us is—LOVE.

205
Henry Heath

Missionary 7.6.7.6.D
(Ewing 90)

L. Mason

HEAD of the new Creation,
  SON of the living GOD!
Captain of our salvation,
  Who shed'st for us Thy blood;
EMMANUEL, Son of David,
  The woman's blessèd Seed;
Thy heel the serpent bruisèd,
  While Thou didst bruise his head.

Thy cross and shame are over,
  And all redemption's toil;
Thy conquests are eternal—
  Unfading is the spoil:
The fame of Thy achievements
  Dies not upon the ear
Of friend or foe for ever,
  For both that fame must hear.

Our great High Priest e'er living,
  With tenderness and might;
Our Shepherd, ever feeding
  Thy sheep—all Thine by right;
Firstfruits of all the sleeping,
  Who rest from toil and strife,
And wait, while we are watching,
  To wear the crown of life—

Soon shall the heavens reveal Thee
  In all Thy glorious might,
In all Thy FATHER'S glory,
  And that of angels bright!
Then shall the Church, beside Thee—
  Bride of Thy heart's delight—
Sit on Thy throne of glory,
  All beauteous in Thy sight!

206   Diadem C.M.

Edward Perronet   (Miles Lane 903)   J. Ellor

ALL hail the power of JESU'S name!
  Let angels prostrate fall;
Bring forth the royal diadem,
  And crown Him LORD of all!

Ye risen saints, attune the lyre,
  And, as ye tune it, fall
Before His face who formed the choir,
  And crown Him LORD of all!

Ye chosen seed of Israel's race,
  Redeemed from Israel's fall,
Adore Him for His wondrous grace,
  And crown Him LORD of all!

Ye Gentiles, come, with all your kings,
  Throughout this earthly ball;
To Zion come, behold Him there,
  And crown Him LORD of all!

All, all above, on earth below,
  In wondering rapture fall;
Join in the universal song,
  And crown Him LORD OF ALL!

207
St. Alphege 7.6.7.6

R.C. Chapman (Barton 392) H.J.Gauntlett

MY Well-beloved is holy,
　　The FATHER'S spotless Lamb,
The Captain of salvation,
　　The omnipotent I AM.

Unsearchable His wisdom—
　　By Him were all things made;
His cross, by perfect weakness,
　　His power to save displayed.

He tells me what temptations
　　In days of flesh He bore;
His bitter death He shews me—
　　He lives for evermore!

By Him are all things ordered,
　　His hand I ever bless;
His sympathy, how tender,
　　Through His own deep distress!

He holds a righteous sceptre,
　　He died to reach His throne;
Enduring is the kingdom
　　Of GOD's belovèd SON!

Westminster C.M.
(Albano 118)

208
R.C. Chapman

Jas. Turle

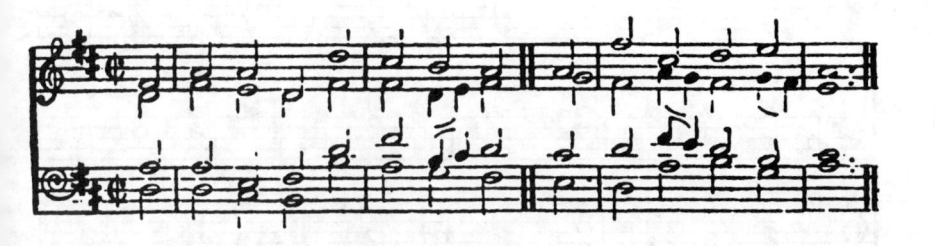

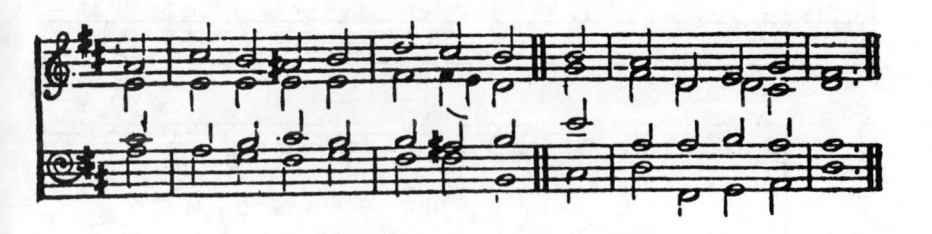

FATHER, how great is Thy delight
  And joy in CHRIST the LORD,
Thy SON, whom once Thy justice smote
  With sin-avenging sword!

He gave Himself the curse to bear;
  He lives, our great High Priest;
Thy bosom, whence He came, is now
  His everlasting rest.

Thy children by Thy SPIRIT learn
  With CHRIST our LORD to sing—
To follow Him, and wait till He
  Our full redemption bring.

Oh, let Thy SPIRIT keep our hearts;
  May we with Thee be one,
Walking in holy fellowship
  With Thee and with Thy SON!

209
Russell Hurditch

Finlandia 11.10.11.10
(Montreal 934)

Jean Sibelius

Omit these two lines or repeat last two lines of each verse

HE dies! He dies! the lowly Man
of sorrows,
On whom were laid our many griefs
and woes;
Our sins He bore, beneath GOD'S
awful billows,
And He hath triumphed over all
our foes.

He lives! He lives! what glorious
consolation!
Exalted at His FATHER'S own right
hand,
He pleads for us, and by His intercession
Enables all His saints by grace to
stand.

He comes! He comes! Oh, blest anticipation!
In keeping with His true and faithful word,
Fulfilling all our holy expectation—
Caught up, to be *"for ever with the
LORD!"*

He comes! He comes! full soon, to
break oppression,
And set the wretched captive prisoners free;
He comes to hush the groaning of
creation,
And reign in righteousness and
equity.

210   Sussex 8.7.8.7

Joseph F. Thrupp   (St. Oswald 152)   English Trad. Melody

FATHER, we commend our spirits
To Thy love in JESU'S name,
Love that His atoning merits
Give us confidence to claim.

Oh, how sweet, how true a pleasure
Flows from love so full and free!
Oh, how great, how rich a treasure,
Saviour, we possess in Thee!

From the world and its confusions,
We now turn to Thee for rest;
From its cares and its delusions,
Turn to Thee, and thus are blest.

Though this scene is ever changing,
Since Thy mercy changes not,
O'er its depths our spirits ranging,
Glory in their happy lot.

By the HOLY GHOST anointed,
May we do our FATHER'S will,
Walk the path by Thee appointed,
All Thy pleasure to fulfil;

Till the welcome signal hearing,
Welcome to Thy saints alone,
We rejoice at His appearing,
Who shall claim us for His own.

211 Lloyd C.M.
Boethia Thompson   (St. Peter 24)   C. Howard

BRIDE of the Lamb, there is for thee
  One only safe retreat;
Where JESUS is, thy heart should be,
  Thy home at His pierced feet.

When Satan tracks thy lonely way,
  When his temptations meet,
In JESU'S presence watch and pray,
  Yea, conquer at His feet.

Since thou hast much to learn, e'en though
  Thou art in CHRIST complete,
In grace and knowledge seek to grow,
  By sitting at His feet.

Through tribulation hasten on;
  With CHRIST the cross is sweet;
The "little while" will soon be gone;
  Keep only at His feet.

Bride of the Lamb, forget the past,
  Prepare thy LORD to greet;
Thou soon shalt share His throne, and cast
  Thy crown before His feet.

212 St. Stephen C.M.
Mary Peters   (Sawley 36)   W. Jones

"PRAISE ye the LORD!" again,
   again,
The SPIRIT strikes the chord;
Nor toucheth He our hearts in vain—
We praise, we praise the LORD.

"Rejoice in Him"—again, again,
The SPIRIT speaks the word;
And faith takes up the happy strain—
Our joy is in the LORD.

"Stand fast" in CHRIST—ah! yet
   again,
He teacheth all the band;
Since human efforts are in vain,
In CHRIST it is we stand.

"Clean every whit"—Thou saidst it,
   LORD;
Shall one suspicion lurk?
Thine, surely, is a faithful word,
And Thine a finished work.

   For ever be the glory given
     To Thee, O Lamb of GOD!
   Our every joy on earth, in heaven,
     We owe it to Thy blood!

213
John Newton   Gounod 8.7.8.7.7.7   C. Gounod
(Requiem 88)

LET us love, and sing, and wonder!
  Let us praise the Saviour's name!
He has hushed the law's loud thunder,
He has quenched mount Sinai's
   flame;
He has cleansed us with His blood,
He has brought us nigh to GOD.

Let us love the LORD that bought us,
  Pitied us when enemies;
Called us by His grace and taught us;
Gave us ears, and gave us eyes;
  He has cleansed us with His blood,
He presents our souls to GOD.

   Let us sing, though fierce temptation
     Threaten hard to bear us down;
   For the LORD, our strong salvation,
     Holds in view the conqueror's
       crown;
   He who cleansed us with His blood,
   Safe will bring us home to GOD.

214 Adoration 6.6.6.6.8.8
W. Pennefather   (Christchurch 81)   W.H. Havergal

THOUSANDS and thousands stand
  Around the throne of light:
With harps in every hand,
  And clothed in virgin white,
They joyfully adore the LAMB,
And magnify the great I AM!

Like ocean's waves that break
  Upon the encircling shore,
The melody rolls on,
  Resounding evermore!
Holy! Most Holy LORD and KING!
With ransomed powers Thy praise they sing.

'Not unto us, O CHRIST,
  Not unto us,' they cry;
'Thou hast salvation wrought,
  Thine is the victory!
To Thee these radiant crowns we owe,
These spotless robes Thou didst bestow!'

LORD! we would blend *our* song
  With *that* triumphant strain,
And as it rolls along
  Echo it back again!
One holy Church—on earth, above—
Unites to sing that "GOD is Love!"

Soon, soon the morn shall break,
  When we shall hear His voice
Calling the dead to wake,
  Bidding His Church rejoice.
LORD JESUS, come, and bear away
Thy Bride to everlasting day!

215 St. John's, Hoxton 6.6.8.4
Mary Peters   (Leoni 247)   E.H.G. Sargent

SALVATION to our God!
    Salvation to the Lamb!
The shedding of His precious blood
    Our only claim.

Our God salvation gives,
    And through the Lamb it flows;
Once slain for us—for us He lives,
    Our sole repose.

The Lamb once slain is seen
    On God's eternal throne,
And His redeemed are white and clean
    Through Him alone.

Salvation's joyful sound
    Bursts from the blood-bought throng;
And holy angels all around
    Take up the song.

Our hearts are tuned for this,
    Such songs our tongues employ—
The Lamb the spring of all our bliss,
    And God our joy

Salvation to our God,
    Thanksgiving, power, and might!
And to the Lamb who shed His blood,
    Our life and light!

216 Kelly 8.8.8.5
Thos. Kelly

PRAISE the Saviour, ye who know Him!
Who can tell how much we owe Him?
Gladly let us render to Him
    All we have and are.

Jesus is the name that charms us,
He for conflict fits and arms us;
Nothing moves, and nothing harms us,
    When we trust in Him.

Trust in Him, ye saints, for ever;
He is faithful, changing never;
Neither force nor guile can sever
    Those He loves from Him.

Keep us, Lord, oh, keep us cleaving
To Thyself, and still believing,
Till the hour of our receiving
    Promised joys in heaven.

Then we shall be where we would be,
Then we shall be what we should be,
Things which are not now, nor could be,
    Then shall be our own.

217
R. Robinson
Stuttgart 8.7.8.7
(Cross of Jesus, Stainer 142)
German

COME, Thou Fount of every blessing!
  Tune my heart to sing Thy grace;
Streams of mercy, never ceasing,
  Call for ceaseless songs of praise.

Teach me, LORD, some rapturous measure,
  Meet for blood-bought hosts above;
Let me sing the countless treasure
  Of my GOD's unchanging love.

JESUS sought me when a stranger,
  Wandering from the fold of GOD;
He, to rescue me from danger,
  Interposed His precious blood.

Oh, to grace how great a debtor
  Daily I'm constrained to be!
Let that grace, LORD, like a fetter,
  Bind my wandering heart to Thee.

Prone to wander, LORD, I feel it,
  Prone to leave the GOD I love:
Keep my heart from wandering, keep it,
  Till I'm perfected above.

Here I raise my Ebenezer,
  Hither by Thy help I'm come;
And I hope, by Thy good pleasure,
  Safely to arrive at home.

218
Samuel Medley
Mainzer L.M.
(Alstone 582(2))
Joseph Mainzer

AWAKE, my soul, in joyful lays,
　To sing thy great Redeemer's
　　praise;
He justly claims a song from thee—
His loving-kindness, oh, how *free!*

He saw us ruined in the fall,
Yet loved us, notwithstanding all;
He saved us from our lost estate—
His lovingkindness, oh, how *great!*

Though numerous hosts of mighty
　foes,
Though earth and hell our way oppose,
He safely leads His saints along—
His lovingkindness, oh, how *strong!*

When trouble, like a gloomy cloud,
Has gathered thick, and thundered
　loud,
He with His church has always stood—
His lovingkindness, oh, how *good!*

　　Soon shall we mount and soar away
　　To the bright realms of endless day,
　　And sing, with rapture and surprise,
　　His lovingkindness in the skies!

219　　　　　　**Luther's Chant L.M.**
Samuel Medley　　　(Gratitude 916)　　　　　H.C. Zeuner

NOW, in a song of grateful praise,
　To our blest LORD the voice we
　　raise;
With all His saints we join to tell—
Our Saviour hath done all things well!

All worlds His glorious power confess;
His wisdom all His works express;
But oh, His love, what tongue can
　tell?—

And since our souls have known His
　love,
What mercies hath He made us prove!
Mercies which all our praise excel—

Though many a fiery, flaming dart
The tempter levels at the heart,
With this we all his rage repel—

　　And when on that bright day we rise,
　　And join the anthems of the skies,
　　Among the rest this note shall swell—
　　Our Saviour hath done all things well!

220
Thos. Kelly

Festus L.M.
(Arizona 834)

From a German Chorale

As sinners saved we praise and sing,
 Salvation's ours, and of the LORD;
We draw from heaven's eternal spring,
 The living GOD our great reward.

As sinners saved we praise and sing,
 Whom grace has kept in dangers past;
And, oh sweet truth! the LORD will bring
 His people safe to heaven at last.

As sinners saved we praise and sing,
 Of JESUS sing through all our days:
In heaven above our harps we'll string,
 And there for ever sing His praise.

221
A. Midlane

Nottingham 7.7.7.7
(University College 149)

From Mozart

SWEET the theme of JESU's love!
Sweet the theme, all themes above;
Love, unmerited and free,
Our triumphant song shall be.

Love so vast that nought can bound;
Love too deep for thought to sound;
Love which made the LORD of all
Drink the wormwood and the gall.

Love which led Him to the cross,
Bearing there unuttered loss;
Love which brought Him to the gloom
Of the cold and darksome tomb.

Love which made Him thence arise
Far above the starry skies;
There, with tender, loving care,
All His people's griefs to share.

Love which will not let Him rest
Till His chosen all are blest;
Till they all for whom He died
Live rejoicing at His side.

222
C. Wesley

Brandenburg 7.7.7.7
(University College 149)

German Melody

LOVE'S redeeming work is done—
Fought the fight, the battle won;
Lo! our Sun's eclipse is o'er;
Lo! He sets in death no more.

Vain the stone, the watch, the seal—
CHRIST has burst the gates of hell;
Death in vain forbids Him rise—
CHRIST has opened paradise.

Lives again the glorious King!
Where, O Death, is now thy sting?
Once He died our souls to save—
Where's thy victory, O Grave?

Hail, Thou LORD of earth and heaven!
Praise to Thee by both be given!
Thee we greet triumphant now;
Hail, the Resurrection THOU!

223
Richard Burnham

Wiltshire C.M.
(Nativity 229)

G. Smart

COME, saints, your grateful voices raise,
  The heavenly Lamb adore,
Dwell on His everlasting love,
  And praise Him evermore!

Spread His blest name through all the earth,
  Sing His eternal power,
Shout the rich fountain of His blood,
  And praise Him evermore!

His mercy, who our ransom paid,
  And all our sorrows bore,
Sing with a note of loftiest joy,
  And praise Him evermore!

Soon shall our LORD appear to reign;
  Then all from shore to shore
Shall see the glory of the Lamb,
  And praise Him evermore!

224
Isaac Watts

Deep Harmony L.M.
(Ombersley 28)

Handel Parker

SWEET is the work, our GOD and
King,
To praise Thy name, give thanks and
sing;
To show Thy love by morning light,
And tell of all Thy truth by night.

Our hearts shall triumph in Thee,
LORD,
And bless Thy works, and bless Thy
word:
Thy works of grace, how bright they
shine!
How deep Thy counsels, how divine!

Soon shall we see, and hear, and know
All we desired or wished below,
And every power find sweet employ
In serving Thee with holy joy.

225   Tuam S.M.
A. Midlane   (Augustine 3)   W. Mason

'TIS heaven where JESUS is,
And nowhere else beside;
'Tis heaven to dwell beneath the gaze
Of JESUS crucified.

Those tender, loving eyes
Unclouded bliss impart;
His gracious smile all fear dispels,
And wins the yielding heart.

Those wounds aloud proclaim
His depth of love for me;
They tell the anguish which He bore
Upon the accursèd tree.

The throne on which He sits,
The glory which He bears,
Alike proclaim how well He won
The Victor's crown He wears.

To Thee, O loving LORD,
My soul in praise expands,
And fain would sing the rapturous [song
Thy deathless love demands.

226 Silchester S.M.
Wm. Hammond (Swabia 615) H.A.C. Malan

AWAKE, and sing the song
  Of Glory to the Lamb!
Wake every heart and every tongue
  To praise the Saviour's name.

Sing of His dying love,
  Sing of His rising power,
Sing how He intercedes above
  For us whose sins He bore.

Sing on your heavenly road,
  Ye heirs of glory, sing;
To the ascended Lamb of GOD,
  Your gladsome praises bring.

Soon shall we hear Him say,
  'Ye blessèd children, come!'
Soon will He call us hence away
  To our eternal home.

There shall each raptured tongue
  His endless praise proclaim,
And sweeter voices tune the song
  Of Glory to the Lamb!

227 Bristol C.M.
G. Burder (Dublin 30) Ravenscroft's Psalter 1621

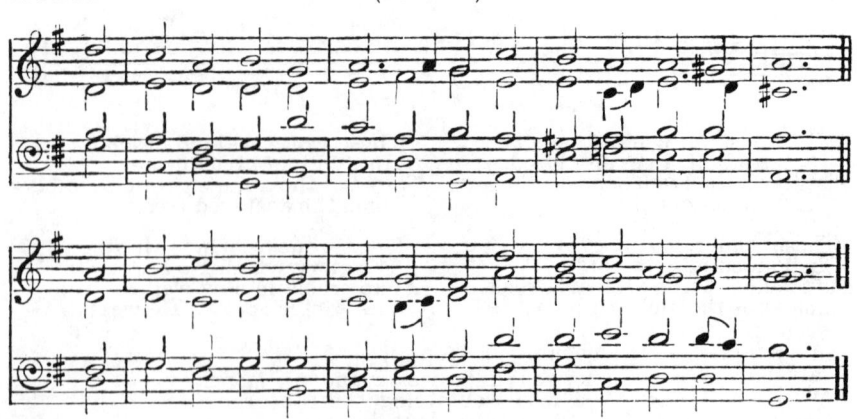

COME, ye that know the Saviour's
  name,
And raise your thoughts above;
Let every heart and voice unite
To sing that GOD is Love!

This precious truth His word reveals,
  And all His mercies prove;
Creation and redemption join
  To shew that GOD is Love!

His patience, bearing much and long
  With those who from Him rove,
His kindness, when He leads them
  home,
Both mark that GOD is Love!

The work begun is carried on
  By power from heaven above;
And every step, from first to last,
  Declares that GOD is Love!

Oh, may we all, while here below,
  This best of blessings prove,
Till nobler songs in brighter worlds
  Proclaim that GOD is Love!

228   **Clarendon Street (I Love Thee) 11.11.11.11**
                (Dilexi 936)   Adoniram J. Gordon

LORD JESUS, I love Thee, I know
  Thou art mine,
My rock and my fortress, my Surety
  divine;
My gracious Redeemer, my song shall
  be now—
'Tis Thou who art worthy, LORD
  JESUS, 'tis Thou!

I love Thee because Thou hast first
  loved me,
And purchased my pardon on
  Calvary's tree;
I love Thee for wearing the thorns on
  Thy brow—

I love Thee in life, I would love Thee
  in death,
And praise Thee as long as Thou
  lendest me breath,
And sing, should the death-dew lie
  cold on my brow—

And when the bright morn of Thy
  glory shall come,
And the children ascend to their
  FATHER'S glad home,
I'll shout, with Thy likeness impressed
  on my brow—

229 Nativity C.M.
Isaac Watts   (Richmond 186)   Hy. Lahee

COME, let us join our cheerful songs
  With all around the throne;
Ten thousand thousand are their tongues,
  But all their joys are one.

'Worthy the Lamb that died,' they cry,
  'To be exalted thus;
'Worthy the Lamb,' our lips reply,
  'For He was slain for us.'

JESUS is worthy to receive
  Honour and power divine;
And blessings, more than we can give,
  Be, LORD, for ever Thine!

Let all that dwell above the sky,
  And air, and earth, and seas,
Conspire to raise Thy glories high,
  And speak Thine endless praise.

Let all creation join in one,
  To bless the sacred name
Of Him who sits upon the throne,
  And to adore the Lamb.

230 Rhodes S.M.
W.P. Mackay   (Huddersfield 180)   C. Warwick Jordan

WITH CHRIST we died to sin,
  Lay buried in His tomb;
But quickened now with Him, our Life,
  We stand beyond our doom.

Our GOD, in wondrous love,
  Has raised us who were dead,
And in the heavenlies made us sit,
  In CHRIST, our living Head.

For us He now appears
  "Within the veil" above;
"Accepted," and "complete in Him,"
  We triumph in His love.

In CHRIST we now are made
  "The righteousness of GOD;"
Born from above, and heirs with Him,
  We follow where He trod.

Rejected and despised,
  He bore the open shame;
As fellow-sufferers, journeying home,
  We glory in His name.

Soon will the Bridegroom come,
  His Bride from earth to call,
With Him in glory then to reign,
  Till GOD be all in all.

231   **Pembroke 8.8.6.D**
Samuel Medley   (Hull 59)   J. Foster

COME, let us sing the matchless
    worth,
  And sweetly sound the glories forth
    Which in the Saviour shine:
To GOD and CHRIST our praise we
    bring,
  The song with which the heavens ring
    We sing by grace divine.

How rich the precious blood He spilt,
Our ransom from the dreadful guilt
    Of sin against our GOD!
How perfect is His righteousness,
In which unspotted, beauteous dress
    His saints have ever stood!

How rich the character He bears,
And all the forms of love He wears,
    Exalted on the throne!
In songs of sweet, untiring praise
We would to everlasting days
    Make all His glories known.

And soon the happy day shall come
When we shall reach our destined
    home,
    And see Him face to face:
Then with our Saviour, LORD, and
    Friend,
The one unbroken day we'll spend
    In singing still His grace!

232 Winchester New L.M.
N.L. Zinzendorf (Ombersley 28) B. Crasselius

JESUS, the LORD, our righteousness!
Our beauty Thou, our glorious dress;
Before the throne, when thus arrayed,
With joy shall we lift up the head.

Bold shall we stand in that great day,
For who aught to our charge shall lay,
Since by Thy blood absolved we are
From sin and guilt, from shame and fear?

Thus Abraham, the friend of GOD,
Thus all the saints redeemed with blood,
Saviour of sinners Thee proclaim,
And all their boast is in Thy name.

This spotless robe the same appears
When ruined nature sinks in years;
No age can change its glorious hue,
The robe of CHRIST is ever new.

Till we behold Thee on Thy throne
We boast in Thee, in Thee alone,
Our beauty this, our glorious dress—
JESUS, the LORD, our righteousness!

233 Love Divine 8.7.8.7
(Sussex 194) J. Stainer

LORD of life and King of glory,
  Now to Thee our hearts we raise,
And we sing the joyful story
  Of the triumphs of Thy grace.

O Thou strength of our salvation,
  None can pluck us from Thy hand;
In the hour of dark temptation,
  Kept by Thee we safely stand.

Grace begun shall end in glory;
  Thou, LORD, hast the victory won;
In Thine own triumphant story
  Is the record of our own.

234

Thos. Kelly

Rhuddlan 8.7.8.7.8.7
(Regent Square 202)

Welsh Trad. Melody

GRACIOUS LORD, my heart is fixed,
  Sing I will, and sing of Thee,
Since the cup that justice mixed
  Thou didst drink, and drink for me:
    Great Deliverer!
  Thou hast set the prisoner free.

Many were the chains that bound me,
  But Thou, Lord, hast loosed them all;
Arms of mercy now surround me—
  Favours these, nor few nor small:
    Saviour, keep me,
  Keep Thy servant, lest he fall.

Fair the scene that lies before me,
  Life eternal JESUS gives;
While He waves His banner o'er me,
  Peace and joy my soul receives:
    Sure His promise,
  I shall live because He lives.

When the world would bid me leave Thee,
  Telling me of shame and loss,
Saviour, guard me, lest I grieve Thee,
  Lest I cease to prize Thy cross;
    This is treasure:
  All beside is only dross.

235   **Eden L.M.**
Edward Denny   (Festus 332)   T.B. Mason

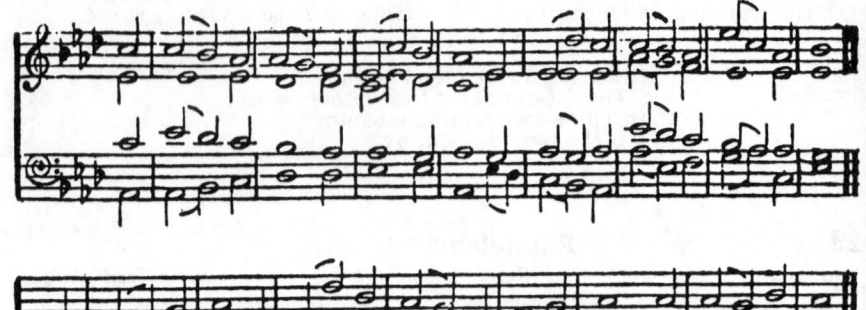

'TIS finished all: our souls to win,
   His life the blessèd JESUS gave;
He died to purge His people's sin,
   And rose triumphant o'er the grave.

Sweet thought! we have a Friend above,
   Our weary, faltering steps to guide,
Who follows with the eye of love
   The little flock for which He died.

Past suffering now, the tender heart
   Of JESUS on His FATHER's throne,
Still in *our* sorrow bears a part,
   And feels it as He felt His own.

LORD JESUS, teach us more and more
   On Thee alone to cast our care,
And, gazing on Thy cross, adore
   The wondrous grace that brought Thee there!

236   **Angels Story 7.6.7.6.D**
Charitie L. Bancroft   (Fairford 913)   A.H. Mann

OH for the robes of whiteness,
　Oh for the undimmed eyes,
Oh for the glorious brightness
　Of the unclouded skies!
Oh for the no more weeping
　Within the land of love,
The endless joy of keeping
　The bridal feast above!

Oh for the bliss of rising,
　Our risen LORD to meet;
On His own breast reclining
　Or sitting at His feet!
Oh for the hour of seeing
　Our Saviour face to face;
The joy of ever being
　In that bright dwelling-place!

JESUS, Thou King of glory,
　We soon shall dwell with Thee;
We soon shall sing the story
　Of love so rich and free;
Meanwhile our thoughts would enter
　E'en now before Thy throne;
That all our love may centre
　On Thee, and Thee alone.

237　　　　Dublin C.M.
John Cennick　　(Manoah 238)　　J. Stevenson

THOU great Redeemer, precious Lamb!
　We love to sing of Thee;
No music like Thy charming name,
　Nor half so sweet can be.

Oh, let us ever hear Thy voice
　To us in mercy speak;
And in our Priest will we rejoice
　Thou great Melchisedec!

Thou, Saviour, shalt be still our theme
　While in this world we stay;
We'll sing our blessèd JESU's name
　When all things else decay,

When we ascend above the cloud,
　With all the favoured throng,
Then shall we sing more sweet, more loud,
　And *THOU* shalt be our song!

238   **Manoah C.M.**
Edward Denny   (Albano 118)   Rossini

O BLESSED JESUS! who but Thou,
  On earth, in heaven above,
May claim from all our willing hearts
  The full response of love?

We love our brethren, LORD, 'tis true,
  Because in them we see
Sweet traces of Thy blessèd self,
  For they are one with Thee;

And one with us—but, oh! 'twas
    Thine,
  Thine only, LORD, to part
With life, and all that love could give,
  To win the wandering heart.

Thus, heirs of endless bliss with Thee,
  We love Thee—we adore,
And ask Thee still for greater grace,
  To love Thee more and more.

239   **It Passeth Knowledge 10.10.10.10.4**
Mary Shekleton   Ira D. Sankey

IT passeth knowledge, that dear love
  of Thine,
O Jesus, Saviour! yet this soul of
  mine
Would of Thy love, in all its breadth
  and length,
Its height and depth, its everlasting
  strength,   Know more and more.

It passeth telling, that dear love of
  Thine,
O Jesus, Saviour! yet these lips of
  mine
Would fain proclaim to sinners, far
  and near,
A love which can remove all guilty
  fear,   And love beget.

It passeth praises, that dear love of
  Thine,
O Jesus, Saviour! yet this heart of
  mine
Would sing that love, so full, so rich,
  so free,
Which brings a rebel sinner, such as
  me,   Nigh unto God.

But though I cannot sing, or tell, or
  know
The fulness of Thy love while here
  below,
My empty vessel I may freely bring:
O Thou, who art of love the living
  spring,   My vessel fill!

Oh, fill me, Jesus, Saviour, with Thy
  love!
Lead, lead me to the living fount
  above!
Thither may I, in simple faith, draw
  nigh,
And never to another fountain fly,
    But unto Thee.

And when my Saviour face to face I
  see,
When at Thy lofty throne I bow the
  knee;
Then of Thy love, in all its breadth
  and length,
Its height and depth, its everlasting
  strength,
    My soul shall sing.

Bentley 7.6.7.6.D

Mary Peters — (Day of Rest 272) — J. Hullah

1 WITHIN the FATHER'S bosom,
  There's even now a home
For every true believer,
  Wherever he may roam
When CHRIST, our Head, ascended,
  His members all arose;
And where He now is seated,
  We may by faith repose.

2 O Risen LORD, Thy SPIRIT
  Doth surely dwell within
The living FATHER'S children,
  Whom Thou hast cleans'd from sin;
Thy blood doth purge our conscience,
  And, though we're self-abhorred,
We trust Thine arm to bring us
  Safe home, Almighty LORD!

3 As risen now in spirit,
  We soon shall really be
In soul and body perfect,
  And glorified with Thee;
Our FATHER'S smiles are cheering,
  Though trying is the way;
Our FATHER'S house the dwelling
  Made ready for that day.

4 The COMFORTER. now present,
  Assures us of Thy love,
And gives us here sweet earnests
  Of all the joys above;
The river of Thy pleasures
  Is what we long for now,
With Thy new name imprinted
  On every sinless brow.

241   Farewell Hymn 11.11.11.11. and Chorus
H.R. Bishop

1. No future but glory, Lord Jesus,
   have we—
How bright is the prospect of being
   with Thee!
O home of all homes, with the
   Father above!
O wonderful dwelling of infinite love!
   Home, home, bright, bright home!
   How blessèd the prospect, Lord
      Jesus, of home!

2. A moment's affliction, Lord Jesus,
      is light,
And works for us glory surpassingly
      bright;
Whilst viewing not things which are
      but for a time,
But objects far brighter in glory
      sublime:
   Home, home, bright, bright home!
   Our future's eternal in Thy blessèd
      home!

3. "One thing" would we do, we would
      press toward the goal,
Thyself, Lord, in glory, the prize of
      our soul—
Forget what's behind, for the bright
      things before,
Since all they who know Thee would
      know Thee still more:
   Home, home, bright, bright home!
   We press on to know Thee and reach
      Thee, at home!

4. In heaven alone is our city and state,
From thence, Lord, as Saviour, Thy-
      self we await,
Our bodies to change and conform
      them to Thine,
That we in Thine image and glory
      may shine:
   Home, home, bright, bright home!
   Soon we shall be with Thee and like
      Thee, at home!

242 Bethany 8.7.8.7.D
W. Williams (Excelling 87) Hy. Smart

1 LEAD us, Saviour, by Thy power,
    Safe into the promised rest:
  Choose the path, the way whatever
    Seems to Thee, O LORD, the best:
  Be our Guide in every peril,
    Watch and keep us night and day,
  Else our foolish hearts will wander
    From the straight and narrow way.

2 Since in Thee we found redemption,
    And salvation full and free,
  Nothing can our souls dishearten
    But forgetfulness of Thee;
  Nought can stay our steady progress,
    More than conquerors we shall be,
  If our eye, whate'er the danger,
    Look to Thee, and none but Thee.

3 In Thy presence we are happy,
    In Thy presence we're secure,
  In Thy presence all afflictions
    We can easily endure;
  In Thy presence we can conquer,
    We can suffer, we can die;
  Far from Thee we faint and languish,
    Oh, our Saviour, keep us nigh!

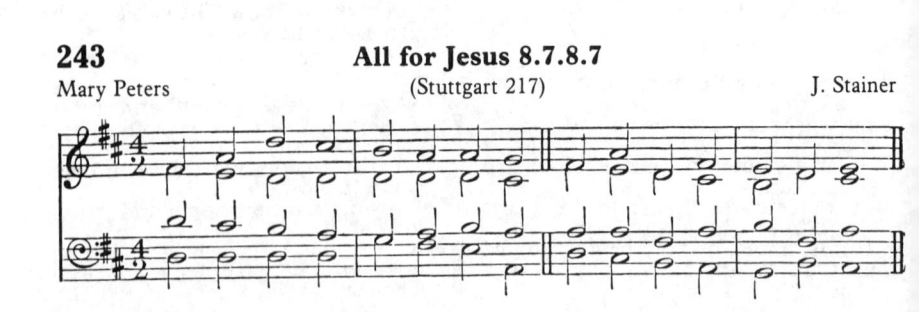

243 All for Jesus 8.7.8.7
Mary Peters (Stuttgart 217) J. Stainer

MANY sons to glory bringing,
  GOD sets forth His heavenly
    name;
On we march, in chorus singing—
  'Worthy the ascended Lamb!'

GOD, who gave the blood to screen us,
  GOD looks down in perfect love;
Clouds may seem to pass between us,
  There's no change in Him above.

Though the restless foe accuses,
  Sins recounting like a flood,
Every charge our GOD refuses—
  CHRIST hath answered with His
    blood.

In the refuge GOD provided, flowers,
  Though the world's destruction
We are safe, to CHRIST confided—
  Everlasting life is ours.

And ere long, when come to glory,
  We shall sing a well-known strain;
This, the never-tiring story—
  'Worthy is the Lamb once slain.'

244   **Meribah 8.8.6.D**
Samuel Davies   (Pembroke 53)   Lowell Mason

ETERNAL praise, our GOD, shall rise
  In mansions far beyond the skies;
Thy name shall be adored!
With joyful hearts our songs we raise,
Our GOD and FATHER, Thee we praise,
  While waiting for our LORD.

When ruined, guilty, and undone,
Thou gav'st for us Thine only SON;
  We trust Thy truthful word:
Rejoicing in Thy love we sing,
Praise for Thy Gift of gifts we bring—
  Thy goodness we record.

We praise Thee in our pathway here—
Far off we were, but now brought near
  Through JESUS CHRIST our LORD:
Fresh grace for every moment here,
Fresh manna in the desert drear,
  Thy SPIRIT doth afford.

When He shall come for whom we wait
We then shall see and know how great
  The gain that love hath stored:
With joyful hearts our songs we raise,
Our GOD and FATHER now we praise,
  While waiting for our LORD.

245
John East

Dawn C.M.D.
(Ellacombe 91)

THERE is a fold where none can stray,
  And pastures ever green,
Where sultry sun or stormy day
  Or night are never seen:
Far up the everlasting hills
  In GOD's own light it lies;
His smile its vast dimension fills
  With joy that never dies.

There is a Shepherd living there,
  The First-born from the dead,
Who tends with sweet, unwearied care
  The flock for which He bled:
There the deep streams of joy that flow,
  Proceed from GOD's right hand;
He made them, and He bids them go
  To feed that happy land.

There congregate the sons of light,
　Fair as the morning sky,
And taste of infinite delight
　Beneath their Saviour's eye :
Where'er He turns, they willing turn ;
　In unity they move ;
Their seraph spirits nobly burn
　In harmony of love.

There, in the power of heavenly sight,
　They gaze upon the throne,
And scan perfection's utmost height,
　And know as they are known :
Their joy bursts forth in strains of love
　And clear, symphonious song,
And all the azure heights above
　The echoes roll along.

　　Oh, may our faith take up that sound,
　　　Though toiling here below ;
　　'Midst trials may our joys abound,
　　　And songs amidst our woe,
　　Until we reach that happy shore,
　　　And join to swell their strain,
　　And from our GOD go out no more,
　　　And never weep again !

246　　　Darwall's 148th 6.6.6.6.8.8

Samuel Barnard　　　(Christchurch 81)　　　John Darwall

JEHOVAH is our strength,
　And He shall be our song ;
We shall o'ercome at length,
　Although our foes be strong ;
In vain doth Satan now oppose,
For GOD is stronger than His foes.

The LORD our refuge is,
　And ever will remain ;
Since He hath made us His,
　He will our cause maintain ;
In vain our enemies oppose,
For GOD is stronger than His foes.

The LORD our portion is,
　What can we wish for more?
By purchase we are His,
　And never can be poor ;
In vain do earth and hell oppose,
For GOD is stronger than His foes.

The LORD our Shepherd is,
　He knows our every need ;
And since we now are His,
　His care our souls will feed ;
In vain do sin and death oppose,
For GOD is stronger than His foes.

247 Leoni 6.6.8.4.D

Thos. Olivers
Hebrew Melody

1 THE God of Abraham praise,
    Who reigns enthroned above,
  Ancient of everlasting days,
    And God of love!
  Jehovah, great "I AM,"
    By earth and heaven confessed—
  I bow, and bless the sacred name,
    For ever blest!

  The God of Abraham praise,
    Whose all-sufficient grace
  Shall guide me all my happy days
    In all His ways;
  He calls a worm His friend,
    He calls Himself my God!
  And He shall save me to the end,
    Through Jesu's blood.

2 The God of Abraham praise,
    At whose supreme command,
  From earth I rise, and seek the joys
    At His right hand;
  I all on earth forsake,
    Its wisdom, fame, and power,
  And Him my only portion make,
    My shield and tower.

  He by Himself hath sworn,
    I on His oath depend;
  I shall, on eagles' wings upborne,
    To heaven ascend;
  I shall behold His face,
    I shall His power adore,
  And sing the wonders of His grace
    For evermore!

248

Jas. G. Deck   **Mackinlay L.M.D.**   Alex. Lee and G.F. Knowles
(Redemption Ground 610)

LORD, we are *Thine:* our GOD Thou art;
  Fashioned and made we were, as clay;
These curious frames, in every part,
  Thy wisdom, power, and love display:
Each breath we draw, each pulse that beats,
  Each organ formed by skill divine,
Each precious sense aloud repeats,
  Great GOD, that we are only Thine.

LORD, we are *Thine:* in Thee we live,
  Supported by Thy tender care:
Thou dost each hourly mercy give—
  Thine earth we tread, we breathe Thine air;
Raiment and food Thy hands supply;
  Thy sun's bright rays around us shine;
Guarded by Thine all-seeing eye,
  We own that we are wholly Thine.

LORD, we are *Thine:* bought by Thy blood—
  Once the poor, guilty slaves of sin;
Thou hast redeemed us unto GOD,
  And made Thy SPIRIT dwell within;
Our sinful wanderings Thou hast borne
  With love and patience all divine:
As brands, then, from the burning torn,
  We own that we are wholly Thine.

LORD, we are *Thine:* Thy claims we own—
  Ourselves to Thee would humbly give;
Reign Thou within our hearts alone,
  And let us to Thy glory live:
Here may we each Thy mind display,
  In all Thy gracious image shine;
So shall we hail that looked-for day,
  When Thou shalt own that we are *Thine!*

249 St. Bernard C.M.
R.C. Chapman (Westminster 270) J. Richardson

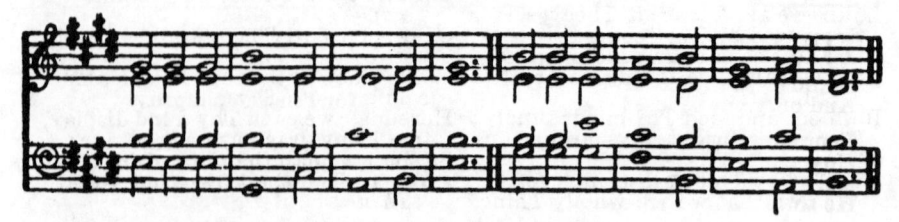

MY GOD and FATHER, I am Thine,
   Teach me to do Thy will;
One business here on earth be mine—
   Thy bidding to fulfil.

To please Thee be my meat and drink,
   To make my FATHER glad;
With wisdom let my heart be filled,
   My soul with beauty clad.

The mind and ways of CHRIST the
     LORD,
   His lowly heart be mine;
That I to all men may declare
   The power of love divine.

Songs in the night Thy SPIRIT gives;
   Thus would I sing to Thee
Of Thy dear SON, whom Thou didst
     bruise
   For sinners on the tree.

250 Whitburn L.M.
Douglas Russell (Antwerp 353) H. Baker

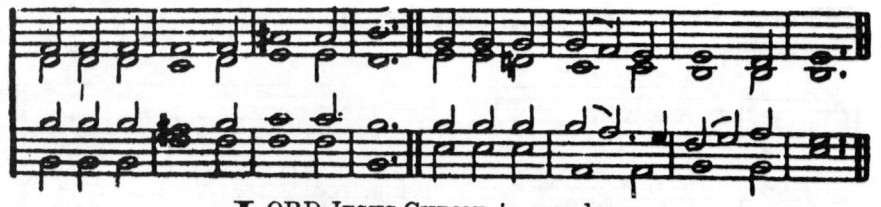

LORD JESUS CHRIST, in wondrous
  grace
    Thou cam'st to earth from heaven's
      high throne;
  As Surety, standing in our place,
    Thou didst for all our sins atone.

Thou wast o'erwhelmed by judgment's flood,
    In whose dark depths our sins were
      drowned;
  Thy love more deep, proved by Thy
    blood,
    Still strong and true is ever found.

LORD, let that love from us draw forth
  A love unfeigned and unreserved
  To Thee, O CHRIST of matchless
    worth,
    As for Thyself we are preserved.

Be Thou the gladness of our joy,
  Thy service here our true delight!
  Soon shall Thy praise our lips employ,
    Thy glories fill our raptured sight!

251   **Woolwich S.M.**
Frances R. Havergal   (Trentham 198)   C.E. Kettle

ONLY one heart to give,   All! for it is His own,
  Only one voice to use,   He gave the tiny store;
Only one little life to live,   All! for it must be His alone;
  And only one to lose!   All! for I have no more.

Poor is my best, and small—   All! for the last and least
  How could I dare divide?   He stoopeth to uplift!
Surely my LORD shall have it all;   The altar of my great High Priest
  He shall not be denied.   Shall sanctify my gift.

Cambridge S.M.
(Tuam 225)

R. Harrison

O SAVIOUR! we are Thine
In everlasting bands;
Our thoughts, ourselves, we would resign
Into Thy gracious hands.

To Thee we fain would cleave,
With ever-growing zeal;
Whenever pressed Thy paths to leave,
Oh, let not sin prevail!

Let nothing from us hide
The glory of Thy day,
But, waiting Thy return, abide
The morning's joyful ray.

Since we with Thee are one,
We know we need not fear;
In heaven Thou wilt not dwell alone,
Thy Bride will soon be there.

Bentley 7.6.7.6.D
(Aurelia 171)

J. Hullah

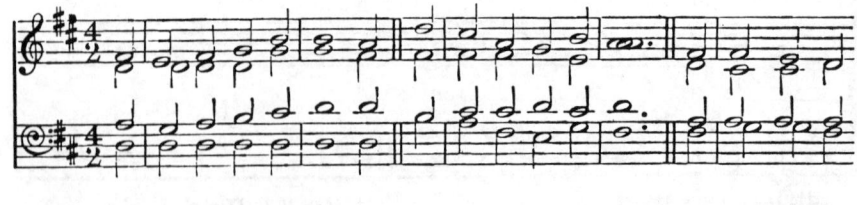

THINE ever—loved and chosen
    In Thy deep thoughts of grace,
Before the world's foundation,
    Or dayspring knew its place:
Thine only—sought and followed,
    When in the far-off land ;
Then kept, and fed, and guided,
    By Thine unwearied hand.

Thine, only Thine, LORD JESUS!
    Whom need we now beside?
For ever in Thy presence
    Our weary souls we hide:
All other refuge faileth,
    All other springs run dry,
Thou, LORD, alone art changeless,
    And Thou art ever nigh.

Thine ever, LORD, Thine only,
    E'en in the glory-light,
When bursts the dawn of heaven
    Upon our raptured sight,
One deep joy shall enfold us,
    Shall swell our highest song—
That we are Thine, Thine only,
    'Mid all the gathered throng!

Thine only, LORD; oh, keep us
    More closely at Thy side!
While here we wait and worship,
    Our hearts would there abide:
We crave no other gladness,
    We seek no other rest,
Till, raised in Thy likeness,
    We shall with Thee be blest!

254   Newcastle 8.6.8.8.6
R.C. Chapman   (Rest, Maker 802)   Henry L. Morley

BY threefold title I am Thine,
    Thou blessèd SON of GOD!
The FATHER'S choice. Thy blood divine,
Thy HOLY SPIRIT'S power combine
    To make me Thine abode.

Companion of my pilgrimage,
    JESUS, exalted LORD ;
Thou art the same from age to age,
My strength, my joy, my heritage
    My glory and reward.

    From idols keep me by Thy grace,
        Pure let my conscience be ;
    And every stain Thine eye can trace,
    Quickly by Thine own blood efface,
        That I may dwell in Thee.

255
A. Midlane

Veni Domine 4.6.8.8.4

THINE, JESUS, Thine!
    No more this heart of mine
Would seek its joy apart from Thee;
The world is crucified to me,
    And I am Thine.

Thine, Thine alone,
    My joy, my hope, my crown!
Now earthly things may fade and die,
They charm my soul no more, for I
    Am Thine alone.

Thine, ever Thine!
    For ever to recline
On love eternal, fixed and sure:
Yes, I am Thine for evermore,
    LORD JESUS, Thine.

Then let me live,
    Continual praise to give
To Thy dear name, my gracious LORD,
Henceforth alone beloved, adored—
    Thine would I live,

Till Thou shalt come
    And bear me to Thy home,
For ever freed from earthly care,
Eternally Thy love to share—
    LORD JESUS, come!

256   **Wells 7.7.7.7.7.7**
Robt. M. McCheyne   (Maidstone 917)   Dmitri Bortnianski

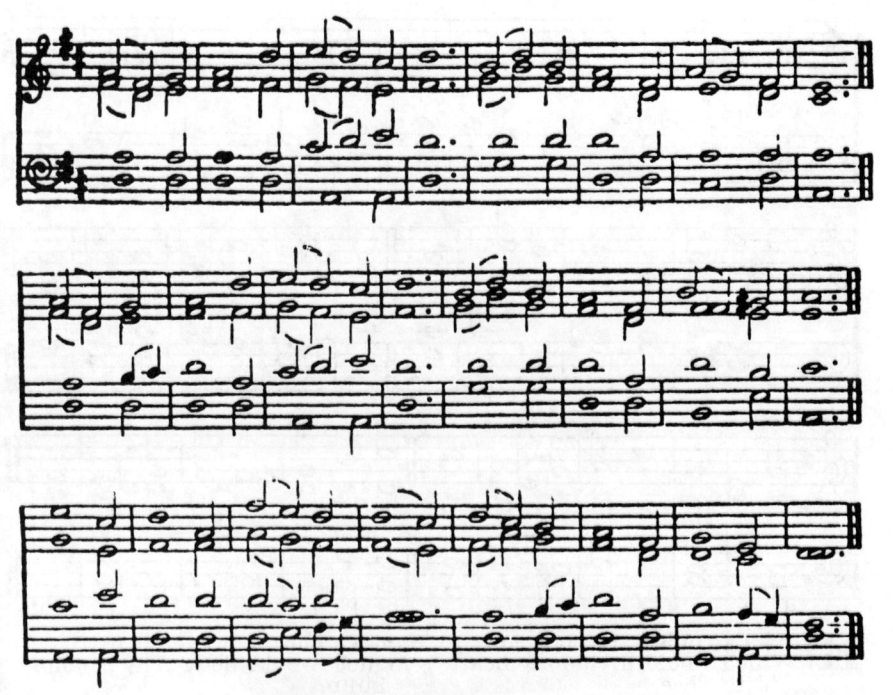

WHEN this passing world is done,
  When has sunk yon radiant sun,
When I stand with CHRIST on high,
Looking o'er life's history—
Then, LORD, shall I fully know,
Not till then, how much I owe.

When I stand before the throne,
Dressed in beauty not my own;
When I see Thee as Thou art,
Love Thee with unsinning heart—
Then, LORD, shall I fully know,
Not till then, how much I owe.

When the praise of heaven I hear,
Loud as thunders to the ear,
Loud as many waters' noise,
Sweet as harp's melodious voice—
Then, LORD, shall I fully know,
Not till then, how much I owe.

Chosen not for good in me,
Wakened up from wrath to flee,
Hidden in the Saviour's side,
By the SPIRIT sanctified—
Teach me, LORD, on earth to show,
By my love, how much I owe.

257   Pater Omnium 8.8.8.8.8.8

G.W. Frazer   (Melita 351)   H.J.E. Holmes

HAVE I an object, LORD, below,
   Which would divide my heart
     with Thee,
Which would divert its even flow
   In answer to Thy constancy?
Oh, may this wandering heart return,
Filled with Thy love afresh to burn!

Have I a hope, however dear,
   Which would defer Thy coming,
     LORD,
Which would detain my spirit here,
   Where nought can lasting joy afford?
From it, my Saviour, set me free,
To look, and long, and wait for Thee.

   Be Thou the object, bright and fair,
     To fill and satisfy my heart;
   My hope to meet Thee in the air,
     And nevermore from Thee to part;
   That I may undistracted be
   To follow, serve, and wait for Thee!

258   Abney C.M.

Macleod Wylie   (St. Peter 24)   Asa Hull

Slow.

A BROKEN and a contrite heart
Thou wilt not, LORD, despise;
Beyond all other offerings,
Be this my sacrifice!

A broken heart, yet cleansed by blood,
Contrite, and yet at rest;
A soul subdued by penitence,
But still by peace possest.

Enable me to render back
This gift of heavenly birth,
So precious in Thy sight, O LORD,
Who knowest well its worth.

259   Abbey C.M.
R.C. Chapman   (St. Fulbert 126)   Scottish Psalter

O JESUS, LORD, whose hands and feet
Declare Thy power to save,
Dominion o'er myself complete—
Full mastery I crave.

May I in body, spirit, soul,
Thy holy vessel be!
Do Thou my every wish control—
Thy sorrows let me see!·

Oh, make me by Thy SPIRIT strong,
Saviour, on Thee to lean,
A pilgrim skilled in heavenly song,
Beholding things unseen;

A perfect image of Thy ways,
A burning, shining light,
A polished jewel to Thy praise,
In GOD the FATHER'S sight!

260   **Hursley L.M.**
J.G. Deck   (Maryton 61)   P. Ritter

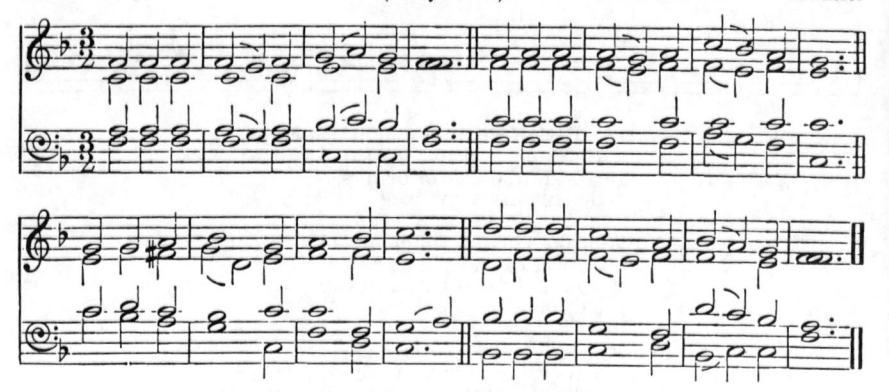

1. MASTER, we would no longer be
Loved by the world that hated Thee;
But patient in Thy footsteps go,
Thy sorrow, as Thy joy, to know.

2. We would—and oh, bestow the power—
With meekness meet the darkest hour;
The shame despise, however tried,
For Thou wast scorned and crucified.

3. Master, to Thee we now would cleave,
Content for Thee all else to leave,
Our cross to bear, Thy steps to trace,
Strong in Thine all-sufficing grace.

4. For soon must pass the "little while,"
And joy shall crown Thy servants' toil;
Our sure reward, to hear Thee own
Our names before the FATHER'S throne.

261   **Blockley L.M.**
Joseph Grigg   (Whitburn 34)   T. Blockley

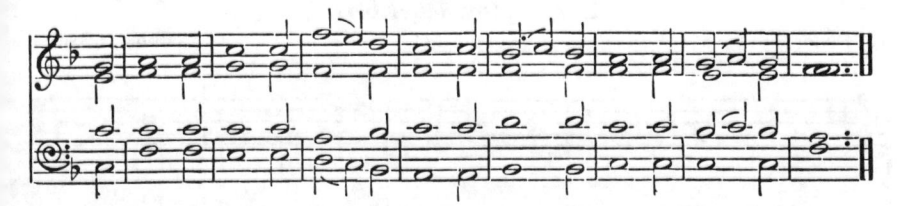

JESUS, and shall it ever be,
    A mortal man ashamed of Thee?
Ashamed of Thee, whom angels praise,
Whose glories shine through endless
    days?

Ashamed of JESUS! sooner far
Let evening blush to own a star;
He shed the beams of light divine
O'er this benighted soul of mine.

Ashamed of JESUS! just as soon
Let midnight be ashamed of noon;
'Twas midnight with my soul till He,
Bright Morning Star, bade darkness
    flee.

Ashamed of JESUS! that dear Friend
On whom my hopes of heaven depend?
No! when I blush, be this my shame,
That I no more confess His name.

In Him I boast, and not in vain—
In Him I boast a Saviour slain!
And oh, may this my glory be,
That CHRIST is not ashamed of me!

262   Claremont C.M.
Edward Denny   (Dalehurst 345)   J. Foster

FORTH from the FATHER'S loving
        breast,
    To bear our sin and shame,
To face a cold, unfeeling world,
    The heavenly Stranger came.

This earth to Him, the LORD of all,
    No kindly welcome gave:
In Judah's land the Saviour found
    No shelter but the grave.

The cross was His: now be it ours
    Its shame on earth to bear,
And glory in the thought that He
    For us once suffered there.

Lymington 7.6.7.6.D
(Aurelia 171)

H. Taylor　　　　　　　　　　　　　　　　　　　　Robt. Jackson

MY Saviour, I would own Thee
　Amid the world's proud scorn—
The world that mocked and crowned
　　Thee
　With diadem of thorn;
The world that now rejects Thee,
　Makes nothing of Thy love,
Counts nought the grace and pity
　That brought Thee from above.

My LORD, my Master, help me
  To walk apart with Thee,
Outside the camp, where only
  Thy beauty I can see;
Far from the world's loud turmoil,
  Far from its busy din,
Far from its praise and honour,
  Its unbelief and sin.

Oh, keep my heart at leisure
  From all the world beside;
In close communion ever,
  With Thee, LORD, to abide,
That I Thy whispered breathings
  Of love and truth may hear,
And hail Thee with rejoicing
  When Thou shalt soon appear.

264
A.M. Toplady

Azmon C.M.
(Abridge 151)

C.G. Glaser

COMPARED with CHRIST, in all
    beside,
  No comeliness I see—
My heart's desire, all-gracious LORD,
  Is to abide in Thee.

Less than Thyself will not suffice,
  But Thou art ample store;
More than Thyself I cannot crave,
  And Thou canst give no more.

Loved of my LORD with love intense
  For Thee my love would burn;
Chosen of Thee ere time began,
  I choose Thee in return.

Whate'er consists not with Thy will
  Oh, teach me to resign;
I'm rich to all the intents of bliss,
  Since my Beloved is mine!

265
Gerhard Tersteegen

Basle 8.8.8.8.8.8
(Pater Omnium 44)

THOU hidden love of GOD, whose height,
Whose depth unfathomed, no man knows,
I see from far Thy beauteous light,
And inly sigh for Thy repose:
My heart is pained, nor can it be
At rest except, my LORD, in Thee.

Is there a thing beneath the sun
  That strives with Thee my heart to share?
Oh, take it thence, and reign alone,
  The LORD of every motion there:
Then shall my heart from earth be free,
  When it has found its all in Thee.

Oh, hide this self from me, that I
  No more, but Thou in me mayst live;
Bid all my vile affections die,
  Nor let one hateful thought survive;
Nothing to tempt me may I see,
  Nor aught desire, or seek, but Thee.

LORD, draw my heart from earth away,
  And make it only know Thy call;
Speak to my inmost soul and say,
  'I am thy Saviour and thine All!'
Oh, dwell in me, fill all my soul,
And all my powers by grace control.

266   Cross of Jesus 8.7.8.7

R.C. Chapman   (Stuttgart 217)   John Stainer

THOU art Love, our GOD and FATHER,
  Who didst from Thy bosom send
Thine own SON, His brethren's Surety,
  Who will love us to the end.

All Thy waves His soul afflicted,
  Death He suffered in our stead;
Then did cease the sea from raging,
  Then He bruised the serpent's head.

Crucified with CHRIST and risen,
  We with JESUS praise Thy name;
He is in Thy bosom resting,
  Whence to ransom us He came.

With the SPIRIT now anointed,
  We present ourselves to Thee;
Bond-slaves once of cruel masters,
  Now we walk at liberty.

267   Fingal C.M.
R.C. Chapman   (Dalehurst 345)   J.S. Anderson

JESUS, the FATHER'S only SON,
  On Thee I fix mine eyes :
Girded by Thee, my race would run,
  And things of earth despise.
I fight Thy battles, glorious LORD !
  Thy SPIRIT'S still small voice
Assures my heart of full reward,
  And warfare is my choice.

I ponder all Thy toil and pain,
  And watch the dawn of day :
Thou, LORD, wilt soon appear again,
  And wipe my tears away.
Thy cross is charging me to care
  For saints and all mankind ;
Grant me to spend myself, nor spare,
  With constant, heavenly mind !

268   Meribah 8.8.6.D
(Hull 517)   Lowell Mason

SAVIOUR, whene'er I think of Thee,
  And of Thy love so full and free,
    In death and suffering shewn ;
All earthly good I would resign,
Follow where'er Thy footsteps shine,
    And cleave to Thee alone.

Thee as my portion I would take,
And suffer all things for Thy sake,
    Who all my woes didst bear :
I would in all things bear my cross ;
In tribulation, shame, and loss,
    Resolved with Thee to share.

What though I meet the worldling's hate,
Thy love will richly compensate
For all my present loss:
What joy with Thee to live and reign!
Oh, may this hope my heart constrain
To count all else but dross!

I can encounter every ill,
If but my heart and mind be still
With Thy loved presence blest:
With joy I then my way pursue,
Assured that Thou wilt bear me thro',
Up to Thy heavenly rest.

269 St. Matthew C.M.D.
H. Bonar   (Ellacombe 91)   W. Croft

FILL Thou my life, O LORD my GOD,
In every part with praise,
That my whole being may proclaim
Thy Being and Thy ways;
Not for the lip of praise alone
Nor e'en the praising heart
I ask, but for a life made up
Of praise in every part;

Enduring wrong, reproach, or loss,
With sweet and steadfast will;
Loving and blessing those who hate,
Returning good for ill;
Surrendering my fondest will
In all things, great or small;
Seeking the good of others still,
Nor pleasing self at all.

So shalt Thou, LORD, from me—e'en me,
Receive the glory due;
And so shall I begin on earth
The song for ever new:
So shall no part of day or night
From sacredness be free,
But all my life, in every step,
Be fellowship with Thee.

270   **Westminster C.M.**

Charitie L. Bancroft   (Belmont 26)   Jas. Turle

LORD, I desire to live as one
  Who bears a blood-bought name,
As one who fears but grieving Thee,
  And knows no other shame;

As one by whom Thy walk below
  Should never be forgot;
As one who fain would keep apart
  From all Thou lovest not.

Grant me to live as one who knows
  Thy fellowship of love;
As one whose eyes can pierce beyond
  The pearl-built gates above;

As one who daily speaks to Thee,
  And hears Thy voice divine
With depth of tenderness declare,
  'Beloved! thou art Mine.'

271   **Nicaea 12.12.12.10**

Douglas Russell   J.B. Dykes

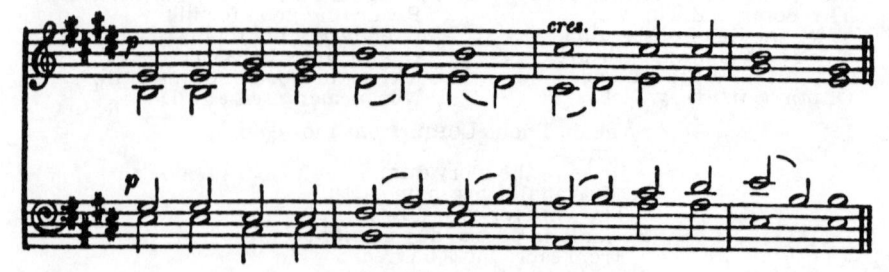

WORTHY, worthy, worthy Thou
    of adoration!
  Glory in the highest! glad praise
    we offer Thee!
  Crowned with glory, honour—worthy
    coronation—
  Thee on the Throne, O Son of God,
    we see!

Worthy, worthy, worthy, Lamb of
    God most holy!
  Blessèd all Thy footprints from
    Bethlehem to the tree;
  Without spot or blemish, ever meek
    and lowly,
  Perfect Thy life—God found repose
    in Thee!

Worthy, worthy, worthy! Perfect
    our salvation!
  Costly was our ransom, once paid
    in blood by Thee;
  We are with Thee risen—past our
    condemnation;
  No longer bondmen—through Thy
    death we're free.

Worthy, worthy, worthy, Lord of
    life and glory!
  Love divine our portion—ours to
    eternity!
  Now we sing Thy praises, theme of
    sacred story!
  Soon in the glory we shall reign
    with Thee.

Thou alone art worthy! Praise from
    every nation,
  Praises loud and lasting, shall yet
    ascend to Thee:
  "Blessing, honour, glory," sings the
    whole creation—
  Heaven, earth and ocean, in full
    harmony.

272 Day of Rest 7.6.7.6.D

J.S.B. Monsell (Bentley 18) J.W. Elliott

Voices in Unison.   *Harmony.*

Man. Ped.

TO Thee, O blessèd Saviour!
  My spirit turns for rest;
My peace is in Thy favour,
  My pillow on Thy breast;
Though all the world deceive me,
  I know that I am Thine,
And Thou wilt never leave me,
  O blessèd Saviour mine!

In Thee my trust abideth,
  On Thee my hope relies,
O Thou whose love provideth
  For all beneath the skies:
'Twas Thou whose mercy found me,
  From bondage set me free,
And then for ever bound me
  With threefold cords to Thee.

Alas, that I should ever
　Have failed in love to Thee,
The only One who never
　Forgot or slighted me!
Oh for a heart to love Thee
　More truly as I ought,
And nothing place above Thee,
　In deed, or word, or thought!

Oh for that choicest blessing
　Of living in Thy love,
And thus on earth possessing
　The peace of heaven above!
Oh for the bliss that by it
　The soul securely knows,
The holy calm and quiet
　Of faith's serene repose!

273　　Albano C.M.
(St. Bernard 5)　　　　V. Novello

NO lips like Thine, most blessèd
　　LORD,
　None ever spake like Thee,
As sweetest honey or as myrrh
　Flows fragrant from the tree.

Thy lips "like lilies!" What so pure,
　So lovely in their grace,
With secret power, in hours of grief,
　To kindle thoughts of praise!

Forth from those lips rich grace is
　　poured,
　To comfort all who mourn;
No tongue like Thine to cheer the
　　faint,
　Thou Friend of the forlorn!

As softening showers upon the grass,
　Gentle as early dew,
Thy speech distils into the soul,
　Its graces to renew.

Ages have passed since at Thy voice
　Men marvelled as they heard;
And still our hearts within us burn
　While listening to Thy word.

274 Sheltered Dale 8.6.8.6.8.6

Anna L. Waring (Spohr 17) German Trad. Melody

1 MY heart is fixed, O GOD, my strength!
  Oh, make me strong to bear;
  I would be joyful in Thy love,
  And peaceful in Thy care:
  Deal with me, for my Saviour's sake,
  According to His prayer.

2 Happy are they who learn of Thee,
  Though patient suffering teach,
  The secret of enduring strength,
  And praise too deep for speech—
  Peace that no pressure from without,
  No strife within, can reach.

3 There is no death for me to fear,
  For CHRIST, my LORD, hath died;
  There is no curse in all my pain,
  For He was crucified;
  And it is fellowship with Him
  That keeps me near His side.

4 Deep unto deep may call, but I
  With peaceful heart would say,
  Thy lovingkindness hath a charge
  No waves can take away;
  So let the storm that speeds me home
  Deal with me as it may.

275   **Morecambe 10.10.10.10**

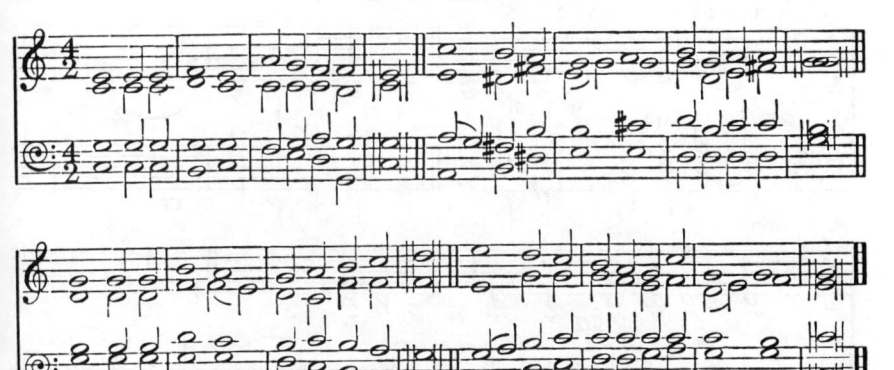

H. Bonar   (St. Agnes, Langran 132)   F.C. Atkinson

NOT what I am, O LORD, but what
   Thou art—
  That, that alone can be my soul's
    true rest;
Thy love, not mine, bids fear and
   doubt depart,
  And stills the tempest of my tossing
    breast.

It is Thy perfect love that casts out
   fear;
  I know the voice that whispers "It
    is I;"
And in Thy well-known words of
   heavenly cheer
  I find the joy that bids each sorrow
    fly.

Thy name is Love! I hear it from Thy
   cross;
  Thy name is Love! I read it in Thy
    tomb;
All meaner love is perishable dross,
  But this shall light me through
    time's thickest gloom.

'Tis what I know of Thee, my LORD
   and GOD,
  That fills my soul with peace, my
    lips with song;
Thou art my health, my joy, my staff
   and rod;
  Leaning on Thee, in weakness I am
    strong.

More of Thyself, oh, shew me, hour
   by hour,
  More of Thy glory, O my GOD and
    LORD;
More of Thyself, in all Thy grace and
   power,
  More of Thy love and truth, Incar-
    nate Word!

276 Thornbury 7.6.7.6.D
S.C.G. Küster (Day of Rest 272) Basil Harwood

L ORD JESUS, Friend unfailing!
   How kind art Thou to me!
Are cares or fears assailing?
   I find my strength in Thee :
Why should my feet grow weary
   Of this my pilgrim way?
Rough though the path and dreary,
   It ends in perfect day!

Nought, nought I court as pleasure,
   Compared, O CHRIST, with Thee !
Thy sorrow without measure
   Earned peace and joy for me!
I love to own, LORD JESUS,
   Thy claims o'er me divine ;
Bought with Thy blood most precious,
   Whose can I be but Thine?

What fills my heart with gladness?
   'Tis Thy abounding grace!
Where can I look in sadness,
   But on my Saviour's face?
My all is Thy providing—
   Thy love can ne'er grow cold ;
In Thee, my refuge, hiding,
   No good wilt Thou withhold.

Why should I droop in sorrow?
   Thou'rt ever by my side!
Why, trembling, dread the morrow?
   What ill can e'er betide?
If I my cross have taken,
   'Tis but to follow Thee ;
If scorned, despised, forsaken,
   Nought severs Thee from me!

From every tribulation,
   From every sore distress,
In Thee I've full salvation,
   Sure help and quiet rest :
No fear of foes prevailing,
   I triumph, LORD, in Thee!
O Saviour, Friend unfailing,
   Be ever near to me!

277 Dublin C.M.
John Ryland (Warwick 340) J. Stevenson

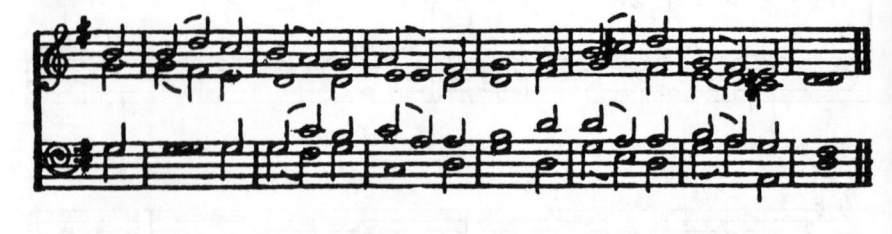

O LORD! I would delight in Thee
  And on Thy care depend;
To Thee in every trouble flee,
  My sure, my steadfast Friend.

When human cisterns all are dried,
  Thy fulness is the same;
May I with this be satisfied,
  And glory in Thy name.

Why should I thirst for aught below,
  While there's a fountain near—
A fountain which doth ever flow,
  The fainting heart to cheer?

Oh that I may by simple faith
  Abide within the veil,
And rest on what my Saviour saith,
  Whose word can never fail!

He that has made my heaven secure,
  Will all I need provide;
While CHRIST is rich, can I be poor?
  What can I want beside?

O LORD, I cast my care on Thee,
  I triumph and adore:
Oh that my great concern may be
  To love and please Thee more!

278 Stracathro C.M.
(Dublin 277) C. Hutcheson

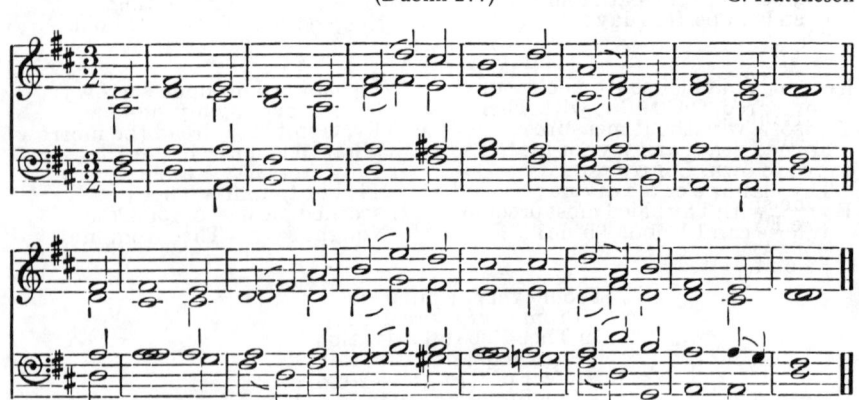

O CHRIST, our living Head, in Thee
What grace and glory meet!
In Thee, in whom all fulness dwells,
Thy members are complete.

Thou true and living Vine, each
branch
Derives its life from Thee,
And while abiding in Thyself
Must ever fruitful be.

Thou Fountain of eternal life,
Thy streams unceasing flow.
And all who come to Thee and drink,
No thirst can ever know.

LORD JESUS, full of grace and truth,
We, who in Thee believe,
Would on Thy fulness ever live,
And grace for grace receive.

On our Belovèd would we lean,
As homeward through this waste—
Still finding Thee our all in all—
With willing steps we haste.

279 Doncaster S.M.
Mary Bowley (Swabia 615) S. Wesley

'ONE spirit with the LORD;'
Oh blessèd, wondrous word!
What heavenly light, what power
divine,
Doth that sweet word afford!

'One spirit with the LORD;'
The FATHER'S smile of love
Rests ever on the members here
As on the Head above.

'One spirit with the LORD
JESUS, the glorified,
Esteems the Church for which He
bled,
His Body and His Bride.

Though now by storms assailed,
And though by trials prest,
Himself our life, He bears us up,
Right onward to His rest.

There we shall drink the stream
Of endless bliss above;
There we shall know, without a cloud,
His full, unbounded love.

280   Canada S.M.

Henry Bennett   (Sandys 431)   W. Mather

I HAVE a home above,
  From sin and sorrow free,
A mansion which eternal love
  Designed and formed for me.

The FATHER'S gracious hand
  Has built this blest abode;
From everlasting it was planned—
  My dwelling-place with GOD,

The Saviour's precious blood
  Has made my title sure;
He passed through death's dark,
    raging flood,
  To make my rest secure.

The COMFORTER is come,
  The earnest has been given;
He leads me onward to the home
  Reserved for me in heaven.

Thy love, most gracious LORD,
  My joy and strength shall be,
Till Thou shalt speak the gladdening
    word
  That bids me rise to Thee.

And then through endless days,
  Where all Thy glories shine,
In happier, holier strains I'll praise
  The grace that made me Thine.

281   Unity P.M.

W. Reid

OURS are peace and joy divine,
 Who are one with CHRIST,
When, like branches in the vine,
 We abide in CHRIST:
As a living, grafted shoot,
Nourished from a hidden root,
We may bear all holy fruit
 Through "the love of CHRIST;"
  Love of CHRIST—love of CHRIST!
 Clusters grow on every branch
  Through "the love of CHRIST."

Christian pity moves our heart,
 Through "the love of CHRIST;"
Others' woes pierce like a dart
 When there's love to CHRIST:
Gospel tidings we must tell,
Sinners warn to flee from hell—
Lure and win—alarm, compel—
 By "the love of CHRIST;"
  Love of CHRIST—love of CHRIST!
 Heaven's ranks we seek to swell
  For "the love of CHRIST."

We would love with tender care,
 Knowing love to CHRIST,
All those who His image bear,
 For "the love of CHRIST:"
"JESUS only" would we know,
That our love to all may flow
In His blood-bought Church below,
 For "the love of CHRIST;"
  Love of CHRIST—love of CHRIST!
 We would love all ransomed ones
  For "the love of CHRIST."

Now we live and walk by faith,
 Through "the love of CHRIST;"
We can triumph over death,
 One in life with CHRIST;
Rooted, settled, knowing more,
Depths and heights of love explore,
Till we gain the heavenly shore,
 Through "the love of CHRIST;"
  Love of CHRIST—love of CHRIST!
 When He comes we then shall know
  All "the love of CHRIST."

282 Rest 8.8.8.8.8.8
(Pater Omnium 44)

J. Stainer

LORD JESUS, Thou who only art
　The endless source of purest joy,
Oh, come and fill this longing heart—
　Do Thou my every thought employ;
Teach me on Thee to fix my eye,
For Thou alone canst satisfy.

The joys of earth can never fill
　The heart that once has known Thy love;
No portion would I seek until
　I reign with Thee, my LORD, above,
When I shall gaze upon Thy face
And know more fully all Thy grace.

Oh, what is all that earth can give,
　To one who shares in GOD'S own joy?
Dead to the world, in Thee I live,
　In Thee is bliss without alloy;
Well may I earthly joys resign—
"All things" are mine, since I am Thine!

Till Thou shalt come to take me home,
　Be this my one ambition, LORD,
Self—sin—the world, to overcome,
　Fast clinging to Thy faithful word;
More of Thyself each day to know,
And more into Thine image grow.

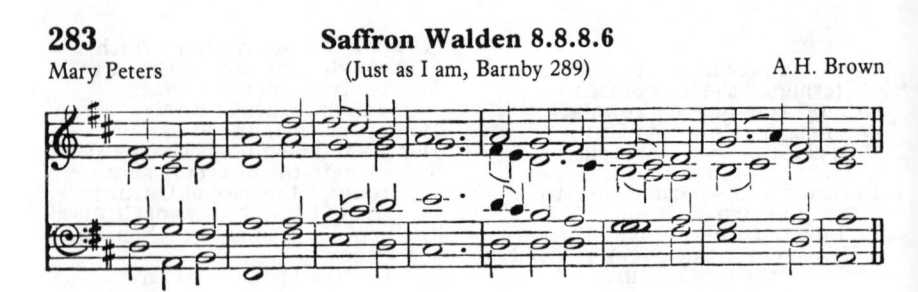

283 Saffron Walden 8.8.8.6
Mary Peters　　(Just as I am, Barnby 289)　　A.H. Brown

O JESUS, LORD, 'tis Thee alone
　　The HOLY SPIRIT would enthrone
In every heart, that we may own
　　Thou art our chiefest joy.

Feebly Thy value we conceive;
Yet with our hearts we do believe,
And would confess from morn to eve,
　　Thou art our chiefest joy.

When unbelief its discord flings
Across our harps, or stills their strings,
Touched by Thy love our spirit sings,
　　Thou art our chiefest joy.

Should this world's dazzling, transient light
Turn from eternal things our sight,
Be Thou than noonday sun more bright;
　　Thou art our chiefest joy.

And when our FATHER'S face we see,
In unveiled brightness, shine in Thee,
We'll sing, in glorious liberty,
　　Thou art our chiefest joy.

284　　Jazer C.M.
R.C. Chapman　　(Attercliffe 902)　　A.E. Tozer

I REST in CHRIST, the SON of GOD,
　　Who took the servant's form;
By faith I flee to JESUS' cross,
　　My covert from the storm.

At peace with GOD no ills I dread,
　　The cup of blessing mine;
The LORD is risen—His precious blood
　　Is new and living wine.

JESUS put all my sins away,
　　When bruised to make me whole;
Who shall accuse, or who condemn
　　A blood-bought, ransomed soul?

285   **Bryn Calfaria 8.7.8.7.8.7**
John Kent   (Cwm Rhondda 200)   W. Owen

SOVEREIGN grace o'er sin abound
  ing!
  Ransomed souls the tidings swell;
'Tis a deep that knows no sounding—
  Who its breadth or length can tell?
    On its glories
  Let my soul for ever dwell!

Souls above, in blest communion,
  Rest from conflict, with their Head;
And we sing the precious union,
  Though in thorny paths we tread;
    One with JESUS,
  By the HOLY SPIRIT led!

On such love, my soul, still ponder—
  Love so great, so rich, so free!
Say, while lost in holy wonder,
  Why, O LORD, such love to me?
    Hallelujah!
  Grace shall reign eternally.

286 Lymington 7.6.7.6.D

J.N. Darby   (Llangloffan 335)   Robt. Jackson

O LORD, Thy love's unbounded,
  So sweet, so full, so free—
My soul is all transported
  Whene'er I think on Thee;
Yet, LORD, alas! what weakness
  Within myself I find;
No infant's changing pleasure
  Is like my wandering mind.

And yet Thy love's unchanging,
  And doth recall my heart
To enjoy in all its brightness
  The peace its beams impart;
But if in Thine own presence
  My soul more constant were,
My eye would, soon familiar,
  Its brighter glories bear.

And thus, Thy deep perfections
  Much better should I know,
And with adoring fervour
  In this Thy likeness grow;
Still, sweet 'tis to discover,
  If clouds have dimmed my sight,
When past, Eternal Lover,
  Towards me, as e'er, Thou'rt bright.

Oh, keep my soul, LORD JESUS,
  Abiding still with Thee:
And if I wander, teach me
  Soon back to Thee to flee,
That all Thy gracious favour
  May to my soul be known;
And versed in this Thy goodness,
  My hopes Thyself shalt crown!

287 Eventide 10.10.10.10
Henry F. Lyte
W.H. Monk

ABIDE with me—fast falls the eventide;
The darkness thickens; LORD, with me abide!
When other helpers fail, and comforts flee,
Help of the helpless, oh, abide with me!

Swift to its close ebbs out life's little day;
Earth's joys grow dim, its glories pass away;
Change and decay in all around I see;
O Thou, who changest not, abide with me!

I need Thy presence every passing hour;
What but Thy grace can foil the tempter's power?
Who like Thyself my guide and stay can be?
Through cloud and sunshine, oh, abide with me!

I fear no foe, with Thee at hand to bless—
Ills have no weight, and tears no bitterness;
Where is Death's sting? or where Grave's victory?
I triumph still if Thou abide with me!

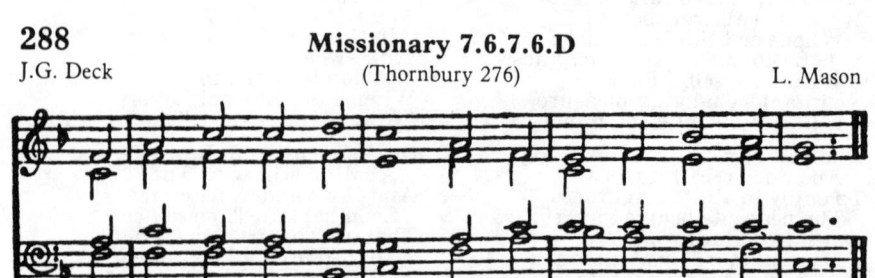

288 Missionary 7.6.7.6.D
J.G. Deck
(Thornbury 276)
L. Mason

O JESUS, gracious Saviour,
  Upon the FATHER'S throne,
Whose wondrous love and favour
  Have made our cause Thine own.
Thy people to Thee ever
  For grace and help repair,
For Thou, we know, wilt never
  Refuse our griefs to share.

O LORD, through tribulation
  Our toilsome journey lies,
Through scorn and sore temptation,
  And watchful enemies;
'Midst never-ceasing dangers
  We press towards our home:
As pilgrims here and strangers,
  We seek the rest to come.

O LORD, Thou too hast hasted
  This dreary desert through,
Hast fully tried and tasted
  Its bitterness and woe;
And hence Thy heart is tender,
  In truest sympathy,
Though now the heavens rende
  All praise to Thee on high.

Oh, by Thy HOLY SPIRIT
  Reveal to us Thy love,
The joy we shall inherit
  With Thee, our Head, above!
May all this consolation
  Our trembling hearts sustain—
Sure, though through tribulation,
  The promised rest to gain!

289 Just As I Am 8.8.8.6
Charlotte Elliott   (Silverstone 928)   Joseph Barnby

O HOLY Saviour, Friend unseen!
　Since on Thine arm Thou bidst
　　me lean,
Help me throughout life's changing
　　scene
　By faith to cling to Thee.

Far from my home, fatigued, opprest,
In Thee I've found my place of rest;
An exile still, yet not unblest
　While I can cling to Thee.

What though the world deceitful
　　prove,
And earthly friends and hopes remove?
With patient, uncomplaining love
　Still would I cling to Thee.

Though faith and hope may oft be
　　tried,
I ask not, need not, aught beside;
So safe, so calm, so satisfied,
　The soul that clings to Thee.

　　Blest is my lot, whate'er befall;
　　What can disturb or who appal,
　　While, as my strength, my rock, my
　　　　all,
　　　Saviour, I cling to Thee?

290 Meribah 8.8.6.D
C. Wesley   (Innsbruck 566)   Lowell Mason

O LOVE divine, how sweet Thou art!
　When shall I find my longing
　　heart
All taken up by Thee?
Oh, may I pant and thirst to prove
The greatness of redeeming love,
　The love of CHRIST to me!

Oh that I may for ever sit,
　Like Mary, at the Master's feet—
　　Be this my happy choice!
My only care, delight, and bliss,
My joy, my heaven on earth, be this—
　To hear the Bridegroom's voice.

　　Oh that I may, like favoured John,
　　Recline my wearied head upon
　　　My dear Redeemer's breast;
　　From care, and sin, and sorrow free,
　　Give me. O LORD, to find in Thee
　　　My everlasting rest!

291　　　　　　**Evan C.M.**
Augustus M. Toplady　　(St. Fulbert 126)　　　W.H. Havergal

　　JESUS! immutably the same,
　　　Thou true and living Vine,
　　Around Thy all-supporting stem,
　　　My feeble arms I twine.

　　Quickened by Thee, and kept alive,
　　　I flourish and bear fruit;
　　My life I from Thy life derive,
　　　My vigour from Thy root.

　　I can do nothing without Thee,
　　　My strength is wholly Thine;
　　Withered and barren should I be
　　　If severed from the Vine.

　　Upon my leaf, when parched with
　　　　heat,
　　　Refreshing dews shall drop;
　　And when the rain and tempest beat,
　　　Thou still wilt bear me up.

　　The object of the FATHER'S care,
　　　And pruned by love divine,
　　Fruit to eternal life shall bear
　　　The feeblest branch of Thine.

292 Whitburn L.M.
Frances R. Havergal (Festus 332) H. Baker

LORD, speak to me, that I may speak
In living echoes of Thy tone;
As Thou hast sought, so let me seek
The erring ones, the lost and lone.

Oh, lead me, LORD, that I may lead
The wandering and the wavering feet;
Oh, feed me, LORD, that I may feed
Thy hungering ones with manna sweet.

Oh, teach me, LORD, that I may teach
The precious things Thou dost impart:
And wing my words, that they may reach
The hidden depths of many a heart.

Oh, fill me with Thy fulness, LORD,
Until my very heart o'erflow,
In kindling thought and glowing word
Thy love to tell, Thy praise to show.

Oh, use me, LORD, use even me,
Just as Thou wilt, and when, and where,
Until Thy blessèd face I see,
Thy rest, Thy joy, Thy glory share!

293 University College 7.7.7.7
G. Burder (Buckland 159) H.J. Gauntlett

GREAT the joy when Christians
  meet!
Christian fellowship how sweet,
When, our theme of praise the same,
We exalt JEHOVAH'S name!

Sing we then eternal love,
Such as did the FATHER move;
He beheld the world undone,
Loved the world, and gave His SON.

Sing the SON'S unbounded love,
How He left the realms above,
To rejoin the FATHER'S side
With a blood-bought, spotless Bride.

Sing we too the SPIRIT'S love,
With our stubborn hearts He strove;
He revealed the SON of GOD,
And the value of His blood.

Sweet the thought, exceeding sweet—
We shall soon in glory meet,
Where, the Saviour still the theme,
We shall ever sing of Him.

294
Mary Peters

Bentley 7.6.7.6.D
(Nyland 185)

J. Hullah

BEHOLD, how good and pleasant,
  As one in CHRIST to meet!
The LORD Himself is present,
  Our blessing to complete;
And, like the pure anointing
  That once o'er Aaron flowed,
The love of GOD'S appointing
  Ascends again to GOD.

Let brother yoked with brother
  Each other's burdens bear;
The joys of one another,
  Or sorrows, let us share;
When knit in love together
  As one in CHRIST our LORD,
'Tis pleasing to the FATHER,
  And well fulfils His word.

Earth's firmest ties will perish,
  Its friendships pass away;
'Tis only safe to cherish
  What cannot so decay;
And brotherly communion,
  Though death and parting break,
Above, in perfect union,
  We shall again partake.

295   **Narenza S.M.**
Mary Peters   (Nearer Home 432)   German

O LORD, what hast Thou wrought!
  How full of power Thy name!
Subdue in us each differing thought,
And light up love's pure flame.

Our faith, O LORD, increase!
  Fast knit to Thine and Thee,
Around us bind the bond of peace—
The SPIRIT'S unity.

One GOD and FATHER ours,
  One CHRIST—His gift of love;
One SPIRIT, shed in living showers;
  One home, prepared above.

To one glad hope we cling,
  Through Thine own life and death;
As Thy redeemed, one song we sing,
  And ours one common faith.

One judgment and one mind
  We seek in all our ways,
One heart to GOD'S own truth inclined,
  One mouth to speak His praise.

Oh, make the Church below
  In love and purpose one,
That so a faithless world may know
  The FATHER sent the SON.

---

296   **St. Saviour C.M.**
R.C. Chapman   (Bristol 227)   F.G. Baker

OUR FATHER, Thou art Light and Love,
We bless Thy holy name!
Our songs Thy heart to gladness move,
Our joy is in the Lamb.

Raised up with JESUS from the dead,
We by the SPIRIT bring
Our offering, and with CHRIST our Head,
To Thee, our GOD, we sing!

Oh, fill our hearts with joy like Thine,
To walk as children dear;
As lights in this dark world to shine,
Thy SPIRIT'S voice to hear!

Thy children in a little while
Shall all in glory meet,
And praise Thy name with perfect skill,
With harmony complete.

297   Carlisle S.M.
S.W. Gandy   (Rhodes 298)   C. Lockhart

PART I.

WHY did the paschal beast,
  Of old, for Israel bleed?
To be their safeguard and their feast,
  To sprinkle and to feed.

Dwell not, my searching soul,
  On ritual shadows now,
CHRIST is the Lamb all pure and whole,
  The ransomed first-born thou.

I hear the accuser roar
  Of ills that I have done;
I know them well and thousands more;
  JEHOVAH findeth none.

Sin, Satan, death, press near
  To harass and appal;
Let but my risen LORD appear,
  Backward they go, and fall.

Before, behind, around,
  They set their fierce array,
To fight, and force me from my ground,
  Along IMMANUEL'S way.

I meet them face to face,
  Through JESU'S conquest blest,
March in the triumph of His grace
  Right onward to my rest.

PART II.

His be the Victor's name,
  Who fought our fight alone;
Triumphant saints no honour claim;
  Their conquest was His own.

Through weakness, like defeat,
  He won the meed and crown;
Trod all our foes beneath His feet,
  By being trodden down.

He hell in hell laid low;
  Made sin, He sin o'erthrew;
Bowed to the grave, destroyed it so,
  And death, by dying, slew.

Bless, bless the Conqueror slain,
  Slain by divine decree!
Who lived, who died, who lives again,
  For thee, my soul, for thee!

298 Rhodes S.M.
W.N. Tomkins   (Carlisle 297)   C. Warwick Jordan

CHRIST'S grave is vacant now,
  Left for the throne above;
His cross asserts GOD's right to bless
  In His own boundless love.

'Twas there His Blood was shed,
'Twas there His Life was poured,
There Mercy gained her diadem,
  Whilst Justice sheathed her sword.

And thence the child of faith
  Sees judgment all gone by,
Perceives the sentence fully met—
  'The soul that sins shall die!'

For He has purged our guilt
  By His own precious blood,
And such its value, not a spot
  E'er meets the eye of GOD.

299 Lloyd C.M.
R.C. Chapman   (Stroudwater 471)   C. Howard

THE Prince of Life, once slain for us,
　　Ascended up on high ;
Captivity was captive led,
　And CHRIST no more can die.

With JESUS we were crucified,
　With CHRIST our Head we live ;
The glory, first by Him obtained,
　To us the LORD shall give.

His word is faithfulness and truth—
　"Behold I quickly come ; "
And faith, that counts the promise sure,
　Can pierce the midnight gloom.

Far spent already is the night:
　In hope we hail the day
Of our belovèd LORD'S return,
　To wipe all tears away.

　　JESUS, at His appointed hour,
　　　In glory shall appear ;
　　Then, fashioned by His mighty hand,
　　　We shall His image bear.

300　　　　Veni Domine 4.6.8.8.4
A. Midlane

CHRIST ever lives!
　What joy the assurance gives:
He lives! and lives no more to die,
My present portion, future joy—
　　He ever lives!

CHRIST ever lives!
　This truth my soul relieves
From all anxiety and fear ;
On Him I roll my every care—
　　He ever lives!

CHRIST ever lives!
　This truth my soul receives,
And glories in its risen LORD,
Alike on earth, in heaven, adored—
　　He ever lives!

CHRIST ever lives!
　This truth my soul believes.;
Farewell then sorrow, doubt, and woe.
I sing with triumph while below—
　　He ever lives!

　　CHRIST ever lives!
　　And blessèd triumph gives
　To all who on Himself rely ;
　For those, upon the throne on high,
　　　He ever lives!

301
R.C. Chapman
St. Bernard C.M.
(Azmon 264)
J. Richardson

1 "No condemnation!" O my soul,
   'Tis GOD that speaks the word;
   Perfect in comeliness art thou,
   In CHRIST, thy glorious LORD.

2 In heaven His blood for ever speaks
   In GOD the FATHER's ear;
   His Church, the jewels on His heart,
   JESUS will ever bear.

3 "No condemnation!" precious word!
   Consider it, my soul;
   Thy sins were all on JESUS laid,
   His stripes have made thee whole.

4 Teach us, O GOD, to fix our eyes
   On CHRIST, the spotless Lamb;
   So shall we love Thy gracious will,
   And glorify Thy name.

302
Sussex 8.7.8.7
(Newton Ferns 411)
English Trad. Melody

SAFE enrolled, the promise ever,
  Writ in hallowed pages, stands.
'I will never leave thee, never;
  None shall pluck thee from My hands.'

No, my Saviour! never, never!
  Thou hast bought me, I am Thine;
Nothing shall prevail to sever
  From Thy love this soul of mine.

Never wilt Thou leave me, never!
  I can trust my all with Thee—
Past, and present, and for ever—
  Loved throughout eternity.

Not the shadow of a turning
  Knows eternal grace divine;
Pure love, in Thy bosom burning,
  Made me, keeps me, ever Thine!

303 St. Saviour C.M.
R.C. Chapman   (Richmond 186)   F.G. Baker

O LORD, amidst the gloom of night,
  We will rejoice with Thee
Who now art dwelling in the light,
  From death and sorrow free.

Thou sittest on the FATHER'S throne
  By Thine own blood divine;
On Thee, His well-belovèd SON,
  His face shall ever shine.

In our adversity Thou art
  Our Brother and our Friend,
And soon, to show us all Thy heart,
  Thou wilt from heaven descend.

Thy members, LORD, though tears
    they shed
  Until that glorious day,
Rejoice with Thee their living Head,
  Whose griefs are fled away.

304
Heathlands 7.7.7.7.7.7

Thos. Kelly (All Red The River 700(2)) Henry Smart

"SING aloud to God our strength:"
　He has brought us hitherto;
He will bring us home at length,
　Every danger bear us through:
Doubt not—stable is His word;
Fear not—He alone is Lord.

"Sing aloud to God our strength:"
　Sing, with wonder, of His love;
Who can tell its breadth and length?
　Who below, or who above?
Who its depth and height explore?
'Tis unbounded evermore.

"Sing aloud to God our strength:"
　He is with us where we go;
Fear we not the journey's length,
　Fear we not the mighty foe:
All our foes He will defeat,
We our journey shall complete.

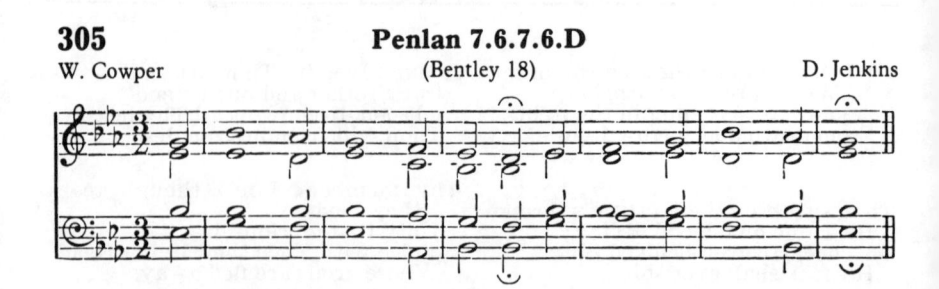

305
Penlan 7.6.7.6.D

W. Cowper (Bentley 18) D. Jenkins

IN holy contemplation,
  We sweetly would pursue
The theme of GOD's salvation,
  And find it ever new:
Set free from present sorrow,
  We cheerfully would say,
E'en let the unknown morrow
  Bring with it what it may—

It can bring with it nothing
  But He will bear us through;
Who gives the lilies clothing
  Will clothe His people too;
Beneath the spreading heavens
  No creature but is fed,
And He who feeds the ravens
  Will give His children bread.

Though vine nor fig-tree neither
  Their wonted fruit shall bear,
Though all the field should wither,
  Nor flocks nor herds be there,
Yet GOD the same abiding,
  His praise shall tune our voice,
For while in Him confiding
  We cannot but rejoice.

306 Llef L.M.
(Saxby 593)

G.H. Jones

1 My Father, when I hear Thy voice,
These accents make my heart rejoice,
And darkness from my soul remove—
'Loved with an everlasting love.'

2 Though tossed on life's dark, stormy wave,
The billows foam, and tempests rave,
I hear Thy voice, the storm above—
'Loved with an everlasting love.'

3 When sore the combat, sharp the strife,
These words renew my strength and life,
And I shall more than conqueror prove—
'Loved with an everlasting love.'

4 And when the tempter's wiles are tried
To lure me from my Saviour's side,
These words forbid my feet to move—
'Loved with an everlasting love.'

5 My Father, in Thy smile of light
The darkest path on earth looks bright;
And this shall be my heaven above—
'*Loved with an everlasting love!*'

307 Abridge C.M.
(Azmon 264)

R.C. Chapman

Isaac Smith

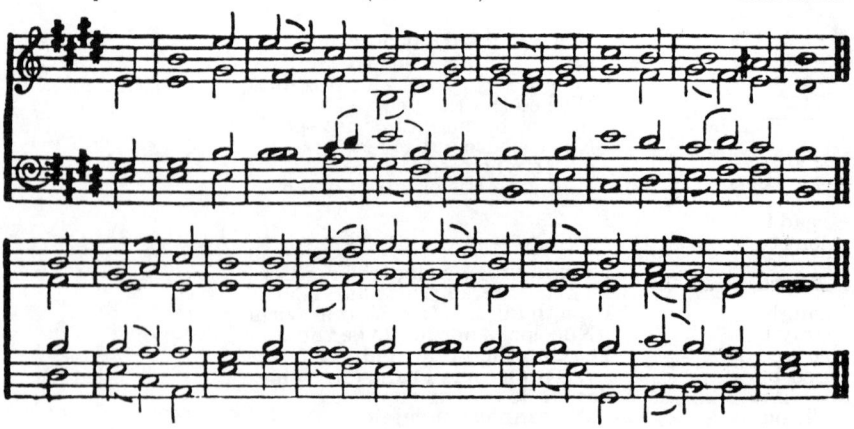

I PRAISE Thy name, O JESUS, LORD,
　Almighty SON of GOD !
The world's Creator, by Thy word—
　My Saviour, by Thy blood.

The waves of hell why should I fear,
　Though I am but a worm?
In every wave Thy voice I hear,
　Thy mercy wings the storm.

Thy SPIRIT whispers to my soul
　That all in heaven is peace ;
Then, with a kingly power and rule,
　Faith bids the tempest cease.

Faith quells it by Thy glorious name,
　And makes Thy tender breast
My welcome haven, safe and calm,
　My heavenly port of rest.

　　Thy wonders in the floods I see,
　　　Thy throne is on the deep ;
　　And I would sit and reign with Thee,
　　　Let storms awake or sleep.

308　　　　　Rhuddlan 8.7.8.7.8.7
Thos. Kelly　　　(St. Raphael 937)　　　Welsh Trad. Melody

WHY those fears? Behold, 'tis JESUS
　Holds the helm, and guides the ship !
Spread the sails, and catch the breezes
　Sent to waft us through the deep,
　　To the regions
Where the mourners cease to weep.

Though the shore we hope to land on
　Only by report is known,
Yet we freely all abandon,
　Led by that report alone ;
　　And with JESUS
Through the trackless deep move on.

Rendered safe by His protection,
　We shall pass the watery waste ;
Trusting to His wise direction,
　We shall gain the port at last ;
　　And with wonder
Think on toils and dangers past.

Oh, what pleasures there await us !
　There the tempests cease to roar ;
There it is that they who hate us
　Can molest our peace no more ;
　　Trouble ceases
On that tranquil, happy shore !

309   **St. Michael S.M.**

Paul Gerhardt   (Woolwich 251)   Day's Psalter 1562

THROUGH waves, through clouds
   and storms,
GOD gently clears the way;
We wait His time, so shall the night
   Soon end in blissful day.

He everywhere hath sway,
   And all things serve His might;
His every act pure blessing is,
   His path unsullied light.

When He makes bare His arm,
   Who shall His work withstand?
When He His people's cause defends,
   Who then shall stay His hand?

We leave it to Himself
   To choose and to command;
With wonder filled, we soon shall see
   How wise, how strong His hand.

We comprehend Him not,
   Yet earth and heaven tell,
GOD sits as Sovereign on the throne,
   And ruleth all things well!

310(1)   **Irish C.M.**

W. Cowper   Dublin Collection 1749

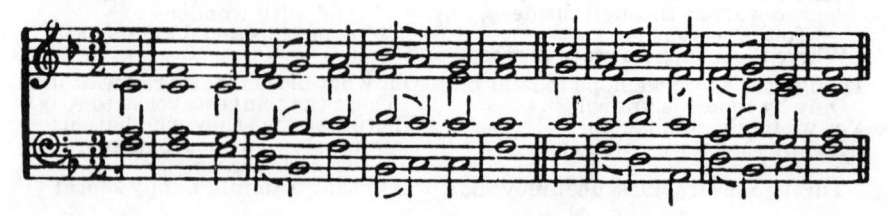

GOD moves in a mysterious way
  His wonders to perform;
He plants His footsteps in the sea,
  And rides upon the storm.

Deep in unfathomable mines
  Of never-failing skill,
He treasures up His bright designs,
  And works His sovereign will.

Ye fearful saints, fresh courage take;
  The clouds ye so much dread
Are big with mercy, and shall break
  In blessings on your head.

Judge not the LORD by feeble sense,
  But trust Him for His grace;
Behind a frowning providence
  He hides a smiling face.

His purposes will ripen fast,
  Unfolding every hour;
The bud may have a bitter taste,
  But sweet will be the flower.

Blind unbelief is sure to err,
  And scan His work in vain;
GOD is His own interpreter,
  And He will make it plain.

310(2)   **Dundee C.M.**   Andeo Hart's Psalter 1615

311
J.G. Deck

Petition 7.6.7.6.D
(Wolvercote 915)

From Haydn

O JESUS CHRIST, our Saviour,
  We only look to Thee;
'Tis in Thy love and favour
  Our souls find liberty;
While Satan fiercely rages,
  And shipwreck we may fear,
'Tis this our grief assuages,
  That Thou art always near.

Yea, though the tempest round us
  Seems safety to defy;
Tho' rocks and shoals surround us,
  And swell the billows high;
Thou dost from all protect us,
  And cheer us by Thy love;
Thy counsels, too, direct us
  Safe to the rest above.

There, with deep joy reviewing
  Past conflicts, dangers, fears—
Thy hand our foes subduing,
  And drying all our tears—
Our hearts with rapture burning,
  The path we shall retrace
Where now our souls are learning
  The riches of Thy grace.

Oh, then, how loud the chorus
  Shall to Thy name resound,
From all at rest before us,
  From all who grace have found!
One joyful song for ever
  Each heart, each lip, shall raise—
The praise of our Redeemer,
  Our GOD and Saviour's praise!

312 Southport S.M.
W. Freeman Lloyd (Canada 280) J. Davies

"My times are in Thy hand;"
  My GOD, I wish them there!
My life, my soul, my all I leave
  Entirely to Thy care.

My times are in Thy hand,
  Whatever they may be—
Pleasing or painful, dark or bright,
  As best may seem to Thee.

My times are in Thy hand;
  Why should I doubt or fear?
My FATHER'S hand will never cause
  His child a needless tear.

My times are in Thy hand,
  JESUS, the Crucified!
The hand my many sins once pierced
  Is now my guard and guide.

My times are in Thy hand,
  JESUS, my Advocate!
Nor can that hand be stretched in vain,
  For me to supplicate.

My times are in Thy hand,
  And I would trust in Thee
Till I have left this weary land,
  And all Thy glory see.

313 Dennis S.M.
Philip Doddridge   (Cambridge 252)   H.G. Nageli arr.

How gentle God's commands,
How kind His precepts are—
Cast thou thy burden on the Lord,
And trust His constant care!

Beneath His watchful eye
His saints securely dwell;
The hand which bears creation up
Shall guard His children well.

Why should an anxious load
Press down our weary mind,
When at our heavenly Father's throne
Refreshment we may find?

His goodness stands approved,
Unchanged from day to day:
We cast our burden at His feet,
And bear a song away.

314 Bryn Calfaria 8.7.8.7.8.7
Thos. Kelly   (Corinth 536)   W. Owen

HAPPY they who trust in JESUS,
 Sweet their portion is, and sure;
When the foe on others seizes,
 He will keep His own secure:
   Happy people!
 Happy, though despised and poor.

Since His love and mercy found us,
 We are precious in His sight;
Thousands now may fall around us,
 Thousands more be put to flight:
   But His presence
 Keeps us safe by day and night.

Lo! our Saviour never slumbers,
 Ever watchful is His care;
Though we cannot boast of numbers,
 In His strength secure we are;
   Sweet our portion
 Who the Saviour's kindness share.

As the bird, beneath her feathers,
 Guards the objects of her care,
So the LORD His loved ones gathers,
 Spreads His wings, and hides them there;
   Thus protected,
 All our foes we boldly dare.

315 **Trewen 8.8.8.8.D**

Augustus M. Toplady (Celeste 427) D.E. Evans

A DEBTOR to mercy alone,
  Of covenant mercy I sing;
Nor fear, with Thy righteousness on,
  My person and offering to bring:
The terrors of law, and of GOD,
  With me can have nothing to do,
My Saviour's obedience and blood
  Hide all my transgressions from view.

The work which His goodness began,
  The arm of His strength will complete;
His promise is Yea and Amen,
  And never was forfeited yet:
Things future, nor things that are now—
  Not all things below nor above,
Can make Him His purpose forego,
  Or sever my soul from His love.

My name from the palms of His hands,
  Eternity will not erase;
Impressed on His heart it remains
  In marks of indelible grace:
Yes, I to the end shall endure,
  As sure as the earnest is given;
More happy, but not more secure,
  The souls of the blessèd in heaven.

316
Anna L. Waring

Penlan 7.6.7.6.D
(Llangloffan 335)

D. Jenkins

1. IN heavenly love abiding,
   No change my heart shall fear,
And safe, in GOD confiding,
   I dread no changes here;
The storm may roar without me
   My heart may low be laid;
But GOD is round about me,
   And can I be dismayed?

2. Wherever He may guide me,
   No want shall turn me back;
My Shepherd is beside me,
   And nothing can I lack;
His wisdom ever waketh,
   His sight is never dim;
He knows the way He taketh,
   And I will walk with Him.

3. Green pastures are before me,
   Which yet I have not seen;
Bright skies will soon be o'er me,
   Where dark the clouds have been;
My hope I cannot measure,
   My path to life is free;
My Saviour is my treasure,
   And He will walk with me.

317 **St. Denio 11.11.11.11**
J.N. Darby   (Maryport 347)   Welsh Hymn Melody

THOUGH faint, yet pursuing, we
   go on our way,
The LORD is our Leader, His strength
   is our stay;
Though suff'ring, and sorrow, and trial
   be near,
The LORD is our refuge—why then
   should we fear?

He raiseth the fallen, He cheereth
   the faint;
If the weak are opprest, He hears
   their complaint;
The way may be dreary, and thorny
   the road,
But let us not falter; our help is in
   GOD.

And to His green pastures our footsteps He leads;
His flock in the desert how kindly He
  feeds!
The lambs in His bosom He tenderly
  bears,
And brings back the wanderer safe
  from the snares.

Though clouds may surround us, our
  GOD is our light;
Though foes are around us, our GOD
  is our might;
So, faint yet pursuing, whatever may
  come,
The LORD is our Leader, and heaven
  our home!

318   **Richmond C.M.**
John Newton   (Stracathro 278)   Thos. Haweis

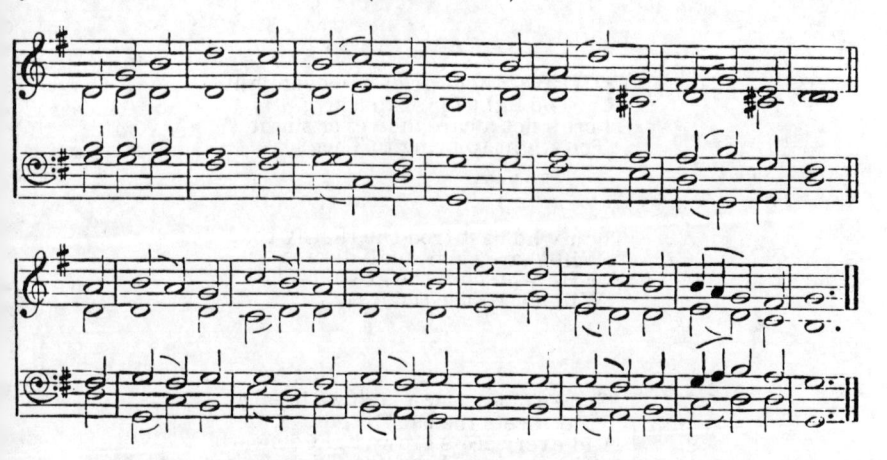

LET us rejoice in CHRIST the LORD,
  Who makes our cause His own;
The hope that's built upon His word
  Can ne'er be overthrown.

Though many foes beset us round,
  And feeble is our arm,
Our life is hid with CHRIST in GOD,
  Beyond the reach of harm.

Weak as we are, we need not faint,
  Or fainting, cannot fail;
JESUS, the strength of every saint,
  Will to the end prevail.

Though now He's unperceived by
  sense,
Faith sees Him always near;
A guide, a glory, a defence,
  To save from every fear.

As surely as He overcame,
  And conquered death and sin,
So surely those that trust His name
  Will all His triumph win.

319
Jane Crewdson

St. Flavian C.M.
(Tiverton 63)

Day's Psalter 1562

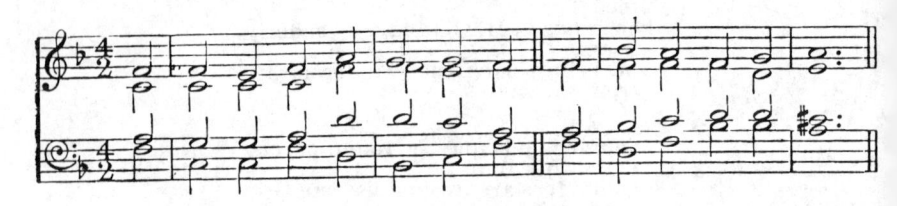

THERE'S not a grief, however light,
　　Too light for sympathy;
There's not a care, however slight,
　　Too slight to bring to Thee!

Thou who hast trod the thorny road
　　Wilt share each small distress;
For He who bore the greater load
　　Will not refuse the less.

There's not a secret sigh we breathe,
　　But meets the ear Divine;
And every cross grows light beneath
　　The shadow, LORD, of Thine.

Life's woes without, sin's strife within,
　　The heart would overflow,
But for that love which died for sin,
　　That love which wept for woe.

All human sympathy but cheers
　　When it is learned from Thee;
Alas for grief, but for those tears
　　Which fell at Bethany!

320   **Carlisle S.M.**
Augustus M. Toplady   (Dominica 496(2))   C. Lockhart

1. YOUR harps, ye trembling saints,
      Down from the willows take;
   Loud to the praise of CHRIST our LORD.
      Let every string awake.

2. Though in a foreign land,
      We are not far from home;
   And nearer to our rest above
      We every moment come.

3. GOD's grace will to the end
      Clearer and brighter shine;
   Nor present things, nor things to come,
      Can change His love divine.

4. Secure within the veil,
      CHRIST is our anchor strong;
   While power supreme and love divine
      Still guide us safe along.

5. And should the surges rise,
      Should sore afflictions come,
   Blest is the sorrow, kind the storm.
      That drives us nearer home.

6. Soon shall our pains and fears
      For ever pass away,
   And we shall then our Saviour see
      In everlasting day.

321
Paul Gerhardt

Zoan 7.6.7.6.D
(Day of Rest 166)

W.H. Havergal

A ROCK that stands for ever
  Is CHRIST my Righteousness,
And there I rest, unfearing,
  In everlasting bliss;
No earthly thing is needful
  To this my life from heaven,
And nought of love is worthy
  Save that which He has given.

There is no condemnation,
  There is no hell for me;
The torment and the fire
  Mine eyes shall never see;
For me there is no sentence,
  For me death has no sting,
Because the LORD who loves me
  Shall shield me with His wing.

His SPIRIT to my spirit
  Sweet words of comfort saith,
How GOD the weak one strengthens,
  Who leans on Him in faith;
How He hath built a city
  Of love, and light, and song,
Where the eye at last beholdeth
  What the heart has loved so long.

The world may pass and perish,
  Thou, LORD, wilt not remove;
No hatred of all devils
  Can part me from Thy love;
No height, nor depth, no creature
  That has been or can be,
Can drive me from Thy bosom,
  Can sever me from Thee!

322   Cross of Jesus 8.7.8.7
H. Bonar   (Sussex 194)   J. Stainer

YES, for me my Saviour careth
  With a brother's tender care;
Yes, with me, with me He shareth
  Every burden, every fear.

Yes, o'er me, o'er me He watcheth,
  Ceaseless watcheth, night and day;
Yes, e'en me, e'en me He snatcheth
  From the perils of the way.

Yes, for me He now is pleading
  At the mercy-seat above;
Ever for me interceding,
  Constant in untiring love.

Yes, in me abroad He shed'deth
  Joys unearthly, love and light,
And to cover me He spreadeth
  His eternal wing of might.

Yes, in me, in me He dwelleth,
  I in Him, and He in me!
And my empty soul He filleth,
  Here and through eternity.

Thus I wait for His returning,
  Singing all the way to heaven;
CHRIST my joyful song each morning
  Still HIMSELF my song at even!

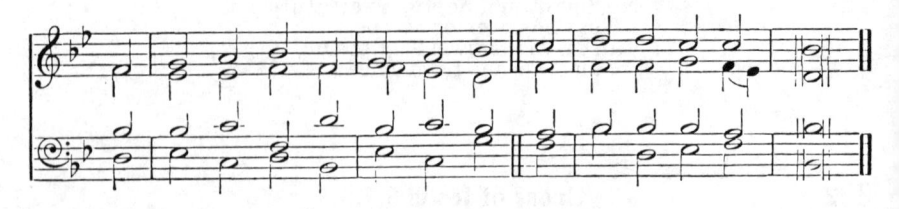

323 Nativity C.M.
Fredk. Whitfield (University 466) H. Lahee

JESUS! O name of power divine
  To all of heavenly birth!
JESUS! the never-failing mine
  Of richest, sweetest worth!

With Thee I cannot feel alone,
  I cannot be forgot;
Tho' friends are changing one by one
  Thou, Saviour, changest not!

My future path, I know, may be
  A path of pressing care;
But love has planned that path for
    me—
  That love in which I share.

The Shepherd's bosom bears each
    lamb
  O'er rock, and waste, and wild;
The object of that love I am,
  And carried like a child.

And is not this, O LORD, enough,
  Thy perfect love to share,
Till Thou shalt call Thy Bride above,
  To meet Thee in the air?

It *is* enough: Thy tender smile—
  Till I behold Thee there—
Shall cheer me through the "little
    while"
  I'm waiting for Thee here.

324
R.C. Chapman St. Mathias 8.8.8.8.8.8 W.H. Monk
(Credo 349)

O GOD, whose wondrous name is
  Love,
 Whose hands have fashioned us
  anew,
Before Thy face now stands the Lamb,
 Whom sinful man once pierced and
  slew: spare—
Thine own dear SON Thou didst not
How shalt Thou cease for us to care?

Our heavenly FATHER! grant us all
 The new-born babe's simplicity;
The doubtful mind be far from us,
 Who boast a GOD who cannot lie:
Arrayed in comeliness divine,
On JESU'S bosom we recline.

Thou art the Potter, we the clay;
 Thy will be ours, Thy truth our light,
Thy love the fountain of our joy,
 Thine arm our safeguard day and
  night,
Till Thou shalt wipe our tears away,
And CHRIST shall bring eternal day.

325   **Laudate Dominum 10.10.11.11**
Isaac Newton   (Hanover 909)   H. Parry

1 THOUGH troubles assail, and dangers affright,
Though friends should all fail and foes all unite;
Yet one thing secures us, whatever betide,
The Scripture assures us, *The* LORD *will provide.*

2 The birds without barn or storehouse are fed,
From them let us learn to trust for our bread;
His saints what is fitting shall ne'er be denied,
So long as 'tis written, *The* LORD *will provide.*

3 We may, like the ships, by tempest be tossed
On perilous deeps, but cannot be lost;
Though Satan enrages the wind and the tide,
The promise engages, *The* LORD *will provide.*

4 His call we obey, like Abra'm of old,
Not knowing our way, by faith made thus bold,
For though we are strangers we have a sure Guide,
And trust, in all dangers, *The* LORD *will provide.*

326 **Montgomery 11.11.11.11**

G. Keith (St Denio 317) J. Stanley

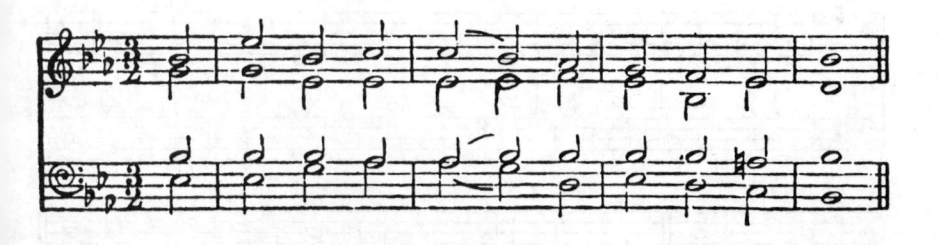

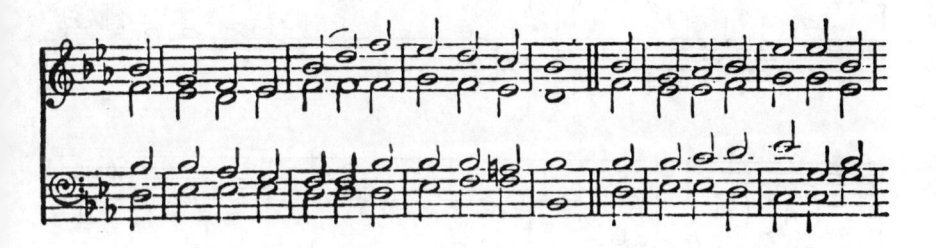

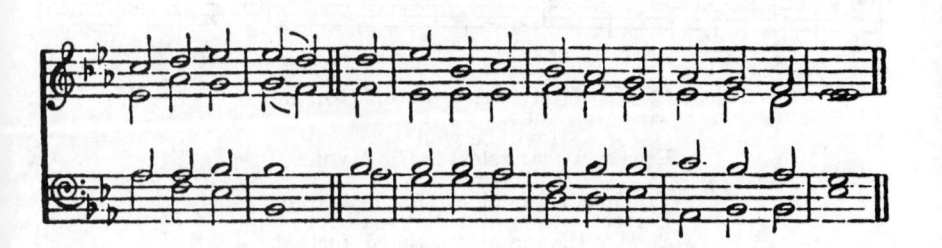

HOW firm a foundation, ye saints of the LORD,
Is laid for your faith in His excellent word!
What more can He say than to you He hath said,
You who unto JESUS for refuge have fled?

'Fear not, I am with Thee; oh, be not dismayed!
I—I am thy GOD, and will still give thee aid;
I'll strengthen thee, help thee, and cause thee to stand,
Upheld by My righteous, omnipotent hand.

'When through the deep waters I call thee to go,
The floods of distress shall not thee overflow;
The flame shall not hurt thee; I only design
Thy dross to consume, and thy gold to refine.

'The soul that on JESUS hath leaned for repose,
I will not, I cannot desert to its foes;
That soul, though all hell should endeavour to shake,
I'll never—no, never—no, never forsake!'

327   **Southgate (Evensong)** 8.4.8.4.8.8.8.4   T.B. Southgate
Mary Peters   (Ar Hyd Y Nos 373)

THROUGH the love of GOD our
   Saviour,
      All will be well;
Free and changeless is His favour,
      All, all is well:
Precious is the blood that healed us,
Perfect is the grace that sealed us,
Strong the hand stretched forth to
   shield us,
      All must be well.

Though we pass through tribulation,
      All will be well;
Ours is such a full salvation,
      All, all is well;
Happy still in GOD confiding,
Fruitful if in CHRIST abiding,
Holy through the SPIRIT's guiding,
      All must be well.

We expect a bright to-morrow,
      All will be well;
Faith can sing through days of sorrow,
      All, all is well;
On our FATHER's love relying,
JESUS every need supplying,
Or in living, or in dying,
      All must be well.

328 Under His Wing 8.8.8.8. and Chorus

Jas. Nicholson　　　　　　　　　　　　　　　　　　　　　Asa Hull

1. In God I have found a retreat,
    Where I can securely abide;
   No refuge nor rest so complete,
    And here I would ever reside:

   *Oh, what comfort it brings,
    As my soul sweetly sings:
    I am safe from all danger
    While under His wings!*

2. I dread not the terror by night,
    No arrow can harm me by day;
   His shadow has covered me quite,
    My fears he has driven away—

3. The pestilence walking about,
    When darkness has settled abroad,
   Can never compel me to doubt
    The presence and power of my God—

4. The wasting destruction at noon
    No fearful foreboding can bring;
   With Jesus my soul doth commune,
    His perfect salvation I sing—

5. A thousand may fall at my side,
    Ten thousand e'en at my right hand;
   Above me His wings are spread wide,
    Beneath them in safety I stand—

329(1)   **St. Fulbert C.M.**
R.C. Chapman   H.J. Gauntlett

OUR GOD, Thou gavest Thine own SON
The curse for us to bear;
Thy Well-belov'd, Thine only SON,
Thy justice did not spare!

Thy SPIRIT teaches us Thy truth,
And leads us in Thy ways;
On CHRIST the LORD our burdens all
We cast, with songs of praise.

Thy SPIRIT gives us fellowship
With Thee and with Thy SON;
His glorious beauty we behold,
With joy our race we run.

To Him, Thy First-born, Thou didst give
Thy Church—His joy and Thine;
FATHER, we each would say, 'Thy will
Be altogether mine!'

Countless Thy thoughts of love to us,
Beyond all searching deep;
E'en as the apple of the eye,
Thy words, oh, may we keep!

Amidst a world of restless pride,
We rest in Thy decrees;
We taste of pleasures evermore,
And in Thee dwell at ease.

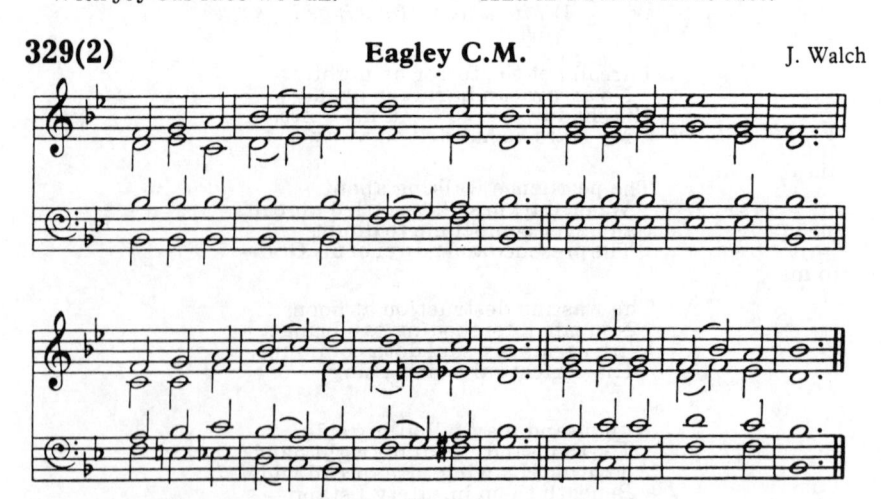

329(2)   **Eagley C.M.**   J. Walch

330
R.M. McCheyne

St. Luke 11.11.11.11
(Lion of Judah 863)

1 ONCE was a stranger to grace and to God;
I knew not my danger, I felt not my load;
Though friends spoke with rapture of Christ on the tree,
Jehovah Tsidkenu was nothing to me.

2 I oft read with pleasure, to soothe or engage,
Isaiah's wild measure, or John's simple page;
But e'en when they pictured the blood-sprinkled tree,
Jehovah Tsidkenu seemed nothing to me.

3 When free grace awoke me, by light from on high,
Then legal fears shook me; I trembled to die:
No refuge, nor safety in self could I see.
Jehovah Tsidkenu my Saviour must be.

4 My terrors all vanished before the sweet name;
My guilty fears banished, with boldness I came,
To drink at the fountain, life-giving and free,
Jehovah Tsidkenu is all things to me!

5 E'en treading the valley, the shadow of death,
This watchword shall rally my faltering breath;
And when from life's conflict my God sets me free,
Jehovah Tsidkenu my triumph shall be!

331   **Silchester S.M.**
Philip Doddridge   (Southport, Davies 312)   H.A.C. Malan

1. GRACE! 'tis a charming sound,
Harmonious to the ear;
Heaven with the echo shall resound,
And all the earth shall hear.

2. Grace taught our wandering feet
To tread the heavenly road;
And new supplies each hour we meet
While travelling home to GOD.

3. 'Twas grace that wrote each name
In life's eternal book;
'Twas grace that gave us to the Lamb,
Who all our sorrows took.

4. Grace saved us from the foe,
Grace taught us how to pray;
And GOD will ne'er His grace forego
Till we have won the day.

5. May grace, free grace, inspire
Our souls with strength divine;
May all our thoughts to GOD aspire,
And grace in service shine!

6. Grace all the work shall crown
Through everlasting days;
It lays in heaven the topmost stone,
And well deserves the praise.

332   Festus L.M.
Charitie L. Bancroft   (Saxby 593)   German

BEFORE the throne of GOD above
   I have a strong, a perfect plea—
A great High Priest, whose name is
     Love,
   Who ever lives and pleads for me.

My name is graven on His hands,
   My name is written on His heart;
I know that while in heaven He
     stands,
   No tongue can bid me thence depart.

When Satan tempts me to despair,
   And tells me of the guilt within,
Upward I look, and see Him there
   Who made an end of all my sin.

Because the sinless Saviour died,
   My sinful soul is counted free;
For GOD, the Just, is satisfied
   To look on Him and pardon me.

Behold Him there—the risen Lamb!
   My perfect, spotless Righteousness,
The great, unchangeable "I AM,"
   The King of glory and of grace!

One with Himself, I cannot die;
   My soul is purchased by His blood;
My life is hid with CHRIST on high,
   With CHRIST, my SAVIOUR, and
     my GOD.

333   **Regent Square 8.7.8.7.8.7**

J. Caspar Schade   (Lewisham 523)   H. Smart

RISE, my soul, with joy and gladness,
  And the praise of JESUS sing;
He removes all cause of sadness—
  Only JESUS life could bring;
    He redeemed me—
  Glory to the eternal King!

Well He knew my lost condition—
  Sinless offering GOD must have;
Vain my tears and deep contrition,
  Nought that I could do would save:
    He redeemed me,
  For His precious life He gave.

Now He lives. He lives for ever,
  And for all His people pleads;
One with Him, now nought can sever
  Those for whom He intercedes:
    He redeemed me,
  And to glory safely leads.

Bright the prospect of that glory,
  Seen by faith at GOD'S right hand;
There we shall recount the story,
  In that happy, happy land:
    He redeemed me—
  Wondrous all His love has planned!

334   Samuel 6.6.6.6.8.8
John Kent   (Harewood 540)   Arthur Sullivan

1. O BLESSÈD GOD! how kind
    Are all Thy ways to me,
  Whose dark, benighted mind
    Was enmity with Thee!
  Yet now, subdued by sovereign grace,
  My spirit joys in Thine embrace.

2. How precious are Thy thoughts,
    That o'er my bosom roll!
  They rise above my doubts,
    And captivate my soul:
  How great their sum, how high they rise,
  Can ne'er be known beneath the skies.

3. Before Thy hands had made
    The sun to rule the day,
  Or earth's foundation laid,
    Or fashioned Adam's clay,
  What thoughts of peace and mercy flowed
  From Thine own bosom, O my GOD!

4. A monument of grace,
    A sinner saved by blood,
  The streams of love I trace
    Up to their source, O GOD,
  And in Thy sacred bosom see
  Eternal thoughts of love to me!

335   **Llangloffan 7.6.7.6.D**

S.P. Tregelles   (Penlan 80)   Welsh Hymn Melody

1. IN Thee, O LORD, believing,
    We now have peace with GOD,
  Eternal life receiving,
    The purchase of Thy blood:
  Our curse and condemnation
    Thou barest in our stead;
  Secure is our salvation
    In Thee, our risen Head.

2. The HOLY GHOST revealing
    Thy work, has made us blest;
  Thy stripes have given us healing,
    Upon Thy love we rest:
  In Thee the FATHER sees us,
    Accepted and complete;
  Thy blood, from sin which frees us,
    For glory makes us meet.

3. We know that nought can sever
    Our souls, O LORD, from Thee;
  And thus united ever
    To all Thy saints are we:
  We know Thy word declaring
    The FATHER'S wondrous love,
  In which we all are sharing
    With Thee, our Head, above.

4. May we this love be shewing
    Until Thou shalt appear—
  Thy love, so freely flowing
    To all Thy members here;
  Till all the Church in union,
    Around the FATHER'S throne,
  Shall rest in full communion,
    For ever joined in one.

336
R.C. Chapman

Bristol C.M.
(Lucius 592)

Ravenscroft's Psalter 1621

MY Shepherd, who for sin atoned,
  When crucified and slain,
Thou with the FATHER art enthroned,
  And soon wilt come again.

Thou art to-day as yesterday,
  And evermore, the same;
Thou art the new and living way,
  How excellent Thy name!

Thy SPIRIT guides me into rest,
  Thy mercies I review;
With all Thy blessings I am blest,
  My song is ever new.

Faithful art Thou, LORD, to restore
  My soul, whene'er it strays;
Then I, more lowly than before,
  More joyful sing Thy praise.

Thy friendship, O my glorious LORD,
  A table spreads for me;
By Thy anointing at Thy board,
  Saviour, I feast with Thee.

Thou hast for Thine prepared a place—
  Thou doest all things well—
There shall I see Thee face to face,
  And in Thy bosom dwell.

337   Leoni 6.6.8.4.D

J. Beaumont   Hebrew Melody

MY Shepherd is the Lamb,
  The living LORD who died;
With all things good I ever am
  By Him supplied;
He richly feeds my soul
  With blessings from above;
And leads me where the rivers roll
  Of endless love.

My soul He doth restore
  Whene'er I go astray;
He makes my cup of joy run o'er
  From day to day;
His love so full, so free,
  Anoints my head with oil;
Mercy and goodness follow me,
  Fruit of His toil.

The day draws on apace
  When He shall claim His own,
Then shall I see Him face to face,
  And know as known;
Still shall I lift my voice,
  His praise my song shall be;
And I will in His love rejoice
  Who died for me.

338
Beloved 11.8.11.8
R.C. Chapman (Belfield 932) Freeman Lewis

MY Shepherd! Thou art, in the
valley of woe,
A Friend and Companion to me:
Through death's darkest shadows
with singing I go,
Emboldened by converse with Thee.

Thy friendship and love, in the face
of my foes,
A banquet before me prepare;
My head Thou anointest, my cup
overflows,
And now in Thy gladness I share.

My days to the end shall with blessings abound,
Of goodness and mercy divine;
In the house of my FATHER I soon
shall be found,
His home shall for ever be mine!

339 Ballerma C.M.

S. Trevor Francis (Lynton 60) Adapted by R. Simpson

LORD JESUS, we would come apart,
  To rest awhile with Thee;
Drawn hither by Thy tender heart
  Of loving sympathy.

We are Thine own, Thy love we sing,
  Held by Thy gracious hand;
His sheep the Shepherd safe will bring
  Home to the Shepherd's land.

We are Thine own, love's treasured
    store,
  By blood, by purchase Thine;
Upon Thy breast for evermore
  As precious gems to shine.

Thine own, yet how unlike Thee now!
  But when Thy face we see,
And in the unclouded glory bow,
  We shall be like to Thee!

340 Warwick C.M.

Isaac Watts (St. Saviour 341) S. Stanley

MY Shepherd will supply my need,
　JEHOVAH is His name;
In pastures fresh He makes me feed,
　Beside the living stream.

He brings my wandering spirit back
　When I forsake His ways,
And leads me, for His own name's
　　sake,
　In paths of truth and grace.

Yea, though I walk through death's
　　dark vale,
　Thy presence is my stay;
Thy rod, Thy staff, will never fail;
　They drive my fears away.

Thy hand, in sight of all my foes,
　Doth now my table spread;
My cup with blessings overflows,
　Thine oil anoints my head.

　　　Goodness and mercy, O my GOD,
　　　　Attend me all my days;
　　　Soon will Thy house be mine abode,
　　　　And all my work be praise!

341　　　　　　　　St. Saviour C.M.
Catesby Paget　　　　　　(Evan 154)　　　　　　　　　F.G. Baker

A MIND at "perfect peace" with
　　GOD—
　Oh, what a word is this!
A sinner reconciled through blood;
　This, this indeed is peace!

By nature and by practice far—
　How very far from GOD!
Yet now by grace brought nigh to
　　Him,
　Through faith in JESU'S blood.

So nigh, so very nigh to GOD,
　I cannot nearer be;
For in the Person of His SON
　I am as near as He.

So dear, so very dear to GOD,
　More dear I cannot be;
The love wherewith He loves the
　　SON—
　Such is His love to me!

　　　Why should I ever careful be,
　　　　Since such a GOD is mine?
　　　He watches o'er me night and day,
　　　　And tells me 'Mine is thine.'

342 Pax Tecum 10.10

E.H. Bickersteth G.T. Caldbeck

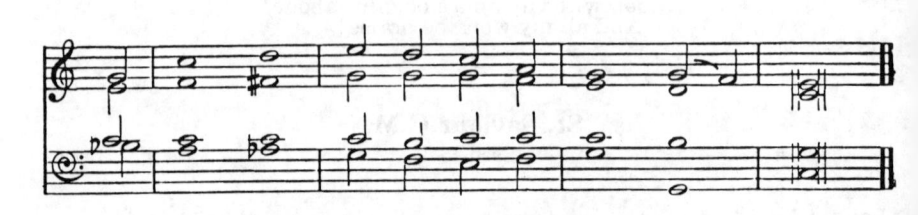

PEACE! perfect peace!—in this
    dark world of sin?
The blood of JESUS whispers peace
    within.

Peace! perfect peace!—by thronging
    duties pressed?
To do the will of JESUS, this is rest.

Peace! perfect peace!—with sorrows
    surging round?
On JESU'S bosom nought but calm is
    found.

Peace! perfect peace!—with loved ones
    far away?
In JESU'S keeping we are safe, and
    they.

Peace! perfect peace!—our future all
    unknown?
JESUS we know, and He is on the
    throne.

Peace! perfect peace!—death shadow-
    ing us and ours?
JESUS has vanquished death and all
    its powers.

It is enough: earth's struggles soon
    shall cease,
And JESUS call to heaven's perfect
    peace.

Chorus Angelorum C.M.
(Fingal 131)

Arthur Somervell

HOW precious were those parting words
 Of our Almighty Friend,
Who loved His own while in the world,
 And loves them to the end:

'I leave you not as orphans here,
 The COMFORTER will come,
And fill your hearts with joy and peace,
 Till I shall take you home.'

And then, as poured on Aaron's head,
 The ointment downward flowed;
So was the SPIRIT'S grace and joy
 From CHRIST our Head bestowed.

As when of old Rebekah trod
 The desert, long and drear,
While Abraham's wealth and Isaac's love
 Rang in her gladdened ear:

So traverse we this wilderness,
 While our blest Guide makes known
The FATHER'S house, the SON'S rich love,
 And all He has, our own!

Sweet thought! our hearts are with Him there,
 We see our glorious home
Made ready for the Bride to share:
 LORD JESUS, quickly come!

344   Worship 6.4.6.4.6.6.6.4

J.G. Deck

JESUS! Thy name we love,
  JESUS, our LORD!
JESUS, all names above,
  JESUS, our LORD!
Thou, LORD, our all must be;
Nothing that's good have we,
Nothing apart from Thee,
  JESUS, our LORD!

Thou, blessèd SON of GOD,
  JESUS, our LORD!
Hast bought us with Thy blood,
  JESUS, our LORD!
Great was indeed Thy love,
All other loves above,
Love Thou didst clearly prove,
  JESUS, our LORD!

When unto Thee we flee,
  JESUS, our LORD!
Thou wilt a refuge be,
  JESUS, our LORD!
Whom, then, have we to fear,
What trouble, grief, or care,
Since Thou art ever near,
  JESUS, our LORD?

Soon Thou wilt come again,
  JESUS, our LORD!
We shall be blessèd then,
  JESUS, our LORD!
When Thine own face we see,
Then shall we like Thee be—
Then evermore with Thee,
  JESUS, our LORD!

345   Dalehurst C.M.

F. Whitfield   (Belmont 26)   Arthur Cottman

THERE is a name I love to hear,
 I love to speak its worth;
It sounds like music in mine ear,
 The sweetest name on earth.

It tells me of a Saviour's love,
 Who died to set me free;
It tells me of His precious blood,
 The sinner's perfect plea.

It tells me of a FATHER'S smile
 Beaming upon His child;
It cheers me through this "little
  while."
 Through desert, waste, and wild.

JESUS! the name I love so well,
 The name I love to hear;
No saint on earth its worth can tell,
 No heart conceive how dear.

This name shall shed its fragrance still
 Along this thorny road,
Shall sweetly smooth the rugged hill
 That leads me up to GOD.

And there, with all the blood-bought
  throng,
 From sin and sorrow free,
I'll sing the new, eternal song
 Of JESUS'S love to me.

346   **Saffron Walden 8.8.8.6**

Jane Crewdson   (Just as I am, Barnby 289)   A.H. Brown

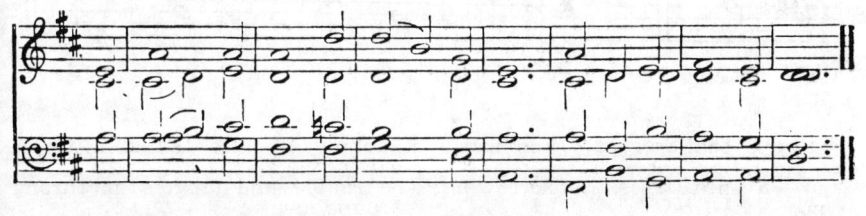

O SAVIOUR, I have nought to plead,
 In earth beneath, or heaven above,
But just my own exceeding need,
 And Thy exceeding love.

The need will soon be past and gone,
 Exceeding great, but quickly o'er;
The love, unbought, is all Thine own,
 And lasts for evermore.

347
Maryport 11.11.11.11

J.N. Darby   (Datchet 935)   John Kitchen

1. OH, eyes that are weary, and hearts that are sore,
Look off unto JESUS, and sorrow no more:
The light of His countenance shineth so bright,
That on earth, as in heaven, there need be no night.

2. "Looking off unto JESUS," my eyes cannot see
The troubles and dangers that throng around me;
They cannot be blinded with sorrowful tears,
They cannot be shadowed with unbelief fears.

"Looking off unto JESUS," my spirit is blest;
In the world I have turmoil, in Him I have rest;
The sea of my life all about me may roar—
When I look unto JESUS I hear it no more.

"Looking off unto JESUS," I go not astray,
My eyes are on Him, and He shews me the way;
The path may seem dark, as He leads me along,
But following JESUS, I cannot go wrong.

And soon, at His coming, the beauty and grace
Of JESUS, my LORD, I shall see in His face,
And His love, which now leads me the desert along,
Shall be in that glory my rest and my song.

348
Dodds Bentley 7.6.7.6.D J. Hullah
(Vox Jesu – Come unto Me, Dykes 670)

MY heart, O LORD, rejoices,
  While on Thy love I dwell;
'Tis like a flowing river,
  A deep, up-springing well—
Ineffable, unchanging,
  Love that no measure knows;
'Tis here, with joy adoring,
  I peacefully repose.

Thy presence, LORD, sustaineth
  Amid the conflict here;
With Thee I ne'er am lonely
  Nor need I yield to fear:
In Thee I well may glory,
  Apart from all below,
My one, my only treasure,
  Surpassing all I know.

My LORD and Saviour! keep me
  Abiding in Thy love,
Till Thou shalt come to take me
  Home to the rest above:
For Thy return I'm waiting,
  When I Thy face shall see,
Shall share Thy throne and glory,
  And be conformed to Thee.

349
J.A. Rothe – John Wesley   **Credo** 8.8.8.8.8.8   J. Stainer
(Pater Omnium 44)

A little slower.
Org.

O LOVE, thou fathomless abyss,
  My sins are swallowed up in Thee!
Covered is my unrighteousness,
  Nor spot of guilt remains on me,
While JESU'S blood, through earth and skies,
  Mercy—free, boundless mercy—cries!

With faith I plunge me in this sea—
  Here is my hope, my joy, my rest;
Hither, when hell assails, I flee,
  I look into my Saviour's breast;
Away, sad doubt, and anxious fear!
  Mercy is all that's written there.

Though waves and storms go o'er my head,
  Though strength, and health, and friends be gone,
Though joys be withered all and dead,
  Though every comfort be withdrawn—
On this my steadfast soul relies,
FATHER, Thy mercy never dies!

350 St. Catherine 8.8.8.8.8.8

P. Gerhardt – John Wesley   (St. Matthias 549)   J.G. Walton

MY Saviour, Thou Thy love to me
　In shame, in want, in pain, hast
　　shewed;
For me upon the shameful tree
　Thou pouredst forth Thy precious
　　blood;
Thy wounds upon my heart impress,
Let nought the stamp of love efface.

From all eternity with love
　Unchangeable Thou hast me viewed;
Ere knew this beating heart to move,
　Thy tender mercies me pursued;
Ever with me may they abide,
And close me in on every side.

What in Thy love possess I not?
　My star by night, my sun by day,
My spring of life when parched with
　　drought,
　My wine to cheer, my bread to stay,
My strength, my shield, my safe abode,
My robe before the throne of GOD!

Still let Thy love guide all my way—
　Such wondrous things Thy love
　　hath wrought—
Still lead me, lest I go astray,
　Direct my word, inspire my thought,
Till soon from heaven Thy voice I
　　hear,
And to Thyself be ever near.

351   **Melita 8.8.8.8.8.8**
P. Gerhardt – John Wesley   (Rest, Stainer 282)   J.B. Dykes

JESUS, Thy boundless love to me
   No thought can reach, no tongue declare!
Then bend my wayward heart to Thee,
   And reign without a rival there;
Thine wholly, Thine alone, I'd live,
Myself to Thee entirely give.

Oh, draw me, Saviour, after Thee,
   So shall I run and never tire;
With gracious words still comfort me,
   Be Thou my hope, my sole desire;
Free me from every weight and fear,
No sin can come if Thou art near.

O LORD, how gracious is Thy way!
   All fear before Thy presence flies;
Care, anguish, sorrow, pass away
   Where'er Thy healing beams arise;
O Saviour, nothing may I see,
Nothing desire, apart from Thee!

In suffering be Thy love my peace,
   In weakness be Thine arm my strength;
And when the storms of life shall cease,
   And Thou from heaven shalt come at length,
LORD JESUS, then this heart shall be
For ever satisfied with Thee.

352
W. Cowper

St. Bees 7.7.7.7
(Vienna 410(2))

J.B. Dykes

HARK! my soul; it is the LORD;
'Tis thy Saviour, hear His word;
JESUS speaks, and speaks to thee—
'Say, poor sinner, lov'st thou Me?

'I delivered thee when bound,
And when wounded healed thy wound;
Sought thee wandering, set thee right,
Turned thy darkness into light.

'Can a woman's tender care
Cease towards the child she bare
Yes, she may forgetful be,
Yet will I remember thee!

'Mine is an unchanging love,
Higher than the heights above;
Deeper than the depths beneath
Free and faithful, strong as death.

'Thou shalt see My glory soon,
When the work of grace is done;
Partner of My throne shalt be!
Say, poor sinner, lov'st thou Me?'

LORD, it is my chief complaint
That my love is weak and faint;
Yet I love Thee and adore,
Oh for grace to love Thee more!

353 Antwerp L.M.
(Saxby 593)

W. Smallwood

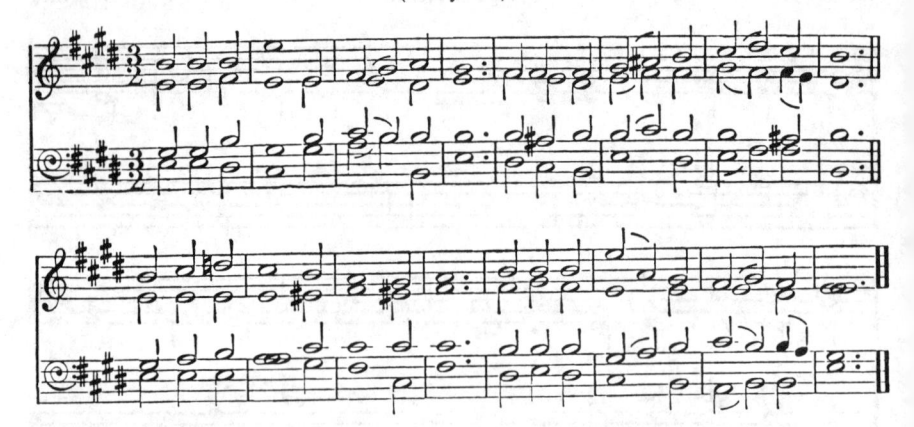

JESUS, my LORD, 'tis sweet to rest
  Upon Thy tender, loving breast,
Where deep compassions ever roll
Towards the helpless, weary soul.

Thy love, O Saviour, dries our tears,
Expels our griefs, and calms our fears;
Sheds light and gladness o'er the heart,
And bids each anxious thought depart.

Blest foretaste this of joys to come
In Thy eternal, heavenly home,
Where we shall see Thy glorious face,
And know Thy rich, unfathomed grace!

That grace sustains our spirits now,
While we are pilgrims here below;
That grace suffices, comforts, guides,
Upholds, defends, preserves, provides.

Yes! Thou art with us, gracious LORD,
To bear us on to Thine abode,
Where we shall never cease to prove
Thy deep, divine, unfailing love.

Help us to praise Thee day by day,
Till earth's dark scenes are passed away—
Till in Thine own unclouded light
Thy glory satisfies our sight!

354 Bristol C.M.
Philip Doddridge (St. Agnes, Durham 21) Ravenscroft's Psalter 1621

O GOD, what cords of love are Thine!
  How gentle, yet how strong!
Thy truth and grace their strength
    combine
  To draw our souls along.

The guilt of twice ten thousand sins
  One moment takes away;
And when the fight of faith begins,
  Our strength is as our day.

Comfort through all this vale of tears
  In rich profusion flows,
And glory of unnumbered years
  Eternity bestows.

Drawn by such cords we'll onward
    move
  Till round Thy throne we meet,
And, captives in the chains of love,
  Embrace our Conqueror's feet.

355   Byzantium C.M.   T. Jackson
Isaac Watts   (Attercliffe 902)

MY GOD, the spring of all my joys,
  The life of my delights,
The glory of my brightest days,
  And comfort of my nights!

In darkest shades if CHRIST appear,
  My dawning is begun;
He is my soul's bright Morning Star,
  And He's my rising Sun.

The opening heavens around me shine
  With beams of sacred bliss,
While JESUS tells me *He is mine*,
  And whispers *I am His*.

My soul would leave this heavy clay
  At that transporting word,
Ascend with joy the shining way,
  To see and praise my LORD!

356   **Rhodes S.M.**
R.C. Chapman   (Canada 280)   C. Warwick Jordan

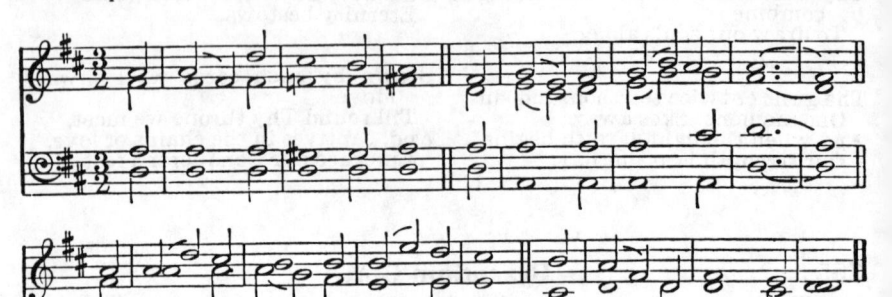

TO GOD, my thirsty soul
   In JESU'S name draws nigh;
Thou art my portion, GOD of love!
   All else is vanity.

My living Fountain, Thou!
   Send forth the plenteous stream;
Each bitter cup I drink shall then
   My FATHER'S kindness seem.

Thy SPIRIT'S still, small voice
   Makes loss of all my gain,
While I by faith of JESUS live,
   Who once for me was slain.

357   **Morningside P.M.**
C. Wesley   English Air

CHORUS

M Y GOD, I am Thine,
What a comfort divine;
What a blessing to know
That CHRIST JESUS is mine!

 Hallelujah! Thine the glory,
  Hallelujah! Amen.
 Hallelujah! Thine the glory.
  Revive us again.

My Saviour to know,
And feel His love flow,
Is life everlasting,
'Tis heaven below—

Yet onward I haste
To the heavenly feast;
That, *that* is the fulness,
But this is the taste—

  And this I shall prove,
  Till with joy I remove
  To the heaven of heavens,
  In JESU'S own love—

358   Gräfenberg C.M.
R.C. Chapman   (St. Fulbert 120)   Praxis Pietatis Melica 1653

G OD of all grace, Thou only wise!
Before Thy throne I wait;
Should yet Thy furnace prove my faith,
Thy love can ne'er abate.

In patience I possess my soul;
The gold must be refined,
The image of Thy SON to show:
Mine be His perfect mind!

The cup Thou givest me I drink,
And bless Thy holy name;
No gall I taste; the curse—my due—
Fell on the spotless Lamb.

One thing, my FATHER and my GOD,
Desires Thy weanèd child—
May I be found from day to day
Blameless and undefiled!

359   **Hereford L.M.**
Isaac Watts   (Abends 571)   S.S. Wesley

O GOD! we see Thee in the Lamb
    To be our hope, our joy, our rest;
The glories that compose Thy name,
    All stand engaged to make us blest.

Thou Great and Good! Thou Just
    and Wise!
Thou art our FATHER and our GOD!
And we are Thine by sacred ties,
    Thy sons and daughters bought
    with blood.

Then, oh! to us this grace afford,
    That from Thyself we ne'er may
    rove;
Our guard, the presence of the LORD,
    Our joy, the sense of pardoning love.

For this will make our hearts rejoice,
    And turn to light our darkest days;
Yea, this will nerve each feeble voice,
    While we have breath, to pray or
    praise.

360   **St. Saviour C.M.**
R.C. Chapman   (Beatitudo 78)   F.G. Baker

FATHER, Thy children all are blest,
　Thy SPIRIT is their Guide;
Thy SON their everlasting rest,
　For on the cross He died.

Joint-heirs with CHRIST, we dwell at
　ease,
And seek our heavenly land;
Our occupation is to please
　The Man of Thy right hand.

　　Our GOD and FATHER, purify
　　Our hearts with hope divine,
　　And let our light to every eye
　　Amid the darkness shine.

361　　　　　**Festus L.M.**
　　　　　　(Antwerp 353)　　　　　　German

"OUR FATHER!" Oh, what gracious
　　ways
And thoughts of love that name conveys!
It tells us of the tender care
Belovèd children ever share.

"Our FATHER!" By Thy mercies past
We learn on Thee our care to cast;
And while our wants are known to
　Thee,
We need not fear, nor anxious be.

How oft when wandering far away,
Thy care has hedged up all our way—
So bidding us return, and live,
And learn how much Thou canst
　forgive.

And though we came with tardy feet,
It was our FATHER ran to meet;
It was upon our FATHER'S breast
We found again a place of rest.

　　How precious are Thy thoughts to us,
　　By Thine own SON revealèd thus!
　　Oh, make us followers of Thee,
　　Thy pleasant children may we be!

362 Sheltered Dale 8.6.8.6.8.6
Anna L. Waring   (Spohr 17)   German Trad. Melody

FATHER, I know that all my life
  Is portioned out for me,
And changes that are sure to come
  I do not fear to see;
I ask Thee for a present mind
  Intent on pleasing Thee.

I ask Thee for a thoughtful love,
  Through constant watching wise,
To meet the glad with joyful smiles,
  And wipe the weeping eyes;
A heart at leisure from itself,
  To soothe and sympathize.

I would not have the restless will
  That hurries to and fro,
Seeking for some great thing to do,
  Or secret thing to know;
I would be treated as a child,
  And guided where I go.

Wherever in the world I am,
  In whatsoe'er estate,
I have a fellowship with hearts
  To keep and cultivate;
A work of lowly love to do
  For Him on whom I wait.

I ask Thee for the daily strength,
  To none that ask denied;
A mind to blend with outward life,
  While keeping at Thy side;
Content to fill a little space,
  If Thou be glorified.

In service which Thy will appoints,
  There are no bonds for me;
My inmost heart is taught the truth
  That makes Thy children free—
A life of self-renouncing love
  Is a life of liberty!

363(1)   **Southport** 8.8.8.4   G. Lomas

Charlotte Elliott

MY GOD, my FATHER, while I stray
   Far from my home on life's
     rough way,
Oh, teach me from my heart to say—
   "Thy will be done!"

Though dark my path and sad my lot,
Let me be still and murmur not,
But breathe the prayer divinely taught—
   "Thy will be done!"

If Thou shouldst call me to resign
What most I prize, it ne'er was mine;
I only yield Thee what was Thine—
   "Thy will be done!"

Renew my will from day to day,
Blend it with Thine, and take away
All that now makes it hard to say—
   "Thy will be done!"

And when on earth I breathe no more
The prayer oft mixed with tears before,
I'll sing upon a happier shore—
   "Thy will be done!"

363(2)   **In Memoriam** 8.8.8.4   F.C. Maker

364
Thos. Kelly

Lloyd C.M.
(Dublin 30)

C. Howard

OUR FATHER sits on yonder throne,
  Amidst the hosts above;
He rules throughout the world alone,
  He reigns, the GOD of Love.

He keeps us now, securely keeps,
  Whatever foe assails,
With vigilance that never sleeps,
  With power that never fails.

He knew us when we knew Him not,
  Was with us, though unseen;
His favour came to us unsought,
  His love has wondrous been.

He gives us hope that we shall be
  Ere long with CHRIST above;
That we shall all His glory see,
  And celebrate His love.

Then let us, while we dwell below,
  Obey our FATHER'S voice;
To all His dispensations bow,
  And in His name rejoice.

365
G.W. Doane

Canada S.M.
(Augustine 3)

W. Mather

OUR FATHER, "it is well;"
　　Thy ways are always right,
And perfect love is o'er them all,
　　Though far above our sight.

Our FATHER, "it is well;".
　　Though deep and sore the smart,
The hand that wounds knows how to
　　　bind,
　　And heal the broken heart.

Our FATHER, "it is well;"
　　Though sorrow cloud the way,
'Twill only make our joy more full
　　When we behold "that day."

Our FATHER, "it is well;"
　　Though rough our way may be,
It is the path that JESUS trod,
　　And leads us home to Thee.

366　　　All For Jesus 8.7.8.7
J.R. Macduff　　(Newton Ferns 411)　　J. Stainer

IF the way seem but to darken,
　　And life's shadows deepened be,
Let me to the promise hearken,
　"As thy days thy strength shall be."

O my FATHER, like my Master,
　　Let me own Thy hand divine,
Since there can be no disaster
　　When the way and will are Thine.

367 Azmon C.M.
R.C. Chapman   (St. Fulbert 120)   C.G. Glaser

ONE thing, my FATHER, only one
  My heart desires of Thee—
To know Thy well-beloved SON,
  And all His beauty see.

His resurrection power and might,
  His cross and depths of woe—
My GOD! unveil them to my sight,
  Their mysteries let me know.

Teach me in JESUS to abide,
  And in Thy bosom dwell,
Unstained by unbelief or pride,
  Unhurt by darts of hell.

May I no more Thy SPIRIT grieve,
  But all His whispers hear;
Thy words into my heart receive,
  And walk in godly fear.

Then, skilful, I with solemn song
  Shall praise the spotless Lamb:
In perfect weakness He was strong—
  His cross declares Thy name.

368 St. Bernard C.M.
Anne Steele   (Sawley 36)   J. Richardson

FATHER, whate'er of earthly bliss
  Thy sovereign will denies,
Accepted at Thy throne of grace
  Let this petition rise:

Give me a calm, a thankful heart,
  From every murmur free;
The blessings of Thy grace impart,
  That I may live to Thee.

Let the sweet truth that CHRIST is
    mine
  My life or death attend,
Thy presence through my journey
    shine,
  And crown my journey's end.

369 Kilmarnock C.M.
R.C. Chapman   (St. Botolph 377)   N. Dougall

OUR GOD and FATHER, dost Thou
    try
  Thy children's patient mind?
Shall we forget Thy name is Love,
  Or deem our GOD unkind?

Thine own dear SON Thou gavest up,
  A Ransom for us all,
And this immeasurable Gift
  Thou never canst recall.

With aught beside if called to part,
  Shall we with GOD contend?
If darkness hide His face, shall we
  Mistrust our heavenly Friend?

Our murmuring we will chide, and say,
  'Our GOD gave up His SON;
Our tears are written in His book—
  His will, not ours, be done!'

370(1) Dalehurst C.M.

Edward Denny   Arthur Cottman

WHERE in this waste, unlovely world,
  May weary hearts, opprest
With thoughts of sorrows yet to come
  In calm assurance rest?

In Him, who, of the FATHER's love
  The gracious Herald came,
Of mercy to a guilty world,
  Of blessing through His name.

In Him, who, with unsullied feet
  And guileless spirit, trod
The paths of this unquiet earth,
  In fellowship with GOD.

In JESUS, who, ascended now,
  Looks backward on the past;
Feels for His suffering members here,
  And loves us to the last.

'Tis only in His changeless love
  Our waiting spirits, blest
With the sweet hope of glory, find
  Their dwelling-place of rest.

In the same track where He of old
  The dreary desert trod,
Led onward by His grace, we learn
  The fulness of our GOD.

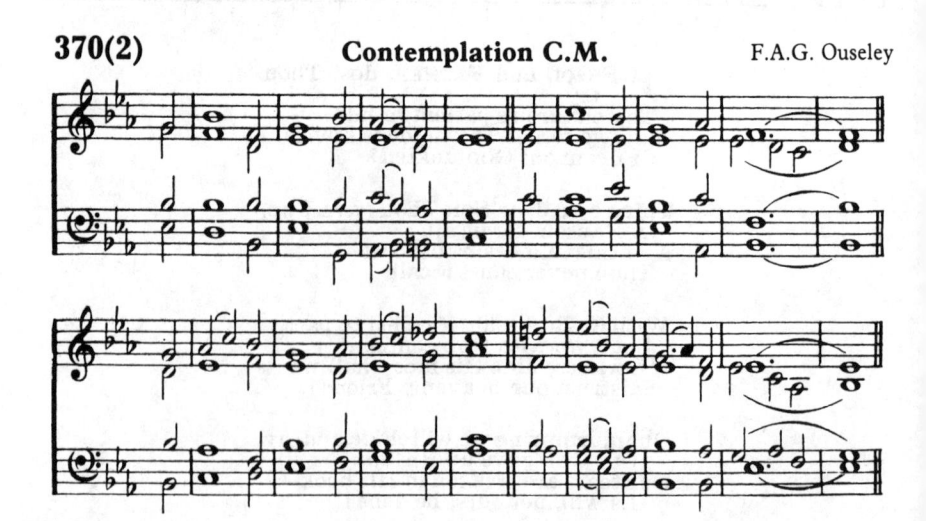

370(2) Contemplation C.M.

F.A.G. Ouseley

371
H. Bonar

St. Cecilia 6.6.6.6.
(Ibstone 434(2))

L.G. Hayne

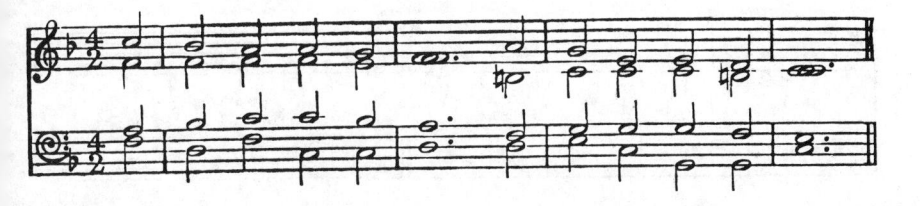

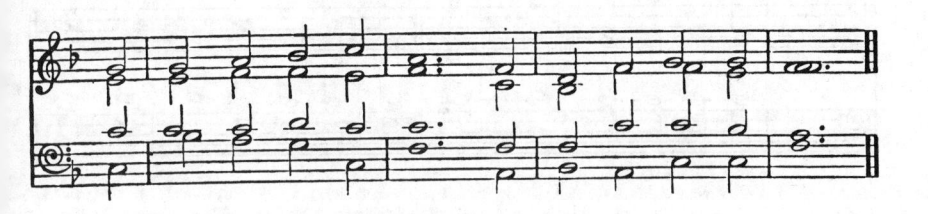

1 THY way, not mine, O LORD,
However dark it be!
Lead me by Thine own hand,
Choose out the path for me.

2 Smooth let it be or rough,
It will be still the best;
Winding or straight, it leads
Right onward to Thy rest.

3 I dare not choose my lot,
I would not if I might;
Choose Thou for me, my GOD,
So shall I walk aright.

4 The kingdom that I seek
Is Thine; so let the way
That leads to it be Thine,
Else I must surely stray.

5 Take Thou my cup, and it
With joy or sorrow fill,
As best to Thee may seem;
Choose Thou my good and ill.

6 Not mine, not mine the choice,
In things or great or small:
Be Thou my guide, my strength,
My wisdom and my all.

372   **Bishopsgarth 8.7.8.7.D**

J.S. Small   (Amicus Divinus 924)   Arthur S. Sullivan

Stately.

I'VE found a Friend, oh, such a Friend!
  He loved me ere I knew Him;
He drew me with the cords of love
  And thus He bound me to Him:
And round my heart still closely twine
  Those ties which nought can sever;
For I am CHRIST's, and He is mine,
  For ever and for ever.

I've found a Friend, oh, such a Friend!
  He bled, He died to save me;
And not alone the gift of life,
  But His own self He gave me:
Nought that I have, my own I call;
  I hold it for the Giver:
My heart, my strength, my life, my all,
  Are His, and His for ever.

I've found a Friend, oh, such a Friend!
  All power to Him is given
To guard me on my onward course
  And bring me safe to heaven:
Eternal glories gleam afar,
  To nerve my faint endeavour;
So now to watch, to work, to war—
  And then to rest for ever!

I've found a Friend, oh, such a Friend!
  So kind, and true, and tender;
So wise a counsellor and guide,
  So mighty a defender:
From Him who loves me now so well,
  What power my soul can sever?
Shall life or death, shall earth or hell?
  No; I am His for ever!

373 Ar Hyd Y Nos 8.4.8.4.8.8.8.4
J. Denham Smith (Southgate, Evensong 140) Welsh Air

G OD'S almighty arms are round me,
   Peace, peace is mine!
Judgment scenes need not confound me,
   Peace, peace is mine!
JESUS came Himself and sought me,
Slave of sin, He found and bought me,
Then my blessèd freedom taught me,
   Peace, peace is mine!

While I hear life's surging billows,
   Peace, peace is mine!
Why suspend my harp on willows?
   Peace, peace is mine!
I may sing with CHRIST beside me,
Though a thousand ills betide me,
Safely He hath sworn to guide me,
   Peace, peace is mine!

Every trial draws Him nearer,
   Peace, peace is mine!
All His strokes but make Him dearer,
   Peace, peace is mine!
Bless I then the hand that smiteth
And in grace to heal delighteth;
'Tis against my sins He fighteth,
   Peace, peace is mine!

Welcome, every morning sunlight,
   Peace, peace is mine!
Nearer home each passing midnight,
   Peace, peace is mine!
Death and hell cannot appal me,
Safe in CHRIST whate'er befall me,
Calmly wait I, till He call me,
   Peace, peace is mine!

374 St. Matthew C.M.D.
Mary Whately   (Lucius 592)   W. Croft

HE sitteth o'er the waterfloods,
   And He is strong to save;
He sitteth o'er the waterfloods,
   And guides each drifting wave.

Though loud around the vessel's prow
   The waves may toss and break,
Yet at His word they sink to rest,
   As on a tranquil lake.

He sitteth o'er the waterfloods
   When waves of sorrow rise,
And, while He holds the bitter cup,
   He wipes the tearful eyes.

He knows how long the wilful heart
   Requires the chastening grief,
And soon as sorrow's work is done
   'Tis He who sends relief.

He sitteth o'er the waterfloods,
  As in the days of old,
When o'er the Saviour's sinless head
  The waves of judgment rolled.

Yea, *all* GOD's *billows* passed o'er Him.
  Our sins—they bore Him down;
For us He met the crushing storm,
  He met the Almighty's frown!

375 **Stroudwater C.M.**
(Evan 154)   Wilkins' Psalmody 1730

GRANT, LORD, the *faith* that over-
    comes
  The world with all its snares,
That steadfast faith which rests on
    GOD,
  At ease from all our cares.

Grant us the *hope* that cheers the soul,
  Though earthly things decay;
And patience, too, which calmly waits
  The dawn of heaven's day.

Grant us the wise and tender *love*
  Which suffers and is kind;
That love "in truth" which manifests
  Thy meek and lowly mind.

Grant us the joy, of heavenly birth,
  Which sings in darkest hours,
And thankfulness, which dwells with
    tears
  On mercy's boundless stores.

Thus would we pass along life's way,
  Nor count the journey long,
And thus attune our souls to join
  The saints' adoring song.

376 Southwell C.M.
J.G. Deck   (Chorus Angelorum 343)   H.S. Irons

L ORD JESUS, when I think of Thee,
  Of all Thy love and grace,
My spirit longs, and fain would see
  Thy beauty, face to face.

And though the wilderness I tread,
  A barren, thirsty ground,
With thorns and briers overspread,
  Where foes and snares abound;

Yet in Thy love such depths I see,
  My soul o'erflows with praise;
Contents itself, while, LORD, to Thee
  My joyful song I raise.

My Lord, my Life, my Rest, my Shield,
  My Rock, my Food, my Light—
Each thought of Thee doth constant yield
  Unchanging, fresh delight.

My Saviour, keep my spirit stayed,
  Hard following after Thee,
Till I, in robes of white arrayed,
  Thy face in glory see!

377 St. Botolph C.M.
(Bristol 336)   Gordon Slater

THY heart, O LORD, with love o'er-
  flowed,
 Love spoke in every breath;
Unwearied love Thy life displayed,
  And triumphed in Thy death.

And Thou hast taught Thy followers
    here
  Their faithfulness to prove,
By yielding to Thy sweet command,
  That we each other love.

May we this sacred law fulfil
  In every act and thought;
Each angry passion be o'ercome,
  Each selfish wish forgot.

Teach us to help each other, LORD,
  Each other's burdens bear,
Let each his willing aid afford,
  And feel his brother's care.

But if from paths of love we stray,
  Our souls restore again;
Direct our footsteps in Thy way,
  And by Thy love sustain.

378   Southport S.M.
Andreas Bernstein   (St. Beuno 433)   J. Davies

O PATIENT, spotless One!
  Our hearts in meekness train
To bear Thy yoke, and learn of Thee,
  That we may rest obtain.

JESUS! Thou art enough
  The mind and heart to fill;
Thy word, to calm the anxious soul;
  Thy love, its fear dispel.

Oh, fix our earnest gaze
  So wholly, LORD, on Thee,
That with Thy beauty occupied
  We elsewhere none may see.

379 Kilmarnock C.M.

R.C. Chapman (Ballerma 339) N. Dougall

THY children, GOD of love, unite
　To bless Thy hallowed name;
We render praises with delight
　To Thee and to the Lamb.

If Thou dost try us or reprove,
　Or smite with chastening rod,
It is a token of Thy love,
　Our FATHER and our GOD.

The song of heaven we sing to Thee,
　For CHRIST our LORD is there;
Soon like Him all Thy saints shall be,
　And meet Him in the air.

Oh, let Him come, that we may know
　Thy wondrous works and ways;
That He may teach Thy children how
　Thy hallowed name to praise!

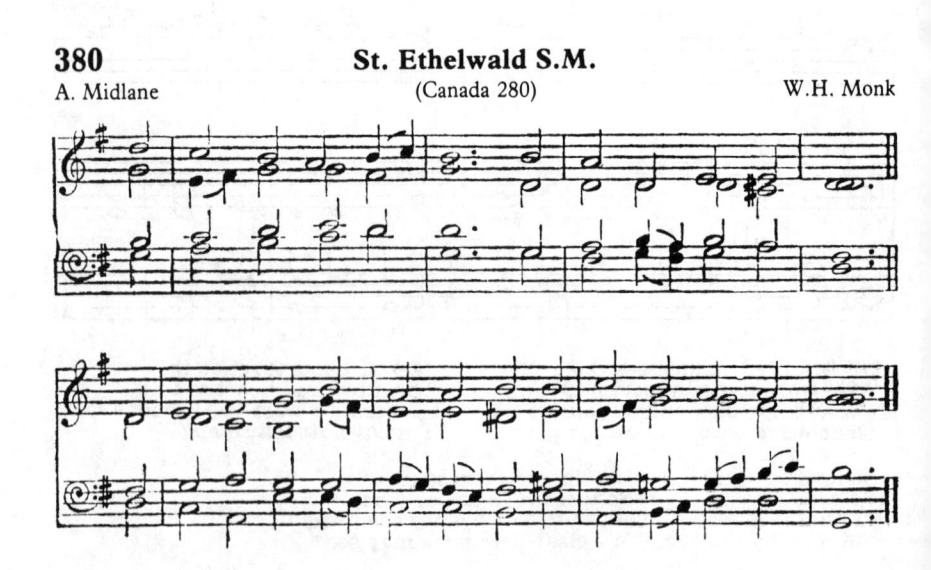

380 St. Ethelwald S.M.

A. Midlane (Canada 280) W.H. Monk

"KEPT by the power of GOD;"
How blessèd 'tis to know
That GOD's sure, gracious hand is o'er
Our chequered path below.

"Kept by the power of GOD;"
It tells of One above
Who bears us on our way, upheld
By His strong arm of love.

"Kept by the power of GOD;"
It tells us we are weak,
And all unable of ourselves
The shortest step to take.

"Kept by the power of GOD;"
It tells us we're secure,
That glory shall at length be ours,
And life for evermore.

381   Melita L.M. and Chorus

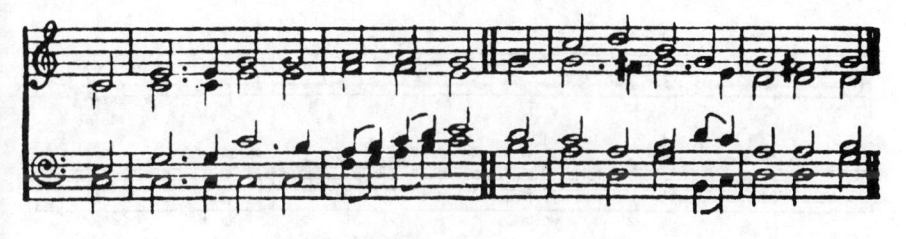

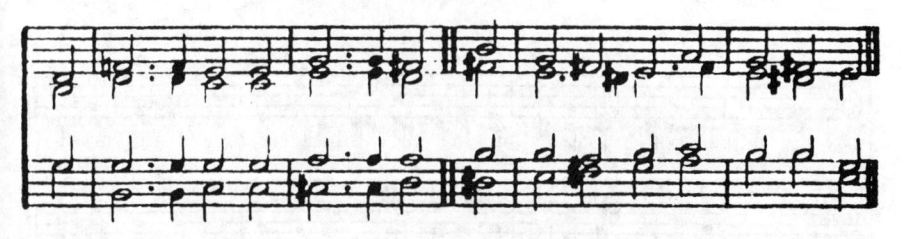

J. Evans   J.B. Dykes

REJOICE, ye saints, rejoice and praise
The blessings of redeeming grace;
JESUS, your everlasting tower,
Mocks at the angry tempest's power—
*On CHRIST, the solid rock, we stand:
All other ground is sinking sand.*

His love's a refuge ever nigh,
His watchfulness, a mountain high;
His name's a rock, which winds above
And waves below can never move—

His faithfulness, for ever sure,
For endless ages will endure;
His perfect work will ever prove
The depth of His unchanging love—

While all things change, He changes not,
He ne'er forgets, though oft forgot;
His love's unchangeably the same,
And as enduring as His name—

382 Overstrand P.M.

Ellen Willis · English Air

Moderato.

I LEFT it all with JESUS long ago;
  All my sins I brought Him, and
    my woe:
When by faith I saw Him on the tree,
Heard His small, still whisper, ''Tis
    for thee,'
From my heart the burden rolled
    away—
          Happy day!

I leave it all with JESUS, for He knows
How to steal the bitter from life's woes,
How to gild the tear-drop with His
    smile.
Make the desert garden bloom a while;
When my weakness leaneth on His
    might,
          All seems light!

I leave it all with JESUS day by day;
   Faith can firmly trust Him, come
      what may;
   Hope has dropped her anchor, found
      her rest
   In the calm, sure haven of His breast;
   Love esteems it heaven to abide
            At His side!

Oh, leave it all with JESUS, drooping
      soul!
   Tell not *half* thy story, but the whole;
   Worlds on worlds are hanging on His
      hand,
   Life and death are waiting His com-
      mand;
   Yet His tender bosom makes *thee*
      room—
            Oh, come home!

383   **Huddersfield S.M.**
C. Russell Hurditch   (Dominica 496(2))   Maurice Green

O CHRIST, Thou heavenly Lamb,
   Joy of the FATHER'S heart,
Let Thine own love my soul inflame—
   Fresh power to me impart!

Power to feel Thy love,
   And all its depths to know;
Power to fix the heart above,
   And die to all below.

Power to keep the eye
   For ever fixed on Thee;
Power to lift the warning cry
   To souls from wrath to flee.

Power lost souls to win
   From Satan's mighty hold;
Power the wanderers to bring
   Into the heavenly fold.

Power to watch and pray,
   'LORD JESUS, quickly come!'
Power to hail the happy day,
   Destined to bear me home.

384
A. Dober

Theodora 7.7.7.7.
(Ellingham 480)

Handel

1. Holy Lamb, who Thee receive,
Who in Thee begin to live,
Day and night should cry to Thee,
'As Thou art, so let us be!'

2. Fix, oh fix each wavering mind,
To Thy cross our spirits bind;
Earthly passions far remove,
Fill our souls with fervent love.

3. Weak and failing though we be,
Strength and life we find in Thee;
Thine we are, Thou Son of God,
Purchased by Thy precious blood.

4. Boundless wisdom, power divine,
Love unspeakable are Thine;
Praise by all to Thee be given,
Son of God, enthroned in heaven!

385
C. Frances Alexander

Lynton C.M.
(Binchester 620)

A.J. Jamouneau

THOU art gone up before us, LORD,
  Thou hast prepared a place,
That we may be where now Thou art.
  And see Thee face to face.

Thus ever on our earthly path
  A gleam of glory lies;
A light still breaks behind the cloud
  That veils Thee from our eyes.

Uplift our hearts, uplift our minds,
  And let Thy grace be given,
That while we wait for Thee below,
  Our hearts may be in heaven;

That where Thou art, at GOD'S right hand,
  Our hope, our love may be;
Dwell in us now, and let us dwell
  For evermore in Thee.

386 St. Alphege 7.6.7.6
S. Trevor Francis   (Barton 392)   H.J. Gauntlett

LORD JESUS, we are waiting
  To know Thy gracious will;
Our hearts, once wildly beating,
  Would restful be, and still.

Into Thy mighty fulness
  We, Saviour, filled would be;
And know the blessèd secret
  Of drawing all from Thee.

Thus daily, hourly trusting—
  Thy love the binding cord—
We work as we are waiting.
  For Thee, our absent LORD.

387 Pass Me Not 8.5.8.5
H.M. Warner
W.H. Doane

"TRUST ye in the LORD for ever,"
  Trust with all thine heart;
He will ne'er forsake thee, never
  From His weak one part.

"Trust ye in the LORD for ever,"
  Though He try thee sore;
Breast the tide, the morning breaketh,
  Thou shalt reach the shore.

"Trust ye in the LORD for ever,
  Trust by day and night;
He is near thee, and, moreover,
  He will give thee light.

Soon shall dawn a cloudless morrow;
  Sunlight then shall show,
Faithful was the hand that led thee
  All the darkness through.

Sing the song that now He giveth
  In the midnight hour,
Till the shadows at His presence
  Flee for evermore.

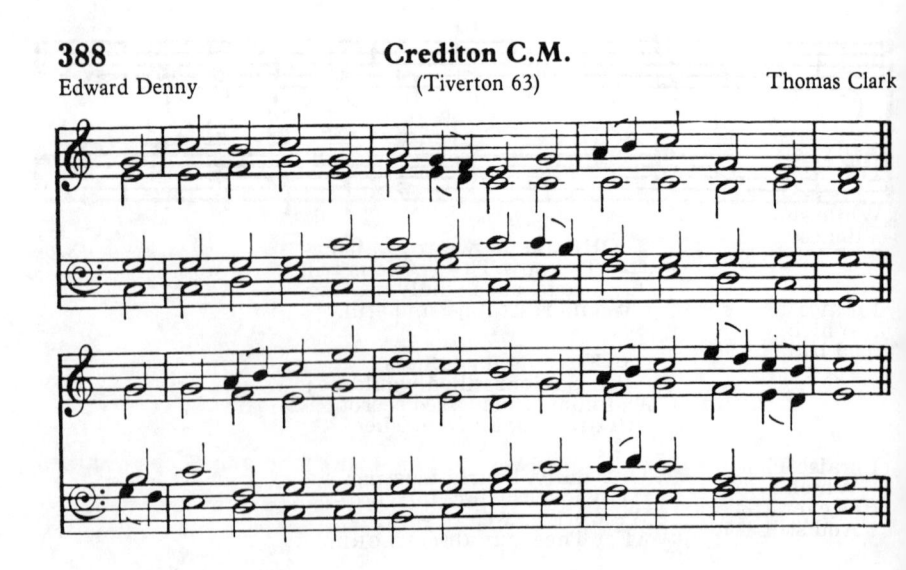

388 Crediton C.M.
Edward Denny
(Tiverton 63)
Thomas Clark

OH, what a lonely path were ours,
   Could we, O FATHER, see
No home or rest beyond it all,
   No guide or help in Thee!

But Thou art near and with us still,
   To keep us on the way
That leads along this vale of tears
   To the bright world of day.

There shall Thy glory, O our GOD!
   Break fully on our view;
And we, Thy saints, rejoice to find
   That all Thy word was true!

There JESUS, on His heavenly throne,
   Our wondering eyes shall see,
While we the blest associates there
   Of all His joy shall be.

   Sweet hope! may we, without a sigh,
     Turn from a world like this,
   To bear the cross, despise the shame,
     For all that weight of bliss!

389   Fingal C.M.
W. Pennefather   (Lynton 60)   J.S. Anderson

MY blessèd SAVIOUR, Thou hast taught
   A grateful heart to sing,
While sheltering my weary soul
   Beneath Thy loving wing.

I praise Thee for that look divine
   Which broke my stony heart,
And bade its sorrows and its fears
   For ever to depart.

I praise Thee for that arm of power,
   Which round my feeble frame
Has ever and anon been thrown,
   And still abides the same.

In adoration I would bow,
   O LORD, before Thy throne,
And yield myself a sacrifice
   To Thee and Thee alone,

For Thou hast bought me with Thy blood,
   Hast made me GOD's own child;
Thou now dost walk the path with me,
   Across this desert wild.

LORD, I am Thine, and Thou art mine;
   Oh, help me, by Thy grace,
To glorify Thee day by day
   Till I shall see Thy face.

390 Glasgow C.M.
Mary Peters (Chorus Angelorum 343) Moore's Companion 1756

JESUS! of Thee we ne'er would tire;
  The new and living food
Can satisfy our hearts' desire,
  And life is in Thy blood.

If such the happy midnight song
  Our fettered spirits raise,
What boundless joys will cause ere long
  Eternal bursts of praise!

To look within and see no stain—
  Abroad no curse to trace;
To shed no tears, to feel no pain,
  But see Thee face to face;

To find each hope of glory gained,
  Fulfilled each precious word;
And fully all to have attained
  The image of our LORD!

For this we're pressing onward still,
  And in this hope would be
More subject to the FATHER'S will
  E'en now much more like Thee.

391 Marching 8.7.8.7
R.C. Chapman (Laus Deo 498) Martin Shaw

HEAVENLY FATHER, by Thy SPIRIT,
Strengthen us with inward might;
We with powers of darkness wrestle,
As the blood-bought sons of light.

Oh, may we be ever faithful,
Ever by Thy SPIRIT led;
Armed by Him, Thy battles fighting,
Knit together in our Head!

Oh that for the Bridegroom watching,
As becomes the ransomed Bride,
JESU'S word of patience keeping,
We may in His love abide!

We who shall appear with JESUS,
In His glorious beauty clad,
Fain would now be wise to please Thee,
Wise to make our FATHER glad.

Thou, the living GOD, art resting
In Thy SON, the spotless Lamb;
We with Him, in song uniting,
Magnify Thy holy name.

392   **Barton 7.6.7.6**
R.C. Chapman   (St. Alphege 109)   J.H. Knecht

HARD after Thee I follow,
My light, and life, and joy;
This world, so false and hollow,
Allures but to destroy.

Thy death and resurrection
Have bound my heart to Thee;
Secure by Thy protection,
I hope Thy face to see.

Thy battles daily fighting,
I prove how strong Thine arm;
My soul, in Thee delighting,
Sees war without alarm.

With patience I am running
My race to win the prize;
The way of error shunning,
On Thee I fix mine eyes.

A foreign land I'm treading,
A wilderness unblest;
On hidden manna feeding,
I journey to my rest.

I publish Thy salvation,
My cross I gladly bear,
In steadfast expectation
My promised crown to wear.

393   **Huddersfield S.M.**   Maurice Green
(Dominica 496(2))

1 "THE battle is the LORD'S!"
    Then victory's secure:
Warriors of CHRIST, march on, march on,
    And to the end endure.

2 "The battle is the LORD'S!"
    Then sing and praise His name;
Join with the hosts of old and praise,
    For GOD is still the same.

3 "The battle is the LORD'S!"
    All power belongs to Him;
Since He His mighty grace affords,
    Let us go on and win.

4 "The battle is the LORD'S!"
    The land before us lies;
For faith can realize her store
    Before she grasps the prize.

5 "The battle is the LORD'S!"
    His is the spoil and prey;
Shout! for His hand is lifted up,
    And we shall win the day.

394   **University College 7.7.7.7**
Hy. Kirke White   (Theodora 384)   H.J. Gauntlett

MUCH in sorrow, oft in woe,
  Onward, Christian, onward go!
Fight the fight, though worn with strife,
Strengthened with the bread of life.

Onward, Christian, onward go!
Join the war, and face the foe;
Faint not, little doth remain
Of the drear and long campaign.

Shrink not, Christian! will you yield?
Will you quit the battle-field?
Will you flee in danger's hour?
Call to mind our Captain's power!

Let your drooping heart be glad;
March, in heavenly armour clad;
Fight, nor think the battle long,
Victory soon shall tune your song.

Let not sorrow dim your eye,
Soon shall every tear be dry;
Let not fears your course impede,
Great your strength, if great your need.

Onward then to battle move;
More than conqueror thou shalt prove;
Though opposed by many a foe,
Christian soldier, onward go!

395 Resolution P.M.

Jane E. Leeson   Anon. 1867

HAVE ye counted the cost,
  Have ye counted the cost,
Ye warriors of the cross?
Are ye fixed in heart for your Master's
    sake
  To suffer all earthly loss?
Can ye bear the scoff of the worldly-
    wise,
  As ye pass by pleasure's bower,
To watch with your LORD on the
    mountain top,
  Through the dreary midnight
    hour?

Ye may drink of His cup,
  Ye may drink of His cup,
And in His baptism share;
Ye shall not fail, if ye tread in His steps,
  A blood-stained cross to bear:
But count ye the cost; oh, count ye
    the cost,
  That ye be not unprepared!
And know ye the strength that alone
    can stand
  In the conflict ye have dared!

In the power of His might,
In the power of His might,
Who was made through weakness strong,
Ye shall overcome in the fearful fight,
And sing His victory song!
By the "blood of the Lamb," by the "blood of the Lamb,"
By the faithful witness Word,
Not loving your lives unto death for Him,
Ye shall triumph with your Lord!

Oh, the banner of love!
Oh, the banner of love!
It will cost you a pang to hold;
But 'twill float in triumph the field above,
Though your heart's blood stain its fold!
Ye may count the cost, ye may count the cost
Of all Egyptia's treasure;
But the riches of Christ ye cannot count—
His love ye cannot measure!

396
Isaac Watts

Nativity C.M.
(Attercliffe 902)

H. Lahee

AM I a soldier of the cross,
A follower of the Lamb?
And shall I fear to own His cause,
Or blush to speak His name?

Must I be carried to the skies
On flowery beds of ease,
While others fought to win the prize,
And sailed through bloody seas?

Are there no foes for me to face?
Must I not stem the flood?
Is this vile world a friend to grace,
To help me on to God?

Since I must fight if I would reign;
Increase my courage, Lord,
To bear the toil, endure the pain,
Supported by Thy Word.

397 St. Ethelwald S.M.
C. Wesley (Day of Praise 899) W.H. Monk

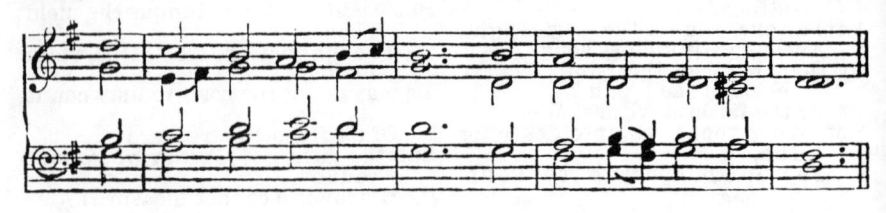

1 SOLDIERS of CHRIST! arise,
And put your armour on,
Strong in the strength which GOD
supplies
Through His eternal SON.

2 Strong in the LORD of hosts,
And in His mighty power;
Who in the strength of JESUS trusts
Is more than conqueror.

3 Stand, then, in His great might,
With all His strength endued;
And take, to arm you for the fight,
The panoply of GOD.

4 To keep your armour bright,
Attend with constant care,
Still walking in your Captain's sight,
And watching unto prayer.

5 And, having all things done,
With all your conflicts past,
Your joy shall be in CHRIST alone,
In Him complete at last.

398 St. Matthew C.M.D.
W. Pennefather (Rex Regum 607) W. Croft

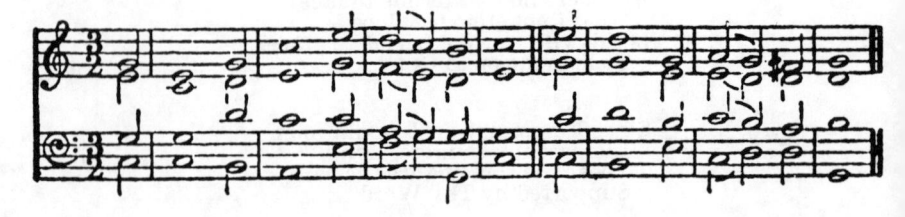

O GOD of glorious majesty,
  Messiah, King of grace,
Unveil to us Thy loveliness,
  And let us see Thy face!
Obedient to Thy loving voice,
  We've turned aside awhile,
To wait beside Thy guiding feet,
  And rest beneath Thy smile.

Oh, nerve us for the conflict, LORD,
  That thickens day by day,
That we, amidst our alien foes,
  Thy banner may display!
We've but a little while to fight,
  To work, to wait for Thee;
Help us to labour in Thy cause
  With holy energy.

Help us upon our watch to stand,
  And never quail for fear,
Till in the glowing eastern sky
  The Morning Star appear;
Then with Thy waiting saints above,
  Thine advent, LORD, we'll hail,
And over death, and sin, and woe,
  We'll joyfully prevail.

399
J.N. Darby

Celeste 8.9.9.9.

1 THIS world is a wilderness wide;
   I have nothing to seek or to choose;
 With no thought in the waste to abide,
   I have nought to regret nor to lose.

2 The LORD has Himself gone before:
   He has marked out the path that I tread;
 'Tis as sure as the love I adore—
   I have nothing to fear nor to dread.

3 For the path where my Saviour has gone
   Leads me up to His FATHER and GOD,
 To the place where He's now on the throne,
   And His strength shall be mine on the road.

4 With Him shall my rest be on high,
   When in holiness bright I sit down,
 In the joy of His love ever nigh,
   In the peace that His presence shall crown.

5 'Tis the treasure I've found in His love
   That has made me a pilgrim below,
 And 'tis there, when I reach Him above,
   As I'm known, all His fulness I'll know.

6 And, Saviour, 'tis Thee from on high
   I await till the time Thou shalt come,
 To take him Thou has led by Thine eye
   To Thyself in Thy heavenly home.

7 Till then, 'tis the path Thou hast trod.
   My delight and my comfort shall be;
 I'm content with Thy staff and Thy rod,
   Till, with Thee, all Thy glory I see.

400

St. Denio 11.11.11.11
(Montgomery 326)

Welsh Hymn Melody

PRESS forward and fear not,
though billows may roll,
The Word of JEHOVAH their rage can
control;
Though waves rise in anger, their
tumults shall cease,
One word of His bidding shall hush
them to peace.

Press forward and fear not, though
trial be near,
The LORD is our refuge, whom then
shall we fear?
His staff is our comfort, our safeguard His rod,
Then let us be steadfast, and trust in
our GOD.

Press forward and fear not, be strong
in the LORD,
In the power of His promise, the truth
of His word;
Through the sea and the desert our
pathway may tend,
But He who hath saved us will save
to the end.

Press forward and fear not, though
rough be our way,
Why should we e'er shrink from our
path in dismay?
We tread but the road which our
Leader has trod,
Then let us press forward, and trust
in our GOD.

401(1)   Yarmouth P.M.   Anon. 1863
Miln

THE cross! the cross!
　　The Christian's only glory;
　I see the standard rise:
March on, march on,
The cross of CHRIST before thee,
　That cross all hell defies.

The cross! the cross!
Redemption's standard raising;
　I see the banner wave:
Sing on, sing on,
Salvation's Captain praising,
　'Tis CHRIST alone can save.

The crown! the crown!
Ah, who at last shall gain it?
　That cross a crown affords:
Press on, press on,
With courage to obtain it,
　The battle is the LORD'S.

401(2)　　　　　　　　**Latimer P.M.**　　　　　　　Latimer James Short

402   **Calon Lan 8.7.8.7.D**

S.P. Tregelles   (Deerhurst 48)   John Hughes

FATHER, we, Thy children, bless Thee
For Thy love on us bestowed ;
As our FATHER we address Thee,
Called to be the sons of GOD :
Wondrous was Thy love in giving
JESUS for our sins to die !
Wondrous was His grace in leaving,
For our sakes, His home on high !

Now the sprinkled blood has freed us,
Onward go we to our rest,
Through the desert Thou dost lead us,
With Thy constant favour blest ;
By Thy truth and SPIRIT guiding—
Earnest He of joys to come—
And, with daily food providing,
Thou dost lead Thy children home.

Though our pilgrimage be dreary,
This is not our resting place ;
Shall we of the way be weary,
When we see our Master's face?
Now, by faith anticipating,
In this hope our souls rejoice ;
We, His promised advent waiting,
Soon shall hear His welcome voice.

FATHER, oh how vast the blessing,
When Thy SON returns again !
Then Thy saints, their rest possessing,
O'er the earth with Him shall reign :
For the fathers' sake beloved,
Israel, in Thy grace restored,
Shall, on earth, the curse removèd,
Be the people of the LORD.

Then shall countless myriads, wearing
  Robes made white in JESU's blood,
Palms, like rested pilgrims, bearing,
  Stand before the throne of GOD:
These, redeemed from every nation,
  Shall in triumph bless Thy name;
Every voice shall cry, "Salvation
  To our GOD, and to the LAMB!"

403 **University College 7.7.7.7**
J.H. Evans   (Newington 563)   H.J. Gauntlett

FAINT not, Christian, though the road
Leading to thy blest abode
Darksome be, and dangerous too,
CHRIST, thy Guide, will bring thee through.

Faint not, Christian, though in rage,
Satan would thy soul engage;
Take thee faith's anointed shield,
Bear it to the battle-field.

Faint not, Christian, though the world
Hath its hostile flag unfurled;
Hold the cross of JESUS fast,
Thou shalt overcome at last.

Faint not, Christian, though within
There's a heart so prone to sin;
CHRIST, the LORD, is over all—
He'll not suffer Thee to fall.

Faint not, Christian, though thy GOD
Smite thee with the chastening rod;
Smite He must, with FATHER's care,
That He may His love declare.

Faint not, Christian, CHRIST is near;
Soon in glory He'll appear:
Then shall cease thy toil and strife;
Thou shalt wear the crown of life.

404 **Houghton 10.10.11.11**
J.G. Deck (Laudate Dominum 325) H.J. Gauntlett

1 WE'RE not of the world that fadeth away,
We're not of the night, but children of day;
The chains that once bound us by JESUS are riven,
We're strangers on earth, and our home is in heaven.

2 Our path is most rugged, and dangerous too,
A wide, trackless waste our journey lies through;
But the pillar of cloud, that shews us our way,
Is our sure light by night, and shades us by day.

3 Our Shepherd is still our Guardian and Guide,
Before us He goes to help and provide;
We drink of the streams from the rock that was riven,
Our bread is the manna that came down from heaven.

4 'Mid mightiest foes, most feeble are we,
Yet in each encounter they tremble and flee;
The LORD is our banner, the battle is His,
The weakest of saints more than conqueror is.

5 Soon, soon shall we enter our own promised land,
Before His bright throne in glory shall stand;
Our song then for ever and ever shall be,
'All glory and blessing, LORD JESUS, to Thee!'

405 **Cwm Rhondda 8.7.8.7.8.7**
W. Williams John Hughes

GUIDE us, O Thou great JEHOVAH!
   Pilgrims through this barren
     land;
We are weak, but Thou art mighty;
   Hold us with Thy powerful hand:
     Bread of heaven!
     Feed us now and evermore.

Open wide the living fountain,
   Whence the healing waters flow;
Be Thyself our cloudy pillar
   All the dreary desert through:
     Strong Deliverer!
     Be Thou still our strength and
     shield.

While we tread this vale of sorrow,
   May we in Thy love abide:
Keep us, O our gracious Saviour,
   Cleaving closely to Thy side!
     Still relying
     On our FATHER'S changeless love.

Saviour, come! we long to see Thee,
   Long to dwell with Thee above,
And to know, in full communion,
   All the sweetness of Thy love:
     Come, LORD JESUS!
     Take Thy waiting people home.

406   **Montgomery 11.11.11.11**

Henry F. Lyte   (St. Denio 317)   J. Stanley

OUR rest is in heaven, our rest is not here,
Then why should we tremble when trials are near?
Be hushed our sad spirits, the worst that can come
But shortens the journey, and hastens us home.

It is not for us to be seeking our bliss,
And building our hopes in a region like this;
We look for a city which hands have not piled,
We pant for a country by sin undefiled.

Let trial and danger our progress oppose,
'Twill only make heaven more sweet at the close;
Come joy or come sorrow, whate'er may befall,
A home with our GOD will make up for it all.

With a scrip on the back, and a staff in the hand,
We march on in haste through an enemy's land:
The road may be rough, but it cannot be long,
And we'll smooth it with hope, and cheer it with song.

407 Manna P.M.

Hannah K. Burlingham

Words over

Heirs of salvation, chosen of God:
Past condemnation, sheltered by blood:
Even in Egypt feed we on the Lamb,
Keeping the statute of God the I AM!
   In the world around, 'tis night,
   Where the feast is spread, 'tis bright,
     Israel's Lord is Israel's light:
'Tis Jesus, 'tis Jesus, our Saviour from above,
'Tis Jesus, 'tis Jesus, 'tis Jesus whom we love!

Pilgrims and strangers, captives no more!
Wilderness rangers—sing we on the shore!
God in His power parted wide the sea,
Foes all have perished—His people are free!
   By the pillar safely led,
   With the manna daily fed,
     Now the homeward way we tread:
'Tis Jesus, 'tis Jesus, our Shepherd here below,
'Tis Jesus, 'tis Jesus, 'tis Jesus whom we know!

Canaan-possessors, safe in the land,
Victors, confessors, banner in hand!
Jordan's deep river evermore behind,
Cares of the desert no longer in mind!
   Egypt's stigma rolled away,
   Canaan's corn our strength and stay,
     Triumph we the livelong day!
'Tis Jesus, 'tis Jesus, the Christ of God alone,
'Tis Jesus, 'tis Jesus, 'tis Jesus whom we own!

Egypt S.M. and Chorus
(Deliverance 901)

Thos. Kelly

F ROM Egypt lately come,
　　Where death and darkness reign,
We seek our new, our better home,
　　Where we our rest shall gain :
　　　Hallelujah!
　　We are on our way to GOD.

There sin and sorrow cease,
　　And every conflict's o'er;
There shall we dwell in endless peace,
　　And never hunger more—

There, in celestial strains,
　　Enraptured myriads sing;
There love in every bosom reigns,
　　For GOD Himself is King—

We soon shall join the throng,
　　Their pleasures we shall share,
And sing the everlasting song,
　　With all the ransomed there—

How sweet the prospect is !
　　It cheers the pilgrim's breast;
We're journeying through the wilderness,
　　But soon shall gain our rest—

409   Abbey C.M.

Isaac Newton   (Abridge 98)   Scottish Psalter 1615

WHEN Israel, by divine command,
  The pathless desert trod,
They found, through all that barren land,
  A sure resource in GOD.

A cloudy pillar marked the road,
  And screened them from the heat;
From the hard rock the water flowed,
  And manna was their meat.

Like them we have a rest in view,
  Secure from adverse powers;
Like them we pass a desert too,
  But Israel's GOD is ours.

His word a light before us sheds,
  By which our path we see;
His love, a banner o'er our heads,
  From harm preserves us free.

JESUS, the Bread of Life, is given
  To be our daily food;
And from the Rock that once was riven,
  We drink the streams of GOD.

410(1)   Melling 7.7.7.7

John Cennick   J. Fawcett

CHILDREN of the heavenly King,
As ye journey, sweetly sing;
Sing your Saviour's worthy praise,
Glorious in His works and ways.

Shout ye little flock and blest,
Ye on JESU'S throne shall rest;
There your seat is now prepared,
There your kingdom and reward.

Ye are travelling home to GOD
In the way the fathers trod;
They are happy now, and ye
Soon with CHRIST your LORD shall be.

Fear not, though a feeble band,
'Mid the conflict boldly stand;
CHRIST your LORD, the day who won,
Bids you undismayed go on.

LORD, we would obedient go,
Gladly leaving all below;
Since Thou wilt our Leader be,
We would ever follow Thee.

410(2)   **Vienna 7.7.7.7**   J.H. Knecht

411 Newton Ferns 8.7.8.7
J.N. Darby   (All for Jesus 243)   *Samuel Smith*

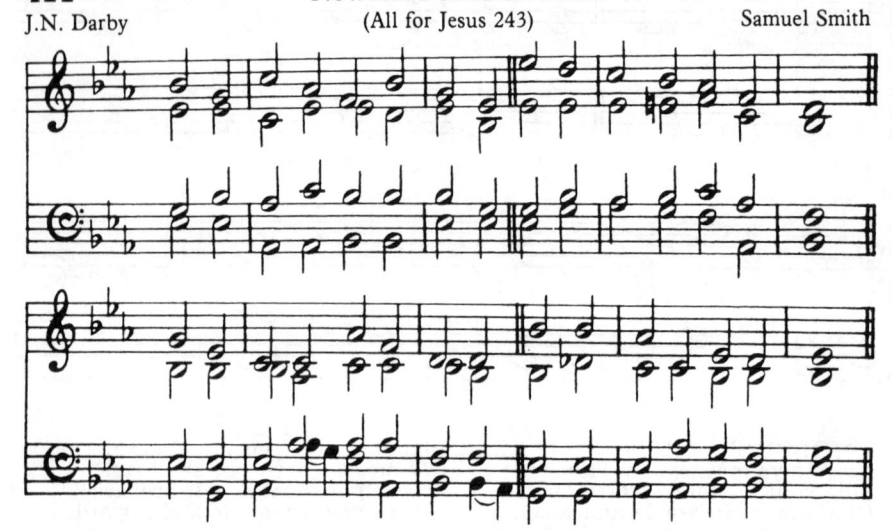

RISE, my soul, thy GOD directs thee,
  Stranger-hands no more impede;
Pass thou on, His hand protects thee—
  Strength, that has the captive freed.

Is the wilderness before thee—
  Desert lands where drought abides?
Heavenly springs shall there restore thee,
  Fresh from GOD'S exhaustless tides.

Light divine surrounds thy going,
  GOD Himself shall mark thy way;
Secret blessings, richly flowing,
  Lead to everlasting day.

Art thou weaned from Egypt's pleasures?
  GOD in secret thee shall keep,
There unfold His hidden treasures,
  There, His love's exhaustless deep.

In the desert GOD will teach thee
  What the GOD that thou hast found,
Patient, gracious, powerful, holy—
  All His grace shall there abound.

Though thy way be long and dreary,
  Eagle strength He'll still renew;
Garments fresh and foot unweary
  Tell how GOD doth bring thee through.

When to Canaan's long-loved dwelling
  Love divine thy foot shall bring,
There, with shouts of triumph swelling,
  Zion's songs in rest to sing—

There no stranger-GOD shall meet thee—
  Stranger thou in courts above—
He who to His rest shall greet thee,
  Greets thee with a well-known love.

412 Lymington 7.6.7.6.D
Mary Peters   (Nyland 185)   *Robt. Jackson*

WE'RE pilgrims in the wilderness,
  Our dwelling is a camp;
Created things, once pleasant,
  Are bearing death's sad stamp;
Yet on, LORD, we are speeding,
  Though sorely let and tried:
The HOLY GHOST is leading
  Thy well-belovèd Bride.

How sweet these frequent meetings,
  As through the waste we roam;
'Tis well to sing together,
  We are not far from home;
For when we've learned obedience,
  Our work in suffering done,
Our ever-loving FATHER
  Will welcome every one.

We look to meet our brethren
  From every distant shore;
Not one will seem a stranger,
  Though never seen before;
While angel hosts attending,
  In myriads throng the sky,
Amidst them all, Thou only,
  O LORD, wilt fix our eye.

LORD, since we sing as pilgrims,
  May we have pilgrims' ways,
Low thoughts of self, befitting
  Proclaimers of Thy praise!
Oh, make us each more holy,
  In spirit pure and meek,
Like citizens of heaven,
  As we of heaven speak!

413 Azmon C.M.
R.C. Chapman (Southwell 478) C. G. Glaser

WELL known, O LORD, this land to Thee,
Through which we hasten home;
Here Thou wast slain upon the tree,
Here buried in the tomb!

Upon Thy bosom we repose,
And weariness forget;
Thy voice beguiles us of our woes,
And makes the bitter sweet.

Thy grace our failing strength renews,
Thy paths are paths of peace;
If thence we stray Thy love pursues,
Thy mercies never cease.

Thou SON of GOD, our great High Priest,
Unchangeably the same,
In hope of our eternal rest
We bless and praise Thy name!

414 Leadeth L.M. and Chorus
Joseph H. Gilmore Wm. B. Bradbury

CHORUS

HE leadeth me, O blessèd thought!
O words with heavenly comfort
fraught!
Whate'er I do, where'er I be,
Still 'tis GOD's hand that leadeth me!
*He leadeth me! He leadeth me!
By His own hand He leadeth me;
His faithful follower would I be,
For by His hand He leadeth me!*

Sometimes 'mid scenes of deepest
gloom,
Sometimes where Eden's bowers
bloom,
By waters still, o'er troubled sea,
Still 'tis His hand that leadeth me—

LORD, I would place my hand in Thine,
And never murmur or repine,
Content, whate'er my lot may be,
Since 'tis my GOD that leadeth me—

415   **Ballerma C.M.**
R.C. Chapman   (Lucius 592)   Adapted by R. Simpson

OUR life is now no more a dream,
  Nor shadows we pursue;
Our joys are now a living stream,
  Our song is ever new.

The LORD who stooped from heaven to die,
  The Mighty One to save,
Now sits with GOD enthroned on high,
  Triumphant o'er the grave.

The Prince of Life by faith we see,
  And now with Him are one;
For us GOD's hand, upon the tree,
  Did bruise His only SON!

We have no home nor city here,
  This earth is all unblest;
Let CHRIST the LORD again appear,
  And give us perfect rest!

Our GOD, Thy holy name we bless,
  And drink our cup of woes;
Hope makes this barren wilderness
  To blossom like the rose.

416   **Mainzer L.M.**
Edward Denny   (Berkshire 567(2))   Joseph Mainzer

WE go with the redeemed to taste
  Of joy supreme that never dies:
Our feet still press the weary waste;
  Our hearts, our home are in the skies.

And oh, while on to Zion's hill
  The toilsome path of life we tread,
Around us, loving FATHER, still
  Thy circling wings of mercy spread!

From day to day, from hour to hour,
  Oh, let our rising spirits prove
The strength of Thine almighty power,
  The sweetness of Thy saving love.

417   **Broomsgrove 6.4.6.4.6.6.6.4**

T.R. Taylor   F.C. Maker

WE are but strangers here;
  Heaven is our home!
Earth is a desert drear;
  Heaven is our home!
Danger and sorrow stand
Round us on every hand;
Heaven is our father-land,
  Heaven is our home!

What though the tempest rage?
  Heaven is our home!
Short is our pilgrimage;
  Heaven is our home!
And time's wild, wintry blast
Soon will be overpast;
We shall reach home at last—
  Heaven is our home!

There at our Saviour's side,
  Heaven is our home!
We shall be glorified,
  Heaven is our home!
There with the good and blest,
Those we've loved most and best,
We shall for ever rest—
  Heaven is our home!

Therefore we'll murmur not;
  Heaven is our home!
Whate'er our earthly lot,
  Heaven is our home!
For we shall surely stand
There at our LORD's right hand;
Heaven is our father-land,
  Heaven is our home!

418 Bishopsgarth 8.7.8.7.D

David Nelson (Sweetest Name 926) Arthur S. Sullivan

Stately.

MY days are gliding swiftly by,
　And I, a pilgrim stranger,
Would not detain them as they fly,
　These hours of toil and danger:
　　*For, oh, we stand on Jordan's
　　　strand,
　　Our friends are passing over,
　　And just before, the shining shore
　　We may almost discover.*

Then let us gird our loins afresh,
　Our distant home discerning;
Our absent LORD has left us word,
　Let every lamp be burning—

Should coming days be cold and dark,
　We need not cease our singing;
That perfect rest none can molest,
　Where golden harps are ringing—

Should sorrow's rudest tempest blow,
　Each cord on earth to sever,
Our LORD's word "*Come*" tells of a
　home
　For ever—aye, for ever!—

419   Clarendon Street 11.11.11.11
Carter   (St. Luke 330)   A.J. Gordon

THROUGH the dark path of sorrow which JESUS once trod,
Thy feeble ones wander, our FATHER and GOD;
And the thick clouds that gather but turn us away
From the waste, howling desert where He could not stay.

In the fierce hour that trieth the children of men—
In the hour of temptation, oh, succour us then!
Let the weak and the feeble find under Thine arm
A shelter and rest in the terrible storm.

Through the cold world that knoweth and loveth its own,
Where JESUS was hated, rejected, unknown,
We would cheerfully hasten, rejoicing to be
Counted worthy to suffer, LORD JESUS, for Thee.

When the proud are exalted, and seated on high,
When trouble and desperate sorrow draw nigh,
When the hearts of all others are failing for fear—
Then we lift up our heads, for the glory is near.

Oh, hasten Thy coming! we look for the day;
Bright Star of the morning, no longer delay;
Let the groaning creation from sorrow be free;
Let Thy purchased possession be gathered to Thee!

420 Homeward 6.6.6.6.4
Anon. Anon.

1 I AM a stranger here,
　No home, no rest I see;
Not all that men count dear
　Should win a sigh from me—
　　I'm going home.

2 SAVIOUR, Thy home is mine,
　And I, Thy FATHER'S child,
With hopes and joys divine;
　The world's a weary wild—
　　I'm going home.

3 Home, oh how soft and sweet,
　It thrills upon the heart!
Home, where the brethren meet,
　And never, never part—
　　I'm going home.

4 Home, where the BRIDEGROOM takes
　The purchase of His love;
Home, where the FATHER waits
　To welcome her above—
　　I'm going home.

5 Ah, gently, *gently* lead
　Along the painful way;
Bid every word and deed,
　And every look to say—
　　I'm going home.

421   **Rhuddlan 8.7.8.7.8.7**
Thos. Kelly   (The Good Shepherd 467)   Welsh Trad. Melody

SAVIOUR, through the desert lead us!
  Without Thee we cannot go;
Thou from cruel chains hast freed us,
  Thou hast laid the tyrant low;
    Let Thy presence
Cheer us all the journey through.

Through the desert, waste and cheerless,
  Though our destined journey lie.
Rendered by Thy presence fearless,
  We may every foe defy;
    Nought shall move us
While we see Thee, Saviour, nigh.

With a price Thy love has bought us—
  Saviour, what a love is Thine!
Hitherto Thy power has brought us,
  Power and love in Thee combine;
    LORD of glory,
Ever on Thy people shine!

When we halt, no track discovering,
  Fearful lest we go astray,
O'er our path Thy pillar hovering—
  Fire by night, and cloud by day—
    Shall direct us,
Thus we shall not miss our way.

When we hunger, Thou wilt feed us,
  Manna shall our camp surround;
Faint and thirsty, Thou wilt heed us,
  Streams shall from the Rock abound;
    Happy people,
What a Saviour we have found!

422
Anne Steele

Richmond C.M.
(Binchester 620)

Thos. Haweis

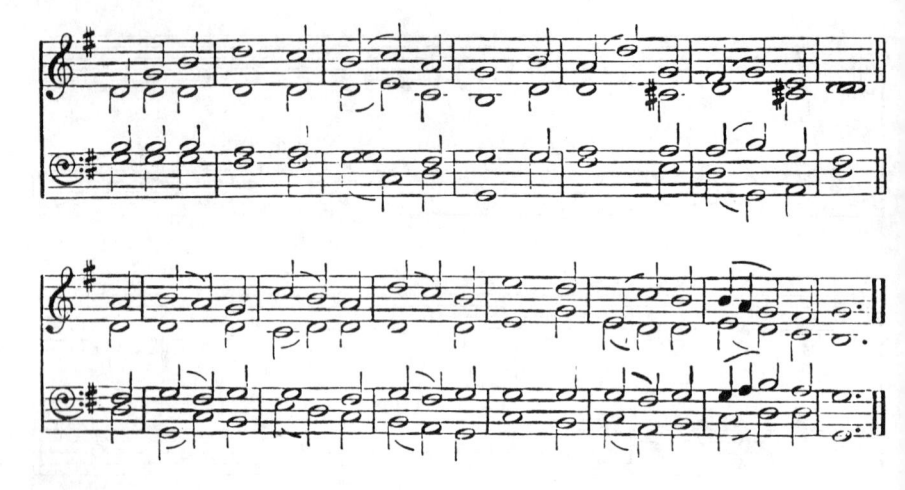

THY gracious presence, O our GOD,
 Our happiness maintains;
With this, beneath temptation's load,
 The heart no more complains.

Happy those scenes of pure delight
 Where JESU'S beams impart
Unclouded beauty to the sight,
 And gladness to the heart.

Our part with Him in realms of bliss
 Our spirits long to know;
Our wishes onward reach to this,
 Nor can they rest below.

Nor can these wishes of our heart
 Be told in vain to Thee;
We know, O LORD, that where Thou art
 We shall for ever be.

Thus would our cheerful spirits sing
 The darkest hours away,
And rise on faith's expanded wing
 To everlasting day.

423
G.B.P.

Tours 7.6.7.6.D
(Nyland 185)

Berthold Tours

"THEY wandered in the desert—
  A solitary way;"
Alone with GOD they journeyed
  For many a night and day;
They wandered on—He kept them
  Throughout that desert wide,
From human friendships severed,
  All human help denied.

And yet it was "the right way,"
  No cause had they to fear;
Although 'twas not the bright way,
  Yet GOD Himself was near;
The rock gave forth the water,
  The heaven gave them bread,
With cloud and pillar o'er them
  The LORD JEHOVAH led.

Each resting-place, each journey
  Were all upon the road
Which led unto "the city"
  For them "prepared" by GOD·
Their enemies He conquered,
  Their needs He well supplied,
And from distress delivered
  When unto Him they cried.

We're pilgrims, too, and strangers,
  But GOD Himself is nigh;
No dwelling here to rest in,
  Our city is on high;
From Egypt unto Canaan
  Each step, marked by His love,
Leads to our land of promise—
  Jerusalem above.

When there we meet the SAVIOUR,
  And see Him face to face,
And there behold His glory,
  So full of truth and grace—
We then shall know our pathway
  Was ordered for the best,
It was our FATHER'S "*right way*"
  To everlasting rest.

424 Behold What Love C.M. and Chorus

M.S. Sullivan
J. McGranahan

BEHOLD what love, what boundless love,
The FATHER hath bestowed
On sinners lost, that we should be
Now called "the sons of GOD!"

"Behold... what manner of love...
what manner of love the FATHER hath
bestowed upon us, that we... that we
should be called... should be called
the sons of GOD!"

No longer far from Him, but now
  By "precious blood" made nigh
"Accepted" in the Well-beloved,
  Near to GOD's heart we lie—

What we in glory soon shall be,
  "It doth not yet appear;"
But when our precious LORD we see,
  We shall His image bear—

With such a blessèd hope in view,
  We would more holy be,
More like our risen, glorious LORD,
  Whose face we soon shall see—

425   Silchester S.M.

Isaac Watts   (Diademata 900)   H.A.C. Malan

COME all who love the LORD,
  And let our joys be known;
Join in a song with sweet accord,
  And thus surround the throne.

Let those refuse to sing
  Who never knew our GOD;
But children of the heavenly King
  Should sound their joys abroad

The GOD who rules on high,
  Whose thunder rends the clouds,
Who rides upon the stormy sky,
  And calms the raging floods—

This holy GOD is ours,
  Encircling us with love;
He shall put forth His mighty powers
  To carry us above.

There shall we see His face,
  And never, never sin;
And from the rivers of His grace
  Drink endless pleasures in.

Then let our songs abound,
  And every tear be dry;
We're marching through this barren
    ground
  To fairer worlds on high.

426 Goshen 6.5.6.5. and Chorus

A. Midlane (Norfolk Park 910) Marchel Davis

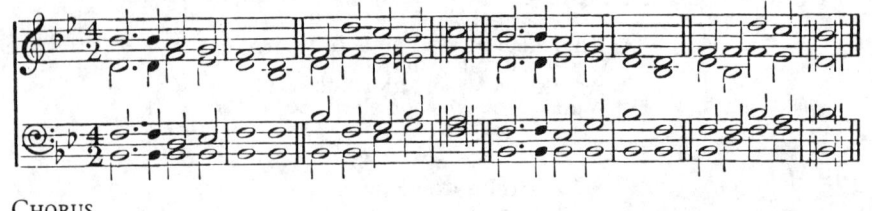

CHORUS

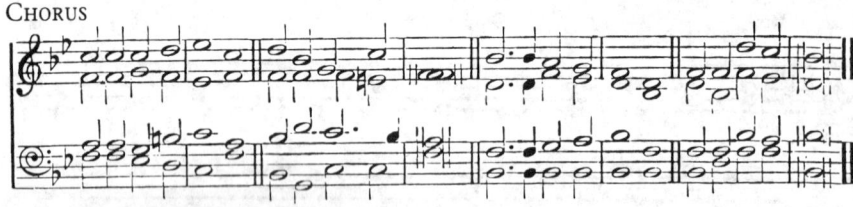

O NWARD! upward! homeward!
 Joyfully we flee
From this world of sorrow,
 With our LORD to be:
  Onward to the glory,
  Upward to the prize,
  Homeward to the mansions
  Far above the skies!

Onward! upward! homeward!
 Here we find no rest,
Treading o'er the desert
 Which our Saviour pressed—

Onward! upward! homeward!
 We shall soon be there;
Soon its joys and pleasures
 We through grace shall share—

Onward! upward! homeward!
 Press with vigour on;
Yet "a little while,"
 And the race is won—

427 Celeste 8.8.8.8

E. Mills (David 930)

W E sing of the realms of the blest,
 That country so bright and so fair,
And oft are its glories confest;
 But what must it be to be there!

We speak of its freedom from sin,
 From sorrow, temptation, and care,
From trials without and within;
 But what must it be to be there!

We speak of its service of love,
 Of the robes which the glorified wear—
The Church of the first-born above;
 But what must it be to be there!

Do Thou, LORD, midst pleasure or woe,
 For heaven our spirits prepare,
And shortly we also shall know
 And feel what it is to be there!

428   Truro L.M.
Thos. Kelly   (Hereford 359)   C. Burney

W E'VE no abiding city here—
 This may distress the worldly mind,
But should not cost the saint a tear,
 Who hopes a better rest to find.

We've no abiding city here—
 Sad thought, were this to be our home!
But let this hope our spirits cheer,
 We seek a city yet to come.

We've no abiding city here—
 Then let us live as pilgrims do;
Let not the world our rest appear,
 But let us haste from all below.

We've no abiding city here—
 We seek a city out of sight;
It needs no sun—"The LORD is there;"
 It shines with everlasting light.

JEHOVAH is her joy and strength;
 Secure, she smiles at all her foes,
And weary travellers at length
 Within her sacred walls repose.

O sweet abode of peace and love,
 Where pilgrims freed from toil are blest,
Soon shall we, with our LORD above,
 In thy blest mansions find our rest!

429 Paradise No. 2 C.M. and Chorus
W.P. Mackay

O HAPPY home! O happy home!
  Prepared by Jesu's hand;
We soon shall be within thy walls,
  With all the ransomed band,
    Where sinners saved by grace,
    Redeemed by Jesu's blood,
    Shall see Him face to face—
    Their Saviour and their God.

O happy home! O happy home!
  Where come no cares nor fears,
Nor death, nor sorrows, for God's hand
  Shall wipe away all tears—

O happy home! O happy home!
  Where we shall sin no more;
Where spotless, sinless, perfect, pure
  We'll dwell for evermore—

O happy home! O happy home!
  Where Jesus we shall see;
When He appears in glory bright,
  Like Him we all shall be—

O happy home! O happy home!
  May thy bright, glorious ray
Pierce through the clouds, and cheer
  our steps
Here on our pilgrim way!—

430 Hasten (Break of Day) P.M.

Denham Smith American Melody

Chorus

1 RISE up and hasten, my soul, haste along!
And speed on thy journey with hope and with song;
Home, home is nearing; 'tis coming into view;
A little more of toiling, and then to earth adieu!
   Come, then, come! and raise the joyful song,
   As children in the wilderness our time cannot be long;
   Home, home, home! oh, why should we delay?
   The morn of heaven is dawning; we're near the break of day!

2 Why should we linger when heaven lies before?
Earth's fast receding, and soon will be no more;
Its joys and its treasures, which once here we knew,
Now nevermore can charm us, with such a goal in view—

3 Loved ones in JESUS have passèd on before;
Resting in glory, they weary are no more;
Desert toils are ended, nothing now but joy,
And praises loud ascending their ever glad employ—

4 No condemnation! blessèd is the word;
No separation! for ever with the LORD:
By His blood He bought them, washed their every stain;
With rapture now they praise Him, the Lamb that once was slain—

5 Soon we shall join them, see Him with these eyes;
Sing Hallelujahs triumphant in the skies;
He will be with us, who loved us long before,
And JESUS, blessèd JESUS, is ours for evermore!—

431 **Sandys S.M.**

Phoebe Carey (Southport, Davies 312) Sandys' Collection 1833

ONE sweetly solemn thought
  Comes to me o'er and o'er—
I'm nearer to my home to-day
Than e'er I've been before.

Nearer my FATHER'S house,
  Where many mansions be;
Nearer my blessèd Saviour's throne
Nearer the crystal sea.

Nearer the bound of life,
  To lay my burden down;
Nearer to giving up my cross,
Nearer the promised crown.

For even now my feet
  May stand on Jordan's brink;
It may be now I'm nearer home,
Much nearer, than I think.

432 **Nearer Home S.M.D.**

James Montgomery (Llanllyfni 573) Isaac B. Woodbury

"For ever with the Lord!"
  Amen! so let it be:
Life from the dead is in that word,
  'Tis immortality:
Here in the body pent,
  Absent from Him I roam,
Yet nightly pitch my moving tent
  A day's march nearer home.

My Father's house on high,
  Home of my soul, how near
At times to faith's transpiercing eye
  Thy golden gates appear!
My thirsty spirit faints
  To reach the land I love,
The bright inheritance of saints,
  Jerusalem above.

And though there intervene
  Rough roads and stormy skies,
Faith will not suffer aught to screen
  Thy glory from mine eyes :
There shall all clouds depart,
  The wilderness shall cease,
And sweetly shall each gladdened heart
  Enjoy eternal peace.

433 St. Beuno S.M.
J.N. Darby (Tuam 225) J.C. Bridge

Rest of the saints above,
  Jerusalem of God!
Who, in thy palaces of love,
  Thy golden streets have trod?

Who shall to me the joy
  Of saint-thronged courts declare,
Tell of that constant, sweet employ
  My spirit longs to share?

The Lamb is there, my soul!
  There God Himself doth rest
In love divine, diffused through all—
  With Him supremely blest.

God and the Lamb! 'tis well;
  I know that source divine
Of joy and love no tongue can tell,
  And know that all is mine.

There on the hidden bread,
  E'en Christ once humbled here—
God's treasured store—for ever fed,
  His love my soul shall cheer.

There in effulgence bright,
  Saviour and Guide, with Thee
I'll walk, and in Thy heavenly light
  Whiter my robe shall be!

God and the Lamb shall there
  The light and temple be,
And radiant hosts for ever share
  The unveiled mystery.

434(1) St. Cecilia 6.6.6.6.
L.G. Hayne

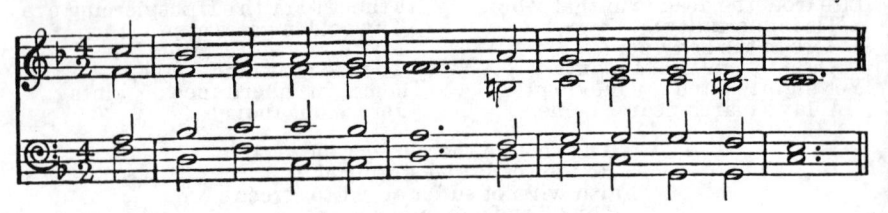

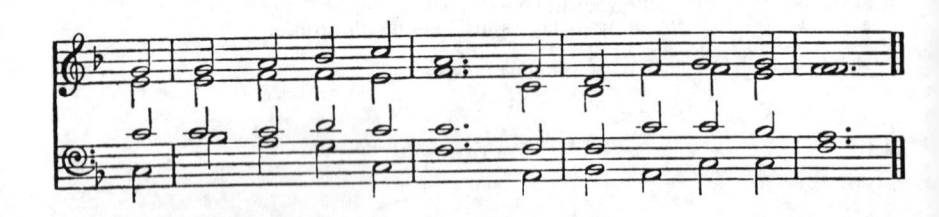

All, all beyond is bright;
  'Tis but "a little while,"
And then eternal light
  Will cheer us with its smile.

All, all beyond is sure;
  Earth's pleasures pass away;
The joys of heaven endure
  Through never-ending day.

All, all beyond is peace;
  Here we no rest may find;
But *there* our conflicts cease,
  All foes are left behind.

All, all beyond is pure;
  Sin ne'er shall enter there;
No tempter shall allure,
  Or spread the fatal snare.

All, all beyond is love;
  Strife and dissension o'er,
The happy host above
  Are *one* for evermore.

And all this bliss is mine,
  Since JESUS died for me,
And I am one with Him
  Throughout eternity!

434(2) Ibstone 6.6.6.6
Maria Tiddeman

435   Homeland 9.9.9

H. Bonar   D. Russell

NO shadows yonder! all light and song!
Each day I ponder and say, 'How long
Shall time me sunder from that glad throng?'

No partings yonder! no space or time
Hearts e'er shall sunder in that fair clime,
Dearer and fonder, friendships sublime!

None wanting yonder bought by the Lamb!
All gathered under the sheltering palm—
Loud as the thunder swells the glad psalm!

436 Morgenlied 8.7.8.7.D and Chorus

Anne R. Cousin

F.C. Maker

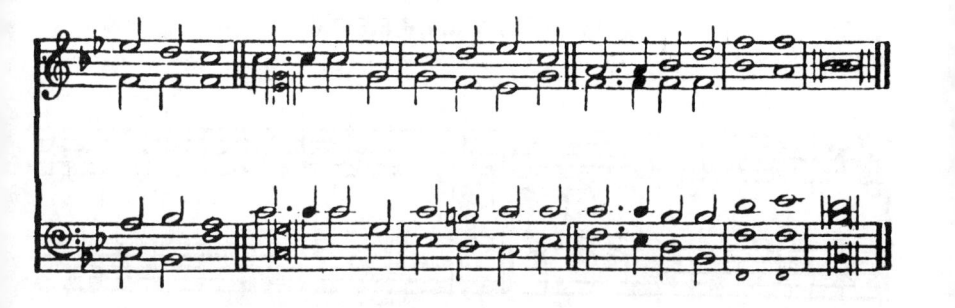

WHEN we reach our peaceful
    dwelling,
On the strong, eternal hills,
And our praise to Him is swelling
Who the vast creation fills;
When the paths of prayer, and duty,
And affliction, all are trod,
And we wake and see the beauty
Of our SAVIOUR and our GOD:
  Oh, 'twill be a glorious morrow
    To a dark and stormy day,
  When we smile upon our sorrow,
    And the storms have passed
        away!

With the light of resurrection,
  When our changed bodies glow,
And we gain the full perfection
  Of the bliss begun below;
When the life which flesh obscureth
  In each radiant form shall shine,
And the joy that aye endureth
  Flasheth forth in beams divine—

Shall the memory be banished
  Of His kindness and His care,
When the wants and woes are vanished
  Which He loved to soothe and share?
All the way by which He led us,
  All the grievings which He bore,
All the patient love He taught us,
  Shall we think of them no more?—

We shall read the tender meaning
  Of the sorrows and alarms,
As we trod the desert, leaning
  On His everlasting arms;
And His rest will be the dearer
  When we think of weary ways,
And His light will shine the clearer
  As we muse on cloudy days—

437
H.K.B.

Ellacombe 7.6.7.6.8.6.7.6

German

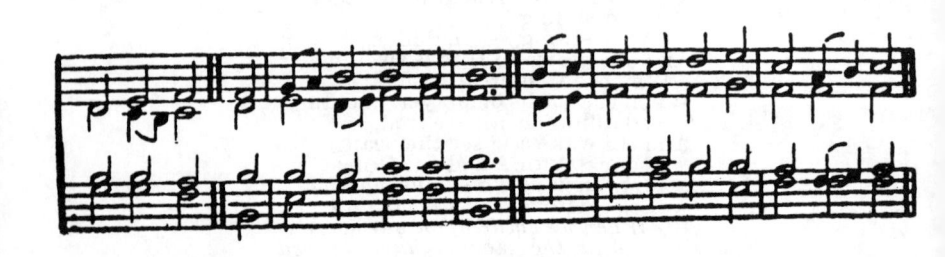

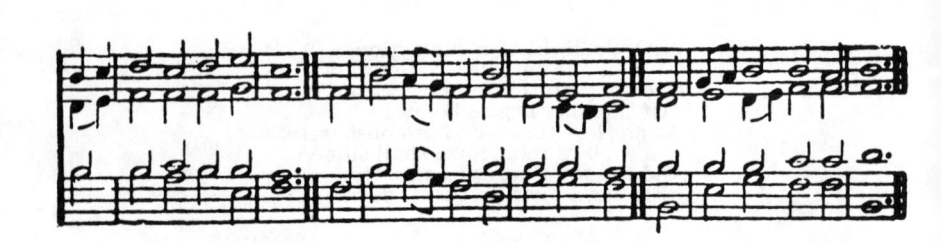

THE glory shines before me—
　I cannot linger here!
Though clouds may darken o'er me.
　My FATHER'S house is near;
If through this barren wilderness
　A little while I roam,
The glory shines before me,
　I am not far from home!

Beyond the storms I'm going,
　Beyond this vale of tears,
Beyond the floods o'erflowing,
　Beyond the changing years;
I'm going to the better land,
　By faith long since possest:
The glory shines before me,
　And this is not my rest.

The Lamb is there the glory!
　The Lamb is there the light!
Affliction's grasp but tears me
　From phantoms of the night;
The voice of JESUS calleth me,
　My race will soon be run;
The glory shines before me,
　The prize will soon be won!

The glory shines before me!
　I know that all is well!
My FATHER'S care is o'er me,
　His praises I would tell;
The love of CHRIST constraineth me,
　His blood hath washed me white;
Where JESUS is the glory,
　'Tis home, and love, and light!

438
L. Laurenti

Nyland 7.6.7.6.D
(Lymington 16)

Finnish Hymn Melody

1 REJOICE, rejoice, believers!
    And let your lights appear;
The evening is advancing,
    The darker night is near:
The Bridegroom soon arising
    Will unto you draw nigh;
Up! pray, and watch, and wrestle—
    At midnight comes the cry.

2 See that your lamps are burning,
    Replenish them with oil;
Look now for your salvation—
    The end of sin and toil:
The watchers on the mountain
    Proclaim the Bridegroom near;
Go, meet Him, as He cometh,
    With Hallelujahs clear.

3 O wise and holy virgins,
    Now raise your voices higher,
Till in your exultation
    Ye meet the angel choir!
The marriage feast is waiting,
    The gates wide open stand;
Up! up! ye heirs of glory,
    The Bridegroom is at hand!

4 Our hope and expectation,
    LORD JESUS, now appear!
Arise, Thou Sun, long looked for,
    O'er this benighted sphere!
With heart and voice uplifted,
    We long, O LORD, to see
The day of our redemption,
    And ever be with Thee.

439 Ewing 7.6.7.6.D
Bernard of Cluny   (Zoan 321)   A. Ewing

JERUSALEM the golden,
　The city of the blest,
The sum of all perfection,
　The home of peace and rest!
I know not, oh! I know not,
　What height of joy is there,
What radiancy of glory,
　What bliss beyond compare!

The cross is all thy splendour,
　The Crucified thy praise;
His laud and benediction
　Thy ransomed people raise:
Upon the Rock of Ages
　They raise thy holy tower;
His is the Victor's laurel,
　And thine the golden dower.

There is His throne of glory,
　And there, from care released,
The song of them that triumph,
　The shout of them that feast;
And they who with their Leader
　Have conquered in the fight,
For ever and for ever
　Are clad in robes of white!

The light hath there no evening,
　The health hath there no sore,
The life hath there no ending,
　But lasteth evermore!
Exult, O dust and ashes,
　The LORD shall be thy part!
His only, His for ever,
　Thou shalt be, and thou art!

440   Addiscombe 10.8.10.8.D and Chorus
W.P. Mackay   E.D.J. Tapson

CHORUS accel.

a tempo.

Words over

WE'RE a pilgrim band in a stranger
land,
Who are marching from Calvary,
Where the wondrous cross, with its
gain and loss,
Is the sum of our history:
There we lost our stand in a death-
doomed land,
As children of wrath by the fall.
There we gained a place as heirs of
grace,
At the feast in the heavenly hall:

*So we sing, while we haste o'er the
wide world's waste,
Of our home with its crystal sea,
Where the new, glad song and the
joyful psalm
Fill the air of eternity.*

We read our guilt in the blood that
was spilt,
And we weep o'er the crimson flow;
But we joy in the grace of the unveiled
face
Of our FATHER, here below;
And as sons of GOD, redeemed by
blood,
We hasten from Egypt away;
We cross the sand to the pleasant land,
And the joys of an endless day—

We were children of night, kept far
from the light,
Enslaved by a cruel foe,
But JESU's pains broke the iron chains,
And redeemed our souls from woe:
Now as children of light we walk and
we fight,
In a path of triumphant joy;
For our strength is the LORD, whose
word is our sword,
While faith is the shield we employ—

Our home is with GOD, and our path
has been trod
By the faithful of ages all,
And us He will bring as on eagle wing
To our place in the marriage hall:
Then, then shall we sing, as the Bride
of the King,
Of the blood that has brought us so
nigh,
To bask in the rays of the Ancient of
days,
Enthronèd above the sky—

441   Fountain C.M. and Chorus

C. Wesley   Old Melody

Chorus

OUR souls are in GOD's mighty hand,
   We're precious in His sight;
And you and I shall surely stand
   With Him in glory bright:
*We'll stem the storm, it won't last
   long;
We'll anchor by-and-by
In the haven of eternal rest,
   With JESUS ever nigh!*

Him eye to eye we soon shall see,
   Our face like His shall shine;
Oh, what a glorious company,
   When saints and angels join!—

Oh, what a joyful meeting there,
   In robes of white arrayed!
We'll all unite in praising Him
   Whose glories never fade—

Then let us hasten to that day
   When all shall be brought home;
Come, O Redeemer, come, we pray,
   LORD JESUS, quickly come!—

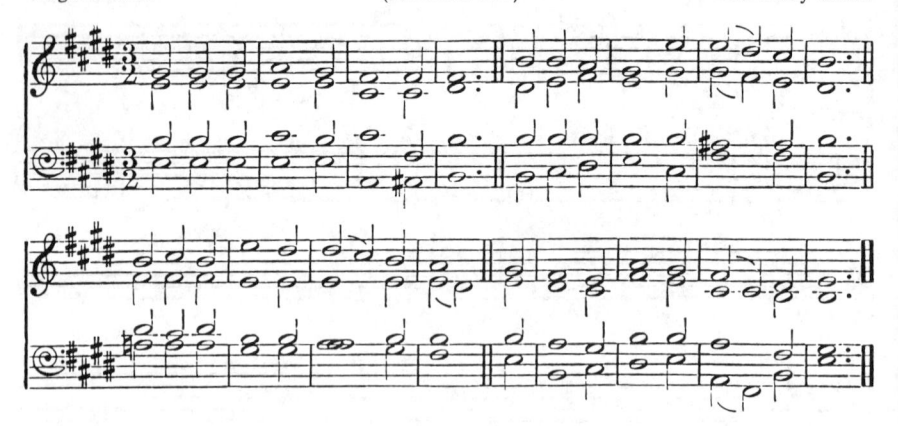

442 Maryton L.M.
Hugh Stowell   (Hereford 359)   H. Percy Smith

FROM every stormy wind that blows,
From every swelling tide of woes,
There is a calm, a safe retreat—
'Tis found beneath the mercy-seat.

There is a place where JESUS sheds
The oil of gladness on our heads;
A place than all besides more sweet—
It is the blood-stained mercy-seat.

There is a spot where spirits blend,
And friend holds fellowship with friend;
Tho' sundered far, by faith they meet
Around one common mercy-seat,

Ah! whither could we flee for aid
When tempted, desolate, dismayed,
Or how the hosts of hell defeat,
Had suffering saints no mercy-seat?

There we on eagles' wings would soar,
Where time and sense are all no more;
There heavenly joys our spirits greet,
For glory crowns the mercy-seat!

443 Warrington L.M.
Wm. Cowper   (Antwerp 353)   Ralph Harrison

JESUS! where'er Thy people meet,
  There they behold Thy mercy-seat;
Where'er they seek Thee, Thou art found,
And every place is hallowed ground.

Here may we prove the power of prayer
To strengthen faith and banish care,
To teach our faint desires to rise,
And bring all heaven before our eyes.

Great Shepherd of Thy chosen few,
Thy former mercies here renew;
Here to our waiting hearts proclaim
The sweetness of Thy saving name.

LORD! we are weak, but Thou art near,
Nor short Thine arm, nor deaf Thine ear;
Oh, fill us with Thy grace divine,
And may our hearts be wholly Thine!

444   Rhodes S.M.
John Newton   (Sandys 431)   C. Warwick Jordan

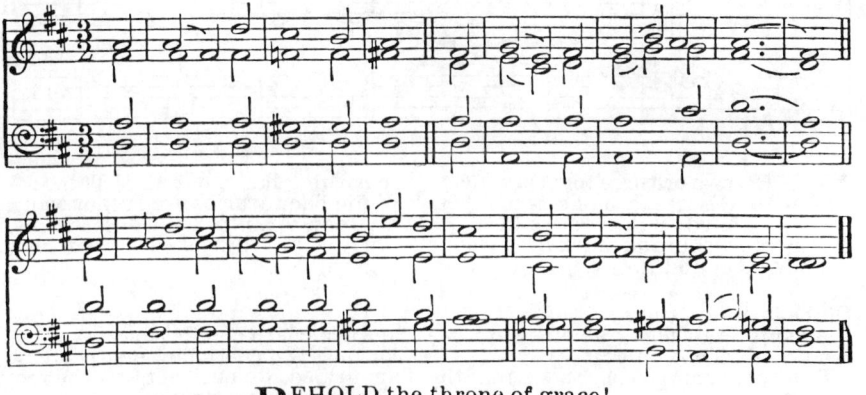

BEHOLD the throne of grace!
  The promise calls us near,
To seek our GOD and FATHER'S face,
  Who loves to answer prayer.

That rich, atoning blood,
  Which sprinkled round we see,
Provides for those who come to GOD
  An all-prevailing plea.

My soul, ask what thou wilt,
  Thou canst not be too bold;
Since His own blood for Thee was spilt,
  What else can He withhold?

Beyond our utmost wants
  His love and power can bless;
To praying souls He always grants
  More than they can express.

Since 'tis the LORD'S command,
  Our mouth we'll open wide:
LORD, open Thou Thy bounteous hand,
  That we may be supplied.

Thine image, LORD, bestow,
  Thy presence and Thy love:
We seek to serve Thee here below,
  And reign with Thee above.

445 Ombersley L.M.
Thos. Kelly. (Nicomachus 526) W.H. Gladstone

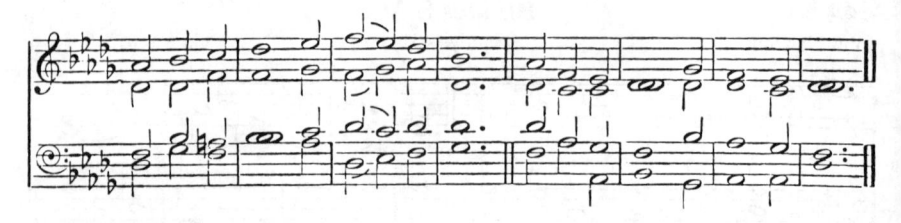

WHEN two or three together meet
 In His great name who lives above,
Their fellowship and work are sweet,
 They meet and they depart in love.

Oh be it, LORD, to us this day,
 According to Thy gracious word,
And send us not unblest away,
 But joy, and peace, and strength afford!

We nothing have, but all is Thine;
 While Thou art rich, we cannot want;
Thine ear, O LORD, Thou dost incline,
 And what Thy people need dost grant.

Thus armed, to conflict may we go,
 And boldly meet the adverse powers;
Thus armed, we need not fear the foe,
 For everlasting strength is ours.

446 Buckland 7.7.7.7
J.S.B. Monsell (Brandenburg 222) L.G. Hayne

LORD, wherever two or three
    Gathered are in Thy blest name,
Thou hast promised Thou wilt be,
    And that promise now we claim.

'Tis not number, time, nor place,
    Can affect our feeble prayer;
Where Thy people seek Thy face,
    Thou hast told us Thou art there.

On the ocean, in the field,
    Mountain, valley, or at home,
Thou to us wilt be revealed,
    As to Thee in faith we come.

Fewest voices that can meet,
    Feeblest accents that can rise,
Carried to the mercy-seat,
    Thou, O LORD, wilt not despise.

447   Rhodes S.M.

W. Pennfather   (Southport, Davies 312)   C. Warwick Jordan

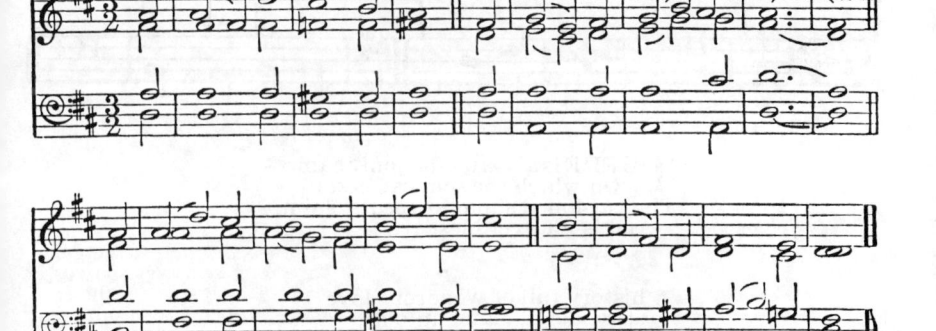

JESUS! in Thy blest name
    With joyful hearts we meet,
In fellowship with saints above,
    Around the mercy-seat!

LORD! make our hearts to burn
    With fervent love to Thee,
And nerve each fainting warrior here
    With holy energy!

With joyfulness we wait
    To see our Master's face:
Come, Saviour, to Thy waiting ones,
    And fill us with Thy grace.

Fill us with light and love,
    Fill us with power divine;
And may Thy people hence depart,
    Fresh sealed and signed as Thine'

St. Bernard C.M.
(Fingal 131)

J. Richardson

1 THERE is a NAME—one only name—
   On which the soul can rest;
The pardoned sinner owns its claim,
   And is for ever blest.

2 A history full of wondrous love
   That sacred name unfolds,
And still that sacrifice of blood
   The FATHER'S eye beholds.

3 There is a name, the sweetest name;
   Let us in this draw nigh!
The veil is rent, the way is made
   To GOD beyond the sky.

4 There is a name—it is our plea
   Before the FATHER'S throne;
Of all His treasures, 'tis the key
   Which makes them all our own.

5 No burning mount, no thunder's roar,
   Shall scare a soul away;
No foe can shut that open door,
   Since JESUS is the way.

6 Oh, plead His name, His precious name,
   With boldness at the throne;
Then all He has, and all we need,
   Will surely be our own.

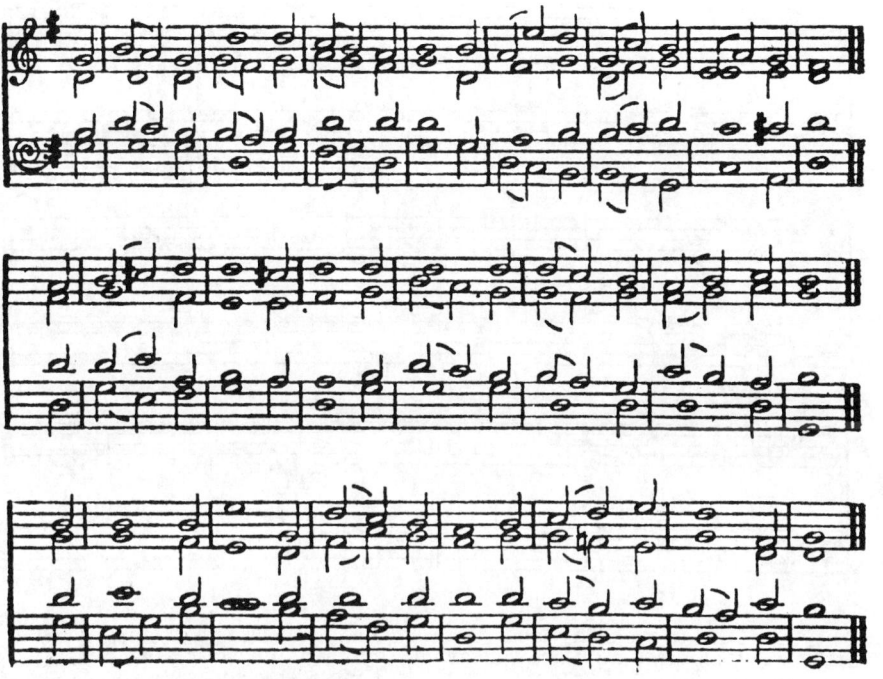

449   Pembroke 8.8.6.D
John Walker   (Manoah 238)   J. Foster

1 THOU GOD of power, and GOD of love!
The seraphs in the realms above
   To Thee their praises bring,
And veil their faces while they cry
Thrice Holy! to their GOD Most High,
   Thrice Holy! to their King.

2 Thee, as our GOD, we now can claim,
And bless the precious Saviour's name,
   Through whom this grace is given;
Who bore the wrath to sinners due,
Who formed our ruined souls anew,
   And made us heirs of heaven.

3 While we in supplication join
Before the throne of grace divine,
   Thou dost incline Thine ear;
LORD, while we listen to Thy word,
And praise Thy name with glad accord
   Display Thy presence here!

4 Give us to know the joy and love
With which all worship Thee above,
   In heaven, Thy blest abode:
Here to our hearts Thyself reveal,
And all assembled cause to feel
   Thy presence, O our GOD!

450 Samuel 6.6.6.6.8.8
J.G. Deck   (Christchurch 81)   *Arthur Sullivan*

FATHER, to seek Thy face,
  Thy children now draw near;
Before the throne of grace
  With boldness we appear;
We plead His name, His precious blood
Who loved, and made us priests to God.

No more we shun the light,
  No more Thy presence fear;
In robes of spotless white
  Before Thee we appear;
Our great High Priest for us is there,
And He presents our praise and prayer.

No power have we to praise
  Thy name, O God of Love,
Unless Thy Spirit raise
  Our thoughts and hearts above;
His grace avails in all our need—
May He our priestly worship lead.

Lord, give us faith to plead
  Thy true and faithful word—
Grace for each time of need,
  And help to us afford:
Thy promises in Christ are yea,
In Him, Amen! to endless day.

451 St. Ann C.M.
Isaac Watts   *Wm. Croft*

O GOD, our help in ages past,
  Our hope for years to come,
Our shelter from the stormy blast,
  And our eternal home!

Under the shadow of Thy throne
  Thy saints have dwelt secure;
Sufficient is Thine arm alone,
  And our defence is sure.

Before the hills in order stood,
  Or earth received her frame,
From everlasting Thou art GOD,
  To endless years the same.

A thousand ages in Thy sight
  Are like an evening gone,
Short as the watch that ends the night
  Before the rising sun.

O GOD, our help in ages past,
  Our hope for years to come,
Be Thou our guard while life shall last,
  And our eternal home!

452 **Meribah 8.8.6.D**
J.G. Deck (Pembroke 449) Lowell Mason

THOU SON of GOD! the woman's
  Seed,
Who didst for us on Calvary bleed,
And bear sin's heavy load:
Spoiler of all the power of hell,
Who conquered death invincible,
  Thou Holy One of GOD!

Thy blood we sing; by that alone,
With boldness to the eternal throne,
  Through Thee we now draw nigh;
It silences the voice of sin,
Washes the guilty conscience clean,
  And makes the accuser fly.

Behold us, LORD, a feeble band!
In conflict with the foe we stand,
  The ransomed of Thy cross:
We sing the triumphs of Thy name;
All other glory here is shame,
  All other gain's but loss.

453 Farrant C.M.
R.C. Chapman (Fingal 131) R. Farrant

JESUS, whose blood was shed on earth,
  Is now raised up on high;
We also rise with Him by faith,
  And unto GOD draw nigh.

See how within the holiest
  By His own blood He stands;
JESUS prepares for us the place,
  With incense in His hands.

Brethren, His glory now is ours,
  His fellowship with GOD;
As seated now with CHRIST the LORD,
  We sing of precious blood.

Whate'er the bosom's joy or grief,
  Our matters, great or small,
Are but an errand to the throne—
  There come and tell out all.

454 Luther's Chant L.M.
Samuel Medley (Nicomachus 526) H.C. Zeuner

JESUS, before Thy face we fall,
  Our LORD, our Life, our Hope, our All!
For we have nowhere else to flee,
No sanctuary, LORD, but Thee!

In Thee we every glory view,
Of safety, strength, and beauty too;
'Tis all our rest and peace to see
Our sanctuary, LORD, in Thee!

Whatever foes or fears betide,
In Thine own presence let us hide;
And, while we rest our souls on Thee,
Do Thou our sanctuary be!

Through time, with all its changing scenes,
And all the grief that intervenes,
Let this support each fainting heart,
That Thou our sanctuary art!

455 Winchester New L.M.
Michael Bruce   (Truro 428)   B. Crasseluis

WHERE high the heavenly temple stands,
The house of GOD not made with hands,
A great High Priest for us appears,
And lives to silence all our fears.

He who for us as Surety stood,
And poured on earth His precious blood,
Pursues in heaven His gracious plan—
The Saviour and the Friend of man.

Partaker of the human name,
He knows the frailty of our frame,
And still remembers, in the skies,
His tears, and griefs, and agonies.

In every pang that rends the heart,.
The "Man of sorrows" bears a part;
He knows and feels our every grief,
And gives the suffering saint relief.

With boldness, therefore, at the throne,
Let us make all our sorrows known.
And seek His grace and heavenly power,
To help us in each trying hour.

456
Anne Steele

Rimington L.M.
(Truro 428)

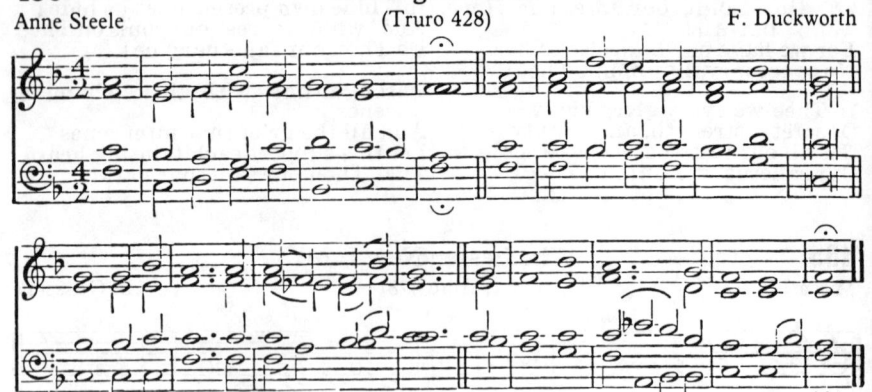

F. Duckworth

1. HE lives, the great Redeemer lives!
   What joy the blest assurance gives!
   And now, enthroned above the skies,
   He pleads His holy sacrifice.

2. Great Advocate, Almighty Friend!
   On Thee do all our hopes depend;
   Our cause can never, never fail,
   For Thou dost plead and must prevail.

3. In every dark, distressing hour,
   When sin and Satan join their power,
   Let this blest truth repel each dart,
   That thou dost bear us on Thy heart!

457
Isaac Watts

Abbey C.M.
(Westminster 160)

Scottish Psalter 1615

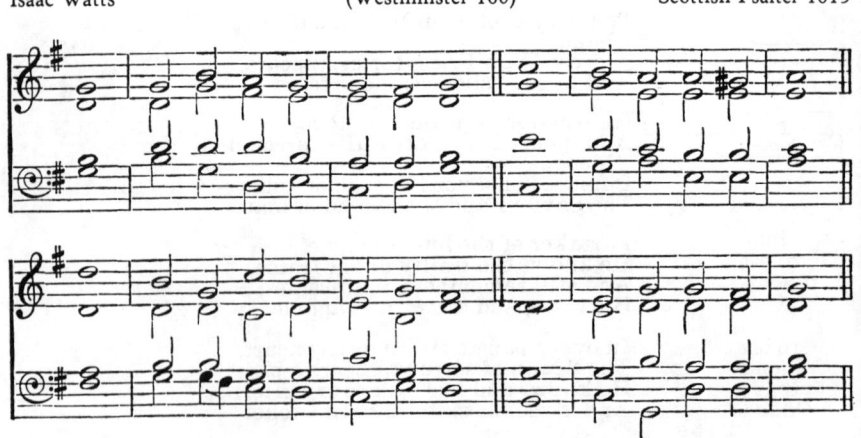

1. WITH joy we meditate the grace
   Of our High Priest above;
   His heart is filled with tenderness,
   His very name is Love.

2. Touched with a sympathy within,
   He knows our feeble frame;
   He knows what sore temptations mean,
   For He has felt the same.

But spotless, undefiled, and pure,
  Our great Redeemer stood;
While Satan's fiery darts He bore,
  And did resist to blood.

He in the days of feeble flesh
  Poured out His cries and tears,
And, though exalted, feels afresh
  What every member bears.

    Then boldly let our faith address
      His mercy and His power;
    We shall obtain delivering grace
      In each distressing hour.

458   Belgrave C.M.

J.C. Wallace   (St. Saviour 296)   W. Horsley

1. THERE is an eye that never sleeps
  Beneath the wing of night;
There is an ear that never shuts
  When sink the beams of light.

2. There is an arm that never tires
  When human strength gives way;
There is a love that never fails
  When earthly loves decay.

3. That eye is fixed on seraph throngs,
  That arm upholds the sky,
That ear is filled with heavenly songs,
  That love is throned on high.

4. But there's a power which faith can wield,
  When mortal aid is vain,
That eye, that arm, that love to reach,
  That listening ear to gain.

5.   That power is prayer, which soars on high,
      Through JESUS to the throne,
    And moves the hand which moves the world,
      To bring deliverance down.

459   **Converse 8.7.8.7.D**
Joseph Scriven   (Calon Lan 86)   C.C. Converse

WHAT a Friend we have in Jesus,
    All our sins and griefs to bear!
What a privilege to carry
    Everything to God in prayer!
Oh, what peace we often forfeit,
    Oh, what needless pain we bear,
All because we do not carry
    Everything to God in prayer!

Have we trials and temptations?
    Is there trouble anywhere?
We should never be discouraged,
    Take it to the Lord in prayer!
Can we find a friend so faithful,
    Who will all our sorrows share?
Jesus knows our every weakness—
    Take it to the Lord in prayer.

Blessèd Jesus, Thou hast promised
    Thou wilt all our burdens bear;
May we ever, Lord, be bringing
    All to Thee in earnest prayer:
Soon in glory, bright, unclouded,
    There will be no need for prayer;
Rapture, praise, and endless worship,
    Shall be our sweet portion there.

460   **Bodmin L.M.**
(Breslau 560)   Alfred Scott-Gatty

S WEET are the seasons when we
   wait
  To hear what GOD our LORD will
   say,
For they who watch at Wisdom's gate
  Are never empty sent away.

Behold us, LORD, a few of Thine,
  Who hither come to seek Thy face;
In mercy on Thy people shine,
  And let Thy presence fill the place.

How sweet, how blessèd is the thought
  That Thou dost hear Thy people's
   cries!
And whether Thou dost give, or not,
  'Tis love that grants, and love denies.

Oh, teach us, LORD, to wait Thy will,
  To be content with all Thou dost:
For us Thy grace sufficient still,
  With most supplied when needing
   most.

461   **Laudate Dominum 5.5.5.5.6.5.6.5**

John Fawcett   (Hanover 909)   H. Parry

1. A FULNESS resides
In JESUS, our Head,
And ever abides
To answer our need;
The FATHER'S good pleasure
Has laid up in store
A plentiful treasure,
To give to the poor.

2. Whate'er be our wants,
We need not to fear,
Our every petition
His mercy will hear;
His fulness shall yield us
Abundant supplies,
His power shall shield us
When dangers arise.

3. This fountain o'erflows
Our wants to redress,
Still more He bestows,
And grace upon grace;
His gifts in abundance
We daily receive;
He has a redundance
For all who believe.

4. Whatever distress
Awaits us below,
Such plentiful grace
Will JESUS bestow
As still shall support us,
And silence our fear,
For nothing can hurt us
While JESUS is near.

5. When troubles attend,
Or dangers, or strife,
His love will defend
And guard us through life;
And when we are fainting,
And ready to die,
Whatever is wanting
His hand will supply.

462 Monkland 7.7.7.7
(Ellingham 480)

J.B. Wilkes

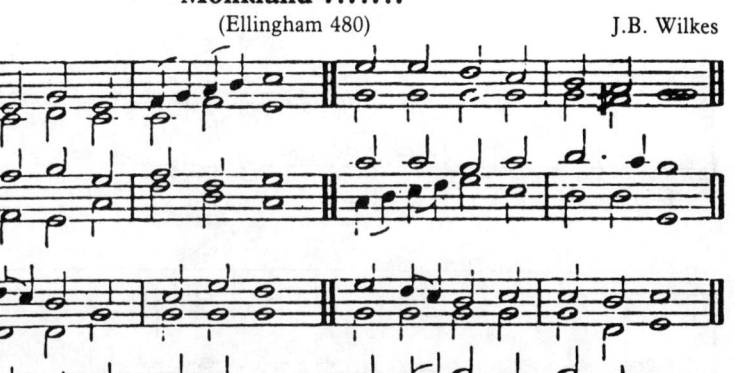

EVER, LORD, our souls to Thee
Would in grateful praises flow,
And our hearts' desire would be
By our deeds, our love to shew.

Give us then, our faithful LORD,
Grace and strength to do Thy will;
Power, in every work and word,
All Thy purpose to fulfil.

463 Bristol C.M.

Ravenscroft's Psalter 1621

O LORD, we would abound in praise;
What cause have we to sing!
The full, deep joy of endless days
Begins, e'en now, to spring.

Our cry for pardon reached Thine ear,
Thy grace how swift to flow!
And now, delivered from all fear,
What ceaseless thanks we owe!

As poor and needy, we rejoice
That prayer to us belongs;
As sinners saved, praise suits our voice—
Ours are eternal songs.

464   **St. Flavian C.M.**

Joseph Dacre Carlisle   (Azmon 264)   Day's Psalter 1562

LORD, when we bend before Thy throne,
And our confessions pour,
Teach us to feel the sins we own,
And hate what we deplore.

When we make known our wants in prayer,
May we our wills resign;
And may no thought our bosoms share,
Which is not truly Thine.

Let faith each meek petition fill,
And bear it to the skies;
Teach Thou our hearts 'tis goodness still
That grants it, or denies.

465   **Weber 7.7.7.7**

John Withy   From Weber

HOLY FATHER, through Thy grace,
  Now we come before Thy face ;
JESU'S worthy name alone
  Is our plea before Thy throne.

For our children, LORD, we pray ;
Shield them in this evil day
From the world's attractive glare,
From each seen or hidden snare.

From the heart that lusts within,
Pride and every lurking sin,
From the subtle tempter's charm,
Save them by Thy mighty arm.

By the sorrows of Thy SON,
By His grace may they be won ;
By the SPIRIT'S quickening power
Give them life for evermore.

As Thou wilt, their lot to-day ;
Not earth's heritage, we pray,
But the portion kept above
For the children of Thy love.

Thus enriched, our children be
Sons and servants, LORD, to Thee ;
JESU'S name on earth to bear,
And His yoke of love to wear.

466 University C.M.
Thos. Hastings   J. Randall

OUR GOD, for children dear we
    plead,
  For young ones Thou hast given ;
Where shall we go in this our need
  But to our GOD in heaven?

We ask not for them wealth or fame,
  Amid the worldly strife :
But in the all-prevailing Name
  We ask eternal life.

We crave the SPIRIT'S quickening
    grace
  To make them Thine in heart,
That they may stand before Thy face,
  And see Thee as Thou art.

467 The Good Shepherd 8.7.8.7.8.7

W.B. Bradbury

GRACIOUS Shepherd! loving
Saviour!
Draw our children's hearts to Thee;
Safe within Thy bosom folded,
May they quickly gathered be:
Gracious Shepherd!
Draw our children's hearts to Thee.

On Thy love and care we cast them,
Bringing them in faith to Thee;
Teach them, LORD, what peace and
pleasure
In Thyself and ways must be—

From the world and Satan's bondage,
From the flesh, oh, set them free!
In their hearts be faith implanted,
Love, and holiness, by Thee—

468 Albano C.M.

Philip Doddridge

V. Novello

SEE! Israel's gentle Shepherd stands,
With all-engaging charms;
Hark! how He calls the tender lambs,
And folds them in His arms.

We bring them, LORD. in loved embrace,
And yield them up to Thee,
Joyful that we ourselves are Thine;
Thine let these children be!

469   Deerhurst 8.7.8.7.D

W.A. Mühlenberg   J. Langran

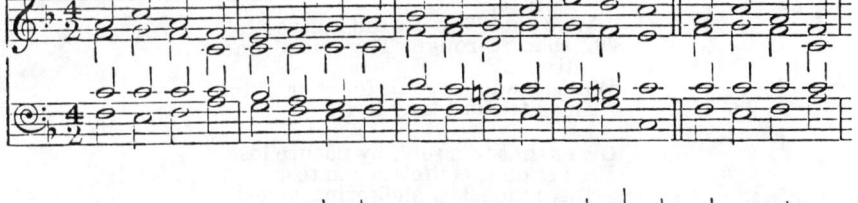

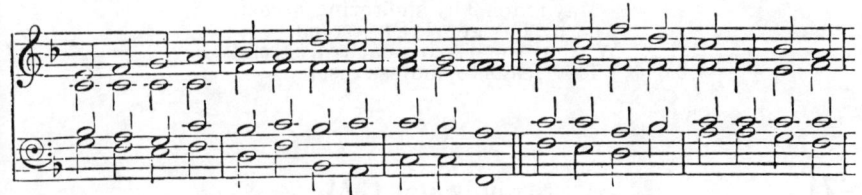

SAVIOUR, who Thy flock art feeding
With a shepherd's kindest care,
All the feeble gently leading,
While the lambs Thy bosom share—
Now, this little one receiving,
Fold it in Thy gracious arm;
There, we know, Thy word believing,
Only there, secure from harm.

470   **Meribah 8.8.6.D**
Carter   Lowell Mason

A CHILD of Adam's sinful race,
  Saviour, we bring before Thy face,
    Who once Thy life didst give:
Oh that, through Thy rich grace divine,
Which made our souls for ever Thine,
    This little one may live!

Grant that this soul, by nature lost,
Ere yet on this life's ocean tost,
    May reach Thy sheltering breast,
And by Thy gentle SPIRIT led,
With us the narrow pathway tread,
    That leads to endless rest!

471   **Stroudwater C.M.**
Carter   Wilkins' Psalmody 1730

L ORD JESUS! at whose glorious feet
   The angels worship now,
And there before Thy lofty seat
   In lowly reverence bow;

When mothers for their infants sought
   The grace of life divine,
The yearning heart, the tender thought,
   Found sweet response in Thine.

And gently, as the dew is shed
   From evening's balmy air,
Thy hand on every infant head
   Left heavenly blessing there.

O Saviour! changeless in Thy love,
   Our hearts now turn to Thee,
And still we hear Thee from above
   Say, 'Bring the babes to Me.'

Once more, Thou Shepherd good and kind,
   The gracious answer speak;
Grant that this little one may find
   The blessing which we seek.

472   **Gräfenberg C.M.**   Praxis Pietatis Melica 1653
Hugh Stowell   (Contemplation 370(2))

J ESUS, our Saviour and our LORD!
   To Thee we lift our eyes;
Teach and instruct us by Thy word,
   And make us truly wise.

Make us to know and understand
   Thy whole revealed will;
Fain would we learn to comprehend
   Thy love more clearly still.

LORD! may Thy word our thoughts engage
   In each perplexing case;
Help us to feed on every page,
   And grow in every grace.

Oh, let it purify our heart,
   And guide us all our days;
Thy wonders, LORD, to us impart,
   And Thou shalt have the praise!

473   **Glasgow C.M.**
Daniel Webley   Moore's Companion 1756

JESUS, our Saviour Thou and LORD,
  How precious is Thy word!
To lowly and believing hearts
  What joy it doth afford!

Thy word of pure, eternal truth
  Shall yet unshaken stay,
When all that man has thought or
    planned,
  Like chaff has passed away.

Thy word, LORD, speaks to us of Thee,
  And Thine exceeding grace;
In it Thy thoughts and ways of love
  With wondering joy we trace.

Thy word upon our daily path
  Its light divine doth shed;
By it our feet through Satan's snares
  In safety may be led.

Oh, may it richly dwell within,
  And mould our every thought;
And be each heart to Thy blest sway
  In full subjection brought!

LORD, by Thy SPIRIT teach and lead,
  While seated at Thy feet,
That we may in Thy holy will
  Stand perfect and complete.

474   Evan C.M.

Anne Steele   W.H. Havergal

JESUS, Thou source of true delight,
   Whom we, unseen, adore,
Unveil our souls to all Thy light,
   That we may love Thee more.

Thy glory o'er creation shines,
   But in the sacred word
We read in fairer, brighter lines
   The glories of our LORD.

'Tis here, whene'er our comforts droop,
   And sins and sorrows rise,
Thy love, with cheerful beams of hope,
   Each fainting heart supplies.

JESUS, our LORD, our life, our light,
   Oh, come with blissful ray,
Break through the gloomy shades of night,
   And bring the looked-for day!

Then shall each soul with rapture trace
   The wonders of Thy love,
And the full glories of Thy face,
   As known to those above.

475 St. Magnus C.M.
W.H. Bathurst — J. Clark

BEFORE Thy mercy-seat, O LORD,
  Behold Thy servants stand,
To seek the knowledge of Thy word,
  The guidance of Thy hand.

Let Thy eternal truths, we pray,
  Dwell richly in each heart,
That from the safe and narrow way
  We never may depart.

Help us to see a Saviour's love
  Shining in every page,
And let the thought of joys above
  With power our hearts engage.

476 Rhodes S.M.
Daniel Webley — C. Warwick Jordan

NONE teacheth, Lord, like Thee,
  None can such truth impart,
Such treasures from Thy word unfold,
  Nor so impress the heart.

How blest Thy servants were,
  When with them on their way
Thou didst commune, and sweetly
    chase
  Their sorrows all away!

So now to us draw near,
  And speak to every heart;
Our light in darkness, joy in grief,
  Our "All in all," Thou art.

Open to us Thy word,
  Thy precious thoughts reveal,
Thy purposes and ways explain,
  And teach us all Thy will.

So shall our doubt and fear,
  Our care and grief subside,
And each enraptured heart exclaim,
  O Lord, with us abide!

477   Meribah 8.8.6.D

J.B. Isbell   Lowell Mason

TO those who love Thee, gracious
    Lord,
How bright, how precious is the word
  By God in mercy given!
A guide to all who, travelling here
'Mid sin and darkness, death and fear,
  Are pressing on to heaven.

O gracious Saviour, God of love!
  Let Thine own Spirit from above
    Now fill us with desire
To read, to mark, to learn Thy will;
And with Thy truth our spirits fill,
  With grace our hearts inspire.

And, till from heaven Thou dost come
To take Thy waiting people home,
  May we obedient be,
Doing Thy will till that blest day
When from this earth we're called
    away
  To dwell above with Thee.

478 Southwell C.M.

Edward Bickersteth   H.S. Irons

LIGHT of the world! shine on our souls;
Thy grace to us afford;
And while we meet to learn Thy truth,
Be Thou our Teacher, LORD!

May we its riches, power, and depth,
Its holiness discern;
Its joyful news of saving grace
By blest experience learn.

Thus may Thy word be dearer still,
And studied more each day;
And, as it richly dwells within,
Thyself to us display.

479 Lancashire 7.6.7.6.D

John Withy   Henry Smart

1 LORD JESUS, on Thy promise
   Our hearts, believing, rest,
And with Thee here among us
   We have a portion blest;
Thy name, as precious ointment,
   Pours forth its fragrance now—
Our life, and light, and gladness,
   Our strength and wisdom, Thou!

2 We own Thee as our Saviour,
   We bow to Thee as LORD,
And round Thy feet we gather,
   To listen to Thy word;
Thee only would we follow;
   Thy paths no darkness know—
There light is ever shining,
   And springs refreshing flow.

3 Thou art to GOD well pleasing,
   His soul delights in Thee;
And to Thy glorious likeness
   We shall conformèd be:
Oh, be it ours, now sharing
   Thy fellowship, to prove
The SPIRIT'S power transforming,
   To perfect us in love!

480 **Ellingham 7.7.7.7**
Thos. Kelly (Nottingham 221) S.N. Godfrey

1 ERE Thy word our hearts engage,
   LORD, a blessing we implore;
Shine upon the sacred page,
   And unlock its precious store.

2 May each child of GOD be fed,
   While Thy truth we ponder o'er;
May the wandering heart be led
   Captive by its saving power.

481   **Purleigh 8.8.6.D**
(Hull 59)
A.H. Brown

OUR FATHER! we adore and praise,
  We bless Thee for Thy wondrous
    grace
  To us in JESUS shewn;
For all the gifts and blessings shed
From CHRIST, our Saviour, LORD,
    and Head,
  Exalted to Thy throne.

Now, thro' the COMFORTER bestowed,
Who dwells in all the sons of GOD,
  And seals them as Thine own,
To Thee we "ABBA, FATHER" cry,
With filial love to Thee draw nigh,
  And worship at Thy throne.

May He into Thy truth now lead,
And teach us on Thy word to feed,
  And shew us things to come:
As He reveals to us our need,
May we the promises still plead
  Before our FATHER'S throne.

482   Sawley C.M.   James Walch
Anne Steele

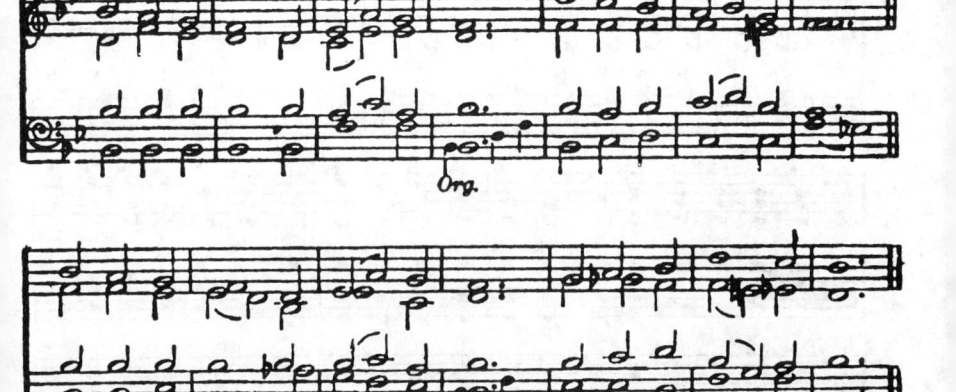

FATHER of mercies, in Thy word
   What endless glory shines!
For ever be Thy name adored
   For these celestial lines.

Here the Redeemer's welcome voice
   Spreads heavenly peace around;
And life and everlasting joys
   Attend the blissful sound.

Oh, may these heavenly pages be
   Our ever fresh delight;
And still new beauties may we see,
   And still increasing light!

483   Buckland 7.7.7.7   L.G. Hayne

MAY the shining of GOD's word
   Light unto our path afford;
May we in His truth and grace
Still with patience run our race!

484 Scatter Seeds of Kindness 8.7.8.7.D and Chorus

J.W. McClure
S.J. Vail

THERE are moments quickly passing,
   Precious moments passing by,
Moments of the brightest service,
   Service for the LORD on high:
Shall we let them pass unheeded?
   Shall our helpless hands hang down,
While for us each treasured moment
   Treasures up a golden crown?

Then let us seize the moments,
Then let us seize the moments,
Then let us seize the moments
   For the service of the King.

There are moments quickly passing,
  Opportunities which rise,
Nevermore to cross our pathway
  As we journey to the skies;
Opportunities, GOD-given,
  With these precious moments flow,
Oh, if we are watching, waiting,
  We shall seize them as they go—

There are moments quickly passing,
  Soon our little day is done;
Soon beyond the far horizon
  Fast will fade the setting sun:
Let us use these golden moments,
  Which the LORD to us doth give,
Till at length with Him in heaven,
  We the life of lives shall live—

485 Broomsgrove 6.4.6.4.6.7.6.4

Anon.   F.C. Maker

H ARK! 'tis the watchman's cry,
    Wake, brethren, wake!
JESUS our LORD is nigh,
    Wake, brethren, wake!
Sleep is for sons of night,
Ye are children of the light,
Yours is the glory bright,
    Wake, brethren, wake!

Call to each wakening band,
    Watch, brethren, watch!
Clear is our LORD's command—
Be ye as men that wait
Always at their Master's gate,
E'en though He tarry late—

Heed we the Steward's call,
    Work, brethren, work!
There's room enough for all—
This vineyard of the LORD,
Constant labour doth afford;
Yours is a sure reward—

Hear we the Shepherd's voice,
    Pray, brethren, pray!
Would ye His heart rejoice?—
Sin calls for constant fear,
Weakness needs the strong One near,
Long as ye struggle here—

Sound now the final chord,
    Praise, brethren, praise!
Thrice holy is the LORD,
    Praise, brethren, praise!
What more befits the tongues,
Soon to lead the angels' songs,
Whilst heaven the note prolongs?
    Praise, brethren, praise!

486 Bishopsgarth P.M.

S. Trevor Francis
Arthur S. Sullivan

Stately.

ARISE! ye warriors of the cross,
  The Master's word obeying,
Gird on the sword, count all things
    loss,
  Go forth without delaying;
Still forward, 'tis our LORD'S
    command,
  He will forsake us never;
His mighty hand none can withstand,
  And He is with us ever.

Arise! "the battle is the LORD'S,"
  The foe must fly before thee;
Shout, warrior, shout the battle cry—
  'For JESUS and for victory!'
The hosts of hell are camped around,
  The cross of CHRIST defying,
In armour bright, forth to the fight,
  Upon the LORD relying.

Unfurl the banner of His love,
  Who died to bring salvation
To rich and poor, to high and low,
  To men of every station;
Yet onward to the glorious fight,
  The foe-men nothing fearing;
Soon victory won, the conflict done—
  Then rest, at His appearing.

487 Morning Light 7.6.7.6.D

George Duffield   G.J. Webb

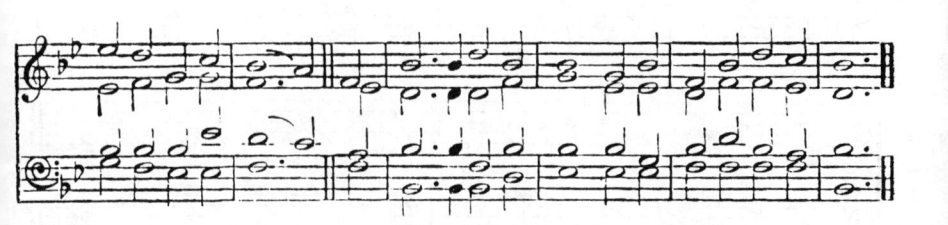

STAND up! stand up for JESUS!
As soldiers of the cross;
Lift high His royal banner,
It must not suffer loss:
From victory unto victory
His army shall He lead,
Till every foe is vanquished,
And CHRIST is LORD indeed.

Stand up! stand up for JESUS!
Stand in His strength alone;
The arm of flesh will fail you—
Ye dare not trust your own:
Put on the heavenly armour,
And, watching unto prayer,
Where duty calls, or danger,
Be never wanting there.

Stand up! stand up for JESUS!
The trumpet-call obey;
Forth to the mighty conflict
In this His glorious day!
"Quit you like men" and serve Him
Against unnumbered foes;
Let courage rise with danger,
And strength to strength oppose.

Stand up! stand up for JESUS!
The strife will not be long;
This day the noise of battle,
The next the victor's song:
To him that overcometh
A crown of life shall be;
He with the King of glory
Shall reign eternally.

488   **Alleuluia 8.7.8.7.D**
D. March   (Calon Lan 86)   S.S. Wesley

HARK the voice of JESUS crying—
  'Who will go and work to-day?
Fields are white, and harvests wait-
  ing:
  Who will bear the sheaves away?'
Loud and strong the Master calleth,
  Rich reward He offers thee:
Who will answer, gladly saying—
  'Here am I; send me, send me'?

If you cannot cross the ocean,
  And the heathen lands explore,
You can find the heathen nearer,
  You can help them at your door:
If you cannot give your thousands,
  You can give the widow's mite;
And all service for the Saviour
  Will be precious in His sight.

If you cannot speak like angels,
  If you cannot preach like Paul,
You can tell the love of JESUS,
  You can say He died for all:
If you cannot rouse the wicked
  With the Judgment's dread alarms,
You can lead the little children
  To the Saviour's waiting arms.

489   **Work, For The Night Is Coming 7.6.7.5.D**

Anna L. Coghill   L. Mason

WORK, for the night is coming,
   Work through the morning
      hours;
Work while the dew is sparkling,
   Work 'mid springing flowers;
Work when the day grows brighter,
   Work in the glowing sun;
Work, for the night is coming,
   When man's work is done.

Work, for the night is coming,
   Work through the sunny noon;
Fill brightest hours with labour,
   Rest comes sure and soon:
Give every flying minute
   Something to keep in store;
Work, for the night is coming,
   When man works no more.

Work, for the night is coming,
   Under the sunset skies;
While their bright tints are glowing,
   Work, for daylight flies;
Work till the last beam fadeth—
   Fadeth to shine no more;
Work while the night is darkening
   When man's work is o'er.

490 Antwerp L.M.
(Williams 759)

W. Smallwood

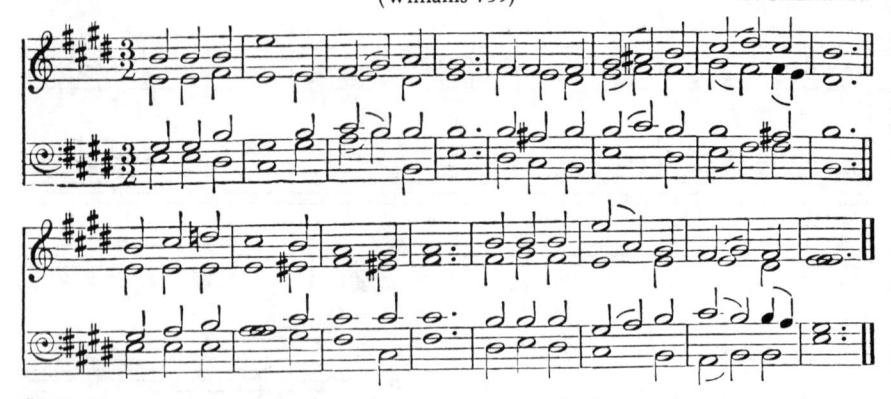

BEAR forth the banner! raise it high
  O'er every region far and wide;
Proclaim to men of every clime
  The cross—the death the Saviour died.

Unfurl the banner! heathen lands
  Shall see from far the glorious light,
And sinners, to the Saviour drawn,
  Shall have their crimson stains made white.

Display the banner! weary souls,
  About to perish in sin's strife,
Shall trust the risen CHRIST of GOD,
  And take His gift—eternal life.

Uphold the banner! let it float
  O'er darkest regions, far and wide;
Our only glory is the cross,
  Our only hope, the CRUCIFIED!

491(1) Zoan 7.6.7.6.D
U.R.N.

W.H. Havergal

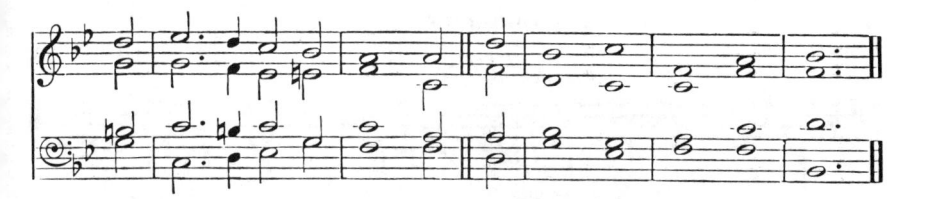

UPLIFT the gospel banner,
  And take the SPIRIT'S sword;
Put on the Christian's armour,
  The armour of the LORD—
The helmet of salvation,
  And faith's victorious shield;
Go forth to every nation,
  The world your battle-field.

Uplift the gospel banner
  And shout, with trumpet sound,
Deliverance to the captive,
  And freedom to the bound—
Earth's jubilee of glory,
  The year of full release:
Oh, tell the wondrous story,
  Go forth and publish peace!

Go forth, confessors, martyrs,
  With zeal and love unpriced,
And preach the blood of sprinkling,
  And live, or die, for CHRIST;
Preach Him to every nation,
  Your banners wide unfurled;
Go forth and preach salvation—
  Salvation to the world!

491(2)   St. Theodulph 7.6.7.6.D   Melchior Teschner c.1600

492   **Missionary 7.6.7.6.D**
Reginald Heber   L. Mason

FROM Greenland's icy mountains,
   From India's coral strand,
Where Afric's sunny fountains
   Roll down their golden sand ;
From many an ancient river,
   From many a palmy plain.
They call us to deliver
   Their land from error's chain.

What though the spicy breezes
   Blow soft on Ceylon's isle ;
Though every prospect pleases,
   And only man is vile—
In vain, with lavish kindness,
   The gifts of GOD are strown ;
The heathen, in his blindness,
   Bows down to wood and stone.

Shall we, whose souls are lighted
   With wisdom from on high,
Shall we to man benighted
   The lamp of life deny ?
Salvation ! oh, salvation !
   The joyful sound proclaim,
Till each remotest nation
   Has heard MESSIAH's name.

493
Thos. Kelly

God Is Love 8.7.8.7.4

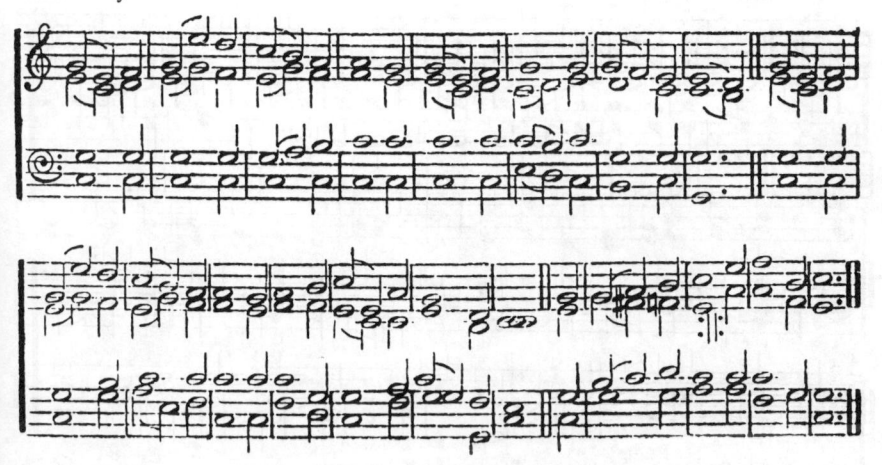

"GOD IS LOVE!" His word has said
  it—
This is news of heavenly birth:
Speed abroad and widely spread it,
  Make it known through all the earth
    That "GOD is LOVE."

Not in yonder blessèd regions,
  Where the LORD, with glory
    crowned,
Reigns amid angelic legions,
  Will the brightest proof be found
    That "GOD is LOVE."

'Tis that "Man of sorrows" yonder,
  Object of contempt beneath,
But, in heaven, of highest wonder,
  Teaches fully by His death
    That "GOD is LOVE."

His a throne—the throne of heaven,
  Yet He comes on earth to bleed.
And for man His life is given:
  This is what declares indeed
    That "GOD is LOVE."

Not for those who ever loved Him
  Did the LORD of glory die;
Pity to the wretched moved Him:
  Who that hears it will deny
    That "GOD is LOVE"?

'Tis a truth: away and spread it—
  Spread the tidings far and near;
Oh, may sinners give it credit,
  And be joyful when they hear
    That "GOD is LOVE."

494 Plainfield 7.6.7.6.D and Chorus

E.M.H. Gates
R. Lowry

1. HOW many sheep are straying,
    Far from the Saviour's fold,
   Upon the lonely mountains,
    Helpless and weak and cold!
   Within the tangled thickets
    Where beasts of prey do creep,
   And over rocky ledges
    Wander the poor, lost sheep:

   Oh come, let us go and find them—
    In the paths of death they roam;
   At the close of the day 'twill be
    sweet to say,
    'I have brought some lost one
    home.'

2. Oh, who will go to find them?
    Who, for the Saviour's sake,
   Will search with tireless patience
    Through brier and through brake?
   Unheeding thirst or hunger,
    Who still, from day to day,
   Will seek as for a treasure
    The sheep that went astray?—

3. Say, will *you* seek to find them?
    From pleasant bowers of ease
   Will you go forth determined
    To find the "least of these"?
   For still the Saviour calls them,
    And looks across the wold;
   And still He holds wide open
    The door into His fold—

495   Zenana P.M.
Sarah G. Stock

A CRY, as of pain,
   Again and again,
Is borne o'er the deserts and wide-spreading main;
A cry from the lands that in darkness are lying,
A cry from the hearts that in sorrow are sighing:
   It comes unto me;
   It comes unto thee;
Oh, what—oh, what shall the answer be?

Oh, hark to the call!
   It comes unto all
Whom JESUS hath rescued from sin's deadly thrall—
'Come over and help us—in bondage we languish!
Come over and help us—we die in our anguish!'
   It comes unto me;
   It comes unto thee;
Oh, what—oh, what shall the answer **be?**

Words continued over

It comes to the soul
 That CHRIST hath made whole,
The heart that is longing His name
 to extol,
It comes with a chorus of pitiful
 wailing;
It comes with a plea which is strong
 and prevailing,
 "For CHRIST's sake," to me;
 "For CHRIST's sake," to thee;
Oh, what—oh, what shall the answer
 be?

We come, LORD, to Thee;
 Thy servants are we;
Inspire Thou the answer, and true it
 shall be!
If here we should work, or afar Thou
 shouldst send us,
Oh, grant that Thy mercy may ever
 attend us,
 That each one may be
 A witness for Thee,
Till all the earth shall Thy glory see!

496(1) St. George S.M.
James Montgomery H.J. Gauntlett

SOW in the morn thy seed,
 At eve hold not thy hand;
To doubt and fear give thou no heed,
Broadcast it o'er the land.

Sow thou with loving care,
 With steadfast faith, with tears;
Sow on in patient hope, with prayer,
Sow till the LORD appears.

Beside all waters sow,
 The highway furrows stock;
Drop it where thorns and thistles
 grow,
Scatter it on the rock.

Thou canst not toil in vain;
 The SPIRIT from on high
Shall quicken and mature the grain
For garners in the sky.

The good, the fruitful ground,
 Expect not here nor there;
O'er hill and dale by plots 'tis found—
Go forth, then, everywhere.

Look to the glorious end!
 The LORD Himself shall come,
And thou, with gathered sheaves,
 ascend
To shout the Harvest-home!

496(2)   Dominica S.M.   H.S. Oakeley

497   Whitburn L.M.   H. Baker
H. Bonar   (Saxby 593)

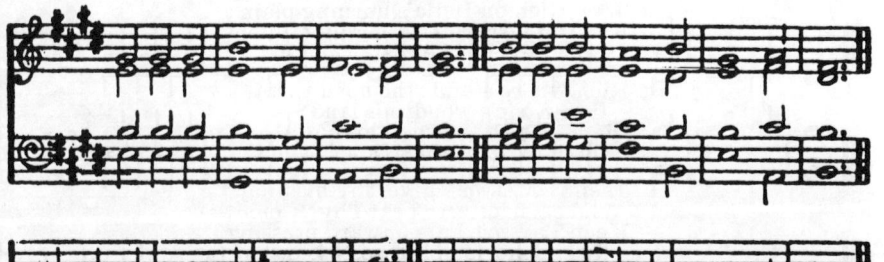

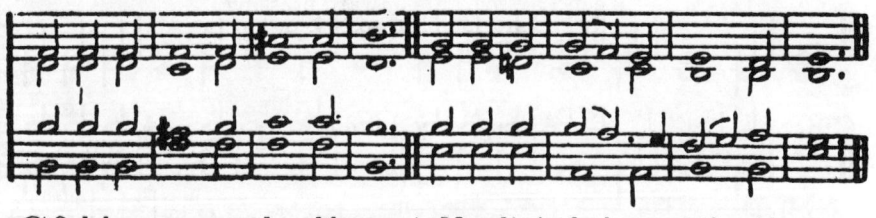

GO, labour on—spend, and be spent,
  Thy joy to do the FATHER's will;
It is the way the Master went—
  Should not the servant tread it still?

Go, labour on—'tis not for nought;
  Thy earthly loss is heavenly gain;
Men heed thee, love thee, praise thee not;
  The Master praises—what are men?

Go, labour on while it is day,
  The world's dark night is hastening on;
Speed, speed thy work, cast sloth away—
  It is not thus that souls are won.

Men die in darkness at thy side,
  Without a hope to cheer the tomb;
Take up the torch and wave it wide—
  The torch that lights time's thickest gloom.

Toil on, faint not, keep watch and pray;
  Be wise the erring soul to win;
Go forth into the world's highway,
  Compel the wanderer to come in.

Toil on, and in thy toil rejoice;
  For toil comes rest, for exile home:
Soon shalt thou hear the Bridegroom's voice,
  The midnight peal—"Behold, I come!"

498   **Laus Deo 8.7.8.7**
Sarah G. Stock   R. Redhead

RICH and plenteous is the harvest—
  Rich on India's burning plain;
Rich 'mid China's thronging millions;
  Rich beyond the eastern main;

Rich where stands the open portal
  Into Afric's wondrous land:
Oh, how rich the spoil immortal!
  Oh, how small the reaper band!

JESUS! Master! give Thy blessing,
  Bid each loiterer hear Thy "Come!"
Keep Thy servants onward pressing
  To the glorious Harvest-home!

499   **Almsgiving 8.8.8.4**
C. Wordsworth   J.B. Dykes

O LORD of heaven, and earth, and sea!
To Thee all praise and glory be:
How shall we shew our love to Thee,
    Who givest all?

For peaceful homes and healthful days,
For all the blessings earth displays,
Our GOD we owe Thee thanks and praise,
    Who givest all.

Thou didst not spare Thine only SON,
But gav'st Him for a world undone,
And freely with that Blessèd One
    Thou givest all.

Thou gav'st the HOLY SPIRIT'S dower,
SPIRIT of life, of love and power,
And dost His sevenfold graces shower
    Upon us all.

For souls redeemed, for sins forgiven,
For present grace and hopes of heaven,
FATHER, what can to Thee be given,
    Who givest all?

We lose what on ourselves we spend,
We have as treasure without end
Whatever, LORD, to Thee we lend,
    Who givest all.

As from Thyself we all derive—
Our life, our gifts, our power to give,
Oh, may we ever to THEE live,
    Who givest all!

500   **Silchester S.M.**
        (Day of Praise 899)   H.A.C. Malan

REVIVE Thy work, O LORD,
    Thy work of quickening power;
O'er earth's parched wilderness pour down
    A pentecostal shower.

Revive Thy work, O LORD,
    In far-off Eastern lands;
Bid Ethiopia's myriad tribes
    Stretch forth to Thee their hands.

Revive Thy work, O LORD,
    Amid the polar snows;
Let Nature's frozen wastes rejoice
    And blossom as the rose.

Revive Thy work, O LORD,
    Among the long-lost sheep
Israel's house, and bid them look
    On Him they pierced, and weep!

Revive Thy work, O LORD,
    In this our native isle,
With floods of light and life divine
    Make all her borders smile.

Revive Thy work, O LORD,
    In our own souls, we pray;
May all for the great Harvest-home
    Be ripening day by day.!

501
Sarah G. Stock

Bethany 8.7.8.7.D
(Alleluia 488)

Henry Smart

1 LORD, Thy ransomed Church is waking
Out of slumber far and near,
Knowing that the morn is breaking,
When the Bridegroom shall appear;
Waking up to claim the treasure
With Thy precious life-blood bought,
And accept in fuller measure
All Thy wondrous death hath wrought.

2 Praise to Thee for this glad shower,
Precious drops of latter rain;
Praise, that by Thy SPIRIT's power
Thou hast quickened us again,
That Thy gospel's priceless treasure
Now is borne from land to land,
And that all the FATHER's pleasure
Prospers in Thy piercèd hand.

3 Praise to Thee for saved ones yearning
O'er the lost and wandering throng;
Praise for voices daily learning
To upraise the glad, new song;
Praise to Thee for sick ones hasting
Now to touch Thy garment's hem;
Praise for souls believing, tasting
All Thy love has won for them.

4 Set on fire our hearts' devotion
With the love of Thy dear name;
Till o'er every land and ocean
Lips and lives Thy cross proclaim:
Fix our eyes on Thy returning,
Keeping watch till Thou shalt come;
Loins well girt, lamps brightly burning:
Then, LORD, take Thy servants home!

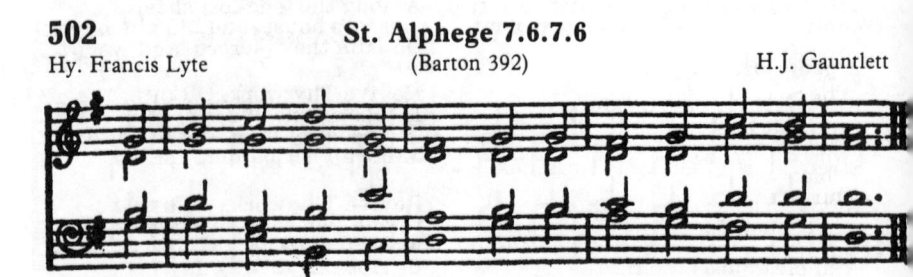

502
Hy. Francis Lyte

St. Alphege 7.6.7.6
(Barton 392)

H.J. Gauntlett

OH that the LORD'S salvation
 Were out of Zion come,
To heal His ancient nation,
To lead His outcasts home!

How long the holy city
 Shall heathen feet profane?
Return, O LORD, in pity;
Rebuild her walls again.

Let Israel, home returning,
 Her lost MESSIAH see;
Give oil of joy for mourning;
Take, LORD, Thy Church to Thee.

503 Albano C.M.
(St. Fulbert 120)

V. Novello

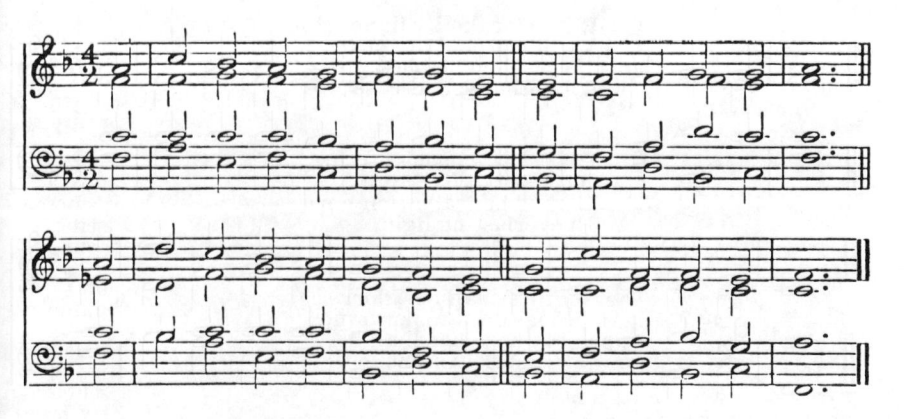

WE would the debt of love repay
 To Israel's seed we owe;
Thro' them has shone salvation's ray
On realms of sin and woe.

JEHOVAH'S covenant first was sealed
 To patriarchs of old;
To Jewish prophets was revealed
The Saviour they foretold.

'Twas Abraham's Seed who gave His
  blood
 Our pardon to ensure;
'Tis Abraham's Seed now pleads with
  GOD,
Our blessings to procure.

By Jews to Gentiles were proclaimed
 The words of life and peace;
By them our fathers were reclaimed
From sin to holiness.

Our Saviour's kinsmen let us love,
 And point them to the way
That leads to purest joys above,
To realms of perfect day.

Blest JESUS! let Thy favour shine
 On Judah's scattered race,
That they, ere long, with us may join
To sing redeeming grace!

504 **Azmon C.M.**
(Nativity 229)

C.G. Glaser

1 FOR Zion's sake I will not rest,
    I will not hold my peace
  Until Jerusalem be blest,
    And Judah dwell at ease;

2 Until her righteousness return,
    As day-break after night;
  The lamp of her salvation burn
    With everlasting light.

3 The Gentiles shall her glory see,
    And kings declare her fame;
  Appointed unto her shall be
    A new and holy name.

4 The watchmen on her walls appear,
    And day and night proclaim—
  'Zion's deliverance is near;
    Make mention of her name.'

5 Go through, go through, prepare the ways,
    The gates wide open spread;
  The standard of the people raise,
    To glorious triumph led.

6 In every clime, through every land,
    Proclaim the joyful word;
  "The holy people" are at hand,
    "Redeemèd of the LORD."

505
John Fawcett

Dismissal 8.7.8.7.8.7
(Rhuddlan 147)

W.L. Viner

1. LORD, dismiss us with Thy blessing,
   Fill our hearts with joy and peace;
   Let us each, Thy love possessing,
   Triumph in redeeming grace:
   Still refresh us,
   Travelling through this wilderness.

2. Thanks we give and adoration
   For salvation's joyful sound:
   May the fruits of that salvation
   In our hearts and lives abound:
   Ever faithful
   To the truth may we be found.

3. Then, whene'er the signal's given
   That shall call us hence away,
   Borne aloft by grace to heaven,
   Glad the summons to obey,
   We shall surely
   Reign with Thee in endless day.

506   Triumph 8.7.8.7.8.7
Robert Hawker   H.J. Gauntlett

LORD, dismiss us with Thy blessing,
  Bid us all depart in peace;
Still on heavenly manna feeding,
May our faith and love increase,
  Till we meet Thee,
And our conflicts all shall cease.

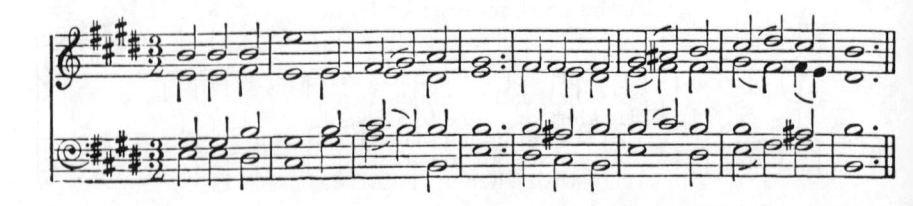

507   Antwerp L.M.
Morshead   W. Smallwood

WE bless our GOD that we have
   met
Once more before the mercy-seat,
As ransomed ones with joy to raise,
In JESU'S name, our songs of praise.

And now Thy blessing we implore,
To guard and keep us evermore;
Into Thine hand ourselves commend,
To guide, to strengthen, and defend.

508 **Blockley L.M.**
(Saxby 593)   T. Blockley

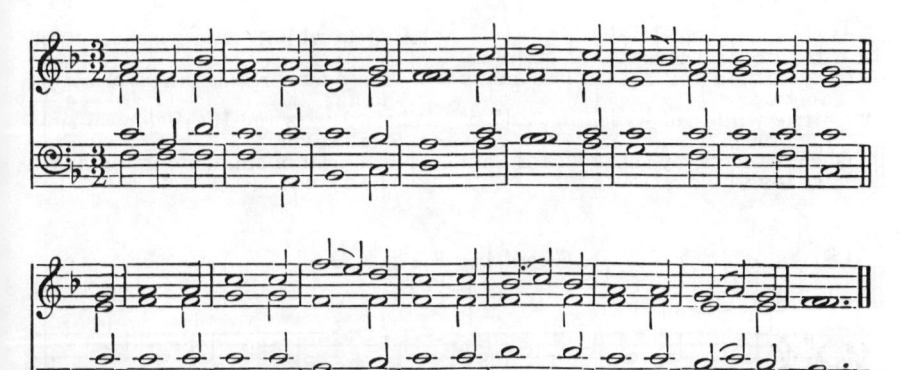

LORD, now we part in Thy blest
   name,
In which we here together came;
Grant us our few remaining days
To do Thy will, and spread Thy praise.

Thee we in life or death would bless
As all our strength and righteousness,
Until we see Thy face above,
And there for ever sing Thy love.

509 Raynolds 11.10.11.10
Charitie L. Bancroft   (O Perfect Love 934)   From Mendelssohn

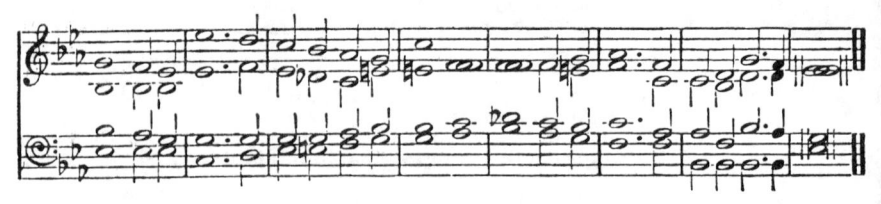

"A LITTLE while" of mingled joy
and sorrow;
"A little while" to love and serve
below,
To wait the dawning of that blissful
morrow,
When morn shall break upon this
night of woe.

A little longer in this vale of weeping,
Of yearning for the sinless home
above;
"A little while" of watching, and of
keeping
Our garments, by the power of Him
we love.

"A little while" to tell the joyful story
Of Him who made our guilt and
curse His own;
"A little while," ere we behold the
glory,
To gather jewels for His heavenly
crown.

"A little while!" and we shall dwell
for ever
Within our bright, our everlasting
home;
Where JESUS and His Bride no time
shall sever,
Nor blight of sin, nor curse of death
shall come.

510 Excelling 8.7.8.7.D
H. Bateman   (Faben 925)   John Zundel

MAY the love of GOD the FATHER,
    And the grace of CHRIST the
        SON,
And communion of the SPIRIT,
    Rest upon us every one ;
Let nought stay the free outflowing,
    Or resist the boundless love
Which through CHRIST, our LORD
        and Saviour,
    Leads us to the rest above.

Though our lot whilst here be conflict,
    GOD abides, our Shield and Guide;
And though sorrow be life's burden,
    Yet the LORD is on our side ;
What so blessèd as to serve Him—
    Let our lives His love proclaim !
What so gracious as His favour—
    Laud and magnify His name !

Ever to our GOD and FATHER,
    GOD and LORD of earth and heaven,
Ever unto CHRIST our Saviour,
    Be all praise and glory given ;
Ever to the HOLY SPIRIT
    Honour and thanksgiving be—
Hallelujah ! Hallelujah !
    Praise our GOD eternally !

511   Love Divine 8.7.8.7

John Newton   (Laus Deo 498)   J. Stainer

MAY the grace of CHRIST our
        Saviour,
    And the FATHER's boundless love,
With the HOLY SPIRIT's favour,
    Rest upon us from above !

Thus may we abide in union
    With each other and the LORD,
And possess in sweet communion,
    Joys which earth can ne'er afford !

512
Thos. Kelly
Mannheim 8.7.8.7.8.7
(Triumph 14)
German

GOD of our salvation, hear us,
  Bless, still bless us, ere we go!
While yet in the world, be near us,
  Lest we cold and careless grow:
    FATHER, keep us,
  Keep us safe from every foe.

As our steps are drawing nearer
  To our true, eternal home,
May our view of heaven grow clearer,
  Hope more bright of joys to come,
    And our hearts say—
  'Come, LORD JESUS, quickly come!'

513
R.C. Chapman
Dalehurst C.M.
(Belmont 26)
Arthur Cottman

THROUGH Jesus *one*, we do not part,
Though now we say "*Farewell;*"
Christ is our Head and risen Lord,
In whom by faith we dwell.

One Father communes with us all;
We have one mercy-seat,
And thither by one Spirit led,
The friends of Jesus meet.

Though from each other far away,
With sea or land between,
Each to the other shall be dear,
As we so long have been.

From Jesu's cross first came the fire
Of mutual love sincere;
Jesus, who makes us pure in heart,
Marks every parting tear.

We shall be gathered to the Lord,
And ever with Him dwell:
Then shall the friends of Jesus meet,
And never say "*Farewell!*"

514   Alleluia 8.7.8.7.D

Charlotte Elizabeth   S.S. Wesley

WHILE to several paths dividing,
We our pilgrimage pursue,
May our Shepherd, safely guiding,
Keep His scattered flock in view;
May the bond of blest communion
Every distant soul embrace,
Till, in everlasting union,
We attain our resting-place!

May we thus, each other aiding,
In companionship still move,
One desire each heart pervading,
One our Lord, our faith, our love;
Oh, how sweet to bend, imploring
Soothing for our brother's pain,
And, the stumbling soul restoring,
Cheer him to the race again!

515   Spanish Hymn 6.6.6.6. and Chorus

J. Hart – R. Hawker   Burgoyne's Collection 1827

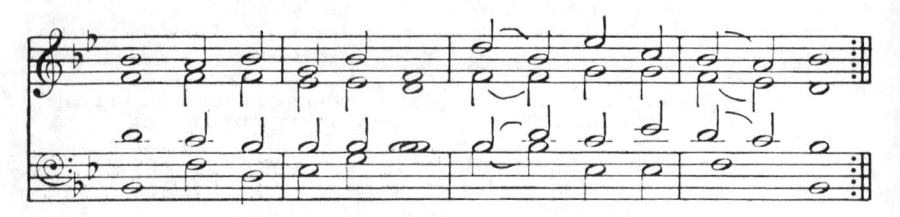

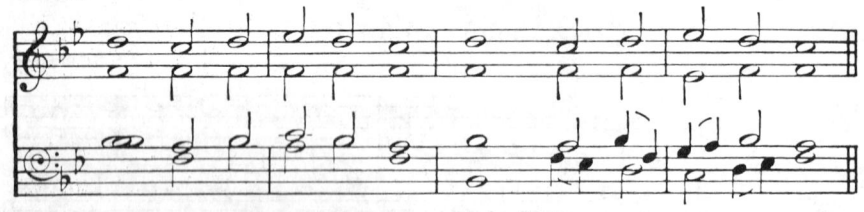

CHORUS

ONCE more before we part,
  We bless the Saviour's name;
Let every tongue and heart
  Join to extol the Lamb:

    JESUS, the sinner's Friend,
      Whom now our souls adore,
    Thy praise shall have no end;
      We'll praise Thee evermore!

LORD, in Thy grace we came,
  Thy blessing still impart;
We met in Thine own name,
  And in Thy name we part—

We on Thy holy word
  Would feed, and live, and grow;
Go on to know Thee, LORD,
  And practise what we know—

516   Praise My Soul 8.7.8.7.8.7
Denham Smith   John Goss

YES, we part, but not for ever—
   Joyful hopes our bosoms swell;
They who love the Saviour never
   Know a long, a last farewell:
      Blissful unions
   Lie beyond this parting vale.

Oh, what meetings are before us,
   Brighter far than tongue can tell—
Glorious meetings to restore us
   Him with whom we long to dwell:
      With what raptures
   Will the sight our bosoms swell!

Now indeed we meet and sever;
   Chequered is our transient day:
Life's best flowers perish, ever
   Tending to a long decay:
      Fairest flowers
   Bud and bloom, and die away.

Soon will cease such short-lived
   pleasures—
Soon will fade this earth away;
Brighter, fairer, nobler treasures
   Wait the full redemption-day:
      Hail its rising,
   Hail the wished-for, new-born ray!

517   **Hull 8.8.6.D**
Robert Hawker   Old Melody

HENCEFORWARD, till the LORD shall come,
To take all His redeemèd home—
With Him for ever then—
May He send blessings from above:
The FATHER, SON, and SPIRIT'S love
Be with us all—Amen!

518   **Penlan 7.6.7.6.D**
J.G. Deck   D. Jenkins

IN love we part as brethren,
　　And, till we see His face,
By faith commend each other
　　To God our FATHER'S grace;
In CHRIST our LORD are treasured
　　Our every day's supplies,
Sufficient is His fulness
　　Whatever wants arise.

Let us His great salvation
　　To every soul proclaim,
As heralds of His mercy,
　　Speak well of JESU's name;
Still labour in His vineyard,
　　Until our Master come,
And occupy our talents
　　Till He shall call us home.

Our souls are not divided,
　　Although our bodies part;
Oceans may roll between us—
　　We still are one in heart;
His SPIRIT dwells within us,
　　As quickened from the dead;
Who can the members sever,
　　United to their Head?

519　Come Unto Me (Vox Jesu) 7.6.7.6.D
N.L. Zinzendorf　　　(Ewing 90)　　　J.B. Dykes

O JESUS CHRIST, most holy,
　　Head of the Church, Thy Bride!
In us each day more fully
　　Thy name be magnified:
Oh, may in each believer
　　Thy love its power display,
And none amongst us ever,
　　From Thee, our Shepherd, stray!

520 What Shall The Harvest Be? P.M.

S. Oakey

P.P. Bliss

SOWING the seed by the dawnlight fair,
Sowing the seed by the noon-day glare,
Sowing the seed by the fading light,
Sowing the seed in the solemn night:
  Oh, what shall the harvest be?
  Oh, what shall the harvest be?

  Sown . . . in the dark . . . ness or
    sown . . . in the light, . . .
  Sown . . . in our weak . . . ness or
    sown . . . in our might ; . . .
  Gathered in time or eternity,
  Sure, ah! sure, will the harvest be! . . .

Sowing the seed by the way-side high,
Sowing the seed on the rocks to die,
Sowing the seed where the thorns will spoil,
Sowing the seed in the fertile soil:
  Oh, what shall the harvest be?—

Sowing the seed with an aching heart,
Sowing the seed while the tear-drops start,
Sowing in hope, till the reapers come
Gladly to gather the harvest home:
  Oh, what shall the harvest be?—

521 Hereford New 6.10.10.6

George Grove

M.K.W.

1. WE part to meet again:
   Our hope looks on to that
      bright, coming day
   When we shall have our tears all
      wiped away;
   We part to meet again.

2. We part to meet again:
   From every clime the ransomed host
      shall come,
   And be together in one glorious home;
   We part to meet again.

3. We part to meet again:
   These partings here, though painful
      now they be,
   Shall have their end when we our
      Saviour see;
   We part to meet again.

4. We part to meet again:
   JESUS, our LORD, for us will quickly
      come,
   Then like Him all—some raised, and
      changèd some—
   We ne'er shall part again.

5. Then evermore to be
   With Him whom now we worship and
      adore,
   We at His feet shall praise Him ever-
      more,
   And never part again.

522   **Old 100th L.M.**

A. Midlane   (Angelus 114)   French/Genevan Psalter 1551

AMEN! one lasting, long Amen!
   Blest anthem of eternal days,
The fulness of the rapturous song
   To CHRIST the Saviour's endless
      praise!

Amen! one lasting, long Amen!
   Heaven's blissful cadence, deep
      and loud,
While every heart before the Throne
   In holy, solemn awe is bowed.

Amen! Amen! it rolls along,
   Re-echoing from the Throne again!
Be ours to mingle with the throng
   In that eternal, loud "Amen!"

523   **Lewisham 8.7.8.7.8.7.**
Thos. Kelly   (Rhuddlan 147)   J. Tilleard

WHO are these that go with gladness,
    Far from friends and native land?
By the world 'tis counted madness,
    But they do not understand—
GOD is with them,
    And they go at His command.

These are bound for heavenly glory;
    Once they loved the world alone:
Now they tell *His* wondrous story,
    Who has claimed them as His own,
And He bids them
    Go, and make His mercy known.

Blessings from the Saviour speed them,
    And make every burden light!
May His hand of mercy lead them
    Safe to yon celestial height,
There for ever
    In His "Well done" to delight!

524   **Albano C.M.**
        (Ballerma 339)   V. Novello

THY servants, LORD, are dear to Thee,
We trust them to Thy care;
Thou wilt their daily succour be,
Their every burden bear.

Far off from friends and native land,
Be Thou their dwelling-place;
Uphold them ever by Thy hand,
Refresh them by Thy grace.

In danger's hour, in sorrow's night,
Be Thou their strength and stay,
Their hope, their shelter, and their light,
Till dawns the endless day.

525 Castle Rising C.M.D.
Sarah G. Stock (Rex Regum 607) F.A.J. Hervey

THE servants of the LORD go forth
To seek a foreign shore:
A wealth of love and prayer behind,
Far-reaching hope before;
And wheresoe'er their footsteps move,
That hope makes sweet the air,
And all the path is paved with love,
And canopied with prayer.

CHRIST in the fondly-loved 'behind,'
CHRIST in the bright 'before'—
Oh, blest are they who start with Him
To seek the foreign shore!
CHRIST is their fair, unfading light,
CHRIST is their shield and sword,
CHRIST is their keeper, day and night,
And CHRIST their rich reward!

526   **Nicomachus L.M.**   A.H. Mann
Madame Guyon   (Antwerp 353)

1 ALL scenes alike engaging prove
   To souls impressed with sacred
      love;
  Where'er they dwell, they dwell in
      Thee,
  In heaven, in earth, or on the sea.

2 To me remains nor place nor time;
  My country is in every clime;
  I can be calm and free from care
  On any shore, since GOD is there.

3 While place we seek, or place we shun,
  The soul finds happiness in none;
  But with my GOD to guide my way,
  'Tis equal joy to go or stay.

4 Could I be cast where Thou art not,
  That were indeed a dreadful lot;
  But regions none remote I call,
  Secure of finding GOD in all.

527   **Rhuddlan 8.7.8.7.8.7**   Welsh Trad. Melody
Thos. Kelly   (Triumph 14)

SPEED Thy servants, Saviour,
 speed them!
Thou art LORD of winds and waves;
They were bound, but Thou hast
 freed them;
 Now they go to free the slaves;
  Be Thou with them,
 'Tis Thine arm alone that saves.

Speed them through the mighty
 ocean;
 In the dark and stormy day,
When the waves, in wild commotion,
 Fill all others with dismay,
  Be Thou with them;
 Drive their terrors far away.

When they reach the land of
 strangers,
 There to sow in faith and tears,
Be their help in toils and dangers,
 And their covert in all fears:
  Be Thou with them
 Till the Harvest Morn appears.

When no fruit appears to cheer them,
 And they seem to toil in vain,
Then in mercy, LORD, draw near them,
 And their sinking hopes sustain:
  Thus supported,
 Let their zeal revive again!

In the midst of opposition
 Let them trust, O LORD, in Thee;
When success attends their mission,
 Let Thy servants humble be:
  Never leave them
 Till Thy face in heaven they see.

528 Verbum Pacis 6.6.8.4
George Watson   (St. John's, Hoxton 125)   George Lomas

1. WITH the sweet word of *peace*
   We bid our brethren go;
   Peace "as a river" to increase,
   And ceaseless flow.

2. With the calm word of *prayer*
   We earnestly commend
   Our brethren to Thy watchful care,
   Eternal Friend!

3. With the strong word of *faith*
   We stay ourselves on Thee,
   That Thou, O LORD, in life or death
   Their help shalt be.

4. With the dear word of *love*
   We give our brief farewell;
   Our love below, and Thine above,
   With them shall dwell.

5. And the bright word of *hope*
   Shall on our parting gleam,
   And tell of joys beyond the scope
   Of earth-born dream.

6. Farewell! in hope, and love,
   In faith, and peace, and prayer;
   Till He whose home is ours above
   Unite us there.

529
Sarah G. Stock

Lucerne 8.7.8.7
(Laus Deo 498)

T.A. Willis

1 ONCE Thy servants toiled in rowing
On the Galilean Sea;
Waves rose high, rough winds were
blowing;
How they longed, O LORD, for Thee!

2 Toiling now, GOD'S sons and daughters,
On the world's dark, troubled sea,
Midst the roar of winds and waters,
Look and long, O LORD, for Thee.

3 Far on high, in glory seated,
Watching from Thy FATHER'S
throne,
Till Thy purpose be completed,
Still uphold and bless Thine own!

4 Let not darkest waters harm them,
Let not rough winds work them ill,
Let not tempest fierce alarm them—
All are subject to Thy will.

5 When the night of toil is ended,
Then we look for Thee to come,
And, by angel-hosts attended,
Bear Thy people safely home.

530 Fountain C.M. and Chorus
Amos Sutton (Blissful Hope 904) Old Melody

CHORUS

Repeat Chorus

HOW blessèd is the tie that binds
   Believers' hearts above!
How sweet the hope that tunes our minds
   In harmony of love!

It is the hope, the blissful hope,
   Which JESUS'S grace hath given,
The hope, when days and years are past,
   That we shall meet in heaven;
We all shall meet in heaven at last,
   With JESUS meet in heaven;
With Him, when days and years are past,
   We all shall meet in heaven.

What though our lot in trial here
   Or poverty be cast!
What though around our sorrowing hearts
   May howl the wintry blast!
Yet still we share the blissful hope—

From Burmah's shores, from India's strand,
   From Afric's burning plain,
From Europe's and Columbia's land,
   We hope to meet again:
Ours is the hope, the blissful hope—

No lingering look, no parting sigh,
   Our meeting then shall know;
There love shall beam from every eye,
   And joy for ever grow:
Oh, sacred hope! oh, blissful hope!—

531 Ballina P.M.

J.E. Rankin
W.G. Tomer

GOD be with you till we meet again!
By His counsels guide, uphold you,
With His sheep securely fold you:
God be with you till we meet again!

Till we meet!... Till we meet!...
Till we meet at Jesus's feet;...
Till we meet!... Till we meet!...
God be with you till we meet again!

God be with you till we meet again!
'Neath His wings securely hide you,
Daily manna still provide you;
God be with you till we meet again!—

God be with you till we meet again!
When life's perils thick confound you,
Put His loving arms around you;
God be with you till we meet again!—

God be with you till we meet again!
Keep love's banner floating o'er you,
Smite death's threatening waves before you;
God be with you till we meet again!—

532 Rimington L.M.

Isaac Watts — F. Duckworth

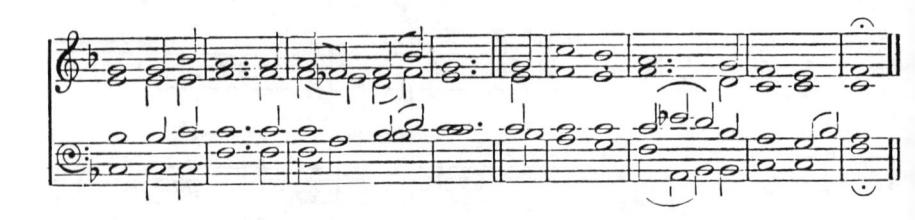

FROM all that dwell below the skies
Let the Creator's praise arise!
Let the Redeemer's name be sung
Through every land by every tongue!

Eternal are Thy mercies, LORD,
Eternal truth attends Thy word:
Thy praise shall sound from shore to shore,
Till suns shall rise and set no more.

533 Old 100th L.M.

Thomas Ken — French/Genevan Psalter 1551

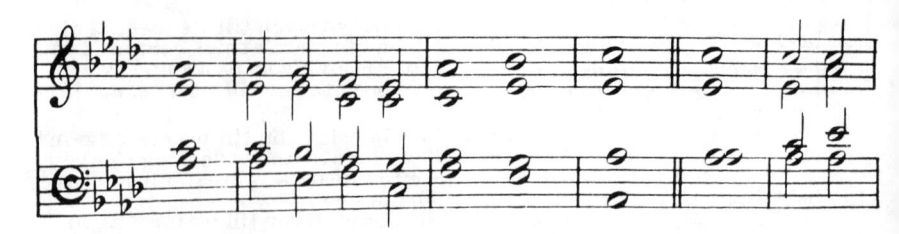

PRAISE GOD, from whom all bless
    ings flow,
Praise Him all creatures here below:
Praise Him above, ye heavenly host,
Praise FATHER, SON, and HOLY
    GHOST!

534 Gräfenberg C.M.
Tate and Brady   (St. Magnus 105)   Praxis Pietatis Melica 1653

TO FATHER, SON, and HOLY GHOST,
    One GOD, whom we adore,
Be glory as it was, is now,
And shall be evermore!

535
Ems P.M.
(Adeste Fideles 150)

F. Naylor   German Chorale

TO Him who is able
  To keep us, His called ones,
Preserved in CHRIST JESUS,
The saints of the FATHER—
To keep us from falling,
And faultless to set us
Before His bright glory
  With fulness of joy:

To the LORD GOD who keepeth
'Midst sin, and in weakness,
Who only hath wisdom—
To GOD and our Saviour
Be majesty, glory,
Dominion, and power,
Both now, and for ever,
　　Amen, and Amen!

536　　　　　　　　Corinth 8.7.8.7.8.7

H. Bonar　　　　　　　　　　　　　　Samuel Webbe

GLORY be to GOD the FATHER,
　Glory be to GOD the SON,
Glory be to GOD the SPIRIT—
　Great JEHOVAH, Three in One!
　　Glory, glory,
　While eternal ages run!

537 Lymington 7.6.7.6.D
Robt. Jackson

WE sing, our GOD and FATHER,
  Of JESUS CHRIST the LORD,
In whom doth dwell all fulness,
  The everlasting Word;
We muse on His perfection,
  His glory and His grace;
And render now our worship
  In grateful, loving praise.

538 Celeste 8.8.8.8.
Joseph Hart

HOW good is the GOD we adore,
  Our faithful, unchangeable Friend,
Whose love is as great as His power,
  And knows neither measure nor end!

'Tis JESUS, the First and the Last,
  Whose SPIRIT shall guide us safe home;
We'll praise Him for all that is past,
  And trust Him for all that's to come.

539   **Woodlands 10.10.10.10**

H. Bonar   W. Greatorex

O CHRIST, we praise Thee for Thy life on earth,
But for Thy death of love we praise Thee most;
We praise Thee, SON of the eternal GOD!
We praise the FATHER and the HOLY GHOST!

540
Harewood 6.6.6.6.8.8
(St. John, Havergal 911)

H. Bonar
S.S. Wesley

PRAISE to the Word made flesh—
True GOD, true man is He:
Praise to the CHRIST of GOD,
To Him all glory be!
Praise to the Lamb that once was slain,
Praise to the King that comes to reign!

541
Firmament 8.8.8.8.D

H. Walford Davies

ALL blessing, honour, glory, power,
  To Him who sits upon the throne,
And to the Lamb for evermore,
  For He is worthy—He alone!
By Him made kings and priests to
    GOD,
  Adoring praises now we bring,
And through eternity will sing—
  'Thou hast redeemed us with Thy
    blood!'

542   **Ashley P.M.**

Theodulph of Orleans   Gospel Magazine 1774

GLORY, honour, praise and power
  Be unto the Lamb for ever!
JESUS CHRIST is our Redeemer,
  Hallelujah! Hallelujah! Hallelujah!
    Praise ye the LORD!

543   Beatitudo C.M.

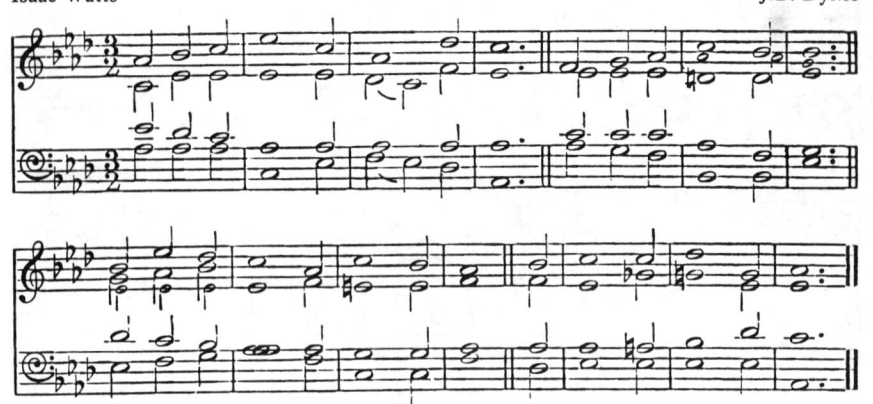

Isaac Watts   J.B. Dykes

UNTO the Lamb that once was slain
   Be endless honours paid!
Salvation, glory, praise remain
   For ever on Thy head!

Thou hast redeemed our souls with
   blood,
Hast set the captives free;
Hast made us kings and priests to GOD,
   And we shall reign with Thee.

544   Regent Square 8.7.8.7.8.7

S.M. Waring   H. Smart

UNTO Him who loved us, gave us
Every pledge that love could give,
Freely shed His blood to save us,
Gave His life that we might live—
Be the kingdom
And dominion,
And the glory evermore!

545
Isaac Watts

Ladywell C.M.

W.H. Ferguson

Stately

TO Him who saved us from the world,
And cleansed us with His blood,
Called us to share His glorious throne,
As kings and priests to GOD—

To Him let every tongue be praise,
And every heart be love,
All grateful honour paid on earth,
And nobler songs above!

546   **Rutherford 7.6.7.6.D**

Margaret C. Campbell   C. D'Urhan

ALL praise and thanks, LORD JESUS,
  Be Thine for evermore;
Thou didst from guilt release us,
  Thy name we now adore;
Still more Thy grace transcending,
  Its fulness will declare,
When, from on high descending,
  We meet Thee in the air.

547   **Credo 8.8.8.8.8.8**

C. Wesley   J. Stainer

A little slower.

FAIRER than all of earth-born race,
Perfect in comeliness Thou art;
Replenished are Thy lips with grace,
And full of love Thy tender heart—
GOD ever blest! We bow the knee,
And own, all fulness dwells in Thee!

548
R.C. Chapman
St. Catherine 8.8.8.8.8.8
(Stella 930)
J.G. Walton

OUR FATHER, let our concord be
An image bright of things above—
A glass to show the unity
Of FATHER, SON, and SPIRIT'S love;
A living picture to display
The love that we can ne'er repay!

549 St. Matthias 8.8.8.8.8.8
W.H. Monk

Lord Jesus, make Thyself to me
A living, bright reality;
More present to faith's vision keen
Than any outward object seen;
More dear, more intimately nigh
Than e'en the sweetest earthly tie.

550 Fulda L.M.
Macleod Wylie

Gardiner's Sacred Melodies 1812

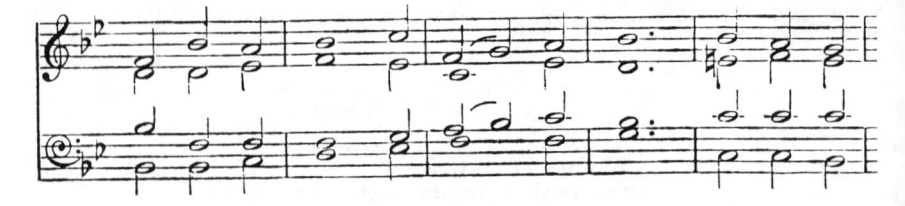

O LORD, as we more fully learn
  Our happy souls' security,
More fervent may our spirits burn
  With deep, adoring love to Thee!

551 Westminster C.M.
Macleod Wylie   James Turle

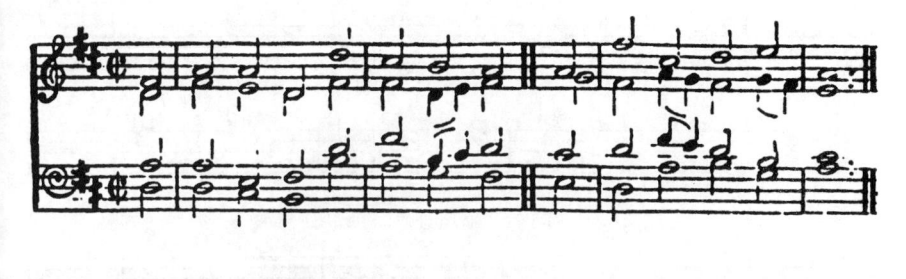

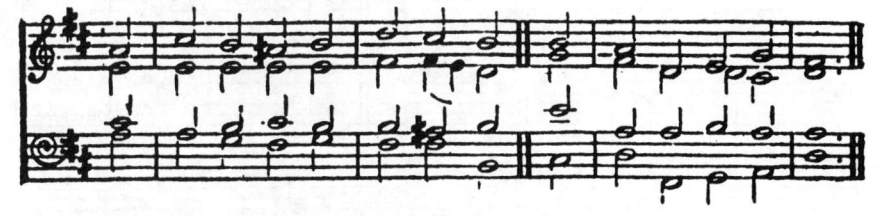

SINCE now we live because CHRIST died,
  And rest at peace with GOD,
May we with glad, submissive hearts
  Pursue the path He trod!

552 Duke Street L.M.

S. Trevor Francis — J. Hatton

I CANNOT tell what may befall—
I know not, but my GOD knows all:
His love will give me what is best;
He lives, He loves—that gives me rest. §

553 Zoan 7.6.7.6.D

J.G. Deck — W.H. Havergal

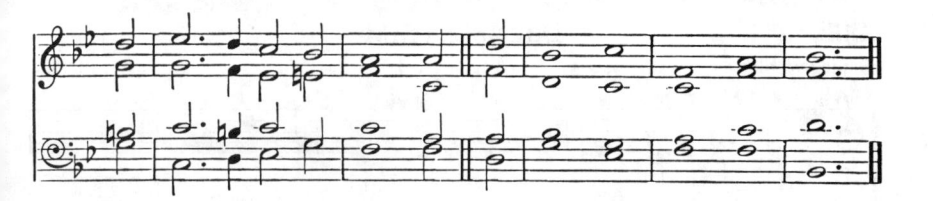

AROUND this grave, Lord Jesus,
    This mystic grave, we stand,
With hearts all full of praises,
    To keep Thy blest command;
By faith, our souls rejoicing,
    We trace Thy path of love,
Through death's dark, angry billows,
    Up to the throne above.

Lord Jesus, we remember
    The travail of Thy soul,
When, through Thy love's deep pity,
    The waves did o'er Thee roll;
Baptized in death's dark waters,
    For us Thy blood was shed;
For us Thou, Lord of glory,
    Wast numbered with the dead.

O Lord, Thou now art risen,
    Thy travail all is o'er;
For sin Thou once hast suffered—
    Thou liv'st to die no more;
Sin, death, and hell are vanquished
    By Thee, the Church's Head;
And lo! we share Thy triumphs,
    Thou First-born from the dead.

Into Thy death baptizèd,
    We own with Thee we died,
With Thee, our Life, are risen,
    And shall be glorified:
From sin, the world, and Satan,
    As ransomed by Thy blood,
We here would walk as strangers
    Alive with Thee to God.

554   Stracathro C.M.
Mary Peters   (Stroudwater 375)   C. Hutcheson

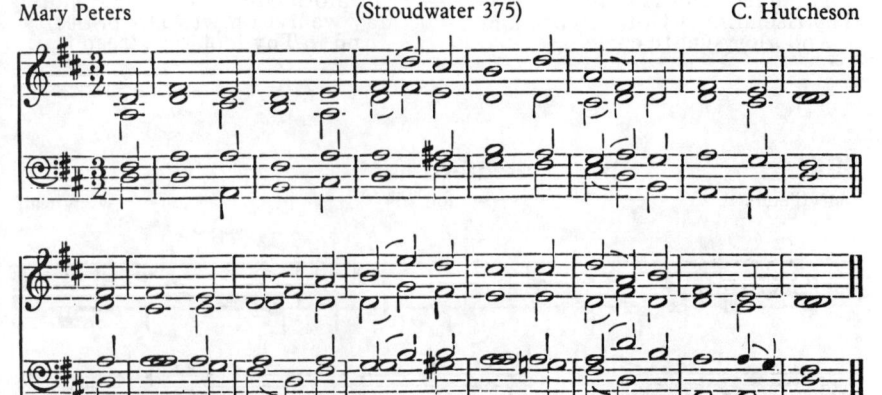

LORD JESUS, meeting in Thy name,
    With joy and thankfulness
We seek our fellowship to claim
    With those who Thee confess.

'Tis sweet to see Thy work set forth
    In this Thine own command;
We gladly own the wondrous worth
    Of all Thy love hath planned.

Here we recall, O blessèd Lord,
    Thine agony and death,
When o'er Thy holy soul were poured
    The floods of righteous wrath.

Thy resurrection from the dead
    We joyfully review,
And, one with Thee, our living Head,
    We praise Thee, Lord, anew!

555   **St. Beuno S.M.**
Daniel Webley   (Augustine 3)   J.C. Bridge

HERE, LORD, we own the truth,
  So precious to the heart,
That all Thy saints are one with Thee,
  That all with Thee have part;

Baptized into Thy death,
  From former bondage free,
We own that to the flesh and sin
  We now have died with Thee.

One with Thee in Thy death,
  Thy burial in the tomb,
Thy risen life at GOD'S right hand
  And glory yet to come.

Partaking of Thy life,
  Conformed to Thee, our Head,
May we live only to Thy praise,
  And in Thy footsteps tread!

556   **Bedford C.M.**
Mary Peters   (Azmon 264)   W. Wheall

O LORD, while we confess the worth
  Of this, the outward seal,
Do Thou the truths herein set forth,
  To every heart reveal.

Death to the world we here avow,
  Death to each fleshly lust;
Newness of life our calling now,
  A risen LORD our trust.

And we, O LORD, who now partake
  Of resurrection life,
With every sin, for Thy dear sake,
  Would be at constant strife.

Baptized into the FATHER'S name,
  To walk as sons of GOD;
Baptized in Thine, to own Thy claim,
  As ransomed by Thy blood;

Baptized into the HOLY GHOST,
  To prove His mighty power;
We would make Thee our only boast,
  And serve Thee hour by hour.

557   Newton Ferns 8.7.8.7
(Love Divine, Stainer 41)   Samuel Smith

"BURIED" in the grave of JESUS—
  Faith accepts what GOD hath said,
In His judgment acquiescing,
  Reckoning now that we are dead.

Death and judgment are behind us,
  Grace and glory are before—
All the billows rolled o'er JESUS,
  And exhausted all their power.

"First-fruits" of the resurrection,
  He is risen from the tomb;
Now we stand in new creation,
  Free, because beyond our doom.

JESUS died, and we died with Him,
  "Buried" in His grave to lie;
One with CHRIST in resurrection,
  "Seated" now in Him on high.

We await the full redemption,
  When the risen One shall come,
And our mortal bodies, changèd,
  Shall be "fashioned" like His own.

LORD, we share in Thy rejection—
  Thy reproach, oh, may we love,
Since we stand in Thine acceptance
  In our FATHER'S sight above!

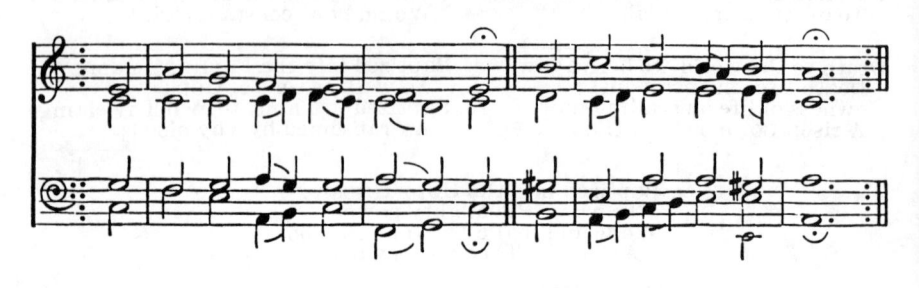

558   Passion Chorale 7.6.7.6.D
       (Nyland 185)   H.L. Hassler

1. BEHOLD Thy servants keeping,
   O LORD, Thy loved command;
   Into Thy death baptizèd,
   May they be strong and stand!
   May all, Thy name confessing,
   Hold fast Thy truth and grace;
   Be blest, and be a blessing,
   Praise Thee, and show Thy praise!

2. As one with Thee, Thy members
   Have endless life begun;
   Nor aught from Thee shall sever
   The least, the feeblest one;
   May we who own our union,
   As dead and raised with Thee,
   Now daily to Thy likeness
   Conformed in spirit be!

3. For ever in remembrance
   May all Thy people keep
   Thy deep humiliation,
   Thy love, Thy sorrows deep!
   So shall we know the gladness
   Of life, O LORD, with Thee;
   Like Thee, in resurrection
   And glory we shall be.

559 Credo 8.8.8.8.8.8
Josiah Conder (Stella 930) J. Stainer

A little slower.

1 O GOD, who didst an equal mate
　For Adam of himself create—
Flesh of his flesh, bone of his bone,
That both might feel and love as one—
Make these Thy children one in heart:
Whom Thou dost join let no man part!

2 LORD of the Church, whose bleeding side
Gave life to Thy redeemèd Bride,
Whose grace, through every member spread,
Joins the whole body to its Head,
Oh, let Thy love the model be
Of this their nuptial unity!

3 O Thou, who once, a Guest divine,
Didst turn the water into wine,
Thy presence, not unsought, afford;
Fill Thou their cup and bless their board,
And, while each heart Thy word obeys,
May all their joy be turned to praise!

560
Breslau L.M.

T. Coleman (Ombersley 28) German

O LORD, when Thou didst man
  create,
Thou didst ordain the marriage state;
And here we learn that mystery—
The union of the Church with Thee.

With grace of life, and love divine,
Upon this union deign to shine,
That hand and heart may faithful
  prove
In duties, prayers, and mutual love.

561
Munich 7.6.7.6.D

John Ellerton (Day of Rest 166) German Melody 1693

O FATHER, all creating,
　Whose wisdom, love and power
First bound two lives together
　In Eden's primal hour,
To-day to these Thy children
　Thine earliest gifts renew—
A home by Thee made happy,
　A love by Thee kept true!

O SAVIOUR, Guest most bounteous
　Of old in Galilee,
Vouchsafe to-day Thy presence
　With those who call on Thee;
Their store of earthly gladness
　Transform to heavenly wine,
And teach them, in the tasting,
　To know the gift as Thine!

O SPIRIT of the FATHER,
　Breathe on them from above,
So mighty in Thy pureness,
　So tender in Thy love,
That, guarded by Thy presence,
　From sin and strife kept free,
Their lives may own Thy guidance,
　Their hearts be ruled by Thee!

Except Thou build it, FATHER,
　The house is built in vain;
Except Thou, SAVIOUR, bless it,
　The joy will turn to pain;
But nought can break the union
　Of hearts in Thee made one,
And love Thy SPIRIT hallows
　Is endless love begun.

562　　St. Bernard C.M.
J. Berridge　　(Binchester 620)　　J. Richardson

SINCE Thou, LORD JESUS, didst appear,
　To grace a marriage feast,
We now would ask Thy presence here,
　To make this wedding blest.

Upon the bridal pair look down,
　Who now are plighting hands;
Their union with Thy favour crown,
　And bless their nuptial bands.

With gifts of grace their hearts endow,
　Of all rich dowries best;
Their substance bless, and peace bestow,
　To sweeten all the rest.

In purest love their souls unite,
　That they, with tender care,
May make domestic burdens light,
　By taking mutual share.

And looking to their heavenly home,
　May trials by the way
But make them long for Thee to come,
　Thy glory to display!

563
W. Bengo Collyer **Newington 7.7.7.7** (Monkland 57) W.D. Maclagan

FATHER, let Thy heavenly grace
　Rest upon us in this place;
Sanction what hath now been done—
Let these twain be truly one;

One in sickness, one in health,
One in poverty or wealth;
And, as year rolls after year,
Each to other still more dear;

　One in purpose, one in heart,
　Never from Thyself to part;
　Soon, around Thy throne to be
　One for ever, LORD, with Thee.

564
M.M. Davis **St. Alphege 7.6.7.6** (Barton 392) H.J. Gauntlett

LORD GOD, Thou didst in Eden
  Lead up to Adam's side,
On that glad, nuptial morning,
  The first and fairest bride.

As hand joined hand, so truly
  In heart Thou mad'st them one,
While Thine own voice upon them
  Breathed blessing from Thy Throne.

Now let that bridal blessing
  Rest on this happy pair,
Who promise here together
  Life's joys and griefs to share,

Until the Heavenly Bridegroom
  Shall bid each be His guest,
To join the "called and chosen"
  At His own marriage feast.

565　　　　　　　　**Angelus L.M.**
Strong　　　　　　　　(Nicomachus 526)　　　　　　　　J. Scheffler

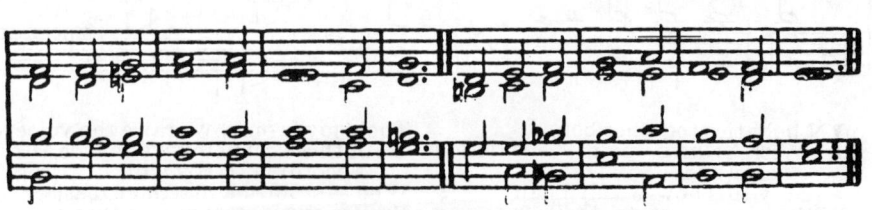

THIS marriage union now complete,
  The twain are one in wedlock sweet;
Oh, guide them, FATHER, with Thine eye,
Until they reach their home on high!

Help them unitedly to shine,
To shed around a light divine,
And may their mutual prayers arise
Like holy incense to the skies.

Grant that their earthly home may be,
Like that of old at Bethany,
Filled with the perfume of true love,
Which has its source in heaven above.

A sanctuary may it be,
From strife and discord ever free
A consecrated, happy place,
Adorned by every Christian grace.

These twain as one we now commend
To Thine own love, which knows no end;
Be Thou their joy in brightest day,
And through night's gloom their light and stay.

566   **Innsbruck 8.8.6.D**
Strong   (Meribah 153)   H. Izaak

IN holy ties together bound,
  With GOD'S own benediction crowned,
May this new-wedded pair
With happy hearts their pathway take,
Resolved to live for JESU'S sake,
  His easy yoke to bear.

Their joy is ours, we raise the voice;
With those rejoicing we rejoice,
  According to His will
Who sanctified a marriage feast
By His own presence as a Guest,
  And who is with us still.

May GOD the FATHER, GOD the SON,
With GOD the SPIRIT, Three in One,
  A triune blessing give,
And speed the LAMB'S great nuptial day,
When we together, caught away,
  With Him shall ever live.

567(1)   **Morning Hymn L.M.**
Thomas Ken   F.H. Barthélémon

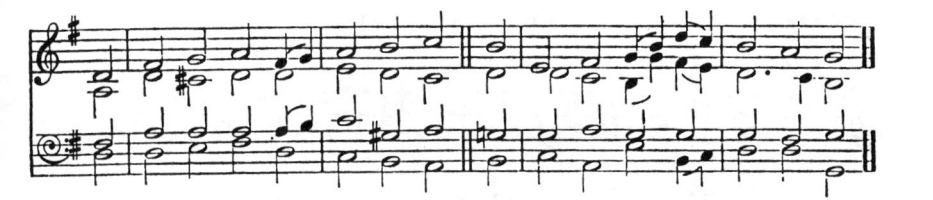

AWAKE, my soul, and with the sun
　Thy daily stage of duty run;
Shake off dull sloth, and early rise
To pay thy morning sacrifice.

All praise to Thee, who safe hast kept,
　And hast refreshed me while I slept!
Guard my first springs of thought and will,
And with Thyself my spirit fill.

In conversation be sincere;
Keep conscience as the noontide clear;
Think how All-seeing God thy ways
And all Thy secret thoughts surveys.

Direct, control, suggest this day
All I design, or do, or say;
That all my powers, with all their might,
For Thy sole glory may unite.

567(2)　　　　**Berkshire L.M.**　　　　S. Wesley

568(1)   **Melcombe L.M.**
John Keble   S. Webbe

NEW every morning is the love
  Our wakening and uprising prove;
Through sleep and darkness safely brought,
Restored to life, and power, and thought.

New mercies, each returning day,
Hover around us while we pray;
Oh, grant us, LORD, with sins forgiven,
New thoughts of GOD, new hopes of heaven.

If on our daily course our mind
Be set to hallow all we find,
New treasures still, of countless price,
Thou wilt provide for sacrifice.

The trivial round, the common task,
Will furnish all we ought to ask—
Room to deny ourselves; a road
To bring us, daily, nearer GOD.

Only, O LORD, in Thy dear love
Fit us for perfect rest above,
And help us, this and every day,
To live more nearly as we pray!

568(2)   **Samson L.M.**   From Handel

569
Thos. Kelly

Ottawa 8.7.8.7.7.7
(Evensong, Summers 619)

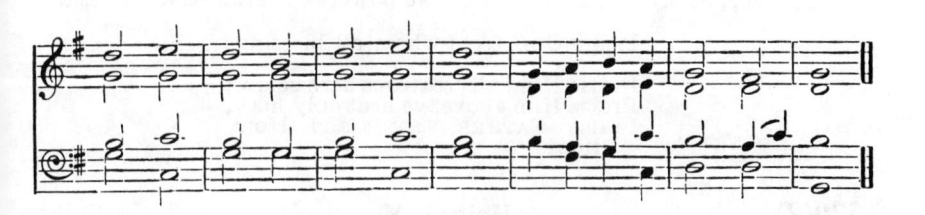

L. Mason

THROUGH the day Thy love has kept us,
　Wearied we lie down to rest;
Through the silent watches guard us
　Let no foe our peace molest:
Lord, do Thou our Guardian be,
Sweet it is to trust in Thee.

Pilgrims here on earth, and strangers,
　Dwelling in the midst of foes,
Us and ours preserve from dangers,
　In Thine arms may we repose;
Soon will life's short day be past,
We shall rest with Thee at last!

570(1) Tallis' Canon L.M.

Thos. Ken — T. Tallis

GLORY to Thee, my GOD, this night,
For all the blessings of the light;
Keep me, oh keep me, King of kings,
Beneath Thine own almighty wings.

Forgive me, LORD, for Thy dear SON,
The ill that I this day have done;
That with the world, myself and Thee,
I, ere I sleep, at peace may be.

Oh, may my soul on Thee repose,
And may sweet sleep mine eyelids close—
Sleep that may me more vigorous make
To serve my GOD when I awake.

If in the night I sleepless lie,
My soul with heavenly thoughts supply;
Let no ill dreams disturb my rest,
No powers of darkness me molest.

Praise GOD, from whom all blessings flow;
Praise Him, all creatures here below;
Praise Him above, ye heavenly host;
Praise FATHER, SON, and HOLY GHOST.

570(2) Holly L.M.

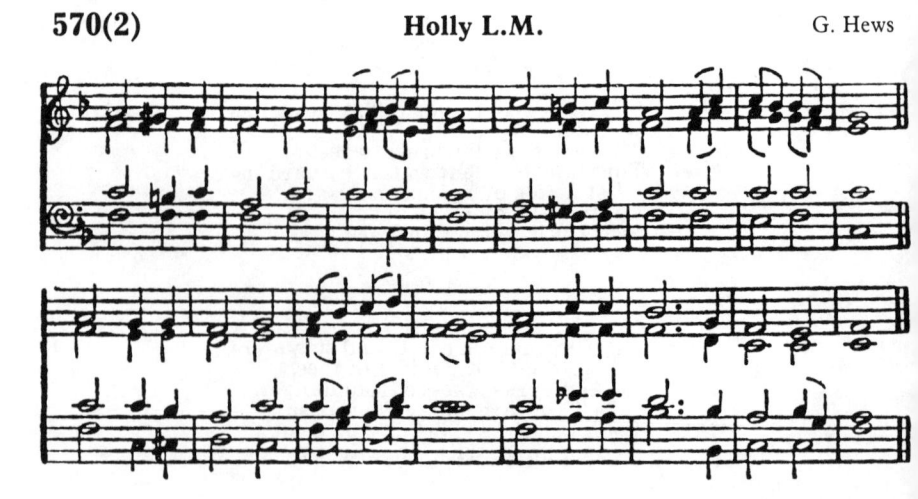

G. Hews

571
John Keble

Abends L.M.
(Hursley 260)

H.S. Oakeley

SUN of my soul, Thou Saviour dear,
It is not night if Thou be near:
Oh, may no earth-born cloud arise
To hide Thee from Thy servant's eyes.

When the soft dews of kindly sleep
My wearied eyelids gently steep,
Be my last thought, how sweet to rest
For ever on my Saviour's breast!

Watch by the sick, enrich the poor
With blessings from Thy boundless store;
Give every mourner sleep to-night,
Like infant's slumbers, pure and light.

Come near and bless us when we wake,
Ere through the world our way we take,
Till in the ocean of Thy love
We lose ourselves in heaven above.

572
Borthwick

Nyland 7.6.7.6.D
(Penlan 80)

Finnish Hymn Melody

STILL on the homeward journey
  Across the desert-plain,
Beside another landmark
  We pilgrims meet again;
We meet in cloud or sunshine
  Beneath a changeful sky,
With calm and storm before us,
  As in the days gone by.

We meet with loving greetings,
  Fond wishes from the heart,
As brothers often parted,
  And soon again to part;
With tender recollections,
  With many a gentle tear
We meet, for some are wanting—
  All loved ones are not here!

Safe in Thy home, LORD JESUS,
  With Thee for ever blest,
How glorious is their portion,
  How undisturbed their rest!
How gladly will they greet us,
  When, all our journey past,
We reach the better country,
  Our FATHER'S house, at last!

Thus round the silent landmark,
  Here on the desert-plain,
We pilgrims meet together
  With loving hearts again:
The storm may gather round us,
  But Thou hast gone before;
We follow in Thy footsteps,
  To meet and part no more.

573

W.H. Bennet

Llanllyfni S.M.D.
(Nearer Home 432)

J. Jones (arr. by D. Jenkins)

O CHRIST, Thou SON of GOD,
  Thou glorious LORD of all,
Thou Living One who once wast slain,
  Before Thy face we fall!
To Thee, O LORD, we look,
  To Thee ourselves we yield;
Be Thou throughout our earthly course
  Our refuge and our shield!

Though all around may change,
  No change Thou e'er shalt know;
The same art Thou upon the throne
  As Thou wast here below;
The same to-day Thou art
  As yesterday Thou wast,
The same e'en to eternal days
  As in the wondrous past.

LORD JESUS, take our hearts,
  From self-love set them free;
Help us, however dark our path,
  To stay our souls on Thee:
Though evil waxes worse,
  And many hearts grow cold,
Help us to cleave unto Thy name.
  Thy faithful Word to hold.

Help us to look beyond
  The dark and gloomy night,
To wait for that blest hour when Thou
  Wilt come in glory bright;
When we Thy voice shall hear,
  Thy glorious face shall see,
And, like Thee, in Thy presence stand,
  And ever worship Thee.

574   **Barton 7.6.7.6**
Frances R. Havergal   (St. Alphege 109)   J.H. Knecht

ANOTHER year is dawning!
  O Master, let it be,
In working or in waiting,
  Another year with Thee;

Another year of mercies,
  Of faithfulness and grace;
Another year of gladness,
  And shining of Thy face;

Another year of progress,
  Another year of praise;
Another year of proving
  Thy presence all the days;

Another year of service,
  Of witness for Thy love;
Another year of training
  For holier work above.

Another year is dawning!
  Our Master, let it be,
On earth or else in heaven,
  Another year for Thee!

575   **Monkland 7.7.7.7**
John Milton   (Melling 410)   J.B. Wilkes

LET us, with a gladsome mind,
  Praise the LORD, for He is kind—
*For His mercies shall endure,
Ever faithful, ever sure.*

All things living He doth feed,
His full hand supplies their need—

He His chosen race did bless
In the dreary wilderness—

He hath with a pitying eye
Looked upon our misery—

Now as those redeemed by blood,
Praise we GOD, for He is good—

576(1)   **Triumph 8.7.8.7.8.7**
J.S.B. Monsell   H.J. Gauntlett

"GOD is Love;" by Him upholden
  Hang the glorious orbs of light,
In their language, glad and golden,
  Speaking to us day and night
    Their great story—
  "GOD is Love," and "GOD is Light."

And the teeming earth rejoices
  In that message from above,
With ten thousand thousand voices
  Telling back from hill and grove
    Her glad story—
  "GOD is Light," and "GOD is Love."

In that precious love He sought us,
  Wand'ring from His holy ways;
With His own SON'S life He bought us;
  Then let all our future days
    Tell this story—
  "GOD is Love"—in lives of praise.

Gladsome is the theme, and glorious,
  Praise to CHRIST, our gracious Head;
CHRIST, the risen CHRIST, victorious,
  Death and hell hath captive led!
    Welcome story!
  JESUS lives who once was dead.

  Up to Him let each affection
    Daily rise, and round Him move,
  Our whole lives one resurrection
    In the Life of life above;
      Their glad story—
    "GOD is Light," and "GOD is Love."

576(2)   **Caer Salem 8.7.8.7.8.7**   Robt. Edwards

577   **Crüger 7.6.7.6.D**   J. Crüger
J.S.B. Monsell   (Llangloffan 335)

LORD, in Thy holy presence
  Thy goodness we adore,
Which crowns the fruitful seed-time
  With Autumn's golden store;
With hearts laid down before Thee,
  We at Thy footstool fall;
And with our lives adore Thee,
  Who art the life of all.

To GOD, our gracious FATHER,
  In whom we live and move;
To CHRIST, our great Redeemer,
  Whose life in us is love;
And to the HOLY SPIRIT,
  Who doth upon us pour
His blessèd dew and sunshine,
  Be praise for evermore!

578   **Mainzer L.M.**   Joseph Mainzer
(Wilton 907)

BLESS thou the LORD, my soul, and
    raise
To Him thy grateful song of praise;
Bless Him for all His love to thee,
For mercies countless, rich, and free.

While from destruction's power
    secure,
Through His redemption, strong and
    sure,
His lovingkindness crowns thy head,
And tender mercies round are shed.

Thy mouth with good things He doth
    fill,
So that thy youth is vigorous still,
E'en as the eagle's strength renewed,
And with fresh grace from heaven
    endued.

Bless Him for all the hourly love,
Gently distilling from above,
Which fills thy soul and makes thee
    blest
Amidst this dreary world's unrest.

Bless Him for hopes of coming peace,
When all thy griefs and pains shall
    cease;
Bless Him that thou His face shalt
    see,
And like Him evermore shalt be.

Bless thou the LORD, my soul, and
    raise
To Him thy grateful song of praise;
Oh, deeply in thy heart record
The unnumbered mercies of thy
    LORD!

579   Peel Castle 10.10.10.10
       (St. Agnes, Langran 132)   Manx Fishermen's Hymn
                                    Adapted by W.H. Gill

SWEET is the work, O LORD Most
   High, to praise,
And Thy great name for evermore
   to bless;
Praise for Thy kindness every morn
   to raise,
And every night Thy faithfulness
   confess.

For Thou, LORD, through Thy work
   hast gladdened me,
And in that work my triumph now
   I make;
Thy mighty arm hath brought salvation free,
Which shall for ever joy and gladness wake.

The men of earth but seek their portion here,
Nor ask thy thoughts, nor seek Thy
   way to trace;
But Thou hast ope'd our eye, and
   waked our ear.
And on our head hast poured Thine
   oil of grace.

Thy saints, O LORD, shall flourish like
   the palm,
Whose root lies deep beneath the
   desert soil;
There secret springs refresh; nor
   storm, nor calm
Shall waste the fruit of Thy most
   patient toil.

Thus to hoar age may we Thy truth
   declare,
Who faithful ever wast, and art
   to be;
Trophies of Thy redeeming grace we
   are,
Thou art our Rock, beneath Thy
   shade we flee.

580   Buckland 7.7.7.7
(Vienna 410(2))   L.G. Hayne

BOUNTEOUS Source of every good,
  Giver of our daily food,
Thou Thy mercy dost reveal,
As we prove, at every meal.

Thou who givest life and breath,
And redeemest us from death,
In Thy tender love dost grant
Full supply for every want.

May these tokens of Thy grace
Wake our hearts to grateful praise;
And these gifts, received from Thee,
Used unto Thy glory be.

For Thy Gift all gifts above,
For Thy ceaseless care and love,
O Thou Fount of blessings, be
Thanks and praise eternally!

581   Abbey C.M.
(Azmon 264)   Scottish Psalter 1615

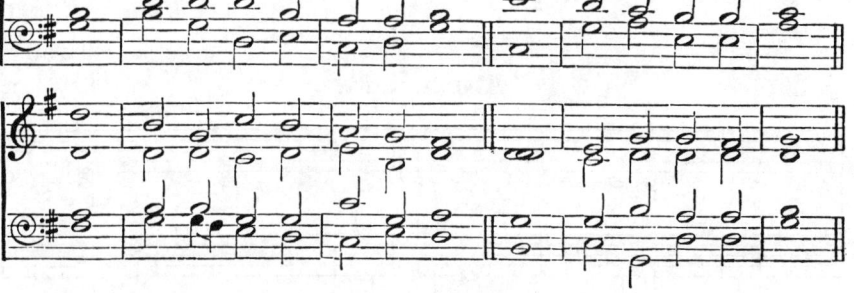

OUR GOD and FATHER, now behold
  Thy children gathered here,
Sweet social fellowship to hold,
  In love and godly fear.

Thy hand this sweet repast has spread,
  Herein Thy love we trace;
'Tis Thou who givest daily bread,
  And all the gifts of grace.

We bless Thee for our portion here,
  And better things above;
With CHRIST Thou givest us to share
  The fulness of Thy love.

582(1)   **Job L.M.**

C.H. Spurgeon   W. Arnold

O UR FATHER, bless the bounteous
store
Wherewith Thou hast our table
spread ;
With grateful songs we would adore,
And bless the hand by which we're
fed.

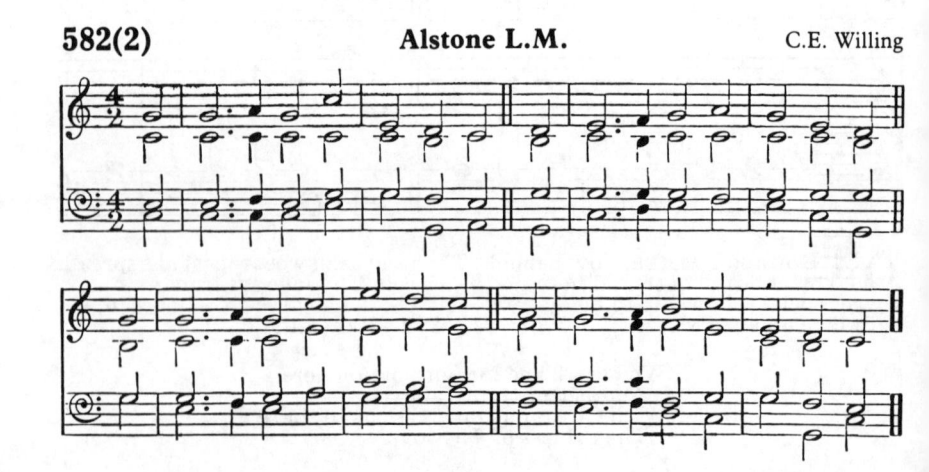

582(2)   **Alstone L.M.**   C.E. Willing

583 Nicomachus L.M.
Edward Denny (Angelus 114) A.H. Mann

O LORD, Thy bounteous hand hath
    spread
  With earthly food our social board;
  Feed Thou our souls with sweeter
    bread,
  The Bread of life—Thyself, O LORD!

Thy grace in all things soars above
  The sweetest songs Thy saints can
    raise;
  Yet, LORD, for this, and all Thy love,
  Accept our grateful note of praise.

584 Antwerp L.M.
John Cennick W. Smallwood

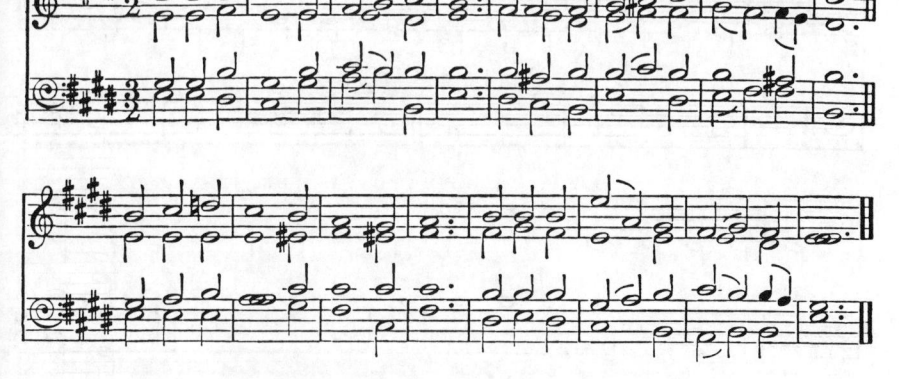

WE thank Thee, LORD, for this our
    food,
  For life, and health, and every good:
  May Manna to our souls be given—
  The Bread of life sent down from
    heaven!

585   **Blockley L.M.**

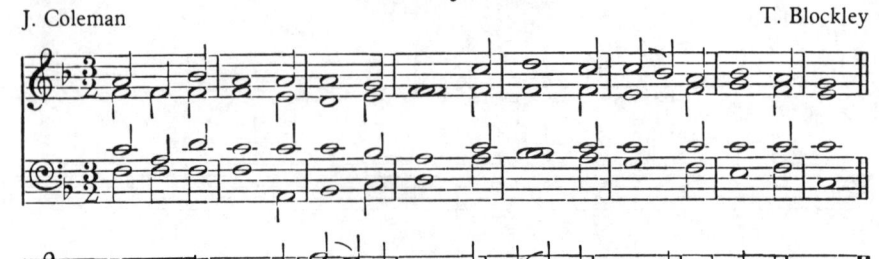

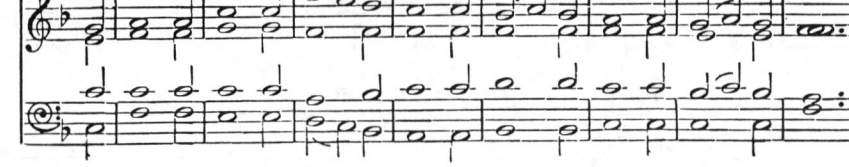

J. Coleman   T. Blockley

LORD, we accept with grateful hearts
These good things that Thy hand imparts:
May we Thy word—that greater good—
Esteem above our daily food!

586   **Church Triumphant L.M.**

John Cennick   J.W. Elliott

BE present at our table, LORD,
Be here and everywhere adored;
These mercies bless, and grant that we
Communion sweet may hold with Thee.

587
J.G. Deck

Penlan 7.6.7.6.D
(Passion Chorale 115)

D. Jenkins

THOU hast *stood* here, LORD JESUS,
  Beside the still, cold grave,
And shewn Thy deep compassion,
  And mighty power to save:
Thy tears of tender pity,
  Thine agonizing groan,
Tell how for us Thou feelest,
  Though seated on the throne.

Thou hast *lain* here, LORD JESUS,
  Thyself the Victim then—
The LORD of life and glory,
  Once slain for wretched men!
From sin and condemnation,
  Thou, only Thou couldst save ;
Thy love than death was stronger,
  And deeper than the grave.

Yes, Thou *wast* here, LORD JESUS,
  But Thou art here no more ;
The terror and the darkness,
  The night of death are o'er :
Great Captain of salvation,
  Thy triumphs now we sing—
"O Grave ! where is thy victory ?"
"O Death ! where is thy sting ?"

We wait for Thine appearing,
  We weep, but we rejoice ;
In all our heartfelt sorrow,
  We still can hear Thy voice:
'I am the Resurrection,
  I live who once was slain ;
Fear not, for this thy loved one
  Shall rise with Me to reign !'

588 Ewing 7.6.7.6.D
J.G. Deck A. Ewing

GREAT Captain of salvation,
   We bless Thy glorious name,
Of death and hell the Victor,
   With all their power and shame:
Weak, helpless, poor, and trembling,
   As in ourselves we stand,
We triumph, more than conquerors,
   Through Thine almighty hand.

Soon Thou wilt come in glory,
   With all Thy Church to shine—
Our bodies raised in honour
   And beauty, LORD, like Thine:
Then, then we'll raise still louder
   The song which now we sing—
"O Grave! where is thy victory?"
"O Death! where is thy sting?"

O SON of GOD, we thank Thee,
   We bless Thy holy name;
Thy love once made Thee willing
   To bear our sin and shame;
And now Thy love is waiting,
   Thy Church, like Thee, to raise;
Firstborn of many brethren
   Thine—Thine be all the praise!

589   **Leoni** 6.6.8.4.D

Mary Peters   Hebrew Melody

By Thee, O CHRIST, redeemed,
  The cost Thy precious blood
Be nothing by our souls esteemed
    Like this great good:
Were the vast world our own,
  With all its varied store,
And Thou, LORD JESUS, wert unknown,
    We still were poor.

Our earthen vessels break,
  The world itself grows old;
But Thou our precious dust wilt take,
    And freshly mould:
Thou wilt these bodies vile
  Then fashion like Thine own,
And bid the whole creation smile,
    And hush its groan.

Thus far by grace preserved,
  Each moment speeds us on;
The crown and kingdom are reserved
    Where Thou art gone:
When cloudless morning shines
  We shall Thy glory share;
In pleasant places are the lines—
    The home how fair!

590 Azmon C.M.

Mary Peters   C.G. Glaser

ALL times are times for praising Thee
When triumphing by faith;
Thy power, O gracious LORD, we see,
Which conquers sin and death.

We thank Thee that this weary one
Hath entered into rest—
His [her] work of faith for ever done—
He [she] leans upon Thy breast.

The perfect spirit droops no more
Beneath its earthly load
His [her] groaning is for ever o'er,
He [she] rests with Thee in GOD.

We praise Thee that Thy mighty hand
Hath helped him [her] through the flood;
And safe before the throne will stand
This purchase of Thy blood.

O blessèd Saviour, quickly come;
Us and the sleepers call;
Make up Thy jewels' perfect sum,
And give Thy joy to all!

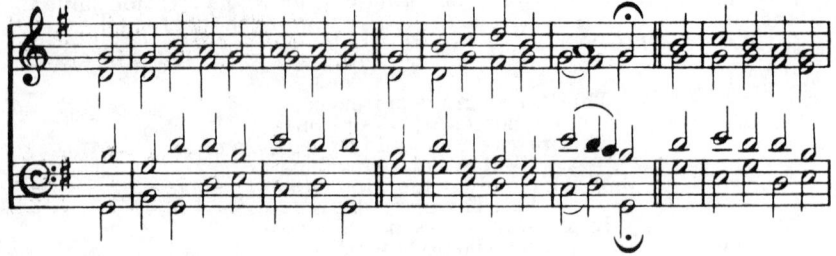

591 Luther's Hymn 8.7.8.8.7

R.C. Chapman   Martin Luther

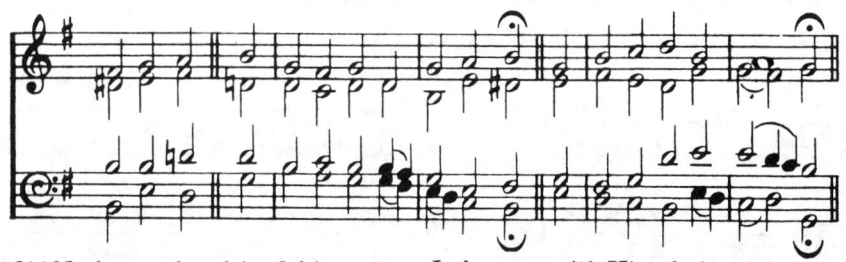

Can heavenly friendships pass
 away,
 So true and tender-hearted?
Can death make any saint his prey,
When from the earthly house of clay
 The spirit has departed?

Behold at God's right hand the Man
 In whom the dead are sleeping:
The Lamb, without a spot or stain,
The Lord, who died and rose again,
 Their dust is safely keeping.

In heaven with Him their spirits rest,
 By angels thither carried;
No foes assail them or molest,
Though oft with cares and sorrows
  prest
 While here on earth they tarried.

In heaven they see the Saviour's face,
 So bright, yet so endearing;
His bosom is their resting-place,
They call to mind their finished race,
 And wait for His appearing.

592   Lucius C.M.

S.P. Tregelles   (Evan 154)   Templi Carmina 1829

'Tis sweet to think of those at rest,
 Who sleep in Christ the Lord;
Whose spirits now with Him are blest,
 According to His word.

How bright the resurrection-morn
 On all the saints will break!
The Lord Himself will then return,
 His ransomed Church to take.

Or raised, or changed, His saints will
  meet,
 All grief and care removed;
What joy 'twill be for us to greet
 Each saint whom here we loved.

Our Lord Himself we then shall see,
 Whose blood for us was shed;
With Him for ever we shall be,
 Made like our glorious Head.

We cannot linger o'er the tomb:
 The resurrection-day
To faith shines bright beyond its
  gloom,
 Christ's glory to display.

593 Saxby L.M.
(Hursley 260)

T.R. Matthews

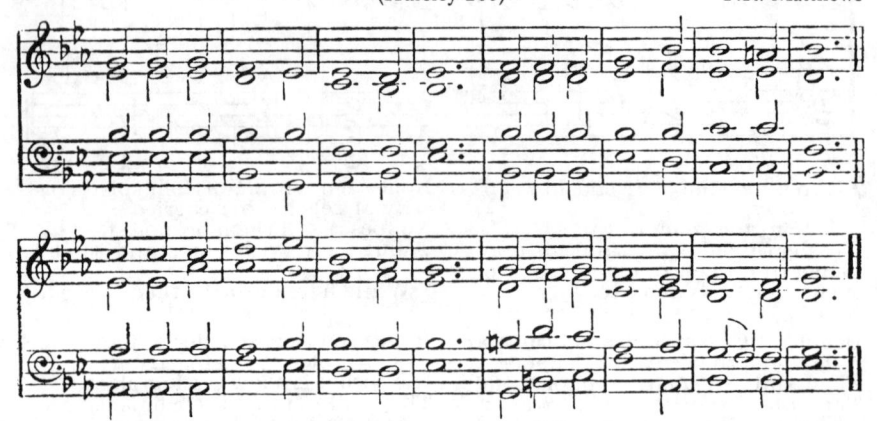

1. THE people of the Lord can say,
   'The friends we mourn are gone before,
   And soon we hope to see the day
   When we shall meet to part no more.'

2. How sweet, how blessèd, thus to see
   The last great foe bereft of power;
   For Jesus sets His people free,
   And gilds with light their dying hour.

3. Oh, may we close to Jesus cleave,
   Who cancelled all our debt of sin;
   May we the world for ever leave,
   And forward press the prize to win!

594 Endemia P.M.

OH, they've reached the sunny shore,
   Over there!
They will never suffer more,
All their pain and grief are o'er,
   Over there!

They will never shed a tear—
For the LORD Himself is near,
And to Him they're ever dear—

There they feel no chilling blast—
For their winter time is past,
And the summers always last—

There they need no lamp at night—
For the day is always bright,
And the Saviour is their light—

We shall form a happy band—
When we hear our LORD'S command,
And in glory round Him stand—
   Over there!

---

595   **Fingal C.M.**   J.S. Anderson
R.C. Chapman

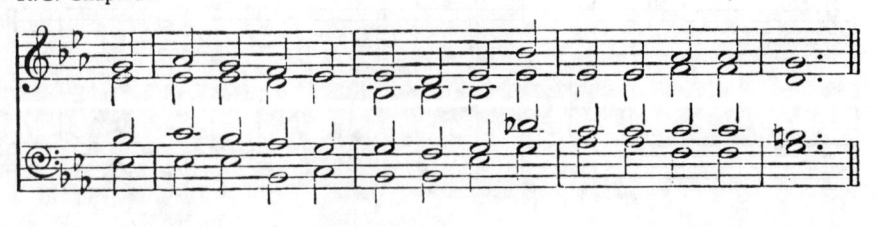

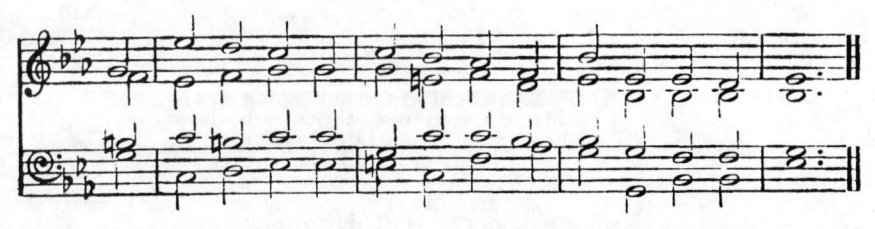

NO more we seek a resting-place
 Where thorns and briers grow:
No Eden now is found on earth,
 But sin and every woe.

Faith sees the Paradise of GOD,
 The better, heavenly land;
That holy city faith discerns,
 Not built by human hand.

O Earth! we only ask of thee,
 When saints in JESUS sleep,
A grave, which, till the Bridegroom come,
 Our brethren's dust shall keep.

Our Sun shall rise without a cloud,
 Shall rise and ne'er go down;
With GOD our FATHER we shall dwell,
 And know as we are known.

596   **Rhuddlan 8.7.8.7.8.7.**
Mary Peters   Welsh Trad. Melody

NOW the silent grave is keeping
   Many a seed in weakness sown;
But the saints in Thee, LORD, sleeping,
   Raised in power, shall share Thy
      throne:
         Resurrection!
LORD of glory! 'tis Thine own.

As we sing, our hearts grow lighter,
   We are children of the day;
Sorrow makes our hope the brighter,
   Faith regards not the delay:
      Sure the promise—
We shall meet Thee on the way.

All the sorrow we are tasting
Is but as the dream of night ;
To the day of CHRIST we're hasting,
Looking for it with delight :
　　Thou art coming—
This will *satisfy* our sight.

597　　　　　　　**Saxby L.M.**

T.R. Matthews

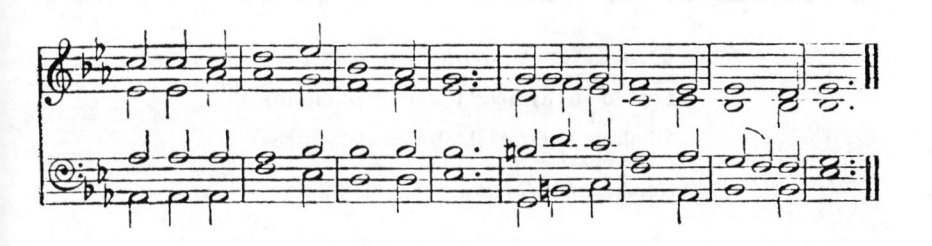

SOON, soon, our LORD, the living
　　One,
　In glory and in light shall come,
And from the grave shall burst a song,
　The death-sealed lips no more be
　　dumb :

'Where, where, O Death, is now thy
　　sting ?
　And where, O Grave, thy victory ?
Death hath been swallowed up in life,
　The grave in immortality.'

598 Artavia 10.10.10.6

S. Doudney

E.J. Hopkins

SLEEP on, belovèd, sleep, and take
   thy rest;
Lay down thy head upon thy Saviour's
   breast:
We love thee well; but JESUS loves
   thee best—

Good night! Good night! Good night!

Until the shadows from this earth
   are cast;
Until He gathers in His sheaves at
   last;
Until the twilight gloom is overpast—

Until the coming glory lights the
   skies;
Till those who sleep in JESUS shall
   arise,
And He shall come, but not in lowly
   guise—

Until, made beautiful by love divine,
Thou in the likeness of thy LORD
   shalt shine,
And He shall bring that golden crown
   of thine—

Only "Good-night," beloved — not "Farewell!"
A little while, and all His saints shall dwell
In hallowed union, indivisible—

Until we meet again before His throne,
Clothed in the spotless robe He gives His own;
Until we know even as we are known—
Good night! Good night! Good night!

599   Huddersfield S.M.

James Montgomery   Maurice Green

THE LORD Himself shall come,
  And shout a quickening word;
Thousands shall answer from the tomb—
  "For ever with the LORD."

Then, as we upward fly,
  That resurrection word
Shall be our shout of victory—
  "For ever with the LORD."

How shall I meet those eyes?
  Mine on Himself I cast,
And own myself the Saviour's prize—
  Mercy from first to last.

Knowing as I am known!
  How shall I love that word,
How oft repeat before the throne—
  "For ever with the LORD!"

That resurrection word,
  That shout of victory—
Once more—"For ever with the LORD:"
  Amen, so let it be!

600 Petherton P.M.

J.S.B Monsell

H. Bennett

SOON and "for ever"—such promise our trust,
Though ashes to ashes, and dust unto dust;
Soon and for ever our union shall be
Made perfect, our glorious Redeemer, in Thee!
Where the sins and the sorrows of life shall be o'er,
Its pains and its partings remembered no more,
Where life cannot fail, and where death cannot sever,
Christians with CHRIST shall be soon and for ever.

Soon and for ever the breaking of day
Shall chase all the night-clouds of sorrow away;
Soon and for ever we'll see as we're seen,
And learn the deep meaning of things that have been:
Where fightings without us and fears from within
Shall weary no more in the warfare of sin,
Where fears, and where tears, and where death shall be never,
Christians with CHRIST shall be soon and for ever.

Soon and for ever our work shall be done,
The warfare accomplished, the victory won;
Soon and for ever the soldier lay down
His sword for a harp, and his cross for a crown:
Then weep not in sorrow, despond not in fear,
A glorious to-morrow is brightening and near;
Where time cannot change, and where death cannot sever,
Christians with CHRIST shall be *soon and for ever!*

601 Love Divine 8.7.8.7

W.H. Bennet
(Newton Ferns 411)
J. Stainer

"GOD is Light"—the cross pro-
   claims it;
See the Just One on the tree,
By the sword of justice smitten
   That the guilty might go free.

"God is Love"—forth from His bosom
   His own SON in grace He gave,
Spared Him not, but e'en forsook Him
   When He died the lost to save.

"GOD is Light"—His SON was
   wounded;
"GOD is Love"—the Lamb has died;
Light and Love—behold the tokens
   In His piercèd hands and side!

Light, in all its glorious brightness,
   Love, in all its depth and height,
Call the sinner out of darkness
   To GOD'S day without a night.

And before His face for ever,
   In the cloudless realms above,
Sinners saved shall sing, exulting,
   "GOD is Light" and "GOD is Love."

602 Tell Me The Old, Old Story 7.6.7.6.D and Chorus

Katherine Hankey
W.H. Doane

Chorus

TELL me the Old, Old Story
　Of unseen things above,
Of JESUS and His glory,
　Of JESUS and His love;
Tell me the Story simply,
　As to a little child,
For I am weak and weary,
　And helpless and defiled:

　　Tell me the Old, Old Story
　　Of JESUS and His love.

Tell me the Story slowly,
　That I may take it in,
That wonderful redemption,
　GOD'S remedy for sin;
Tell me the Story often,
　For I forget so soon;
The "early dew" of morning
　Has passed away at noon—

Tell me the Story softly,
　With earnest tones and grave
Remember I'm the sinner
　Whom JESUS came to save;
Tell me that Story always,
　If you would really be,
In any time of trouble,
　A comforter to me—

Tell me the same Old Story
　When you have cause to fear
That this world's empty glory
　Is costing me too dear;
Yes, and when *that* world's glory
　Is dawning on my soul,
Tell me the Old, Old Story,
　"CHRIST JESUS makes thee whole"—

603 Tichfield 7.7.7.7 and Chorus

Hannah K. Burlingham   (Easter Hymn 918)   J. Richardson

GOD in mercy sent His SON
To a world by sin undone;
JESUS CHRIST was crucified—
'Twas for sinners JESUS died!

   Oh, the glory of the grace
   Shining in the Saviour's face,
   Telling sinners, from above,
   "GOD is Light," and "GOD is Love!"

Sin and death no more shall reign;
JESUS died and lives again!
In the glory's highest height
See Him, GOD'S supreme delight!—

All who in His name believe,
Everlasting life receive;
LORD of all is JESUS now,
Every knee to Him must bow—

   CHRIST the LORD will come again,
   He who suffered once will reign;
   Every tongue at last shall own,
   "Worthy is the LAMB" alone—

604 Ishmael S.M. and Chorus

A. Midlane   (Mercy's Portal 722)   C. Vincent

HOW vast, how full, how free,
The mercy of our GOD!
Proclaim the blessèd news around,
And spread it all abroad:

*The mercy of our GOD
Is vast, and full, and free,
Because the Saviour's blood was
shed
For us on Calvary!*

How *vast!* "Whoever will"
May drink at mercy's stream,
And know that faith in JESUS brings
Salvation e'en to him—

How *full!* It doth remove
The stain of every sin,
And leaves the soul as white and pure
As though no sin had been—

How *free!* It asks no price,
For GOD delights to give;
It only says—a simple thing—
'Believe in CHRIST, and live '–

605 Castle Rising C.M. and Chorus

John Newton   (Dawn 245)   F.A.J. Hervey

GOD'S grace has found the wondrous means
Which can effectual prove
To cleanse us from our countless sins,
And teach our hearts to love:

   In sovereign grace GOD gave His SON
   To bear away our sin,
   And in like grace His SPIRIT sent,
   Our stubborn hearts to win.

JESUS for sinners undertakes;
He dies that we may live;
His blood a full atonement makes,
And cries aloud, "Forgive"—

The HOLY SPIRIT doth reveal
The Saviour's work and worth;
Then the hard heart begins to feel
A new and heavenly birth—

Thus bought with blood, and born again,
Redeemed and saved by grace,
Rebels in GOD'S own house obtain
The sons' and daughters' place—

606
Isaac Watts

Jazer C.M.
(Binchester 620)

A.E. Tozer

1 How condescending and how kind
  Was God's eternal Son!
  Our misery reached His heavenly
      mind,
  And pity brought Him down.

2 When Justice, by our sins provoked,
    Drew forth its dreadful sword,
  He gave His soul up to the stroke
    Without a murmuring word.

3 He sank beneath our heavy woes,
    To raise us to His throne;
  There's ne'er a gift His hand bestows,
    But cost His heart a groan.

4 This was compassion like a God,
    That when the Saviour knew
  The price of pardon was His blood,
    His pity ne'er withdrew.

5 Now, though He reigns exalted high,
    His love is still as great;
  Well He remembers Calvary,
    Nor let my soul forget.

607 Rex Regum C.M. and Chorus
J. Stennett   (The Saviour's Call 656)   J. Stainer

TO us our God His love commends
When by our sins undone;
That He might spare His enemies
He would not spare His Son :

Far, far exceeding human love,
E'en in its tenderest ties,
Is God's own love that gave His Son
For us a Sacrifice.

His only Son, on whom He placed
His whole delight and love
Before He formed the earth below,
Or spread the heavens above—

He sent His well-belovèd Son
To veil His glorious face ;
To take a servant's form, and feel
The pains of human race—

Our sorrows and our sins to bear,
Our heavy load sustain;
Upon the tree of shame to die,
That we might life obtain—

608   St. Matthias L.M. and Chorus

Robert Sandeman   W.H. Monk

CHORUS

SEE *mercy*, mercy from on high,
Descend to rebels doomed to die;
'Tis mercy free, which knows no bound,
How sweet, how joyful is the sound!
*GOD'S mercy doth for aye endure;
Who taste it are from wrath secure.*

Soon as the reign of sin began,
The light of mercy dawned on man,
When GOD announced the blessèd news,
'The woman's Seed thy head shall bruise'—

Brightly it beamed on men forlorn,
When CHRIST, the holy Child, was born;
And brighter still in splendour shone,
When JESUS, dying, cried, ''Tis done!'—

It triumphed when from death He rose,
And broke the power of all His foes;
Then captive led captivity,
And took for us His seat on high—

609 Credo L.M. and Chorus

A. Midlane

J. Stainer

CHORUS *A little slower.*

1 THE perfect righteousness of GOD
  Is witnessed in the Saviour's blood;
  'Tis in the cross of CHRIST we trace
  His righteousness, yet wondrous grace:
    " A just GOD and a Saviour" He,
    Who pardons sin and sets us free.

2 GOD could not pass the sinner by;
  His sin demands that he must die;
  But in the cross of CHRIST we see
  How GOD can save, yet righteous be—

3 The sin alights on JESU's head;
  'Tis in His blood sin's debt is paid:
  Stern Justice can demand no more,
  And Mercy can dispense her store—

4 The sinner who believes is free,
  Can say, 'The Saviour died for me;'
  Can point to the atoning blood,
  And say, 'This made my peace with GOD'—

610 Redemption Ground L.M. and Chorus

H. Bonar
J. McGranahan

1. THE love of God is righteous love,
   Seen in CHRIST'S death upon the tree;
   Love that exacts the sinner's debt,
   Yet, in exacting, sets him free:

   Oh, wondrous love to sinners given,
   To save from hell, and bring to heaven!
   Oh, tell the virtues all abroad
   Of love divine—the love of GOD!

2. Love that condemns the sinner's sin,
   Yet, in condemning, pardon seals;
   That saves from righteous wrath, and yet,
   GOD'S righteousness to faith reveals—

3. 'Tis not the love without the blood;
   That were to me no love at all:
   It could not reach my sinful soul,
   Nor hush the fears that me appal—

4. I need the love, I need the blood,
   I need the grace, the cross, the grave,
   I need the resurrection power,
   A soul like mine to purge and save—

5. This is the love that stills my fears,
   That soothes each conscious pang within,
   That pacifies my troubled heart,
   And frees me from the power of sin—

611 To All Eternity The Same P.M.

D. Russell
J. McGranahan

GOD'S love is *everlasting* love,
  Time never was when it was not;
The stream is here—the Fount above;
Who taste it now, blest is their lot:
  His love's enduring as His name,
  To all eternity the same,
  To all eternity, to all eternity,
  To all eternity the same.

'Tis like an ocean without shore,
  Whose depth no line can ever sound;
And to its height no thought can soar,
  'Tis infinite—it knows no bound—

GOD loved and gave—still loves and gives,
  His love He strews along our path;
He gave His SON, who died and lives
  To save and keep from coming wrath—

In Him believing, life is ours,
  A life that everlasting is;
To spread His fame, wake, all our powers;
  The grace and all the glory His!—

612 Vox Dilecti C.M. and Chorus
W. Robertson   (Ladywell 545)   J.B. Dykes

1 THE Saviour comes! No outward pomp
   Bespeaks His presence nigh;
No earthly beauty shines in Him
   To draw the carnal eye:

    All beauty may we ever see
    In GOD'S beloved SON,
    The chiefest of ten thousand He,
    The only lovely One!

2 Rejected and despised of men,
   Behold a Man of woe!
Grief was His close companion here
   Through all His life below—

3 Yet all the griefs He felt were ours,
   Ours were the woes He bore;
Pangs, not His own, His spotless soul
   With bitter anguish tore—

4 We all, like sheep, had gone astray
   In ruin's fatal road;
On Him were our transgressions laid;
   He bore the mighty load!—

613 Who Is He? P.M.

B.R. Hanby

B.R. Hanby

WHO is He in yonder stall,
At whose feet the shepherds fall?

'Tis the LORD, oh, wondrous story!
'Tis the LORD, the King of glory!
At His feet now let us fall,
Own Him Saviour, LORD of all!

Who is He in deep distress,
Fasting in the wilderness?—

Who is He to whom they bring
All the sick and sorrowing?—

Who is He who stands and weeps
At the grave where Lazarus sleeps?—

Who is He the gathering throng
Greet with loud, triumphant song?—

Lo! at midnight, who is He
Prays in dark Gethsemane?—

Who is He on yonder tree
Dies in grief and agony?—

Who is He who from the grave
Comes to succour, help, and save?—

Who is He who from His throne
Rules through all the worlds alone?—

614
John Newton

Bodmin L.M.
(Arizona 834)

Alfred Scott-Gatty

1. No terrors of the law we hear
From Sinai's top with dread and fear,
But glorious beams of heavenly grace
Appear unveiled in JESU'S face.

2. He wears no terrors on His brow,
He speaks in love from heaven now;
It is the voice of His own blood
That calls the sinner nigh to GOD.

3. Hark! how from Calvary it sounds,
From the Redeemer's bleeding wounds;
Pardon and grace He freely gives:
The sinner looks to Him and lives.

4. O Saviour, let Thy power be felt,
And cause the stony heart to melt;
May trembling, doubting sinners flee,
To find eternal life in Thee!

615   **Swabia S.M.**
A. Midlane   (Cambridge 252)   German

WHAT can the sinner do?
   Where can the sinner fly?
Eternal wrath hangs o'er his head,
   And judgment lingers nigh.

For GOD must visit sin
   With His displeasure sore;
For He is holy, just, and true,
   And righteous evermore.

Yet JESUS died for sin—
   Upon the cross He died;
GOD'S righteousness was there displayed,
   And Justice satisfied.

This can the sinner do—
   Believe in CHRIST and live;
Fly to the shelter of His blood,
   Who only life can give.

The life He gives to those
   Who trust Him ne'er shall end,
Who make Him now by simple faith
   Their Saviour and their Friend!

616   **Ye Must Be Born Again P.M.**
W.T. Sleeper, Arr.   Geo. C. Stebbins

A RULER once came to JESUS by night,
To ask Him the way of salvation and light:
The Master made answer in words true and plain,
"Ye must be born again:"

"*Ye must be born again;*"
"*Ye must be born again;*"
I verily, verily, say unto thee,
"*Ye must be born again.*"

Ye children of men, attend to the word
So solemnly uttered by JESUS the LORD;
And let not this message to you be in vain,
"Ye must be born again"—

O ye who would enter this glorious rest,
And sing with the ransomed the song of the blest;
The life everlasting if ye would obtain,
"Ye must be born again"—

The Saviour who died upon Calvary's tree,
Now seated in glory, is pleading with thee;
To yield thyself to Him no longer refrain:
"Ye must be born again"—

617   Southport S.M.

A. Midlane   (Doncaster 279)   J. Davies

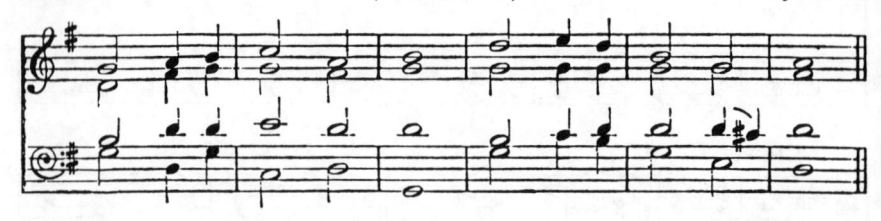

HOW solemn are the words,
And yet to faith how plain,
Which JESUS uttered while on earth—
"*Ye must be born again!*"

"*Ye must be born again!*"
For so hath GOD decreed:
No reformation will suffice—
'Tis *life* poor sinners need.

"*Ye must be born again!*"
And life *in CHRIST* must have:
In vain the soul elsewhere may go—
'Tis He *alone* can save.

"*Ye must be born again!*"
Or never enter heaven;
'Tis only blood-washed ones are there,
The ransomed and forgiven.

"*Ye must be born again!*"
Then look *to CHRIST* and live:
He is the "Life," and waits in heaven
Eternal life to give.

618   Redemption Ground L.M. and Chorus

Isaac Watts   J. McGranahan

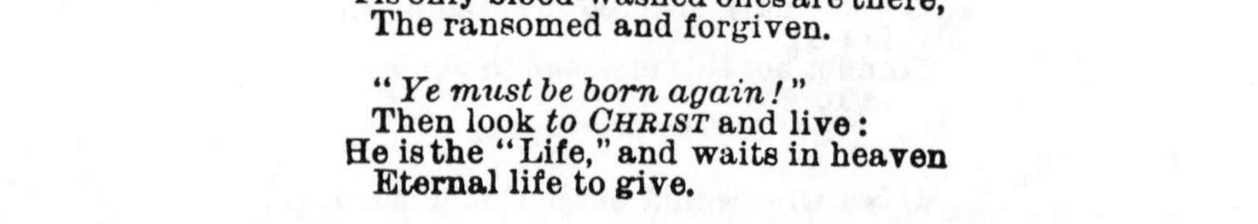

CHORUS

NOT to condemn the sons of men
Did CHRIST, the SON of GOD,
appear;
No weapons in His hands are seen,
No flaming sword nor thunder there:

"Not to condemn" are His own
words,
"No condemnation" we may say;
In our own stead He was condemned,
And thus He bore our sins away,

Such was the pity of our GOD,
He loved our fallen race so well,
He sent His SON to bear our load,
And thus to save our souls from hell—

Give ear, believe the Saviour's word,
Trust in His mighty name, and live !
A thousand joys His lips afford,
His hands a thousand blessings
give—.

619 Evensong 8.7.8.7.7.7

Thos. Kelly
J. Summers

1 WITHOUT blood is no remission;
  Thus the LORD proclaims from heaven:
 Blood must flow—on this condition,
  This alone, are sins forgiven;
 Yes, a victim must be slain,
 Else all hope of life is vain.

2 But the victim, who shall find it—
  Such an one as sinners need?
 To the altar who shall bind it?
  Who shall make the victim bleed?
 Such a victim as must die,
 All the world could not supply.

3 GOD Himself provides the Victim;
  JESUS is the Lamb of GOD;
 Heaven, and earth, and hell afflict Him,
  While He bears the sinner's load;
 JESU'S blood—His blood alone,
 Can for human guilt atone.

4 Joyful truth! He bore transgression
  In His body, on the cross!
 Through His blood there's full remission
  For the vilest, e'en for us:
 JESUS for the sinner bleeds,
 Nothing more the sinner needs.

620 Binchester C.M.
(Crediton 388)

E.M. Hall
W. Croft

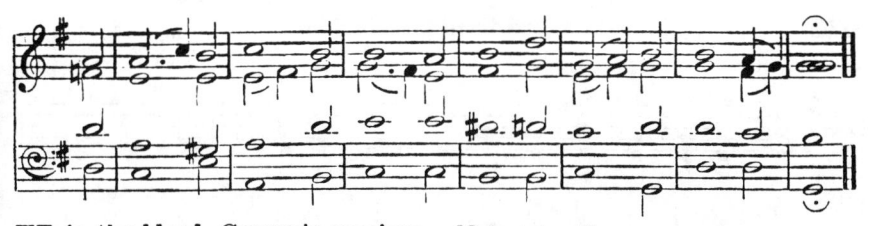

IT is the blood, CHRIST'S precious
  blood,
Which has atonement made;
It is His blood which once for all
Our ransom price has paid.

It was the blood, the mark of blood,
  That Israel's houses bore;
And when that mark by GOD was seen,
  His angel passed the door.

Not water then, nor water now,
  Has ever saved a soul;
Not Jewish rites, but JESU'S stripes,
  Can make the wounded whole.

'I see the blood, I see the blood,'
  A voice from heaven cries;
The soul that owns this token true,
  And trusts it, never dies.

For He who suffered "once for all"
  "Eternal life" doth give;
Because He died we never die,
Because He lives we live.

621 Wimborne 8.7.8.7
Thos. Kelly   (Love Divine 41)   J. Whitaker

'STRICKEN, smitten and afflicted,'
  See Him dying on the tree!
'Tis the CHRIST, by man rejected;
  Yes, my soul, 'tis He! 'tis He!

Many hands were raised to wound
    Him,
  None would interpose to save;
But the awful stroke that bowed Him
  Was the stroke that Justice gave.

Mark the Sacrifice appointed!
  See *Who* bears the awful load!
'Tis the Word, the LORD'S Anointed,
  SON of man, and SON of GOD!

Here we have a firm foundation;
  Here the refuge of the lost:
CHRIST, the rock of our salvation,
  His the name in which we boast.

Lamb of GOD, for sinners wounded!
  Sacrifice to cancel guilt!
None shall ever be confounded
  Who on Thee their hopes have built.

622   Rhuddlan 8.7.8.7.8.7.
Jonathan Evans   Welsh Trad. Melody

HARK! the voice of love and mercy
   Sounds aloud from Calvary!
See! it rends the rocks asunder,
   Shakes the earth and veils the sky!
      "It is finished!"
Hear the dying Saviour cry.

"It is finished!" Oh, what pleasure
   Do these precious words afford!
Heavenly blessings without measure
   Flow to us from CHRIST the LORD:
      "It is finished!"
His own dying words record.

Finished all the types and shadows
   Of the ceremonial law:
Finished all that GOD had promised;
   Death and hell no more shall awe!
      "It is finished!"
Hence we lasting comfort draw.

623 Te Laudant Omnia 7.7.7.7 and Chorus

H. Bonar J.F. Swift

CHRIST has done the mighty work;
  Nothing left for us to do
But to enter on His toil,
  Enter on His triumph too:

His own self upon the tree
Bore our sins to set us free.

His the pardon, ours the sin—
  Great the sin, the pardon great;
His the good and ours the ill,
  His the love and ours the hate—

His the labour, ours the rest,
  His the death and ours the life;
Ours the fruits of victory,
  His the agony and strife—

He has sowed the precious seed,
  Nothing left for us unsown;
Ours it is to reap the fields,
  Make the harvest joy our own—

624. Ellacombe C.M. and Chorus
(Ladywell 545)

German

1 How sweet the gospel trumpet sounds!
  Its notes are grace and love;
  Its echo through the world resounds
  From God's high throne above:

  *It is the sound, the joyful sound
  Of mercy rich and free;
  Pardon it offers, peace proclaims,
  Alone through Calvary.*

2 It tells the weary soul of rest,
  The poor of heavenly wealth,
  Of joy to heal the mourning breast;
  It brings the sin-sick health—

3 It speaks of boundless grace, by which
  The vilest are forgiven,
  To sinners it proclaims a rich
  Inheritance in heaven—

625
C. Cole

Truro L.M.
(Llef 306)

C. Burney

1 HARK, how the gospel trumpet sounds!
  The grace of GOD therein abounds—
  To sinners lost, grace full and free,
  And if free grace, why not for *thee?*

2 The Saviour died, and by His blood
  Brings rebel sinners nigh to GOD;
  He died to set the captive free,
  And why, dear soul, why not for *thee?*

3 The blood of CHRIST alone is found
  To cleanse and heal the sinner's wound;
  The streams thereof are full and free,
  And why, dear soul, why not for *thee?*

4 'Twas sinners JESUS came to bless—
  To clothe them in GOD's righteousness,
  That best of robes, so bright and free,
  And why, dear soul, why not for *thee?*

5 Eternal life by CHRIST is *given,*
  That lost ones might be raised to heaven:
  Accept His grace, so rich and free,
  And know, dear soul, 'tis ALL for *thee!*

626 Better World 8.3.8.3.8.8.8.3

A. Midlane
J. Hayhurst

1 Oh, what a glorious truth is this—
    Jesus died!
Wide open is the path to bliss—
    Jesus died!
God loved the world, His Son He gave,
That all who do in Him believe
Should full and gracious pardon
    have— Jesus died!

2 To save our souls from death and
    hell— Jesus died!
Such love amazing who can tell?—
    Jesus died!
Yes, He for ruined men was slain
That we through Him might life
    obtain,
And everlasting glory gain—
    Jesus died!

3 Soon heaven shall raise the happy
    song— Jesus died!
Which endless ages shall prolong—
    Jesus died!
By virtue of His precious blood,
Believers are brought nigh to God;
Oh, spread the glorious news abroad—
    Jesus died!

627   **Oh, Precious Words! C.M. and Chorus**

F. J. Crosby   Ira D. Sankey

OH, precious words that JESUS said—
  'The soul that comes to Me,
I will in no wise cast him out,
  Whoever he may be;'
    'Whoever he may be,
    Whoever he may be;
  I will in no wise cast him out,
    Whoever he may be.'

Oh, precious words that JESUS said—
  'Behold, I am the Door,
And all that enter in by Me
  Have life for evermore;'
    'Have life for evermore,
    Have life for evermore;
  And all that enter in by Me
    Have life for evermore.'

Oh, precious words that JESUS said—
  'Come, weary souls oppressed,
Come, take My yoke and learn of Me,
  And I will give you rest;'
    'And I will give you rest,
    And I will give you rest;
  Come, take My yoke and learn of Me,
    And I will give you rest.'

Oh, precious words that JESUS said—
  'The world I overcame;
And they who follow where I lead
  Shall conquer in My name;'
    'Shall conquer in My name,
    Shall conquer in My name;
  And they who follow where I lead
    Shall conquer in My name.'

628 Whosoever Will P.M.

P.P. Bliss

P.P. Bliss

Joyfully.

CHORUS

1. "WHOSOEVER heareth," shout, shout the sound,
Send the blessèd tidings all the world around;
Spread the joyful news wherever man is found:
"Whosoever will may come:'

*Whosoever will, whosoever will,
Send the proclamation over vale and hill;
'Tis a loving Saviour calls the wanderer home:
"Whosoever will may come."*

2. Whosoever cometh need not delay;
Now the door is open, enter while you may;
JESUS is the true, the only living way,
"Whosoever will may come."

3. "Whosoever will," the promise is secure;
"Whosoever will," for ever shall endure;
"Whosoever will," 'tis life for evermore;
"Whosoever will may come"—

629   Castle Rising C.M.D.
A. Midlane   (Rex Regum 607)   F.A.J. Hervey

SALVATION—what a precious word!
Salvation—what a theme!
It casts across the sinner's path
A radiant, heavenly beam:
However cheerless, dark and sad
The path before he trod,
Salvation comes with blissful ray
And lights the soul to GOD.

Salvation is the precious boon
Of love divine to man;
Salvation is the grand result
Of GOD's redemption plan:
It finds the sinner far from GOD,
And brings him very nigh;
It finds him full of sin and shame
And makes him full of joy.

Salvation is the song on earth
Of all who love the LORD;
Salvation is the theme of heaven,
Its fullest, sweetest chord:
The Saviour bids each sinner come
And join the glorious train,
Trust in His own most precious blood,
And life and joy obtain.

630 Moment By Moment (Mighty To Save) P.M.

A. Midlane

May Whittle Moody

1. OH, what a Saviour is JESUS the LORD!
   Well may His name by all saints be adored;
   For He redeems them from hell by His blood,
   Saves them for ever, and brings them to GOD:

   CHORUS:
   JESUS the Saviour is "mighty to save,"
   JESUS hath triumphed o'er death and the grave!

2. Now in the glory He waits to impart
   Peace to the conscience and joy to the heart;
   Waits to be gracious, to pardon and heal
   All who their sin and their wretchedness feel—

3. Come, then, to JESUS, no longer delay,
   Come to the Saviour, come *now* while you may;
   So shall your peace be eternally sure,
   So shall your happiness ever endure—

631 Pembroke 8.8.6.D

R.L. Johnston J. Foster

1. LET all who know the joyful sound
   With gladness spread the tidings round,
     And tell that GOD is Love;
   That GOD so loved the world, He gave
   His own dear SON the world to save—
     GOD'S message from above;

2. That all who in the SON believe
   Shall never perish, but receive
     Life, endless and divine;
   No condemnation e'er shall know;
   From death to life they pass below,
     And then in glory shine.

3. The SPIRIT and the Bride say, "Come!"
   Let him that heareth, too, say, "Come!"
     Whoever thirsts may come;
   Water of life is freely given,
   Till CHRIST the LORD descends from heaven—
     Come then, oh, quickly come!

632 Redemption 9.8.9.8 and Chorus

Goodfellow

Peter Bilhorn

CHORUS

1. OH, tell through the breadth of creation
That JESUS, the Saviour, has come
To secure an eternal salvation,
A rest, and a heavenly home!

 'The Saviour has come and He calls thee:'
 This message was given to one
 Who quickly arose and went to Him:
 Fall thou at His feet, as undone!

2. Yea, tell all without an exception,
 'Whoever believeth shall live;'
Though guilt may have stained every action,
"The blood of the Lamb" cries "Forgive!"—

Receive this free mercy—receive it;
 No money, no price, GOD demands;
Yea, GOD in rich grace loves to give it;
 Accept, then, the gift at His hands—

Oh, taste of that precious salvation,
 Which JESUS has bought with His blood;
Then yield Him thy heart's adoration,
 And own Him thy Saviour and GOD!—

633 His Saving Name C.M. and Chorus

D. Russell
F. A. Fillmore

1 WE tell abroad a Saviour's love,
    GOD's wondrous mystery:
  In love He came from heaven above,
    To die on Calvary:

  *We now proclaim . . . His saving
      name: . . .
  On CHRIST alone . . . depend, . . .
  And you shall know, . . . e'en here
      below, . . .
  A life that ne'er . . . . shall end . . . .*

2 He saw us lost and doomed to die
    And, when all hope had fled,
  He came the law to magnify
    By dying in our stead—

3 Our sins had filled a bitter cup
    Which we could never drain;
  In love the Saviour drank it up.
  He died! He lives again!—

4 Glad tidings now to all we bring,
    'Tis GOD's good news we tell;
  Come, trust the Saviour while we sing,
    He saves from death and hell—

634   Millennium 6.6.6.6.8.8

C. Wesley

(Gopsal 10)

1 LET earth and heaven agree,
    Let men with angels join
To praise salvation free,
    The work of grace divine;
To bless the great, atoning Lamb,
And all His wondrous love proclaim.

2 JESUS! life-giving sound,
    The joy of earth and heaven;
No other help is found,
    No other name is given
In which the sons of men can boast,
But His who seeks and saves the lost.

3 That name the sinner hears,
    And is from guilt set free;
'Tis music in his ears,
    'Tis life and victory;
His heart o'erflows with sacred joy,
And songs of praise his lips employ.

635 Wondrous Love C.M. and Chorus
Martha M. Stockton (Castle Rising 525) W.G. Fischer

1 GOD loved the world of sinners lost
   And ruined by the Fall;
Salvation full, at highest cost,
   Is published free to all:

*Oh, 'twas love, 'twas wondrous love,
   The love of GOD to me!
It brought my Saviour from above,
   To die on Calvary.*

2 E'en now by faith I claim Him mine,
   The risen SON of GOD;
Redemption by His death I find,
   And cleansing through His blood—

3 Love brings the glorious fulness in,
   And to His saints makes known
The blessèd rest from inbred sin,
   Through faith in CHRIST alone—

4 Believing souls, rejoicing go!
   There shall to you be given
A glorious foretaste, here below,
   Of endless life in heaven—

5 Of victory now o'er Satan's power
   Let all the ransomed sing,
And triumph in the dying hour
   Through CHRIST the LORD and King—

636 The Ninety and Nine P.M.

Elizabeth C. Clephane — Ira D. Sankey

THERE were ninety and nine that
   safely lay
In the shelter of the fold;
But one was out on the hills away,
   Far off from the gates of gold;
Away on the mountains wild and bare,
Away from the tender Shepherd's
care.

'Lord, Thou hast here Thy ninety
   and nine,
   Are they not enough for Thee?'
But the Shepherd made answer 'This
   of Mine
   Has wandered away from Me;
And although the road be rough and
   steep,
I go to the desert to find My sheep.'

But none of the ransomed ever knew
   How deep were the waters crossed;
   Nor how dark was the night that the
      Lord passed through,
   Ere He found His sheep that was
      lost;
Out in the desert He heard its cry,
Sick, and helpless, and ready to die.

'Lord, whence are those blood-drops
   all the way,
   That mark out the mountain's
      track?'
'They were shed for one who had
      gone astray
   Ere the Shepherd could bring him
      back.'
'Lord, whence are Thy hands so rent
   and torn?'
'They were pierced to-night by many
   a thorn.'

But all through the mountains, thun-
   der riven,
   And up from the rocky steep,
   There arose a cry to the gates of
      heaven,
   'Rejoice! I have found My sheep!'
And the angels echoed around the
   throne,
'Rejoice, for the Lord brings back
   His own!'

637 Joy! Joy! Joy! P.M.

W.B. Bradbury

JOY! joy! joy! there is joy in
   heaven with the angels,
  Joy! joy! joy! for the prodigal's
   return;
He has come, he has come
  To his FATHER'S house at last;
He was lost, he is found,
  And the night of gloom is past:
Blessèd hour of joy and communion
   sweet,
For his heart is full and his love
   complete;
His FATHER sees him and hastes to
   meet,
  And bids him welcome home:

    Joy! joy! joy! there is joy in
     heaven with the angels;
    Joy! joy! joy! for the prodigal's
     return.

Joy! joy! joy! in the courts of heaven
   resounding,
  Joy! joy! joy! o'er the prodigal's
   return;
Hark, the song! hark, the song!
  'Tis a joyful, joyful strain,
Welcome home, welcome home
  To thy FATHER'S house again:
While his eye is dim with the falling
   tears
Of repentant grief, over wasted years,
The pardoning voice of his FATHER
   cheers,
  And bids him welcome home—

Joy! joy! joy! in the radiant fields of
   glory,
  Joy! joy! joy! when a wand'ring
   soul returns;
Let us haste, let us haste,
  While the morning sun is bright;
JESUS calls, JESUS calls
  To a land of love and light:
We will journey on till our pilgrim
   feet
Shall be found at last in the golden
   street;
Our glorious Saviour with smile will
   greet,
  And bid us welcome home—

638   **Speed Away! 12.12.12.12 and Chorus**

H. Wreford   I.B. Woodbury (arr.)

SPREAD the news! spread the news!
   Lift the banner on high!
Tell the story of JESUS; His coming is nigh!
Let the gospel of glory sound clearly to-day,
That the sinner may come, and that CHRIST is the way:

   Spread the news! spread the news!
     Lift the banner on high!
   Speed away! speed away! speed away!

Spread the news! spread the news!
that the sinner may hear;
Let the music of heaven swell loudly
and clear:
We stand 'neath the banner of JESUS
unfurled,
And the gospel of JESUS we give to
the world—

Spread the news! spread the news!
Never tire while 'tis day,
While the voice from the glory says,
"I am the way;"
We shall rest! we shall rest! in the
home of His love,
In the peace of His presence, in
mansions above—

639 The Harvest Is Passing 12.11.12.11 and Chorus

P.P. Bliss

OH, wonder surpassing! that
CHRIST as the Victim,
Should suffer from GOD all the judgment of sin;
Oh, mercy amazing! that GOD should
afflict Him,
That He for lost sinners salvation
might win:
*The harvest is passing, the summer
will end,
The harvest is passing, the summer
will end!*

Now raised from the dead and in
glory ascended,
He sits on the throne who for
sinners was slain,
But soon shall return, by His angels
attended,
To bind all His foes, and in righteousness reign—

"Behold, ye despisers, and wonder,
and perish"—
How solemn the sentence pronounced by the LORD!
The portion of all who their sinfulness cherish,
Despising the Saviour, His work
and His word—

640 Trumpet Call P.M.

1. THE blast of the trumpet, so loud and so shrill,
Will shortly re-echo o'er mountain and hill:
   *When the mighty, mighty, mighty trump sounds,
   Come, come away!
   Oh, may we be ready to hail that glad day!*

2. The earth and the waters will yield up the dead,
And the righteous with joy will awake from their bed—

3. The chorus of angels will burst from the skies,
And blend with the shouts of the saints as they rise—

4. Acknowledged by JESUS, confessed as His own,
Transported to glory, to sit on His throne—

5. Oh, land of the holy, the happy, the free,
In JESUS thy portals are open to me!—

641   **The Gospel Of Thy Grace P.M.**

Arthur T. Pierson

J. McGranahan

1. THE gospel of Thy grace my stubborn heart has won;
For GOD so loved the world He gave His only SON,
That 'Whosoever will believe, shall everlasting life receive!'

2. The serpent "lifted up" could life and healing give,
So JESUS on the cross bids me to look and live:
For 'Whosoever will believe, shall everlasting life receive!'

3. 'The soul that sinneth dies;' my awful doom I heard;
I was for ever lost, but for Thy gracious word,
That 'Whosoever will believe, shall everlasting life receive!'

4. "Not to condemn the world" the "Man of sorrows" came,
But that the world might have salvation through His name:
For 'Whosoever will believe, shall everlasting life receive!'

642 Grace Divine 8.7.8.7 and Chorus

Douglas Russell G.F. Knowles

GRACE, our highest thought transcending,
　Dwells in CHRIST at GOD's right hand,
"Grace and truth" in Him are blending,
　And by faith, in grace we stand :
　　'Tis full and free !
　　'Tis full and free !
　　Grace divine, so full and free !
　　Sing, oh, sing of grace abounding;
　　Grace shall reign eternally.

Grace divine is ever flowing
　Like a river, full and free;
Wondrous grace, no change e'er knowing,
　Reaches us through Calvary—

Grace o'er sin is now abounding,
　And will reign for evermore;
Ransomed saints, the Throne surrounding,
　Forth their songs of praise will pour—

Grace is yet salvation bringing,
　"Without money"—all is free!
Oh, receive it while we're singing;
　"Without price" it comes to thee—

643
Hannah K. Burlingham

Regent Square 8.7.8.7.8.7
(Rhuddlan 147)

H. Smart

1. ON His FATHER'S throne is seated
   CHRIST the LORD, the Living One;
   All His toil on earth completed,
   All His work for sinners done:
       In the glory
   See Him, GOD's eternal SON!

2. Every knee shall bow before Him,
   Every tongue confess His name;
   Ransomed myriads now adore Him
   Who endured the sinner's shame:
       From the glory
   GOD doth now His worth proclaim!

3. Man the cross to Him awarded;
   Man the Saviour crucified;
   Sin's full judgment stands recorded—
   Thus was Justice satisfied:
       To the glory
   GOD exalted Him who died.

644 Stockton P.M.

William Luff G.F. Knowles

IF I could find the *oldest* heart,
  That longest has withstood
The wooings of almighty love,
  My Saviour could and would
Forgive the awful life of sin,
And take the aged offender in—
  My Saviour could and would.

If I could find the *hardest* heart,
  Receiving only good
And yet returning only ill,
  My Saviour could and would,
With one sweet glance of patient love,
The hardened rebel's spirit move—
  My Saviour could and would.

If I could find the *coldest* heart,
  And in its coldest mood,
A stone beneath the brooding wings,
  My Saviour could and would
Put warmth into the icy thing,
And give it life and give it wing—
  My Saviour could and would.

If dark despair had sealed the heart,
  And like a sentry stood,
And, cried 'Life is impossible!'
  My Saviour could and would—
He *could* give life, for He has died;
He *would* give life, though all denied—
  My Saviour could and would.

My heart is charmed to sing this song,
  And if perchance it should
Prove music to a hopeless one,
  My Saviour could and would
That hopeless one this hour forgive,
If but God's message he believe—
  My Saviour could and would.

645   Rutherford 7.6.7.6.D

Lucy A. Bennett   C. D'Urhan

OH, teach me what it meaneth—
  That cross uplifted high
With Thee, the "Man of sorrows,
  Condemned to bleed and die:
Oh, teach me what it cost Thee
  To make a sinner whole;
And teach me, Saviour, teach me
  The value of the soul.

Oh, teach me what it meaneth—
  That sacred crimson tide,
The blood and water flowing
  From Thine own wounded side:
Teach me that if none other
  Had sinned but I alone,
Yet still Thy blood, LORD JESUS,
  Thine only, could atone.

Oh, teach me what it meaneth—
  Thy love beyond compare,
The love that reacheth deeper
  Than depths of self-despair:
Yea, teach me till there gloweth
  In this cold heart of mine
Some faint, yet true reflection
  Of that pure love of Thine!

O Infinite Redeemer,
  I bring no other plea;
Because Thou dost invite me,
  I cast myself on Thee!
Because Thou dost accept me,
  I love Thee and adore!
Because *Thy* love constraineth,
  I'll praise Thee evermore!

646
Lancashire 7.6.7.6.D

Douglas Russell H. Smart

1. TELL out, tell out glad tidings
   In spoken word and song;
 The day of grace is passing,
   Its close will come ere long:
 The Master quickly cometh
   To call away His own;
 Go forth, while yet He tarries,
   And make the gospel known.

2. Lift up the voice of warning,
   For thousands sleep in sin;
 Sound out GOD's invitation
   Above earth's deafening din:
 Proclaim a full salvation
   To those afar from GOD,
 To guilty ones free pardon
   Through JESU's precious blood.

3. Go, speak of life eternal—
   GOD's love-gift in His SON—
 That whoso will may take it,
   For He refuseth none:
 In Him we are accepted,
   In Him are we complete;
 To join with saints in glory
   His blood doth make us meet.

647
John Lyth

Auber 8.3.8.3.8.8.8.3
(Better World 626)

From Weber

THERE is a better world we know,
　　Oh, so bright!
Where never enter sin and woe,
　　Oh, so bright!
Sweet music fills the balmy air,
And angels bright and saints are there,
And harps of gold and mansions fair.
　　Oh, so bright!

No clouds e'er pass along its sky,
　　Happy land!
No tear-drop glistens in the eye,
　　Happy land!
They drink the living streams of grace,
And gaze upon the Saviour's face,
Whose brightness fills the holy place,
　　Happy land!

But though we're sinners, every one,
　　Jesus died!
And though our crown of peace is
　gone,　　Jesus died!
We may be cleansed from every stain,
And peace with God by faith obtain,
And in that land of pleasure reign,
　　Jesus died!

648 St. Flavian C.M.
(Belgrave 458)

Day's Psalter 1562

1 'TIS "he that hath the SON hath
  life,"
 Though dead in sin before,
 And nothing of the wrath of GOD
  Can ever reach him more.

2 'Tis "he that hath the SON hath life,"
 And fears he need have none;
 For into union he is brought
  With GOD's belovèd SON.

3 'Tis "he that hath the SON hath life,"
 And light and joy are his,
 For in the FATHER'S house itself
  His place, his portion is.

4 And if his blessedness is great,
 Who truly "hath the SON,"
 Most surely he who hath Him not
  Is wretched and undone!

649 St. Gertrude 11.11.11.11. and Chorus

Douglas Russell

Arthur Sullivan

CHRIST a full salvation bringeth to the lost,
He by His oblation paid the mighty cost;
Sinai's awful thunder hushed for aye has been,
Now we gaze in wonder: Love alone is seen:
    Hearts attuned and voices, praises let us sing,
    While all heaven rejoices, and its anthems ring.

He who once descended to a death of shame,
Rose and then ascended—Glory to His name!
Now to Him united, and to GOD made nigh,
On we go, delighted, to our home on high—

Home to glory bringing many, many sons,
All triumphant, singing as His ransomed ones,
JESUS keepeth ever all the FATHER gave,
Nought from Him shall sever those He lives to save—

Soon will break the morning—JESUS comes again!
Many crowns adorning, He shall come to reign;
Saints of every nation, mounting up with joy,
Shall with adoration heart and tongue employ—

650
Tweedy

Fingal C.M.
(Abney 2)

J.S. Anderson

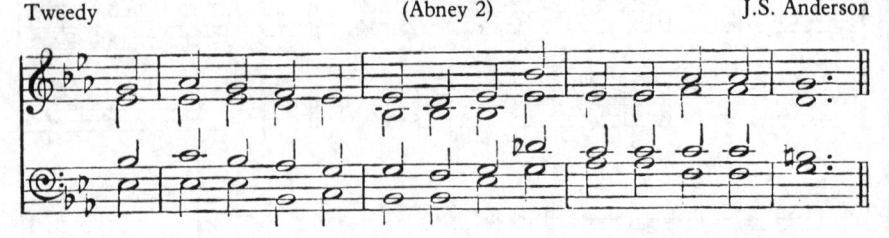

LIKE as the days of Noah were,
 So shall they also be
When CHRIST, the Son of man, shall
 come,
 Whom every eye shall see.

Before the flood, they ate, they drank,
 And married, day by day,
And knew not till the flood was come
 That swept them all away.

So now men live, and buy, and sell,
 And "Peace and safety" cry,
Not knowing, in their unbelief,
 That CHRIST the LORD is nigh.

The ark, the ark, and it alone
 Gave safety in the flood;
So JESUS, and no other name,
 Saves sinners by His blood!

All in the ark were very safe,
 For GOD had shut them in;
So all CHRIST'S sheep are in His hand,
 And none can pluck from Him.

651 Better World 8.3.8.3.8.8.8.3

J. Hoskins
J. Hayhurst

1 BEHOLD, behold the Lamb of GOD,
    On the cross!
For us He shed His precious blood,
    On the cross!
Oh, hear that sad, expiring cry,
"Eli, lama sabachthani;"
Draw near and see the Saviour die,
    On the cross!

2 See, see His arms extended wide—
Behold His bleeding hands and side—
The sun withholds its rays of light,
The heavens are clothed in shades of night,
While JESUS wins the glorious fight—

3 Behold the Saviour lifted up—
He drinks for us the bitter cup—
The rocks do rend, the mountains quake,
While JESUS suffers for our sake,
While He doth full atonement make—

4 And now the mighty deed is done—
The battle's fought, the victory's won—
To heaven He turns His wearied eyes,
"'Tis finished!" now the Conqueror cries,
Then bows His sacred head, and dies,
    On the cross!

652 The Light Of The World P.M.

P.P. Bliss
P.P. Bliss

CHORUS.

THE whole world was lost in the darkness of sin,
The Light of the world is JESUS!
Like sunshine at noonday His glory shone in,
The Light of the world is JESUS!

> Come to the Light! 'tis shining for thee!
> Sweetly the Light has dawned upon me;
> Once I was blind, but now I can see:
> The Light of the world is JESUS!

No darkness have we who in JESUS abide,
The Light of the world is JESUS!
We walk in the light when we follow our Guide,
The Light of the world is JESUS!—

Ye dwellers in darkness, with sin-
blinded eyes,
The Light of the world is JESUS!
Go wash at His bidding, and light
will arise,
The Light of the world is JESUS!—

No need of the sunlight in heaven,
we're told,
The Light of that world is JESUS!
The Lamb is the Light in the city of
gold,
The Light of that world is JESUS!—

653 Even Thee P.M.

W.B. Bradbury

YES, dear soul, a voice from heaven
Speaks a pardon full and free;
Come, and thou shalt be forgiven;
Boundless mercy flows for thee:
Even thee, even thee,
Boundless mercy flows for thee!

See the healing fountain springing
From the Saviour on the tree,
Pardon, peace, and cleansing bring-
ing;
Lost one, loved one, 'tis for thee—

Every sin shall be forgiven,
Thou, through grace, a child shalt
be,
Child of GOD, and heir of heaven,
With a mansion e'en for thee—

There in love for ever dwelling,
JESUS all thy joy shall be,
And thy song shall e'er be telling
All His mercy did for thee—

654   Salvation 7.6.7.6.D

A. Midlane

W.E. Vine

SALVATION! oh, salvation!
  Endearing, precious sound!
Shout, shout the word "*Salvation*"
  To earth's remotest bound:
Salvation for the guilty,
  Salvation for the lost,
Salvation for the wretched,
  The sad and sorrow-tossed.

Salvation for the aged,
  Salvation for the young,
Salvation e'en for children,
  Proclaim with joyful tongue:
Salvation for the wealthy,
  Salvation for the poor,
Salvation for the lowly—
  E'en life for evermore.

Salvation without money,
  Salvation without price,
Salvation without labour—
  Believing doth suffice;
Salvation now—this moment!
  Then why, oh, why delay?
You may not see to-morrow;
  Now is salvation's day!

655 Adeste Fideles 11.11.11.11
(St. Luke 330)

J. Reading

1 AFAR off from God, in the broad,
    downward road
  The soul may have wandered, 'neath
    sin's heavy load;
  Yet still there's a message for Gentile
    and Jew,
  And this is its purport—*There's a
    Saviour for you!*

  Oh, why quench your thirst at the
    rivers of earth,
  By drinking from streams of unsanc-
    tified mirth?
  Oh, why not the world and its
    pleasures eschew,
  And heed the glad tidings—*There's a
    Saviour for you?*

2 Though burdened with sin, and
    though laden with care,
  E'en now there is hope, and none need
    despair;
  For Jesus has met all the penalty
    due,
  And now in the glory—*There's a
    Saviour for you!*

  A Saviour for you! Oh, how precious
    the word,
  That God hath declared Him both
    Saviour and Lord!
  All done is the work God assigned
    Him to do,
  And now rest assured—*There's a
    Saviour for you!*

3 But soon will this day of God's favour
      be o'er,
    When He will for ever have shut to
      the door;
    How bitterly, then, all the past you'll
      review,
    When no longer you hear—*There's a
      Saviour for you!*

656   The Saviour's Call C.M.D.
(Ladywell 545)   Old Melody

O FRIENDS and fellow-sinners, Come,
  Obey the Saviour's call!
Unto His outstretched arms of love
  He now invites you all:
Oh, haste away, nor longer stay
  Where sin and darkness reign,
But flee to Him who died to save,
  And life and peace obtain.

Come, anxious sinner, here's a balm
  For every troubled mind;
In JESU'S full salvation you
  A perfect rest shall find;
For heaviest grief a full relief
  In the atoning blood,   [nigh,
Which brings the trembling sinner
  And seals his peace with GOD.

Come, weary sinner, who in vain
  From day to day hast striven,
By sighs, and tears, and labouring steps,
  To climb the ascent to heaven;
The work is done, the victory's won,
  If Thou wilt but receive
The blessing JESUS doth bestow
  On all who will believe.

Come, careless sinner, sport no more
  Upon the brink of hell!
For who 'midst everlasting fires
  Would be content to dwell?
Forsake thy way, and only stay
  Thy soul on JESU'S love—
A free forgiveness now receive,
  And mercy from above.

657   **Call The Weary Home P.M.**

S. Trevor Francis   G.F. Knowles

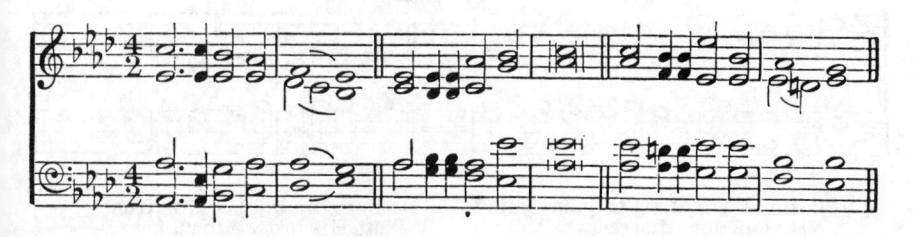

CHORUS

CALL the weary home,
   Home to the rest above,
Home to a gracious Saviour,
Home to His heart of love!

   Call the weary home,
      Home to the rest above,
   Home to a gracious Saviour,
   Home to His heart of love;
   Call the weary home!

Call the weary home!
   JESUS, the Ransom, died;
Hark! 'tis the SPIRIT'S whisper,
   'Come to His bleeding side'—

Call the weary home!
   Sin's captives may be free;
The precious blood of JESUS
   Shall give them liberty—

Call the weary home!
   The night of time sets in;
The world is full of sorrow,
   And hearts are full of sin—

Call the weary home!
   Now they may be forgiven,
Robed in unsullied glory,
   Fit for the light of heaven—

658 Stephanos 8.5.8.3.

J.M. Neale   H.W. Baker

'ART thou weary? art thou languid?
  Art thou sore distrest?
'Come to Me,' saith One; 'and coming,
  Be at rest.'

'Hath He marks to lead me to Him,
  If He be my Guide?'
In His feet and hands are wound-
  prints,
    And His side.

'Is there diadem as Monarch
  That His brow adorns?'
Yea, a crown in very surety,
  But of thorns!

'If I ask Him to receive me,
  Will He say me nay?'
Not till earth, and not till heaven
  Pass away.

'Finding, following, heeding, trust-
    ing,
  Is He sure to bless?'
Saints, Apostles, Prophets, Martyrs,
    Answer—Yes!

659 There is life for a look. P.M.

A.S. Ormsby   E.G. Taylor

ARE you weary and sad 'neath the
burden of sin?
Does it fill all your soul with dismay?
And to meet the just claims of a
sin-hating GOD,
Do you know you have "nothing to
pay?"

    Come! come! come to Him!
    If you own, with repentance,
      you've "nothing to pay,"
    He will freely and 'frankly
      forgive.'

All your tears and your sorrow will
never atone,
Nor by works can you clear away
sin;

Then turn to the One from whom help
comes alone,
To the Saviour in confidence cling—

'Tis He who once came from GOD's
glory above,
To save you from ruin and loss;
And He paid the full debt in His own
precious blood
When He "put away sin" on the
cross—

Then come, ruined sinner, no longer
delay,
Nor in bondage and misery live;
If you own, with repentance, you've
"nothing to pay,"
He will freely and 'frankly forgive'—

660   One There Is Who Loves Thee P.M.

H.C. Ayers   W.H. Doane

CHORUS

ONE there is who loves thee,
   Waiting still for thee;
Canst thou yet reject Him?
   None so kind as He;
Do not grieve Him longer,
   Come, and trust Him now!
He has waited all thy days:
   Why waitest thou?

    One there is who loves thee,
      Oh, receive Him now!
    He has waited all the day;
     · Why waitest thou?

Tenderly He woos thee,
   Do not slight His call:

Though thy sins are many,
   He'll forgive them all.
Turn to Him, repenting,
   He will cleanse thee now;
He is waiting at thy heart:
   Why waitest thou?—

JESUS still is waiting;
   Sinner, why delay?
To His arms of mercy
   Rise and haste away!
Only come believing,
   He will save thee now;
He is waiting at the door:
   Why waitest thou?—

661   There is life for a look. P.M.

Amelia M. Hull   E.G. Taylor

THERE is life in a look at the Crucified One;
There is life at this moment for thee:
Then look, sinner, look unto Him and be saved,
Unto Him who was nailed to the tree:

Look! look! look and live!
There is life in a look at the Crucified One,
There is life at this moment for thee.

It is not thy tears of repentance or prayers,
But THE BLOOD that atones for the soul;
On Him, then, who shed it thou mayest at once
Thy weight of iniquities roll—

His anguish of soul on the cross hast thou seen
His cry of distress hast thou heard?
Then why, if the terrors of wrath He endured,
Should pardon to thee be deferred?—

We are healed by His stripes; wouldst thou add to the word?
And He is our righteousness made;
The best robe of heaven He bids thee put on:
Oh, couldst thou be better arrayed?—

Then take, with rejoicing, from JESUS at once,
The life everlasting He gives;
And know, with assurance, thou never canst die,
Since He as thy righteousness lives—

    There is life in a look at the Crucified One;
      There is life at this moment for thee:
      Then look, sinner, look unto Him
        and be saved,
      And know thyself spotless as He!—

662 I Love To Tell The Story 7.6.7.6.D and Chorus

Katherine Hankey W.G. Fischer

I LOVE to tell the story
  Of unseen things above,
Of JESUS and His glory,
  Of JESUS and His love:
I love to tell the Story,
  Because I know it's true;
It satisfies my longings
  As nothing else would do:

  And so I tell the Story
   Of unseen things above,
   Of JESUS and His glory,
   Of JESUS and His love.

I love to tell the Story;
  More wonderful it seems
Than all the golden fancies
  Of all our golden dreams:
I love to tell the Story;
  It did so much for me!

And that is just the reason
  I tell it now to thee—

I love to tell the Story,
  'Tis pleasant to repeat;
It seems, each time I tell it,
  More wonderfully sweet:
I love to tell the Story,
  For some have never heard
The message of salvation
  From GOD'S own holy Word—

I love to tell the Story,
  For those who know it best
Seem hungering and thirsting
  To hear it like the rest:
And when in scenes of glory
  I sing the NEW, NEW SONG,
'Twill be the OLD, OLD STORY
  That I have loved so long—

663 Only Trust Him C.M. and Chorus

W.P. Mackay
J.H. Stockton

"COME, let us reason," saith the LORD;
Your sins of crimson dye
Shall be like snow, or white as wool,
If you on CHRIST rely:

Only trust Him! Only trust Him!
Only trust Him now!
He will save you! He will save you!
He will save you now!

Come, thirsty one, who oft hast drained
The cup of pleasure dry,
For JESUS only life can give,
A life that ne'er shall die—

Come as thou art, with all thy sins;
Come with thy hardened heart;
Come with thy cares, thy doubts, thy fears:
All grace He will impart—

Come now, while yet His mercy lasts;
Perhaps thou wilt not see
To-morrow's sun: thy soul to-night
May be required of thee!—

664 St. John 6.6.6.6.8.8
A. Midlane (Samuel 334) J. Baptiste Calkin

HIMSELF He could not save!
He on the cross must die,
Or mercy could not come
To ruined sinners nigh;
Yes, CHRIST, the SON of GOD, must bleed,
That sinners might from sin be freed.

Himself He could not save,
For justice must be done,
And sin's full weight must fall
Upon the sinless One;
For nothing less could GOD accept
In payment of our fearful debt.

Himself He could not save,
For He as Surety stood
For all who will rely
Upon His precious blood:
He bore the penalty of guilt
When on the cross His blood was spilt.

Himself He would not save,
And now a *Saviour* He!
Come, sinner, to Him come—
He waits to welcome thee:
Believe in Him, and thou shalt prove
His saving power, His changeless love.

665 There's One Who Has Loved Thee 11.11.11.11

Douglas Russell · A.J. Gordon

THERE'S One who has loved thee,
 who loveth thee yet,
O sinner, though prone Jesu's love to
 forget!
In deepest compassion He came from
 the throne,
And went to the cross for our sins to
 atone.

He saw us all ruined, and guilty, and
 lost;
He came to redeem us at infinite cost;
Our sins were laid on Him, He bore
 them alone—
He died, and arose, and returned to
 the throne.

Salvation, eternal, and present, and
 free,
With life everlasting, is brought nigh
 to thee;
Acceptance unchanging, a place on
 the throne—
Blest portion of all who make Jesus
 their own.

Believe in His love, and enjoy it to-day,
Oh, trust Him—the Life, and the Truth, and the Way;
We publish the tidings: to all be it known—
By the cross is the path that leads up to the throne.

666   Only Trust Him C.M. and Chorus

J.H. Stockton   J.H. Stockton

COME, every soul by sin opprest,
  There's mercy with the LORD;
And He will surely give you rest,
  By trusting in His word:

*Only trust Him! Only trust Him!
  Only trust Him now!
He will save you! He will save you!
  He will save you now!*

For JESUS shed His precious blood
  That you might life obtain,
And those that take Him at His word
  Ne'er find their trust in vain—

He is the Life, the Truth, the Way,
  'Tis He alone gives rest;
By faith in Him this very day
  You may be truly blest—

667 **St. Matthew C.M.D.**
(Land of Rest 905)
W. Croft

POOR, weary wanderer, wilt thou
   come,
 And find in CHRIST thy rest?
Or wilt thou make this earth thy
   home,
 Refusing to be blest?
CHRIST JESUS gave His precious blood
 That thou mightst be forgiven;
And by His death made peace with
   GOD
 That Thou mightst enter heaven.

Is there not, deep within Thy heart,
 A want unsatisfied,
An empty, aching void unfilled,
 A craving unsupplied?
Then come at once to CHRIST the
   LORD,
 For He hath all you need;
Filled with Himself, thy life shall be
 A happy life indeed!

Oh, yield thy heart to JESUS now,
 Who gave His life for thine;
Thou wilt not find His service hard,
 Thy path shall brightly shine:
Not for eternity alone
 A blessing thou shalt gain,
But e'en on earth the peace of GOD
 Deep in thy heart shall reign.

668
L.H. Farrell

St. Denio 11.11.11.11
(Montgomery 326)

Welsh Hymn Melody

1. How wondrous a Saviour is GOD's blessèd SON!
How great and eternal the work He has done!
GOD's glory shines forth through His death on the tree,
And mercy flows freely to you and to me.

2. How free is the pardon His blood has procured!
How blessèd the welcome His name has ensured!
All those who confess Him as Saviour and LORD
Are brought into favour, through faith in His word.

3. On Calvary see Him who died in our stead,
There bearing GOD's judgment when for us He bled;
GOD's wrath He endurèd on Calvary's tree;
Through weakness and dying, the Victor is He.

4. Oh, why remain distant when GOD calls thee near?
His mercy dismisses all bondage and fear:
Oh, why remain Christless when thou may'st be blest?
Oh, why remain weary when CHRIST giveth rest?

5. The moments are fleeting; then make no delay,
Secure GOD's salvation while yet 'tis to-day;
Eternity's ages thy soul has to face—
In blackness of darkness, or sunshine of grace!

669 Triumph 8.7.8.7.8.7
Joseph Hart (Mannheim 29) H.J. Gauntlett

COME, ye sinners, poor and wretched,
  Weak and wounded, sick and sore,
Jesus ready stands to save you,
  Full of pity, joined with power;
    He is able,
  He is willing; doubt no more.

Let not conscience make you linger,
  Nor of fitness fondly dream;
All the fitness He requireth
  Is to feel your need of Him;
    This He gives you,
  'Tis the SPIRIT'S rising beam.

Come, ye weary, heavy laden,
  Lost and ruined in the fall!
If you tarry till you're better
  You will never come at all:
    Not the righteous,
  Sinners JESUS came to call.

Agonizing in the garden,
  Lo, the Saviour prostrate lies!
On the blood-stained tree behold Him!
  Hear Him cry before He dies,
    "It is finished!"
  Sinner, will not this suffice?

Lo, the incarnate GOD, ascended,
  Pleads the merit of His blood;
Venture on Him, venture wholly,
  Let no other trust intrude;
    None but JESUS
  Can do helpless sinners good.

670 Vox Jesu (Come Unto Me) 7.6.7.6.D
W. Chatterton Dix J.B. Dykes

' COME unto Me, ye weary,
  And I will give you rest '—
Oh, blessèd voice of JESUS,
  Which comes to hearts opprest!
It tells of benediction;
  Of pardon, grace, and peace;
Of joy that hath no ending:
  Of love which cannot cease.

And whosoever cometh
  I will not cast him out '—
Oh, patient love of JESUS,
  Which drives away our doubt,
Which calls us, very sinners—
  Unworthy though we be
Of love so free and boundless—
  To come, O LORD, to Thee!

671   Saffron Walden 8.8.8.6.

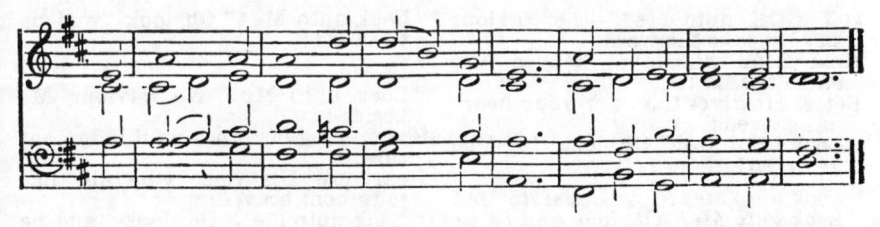

A. Midlane   A.H. Brown

COME, weary, anxious, laden soul,
  To JESUS come, and be made whole;
On Him your heavy burden roll—
  Come, burdened sinner, come!

Behold the cross on which He died;
Behold His wounded, bleeding side;
Come, in His precious love confide—
  Come, doubting sinner, come!

True joy the world can ne'er afford,
'Tis found alone in CHRIST the LORD,
In Him for wretched sinners stored—
  Come, anxious sinner, come!

If to His feet you now repair,
You'll find eternal comfort there,
And soon shall heavenly glory share—
  Come, troubled sinner, come!

672 Look Unto Me 10.10.10.10 and Chorus

Douglas Russell   Geo. C. Stebbins

CHORUS

"LOOK unto Me!"—the Saviour speaks the word;
Hear Him, who is of heaven and earth the LORD;
Better He gives than e'er your heart has craved;
"Look unto Me!" Oh, look "and be ye saved!"

    Look unto Me!.... Look unto Me!
    Look unto Me! Oh, look and be ye saved!
    Look and be ye saved!.... Look and be ye saved!....

"Look unto Me!" And yield not to delay;
Give earnest heed while yet 'tis called to-day!
Though far from GOD, all guilty and depraved,

"Look unto Me!" Oh, look "and be ye saved!"—

"Look unto Me!" No Saviour Me beside!
See, flowing fast, the awful judgment tide!
Hear now His voice who all that judgment braved,
"Look unto Me!" Oh, look "and be ye saved!"—

"Look unto Me!" Let nothing hold you back!
None are refused, though all must fitness lack;
Each one who trusts, upon His heart is graved:
"Look unto Me!" Oh, look "and be ye saved!"—

673
Douglas Russell

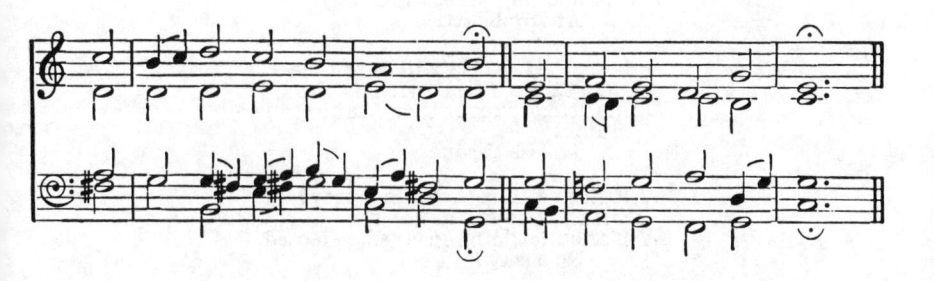

Passion Chorale 7.6.7.6.D

H.L. Hassler

A WAKE, awake, O sleeper!
  There's danger dread at hand;
And Death, like some grim reaper,
  Is stalking through the land:
Asleep, asleep in danger,
  And dreaming while asleep,
Though still to GOD a stranger!
  Will thou but wake to weep?

The day of grace declining,
  Thy sun will soon have set;
Long, long has it been shining,
  Art thou not saved e'en yet?
Thy sand-glass quickly running,
  The die will soon be cast:
Through Satan's art and cunning
  Wilt thou be lost at last?

"Now," "now" there is salvation
  Prepared of GOD for thee,
And from all condemnation
  CHRIST'S death can set thee free:
"To-day," "to-day"—embrace it,
  Press through the open gate:
To-morrow—dare you face it?—
  Your wail may be—'Too late!'

674 Come Thou Weary 8.5.8.3

S.C. Morgan
Ira D. Sankey

COME, thou weary! JESUS calls thee
To His wounded side;
'Come to Me,' saith He, 'and ever
Safe abide.'

Seek'st thou JESUS? JESUS seeks
thee—
Seeks thee as thou art;
He is knocking, ever knocking
At thy heart.

Only trust Him, He will save thee—
Make thee all His own:
Guide thee, keep thee, take thee
quickly
To His throne.

Wilt thou still refuse His mercy?
Wilt thou say Him nay?
Wilt thou let Him, grieved, rejected,
Go away?

Dost thou feel thy life is weary?
Is thy soul distrest?
Take salvation, wait no longer;
Be at rest!

675 Glorious Home P.M.

M.C. Wilson
G.F. Knowles

WE know there's a bright and a
glorious home,
Away in the heavens high,
Where all the redeemed shall with
JESUS dwell:
Will you be there and I?

Will you be there and I?
Will you be there and I?
Where all the redeemed shall with
JESUS dwell:
Will you be there and I?

In robes of white, o'er the streets of
gold,
Beneath a cloudless sky,
They walk in the light of their
FATHER'S smile:
Will you be there and I?—

From every kingdom of earth they
come
To join the triumphal cry,
Singing, 'Worthy the Lamb that
once was slain:'
Will you be there and I?—

If we trust the loving Saviour now,
And on His word rely,
When He gathers His own to that
bright home,
Then you'll be there and I—

If we are ransomed by the cross,
And through His blood brought
nigh,
Our utmost gain we'll count but loss,
Since you'll be there and I—

676   Hear And Obey P.M.

J.P. Webster

1. THERE'S a voice that is calling to thee,
And it pleads with its tenderest tone,
Whilst it bids thee from judgment to flee,
And whispers, 'To JESUS now come!'

Oh, then, hear . . . and obey! . . .
'Tis the voice of the SPIRIT that cries: . .
While He strives . . . yield to Him, . . .
Do not quench the convictions that rise.

2. There's a Saviour now waiting for thee,
With His heart and His arms open wide;
Wilt thou come, and from judgment be free,
Through the Lamb who on Calvary died?—

There's a fountain that's open for thee;
  Go, wash and be clean from thy sin;
Not a spot nor a stain shall there be
  If but once thou art cleansèd there-
    in—

There's a mansion prepared above,
  With its pleasures that none can
    conceive;
And true joy shall be thine in His love,
  If thou wilt but on JESUS believe—

677 Just As I Am 8.8.8.6
R.S. Cook   (Agnes Dei 134)   Joseph Barnby

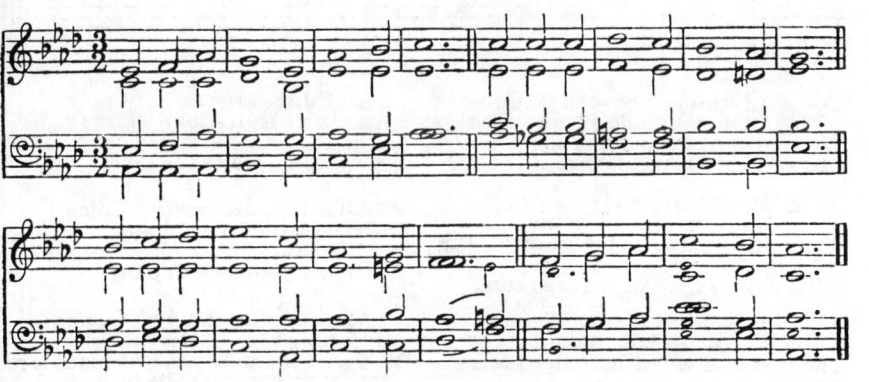

JUST as thou art, without one trace
  Of love, or joy, or inward grace,
Or meetness for the heavenly place,
  O *guilty* sinner, come!

Burdened with guilt, wouldst thou be
  blest?
Trust not the world, it gives no rest;
CHRIST brings relief to hearts opprest:
  O *weary* sinner, come!

Come, leave thy burden at the cross;
Count all thy gains but worthless
  dross;
His grace o'erpays all earthly loss:
  O *needy* sinner, come!

Come, hither bring thy boding fears,
Thy aching heart, thy bursting tears;
'Tis mercy's voice salutes thine ears:
  O *trembling* sinner, come!

The time is short; GOD's word says,
  "Come!"
Rejoicing saints re-echo, "Come!"
Who faints, who thirsts, who will,
  may come:
  The Saviour bids *thee* come!

678 Narenza S.M.
A. Midlane — (St. Beuno 433) — German

1. "All things are ready," Come;
   Oh, make no vain excuse;
   No yoke of oxen, wife, or field,
   Instead of JESUS choose.

2. "All things are ready" now;
   'Tis GOD who bids all come;
   Bring in the poor, the maimed, the blind;
   'Tis done—and yet there's room.

3. "All things are ready," Come;
   Come all, both bad and good;
   The best and worst both need alike
   The Saviour's cleansing blood.

4. "All things are ready," Come,
   And taste GOD's love so free;
   See mercy's door stands open wide—
   A welcome waits for thee.

5. "All things are ready," Come,
   Nor pass that open door;
   Too late you may an entrance seek,
   Too late your loss deplore.

6. "All things are ready," Come;
   GOD calls you by His grace!
   Oh, turn not from such wondrous love
   But seek e'en *now* His face.

679 St. Ethelwald S.M.
A. Midlane — (Swabia 615) — W.H. Monk

"ALL things are ready," Come;
　The heavenly feast is spread;
Come rich and poor, come old and
　young,
　Come and be richly fed.

"All things are ready," Come;
　The invitation's given
By Him who now in glory sits
　At GOD's right hand in heaven.

"All things are ready," Come;
　The door is open wide;
Oh, feast upon the love of GOD,
　For CHRIST, His SON, has died!

"All things are ready," Come;
　All hindrance is removed;
And GOD, in CHRIST, His precious
　love
　To fallen man has proved.

"All things are ready," Come;
　To-morrow may not be;
O sinner, come—the Saviour waits
　This hour to welcome thee!

680　　Olivet 6.6.4.6.6.6.4

J.F. Elwin　　　　　　　　　　　　　L. Mason

PEACE! what a precious sound!
　Tell it the world around:
　　CHRIST hath made peace!
Brought nigh are we to GOD
By His atoning blood,
And crowned with every good—
　　CHRIST hath made peace!

Love was the spring of all,
Love triumphed o'er our fall,
　The love of GOD!
My soul, this love adore,
And praise for evermore;
Yea, sound from shore to shore
　The love of GOD.

681   Ar Hyd Y Nos 8.4.8.4.8.8.8.4

Mary Peters   Welsh Air

1 ARE your souls the Saviour seeking?
   Peace, peace—be still;
'Tis the LORD Himself is speaking,
   Peace, peace—be still;
For before the world's foundation
GOD secured a full salvation,
Happy people—chosen nation!
   Peace, peace—be still.

2 'Tis the blood of CHRIST hath spoken,
   Peace, peace—be still;
The destroyer sees the token—
   Peace, peace—be still;
On GOD'S word we boldly venture,
All our hopes in JESUS centre,
Into rest our souls can enter—
   Peace, peace—be still.

3 Great the calm the Saviour spreadeth,
   Peace, peace—be still;
Whatsoe'er your spirit dreadeth,
   Peace, peace—be still;
Though with mighty foes engaging,
War with sin and Satan waging
Storms of trial fiercely raging,
   Peace, peace be still.

4 JESUS walks upon the ocean,
   Peace, peace—be still;
He shall hush its loud commotion,
   Peace, peace—be still;
Soon shall end our days of sighing,
Pain and sorrow, death and crying;
Till that hour, on GOD relying—
   Peace, peace—be still.

682 Invitation P.M.

J.M. Wigner F.C. Maker

C OME to the Saviour now!
He ready stands to bless,
He bids thee nothing bring—
Only thy guilt confess;
No anger fills His heart,
No frown is on His brow,
His look is perfect grace,
He bids thee trust Him now!
Come! come! come!

Come to the Saviour now!
No longer make delay;
Life's tide is ebbing fast,
Near is the judgment day!
Wouldst thou escape His ire
Who then will fill the throne?
To CHRIST, the LORD, now come,
Henceforth be His alone:
Come! come! come!

Come to the Saviour now!
No barrier stops thy way,
The wrath of GOD He bore
In the atonement day:
For us He sin was made,
For sinners thus He died;
GOD'S claims He fully met
And Justice satisfied:
Come! come! come!

Come to the Saviour now!
"'Tis finished!" once He said;
His work for sinners done,
GOD raised Him from the dead;
Peace unto thee He speaks—
The peace He made by blood;
Believing in His name,
He brings thee nigh to GOD:
Come! come! come!

Come to the Saviour now!
Repose on Him alone,
For quickly He will come
To gather up His own;
If thou on Him wilt rest,
As His thou then shalt rise
To meet Him, and to swell
Sweet anthems in the skies:
Come! come! come!

683
Broomsgrove 6.4.6.4.6.6.6.4

G.W. Frazer
F.C. Maker

HEAR now the gospel sound,
  "Yet there is room!"
It tells to all around,
  "Yet there is room!"
Though guilty, do not fear;
Though vile, you may draw near
With joy this word to hear,
  "Yet there is room!"

GOD'S love in CHRIST we see—
Greater it could not be—
His only SON He gave;
Though righteous He can save
All who on *Him* believe—

"All things are ready: come!"
CHRIST everything hath done—
The work is now complete,
And at the mercy-seat
A Saviour you will meet—

GOD'S house is filling fast—
While mercy's day doth last—
But soon salvation's day
For you will pass away,
Then grace no more will say,
  "Yet there is room!"

684
Fountain C.M. and Chorus

W. Cameron
Old Melody

Chorus

H O! ye that thirst, approach the spring
Where living waters flow;
Free to that sacred fountain all
Without a price may go:

Without a price then go,
Where living waters flow;
Free to that sacred fountain all
Without a price may go.

How long to streams of false delight
Will ye in crowds repair?
How long your strength and substance waste
On trifles light as air?—

Christ's stores afford those rich supplies
That health and pleasure give:
Incline your ear and come to Him;
The soul that hears shall live—

Seek ye the Lord while yet His ear
Is open to your call;
While offered mercy still is near,
Before His footstool fall—

685   Ho! Ye Thirsty, Jesus Calls You   P.M.

P.P. Bliss

HO! ye thirsty, JESUS calls you;
 For He came to give
Wine and milk of free salvation;
Come to Him and live:

> Whosoever will is welcome;
> Hear the gospel cry!
> Without price and without money,
> Come to Him and buy.

Wherefore do ye spend your treasure
For what is not bread?
Only by the living Saviour
Dying souls are fed—

None can be too vile for JESUS,
None can be too poor;
Through His blood are peace and pardon—
Mercies ever sure—

Oh, His tender love and pity!
Still He calls to-day;
Never one to Him who cometh
Will He cast away—

From all sin He came to save us;
Satan's slaves to free:
To His royal feast He bids us;
Come, then, taste and see—

686(1)   Chalvey S.M. and Chorus

Russell Hurditch   L.G. Hayne

TO dying sons of men
   CHRIST calls afresh to-day;
Oh, turn not from His gracious word,
   But heed without delay:

   Sin's burden once He bore
     Upon the dreadful tree;
   The curse, the wrath, the death,
     were His,
   From sin to set us free!

Pardon and peace He gives
   To such as seek His face;
Salvation through His precious blood
   And everlasting grace—

Now risen from the dead,
   Exalted to GOD'S throne,
He gives eternal life to all
   Who trust in Him alone—

When JESUS comes to reign,
   We shall His glory share;
But those who now reject His grace
   The sinner's doom must bear—

686(2)   Moncton S.M.D.   W.E. Vine

687 Rejoice And Be Glad 11.11 and Chorus

H. Bonar
English Air

REJOICE and be glad! the Redeemer has come!
Go look on His cradle, His cross, and His tomb!

Sound His praises! tell the story of Him who was slain!
Sound His praises! tell with gladness He liveth again!

Rejoice and be glad! for the blood hath been shed:
Redemption is finished, the price hath been paid—

Rejoice and be glad! now the pardon is free!
The Just for the unjust has died on the tree—

Rejoice and be glad! for the Lamb that was slain
O'er death is triumphant, and liveth again—

Rejoice and be glad! for He cometh again;
He cometh in glory, the Lamb that was slain:

Sound His praises! tell the story of Him who was slain!
Sound His praises! tell with gladness He cometh again!

688 The Giver Of Rest P.M.
(Repose 938)

G.F. Knowles

WHY 'neath the load of your sins
do ye toil?
CHRIST giveth rest—giveth rest;
Why be in slavery—to Satan a spoil?
You may be blest—may be blest:
CHRIST now invites you His rest to
receive,
Heavy your burden, yet He can
relieve;
If but this moment in Him you believe,
You shall have rest—shall have rest.

Why are you troubled when death
comes in view?
CHRIST giveth rest—giveth rest;
Though after death must come judgment too,
You may be blest—may be blest:
CHRIST bore GOD'S judgment lost sinners to save;
He gained the victory o'er death and
the grave;
Oh, now believe Him, and life you
shall have!
You shall have rest—shall have rest.

Money or price you need not to bring;
CHRIST *giveth* rest—giveth rest;
Why to your rags and your poverty
cling?
Come and be blest—and be blest:
Away with all fear, away with all
doubt,
Hear His own words, which none can
refute—
Whoe'er comes to Him, He will never
cast out,
You shall have rest—shall have rest.

689   The Hem Of His Garment 10.6.10.6. and Chorus

Geo. F. Root   Geo. F. Root

SHE only touched the hem of His garment,
As to His side she stole,
Amid the crowd that gathered around Him;
And straightway she was whole:

Oh, touch the hem of His garment,
And thou too shalt be free!
His saving power this very hour
Shall give new life to thee!

She came in fear and trembling before Him,
She knew her LORD had come,
She felt that virtue from Him had healed her;
The mighty deed was done—

He turned with "Daughter, be of good comfort;
Thy faith hath made thee whole!"
And peace that passeth all understanding
With gladness filled her soul—

690   Ellers 10.10.10.10

E.J. Hopkins

PEACE was *procured* by CHRIST,
   the SON of GOD,
When on the cross He gave His
   precious blood;
It seals a pardon, perfect, full and
   free,
To guilty, rebel sinners such as we.

Peace is *possessed* by those who
   simply hide
In CHRIST alone, and in His word
   confide;
They read their pardon, written full
   and plain,
And GOD Himself beholds them without stain.

Peace is *proclaimed* from heaven's
   bright courts of love,
Where JESUS sits at GOD's right hand
   above;
Now on His brow rest crowns of glory
   bright—
Blest token of acceptance in GOD's
   sight.

"He is our Peace" in glory's highest
   height,
Changeless is He, though clouds may
   dim our sight;
Our peace remains, though joy may
   come and go—
Peace, perfect peace, our portion here
   below.

O sinner, GOD is waiting thee to bless;
   His love now floweth forth in righteousness,
And will bestow on weary, sin-sick
   hearts
That peace divine which He alone
   imparts.

691   **Sussex 8.7.8.7**
A. Midlane   (Lucerne 529)   English Trad. Melody

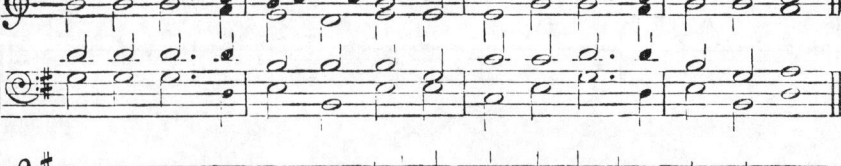

PEACE with GOD—how great a
   treasure!
Peace with GOD—how true a joy!
Peace with GOD—how high a pleasure!
Peace with GOD—heaven's full
   supply.

Peace with GOD must come through
   JESUS,
He the victory has won;
Now 'tis GOD's delight to give us
Peace with Him, through His dear
   SON.

Peace with GOD—all sins forgiven!
Peace with GOD—all guilt removed!
Peace with GOD—foretaste of heaven,
Peace with GOD—His mercy proved!

Why, O friend, art thou delaying?
   Trust in Him who bore sin's load;
And, His gracious call obeying,
   Thou shalt have sweet peace with
      GOD.

692 Limpsfield 7.6.7.6.7.7.7.6

Priscilla J. Owens　　　　　　　　　　　　　　　　J. Booth

WE have heard the joyful sound—
　Jesus saves! Jesus saves!
Tell the message all around—
　Jesus saves! Jesus saves!
Bear the news to every land,
　Climb the steeps and cross the waves;
Onward!—'tis our Lord's command—
　Jesus saves! Jesus saves!

Sing above the toil and strife—
　Jesus saves! Jesus saves!
By His death and endless life
　Jesus saves! Jesus saves!
Sing it softly through the gloom,
　When the heart for mercy craves,
Sing in triumph o'er the tomb—
　Jesus saves! Jesus saves!

Give the winds a mighty voice:
  JESUS saves! JESUS saves!
Let the lost ones now rejoice—
  JESUS saves! JESUS saves!
Shout salvation full and free
  To every strand that ocean laves;
This our song of victory—
  JESUS saves! JESUS saves!

693   **Rest C.M.**
A. Midlane   (Gräfenberg 358)   Handley C.G. Moule

" 'TIS finished," cried the dying
    Lamb;
" 'Tis finished," rends the skies;
" 'Tis finished," Justice sweetly sings;
" 'Tis finished," Love replies.

" 'Tis finished,"—our salvation's toil;
  " 'Tis finished,"—all is done;
" 'Tis finished,"—peace with GOD is
    made;
  " 'Tis finished,"—life is won.

" 'Tis finished;" look thou now to
    CHRIST,
  Upon the cross He dies;
Believe in Him, and thou shalt have
  A home beyond the skies.

694 Tetelestai P.M.

J. Proctor
E.H.G. Sargent

CHORUS

NOTHING either great or small,
  Nothing, sinner, no;
JESUS did it, did it all,
  Long, long ago:

  "*It is finished!*" *Yes, indeed,*
    Finished every jot:
  Sinner, this is all you need;
    Tell me, is it not?

When He, from His lofty throne,
  Stooped to do and die,
Everything was fully done,
  Hearken to *His cry*—

Weary, working, burdened one,
  Wherefore toil you so?
Cease *your* doing; all was done
  Long, long ago—

Till to JESUS CHRIST you cling,
  By a simple faith,
Doing is a deadly thing;
  Doing ends in death—

Cast your deadly doing down,
  Down at JESUS'S feet,
Stand in HIM, in *Him* alone,
  Gloriously *complete*—

695 Would You Taste Of Joy? 8.7.8.7.D and Chorus

Douglas Russell
Ira D. Sankey

WOULD you taste of joy and gladness,
And have sorrow flee away,
Find a solace in your sadness,
And have night give place to day?
GOD invites you to the fountain
Where life flows in ceaseless streams,
Fears shall cease like mist on mountain,
Chased away by sun's bright beams:

Sinner, come! . . The living fount . .
Freely flows . . from Calvary's mount . .
There we see our sins forgiven,
Through the precious blood once shed,
Find, in foretaste, joy of heaven,
Since He liveth who was dead.

Would you share on earth the pleasures
Which shall last for evermore,
Know the earnest, here, of treasures
Drawn from heaven's eternal store?
In abundance they are flowing,
Like a river, full and free:
GOD is still His grace bestowing;
Grace that flows to you and me—

Oh, believe and tell the story,
Sing with joy redeeming love !
'Tis the theme of all in glory—
It will be our joy above:
Not for self, but now for JESUS
We would live—for Him alone,
Till from heaven He comes and frees us,
And we meet around the throne—

696 It Is Finished! 8.7.8.7 and Chorus

M. Fraser
J. McGranahan

"It is finished!" What a gospel!
  Nothing left for you to do,
But to take with grateful gladness
  What the Saviour did for you!

  It is finished, Hallelujah!
  It is finished, Hallelujah!
  Christ the work has fully done;
    Hallelujah!
  All who will may now have pardon
  Through the blood of God's dear
    Son.

"It is finished!" What a gospel!
  Bringing news of victory won,
Telling us of peace and pardon
  Through the blood of God's dear
    Son—

"It is finished!" What a gospel!
 Now each weary, laden breast
That accepts GOD's gracious message
 Enters into perfect rest—

"It is finished!" What a gospel!
 JESUS died to save your soul;
Have you welcomed His salvation?
 Sought His grace to make you whole?—

697 Ballerma C.M.
A. Midlane   (Rest (Moule) 4)   Adapted by R. Simpson

GOD speaks from heaven—in *love* He speaks,
 Inviting sinners near;
No price or money He demands
 Oh, lend a listening ear!

GOD speaks from heaven—in *grace* He speaks;
 'Tis dangerous to delay;
Accept the freely-offered grace—
 Oh, come! while yet 'tis day.

GOD speaks from heaven—in *truth* He speaks;
 Oh, heed the voice divine!
Receive His love, in CHRIST made known,
 And pardon shall be thine.

698 Have You Been To Jesus? P.M.

E.A. Hoffmann
E.A. Hoffmann

Chorus

HAVE you been to Jesus for His cleansing power?
 Are you washed in the blood of the Lamb?
Are you fully trusting in His grace this hour?
 Are you washed in the blood of the Lamb?

Are you washed . . . in the blood . . .
 In the soul-cleansing blood of the Lamb? . . .
Are your garments spotless? Are they white as snow?
 Are you washed in the blood of the Lamb?

Are you walking daily by the Saviour's side?
 Are you washed in the blood of the Lamb?
Do you rest each moment in the Crucified?
 Are you washed in the blood of the Lamb?—

When the Bridegroom cometh, will your robes be white—
 Pure and white in the blood of the Lamb?
Will your soul be ready for the mansions bright,
 As one washed in the blood of the Lamb?—

Lay aside the garments that are stained with sin,
 If you're washed in the blood of the Lamb!
There's a fountain flowing for the soul unclean;
 Oh, be washed in the blood of the Lamb!—

699 'Come,' Is The Lord's Invitation 8.7.8.7 and Chorus

D. Russell
Geo. C. Stebbins

"COME," is the Lord's invitation;
"Come unto Me," hear Him say;
Come now for rest and salvation;
Come, and accept Him to-day!

Come thou away! Trust Him to-day!
Nothing to do, sinner, nothing to pay;
Great was the price, but He paid it!
Come unto Him while you may.

Trust thou alone in the Saviour,
Trust in the blood that He shed;
Trust not thy blameless behaviour,
Trust Him who rose from the dead—

"Look unto Me," He is calling:
Look, light in darkness will shine;
Look, though thy guilt be appalling,
Look, and a pardon is thine—

Come unto Him, as invited;
Trust Him who waiteth to bless:
Look, and thy soul shall be lighted:
Jesus thy Lord then confess—

700(1) Dix 7.7.7.7.7.7

A. Midlane

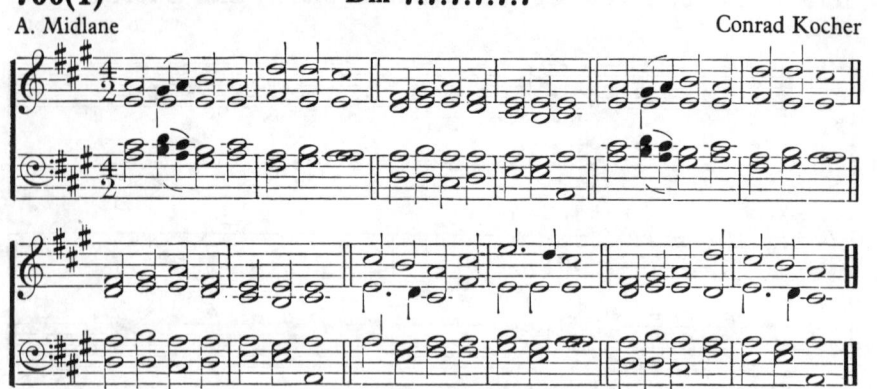

Conrad Kocher

JESUS never answered, "Nay,"
  When a sinner sought His aid;
JESUS never turned away
  When request to Him was made;
No! each weary, needy one
Found a friend in GOD's dear SON.

When the palsied, sick, and sad
  Upward turned to Him the eye,
He rejoiced to make them glad,
  Filling each with peace and joy,
Yes! each weary, needy one
Found a friend in GOD's dear SON.

Now upon the throne above,
  Still the self-same heart is His,
Full of tenderness and love,
  Waiting still to aid and bless;
Still may every needy one
Find a friend in GOD's dear SON.

Weary one, to Him repair,
  Cast thy burden at His feet;
Safety, peace, and bliss are there,
  Now approach the mercy-seat;
Thus each needy, weary one
Finds a friend in GOD's dear SON.

700(2) All Red The River 7.7.7.7.7.7

Chinese verse tune

701   Look And Live 7.6.7.3.D and Chorus

P.P. Bliss   P.P. Bliss

Tenderly.

LOOK to Jesus, weary one,
  Look and live! look and live!
Think of what the Lord hath done,
  Look and live!
See Him lifted on the tree,
  Look and live! look and live!
Hear Him say, "Look unto Me!"
  Look and live!

    Look! the Lord is lifted high;
    Look to Him; He's ever nigh:
    Look and live! why will ye die.
      Look and live!

Though unworthy, vile, unclean—
Look away from self and sin—
Long by Satan's power enslaved—
Look to Jesus and be saved—

Though you've wandered far away—
Harden not your heart to-day—
Soon the Lord will come again—
Would you see His glory then?
    Look and Live!—

702 Look And Thou Shalt Live P.M.

F.T. Watt J.H Stockton

CHORUS

LOOK to the Saviour on Calvary's
  tree;
How He there suffered we plainly see:
Hark, while He lovingly calls to thee.
  'Look, and thou shalt live!'

*Look, and thou shalt live!
Look, and thou shalt live!
Look to the cross where He died
  for thee:
Look, and thou shalt live!*

Hast thou a sin-burdened soul to save?
Life everlasting wouldst thou have?
JESUS Himself a ransom gave:
  Look, and thou shalt live!—

Look to the Saviour who rose from
  the tomb;
Haste now to Him, while there yet is
  room;
His shining face will dispel thy gloom:
  Look, and thou shalt live!—

JESUS on high lives to intercede,
He knows the weary sinner's need;
Surely thy footsteps He will lead
  Look, and thou shalt live!—

703 Kingsfold C.M. and Chorus

W.P. Mackay (St. Matthew 667) English Melody

CHORUS

"LOOK unto Me, and be ye saved!"
  Look, men of nations all;
Look, rich and poor; look, old and
    young;
  Look, sinners, great and small!

Look unto Him, and be ye saved,
  Each weary, troubled soul;
Oh, look to JESUS while you may;
  One look will make you whole!

"Look unto Me, and be ye saved!"
  Look now, nor dare delay;
Look as you are—lost, guilty, vile;
  Look, while 'tis called to-day—

"Look unto Me, and be ye saved!"
  Look from your doubts and fears;
Look from your sins of crimson dye,
  Look from your prayers and tears—

"Look unto Me, and be ye saved!"
  Look to the work all done:
Look to the piercèd Son of man,
  GOD'S well-belovèd SON!—

704. Believe And Be Thou Saved S.M. And Chorus

W.H. Doane

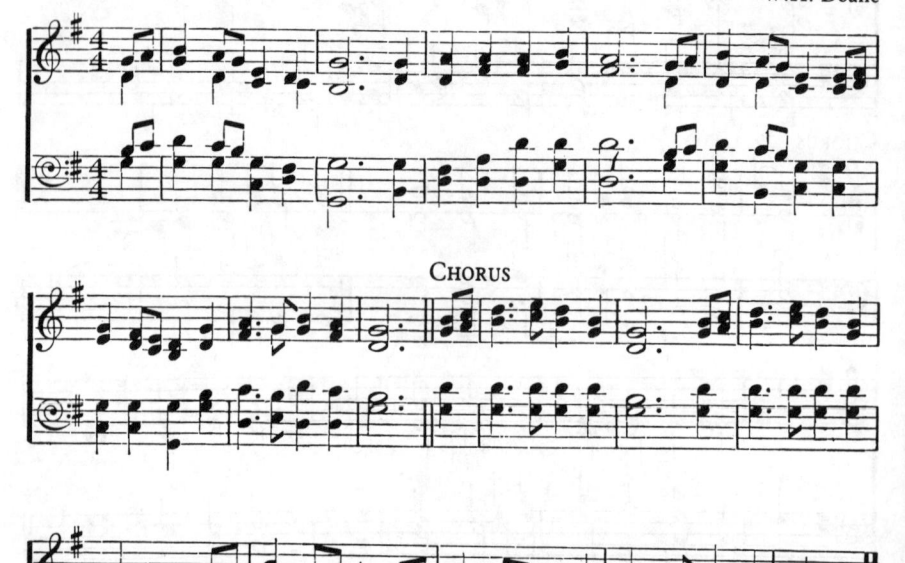

B<small>EHOLD</small> the Lamb of G<small>OD</small>,
Who bore a vile world's sin !
Look unto Him and be thou saved,
The promise takes thee in :

Believe and be thou saved;
The promise takes thee in;
The Saviour see, who died for thee;
The promise takes thee in.

For G<small>OD</small> so loved the world,
His only S<small>ON</small> He gave,
That whosoever Him believes,
Not Wrath, but life shall have—

Gaze on His thorn-wreathed brow,
Behold the crimson tide
Flow from His head, His hands, His feet,
And from His open side—

He gave His precious blood
To cleanse our every stain;
Believing now, He will thee cleanse
Nor shall one spot remain—

705   Fingal C.M.
F. Haweis   (Lucius 592)   J.S. Anderson

BEHOLD the Lamb! 'Tis He who bore
Sin's burden on the tree,
And paid in blood the dreadful score,
The ransom due for thee.

Oh, look to Him till sight endear
The Saviour to thy heart;
Yea, look to Him to calm thy fear,
And ne'er from Him depart.

Oh, look until His precious love
Doth every thought control;
Its vast, constraining influence prove
O'er spirit, body, soul.

706   Better World 8.3.8.3.8.8.8.3

A. Midlane   J. Hayhurst

BEHOLD the manner of GOD'S love
    On the cross!
Expressed in deeds, all words above,
    On the cross!
The world with all its wealth were vain
  To ransom souls from sin's dark stain;
Blood only could remission gain,
    By the cross!

Behold the measure of GOD'S love
    On the cross!
There, there He did its greatness prove,
    On the cross!
Oh, what can with such love compare?
There JESUS did GOD'S love declare,
And all the weight of judgment bear
    On the cross!

Behold the fulness of GOD'S love
    On the cross!
His love to all He then did prove,
    On the cross!
No greater gift could He bestow,
To show His love to man below;
Through His own SON doth mercy flow,
    By the cross!

707 Happy Morn 8.8.6.8.8.8.6

G.W. Frazer
A. Radiger

BEHOLD the Lamb for sinners slain!
  To cleanse them from each guilty
    stain
His precious blood was shed;
He took our place upon the tree,
Made sin, He bore our penalty,
To set the guilty captives free,
  By dying in our stead.

Enduring there GOD'S righteous
    stroke,
O'er Him the waves and billows broke,
  He bowed His head and died;
GOD then forsook His only SON,
The holy, true, obedient One,
By whom alone His will was done,
  And He was crucified!

Behold Him now upon the throne,
The source of life and peace alone—
  No longer in the grave—
Dispensing blessing full and free
To such as lost and ruined be;
Enthroned above He welcomes thee,
  And justly thee can save.

Soon He will rise and close the door,
Glad tidings thou wilt hear no more,
  Thy day of grace then past,
For all who will not bow the knee,
Nor own Him "LAMB of GOD" to be,
Shall shun His call, and from Him
    flee,
  Who comes, as Judge, at last.

708   **Sharon 8.7.8.7**
(Newton Ferns 411)   Wm. Boyce

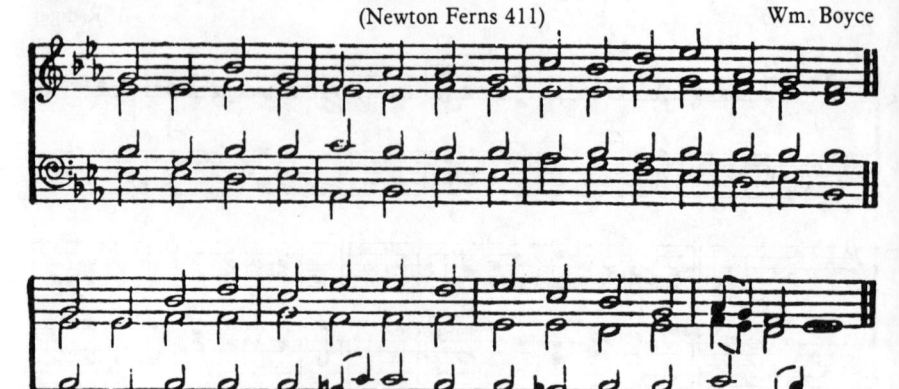

HITHER come, behold and wonder!
  View the sight all sights above;
Fix thy gaze on Calvary yonder,
  See the proof that "GOD is Love."

There, as man in outward fashion,
  GOD's own SON pours out His blood,
Bearing in divine compassion
  All the righteous wrath of GOD.

Yes! He bears it undiminished—
  Hear His GOD-forsaken cry!
Hear Him utter, "It is finished;"
  See Him yield His breath and die!

Trace Him now from earth to heaven,
  Crowned, and seated on the throne;
See, the highest place is given
  To the Lamb who did atone.

GOD can now in mercy pardon
  E'en the chief of sinners here;
But take heed lest sin should harden—
  Seek His mercy while 'tis near.

709   **Deerhurst 8.7.8.7.D**
A. Midlane   J. Langran

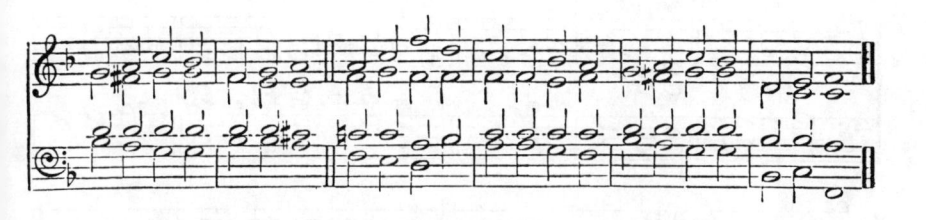

SEE the blessèd Saviour dying
On the cross for ruined man;
See the willing, spotless Victim
Working out redemption's plan!
Listen to His loving accents,
'FATHER, oh, forgive!' He cries;
Hark, again He speaks — "'Tis finished "—
Ere He bows His head and dies!

With this cruel death before Him,
Every insult, pang, foreseen,
Nought could turn Him from His purpose,
No dismay could intervene;
Yea, and through all contradiction,
Nothing could His calmness move
Oh, the wondrous depths eternal
Of His own almighty love!

Love made Him, "the LORD of glory,
Come to die—the "sinners' Friend,
Love beyond the thought of mortals,
Love too deep to comprehend!
Sinner, make this love thy portion,
Slight not love so vast and free,
Still **unblest** if unforgiven,
Come—the Saviour calleth thee!

710 Bethany 8.7.8.7.D

Hannah K. Burlingham
Henry Smart

OH, the love of CHRIST is boundless,
 Broad and long, and deep and high;
Every doubt and fear is groundless,
 Now the word of faith is nigh:
JESUS CHRIST, for our salvation,
 Shed on earth His precious blood,
Clear we stand from condemnation,
 In the risen SON of GOD.

Are you 'waiting' still for pardon?
 Are you 'hoping' to be saved?
Waiting — though your heart will harden?
 Hoping danger may be braved?
If by GOD'S own truth confounded,
 You as guilty stand confest,
Grace will reign where sin abounded,
 GOD will give you perfect rest.

'Tis not doing, 'tis not praying,
 'Tis not weeping, saves the soul;
GOD is now His grace displaying;
 JESUS died to make us whole.
Look to Him, and life-works follow;
 Look to Him without delay!
Trust Him *now*, and all thy sorrow,
 With thy guilt, will pass away.

711(1) Jesus Of Nazareth Passeth By P.M.

Etta Campbell
T.E. Perkins

JESUS the LORD, when here below,
  Man's pathway trod, 'mid pain
    and woe;
And burdened hearts, where'er He
    came,
  Brought out their sick, and deaf, and
    lame;
Blind men rejoiced to hear the cry—
  " JESUS of Nazareth passeth by ! "

Ho ! all ye heavy-laden, come !
Here's pardon, comfort, rest, a home ;
All ye who fear to meet GOD'S face,
Return, accept His proffered grace ;
Ye tempted ones, there's refuge nigh—
  " JESUS of Nazareth passeth by ! "

    But if you still His call refuse,
    And dare such wondrous love abuse,
    Soon will He sadly from you turn,
    Your bitter prayer in justice spurn :
    ' Too late ! too late ! ' will be the cry,
    ' JESUS of Nazareth *has passed by !* '

711(2)   St. Chrysostom 8.8.8.8.8.8   J. Barnby

712 Buckland 7.7.7.7
J. Denham Smith (Brandenburg 222) L.G. Hayne

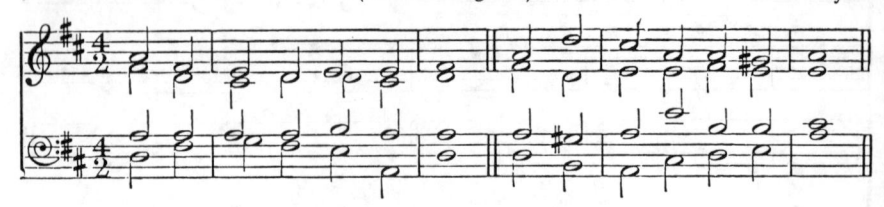

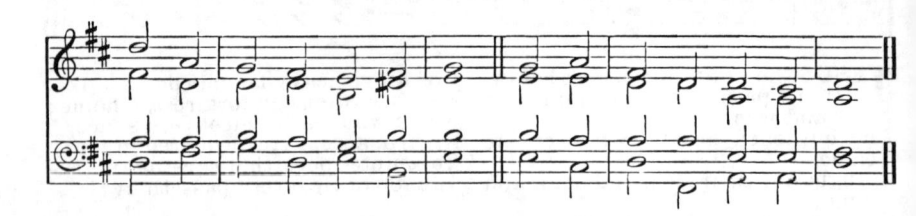

JESUS CHRIST is passing by,
  Sinner, lift to Him thine eye;
As the precious moments flee,
Cry, "Be merciful to me!"

Lo! He stands and calls to thee,
'What wilt thou then have of Me?'
Rise, and tell Him all thy need;
Rise—He calleth thee indeed!

JESUS CHRIST is passing by:
Will He always be so nigh?
Now is the accepted day;
Seek for healing while you may.

Oh, how sweet His touch of power!
With it comes salvation's hour;
JESUS gives from guilt release—
"Faith hath saved thee; go in peace!"

713 Redemption P.M.
E.E.M. Peter Bilhorn

CHORUS

SHALL the prey not be snatched from the mighty
  By Him who is LORD over all?
'It shall!' cry the hosts of the ransomed,
  'The foe shall no longer enthral,
For JESUS, the glorious Redeemer,
  Captivity captive has led;
Salvation He fully accomplished
  For us when He suffered and bled:'
    To Him be the glory for ever,
      To Him who has conquered the grave,
    To Him who is strong to deliver,
      To Him who is "Mighty to save"!

He has come as the Mighty Deliverer
  From bondage, from darkness, from sin!
O ye who are yearning for freedom,
  Let this Mighty Saviour come in,
Come into thy heart so desponding,
  To burst every bond, and set free
The powers of thy spirit and body,
  For Him ever only to be!—

Then, possessed and indwelt by His SPIRIT,
  Let all who behold see in thee
The prey that was snatched from the mighty
  By One who is stronger than he;
By One who is strong to deliver,
  Whose freed ones no foe can enslave:
To Him be the glory for ever,
  For He is the "Mighty to save!"—

714 Weeping Will Not Save Thee P.M.

R. Lowry
R. Lowry

WEEPING will not save thee:
    Though thy face were bathed
      in tears,
That could not allay thy fears,
Could not wash the sins of years;
    Weeping will not save thee:

    JESUS *wept and died for thee;*
    JESUS *suffered on the tree;*
    JESUS *waits to make thee free:*
    HE *alone can save thee!*

Working will not save thee:
Purest deeds that thou canst do,
Holiest thoughts and feelings too,
Cannot form thy soul anew;
    Working will not save thee—

Waiting will not save thee:
Listen not to Satan's lie,
Turn thine ear to mercy's cry;
Wait not, sinner, lest thou die;
    Waiting will not save thee—

    Faith in CHRIST *will* save thee:
    Only trust in GOD'S dear SON.
    Trust the work that He has done;
    Look to JESUS, helpless one;
      JESUS CHRIST *will save thee!*—

715. Oh, Come, And Linger Not L.M. and Chorus

Wm. J. Kirkpatrick

1. O WEARY soul, now seeking peace,
O heart distrest, that needs release,
From earth's cold comforts quickly flee,
The Saviour waits, so near, for thee:

Oh, come, . . . sinner come, and linger not!
Oh, come, . . . sinner come, and linger not!
Oh, come, . . . come, . . .
While JESUS waits for thee!

2. O *thirsty* soul, earth's fountain dry
Can neither quench nor satisfy;
Come, take the Living Water free!
GOD's "whosoever" takes in thee—

3. O *sin-sick* soul, for thy disease
Hast thou spent all, yet got no ease?
E'en though thy case may desperate be,
The Great Physician waits for thee—

4. O *burdened* soul—thy load may drop,
Thy burden fall, thy labour stop,
Thy step henceforth be light and free,
For JESUS bore sin's load for thee—

5. O *guilty* soul, though sunk in sin,
The Saviour seeks thy heart to win;
With outstretched arms that Saviour see,
His piercèd hands will welcome thee—

716 **Jesus Is Waiting P.M.**

Douglas Russell

E.S. Ufford

CHORUS

1. JESUS is waiting, O sinner, for you!
Nothing is left you to pay or to do;
For our redemption *His blood* has been paid;
His work is all finished, apart from our aid:

Chorus:
Jesus is waiting, Jesus is waiting,
Waiting and pleading for you!
Jesus is waiting, Jesus is waiting,
Nothing is left you to do!

2. JESUS is waiting, is waiting to save,
For He has triumphed o'er death and the grave;
"Ready to perish!" salvation to-day
He brings you, with nothing to do or to pay!—

3. JESUS is waiting! through Him you may live;
Life everlasting He freely doth give;
Come then, believing; for oh, it is true,
He *gives* it, with nothing to pay or to do!—

4. JESUS is waiting! come now, while you may;
Come empty-handed, there's nothing to pay;
Others are learning, may you learn it too,
That "all things are ready," there's nothing to do!—

717 Choose Ye Today P.M.

F.J. Crosby
W.H. Doane

Legato.

A BLESSING for you—will you take it? *Choose ye to-day!*
A word from the heart—will you speak it? *Choose ye to-day!*
Will you believe, or the Saviour neglect?
Will you receive, or His mercy reject?
Pause, ere you answer, oh pause and reflect: *Choose ye to-day!*

A death to be feared—will you fear it?—
A voice that invites—will you hear it?—
Strait is the portal and narrow the way;
Enter at once, and be saved while you may;
Think what may hang on a moment's delay—

There's life through the cross—will you share it?—
The cross that CHRIST gives—will you bear it?—
Soon will the day of salvation be o'er;
Then will the SPIRIT entreat you no more;
JESUS no longer will stand at the door—

The bondage of sin—will you break it?—
The water of life—will you take it?—
Come to the arms that are open for you;
Hide in the wounds that by faith you may view;
Death ere the morrow your steps may pursue— *Choose ye to-day!*

718 Oh, Be Saved! P.M.

Frances J. van Alstyne — S.J. Vail

1 SINNER, is thy heart now troubled?
  GOD is coming very near;
  Do not hide thy deep emotion,
  Do not check the falling tear:

  Oh, be saved; His grace is free!
  Oh, be saved, CHRIST died for thee!
  Oh, be saved eternally!

2 JESUS now is bending o'er thee:
  JESUS, lowly, meek, and mild;
  To the Friend who died to save thee
  Wilt thou not be reconciled?—

3 Art thou waiting till the morrow?
  Thou may'st never see its light;
  Come at once! accept His mercy:
  He is waiting: come to-night—

4 With a lowly, contrite spirit,
  Kneeling at the Saviour's feet,
  Thou canst have, this very moment,
  Pardon, precious, full, and sweet—

5 Let the angels bear the tidings
  Upward to the court of heaven;
  Let them sing with holy rapture
  O'er another soul forgiven—

719 Dennis S.M.
(Doncaster 279) — H.G. Nageli

CEASE, O thou wandering soul,
　On restless wing to roam ;
All this wide world, to either pole,
　Has not for thee a home.

Behold the Ark of GOD ;
Behold the open Door ;
Haste thee to gain that blest abode,
　And rove, O soul, no more !

　　There safe shalt thou abide,
　　There sweet shall be thy rest,
　　Thy every longing satisfied,
　　With GOD'S salvation blest.

720　　Love's Invitation C.M. and Chorus

Douglas Russell　　　　　　　　　　　　　　　　W.E. Vine

COME, anxious one, and lowly kneel
　Down at the Saviour's feet ;
His word receive—wait not to feel,
And peace thy soul shall greet :
　　Come, rest alone on JESUS'S blood,
　　　Once shed on Calvary ;
　　O'erwhelmed by judgment as a
　　　　flood,
　　He bore our penalty.

In death for us He stood alone,
　For unjust ones, the Just !
And He who did for sin atone
　Now calls for simple trust—

What law demanded JESUS met,
　As Surety in our stead ;
We know His blood has paid the debt;
　He liveth who was dead—

　　Since Justice can no more demand,
　　　And GOD is satisfied,
　　Accepted now in CHRIST we stand ;
　　　We live in Him who died—

721 Wonderful Words of Life 8.6.8.6.6.6 and Chorus

P.P. Bliss   P.P. Bliss

SING them over again to me,
   Wonderful words of Life!
Let me more of their beauty see,
   Wonderful words of Life!
      Words of life and beauty,
      Teaching faith and duty!
Beautiful words! wonderful words!
Wonderful words of Life!

CHRIST, the blessèd One, gives to all
   Wonderful words of Life!
Sinner, list to the loving call,
   Wonderful words of Life!
      All so freely given,
      Wooing us to heaven!—

Sweetly echo the gospel call,
   Wonderful words of Life!
Peace and pardon proclaim to all,
   Wonderful words of Life!
      JESUS, only Saviour,
      Sanctify for ever!—

722 Mercy's Portal S.M. and Chorus
A. Midlane (Chalvey 686) W.E. Vine

HOW sweet the cheering words,
"*Whoever will*" may come!
The door of mercy open stands;
As yet there still is room:

Now is 'salvation's day;'
His message God doth send,
That "whoso will" may surely come,
Ere mercy's day shall end.

'Tis the "accepted time,"
The day of grace and love;
And GOD invites "*whoever will*"
His faithfulness to prove—

The Saviour sits on high,
His work on earth is done;
And sinners GOD will now accept,
Through His belovèd SON—

That Saviour soon will rise,
And close the open door;
Then all who have refused to come,
Will hear of grace no more—

723 Ottawa 8.7.8.7.7.7

Thos. Kelly • L. Mason

SEE the Saviour! sinners slew Him,
  Yet for sinners He was slain;
Sinners now are welcome to Him,
  Such compose the Saviour's train:
Sinners, ransomed by His blood!
Sinners, reconciled to GOD!

See the holy Victim suffering!
  Sinners, here's a sight for you!
Here's an all-sufficient offering;
  Oh, believe the record true!
See the Lamb for sinners slain;
Every other hope is vain.

'Tis a true and "faithful saying,"
  JESUS came to save the lost;
Grace and truth at once displaying—
  GOD, the Saviour, true and just:
Sinners, hear His gracious voice,
In His saving work rejoice!

724 Claremont C.M.

S. Trevor Francis • (St. Peter 24) • J. Foster

HAST Thou not finished all, O GOD,
  For sinners lost, undone?
Has not the burden of their guilt
  Been laid upon Thy SON?

Oh, that this wondrous love of Thine
  May heal the inward smart,
Within the strange, mysterious depths
  Of some poor, broken heart!

Oh, love unmeasured! stretching far
  Beyond our utmost gaze—
Farther than sun, or gleaming star,
  That shineth forth Thy praise;

Deeper than sin's deep depths of woe,
  Higher than heaven above,
More boundless than the ocean's flow—
  Immeasurable love!

725   Lewisham 8.7.8.7.8.7

Thos. Kelly   J. Tilleard

"IT IS FINISHED!" sinners hear it,
  'Tis the dying Victor's cry;
"It is finished!" angels bear it—
  Bear the joyful truth on high:
    "It is finished!"
  Tell it through the earth and sky.

Justice, from her awful station,
  Bars the sinner's peace no more;
Justice views with approbation
  What the Saviour did and bore;
    Grace and mercy
  Now display their boundless store.

"It is finished!" all is over;
  He the cup of wrath has drained;
Such the truth these words discover,
  Thus our victory was obtained:
    'Tis a victory
  None but JESUS could have gained!

726 **Christ Arose 6.5.6.4. and Chorus**

R. Lowry   R. Lowry

CHORUS. *faster.*

L OW in the grave He lay,
   JESUS, my Saviour!
Waiting the coming day,
   JESUS, my LORD!

*Up from the grave He arose . . .
With a mighty triumph o'er His
   foes; . . .
He arose a Victor from the dark
   domain,
And He lives for ever with His saints
   to reign!
         He arose! . . . He arose! . . .
      Hallelujah! CHRIST arose!*

Vainly they watch His bed,
   JESUS, my Saviour!
Vainly they seal the dead,
   JESUS, my LORD!—

Death cannot keep his prey,
   JESUS, my Saviour!
He tore the bars away,
   JESUS, my LORD!—

727
Carter

Cwm Rhondda 8.7.8.7.8.7

John Hughes

1 He who once was dead, now liveth!
　Lo! He lives for evermore—
He who all our sins forgiveth,
　He who all our sorrows bore:
　　Hallelujah!
　We our risen Lord adore!

2 Sing, 'tis done! from heaven's own
　　treasure
　All the fearful debt is paid;
All our sin, in its full measure,
　God has on our Surety laid;
　　And "for ever"
　Is the sacrifice He made!

3 Tell around the wide creation
　　What redeeming love hath done;
Publish full and free salvation
　　Through the blood of God's dear
　　　Son:
　　Hallelujah!
　His the glory—His alone.

728 Zurich S.M.
(Woolwich 251)

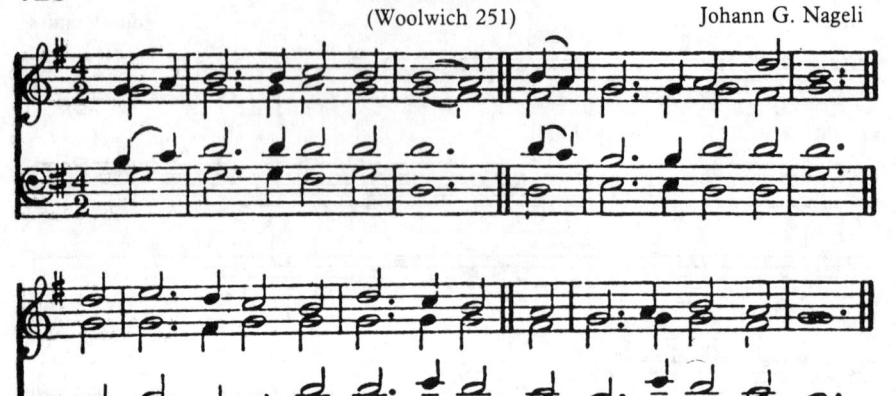

Johann G. Nageli

BEHOLD the empty tomb,
  The place where JESUS lay!
Upon the cross He bore our doom,
  And rolled our curse away.

The ransom fully paid,
  The work completely done,
GOD, who on Him our judgment laid.
  To glory raised His SON.

There, where the sprinkled blood
  Doth in the light abide,
We now rejoice before our GOD,
  For ever satisfied.

We glory in His grace,
  We sing what He hath done;
And sound abroad in every place
  The Gospel of GOD'S SON.

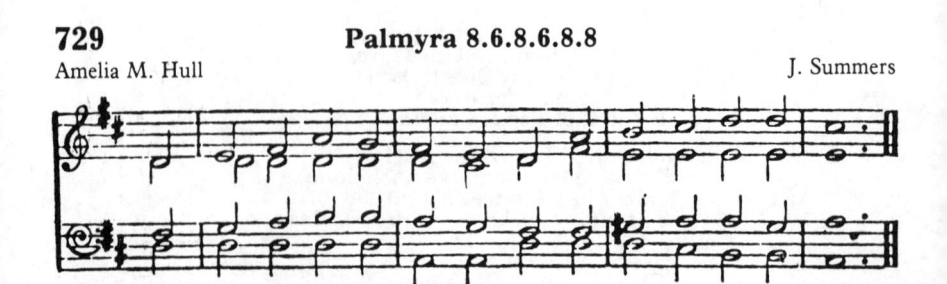

729 Palmyra 8.6.8.6.8.8
Amelia M. Hull

J. Summers

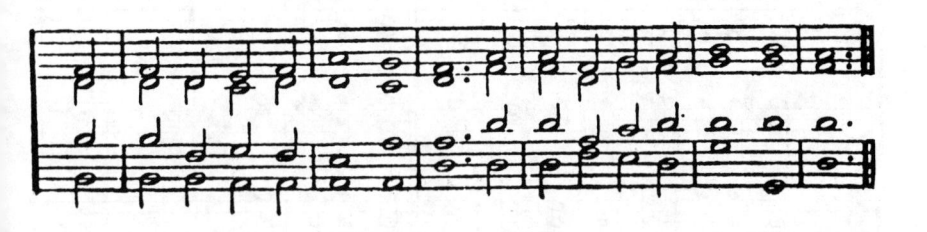

GOD tells me how I may be saved.
He points to something *done,*
Accomplished on Mount Calvary
By His belovèd SON,
In which no works of mine have place;
For grace with works is no more grace.

**Ah, yes; it is His *finished* work
On which my soul relies;
And if my unbelieving heart
Its preciousness denies,
That works of mine might have a place;
Then grace, indeed, is no more grace.**

But, in that He is raised on high
Who came our sins to bear,
I learn that I am seen of GOD
In oneness with Him there,
Where not a spot His eye can trace,
Or aught that mars His work of grace.

Oh, wondrous words! Oh, precious work
By which my soul is saved!
And thou who didst it, blessèd LORD!
Hast in my heart engraved
That Name which must all names displace,
And I now glory in Thy grace!

730   Herein Is Love 8.4.8.4.8.8.8.4

G.W. Frazer   W.E. Vine

GOD sent His only SON to die:
   "*Herein is love!*"
Sent Him from off the throne on high;
   "*Herein is love!*"
Oh, wondrous love, that GOD should give
His only SON, that we might live
Through Him, in whom we now believe:
   "*Herein is love!*"

GOD made Him "sin" upon the tree—
That we His righteousness might be—
Oh, deep and full abounding grace,
Which brought Him to the sinner's place,
The curse to bear in righteousness—

GOD raised Him from amongst the dead—
And set Him over all as Head:—
Redemption's work now fully done,
GOD glorified in His own SON,
We share the victory He hath won—

Soon in the FATHER's house we'll rest—
There with the SON, for ever blest—
As on His blessèd face we gaze,
Our hearts and voices we shall raise,
And fill those courts with ceaseless praise—
   "*Herein is love!*"

731   Evan C.M.

Isaac Watts   (Kilmarnock 369)   W.H. Havergal

SALVATION! oh, the joyful sound!
 What pleasure to our ears!
A sovereign balm for every wound,
A cordial for our fears.

Buried in sorrow and in sin,
 At hell's dark door we lay;
But we were raised by grace divine
 To see a glorious day.

Salvation! let the echo fly
 The spacious earth around,
While heavenly hosts above the sky
 Rejoice to raise the sound.

Salvation! O Thou bleeding Lamb!
 To Thee the praise belongs!
Salvation shall inspire our hearts,
 And dwell upon our tongues.

732   Better World 8.3.8.3.8.8.8.3

H. Kingsbury   J. Hayhurst

COME, let us all unite to sing,
 "GOD IS LOVE!"
Let heaven and earth their praises
 bring;
 "GOD IS LOVE!"
Let this blest truth our hearts inflame
With joy and praise, as we proclaim
The glories of JEHOVAH'S name:
 "GOD IS LOVE!"

Oh, tell to earth's remotest bound—
 In CHRIST we have redemption
 found—
His blood has purged our sins away;
His SPIRIT turned our night to day;
And now we can rejoice to say—

How happy is our portion here!—
His promises our spirits cheer—
He is our sun and shield by day,
Our help, our hope, our strength and
 stay;
He will be with us all the way—

In glory we shall sing again—
Yes, this shall be our lofty strain—
Whilst endless ages roll along,
In concert with the heavenly throng,
This shall be still our sweetest song,
 "GOD IS LOVE!"

733 Let The Saviour In! P.M.

J.B. Atchinson

E.O. Excell

THERE'S a Stranger at the door;
  Let .... Him in! ....
He has been there oft before;
  Let .... Him in! ....
Let Him in, ere He be gone;
Let Him in, the Holy One,
JESUS CHRIST, the FATHER'S SON:
  Let .... Him in! ....

Open now to Him your heart—
If you wait, He may depart—
Let Him in; He is your Friend,
He your soul will e'er defend;
He will keep you till the end—

Hear you now His loving voice?—
Now, oh now, make Him your choice—
He is standing at the door;
Blessings on you He will pour,
And His name you will adore—

Now admit the heavenly Guest—
He will make for you a feast—
He will tell of sins forgiven,
And when earth-ties all are riven,
He will take you home to heaven—
Let .... Him in! ....

734 **Bodmin L.M.**
Joseph Grigg   (Nicomachus 526)   Alfred Scott-Gatty

BEHOLD a Stranger at the door;
He gently knocks, has knocked before;
Has waited long; is waiting still:
Who ever used a friend so ill?

Oh, lovely attitude! He stands
With willing heart and open hands;
Oh, matchless kindness! and He shows
This matchless kindness to His *foes*.

But will He prove a friend indeed?
He will; the very friend you need:
The Friend of sinners, yes, 'tis He,
Who died for sin on Calvary.

Admit Him ere His anger burn,
Lest He depart and ne'er return;
Admit Him, or the hour's at hand
When at His door denied you'll stand.

Admit Him, for the human breast
Ne'er entertained so kind a guest;
No mortal tongue their joys can tell,
With whom He condescends to dwell.

735　　　　Redemption 9.8.9.8 and Chorus

S.M. Sayford　　　　　　　　　　　　　　　　　　　Peter Bilhorn

Chorus

rit.

REDEMPTION! oh, wonderful story,
Glad message for you and for me,
That JESUS has purchased our pardon,
And paid all the debt on the tree:

Believe it, O sinner, believe it;
Receive the glad message—'tis true;
Trust now in the Crucified Saviour,
Salvation He offers to you.

From death unto life He doth bring us,
And make us by grace sons of GOD;
A fountain is opened for sinners,
Oh, wash and be cleansed by His blood!—

No longer shall sin have dominion,
Though present to tempt and annoy,
For CHRIST in His blessèd redemption,
The power of all sin can destroy—

Accept now GOD'S message of mercy;
To JESUS, oh, hasten to-day,
For He will receive him that cometh,
And never will turn him away!—

736 Redeemed by Blood C.M. and Chorus

Macleod Wylie
S.J. Vail

REDEEMED by blood of God's dear
 Son,
 Our sins are all forgiven;
We rest on work which He has done,
 Our perfect claim to heaven:
 Oh, depth of mercy, wide and free,
 That precious blood was shed for
  me,
   For me, . . . for me, . . .
 That blood was shed for me!

Redeemed by blood, we glory now
 In Him who judgment bore;
To Him with grateful hearts we bow,
 We triumph and adore—

Redeemed by blood: oh, let us ne'er
 Forget the debt we owe,
Nor shrink the cross and shame to
  bear,
 For Him who loved us so—

737   Munich 7.6.7.6.D

H.E. Govan   (Llangloffan 335)   German Melody

O SINNERS, come to JESUS!
  All other trust is vain;
Your every hope must fail you
  Unless you're born again:
You need the cleansing fountain
  To purge your heart within,
And purify your conscience
  From all the stains of sin.

You need to come to JESUS,
  And find in Him your rest;
Confiding in His goodness,
  Reclining on His breast;
You need the voice of JESUS
  To whisper, "Go in peace!"
To calm the inward tempest,
  And bid the conflict cease.

Then, will you come to JESUS,
  In spite of fear and doubt?
He's waiting now to save you,
  And will not cast you out;
If but in true repentance
  Before His cross you bow,
He'll give you free forgiveness
  And full salvation—NOW.

738   Come Unto Me 10.10.10.10 and Chorus

Douglas Russell   Geo. C. Stebbins

"COME unto Me!" An echo, soft and clear,
Borne down the ages, falls upon the ear:
Word of all words for weary hearts the best—
"Come unto Me, and I will give you rest:"

"Come unto Me, . . . come unto Me,
Come unto Me, and I will give you rest,
I will give you rest, . . . I will give you rest." . . .

Come, weary one, all vain your labour long,
Come—He will turn your sighing into song;
Why wander on 'neath load of sin opprest?
"Come unto Me, and I will give you rest"—

"Come," list again—sweet word, so fresh and true!
Kind invitation, sent, O soul, to *you!*
Come, find in Him what meets your anxious quest:
"Come unto Me, and I will give you rest"—

Come as you are, for He *gives* rest and peace,
Life and salvation, joys that ne'er shall cease;
Answer His call—of all be now possest:
"Come unto Me, and I will give you rest"—

739 There Is Pardon For You P.M.

Frances J. van Alstyne (arr.) H.P. Main

Slowly.

CHORUS

OH, come to the Saviour, believe in
His name,
And He will your heart now renew:
He waits to be gracious; oh, turn not
away,
For now there is pardon for you:

Yes, there is pardon for you, . . .
Yes, there is pardon for you; . . .
For JESUS has died to redeem you,
And purchased full pardon for
you.

The way of transgression that leads
    unto death,
  Oh, why will you longer pursue?
How can you reject the sweet message of love,
  That brings a full pardon to you?—

Then trust in the Saviour, believe on
    His name,
  Rely on His promise so true;
Your sins, though as scarlet, He'll
    make white as snow,
  And grant a full pardon to you—

740 Kensington New 8.7.8.7.8.7
Andrew Reed   (Praise my soul 155)   J. Tilleard

HEAR, O sinner! mercy hails you,
    Now with sweetest voice she
      calls,
  Bids you haste to seek the Saviour,
    Ere the hand of justice falls:
      Hear, O sinner!
  'Tis the voice of mercy calls.

See the storm of vengeance gathering
    O'er the path you dare to tread!
  Hark! the awful thunder rolling,
    Loud and louder o'er your head:
      Turn, O sinner,
  Unto Him who for us bled!

Haste, O sinner, to the Saviour,
    Seek His favour while you may;
  Mercy's day will soon be over,
    Soon your life will pass away:
      Haste, O sinner!
  Lest you perish through delay.

741 The Master's Call 10.8.11.8 and Chorus
Frances J. van Alstyne   W.E. Vine

Chorus *Slowly.*

" THE Master is come, and calleth for thee,"
He stands at the door of thy heart;
No friend so forgiving, so gentle as He,
Oh say, wilt thou let Him depart?

Patiently waiting, earnestly pleading,
JESUS, the Saviour, knocks at thy heart.

The Master is come, with blessings for thee;
Arise, and His message receive;
Thy ransom is furnished, thy pardon is free,
If thou wilt repent and believe—

The Master is come, and calleth thee now;
This moment what joys may be thine!
How tender the grace that illumines His brow,
A pledge of His favour divine!—

742 St. Agnes 6.4.6.4.D
Smith and Hastings
J. Langran

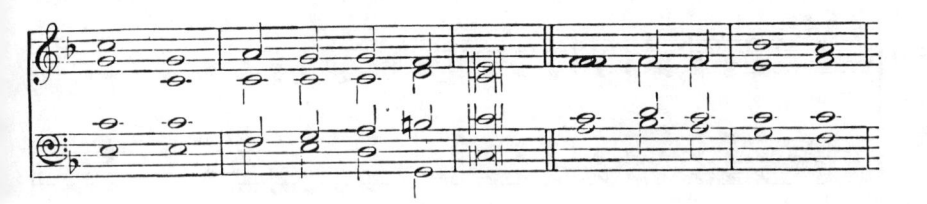

1 TO-DAY, the Saviour calls
    The wanderers home;
  O ye benighted souls,
    Why longer roam?

2 To-day, the Saviour calls—
    Oh, hear Him now;
  While yet within these walls,
    To JESUS bow,

3 To-day, the Saviour calls—
    For refuge fly;
  The storm of justice falls,
    And wrath is nigh.

4 The SPIRIT calls to-day—
    Yield to His power;
  Oh, grieve Him not away,
    'Tis mercy's hour!

743 Mercy Is Boundless P.M.

Henrietta E. Blair

W.J. Kirkpatrick

CHORUS

PRAISE be to JESUS, His mercy is free,
  Mercy is free, mercy is free!
Sinner, that mercy is flowing for thee;
  Mercy is boundless and free!
If thou art willing on Him to believe;
  Mercy is free, mercy is free!
Life everlasting thou mayest receive;
  Mercy is boundless and free!

*JESUS, the Saviour, is seeking for thee,
  Seeking for thee, seeking for thee;
Lovingly, tenderly, calling for thee,
  Calling and seeking for thee.*

Why on the mountains of sin wilt thou roam?
  Mercy is free, mercy is free!
Gently the SPIRIT is calling thee home;
  Mercy is boundless and free!
Art thou in darkness? oh, come to the light;
  Mercy is free, mercy is free!
JESUS is waiting, He'll save you tonight;
  Mercy is boundless and free!—

Yes, there is pardon for all who believe;
  Mercy is free, mercy is free!
Come, and this moment a blessing receive;
  Mercy is boundless and free!
JESUS is waiting, oh, hear Him proclaim;
  Mercy is free, mercy is free!
Cling to His promise, believe on His name;
  Mercy is boundless and free!—

744 Through The Name Of Jesus 11.9.11.9 and Chorus

G.F. Root

CHORUS.

THROUGH the name of JESUS mercy flows to-day,
Fount of lovingkindness sweet and free;
See how JESUS suffered when upon the tree,
All to bring salvation e'en to thee:

> Welcome, welcome, now to JESUS come!
> Welcome, welcome to the FATHER'S home!
> JESUS will receive you; in His love confide;
> 'Twas to save lost sinners JESUS died!

Through the work of JESUS peace is preached to-day,
GOD now sends His message far and wide,
Message of salvation, life eternally,
Righteousness through JESUS now supplied—

Through the blood of JESUS sins are washed away,
Cleansing fount of blessing let it be!
CHRIST endured sin's judgment when upon the tree,
Everlasting favour then for thee—

GOD delights in giving rest and peace to-day,
Sinner, leave your burden while you may:
Mercy still is flowing like a river free,
Pouring forth forgiveness now for thee—

745   **Fading Away 11.11.11.11 and Chorus**

A. Midlane   Ira D. Sankey

1. SING softly; for JESUS is passing this way,
Salvation proclaiming, and mercy's glad day;
The night of this world is fast hasting along,
He speaks ere its last fading shadow is gone:

Fading away; fading away;
Sing softly; earth's glories are fading away!

2. Sing softly; it may be our last closing song,
The moments, so solemn, are passing along;
The sweet, flowing cadence may scarce die away
Ere voices are tuned in the region of day—

3. Sing softly; the star of the morning appears;
It rose in the distance, but see how it nears!
Faith catches its brightness, its summons to soar
To JESU'S bright presence—peace, joy, evermore!—

4. Sing softly; for solemnly closes the day,
The time of acceptance is ebbing away;
Like Sodom's fair morning earth's sun may arise:
Ere evening thick darkness may cover the skies!—

746 Look And Live P.M.

W.A. Ogden
W.A. Ogden

CHORUS.

I'VE a message from the LORD, Hallelujah!
The message unto you I'll give;
'Tis recorded in His Word, Hallelujah!
It is only that you "look and live:"

"Look and live," . . . for ever live!
Look to JESUS now and live;
'Tis recorded in His word, Hallelujah!
It is only that you "look and live!"

I've a message full of love, Hallelujah!
A message, O my friend, for you;
'Tis a message from above, Hallelujah!
JESUS said it, and I know 'tis true—

Life is offered unto thee, Hallelujah!
Eternal life thy soul shall have;
Only look thou unto Him, Hallelujah!
Look to JESUS, who alone can save—

747 Pilgrims 11.10.11.10 and Chorus

Henry Smart

HARK! hark! the voice of CHRIST,
　　the sinner's Saviour,
In glory seated on His FATHER's
　　throne!
It tells of love and everlasting favour
For sinners far from GOD, by sin
　　undone :

Message of JESUS, message of love,
Telling of welcome to that bright
　　home above.

It is the voice of Him now crowned
　　with glory,
That tells of life for "whosoever
　　will;"
How sweet the sound of that entranc-
　　ing story !
It tells of love for guilty sinners
　　still !—

Blest words! they speak to us of GOD's
　　salvation,
Wrought out by CHRIST alone upon
　　the cross,
Who by His blood redeems from
　　every nation,
And saves His people from eternal
　　loss—

Now, weary souls, who rest and peace
　　are seeking,
Who long for One to meet your
　　deepest need,
Hear in the Word the voice of JESUS
　　speaking,
And trust in Him who makes us
　　free indeed !—

748   St. Luke 11.11.11.11

OH, why not, say why not, God's
   message receive?
Why not at this moment believe it
   and live?
It tells, through the Saviour's atonement for sin,
Of grace that no effort of ours e'er
   could win.

'Tis not thy remorse, nor thy sorrow
   and fear,
Nor e'en thy repentance, thy conscience can clear;
These could not atone for or put
   away sin,
Or give thee the peace which thou
   needest within.

Why sorrow, or grieve, or in misery
   stay,
Or wait for more feeling on some
   future day?
What feeling of thine, or what grief,
   can compare
With all He once suffered, thy burden
   to bear?

The anguish for sin that once fell on
   the LORD,
The wrath He endured, as told out in
   His word,
The death which He suffered, the
   life He now lives—
Their infinite worth to the sinner He
   gives!

No longer delaying, the message receive;
'Tis GOD who now bids thee believe
   it and live;
He sends the good tidings to gladden
   thy soul,
And thou, in believing, shalt now be
   made whole.

749 **Abundantly Able To Save** 11.11.11.11 and Chorus

E.A. Hoffman

P.P. Bliss

Chorus

Words over

WHOEVER receiveth the Cruci-
   fied One,
Whoever believeth on GOD'S only SON,
A free and a perfect salvation shall
   have,
For He is abundantly able to save:

Oh, hearken, the Sa . . viour is calling
   for thee ! . .
His grace and His mer . . . cy are
   wondrously free; . . .
His blood as a ran . . . som for sinners He gave, . . .
And He is abun . . . dantly able to
   save.

Whoever receiveth the message of
   GOD,
And trusts in the power of the soul-
   cleansing blood,
A full and eternal redemption shall
   have,
For He is both able and willing to
   save—

Whoever repents and forsakes every
   sin,
And opens his heart for the LORD to
   come in,
A present and perfect salvation shall
   have,
For JESUS is ready this moment to
   save—

750   Hark! Hark! Hark! P.M.
Hannah K. Burlingham

HARK! hark! hark!
   'Tis a message of mercy free;
O sinner, thy crimson sins are dark,
   But JESUS hath died for thee:

   Died for thee, died for thee,
   O sinner, thy crimson sins are dark,
   But JESUS hath died for thee !

Look! look! look!
   The crucified Saviour see!
Thy sins are entered in GOD'S own
      book,
   But JESUS hath died for thee—

Come! come! come!
   For JESUS can rescue thee:
He healeth the leper, the lame, the
      dumb:
   O sinner, He died for thee—

Haste! haste! haste!
   Delay not from death to flee;
Oh, wherefore the moments in mad-
      ness waste
   When JESUS is calling thee?—

Now! now! now!
   To-morrow too late may be;
O sinner, with tears of contrition bow,
   Confessing 'He died for me!'—

751 Jesus Is Calling! P.M.

F.J. Crosby
Geo. C. Stebbins

CHORUS

1. JESUS is tenderly calling thee home,
   Calling to-day, calling to-day;
   Why from the sunshine of love wilt thou roam,
   Farther and farther away?—

   Call . . . ing to-day! . . .
   Call . . . ing to-day! . . .
   JE . . . sus is call . . . ing,
   Is tenderly calling to-day.

2. JESUS is calling the weary to rest,
   Calling to-day, calling to-day;
   Bring Him thy burden and thou shalt be blest;
   He will not turn thee away—

3. JESUS is waiting: oh, come to Him now;
   Waiting to-day, waiting to-day;
   Come with thy sins, at His feet lowly bow,
   Come, and no longer delay—

4. JESUS is pleading: oh, list to His voice,
   Hear Him to-day, hear Him to-day;
   They who believe in His name shall rejoice;
   Quickly arise and away!—

752 Rousseau 8.7.8.7.8.7

A. Midlane
J.J. Rousseau

HARK! the voice of JESUS calling,
'Come, ye laden, come to Me;
I have rest and peace to offer;
Rest, thou labouring one, for thee:
  Take salvation—
  Take it now, and happy be.'

Yes; though high in heavenly glory,
Still the Saviour calls to thee;
Faith can hear His gracious accents,
'Come, ye laden, come to Me'—

Soon that voice will cease its calling,
Now it speaks, and speaks to thee;
Sinner, heed the gracious message,
To His blood for refuge flee—

Life is found alone in JESUS,
Only thus 'tis offered thee,
Offered without price or money,
'Tis the gift of GOD sent free—

753 Christ Is Coming 8.7.8.7 and Chorus

Mary Sullivan
Ira D. Sankey

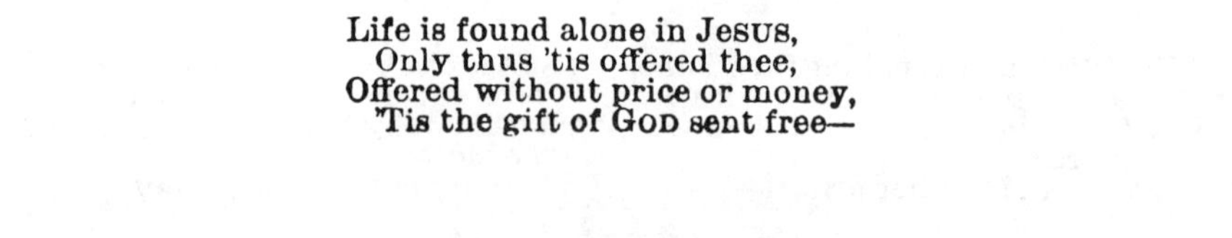

CHRIST is coming, quickly coming,
  Art thou ready for that day?
Are thy crimson sins forgiven,
  In His blood all washed away?

Oh, the bliss, the rest of knowing
  JESUS as thy dearest Friend,
As thy Guide, thy Guard, thy
    Shepherd,
  Who will love thee to the end !

Once on Calvary He suffered,
  Died in grace to set thee free;
Oh, believe the joyful tidings,
  And to CHRIST for pardon flee—

JESUS waiteth to be gracious,
  Waiteth even now for thee;
Listen to His earnest pleading,
  ' Come, ye weary, come to Me '—

Come, and gaze by faith upon Him;
  Lost and dying, look and live;
See, He waiteth to receive thee,
  That He may thy sins forgive—

Then thou wilt not fear His coming,
  But with joy wilt hail that day
When He comes to take His ransomed
  To His FATHER'S house away—

754 Hear God's Blessed Invitation P.M.

G.M.J.

J. McGranahan

HEAR GOD'S blessèd invitation,
　　Come, come, come!
To the fountain of salvation
　　Come, come, come!
Healing streams are flowing still;
Welcome, " whosoever will,
Let him take the water of life freely: "

　　"*Let him take . . . let him take . . .
　　Let him take the water of life freely;
　　Let him take . . . let him take . . .
　　Let him take the water of life freely.*"

'Tis the voice of JESUS saying,
　　Come, come, come!
Now His blest command obeying,
　　Come, come, come!
He will cleanse from every ill:
Welcome, " whosoever will,
Let him take the water of life freely"—

'Tis the HOLY SPIRIT calling,
　　Come, come, come!
Ere the shades of death are falling,
　　Come, come, come!
He the heart with peace will fill;
Welcome, " whosoever will,
Let him take the water of life freely" –

755　　St. Cuthbert 8.6.8.4

Douglas Russell　　　　　　　　　　J.B. Dykes

"COME unto Me!" In tend'rest tone
　　A voice still calls to you;
O labouring one, so sad and lone,
　　CHRIST'S word is true!

"Come unto Me!" Respond to-day—
　　Oh, come with trustful heart;
Come, at His feet your burden lay—
　　With sadness part.

" Come unto Me!" The echo still
　　Falls sweetly on our ear;
Each aching void He, He can fill,
　　And banish fear!

"Come unto Me!" His precious blood
　　Can cleanse each crimson stain;
He died! Beyond the judgment flood
　　He lives again!

Then come to Him—on Him believe,
　　Trust in His death alone;
Life, rest and peace you will receive,
　　And share His throne!

756 None But Christ Can Satisfy C.M. and Chorus

A. Midlane

J. McGranahan

CHORUS

Y ET one more call, belovèd one,
  A solemn call to thee,
With hasty steps still journeying on
  Unto eternity:

  *'Tis CHRIST alone can satisfy,
    And none but He can save;* . . .
  *Pardon of sin is found in Him,
    And triumph o'er the grave.*

One solemn call, the last, may-be,
  That e'er thy soul shall know;
Why choose to spend eternity
  In darkness and in woe?—

From lips long silent still may come
  The words which met thine ear
Ere some belovèd one passed away,
  Still sounding deep and clear!—

Oh, turn thee, turn thee, e'en to-day!
  Love's door is open still;
The dying prayer, the Saviour's call,
  True love's desire, fulfil—

757 Come Believing 8.7.8.7 and Chorus

El Nathan
J. McGranahan

1. ONCE again the gospel message
   From the Saviour you have heard;
   Will you heed the invitation?
   Will you turn and seek the LORD?

   Come, believing; . . . come, believing; . . .
   Come to JESUS: look and live! . . .

2. Many summers you have wasted,
   Ripened harvests you have seen;
   Winter snows by spring have melted:
   Will you linger still in sin?—

3. JESUS for your choice is waiting;
   Tarry not—at once decide;
   While the SPIRIT now is striving,
   Yield, and seek the Saviour's side—

4. Cease of fitness to be thinking;
   Do not longer try to feel:
   It is *trusting* and not *feeling*,
   That will give the SPIRIT'S seal—

5. Let your will to GOD be given;
   Trust in CHRIST'S atoning blood;
   Look to JESUS now, in heaven,
   Rest on His unchanging word—

758   Call Them In 8.7.8.7.D
Anna Shipton   Ira D. Sankey

'CALL them in'—the poor, the wretched,
  Sin-stained wanderers from the fold;
Peace and pardon freely offer:
  Can you weigh their worth with gold?
'Call them in'—the weak, the weary,
  Laden with the doom of sin;
Bid them come and rest in JESUS;
  He is waiting—'call them in!'

'Call them in'—the Jew, the Gentile,
  Bid the stranger to the feast;
'Call them in'—the rich, the noble,
  From the highest to the least:
Forth the FATHER runs to meet them,
  He hath all their sorrows seen;
Robe and ring, and royal sandals,
  Wait the lost ones—'call them in!'

    'Call them in'—the broken-hearted,
      Cowering 'neath the brand of shame;
    Speak love's message, low and tender—
      ''Twas for sinners JESUS came:'
    See! the shadows lengthen round us,
      Soon the day-dawn will begin;
    Can you leave them lost and lonely?
      CHRIST is coming—'call them in!'

759   Williams L.M.
J. Fawcett   (Saxby 593)   From Templi Carmina 1829

BEHOLD the sin-atoning Lamb,
With wonder, gratitude, and love;
To take away our guilt and shame,
See Him descending from above.

Our sins and griefs on Him were laid,
He meekly bore the heavy load,
Our ransom price He fully paid,
In tears, in agony, and blood.

Pardon and peace through Him abound,
He can the richest blessings give;
Salvation in His name is found,
He bids the dying sinner live.

O Lamb of GOD, we look to Thee!
Where else can helpless sinners go?
Oh, may Thy SPIRIT now set free
Those burdened with their guilt and woe!

760   At The Cross There's Room P.M.

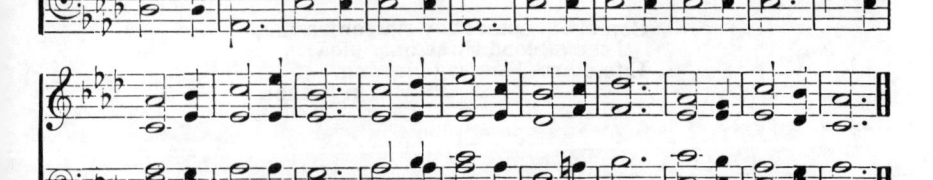

F.J. Crosby   R. Lowry

MOURNER, wheresoe'er thou art,
   At the cross there's room!
Tell the burden of thy heart;
   At the cross there's room!
Tell it in the Saviour's ear,
Cast away thine every fear,
Only speak, and He will hear:
   At the cross there's room!

Haste thee, wanderer, tarry not—
Seek that consecrated spot—
Heavy-laden, sore opprest,
Love can soothe thy troubled breast
In the Saviour find thy rest—

Thoughtless sinner, come to-day—
Hark! the Bride and SPIRIT say—
Now a living fountain see,
Opened there for thee and me,
Rich or poor, or bond or free—

Blessèd thought! for every one—
Love's atoning work is done—
Streams of boundless mercy flow,
Free to all who thither go:
Oh that all the world might know,
   At the cross there's room!

761   **Lost One, Wandering On (Filey) 8.7.8.4**

J.M. Wigner   Lowell Mason

LOST one! wandering on in sadness,
   None to guide or comfort thee,
Vainly seeking rest and gladness,
        To JESUS flee.

Peace He offers, and salvation,
   Pardon, blood-bought, full and free;
Spurn no more His invitation,
        "Come unto Me."

Come, oh, come! thy sin confessing,
   JESU'S blood thine only plea;
Life eternal—every blessing,
        He will give thee.

762   **Yet There Is Room 10.10.4.6**

H.F. Witherby   Ernest E. Courtney

YET there is room! Love, love
eternal waits,
The Master sits within yon golden
gates!
 Come, come, oh! come,
 The CHRIST of GOD receive.

Long-suffering love waits, wanderer,
for thee,
Oh, hear the sounds of heaven's sweet
melody!
 Come, come, oh! come,
 The FATHER'S love believe.

Within those doors the FATHER and
the SON
Rejoice o'er souls to joys eternal won:
 Come, come, oh! come,
 And swell the gladsome song.

The FATHER waits with loving, tender
kiss;
For thee He keeps the ring of endless
bliss:
 Come, come, oh! come,
 Home joys to sons belong.

Thy restless feet with peace may yet
be shod,
And thou be robed with the best
robe of GOD:
 Come, come, oh! come,
 GOD glories in His grace.

With sons in light thou shalt be
glorified,
On golden harp shalt praise the Lamb
who died:
 Come, come, oh! come,
 And see the Saviour's face.

Behold! His hand, once nailed upon
the tree,
To heavenly mansions quickly beck-
ons thee:
 Come, come, oh! come,
 For soon 'twill be too late.

763 Yet There Is Room 10.10 and Chorus

H. Bonar
Ira. D. Sankey

"YET there is room!" The Lamb's
bright hall of song,
With its fair glory, beckons thee
along:
Room, room, still room!
Oh, enter, enter now!

Day is declining, and the sun is low:
The shadows lengthen, light makes
haste to go—

The bridal hall is filling for the feast;
Pass in, pass in, and be the Bridegroom's guest—

It fills, it fills, that hall of jubilee!
Make haste, make haste: 'tis not too
full for thee—

Yet there is room! Still open stands
the gate,
The gate of love; it is not yet too late—

Pass in, pass in! That banquet is for
thee;
That cup of everlasting love is free—

All heaven is there, all joy! Go in, go
in,
The angels beckon thee the prize to
win—

Louder and sweeter sounds the loving
call;
Come, lingerer, come; enter that festal
hall—

Ere night that gate may close, and
seal thy doom:
Then the last low, long cry, 'No room,
no room!'
No room, no room!
Oh, woful cry, 'No room!'

764 Penlan 7.6.7.6.D

D. Jenkins

TO-DAY God's mercy calls thee
　　To wash away thy sin;
However great thy trespass,
　　Whatever thou hast been;
However long from mercy
　　Thou may'st have turned away,
The blood of CHRIST can cleanse thee,
　　And make thee white *to-day.*

To-day the gate is open,
　　And all who enter in
Shall find a gracious welcome,
　　And pardon for their sin:
The past shall be forgotten,
　　And present grace be given,
With future joy in prospect—
　　A glorious home in heaven!

765 There's A Refuge In God 11.11.11.11

Henry Bennett

A.J. Gordon

THERE'S a refuge in GOD for the sin-burdened soul,
And a life-giving fountain whose streams make us whole;
There's a refuge in JESUS, the sinner's true Friend,
Who pardons, and cleanses, and keeps to the end.

There's a refuge in GOD for the care-burdened heart,
That turns in its sorrow from others apart;
There's a refuge in JESUS, whose love and whose power
Can take off the load in the heaviest hour.

Then faint not, and fear not; His presence is nigh,
His arm shall protect thee, His fulness supply;
Oh, trust His assurance; on Him cast thy load;
Oh, come to thy rest, to thy refuge in GOD!

766(1)   Blaenwern 8.7.8.7 and Chorus

El Nathan, arr.   Wm. P. Rowlands

CHORUS

HAVE you any room for JESUS,
   Who once bore our load of sin?
As He knocks and asks admission,
   Sinner, will you let Him in?

   Room for JESUS, King of glory!
      Hasten now, His word obey!
   Swing the heart's door widely open!
      Bid Him enter while you may!

Room for pleasure, room for business;
   But for CHRIST the crucified,
Not a place that He can enter
   In the heart for which He died!—

Have you any time for JESUS,
   As in grace He calls again?
"Now"—"TO-DAY"—is "time accepted;"
To-morrow you may call in vain—

   Room and time now give to JESUS;
      Soon will pass GOD'S day of grace;
   Soon thy heart be cold and silent,
      And the Saviour's pleadings cease—

766(2) Have You Any Room For Jesus?
8.7.8.7 and Chorus

C.C. Williams
Arr. G.C. Stebbins

CHORUS.

767 Cairnbrook 8.5.8.3
R.D. Edwards

E. Prout

WILT thou come, or wilt thou linger?
'Tis the Saviour calls;
Death and darkness are about thee,
Sin enthralls.

Thou may'st come! the vilest sinner
May in CHRIST confide;
Thou art welcome, for to save thee
JESUS died.

Darkness once did shroud the Saviour,
　But 'tis light for thee;
Sacred spot for guilty sinners,
　　Calvary!

See the blood, that still is speaking
　Of redemption done;
And on glory's heights behold Him,
　　God's own Son!

Hear Him speak the word of pardon;
　Trust in Him who died;
And thy heart shall lose its burden
　By His side.

768   **Why Do You Wait? P.M.**

Geo. F. Root   Geo. F. Root

WHY do you wait, O lost one?
　Oh, why do you tarry so long?
The Saviour is waiting to give you
　A place in His heavenly throng:
　　Why not? Why not?
　　Why not come to Him now?

Do you not feel, O lost one,
　The Spirit now striving within?
Oh, why not accept God's salvation?
　Be freed from your burden of sin?—

What do you hope, O lost one,
　To gain by a further delay?
There's no one can save you but Jesus,
　There's no other way but His way—

Why do you wait, O lost one?
　The harvest is passing away:
The Saviour is ready to bless you,
　There's danger, there's death in delay!—

769   **Dismissal 8.7.8.7.8.7**
A. Midlane   W.L. Viner

PASSING onward, quickly passing;
  Yes, but whither, whither bound?
Is it to the many mansions
  Where eternal rest is found?
    Passing onward;
Yes, but whither, whither bound?

Passing onward, quickly passing;
  Nought the wheels of time can stay;
Sweet the thought that some are going
  To the realms of perfect day,
    Passing onward,
CHRIST their Leader—CHRIST their Way.

Passing onward, quickly passing;
  Time its course will quickly run;
Sinner, hear the fond entreaty
  Of the ever-gracious One,
    "Come," and welcome,
Be thy path of life begun!

770 **Ishmael S.M. and Chorus**

Philip Doddridge — C. Vincent

HARMONY.

CHORUS

1. AND will the Judge descend?
   And must the dead arise?
   And not a single soul escape
   His all-discerning eyes?

   *O sinner, seek His grace,
   Whose wrath thou canst not bear;
   Flee to the shelter of His cross,
   And find salvation there!*

2. How will the sinner stand
   The terrors of that day,
   When earth and heaven, before GOD's face,
   Astonished, flee away?—

3. But ere the trumpet shakes
   The mansions of the dead,
   Hark! from the gospel's gentle voice
   What joyful tidings spread!—

4. So shall the curse remove,
   For which the Saviour bled;
   And the bright coming day shall pour
   His blessings on thy head—

771   Kelso P.M.

H. Bonar

REFUSE Him not, O man!
  He bids thee seek His face;
He beckons thee to come and taste
  The riches of His grace:
    Was ever grace like His,
    So full, so free?
    Grace for the guiltiest,
      Abounding grace for thee!

Reject Him not, O man!
  He speaketh from above;
He offers thee Himself and all
  The fulness of His love:
    Was ever love like His,
    So full, so free?
    Love for the sinfulest,
      Love, boundless love for thee!

Resist Him not, O man!
  He lays His hand divine
Upon thy head in love, and says,
  'Let all My peace be thine!'
    Was ever peace like His,
    So full, so free?
    Peace for the fearfulest,
      Abiding peace for thee!

Close not thine ear, O man!
  With sin and toil opprest;
He speaks to thee in love—'O come,
  And I will give you rest!'
    Was ever rest like His,
    So full, so free?
    Rest for the weariest,
      Rest, perfect rest for thee!

772 When The Harvest Is Past P.M.

S.F. Smith

H.H. McGranahan

CHORUS

WHEN the harvest is past and the summer is gone,
And pleadings and prayers shall be o'er;
When for you on this earth light shall ne'er again dawn,
And JESUS invites you no more:

When the har... vest is past,...
and the sum... mer is o'er; ...
When the wheat and the tares
GOD'S judgment declares,
Oh, where wilt thou be evermore?

When the rich gales of mercy no longer shall blow,
The Gospel no message shall bear;
How canst thou endure the deep wailing of woe,
How suffer the night of despair?—

When the holy have gone to the regions of peace,
To dwell in the mansions above;
When their harmony wakes in the fulness of bliss
Their song to the Saviour they love—

Say, O sinner, who livest at rest and secure,
Who fearest no trouble to come;
Can thy spirit the swellings of sorrow endure,
Or bear the impenitent's doom?—

773   **The Harvest Is Passing 12.11.12.11 and Chorus**

H.C. Anstey   P.P. Bliss

H ARK, sinner, while God from on
    high doth entreat thee,
And warnings with accents of mercy
    doth blend:
Give ear to His voice, lest in judg-
    ment He meet thee:
*The harvest is passing, the summer
    will end.*

How oft of thy danger and guilt He
    hath told thee;
How oft still the message of mercy
    doth send;
Haste, haste, while He waits in His
    arms to enfold thee—

Despised and rejected, at length He
    may leave thee:
What anguish and horror thy bosom
    will rend!
Then haste thee, O sinner, while He
    will receive thee—

The Saviour yet waits in His grace to
    receive thee;
Oh, trust in His mercy, and prove
    Him thy Friend;
Now yield thy heart to Him, lest
    Satan deceive thee:
*THY harvest is passing, THY sum-
    mer will end!*

774 Moment By Moment (Just On The Threshold) P.M.

G. Cooper
May Whittle Moody

Chorus.

JUST on the threshold! oh, why not come in,
Leaving the mazes of darkness and sin?
Light is before thee and pardon divine;
Let not sin's darkness and judgment be thine:

Just on the threshold- and CHRIST calls to thee;
Come, with the pardoned for ever to be!
Just on the threshold—why linger so long?
Learn, with the ransomed, eternity's song!

Just on the threshold, and joy near at hand;
Yonder's the gleam of Immanuel's land;
Refuge and rest are now offered to thee;
Sin or salvation—oh, which shall it be?—

Just on the threshold—oh, make now thy choice;
Come with the servants of CHRIST and rejoice!
JESUS is calling, oh, turn not aside!
Come, 'tis the voice of the Saviour who died—

775   Only A Step To Jesus 7.6.7.6 and Chorus

F.J. Crosby   W.H. Doane

CHORUS

ONLY a step to JESUS!
  Then why not take it now?
Come, and thy sins confessing,
  To Him as Saviour bow:

Only a step, only a step;
  Come, He waits for thee;
Come, and thy sins confessing,
  Thou shalt receive a blessing;
Do not reject the mercy
  He freely offers thee.

Only a step to JESUS!
  Believe, and thou shalt live;
Lovingly now He's waiting,
  And ready to forgive—

Only a step to JESUS!
  A step from sin to grace;
What has thy heart decided?
  The moments fly apace—

Only a step to JESUS!
  Oh, why not come, and say,
'Gladly to Thee, my Saviour,
  I give myself away'?—

776   Not Far From The Kingdom P.M.

Frederic Smith (arr.)   Ira D. Sankey

NOT far, not far from the Kingdom;
   Yet in the shadow of sin;
How many are coming and going!
   How few there are entering in!

How few there are entering in!
How few there are entering in!
How many are coming and going!
How few there are entering in!

Not far, not far from the Kingdom,
   Where voices whisper and wait,
Too timid to enter in boldly,
   So linger still outside the gate—

Away in the dark and the danger,
   Far out in the night and the cold,
Though JESUS is waiting to lead you
   So tenderly into His fold—

Not far, not far from the Kingdom,
   'Tis only a little space;
Take heed that you be not for ever
   Shut out from yon heavenly place!—

777 So Near To The Kingdom! 11.11.11.11 and Chorus

F.J. Crosby
R. Lowry

SO near to the Kingdom; yet what dost thou lack?
So near to the Kingdom; what keepeth thee back?
Renounce every idol, though **dear** it may be,
And come to the Saviour now pleading with thee:

Plead . . ing with thee, . . .
The Saviour is pleading, is pleading with thee.

So near, for thou hearest the songs that resound
From those who, believing, a pardon have found;
So near, yet unwilling to give up thy sin,
When JESUS is waiting to welcome thee in!—

To die with no hope; hast thou counted the cost?
To die out of CHRIST, and thy soul to be lost!
So near to the Kingdom; resist, then, no more;
While JESUS is **pleading, come, enter the door**!—

778 Wonderful Love P.M.

1 OH, have you not heard of that
   wonderful love,
That flows from GOD'S heart so free,
Which led Him to give, that sinners
   might live,
His SON to be nailed to the tree?

Believe that wonderful love,
Believe that wonderful love,
The Gospel is free! GOD sends it
   to thee!
Believe GOD'S wonderful love!

2 Ye children of men, so helpless and
   lost,
This love of our GOD now receive;
No heart is too sad for this love to
   make glad,
When once on GOD'S word you
   believe—

3 Oh, sweet is its rest to the weary and
   worn,
Who feel the dread burden of sin;
It seeks for no worth of natural birth,
No goodness without or within—

4 This wonderful love has no measure
   or end,
It ever remaineth the same;
The heart that has known this love
   as its own,
Need have no more sorrow or
   shame—

5 Then will you not prove this wonder-
   ful love,
That flows from GOD'S heart so free,
Which led Him to give, that sinners
   might live,
His SON to be nailed to the tree?—

779 Why Not Tonight? L.M. and Chorus

E. Reed (Saved by grace 908) Ira D. Sankey

1 OH, do not let the word depart,
　And close thine eyes against the light;
O sinner, harden not thy heart:
　Thou wouldst be saved—why not to-night?

2 To-morrow's sun may never rise
　To bless thy long-deluded sight:
This is the time! oh, then, be wise!
　Thou wouldst be saved—why not to-night?

3 The world has nothing left to give—
　It has no new, no pure delight;
Oh, seek the life which Christians live!
　Thou wouldst be saved—why not to-night?

4 Our blessèd LORD refuses none
　Who would to Him their souls unite;
Then be the work of grace begun:
　Thou wouldst be saved—*why not to-night?*

780 St. Cuthbert 8.6.8.4

Douglas Russell J.B. Dykes

'TIS softly breathed by heaven's air,
'Tis murmured by the sea;
One word of import past compare—
Eternity!

And Time, for ever on the wing,
As swift its moments fly,
In earnest tones doth e'er out-ring—
Eternity!

Brief life! a shadow and a span!
A tale, a song, a sigh!
It says to you, O dying man—
Eternity!

From yonder plot of hallowed ground,
Where many loved ones lie,
Unspoken, seems to come a sound—
Eternity!

'Tis echoed 'mid earth's whirl and din,
Where all is vanity;
Oh, hear it, ye who live in sin—
Eternity!

Rest thou on CHRIST, O weary soul,
Stand firm at Calvary!
Then, hail with joy the glorious goal—
Eternity!

781 Where Will You Spend Eternity? L.M. and Chorus

Douglas Russell
J.H. Tenney

CHORUS

WHERE will you be when earth is past?
Where, when the dreaded comes at last?
Where, when to you *Time* is no more,
When shut for ever is the door?

Eternity! Eternity!
Where will you spend Eternity?

All who on earth make CHRIST their choice,
Ever before Him shall rejoice;
But, waking in eternity,
What will your endless portion be?—

Now is salvation brought to *you*,
Freely to all—to Gentile, Jew;
Should you neglect it—ah! *what then?*
No word of grace will sound again!—

Oh, do not linger, rise and flee;
JESUS has died for you, for me;
Haste unto Him, no more delay;
Trust Him alone, to-day! to-day!

And with Him spend Eternity!
Eternity! Eternity!

782   Not Yet Decided P.M.

P.P. Bliss

1 NOT yet decided, not yet forgiven?
   Still on sin's highway, not bound for heaven?
   Oh that thy word may be,
   'JESUS has died for me,
   JESUS has set me free,
       JESUS alone!'

2 Not yet decided, longing for rest?
   Not yet decided; why not be blest?
   Nought need you feel or do,
   Nor need you doctrines new;
   Only the old is true,
       JESUS alone!

3 Not yet decided; why this delay?
   "Come," saith the Saviour, "I am the way:"
   Hoping and fearing still,
   Hindered by stubborn will—
   Oh, think of Calvary's hill,
       Where JESUS died!

4 Not yet decided; time passes on;
   Judgment is coming; life soon is gone:
   Yes, soul, to-night may be
   Mercy's last call to thee;
   Choose for eternity—
       Heaven or hell!

783   Llef L.M.

T. Scott   (Eden 235)   G.H. Jones

HASTEN, O sinner, to be wise,
And stay not for the morrow's
sun;
For if the Saviour you despise,
You will for ever be undone.

Oh, hasten, mercy to implore,
And stay not for the morrow's sun;
Thy day of mercy may be o'er
Before this evening's stage is run.

Oh, hasten, sinner, to return,
And stay not for the morrow's sun,
Lest thy frail lamp should cease to
burn
Before the needful work is done.

Oh, hasten, sinner, to be blest,
And stay not for the morrow's sun;
Lest sudden death thy soul arrest
Before the morrow is begun.

O LORD, do Thou the sinner turn,
Nor let him wait the morrow's sun;
Oh, let him not Thy mercy spurn,
Nor slight the work on Calvary done!

784   **Not Yet Decided P.M. (Tune opposite 782)**
P.P. Bliss

'ALMOST persuaded' now to
believe;
'Almost persuaded' CHRIST to receive:
Seems now some soul to say,
'Go, SPIRIT, go Thy way:
Some more convenient day
On Thee I'll call'?

'Almost persuaded': come, come
to-day!
'Almost persuaded:' turn not away!
JESUS invites you here,
Angels are lingering near,
Prayers rise from hearts so dear—
O wanderer, come!

'Almost persuaded': harvest is past!
'Almost persuaded': doom comes at
last!
'Almost' cannot avail;
'Almost' is but to fail:
Sad, sad, that bitter wail—
'Almost'—*but lost!*

785(1)   Too Late! Too Late (Abney) C.M.

Asa Hull

'Too late, too late!' how sad the sound
On anxious, loving ears,
When those who, waiting long in hope,
At last must yield to fears!

But there's a time when sadder far
Shall sound in mortal ears
A dread 'too late,' which, quenching hope,
Will turn to truth *all fears!*

'Too late!' for mercy's door will shut,
Which now stands open wide:
'Too late!' for all must meet their God,
With no place *then* to hide!

O sinner! pause, ere yet 'too late'—
Now is the day of grace;
Now Jesus calls—oh, yet obey,
And truly seek His face!

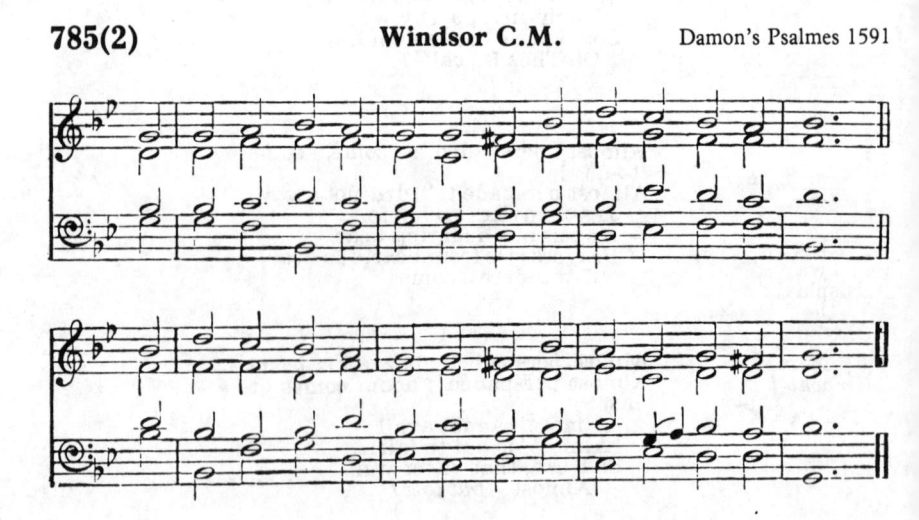

785(2)   Windsor C.M.

Damon's Psalmes 1591

786 Sovereignty 8.8.8.8.8.8

S. Davies
J. Newton

GREAT GOD of wonders! all Thy ways
Display Thine attributes divine;
But the fair glories of Thy grace
Beyond Thine other wonders shine:
Such deep transgressions to forgive!
Such guilty, daring worms to spare!
This is Thine own prerogative,
And in that honour none shall share—

Who is a pardoning GOD like Thee?
Or who has grace so rich and free?

Pardon—from an offended GOD!
Pardon—for sins of deepest dye!
Pardon—bestowed through JESU'S blood!
Pardon—that brings the rebel nigh!—

787 Fully Persuaded P.M.

J.B. Atchinson G.F. Knowles

FULLY persuaded—LORD, I believe!
Fully persuaded—Thee to receive!
I would obey Thy call,
Low at Thy feet would fall,
Here would surrender all,
And Thee receive.

Fully persuaded—no more opprest!
Fully persuaded—and ever blest!
LORD, be Thou now my Guide,
I would in Thee abide;
My soul is satisfied
In Thee to rest.

Fully persuaded—JESUS is mine!
Fully persuaded—LORD, I am Thine!
Oh, make my love to Thee
Like Thine own love to me,
So rich, so full, and free,
Saviour divine!

788 Augustine S.M.
(Canada 280)

H. Bonar J.S. Bach (arr.)

NOT what these hands have done
Could save my guilty soul;
Not what this toiling flesh has borne
Could make my spirit whole.

Not what I feel or do
Could give me peace with GOD;
Not all my prayers, and sighs, and tears,
Could move my awful load.

Thy work alone, O CHRIST,
Removes my weight of sin;
Thy blood alone, O Lamb of GOD,
Doth give me peace within.

Thy love to me, O GOD,
Not mine, O LORD, to Thee,
Doth rid me of my dark unrest,
And set my spirit free.

Thy grace alone, O GOD,
To me doth pardon speak;
Thy power alone, O SON of GOD,
Doth my sore bondage break.

No other work save Thine,
No meaner blood will do;
No strength save that which is divine
Can bear me safely through.

789   **Darwall's 148th 6.6.6.6 and Chorus**

H. Bonar   (Harewood 540)   J. Darwall

CHORUS

THY work, not mine, O CHRIST,
  Speaks gladness to this heart;
It tells me all is done;
It bids my fear depart:
    To none save Thee,
    Who didst alone
    For sin atone,
    LORD, *could I flee!*

Thy wounds, not mine, O CHRIST,
Have healed my bruisèd soul;
Thy stripes, not mine, contain
The balm that makes me whole—

Thy blood, not mine, O CHRIST,
Thy blood so freely spilt,
Has blanched my blackest stains,
And purged away my guilt—

Thy cross, not mine, O CHRIST,
Has borne the awful load
Of sins, that none in heaven
Or earth could bear, but GOD—

Thy death, not mine, O CHRIST,
Has paid the ransom due;
Ten thousand deaths like mine
Would have been all too few—

    Thy righteousness, O CHRIST,
    Alone doth cover me;
    No righteousness avails
    Save that which is of Thee—

790 St. Michael S.M.
H. Bonar   (Cambridge 252)   Day's Psalter 1562

I HEAR the words of love,
  I gaze upon the blood,
I see the mighty sacrifice,
  And I have peace with GOD.

'Tis everlasting peace!
  Sure as JEHOVAH'S name;
'Tis stable as His steadfast throne,
  For evermore the same.

The clouds may go and come,
  And storms may sweep my sky,
This blood-sealed friendship changes not,
  The cross is ever nigh.

My love is oft-times low,
  My joy still ebbs and flows,
But peace with Him remains the same,
  No change JEHOVAH knows.

That which can shake the cross
  May shake the peace it gave,
Which tells me CHRIST has never died,
  Or never left the grave!

Till then my peace is sure,
  It will not, cannot yield;
JESUS, I know, has died and lives—
  On this firm rock I build.

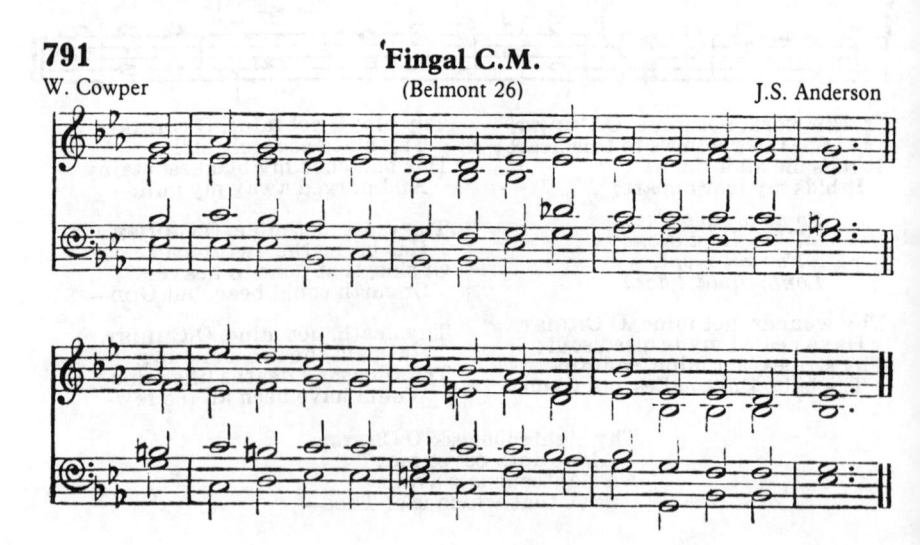

791 Fingal C.M.
W. Cowper   (Belmont 26)   J.S. Anderson

THERE is a fountain filled with
    blood,
Drawn from IMMANUEL'S veins, .
And sinners plunged beneath that
    flood
Lose all their guilty stains.

The dying thief rejoiced to see
    That fountain in his day;
And there have I, as vile as he,
    Washed all my sins away.

Dear dying Lamb! Thy precious blood
    Shall never lose its power
Till all the ransomed saints of GOD
    Are saved to sin no more.

E'er since, by faith, I saw the stream
    Thy wounds supplied for me,
Redeeming love has been my theme,
    And shall for ever be.

Soon in a nobler, sweeter song,
    I'll sing Thy power to save;
No more with lisping, stammering
    tongue,
But conqueror o'er the grave.

792   **The Quiet Hour 6.5.6.5**

H. Green

SAVIOUR, loving Saviour,
    Slain on Calvary,
Slain to bring salvation,
    Present, full and free'

Here are hearts so weary,
    Sick with self and sin—
Life all dark and dreary
    From the war within.

By Thy blood so precious,
    Once for sinners spilt,
Shed to bring us pardon
    From our sin and guilt;

By Thy glorious triumph
    O'er the gloomy grave,
By Thy risen power,
    Save, O JESUS, save!

793   **Just As I Am 8.8.8.6**

Charlotte Elliott   W.B. Bradbury

JUST as I am—without one plea,
But that Thy blood was shed for me,
And that Thou bidst me come to Thee,
    O LAMB of GOD, I come!

Just as I am—and waiting not
To rid my soul of one dark blot,
To Thee, whose blood can cleanse each spot,
    O LAMB of GOD, I come!

Just as I am—though tossed about
With many a conflict, many a doubt,
Fightings within, and foes without,
    O LAMB of GOD, I come!

Just as I am—poor, wretched, blind—
Sight, riches, healing of the mind,
Yea, all I need, in Thee to find,
    O LAMB of GOD, I come!

Just as I am—Thou wilt receive,
Wilt welcome, pardon, cleanse, relieve:
Because Thy promise I believe,
    O LAMB of GOD, I come!

Just as I am—Thy love I own
Has broken every barrier down;
Now to be Thine, yea, Thine alone,
    O LAMB of GOD, I come!

794 Redhead No.76 7.7.7.7.7.7

Augustus M. Toplady

R. Redhead

1 Rock of Ages, cleft for me,
  Let me hide myself in Thee!
  Let the water and the blood,
  From Thy riven side which flowed,
  Be of sin the double cure,
  Cleansing from its guilt and power!

2 Not the labour of my hands
  Can fulfil Thy law's demands:
  Could my zeal no respite know,
  Could my tears for ever flow,
  All for sin could not atone:
  Thou must save, and Thou alone.

3 Nothing in my hand I bring,
  Simply to Thy cross I cling;
  Naked, come to Thee for dress;
  Helpless, look to Thee for grace;
  Vile, I to the fountain fly;
  Wash me, Saviour, or I die.

4 While I draw this fleeting breath,
  If mine eyelids close in death,
  When I soar to heights unknown,
  See Thee on Thy judgment-throne—
  Rock of Ages, cleft for me,
  Let me hide myself in Thee!

795

C. Wesley

Aberystwyth 7.7.7.7.D
(Hollingside 919)

J. Parry

JESUS! Lover of my soul,
  Let me to Thy bosom fly,
While the billows near me roll,
  While the tempest still is high!
Hide me, O my Saviour! hide,
  Till the storm of life be o'er;
Safe into the haven guide,
  Where the tempest's heard no more.

Other refuge have I none;
  Hangs my helpless soul on Thee;
Leave, ah, leave me not alone,
  Still support and comfort me:
All my trust on Thee is stayed,
  All my help from Thee I bring;
Cover my defenceless head
  With the shadow of Thy wing.

Thou, O CHRIST, art all I want;
  More than all in Thee I find;
Raise the fallen, cheer the faint,
  Heal the sick, and lead the blind:
Just and holy is Thy name;
  I am all unrighteousness:
Vile and full of sin I am;
  Thou art full of truth and grace.

Plenteous grace with Thee is found,
  Grace to pardon all my sin:
Let the healing streams abound;
  Make and keep me pure within!
Thou of life the fountain art;
  Freely let me take of Thee;
Spring Thou up within my heart,
  Now, and to eternity.

796   Missionary 7.6.7.6.D

H. Bonar   (Nyland 185)   Lowell Mason

1. I LAY my sins on JESUS,
The spotless Lamb of GOD;
He bears them all and frees us
From the accursèd load:
I bring my guilt to JESUS,
To wash my crimson stains
White in His blood most precious,
Till not a spot remains.

2. I lay my wants on JESUS:
All fulness dwells in Him;
He heals all my diseases,
He doth my soul redeem:
I lay my griefs on JESUS,
My burdens and my cares;
He from them all releases,
He all my sorrows shares.

3. I rest my soul on JESUS,
This weary soul of mine;
His right hand me embraces,
I on His breast recline:
I love the name of JESUS,
IMMANUEL, CHRIST, the LORD!
Like fragrance on the breezes,
His name abroad is poured.

4. I long to be like JESUS,
Meek, loving, lowly, mild;
I long to be like JESUS,
The FATHER'S holy Child;
I long to be with JESUS
Amid the heavenly throng,
To sing with saints His praises,
In one eternal song.

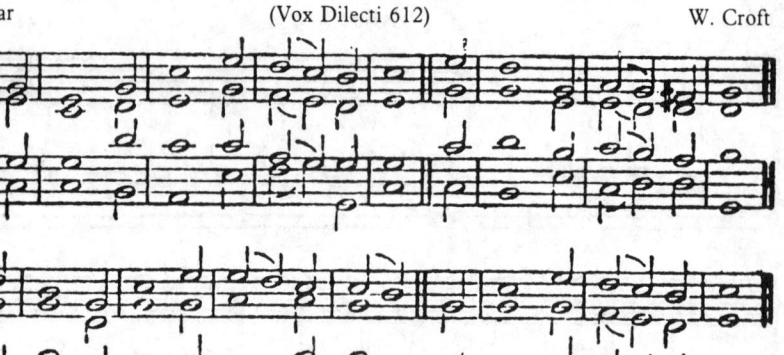

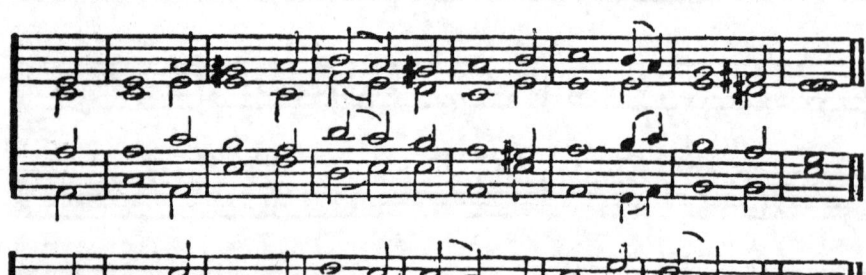

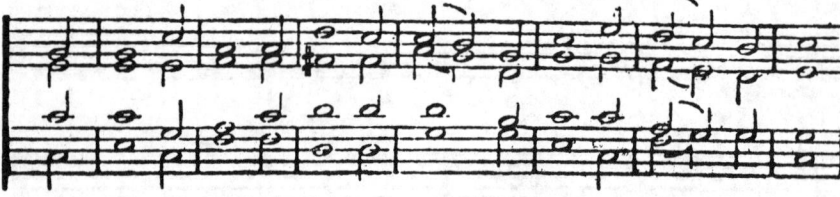

797 St. Matthew C.M.D.
H. Bonar (Vox Dilecti 612) W. Croft

1. I HEARD the voice of JESUS say,
   'Come unto Me and rest;
Lay down, thou weary one, lay down
   Thy head upon My breast!'
I came to JESUS as I was,
   Weary, and worn, and sad,
I found in Him a resting-place,
   And He has made me glad.

2. I heard the voice of JESUS say,
   'Behold, I freely give
The living water—thirsty one,
   Stoop down, and drink, and live!'
I came to JESUS, and I drank
   Of that life-giving stream,
My thirst was quenched, my soul revived,
   And now I live in Him.

3. I heard the voice of JESUS say,
   'I am this dark world's light;
Look unto Me, thy morn shall rise,
   And all thy day be bright!'
I looked to JESUS, and I found
   In Him my Star, my Sun;
And in that light of life I'll walk,
   Till travelling days are done.

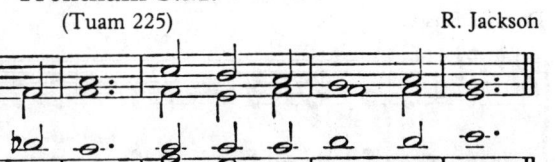

798   **Trentham S.M.**
W. Pennefather   (Tuam 225)   R. Jackson

JESUS! the sinner's Friend,
  We hide ourselves in Thee!
GOD looks upon Thy sprinkled blood;
  It is our only plea.

He hears Thy precious name;
  We claim it as our own;
The FATHER must accept and bless
  His well belovèd SON.

He sees Thy precious blood;
  It cleanses all our sin;
The golden gates have welcomed
    Thee,
  And we may enter in.

JESUS! the sinner's Friend,
  We cannot speak Thy praise;
No mortal voice can sing the song
  That ransomed hearts would raise.

But when before the throne,
  Upon the glassy sea,
Clothed in our blood-bought robes of
    white
  We stand complete in Thee—

O LORD, we'll give Thee then
  Such praises as are meet;
With all Thy saints we'll cast our
    crowns
  Adoring at Thy feet!

799 'Tis The Blood C.M. and Chorus

Douglas Russell
R.E. Hudson

IN nought of goodness dare I trust,
  My *best* is stained with sin;
My place is prostrate in the dust,
  All vile, without, within!

  *'Tis the blood, 'tis the blood that can
    cleanse me from sin,
  And for ever give the soul settled
    peace;
  With atonement made, I may enter
    in,
  And rest where all fears for ever
    cease.*

For what I am, what I have done,
  My Saviour bled and died,
I see Him now, the risen One,
  Ascended, glorified—

For ever gone, the sins He bore,
  His work is all complete,
They ne'er will be remembered more;
  I worship at His feet—

800 Boylston S.M.
Isaac Watts   (St. George 145)   Lowell Mason

NOT all the blood of beasts
  On Jewish altars slain,
Could give the guilty conscience peace
  Or wash away its stain.

But CHRIST, the heavenly Lamb,
  Took all our sins away,
A sacrifice of nobler name,
  And richer blood than they.

Our souls look back to see
  The burden Thou didst bear
When made a curse upon the tree,
  For all our guilt was there.

Believing, we rejoice
  To see the curse remove;
We bless the Lamb with cheerful voice,
  And sing redeeming love.

801 Dominus Regit Me 8.7.8.7 (Iambic)
J.B. Dykes

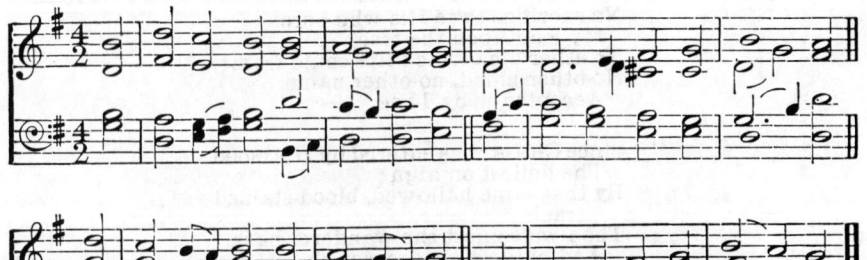

'TIS JESU'S precious blood alone
  Can fit the soul for glory:
A truth which far and wide is known,
  An oft-repeated story.

And still 'tis true GOD'S grace is free,
  O sinner, now believe it!
Eternal life is brought to thee,
  Then haste thee to receive it.

"*Eternal life*"! Oh ponder well
  The meaning of that sentence;
Deep in thy heart now let it dwell,
  And lead thee to repentance.

No longer think the blessèd GOD
  Is One who does not love thee;
He waits to free thee of thy load,
  Oh, may His mercy move thee!

802

W.S.W. Pond

Rest 8.6.8.8.6

F.C. Maker

1 THE blood of CHRIST, Thy spotless
        Lamb,
    O GOD, is all my plea;
  Nought else could for my sin atone;
  I have no merit of my own
        Which I can bring to Thee.

2 No sacrifice save His who bore
        My load upon the tree,
  No other plea which lips could frame,
  No other blood, no other name,
        Accepted is by Thee.

3 Since CHRIST has entered by *His* blood
        The holiest on high;
  By that same hallowed, blood-stained
        track
  Thou welcomest the wanderer back,
        And biddest me draw nigh.

4 Oh, wondrous cross! Oh, precious
        blood!
    Oh, death by which I live!
  The sinless One, for me made sin,
  Doth now His wondrous heart within
        Eternal refuge give!

5 By that blest cross, that cleansing
        blood,
    I know His power to save;
  The merits of *His* work confest,
  I stand in Him completely blest,
        A conqueror o'er the grave!

803   Nothing But The Blood of Jesus 7.8.7.8 and Chorus

R. Lowry   Geo. F. Knowles

WHAT can wash away my stain?
   Nothing but the blood of JESUS:
What can make me whole again?
   Nothing but the blood of JESUS:

    *No other fount I know
    That makes me white as snow;
    No other fount I know—
       Nothing but the blood of JESUS!*

For my cleansing this I see—
For my pardon, this my plea—

Nothing can for sin atone—
Nought of good that I have done—

This is all my hope and peace—
This is all my righteousness—

Now by this I overcome—
And by this will reach my home—

Glory! glory! thus I sing—
All my praise for this I bring—

804   Precious Blood of Jesus (Pater Meus) P.M.

Frances R. Havergal   (Precious Blood of Jesus, Mountain 938)   J.H. Burke

PRECIOUS, precious blood of JESUS,
  Shed on Calvary;
Shed for rebels, shed for sinners,
  Shed for thee!

  Precious, precious blood of JESUS,
    Message ever free;
  Oh, believe it, oh, receive it,
    'Tis for thee.

Though thy sins are red like crimson,
  Deep as scarlet glow,
JESU'S precious blood can wash thee
  White as snow—

Then the holiest with boldness
  Thou may'st enter in;
For the open fountain cleanseth
  From all sin—

Precious blood! by this we conquer
  In the fiercest fight,
Sin and Satan overcoming
  By its might—

Precious blood! its full atonement
  Makes us nigh to GOD!
Gracious Saviour, Thee we worship,
  Praise and laud!—

805 Safe In The Arms Of Jesus 7.6.7.6.D and Chorus
W.H. Doane

SAVED through the blood of JESUS,
  Saved from all guilt and shame;
Saved is the soul that trusts Him,
  Trusts in His precious name:
Safe in the Rock of Ages
  Fearlessly he may hide;
Safe from the storm of judgment,
  Safe from its swelling tide:

    Saved through the blood of JESUS;
      Perfect and only plea;
    Nought else avails for sinners,
      Nought else avails for me

Saved through the blood of JESUS,
  Saved from the wrath to come,
Saved too to dwell for ever
  Safe in the FATHER'S home:
Joy is among the angels,
  Joy in the heart of GOD,

When an unworthy sinner
  Trusts in the precious blood—

Saved through the blood of JESUS,
  Saved from eternal doom,
Saved too to share CHRIST'S glory,
  Saved until He shall come:
Saved from o'erwhelming sorrow,
  Saved from distracting care,
Saved from a world of evil,
  Saved from all doubt and fear—

Saved for the day of glory,
  Redemption's song to sing;
Still of the blood of JESUS
  Loudly our praise will ring:
Saved now to wait with patience,
  Looking by faith afar,
Till, just before the dawning,
  Rises the Morning Star—

806 At The Cross C.M. and Chorus

J.H. Stockton
R.E. Hudson

THE cross! the cross! the wondrous cross!
'Twas there the Saviour died:
I gaze upon that thorn-clad brow,
That pierced and bleeding side!

At the cross! at the cross! there I first saw the light,
And the burden of my heart rolled away.
It was there by faith I received my sight,
And now I am happy all the day.

I see the burden of my sin,
   By GOD upon Him laid;
And He, the spotless Lamb of GOD,
   My sacrifice was made!—

The cross of CHRIST is all my boast,
   His blood my only plea:
My passport to the realms of bliss
   Is—JESUS died for me!—

807   Sawley C.M.
Augustus M. Toplady   (Warwick 340)   J. Walch

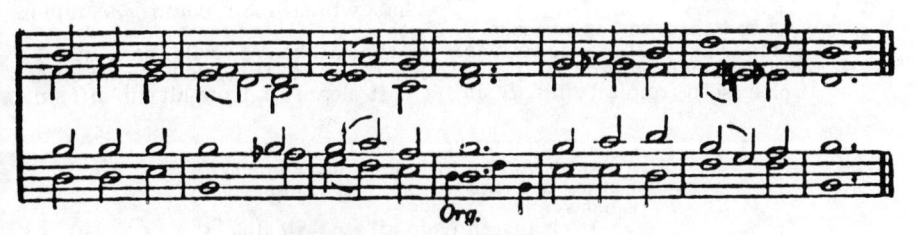

OH, precious blood, oh, glorious death,
   By which the sinner lives!
When stung with sin, this blood we view,
   And all our joy revives.

CHRIST'S blood doth make His glorious church
   From every blemish free;
And oh, the riches of His love,
   He poured it out for me!

Guilty and worthless as I was,
   It all for me was given;
And boldness through His blood I have
   To enter into heaven.

The FATHER'S everlasting love,
   And JESU'S precious blood,
Shall be our endless themes of praise
   In yonder blest abode.

808   It Cleanseth From All Sin (Just as I am) L.M.

Douglas Russell   W.B. Bradbury

NO theme on earth I love so well—
   Christ's "precious blood" all
fears can quell:
  Its cleansing power I love to tell;
    It cleanseth from all sin—*all* sin.

I sought in vain from sin to cease—
The Saviour came and gave release:
Redeeming blood secured my peace;
    It cleanseth from all sin—*all* sin.

By Calvary we reach the throne;
There Jesus is—no more alone:
Made nigh by blood are all His own;
    It cleanseth from all sin—*all* sin.

That which men count a common
   thing—
Of that all heaven will ever sing:
His blood—to this one hope we cling;
    It cleanseth from all sin—*all* sin.

O ye, who long your *sins* have seen,
Who *trying, hoping,* long have been;
Come, see *the blood,* with nought
   between;
    It cleanseth from all sin—*all* sin.

809   Evensong 8.7.8.7.7.7

A. Midlane   J. Summers

SOFT the voice of mercy soundeth,
  Sweet as music to the ear:
'Grace abounds where sin aboundeth'—
This the word that soothes our fear;
Grace, the sweetest sound we know,
Grace to sinners here below!

Grace, we sing, GOD'S grace through JESUS;
Grace, the spring of peace to man;
Grace, that from each sorrow frees us;
Grace, too high for thought to scan;
Grace, the theme of GOD'S own love,
Grace, the theme all themes above!

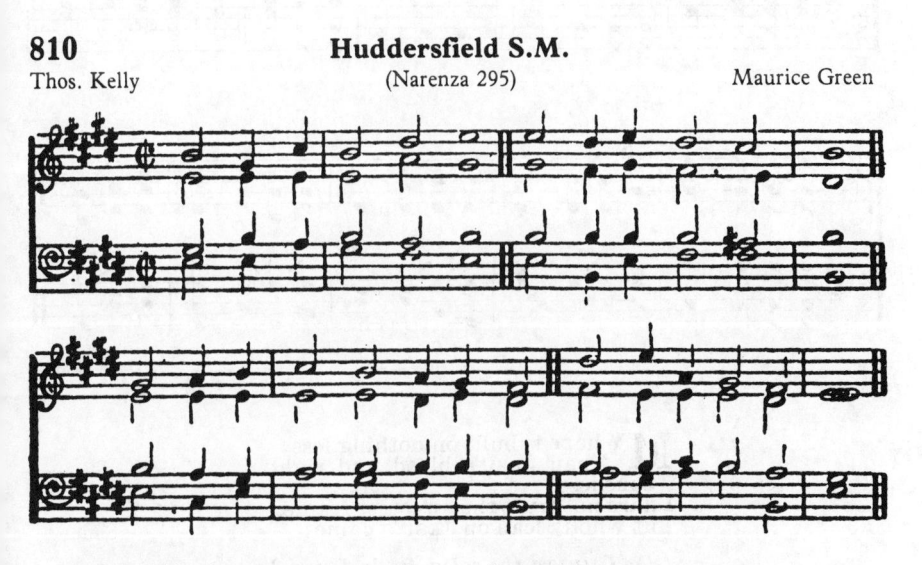

810 Huddersfield S.M.
Thos. Kelly (Narenza 295) Maurice Green

GRACE is the sweetest sound
  That ever reached our ears;
When conscience charged and justice frowned,
'Twas grace removed our fears.

'Tis freedom to the slave,
  'Tis light and liberty;
It takes its terror from the grave,
From death its victory.

Grace is a mine of wealth,
  Laid open to the poor;
Grace is the sovereign spring of health;
'Tis life for evermore.

Of grace then let us sing,
  Oh, joyful, wondrous theme!
Who *grace* has brought shall *glory* bring,
And we shall reign with Him.

Then shall we see His face
With all the saints above,
And sing for ever of His grace,
For ever of His love.

811 The Solid Rock L.M. and Chorus
E. Mote
W.B. Bradbury

CHORUS.

MY hope is built on nothing less
Than JESU'S blood and right-
eousness;
I dare not trust the sweetest frame,
But wholly lean on JESU'S name:

*On CHRIST, the solid Rock, I stand,
All other ground is sinking sand.*

When darkness seems to veil His face,
I rest on His unchanging grace;
In every high and stormy gale,
My anchor holds within the veil—

His oath, His covenant, and blood,
Support me in the whelming flood:
When all around my soul gives way,
He then is all my hope and stay—

812 Fountain C.M.D. and Chorus

A. Midlane
Old Melody

Chorus

D.S.

I ONCE was bound by Satan's chains,
  And blinded by his power;
But JESUS broke my fetters off:
  Oh, blessèd, wondrous hour!
He told me of His love, and drove
  My unbelief away,
And now I see His face with joy,
  And bow beneath His sway:

> *Yes, JESUS did it—did it all;*
>   *He saved e'en sinful me;*
> *Nor will He rest till I am blest,*
>   *And His full glory see.*

Salvation is my happy song,
  The cross of CHRIST my theme;
I now enjoy His blessèd smile,
  And drink at life's pure stream;
And in a little while I'll go
  To dwell with Him on high,
Where not a cloud shall intercept
  The full tide of my joy!—

813 Ever, My Heart, Keep Clinging 8.6.8.6.8.8 and Chorus
Douglas Russell   W.A. Ogden

THE Saviour's blood, on Calvary shed,
  Has full atonement made;
Captivity He captive led,
  My ransom price He paid;
The crown has found a worthy brow:
As "LORD of all" behold Him now!

*Ever, my heart, keep cling . . ing, . .
Cling to the LORD alone; . .
His work is done, His victory won;
Well may my heart keep singing,
Well may my heart keep singing!*

In Him "accepted" and "complete,"
　As He is, so am I;
The judgment storm on Him did beat
　He lives, no more to die!
Atoning blood—I hear its voice!
It speaketh peace! my heart, rejoice!—

The great High Priest within the veil,
　Both Priest and Sacrifice,
To keep His own will never fail,
　Made His at such a price!
They soon will see Him coming out;
With rapture greet His welcome shout!—

814　　　Abends L.M.
Mary J. Walker　　　(Fulda 550)　　　H.S. Oakeley

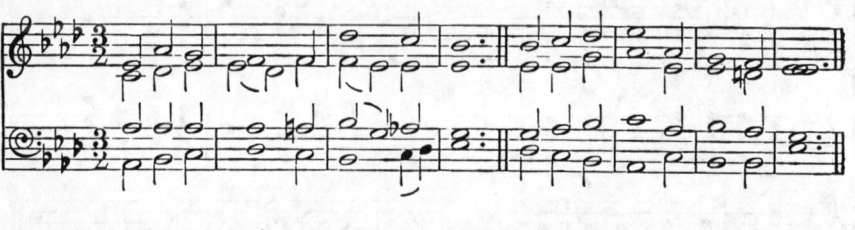

O SPOTLESS Lamb of God, in Thee
　The FATHER'S holiness we see;
And with delight Thy people trace
In Thee His wondrous love and grace.

When we behold Thee, Lamb of God,
Beneath our sins' tremendous load,
Bearing our curse upon the tree,
How great our guilt with grief we see!

Once Thou didst leave Thy throne above
To teach us that our "GOD IS LOVE;"
And now we see His glory shine
In every word and deed of Thine.

Yet there with joy that grace behold,
Whose height and depth can ne'er be told;
It burst our chains, and set us free,
And sweetly draws our souls to Thee.

The cross reveals Thy love below,
But better soon our hearts shall know—
When we behold Thy face above—
The fulness of our FATHER'S love.

815 Seeking For Me P.M.

A.N.
E.E. Hasty (arr.)

1 JESUS, my Saviour, to Bethlehem came,
  Born in a manger to sorrow and shame;
  Oh, it was wonderful—blest be His name!
    Seeking for me, for me!
    Seeking for me! for me! . . .
    Seeking for me! for me! . . .
  Oh, it was wonderful—blest be His name!
    Seeking for me, for me!

2 JESUS, my Saviour, on Calvary's tree,
  Paid the great debt, and my soul He set free;
  Oh, it was wonderful—how could it be?
    Dying for me, for me!—

JESUS, my Saviour, the same as of old,
While I was wand'ring afar from the
  fold,
Gently and long did He plead with
  my soul,
  Calling for me, for me!—

JESUS, my Saviour, shall come from
  on high:
Sweet is the promise as weary years
  fly;
Oh, I shall see Him descending the sky,
  Coming for me, for me!—

816 Bodmin L.M.
John Newton   (Antwerp 353)   Alfred Scott-Gatty

POOR, weak, and worthless though
    I am,
I have a rich, almighty Friend;
JESUS, the Saviour, is His name;
He freely loves, and without end.

He ransomed me from hell with blood,
And by His power my foes o'ercame;
He found me wandering far from GOD,
And bore in grace my sin and shame.

He cheers my heart, my wants supplies,
And says that I shall shortly be
Enthroned with Him above the skies:
Oh, what a Friend is CHRIST to me!

817 Safe In The Arms Of Jesus 7.6.7.6.D and Chorus

Frances J. van Alstyne   W.H. Doane

SAFE in the arms of JESUS,
    Safe on His gentle breast!
There by His love o'ershaded,
    Sweetly my soul shall rest:
Hark, 'tis the voice of angels
    Borne in a song to me,
Over the fields of glory
    Over the crystal sea!

Safe in the arms of JESUS,
    Safe on His gentle breast!
There by His love o'ershaded,
    Sweetly my soul shall rest.

Safe in the arms of JESUS,
    Safe from corroding care,
Safe from the world's temptations,
    Sin cannot harm me there!
Free from the blight of sorrow,
    Free from my doubts and fears;
Only a few more trials,
    Only a few more tears!—

JESUS, my heart's dear refuge!
JESUS has died for me;
Firm on the Rock of Ages
Ever my trust shall be:
Here let me wait with patience,
Wait till the night is o'er,
Wait till I see the morning
Break on the golden shore!—

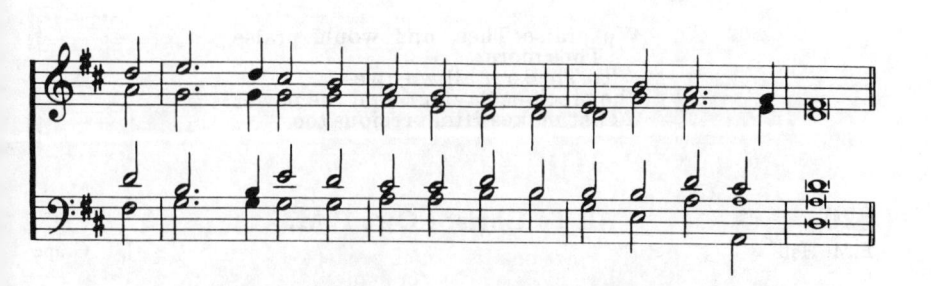

818 St. Beuno S.M.
(St. George 145)

H. Bonar J.C. Bridge

I BLESS the CHRIST of GOD,
  I rest on love divine,
And with unfaltering lip and heart
  I call this Saviour mine!

In Him is only good,
  In me is only ill;
My ill but draws His goodness forth.
  And me He loveth still.

His cross dispels each doubt;
  I bury in His tomb
Each thought of unbelief and fear,
  Each lingering shade of gloom.

'Tis He who saveth me,
  And freely pardon gives;
I love because He loveth me,
  I live because He lives.

I praise the GOD of grace;
  I trust His truth and might;
He calls me His, I call Him mine,
  My GOD, my joy, my light!

My life with Him is hid,
  My death has passed away;
My clouds have melted into light,
  My midnight into day!

819   **Byzantium C.M.**
W. Cowper   (Evan 154)   T. Jackson

OF all the gifts Thy love bestows,
  Thou Giver of all good,
Not heaven itself a richer knows
  Than the Redeemer's blood.

Faith, too, that trusts the blood through grace,
  From that same love we gain;
Else, sweetly as it suits our case,
  That gift had been in vain.

We praise Thee, and would praise Thee more;
  To Thee our all we owe—
The precious Saviour, and the power
  That makes Him precious too.

820   **All To Christ I Owe P.M.**
E.M. Hall   J.T. Grape

I HEAR the Saviour say,
  'Thy strength indeed is small;
Child of weakness, watch and pray,
  Find in Me thine all in all:'

    JESUS paid it all;
      All to Him I owe!
    Sin had left a crimson stain,
      He washed it white as snow!

LORD, true it is, we know,
  Thy power, and Thine alone,
Can change the leper's spots,
  And melt the heart of stone—

For nothing good have we
  Whereby Thy grace to claim;
We trust in Thee, Thou LAMB of GOD,
  And glory in Thy name—

821   Rhodes S.M.
Isaac Watts   (Woolwich 251)   C. Warwick Jordan

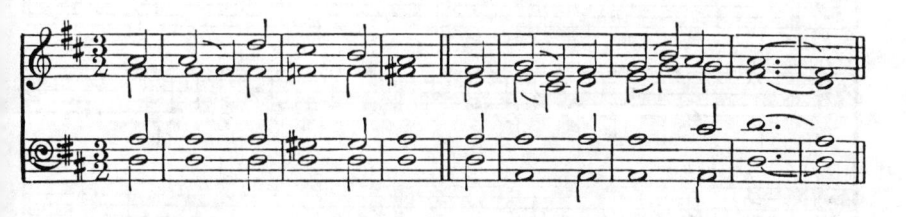

LIKE sheep we went astray
  Far from the fold of GOD,
Each wandering in a different way,
  But all the downward road.

How dreadful was the hour
  When GOD our wanderings laid,
And did at once His vengeance pour,
  Upon the Shepherd's head!

How glorious was the grace
  When CHRIST sustained the stroke!
His precious blood the Shepherd pays,
  A ransom for the flock.

He bowed His willing head,
  He drank the bitter gall;
But GOD hath raised Him from the dead,
  And made Him LORD of all.

822 Ich Halte Treulich Still S.M.D.

H. Bonar (Chalvey 686) J.S. Bach

I WAS a wandering sheep,
  I did not love the fold;
I did not love my Shepherd's voice,
  I would not be controlled:
I was a wayward child,
  I did not love my home,
I did not love my FATHER's voice,
  I loved afar to roam.

JESUS my Shepherd is,
  'Twas He that loved my soul;
'Twas He that washed me in His blood,
  'Twas He that made me whole;
'Twas He that sought the lost,
  That found the wandering sheep;
'Twas He that brought me to the fold,
  'Tis He that still doth keep.

I was a wandering sheep,
  I would not be controlled;
But now I love my Shepherd's voice,
  I love, I love the fold:
I was a wayward child,
  I once preferred to roam;
But now I love my FATHER's voice,
  I love, I love His home.

823 Winchester New L.M.
W.S.W. Pond (Truro 428) B. Crasselius

1 AWAKE, my soul, awake and raise
    Thy tribute to JEHOVAH's praise;
  His glorious name adoring bless,
  "According to His righteousness."

2 High as the highest mountain's head
  From the deep ocean's deepest bed,
  And ever steadfast, strong and sure—
  So doth His righteousness endure.

3 Thy righteousness is "very high,"
  Yet Thou, O GOD, hast brought it nigh;
  And now with joy my lips confess
  JEHOVAH as my righteousness.

4 What though temptations strong assail?
  He who is stronger shall prevail!
  What though their waves as mountains rise?
  My righteousness is in the skies!

5 Sing on, my soul; thy song of praise
  Shall last through time and endless days,
  For e'en when with Him thou shalt bless
  JESUS, "the LORD our righteousness."

824   **Lyngham C.M.**

C. Wesley   (Chorus Angelorun 343)   T. Jarman

OH for a thousand tongues to sing
   My great Redeemer's praise,
The glories of my GOD and King,
   The triumphs of His grace!

JESUS, the name that calms our fears,
   That bids our sorrows cease;
'Tis music in the sinner's ears;
   'Tis life, and health, and peace.

He breaks the power of cancelled sin,
   And sets the prisoner free:
His blood can make the foulest clean;
   His blood availed for me.

He speaks; and listening to His voice,
   New life the dead receive;
The mournful, broken hearts rejoice,
   The humble poor believe.

    Hear Him, ye deaf; His praise, ye dumb,
       Your loosened tongues employ;
    Ye blind, behold your Saviour come;
       And leap, ye lame, for joy!

825 Williams L.M.
W.J. Govan   (Wilton 907)   From Templi Carmina 1829

THE Son of God is come to save;
  From highest heaven the Light
    has shone:
O Life, that overcomes the grave!
O Love, that bids our fears be gone!

He bears away our load of guilt,
  The Lamb of God for sinners slain;
For us the precious blood is spilt,
  That washes white our darkest
    stain.

O Life, that overcomes the grave!
  O Love, that bids our fears be gone!
The Son of God is come to save;
  Through deepest dark the Light
    has shone.

His grace and love are still the same,
  Victorious on the Father's throne;
And every soul that pleads His name,
  He gladly welcomes as His own.

None other hope nor help have we,
  Behold, we come with all our sin;
O Christ! from darkening skies we
    flee,
  Thy wounded hand will take us in.

O Love, that bids our fears be gone!
  O Life, that overcomes the grave!
Within our hearts the Light has
    shone;
  The Son of God is come to save!

826 Look To Me And Be Ye Saved 7.7.7.7

W.J. Govan   (Theodora 384)   W.E. Vine

"LOOK to Me, and be ye saved!"
  Sound the glorious word abroad;
Break the bonds of souls enslaved,
  Bring the wanderers back to GOD!

Look to JESUS on the tree,
  Dead for thee! How vast thy guilt!
Wilt thou then from sin go free?
  Thou canst surely, if thou wilt.

Look to Him in heaven enthroned,
  Clothed with might, with glory crowned,
Him, who once for sin atoned,
  Girt with praise—His lost are found!

Look! thou need'st not mount on high;
  Lo, the word within thine heart!
Longing, seeking, He is nigh:
  Wilt thou bid the LORD depart?

"Look to Me, and be ye saved!"
  Joyfully the word obey;
Thou hast long salvation craved,
  Look, and CHRIST is thine to-day!

827 University College 7.7.7.7

Thos. Kelly   H.J. Gauntlett

CROWNS of glory ever bright
    Rest upon the Victor's head;
Crowns of glory are His right—
    His, who liveth, and was dead.

JESUS fought and won the day;
    Such a victory ne'er was won;
Well His people now may say,
    'See what GOD in grace has done!

He subdued the powers of hell,
    In the fight He stood alone;
All His foes before Him fell,
    By His single arm o'erthrown.

His the fight, the arduous toil,
    His the honours of the day,
His the glory and the spoil—
    JESUS bears them all away.

Now proclaim His deeds afar,
    Fill the world with His renown;
His alone the Victor's car,
    His the everlasting crown.

828   I Looked To Jesus 8.7.8.7 and Chorus

El Nathan   J. McGranahan

I LOOKED to JESUS in my sin,
    My want and woe confessing;
Undone and lost, I came to Him,
    I sought and found a blessing:

    I looked . . to Him; . . ;
    'Twas true, His "Whosoever;"
    He looked . . on me, . .
    And we were one for ever.

I looked to JESUS on the cross;
    For me I saw Him dying;
GOD's word believed, that all my sins
    Were then upon Him lying—

I looked to JESUS raised on high,
    From death enthroned in glory:
I trusted in His power to save,
    Believed the old, old story—

He looked on me, oh, look of love!
    My heart by it was broken;
And with that look of love He gave
    The HOLY SPIRIT'S token—

Now one with CHRIST, I find my peace
    In Him to be abiding;
And His own love meets all my need,
    In child-like faith confiding.

829
F. Whitfield

Nyland 7.6.7.6.D
(Fairford 913)

Finnish Hymn Melody

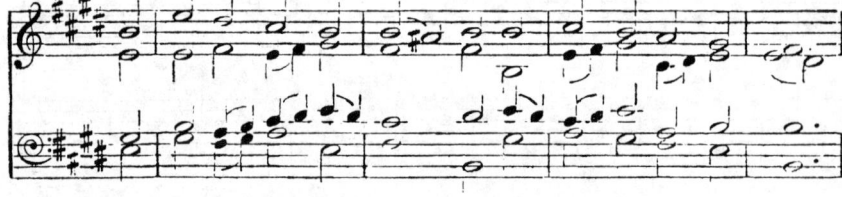

I SAW the cross of JESUS,
  When burdened with my sin;
I sought the cross of JESUS
  To give me peace within;
I brought my sins to JESUS,
  He cleansed them in His blood;
And in the cross of JESUS
  I found my peace with GOD.

I love the cross of JESUS;
  It tells me what I am—
A vile and guilty creature,
  Saved only through the Lamb;
No righteousness, no merit,
  No beauty can I plead;
Yet in the cross I glory,
  My title there I read.

Sweet is the cross of JESUS;
There let my weary heart
Still rest in peace unshaken,
Till *with Him*—ne'er to part;
And then in strains of glory
I'll sing His wondrous power,
Where sin can never enter,
And death is known no more.

830   Westminster C.M.
(St. Stephen 64)   James Turle

O LORD, in nothing would I boast
  Save in Thy glorious name;
Though in myself all vile and lost,
  In Thee all fair I am.

Of sin and Satan once the slave,
  My chains were burst by Thee;
In Thee I now redemption have,
  Thou, LORD, hast set me free.

I glory only in Thy name,
  'Gainst sin, and death, and hell;
I own my guilt, confess my shame,
  But Thy salvation tell.

And when I stand before the throne,
  And in Thy presence shine,
Still of Thy name I'll boast alone,
  For all the praise is Thine.

831   I Am The Way C.M. and Chorus

Douglas Russell   J. McGranahan

"I AM the *Way*," the Saviour said,
    The only way to GOD;
That "new and living way" we tread,
    Made by His precious blood:

    "I . . . . am the Way, ... the
      Truth, ... and the Life: . . . .
    No man cometh unto the FATHER
      but by Me."

"I am the *Truth*." We rest in Him;
His word shall aye endure,
And nought can e'er its lustre dim,
Eternal, fixed, and sure—

"I am the *Life*." From heaven He came,
His life for us laid down;
He lives again, for e'er the same,
Our joy, our hope, our crown!—

832 Benediction 8.7.8.7.8.7
(Lewisham 523) S. Webbe

THOU, O GOD, Thy love commendest,
In that CHRIST for sinners died;
Thou hast raised Him and Thou sendest
Thy glad tidings far and wide:
Now believing,
By His blood we're justified.

Now Thine eye no longer sees us
Enemies, by sin defiled,
For we stand complete in JESUS;
Through His blood we're reconciled:
Nought can sever
From Thy love one blood-bought child.

Since on high the Saviour liveth,
In Him now our life's secure,
And Thy SPIRIT witness giveth
That our blessing standeth sure:
CHRIST'S redemption
Shall eternally endure.

833 Mighty Love 11.11.11.11 and Chorus

F. Bottome
W.B. Bradbury

OH, joy of the justified, joy of the free!
I'm cleansed by that precious blood once shed for me!
In CHRIST my Redeemer rejoicing I stand,
And point to the print of the nails in His hand:

> Oh, sing of His mighty love,
> Sing of His mighty love,
> Sing of His mighty love,
> Mighty to save!

O JESUS, the Crucified! JESUS is mine!
Though once a lost sinner, yet now I am Thine;
In conscious salvation I sing of Thy grace,
Which now lifts upon me the smile of Thy face—

O JESUS, my Saviour, I'll still sing of
  Thee,
Yes, sing of Thy precious blood poured
  out for me;
And when in the mansions of glory
  above,
I'll praise and adore Thine unchangeable love-

O ye who are guilty and wretched
  within,
Who feel the sad burden and sorrow
  of sin,
Oh, look unto JESUS, and yield not to
  fear,
The sigh of the contrite He ever will
  hear—

834 Arizona L.M.

Thos. Kelly (Duke Street 843) R.H. Earnshaw

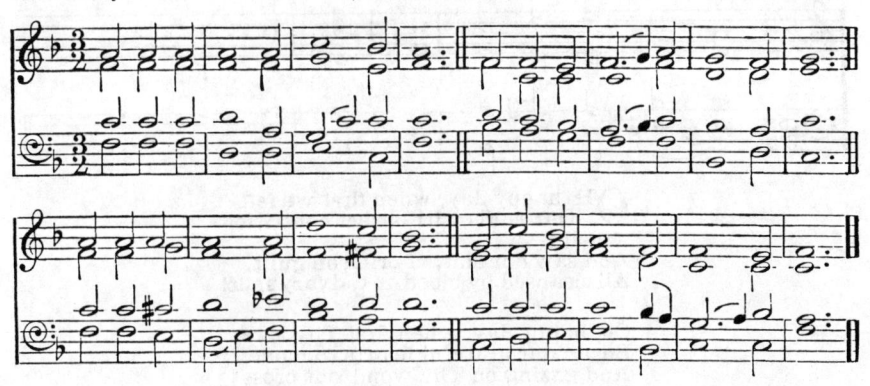

WE sing the praise of Him who died,
  Of Him who died upon the cross!
The sinner's Hope, though men deride;
  For Him we count the world but loss.

The cross—it takes our guilt away;
  It holds the fainting spirit up;
It cheers with hope the gloomy day,
  And sweetens every bitter cup.

Inscribed upon the cross we see,
  In shining letters, "GOD IS LOVE!"
The Lamb who died upon the tree
  Has brought us mercy from above.

It makes the coward spirit brave,
  And nerves the feeble arm for fight;
It takes its terror from the grave,
  And gilds the bed of death with light.

The balm of life, the cure of woe,
  The measure and the pledge of love,
The sinner's refuge here below,
  The angels' theme in heaven above.

835   **Bodmin L.M.**
J.G. Deck   (Job 582)   Alfred Scott-Gatty

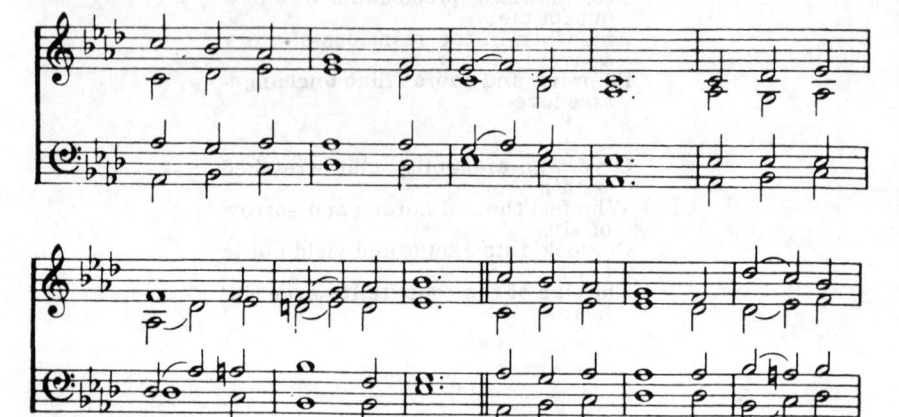

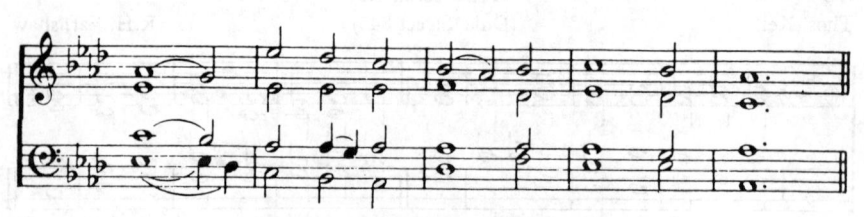

OH, happy day, when first we felt
   Our souls with sweet contrition melt,
And saw our sins, of crimson guilt,
All cleansed by blood on Calvary spilt!

Oh, happy day, when first Thy love
Began our grateful hearts to move,
And gazing on Thy wondrous cross
We saw all else as worthless dross!

Oh, happy day, when we no more
Shall grieve Thee whom our souls adore,
When sorrows, conflicts, fears shall cease,
And all our trials end in peace!

Oh, happy day, when we shall see
And fix our longing eyes on Thee—
On Thee, our Light, our Life, our Love,
Our All below, our Heaven above!

Oh, happy day of cloudless light,
Eternal day without a night!
LORD, soon may we its dawning see,
And spend it all in praising Thee!

836   Oh, Happy Day! L.M. and Chorus

Philip Doddridge   Anon.

OH, happy day that fixed my choice
   On Thee, my Saviour and my
    GOD!
Well may this glowing heart rejoice,
And tells its raptures all abroad:
   Happy day! happy day!
     When Jesus washed my sins
      away.
   He taught me how to watch and
     pray
   And live rejoicing every day,
   Happy day! happy day!
     When Jesus washed my sins
      away.

'Tis done—the great transaction's
   done;
I am my Lord's, and He is mine!
He drew me, and I followed on,
   Charmed to confess the voice
    divine—

Now rest, my long-divided heart;
   Fixed on this blissful centre, rest;
With ashes who would grudge to part,
   When called on heavenly bread to
    feast?—

837 Love Divine 8.7.8.7

J.M. Neale (tr.)   J. Stainer

"JESUS" is the name we treasure,
  Saving us from sin and hell;
Name of gladness, name of pleasure,
Ear and heart delighting well.

Tis the name for adoration,
  Name for songs of victory,
Name for holy meditation
In this world of misery.

'Tis the name that whoso preacheth,
  Speaketh music to the ear:
In this name whoe'er believeth,
  Is delivered from all fear.

838 Look Away To Jesus 11.11.11.11

Mary J. Walker   P.P. Bliss

JESUS, LORD, I trust Thee—name
  of matchless worth!
Spoken by the angel at Thy wondrous
  birth;
Written, and for ever, on Thy cross
  of shame,
LORD, I bow and worship, trusting
  in that name!

JESUS, LORD, I trust Thee—pondering
  Thy ways,
Full of love and mercy all Thine
  earthly days;
Sinners gathered round Thee, lepers
  sought Thy face,
None too vile or loathsome for a
  Saviour's grace.

JESUS, LORD, I trust Thee—trust Thy
  written word,
Though Thy tones of mercy I have
  never heard;
When•Thy SPIRIT teacheth, to my
  taste how sweet!
Ever would I hearken, sitting at Thy
  feet.

JESUS, LORD, I trust Thee—trust
  Thee with my soul;
Guilty, lost, and helpless, Thou canst
  make me whole.
There is none in heaven, or on earth
  like Thee;
Thou hast died for sinners—therefore,
  LORD, for me.

    JESUS, LORD, I trust Thee—trust
      without a doubt:
    'Whosoever cometh, Thou wilt not
      cast out;'
    Faithful is Thy promise, precious is
      Thy blood:
    These my soul's salvation, Thou my
      SAVIOUR-GOD.

839   **Bristol C.M.**
         (Gräfenberg 534)   Ravenscroft's Psalter 1621

THE Saviour bears a lovely name,
  Of saving power possest;
It takes away the sinner's shame,
  And gives his conscience rest.

However sweet the flower that
  spreads
Its perfume o'er the fields,
His name a richer fragrance sheds,
  And more refreshment yields.

No name on earth is half so great,
  Howe'er extolled by fame;
Nor can celestial tongues repeat
  A more exalted name.

Sweet name! the sinner's sure relief,
  His medicine, food, and joy!
'Tis help in trouble, ease in grief,
  'Tis gold without alloy.

    JESUS! Thy name to us is dear,
      It saves us from our foes;
    Armed with its power, we need not
      fear,
      Though earth and hell oppose.

840 Lynton C.M.
Edward Denny (Azmon 590) A.J. Jamouneau

1 SWEET was the hour, O LORD, to Thee
   At Sychar's lonely well,
  When a poor outcast heard Thee there
   Thy great salvation tell.

2 Thither she came, but oh, her heart,
   All filled with earthly care,
  Dreamed not of Thee, nor thought to find
   The hope of Israel there.

3 LORD, 'twas Thy power unseen that drew
   The stray one to that place,
  In solitude to learn from Thee
   The secrets of Thy grace.

4 There Jacob's erring daughter found
   Those streams unknown before,
  The waterbrooks of life, that make
   The weary thirst no more.

5 And, LORD, to us, as vile as she,
   Thy gracious lips have told
  That mystery of love revealed
   At Jacob's well of old!

841 Lucius C.M.
Edward Denny   (Farrant 453)   Templi Carmina 1829

1 Sweeter, O Lord, than rest to Thee,
   While seated by the well,
  Was the blest work that led Thee there,
   Of grace and peace to tell.

2 One thoughtless heart, that never knew
   The pulse of life before,
  There learned to love—was taught to sigh
   For earthly joys no more.

3 Friend of the lost, O Lord, in Thee
   Samaria's daughter there
  Found One whom love had drawn to earth,
   Her weight of guilt to bear.

4 Fair witness of Thy saving grace!
   In her, O Lord, we see
  The wandering soul by love subdued,
   The sinner drawn to Thee.

5 Through all that sweet and blessèd scene,
   O Saviour, by the well,
  More than enough the trembler finds
   All guilty fears to quell.

6 There, in the blest repose of faith,
   The soul delights to see,
  Not only One who fully loves,
   But Love *itself* in Thee!

842 Lord, Thou Art Worthy 11.10.11.10 and Chorus

Henry d'A. Champney Ira D. Sankey

1 JESUS, our LORD, with what joy
    we adore Thee,
  Chanting our praise to Thyself on
    the throne!
  Blest in Thy presence, we worship
    before Thee,
  Own Thou art worthy, and worthy
    alone:

  LORD, Thou art worthy; LORD,
    Thou art worthy;
  LORD, Thou art worthy, and
    worthy alone!
  Blest in Thy presence, we worship
    before Thee,
  Own Thou art worthy, and
    worthy alone!

2 Verily GOD, yet become truly human—
    Lower than angels—to die in our
      stead;
  How hast Thou, long-promised "Seed
    of the woman,"
  Trod on the serpent, and bruisèd
    his head!—

How didst Thou humble Thyself to
  be taken,
    Led by Thy creatures, and nailed
    to the cross!
Hated of men, and of GOD, too, forsaken,
    Shunning not darkness, the curse,
    and the loss!—

How hast Thou triumphed, and triumphed with glory,
    Battled death's forces, rolled back
    every wave!
Can we refrain, then, from telling
  the story?
    LORD, Thou art Victor o'er death
    and the grave!—

843   Duke Street L.M.
S. Medley   (Antwerp 584)   J. Hatton

THE Saviour lives, no more to die;
  He lives our Head, enthroned
  on high;
He lives triumphant o'er the grave;
He lives eternally to save!

The chief of sinners He receives;
His saints He loves, and never leaves;
He'll guard us safe from every ill,
And all His promises fulfil.

Abundant grace will He afford
Till we are present with the LORD,
And prove what we have sung before,
That JESUS lives for evermore.

Then let our souls in Him rejoice,
  And sing His praise with cheerful
  voice;
All doubts and fears for ever gone,
For CHRIST is on the FATHER'S throne.

844 Tours 7.6.7.6.D
Frances J. van Alstyne   (My song shall be of Jesus 914)   Berthold Tours

M Y song shall be of JESUS,
   The precious Lamb of GOD,
Who gave Himself my ransom,
   And bought me with His blood:
My song shall be of JESUS,
   His mercy crowns my days;
He fills my cup with blessings,
   And tunes my heart to praise.

My song shall be of JESUS,
   When, sitting at His feet,
I call to mind His goodness,
   In meditation sweet:
My song shall be of JESUS,
   Whatever ill betide;
I'll sing the grace that saves me,
   And keeps me at His side.

My song shall be of JESUS,
  While pressing on my way
To reach the blissful region
  Of pure and perfect day:
And when by grace I enter
  The heavenly mansions fair,
A song of praise, LORD JESUS,
  I'll sing for ever there.

845   **Forgiveness L.M.**   W.E. Vine
T. Gibbons   (Nicomachus 526)

FORGIVENESS! 'twas a joyful sound
  To us when lost and doomed to die:
Oh, publish it the world around,
  And let it echo through the sky.

'Tis the rich gift of love divine;
  'Tis full, effacing every crime;
Unbounded shall its glories shine,
  And know no change by changing time.

For this, the blood-bought gift of heaven,
  Our gratitude how shall we show?
Where much transgression is forgiven,
  May love to CHRIST in each heart glow!

By love inspired, may all our days
  With every heavenly grace be crowned;
May truth and goodness, joy and praise,
  In all abide, in all abound!

846. Since I Have Been Redeemed C.M. and Chorus

E.O. Excell

CHORUS

I HAVE a song I love to sing
  Since I have been redeemed,
Of my Redeemer, Saviour, King,
  Since I have been redeemed:

  Since I have been redeemed,
  Since I have been redeemed,
    I will glory in His name;
  Since I have been redeemed,
    I will glory in the Saviour's name.

I have a CHRIST who satisfies—
To do His will my highest prize—

I have a witness bright and clear—
Dispelling every doubt and fear—

I have a joy I can't express—
Through His own blood and righteousness—

I have a home prepared for me—
Where I shall dwell eternally—

847   My Redeemer 8.7.8.7 and Chorus

P.P. Bliss   J. McGranahan

CHORUS.

Words over

I WILL sing of my Redeemer,
  And His wondrous love to me;
How upon the cross He suffered,
  From the curse to set me free:

> Sing, oh, sing . . . of my Redeemer! . . .
> With His blood . . . He purchased me! . . .
> On the cross . . . He sealed my pardon, . . .
> Paid my debt . . . and made me free! . . .

I will tell the wondrous story,
  How my ruined soul to save,
In His boundless love and mercy,
  He the ransom freely gave—

I will praise my dear Redeemer,
  His triumphant power I'll tell;
How the victory He giveth
  Over sin, and death, and hell—

I will sing of my Redeemer,
  And His heavenly love to me;
He from death to life hath brought me,
  SON of GOD, with Him to be—

848 Celeste 8.8.8.8

C. Wesley

Lancashire Sunday School Songs

LORD JESUS, to tell of Thy love
  Our souls would for ever delight,
And join with the blessed above
  In praises by day and by night.

Wherever we follow Thee, LORD,
  Admiring, adoring, we see
That love which was stronger than death,
  Flow out without limit and free.

Descending from glory on high,
  With men Thy delight was to dwell;
Contented, our Surety to die,
  By dying to save us from hell;

Enduring the grief and the shame,
  And bearing our sins on the cross—
Oh, who would not boast of Thy love,
  And count the world's glory but loss!

849 Praise Him! Praise Him! P.M.

F.J. Crosby

Chester G. Allen

PRAISE Him! praise Him! JESUS,
  our blessèd Redeemer!
Sing, O earth—His wonderful love
  proclaim!
Hail Him! hail Him! highest arch
  angels in glory,
Praise and honour give to His holy
  name!
Like a Shepherd JESUS will guard
  His loved ones,
In His arms He carries them all
  day long:

  *Praise Him! praise Him! tell of
    His excellent greatness:
  Praise Him! praise Him! ever
    in joyful song!*

Praise Him! praise Him! JESUS, our
  blessèd Redeemer!
For our sins He suffered, and bled,
  and died:
He our Rock, our hope of eternal
  salvation:
Hail Him! hail Him! JESUS, the
  Crucified!
Sound His praises—JESUS who bore
  our sorrows!
Love unbounded, wonderful, deep,
  and strong—

Praise Him! praise Him! JESUS, our
  blessèd Redeemer!
Heavenly portals, loud with
  hosannas ring!
JESUS, Saviour, reigneth for ever
  and ever:
Crown Him! crown Him! Prophet,
  and Priest, and King!
CHRIST is coming, over the world
  victorious,
Power and glory unto the LORD
  belong—

850 Better World 8.3.8.3.8.8.8.3

W.P. Mackay
J. Hayhurst

1. As sinners saved, we love to sing
   Jesus died!
   God's grace doth now salvation bring;
   Jesus died!
   To seek and save the lost He came,
   He glorified the FATHER's name:
   With joyful lips we spread His fame;
   Jesus died!

2. Victorious over every foe
   Jesus rose!
   Sin, death, and Satan all laid low—
   And He is mighty now to save,
   Since for our sins Himself He gave;
   And then, triumphant o'er the grave—

3. And now in glory bright on high
   Jesus lives!
   Himself our life, we cannot die—
   The CHRIST who once on Calvary died,
   Hath GOD the FATHER glorified;
   In Him we now rest satisfied—

851 The Half Was Never Told C.M. and Chorus

P.P. Bliss
P.P. Bliss

CHORUS.

REPEAT the story o'er and o'er,
   Of *grace* so full and free:
I love to hear it more and more,
   Since grace has rescued me:

    The half . . . was never told, . . .
    The half . . . was never told, . . .
    Of grace divine, so wonderful, . . .
    The half . . . was never told. . . .

Of *peace* I only knew the name,
   Nor found my soul its rest,
Until the voice of JESUS came
   To soothe my troubled breast—

    Of peace divine, so wonderful, . . .

My highest place is—lying low
   At my Redeemer's feet;
No real *joy* in life I know
   But in His service sweet—

    Of joy divine, so wonderful, . . .

And oh, what rapture will it be,
   With all the hosts above,
To sing through all eternity
   The wonders of His love!—

    Of love divine, so wonderful, . . .
    The half . . . was never told. . . .

852 'Verily, Verily!' 10.10.10.6 and Chorus

J. McGranahan   J. McGranahan

OH, what a Saviour—that He died for me!
From condemnation He hath made me free!
"He that believeth on the SON," saith He,
    "*Hath* everlasting life!"

  "*Verily, verily, I say unto you:*"
  "*Verily, verily*"—*message ever new!*
  "*He that believeth on the* SON"—'*tis true!*
    "*Hath everlasting life!*"

All my iniquities on Him were laid,
All my indebtedness by Him was paid;
All who believe on Him, the LORD hath said,
    "*Have* everlasting life"—

Though poor and needy, I can trust my LORD,
Though weak and sinful, I believe His word;
Oh, glad message—every child of GOD
    "*Hath* everlasting life!"—

Though all unworthy, yet I will not doubt;
For him that cometh He will not cast out:
"He that believeth"—oh, the good news shout!
    "HATH everlasting life!"—

853   One Half Has Not Been Told C.M. and Chorus

Douglas Russell   R.E. Hudson

THY love to me, my LORD, I own
   No mortal tongue can tell;
As it becomes more fully known,
   My grateful praises swell:
    *One half Thy love has not been
      told,* . . .
    Nor e'er on earth can be;
    That love the SPIRIT *doth un-*
      fold; . . .
    Thy blood now cleanseth me! . . .

'Twas love that brought Thee from
   the throne
To tread a thorny path,
To die, and for my sins atone,
To rescue me from wrath—

To wipe away my sins' dark blot
   I tried, and tried again;
Thy precious blood leaves not a spot:
   It cleanseth every stain—

      To Thee alone my heart would cling
         Till earthly life is past;
      Thy blood, of which the ransomed
         sing,
         My song from first to last—

854 Saviour, Keep Me Near The Cross 7.7.7.7 and Chorus

Douglas Russell
Frank M. Davis (Arr.)

JESUS, LORD, Thy love to me . . .
Led Thee to the shameful tree, . . .
There to take my bitter cup, . . .
And its dregs Thou drankest up: . . .

Keep me, keep me,
  Saviour, keep me near the cross! . . .
There is centred all my hope, . . .
  All for Thee I'd count but loss. . . .

Judgment threatened like a flood,
'Neath it, guilty, vile, I stood;
All its billows beat on Thee,
Thou didst sink! Now peace for me!—

Sin, in all its crimson hue,
Marked against me, did pursue;
Thine own blood, by grace so free,
Shed for sinners, cleanseth me!—

Death and judgment left behind,
Now Thy glory fills the mind;
Saviour, Thou wilt come for me,
I shall ever dwell with Thee!—

855 Main 8.4.8.4.8.8.8.4

Marianne Nunn   H.P. Main

ONE there is above all others—
  Oh, how He loves!
His is love beyond a brother's,
  Oh, how He loves!
Earthly friends may fail or leave us,
One day soothe, the next day grieve us,
But this Friend will ne'er deceive us;
  Oh, how He loves!

'Tis eternal life to know Him—
Think, oh, think how much we owe Him—
With His precious blood He bought us,
In the wilderness He sought us,
To His fold He safely brought us—

We have found a Friend in JESUS—
'Tis His great delight to bless us—
How our hearts delight to hear Him
Bid us dwell in safety near Him!
Why should we distrust or fear Him?—

Through His name we are forgiven—
Backward shall our foes be driven—
Best of blessings He'll provide us,
Nought but good shall e'er betide us,
Safe to glory He will guide us—
  Oh, how He loves!

856   Requiem 8.7.8.7.7.7

John Newton   W. Schulthes

1. ONE there is, above all others,
    Well deserves the name of Friend;
 His is love beyond a brother's,
    Costly, free, and knows no end:
 They who once His kindness prove
 Find it everlasting love.

2. Which of all our friends to save us
    Could or would have shed his blood!
 But our Saviour died to have us
    Reconciled in Him to GOD:
 This was boundless love indeed;
 JESUS is a Friend in need.

3. When He lived on earth abasèd,
    "Friend of sinners" was His name;
 Now above all glory raisèd,
    He rejoices in the same,
 For He calls us "brethren," "friends,"
 And to all our wants attends.

4. Oh for grace our hearts to soften!
    Teach us, Saviour, love for love;
 We, alas! forget too often
    What a Friend we have above:
 But when home to glory brought,
 We shall love Thee as we ought.

857 The Love That Gave Jesus To Die P.M.

El Nathan　　　　　　　　　　　　　　　　　　　　J. McGranahan

1 LET us sing of the love of the LORD,
　　As now to the cross we draw nigh;
　Let us sing to the praise of the GOD
　　of all grace,
　　For the love that gave JESUS to die!

Oh, the love that gave JESUS to die!
　The love that gave JESUS to die!
Praise GOD, it is mine, this love so
　divine,
　The love that gave JESUS to die!

2 Oh, how great was the love that was
　　shown
　　To us—we can never tell why!
　Not to angels, but *men*—let us praise
　　Him again
　　For the love that gave JESUS to die!—

3 Now this love unto all GOD commends,
　　Not one would His mercy pass by;
　"Whosoever shall call"—there is pardon for all
　　In the love that gave JESUS to die!—

4 Who is he that shall ever condemn
　　Those GOD doth in love justify?
　Whatsoever we need He includes in
　　the deed,
　　In the love that gave JESUS to die!—

858 Always More To Follow 7.6.7.6.D and Chorus

P.P. Bliss   P.P. Bliss

HAVE you on the LORD believed?
   Still there's more to follow;
Of His grace have you received?
   Still there's more to follow;
Oh, the grace the FATHER shows!
   Still there's more to follow;
Freely He His grace bestows,
   Still there's more to follow:

   More and more, more and more,
     Always more to follow;
   Oh, His matchless, boundless love!
     Still there's more to follow.

Have you felt the Saviour near?—
Does His blessèd presence cheer?—
Oh, the love that JESUS shows!—
Freely He His love bestows—

Have you felt the SPIRIT'S power—
Falling like the gentle shower?—
Oh, the power the SPIRIT shows!—
Freely He His love bestows—

859 Come Unto Me 10.10.10.6 and Chorus

E.E. Hasty (arr.)

CHORUS

Repeat third line

1. JESUS, our LORD, with what joy
Thou didst show
Infinite love amidst sorrow and woe,
When, for the first time, was heard here below,
"Come unto Me, to Me."

2. Not even *one* was sent empty away,
Ne'er could Thy heart to the needy say 'Nay!'
Sweetly Thy words sounded day after day—
"Come unto Me, to Me."

3. Oh, how the leper, the lame, and the blind,
Weary ones, troubled in body or mind,
Oh, how they gathered a Saviour to find,
Trusting in Thee, in Thee!

4. Words of eternal life, well do we know,
Found their deep spring in *Thyself* here below,
Where and to whom, blessèd LORD, could we go?
Only to Thee, to Thee.

Words continued over

Who but Thyself, LORD, the blest SON of GOD,
Ever could take away sin's heavy load,
Purging the conscience by shedding Thy blood,
    Dying for me, for me?

Thou the fierce battle with Satan hast won,
Rising, hast proved Thyself truly GOD'S SON;
Life—yes, *eternal* life—find we alone,
    Only in Thee, in Thee.

Keep us, O LORD, whilst on earth here we roam,
Filled with *Thyself* and the prospect of home,
Waiting and watching until Thou shalt come,
    Watching for Thee, for Thee.

860   Sound His Praise P.M.

R.D. Edwards   W.H. Doane

How sweet is the story of GOD'S
   boundless love,
That brought His own SON from the
   glory above,
Who died in our stead upon Calvary's
   tree,
Obtaining redemption that we might
   be free!

> Sound His praise! sound His
>   praise! all the work has been
>   done;
> Praise His name! praise His name!
>   GOD'S own blessed SON!
> We give Him the glory, our Saviour
>   and Friend!
> Our song is of JESUS, and never
>   will end.

How wondrous the story! The claims
   of GOD'S throne
Were met by that blood which for
   guilt did atone;
The judgment of sin has been borne
   by the SON,
Who glorified GOD by the work He
   has done—

How brilliant the glory where CHRIST
   is enthroned!
How rightly His name above all
   names is owned!
Yes; JESUS, the Saviour, the glory-
   crowned LORD,
Is worthy by all to be ever adored—

How blessèd the hope of all those
   who believe,
That JESUS is coming, "His own" to
   receive!
What rapture, what glory, for ever
   will be,
When "caught up" to meet Him,
   their Saviour they see!—

861 There Is A Love P.M.

Douglas Russell — Geo. C. Stebbins

1. THERE is a *love* our souls have only tasted—
A love whose length and breadth, whose depth and height,
None fully know! When darkness reigned, it hasted
To bring us light—to bring us light!
'Tis love divine that hath from heaven descended:
In CHRIST in all its glory see it shine!
'Tis love unchanged, though now He hath ascended—
Oh, make it thine—oh, make it thine!

2. There is a *life*—a life that GOD bestoweth,
A life that's everlasting, costly, free;
Its source above, it as a river floweth—
It flows to thee—it flows to thee!
'Tis life divine, foretold in by-gone ages:
'Tis found in Him whose cross led to the throne;
It reaches men, as told in sacred pages,
Through death alone — through death alone!

3. There is a *home* we're now anticipating,
A home of love and peace past human ken;
For Him to take us there we now are waiting—
True Friend of men—true Friend of men!
That home above knows nought of earthly grieving,
And there from Him our feet shall never roam;
With friends beloved who passed away believing,
We'll meet at home—we'll meet at home!

862   To God Be The Glory 11.11.11.11 and Chorus

Frances J. van Alstyne (F.J. Crosby)   W.H. Doane

TO GOD be the glory! Great things
   He hath done!
So loved He the world that He gave
   His own SON,
Who yielded His life an atonement
   for sin,
And opened the Life-gate that all
   may go in:

Praise the LORD! *praise the* LORD!
   Let the earth hear His voice!
Praise the LORD! *Praise the* LORD!
   Let His people rejoice!
We come to the FATHER, *through*
   JESUS *the* SON,
And give Him the glory! Great things
   He hath done!

Oh, perfect redemption, the purchase
   of blood!
To every believer, the promise of GOD;
The vilest offender who truly believes,
That moment from JESUS a pardon
   receives—

Great things He hath taught us,
   great things He hath done,
And great our rejoicing through
   JESUS the SON;
But purer, and higher, and greater
   will be
Our wonder, our transport, when
   JESUS we see!—

863 Lion Of Judah (Will you be there?) 11.11.11.11

Henry Tucker (arr.)

1 BY faith in a glorified CHRIST on the throne,
We give up the joys of the world to its own,
As strangers and pilgrims we plainly declare,
Our home is up yonder; *but will you be there?*

2 We're watching for JESUS, who entered within
The holiest of all, having put away sin;
A place in the glory He's gone to prepare,
Where we shall be with Him; *but will you be there?*

3 We're waiting for JESUS—His promise is plain,
His word sure and steadfast—He's coming again;
A numberless people will meet in the air
The LORD who redeemed them; *but will you be there?*

4 For the guilty and needy the banquet is spread;
And the naked are clothed, and the hungry are fed:
The house is fast filling—there is yet room to spare;
Not a seat will be vacant; *but will you be there?*

864   Yet There Is Room (Peace! Blessed Peace!)
10.10 and Chorus   Ira D. Sankey

PEACE! blessèd peace! yes, peace
for all who trust
In Him who came to seek and save
the lost:

Peace, peace! sweet peace!
'Tis everlasting peace!

Peace! perfect peace! word fraught
with sweetest rest,
To meet deep longings breathed by
souls distrest—

Peace! cloudless peace! no mists of
doubt or fear;
All bright and joyous, wondrous portion here!—

Peace! peace eternal! made by JESU'S
blood,
As steadfast as the Eternal Throne
of GOD—

Peace! changeless peace! through
Thee, LORD, this is mine
Midst changing scenes so marred
with wrecks of time—

Yes; tranquil peace! till blissful moment dawn,
When peace surrounds in heaven's
eternal calm—

865 Peace, Peace Is Mine 11.10.11.10

Douglas Russell H.P. Main

PEACE, peace is mine! 'Tis peace
  of JESU's making,
 The purchase of His own most
  precious blood;
He bore my sins, and suffered GOD's
  forsaking,
 While judgment poured on Him
  its whelming flood.

Peace, peace is mine, for He who
  once descended
 Has passed in triumph through
  death's dark domain;
As Victor He to GOD's right hand
  ascended,
 And now is seen, the Lamb who
  once was slain.

Peace, peace is mine! On high is
  CHRIST appearing,
 Within the veil my great High
  Priest is He;
Honour and glory as a crown He's
  wearing,
 Who wore on earth the crown of
  thorns for me.

Peace, settled peace—a foretaste here
  of glory!
 May mine e'er as an even river flow!
His love constrains me now to tell
  the story—
 The story old, whose fulness none
  can know.

Thus too may others come and share
  the blessing—
 Peace, peace divine—then raise the
  anthem high,
The name of JESUS "Lord of all"
  confessing,
 And live for Him whose coming
  draweth nigh!

866   Malvern 6.6.4.6.6.6.4
James Allen   The Hallelujah 1849

GLORY to GOD on high!
   Let heaven and earth reply,
     "Praise ye His name!"
Angels His love adore
Who all our sorrows bore,
And saints cry evermore,
   "Worthy the Lamb!"

Join, all the ransomed race,
Our LORD and GOD to bless—
Tell what His arm hath done,
What spoils from death He won;
Sing His great name alone—

JESUS, our LORD and GOD,
Bore sin's accursèd load—
Now we, who know His blood
Hath made our peace with GOD,
Would sound His praise abroad—

Let all the hosts above
Join in one song of love—
To Him ascribèd be,
Honour and majesty,
Through all eternity—
   "Worthy the Lamb!"

867 Moscow 6.6.4.6.6.6.4

Thos. Kelly
F. Giardini

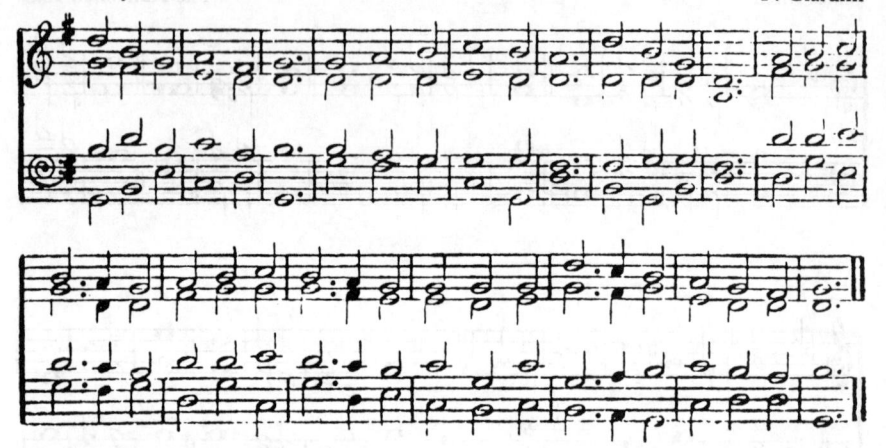

GLORY to God on high!
  Peace upon earth and joy!
  Good will to man!
We who His blessing prove
Join with the hosts above
To praise the Saviour's love—
  Too vast to scan.

Mercy and truth unite;
Oh, 'tis a wondrous sight,
  All sights above!
JESUS the curse sustains!
Bitter the cup He drains!
Nothing for us remains,
  Nothing but love;

Love that no tongue can teach,
Love that no thought can reach:
  No love like His!
GOD is its blessèd source;
Death could not stop its course;
Nothing can stay its force;
  Matchless it is.

Blest in this love we sing;
To GOD our praise we bring;
  All sins forgiven!
JESUS, our LORD, to Thee
Honour and majesty
Now and for ever be,
  Here, and in heaven!

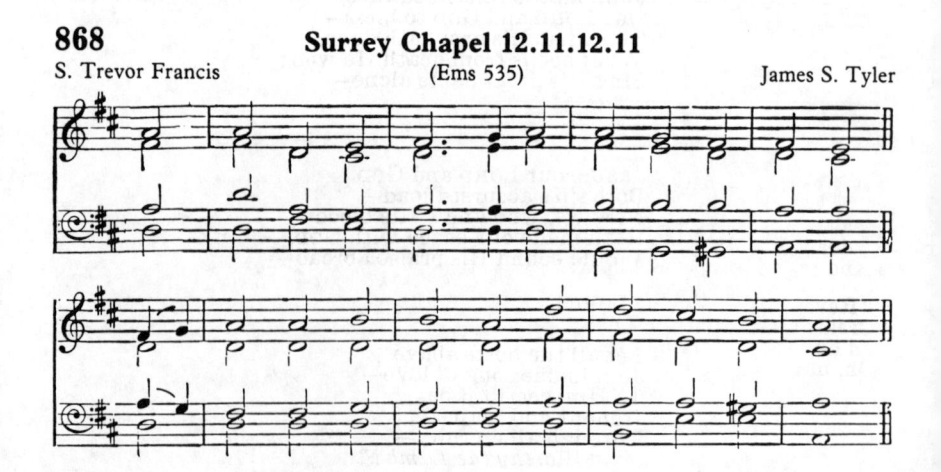

868 Surrey Chapel 12.11.12.11

S. Trevor Francis
(Ems 535)
James S. Tyler

REVIVE us, Lord Jesus, give
times of refreshing,
Oh, put forth Thy power, or our
service is vain;
We humble ourselves, as we plead
for Thy blessing;
Revive us, O Lord, ere Thy coming
again!

Revive us again, O our God, send the
shower;
Let heavenly blessing sweep over
our land,
Let sin-wearied hearts feel the might
of Thy power,
The touch of Thy tender, omnipotent hand!

869 Huddersfield S.M.
A. Midlane   (Silchester 500)   Maurice Green

"REVIVE Thy work, O Lord!"
Thy mighty arm make bare;
Speak with the voice that wakes the
dead,
And make Thy people hear.

"Revive Thy work, O Lord!"
Create soul-thirst for Thee;
And hungering for the bread of life,
Oh, may our spirits be!

"Revive Thy work, O Lord!"
Exalt Thy precious name,
And by the Holy Ghost our love
For Thee and Thine inflame.

"Revive Thy work, O Lord!"
Give power unto Thy word,
Grant that Thy blessed gospel may
In living faith be heard.

"Revive Thy work, O Lord!"
Give Pentecostal showers:
The glory shall be all Thine own,
The blessing, Lord, be ours!

870 Bodmin L.M.
(Llef 783)
Alfred Scott-Gatty

LORD of the Harvest! GOD of love!
  Spring of eternal blessing, Thou!
Oh, by Thy SPIRIT from above,
  Speed forth salvation's message now!

Oh, let Thy doctrine drop as rain,
  Thy speech distil as gentlest dew,
Thy word be sown, as precious grain,
  To root, and spring in life anew.

Thy SPIRIT'S grace and power be known,
  As still small voice, or rushing wind,
To break or melt the heart of stone,
  The bruised and broken heart to bind.

Thy Holy One be honoured now,
  Who on the cross was put to shame:
Some trophies to adorn His brow
  Win by the music of His name.

Now may that wondrous joy be Thine—
  The FATHER'S joy when sons are born;
Be jewels wrought, by grace divine,
  Thy heavenly temple to adorn!

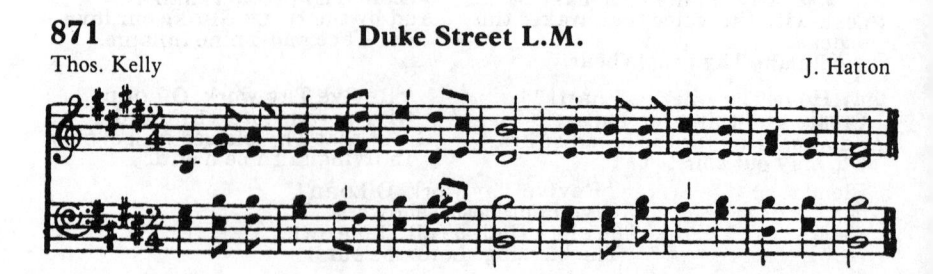

871 Duke Street L.M.
Thos. Kelly
J. Hatton

Now may the gospel's conquering
    power
Be felt by all assembled here!
So shall this prove a joyful hour,
And God's own arm of power appear.

Lord, let Thy mighty voice be heard;
    Speak in the Word, and speak with
    power;
So shall Thy glorious name be feared
By those who never feared before!

Oh, pity those who sleep in sin;
    Preserve them from the sinner's
    doom;
Show them the Ark, and take them in,
And save them from the wrath to
    come!

So shall the angels joyful be,
    And saints below more loudly sing;
And both ascribe the praise to Thee,
To Thee—the Everlasting King!

872 Rhodes S.M.
Macleod Wylie   (Silchester 500)   C. Warwick Jordan

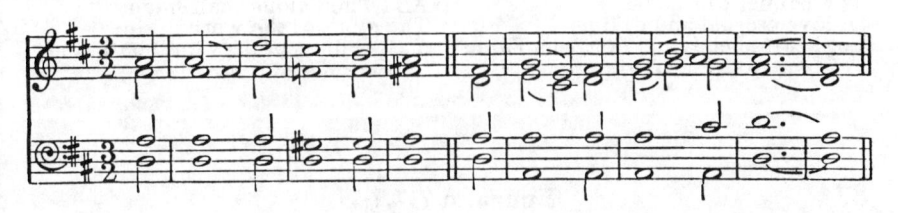

Oh for the Spirit's breath
    To breath upon the slain!
May He who wrought at Pentecost
Speak now in power again!

Unite Thy people, Lord;
    Blend all our hearts in one;
Hear Thou our prayer—let conquered
    souls
Bring glory to Thy Son!

Send forth afar Thy voice—
    A mighty voice indeed;
May dead arise, may slumberers
    wake,
And prisoners be freed!

May we have harvest joy,
    And reap the fruits of love,
While listening angels hear the sound
Of higher joy above!

873 Patience 4.6.8.8.4
A. Midlane

LORD JESUS, save!
　Thy blessing now we crave
For every anxious sinner here:
Oh, let Thy mercy now appear!
　LORD JESUS, save!

LORD JESUS, save!
Thy banner e'er us wave
Of love eternal and divine,
Let hearts believing, LORD, be Thine!
　LORD JESUS, save!

LORD JESUS, save!
Thou Conqueror o'er the grave,
Give every fettered soul release,
And whisper to the troubled, "Peace!"
　LORD JESUS, save!

LORD JESUS, save!
And Thou alone shalt have
The glory of the work divine:
Yea, endless praises shall be Thine;
　LORD JESUS, save!

874 Ephraim 7.7.7.7
A. Midlane　　　　　　　　　　　　　　H. Leslie

LET the waves of blessing roll,
  Far and wide, from pole to pole—
Blessing deep, exhaustless, free,
Bringing glory, LORD, to Thee!

Let the waves of blessing roll,
Lightening many a darkened soul,
Giving to the bound release,
Whispering to the troubled, "Peace!"

Let the waves of blessing roll,
Mighty, irresistible,
Bearing on their waters clear,
'CHRIST inviteth sinners near!'

Let the waves of blessing roll,
Far and wide, from pole to pole;
Over every land and sea,
Bringing glory, LORD, to Thee!

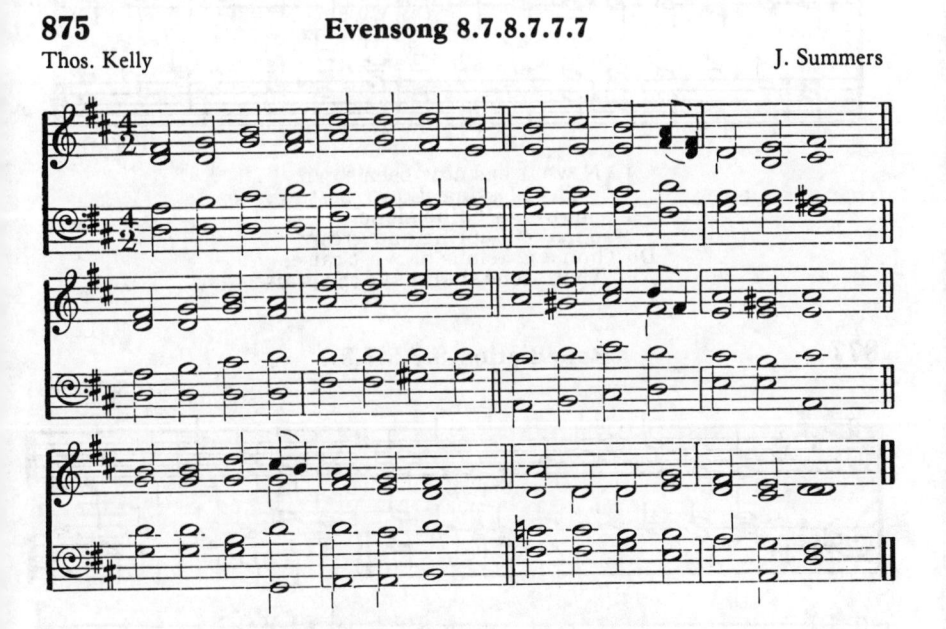

875 **Evensong 8.7.8.7.7.7**
Thos. Kelly   J. Summers

SAVIOUR, follow with Thy blessing
  Truths delivered in Thy name!
Thus the Word, Thy power possessing,
  Shall declare from whom it came:
Mighty let the gospel be,
Bringing souls, O LORD, to Thee!

876 Adoration 6.6.6.6.8.8
John Newton — W.H. Havergal

ON what has now been sown,
  Thy blessing, LORD, bestow;
The power is Thine alone,
  To make it spring and grow:
Do Thou a gracious harvest raise,
And Thou alone shalt have the praise!

877 Benediction 8.7.8.7.8.7
S. Webbe

May the power that brings salvation
Now accompany the word,
By its quickening operation
Life impart and joy afford—
Life to sinners,
Joy to those who know the Lord!

878   Ellacombe C.M. and Refrain
A. Midlane   German

Chorus

Words over

'TWAS GOD who gave the precious name
Of "JESUS" to His SON,
Because He knew redemption's work
By Him would well be done:

The SON of GOD, the LORD of Life,
How wondrous are His ways!
Not e'en a harp of thousand strings
Could sound out all His praise!

The name of "JESUS" Saviour means;
And such He is indeed
To all who feel the weight of sin,
And peace and pardon need—

His name was JESUS when on earth,
His name is JESUS now;
And GOD declares that to that name
All heaven and earth shall bow—

And truly happy is the soul
That loves His precious name;
He soon shall Him in glory see
Who once in mercy came—

879   Sandys S.M.
A. Midlane   (Augustine 788)   Sandys' Collection 1833

IN heathen lands they bow
To blocks of wood and stone,
And worship what their hands have made,
For GOD is there unknown.

There JESU'S precious name
Is never lisped in prayer;
Darkness and cruelty abound,
And sin and suffering there.

Here we are taught to read
The blessèd word of GOD,
Which tells us of the cleansing power
Of JESU'S precious blood.

It tells us of the home
For all who know the LORD,
Oh, may we greatly prize and love
GOD'S blessèd, holy Word!

880

A. Midlane

Albano C.M.
(Stroudwater 471)

V. Novello

1 THE Bible tells us JESUS *came*
 From glory bright and fair—
 GOD'S perfect, sinless, spotless Lamb,
 His mercy to declare.

2 The Bible tells us JESUS *died*,
 A sacrifice for sin,
 The gates of heaven to open wide,
 That we may enter in.

3 The Bible tells us JESUS *rose*,
 And left the silent grave,
 Triumphant over all His foes,
 The mighty One to save.

4 The Bible tells us He *will come*,
 And take His saints away,
 To dwell with Him in His sweet home
 Through everlasting day.

5 The Bible tells us He *will reign*
 O'er all the earth, ere long,
 When heaven and earth shall wake
  the strain
 Of one eternal song.

6 The Bible tells us *all* may come
 And drink at mercy's stream;
 That JESUS soon *will share His home*
 With all who trust in Him.

881　　　　　　　　Hereford L.M.
Ann Gilbert　　　　　　(Truro 625)　　　　　　　S.S. Wesley

JESUS, who lived above the sky,
　Came down to be a man and die,
And in the Bible we may see
How very good He used to be.

He went about, He was so kind,
To cure poor people who were blind;
And many who were sick and lame,
He pitied them, and did the same.

And more than that, He told them too
The things that GOD would have them do,
And was so gentle and so mild,
He would have listened to a child.

But such a cruel death He died—
He was cast out and crucified;
And those kind hands, that did such good,
They nailed them to a cross of wood.

And so He died; and this is why
He came to be a man and die—
The Bible says He came from heaven
That we might have our sins forgiven.

He knew how wicked all had been,
And knew that GOD must punish sin;
So, out of pity, He was led
To bear the punishment instead.

882   We Sing Of A Saviour's Love P.M.

1. COME, sing once again the sweet story of old,
Which tells of a Saviour's love,
Of JESUS who came and died as the Lamb,
To bring us to heaven above:

*We sing of a Saviour's love,
We sing of a Saviour's love—
Of JESUS who came and died as the Lamb,
To bring us to heaven above.*

2. He came as a babe; in a manger was laid—
CHRIST JESUS, the blest SON of GOD:
He came from on high, that here He might die,
To ransom us by His own blood—

3. He lived upon earth, as a child, as a man,
So gentle, and loving, and kind,
So spotless and pure, so ready to cure
The deaf, and the dumb, and the blind—

4. But oh, how He loved little children when here!
They brought them to Him, and we see
His hands on them laid, as He tenderly said,
'Let the little ones come unto Me'—

5. And now He has gone to His FATHER'S bright home,
And if our hearts trust in His love,
Then, if we should die, He will take us on high,
To be with Him in heaven above—

883 Sunnyside 6.5.6.5 and Chorus

Franes J. van Alstyne
W.O. Gibb

IF I come to JESUS
  He will make me glad;
He will give me pleasure
  When my heart is sad:

If I come to JESUS
  Happy I shall be;
He is gently calling
  Little ones like me.

If I come to JESUS
  He will hear my prayer,
For He truly loves me;
  He my sins did bear—

If I come to JESUS
  He will take my hand,
He will kindly lead me
  To the better land—

There with happy children,
  Robed in snowy white,
I shall see my Saviour
  In that world so bright—

884 Mothers Of Salem P.M.

W.M. Hutchings

German Air
arr. by A. Rhodes

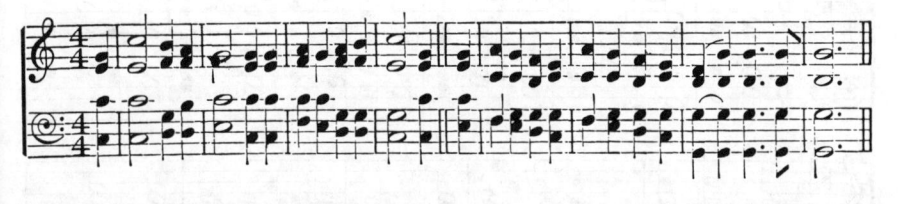

1. WHEN mothers of Salem their
   children brought to JESUS,
   The stern disciples drove them back,
   and bade them depart;
   But JESUS saw them ere they fled,
   And sweetly smiled and kindly said,
   "*Suffer the children to come unto
   Me.*"

2. 'For I will receive them, and fold
   them to My bosom;
   I'll be a Shepherd to those lambs, oh,
   drive them not away;
   For if their hearts to Me they give
   They shall with Me in glory live;'
   "*Suffer the children to come unto
   Me.*"

3. How happy the children who rest on
   JESU'S bosom,
   And there, like little folded lambs, lie
   safely and at rest!
   Thence none can pluck them e'er
   away,
   For He who keeps them loves to say,
   "*Suffer the children to come unto
   Me.*"

4. And still the kind Saviour bids little
   children welcome,
   For JESU'S loving, tender heart to
   children is the same;
   Though here His voice is no more
   heard,
   From heaven itself He speaks this
   word,
   "*Suffer the children to come unto
   Me.*"

885 In Memoriam 8.6.7.6.7.6.7.6
A. Midlane J. Stainer

1. THERE'S a FRIEND for little children,
Above the bright blue sky;
A Friend who never changes,
Whose love can never die;
Unlike our friends by nature,
Who change with changing years,
This Friend is always worthy
The precious name He bears.

2. There's a *home* for little children,
Above the bright blue sky,
Where JESUS reigns in glory,
A home of peace and joy;
No home on earth is like it,
Or can with it compare,
For every one is happy,
Nor could be happier there.

3. There's a *crown* for little children,
Above the bright blue sky,
And all who look for JESUS
Shall wear it by-and-by;
A crown of brightest glory,
Which He will then bestow
On all who've found His favour
And loved His name below.

4. There's a *robe* for little children,
Above the bright blue sky,
And a *harp* of sweetest music,
And a *palm* of victory;
All, all above is treasured,
And found in CHRIST alone:
If we as Saviour trust Him
Then all will be our own!

886 Suffer Them To Come 10.10.10.6 and Chorus
A. Midlane J. McGranahan

OH, what a welcome little children
found,
When, with the arms of JESUS thrown
around,
From His own lips they heard the
happy sound—
'Oh, suffer them to come!'

*'Suffer them, suffer them—let the
children come,
Suffer them, suffer them—bid them
not to roam,
Come to My loving arms, and to My
home,
Oh, suffer them to come!'*

Joyous and happy were the children
dear,
Smiles from the Saviour chased away
all fear;
Yes, it was sweet for them His words
to hear—
'Oh, suffer them to come!'

Still doth His loving heart a welcome
give,
Still all who come to Him His smiles
receive;
Hark! 'Look to Me,' He says, 'and
looking, live;'
'Oh, suffer them to come!'

887 Lymington 7.6.7.6.D

J. King
Robt. Jackson

1. WHEN, His salvation bringing,
    To Zion JESUS came,
   The children all stood singing,
    "Hosanna" to His name;
   Nor did their zeal offend Him;
   But, as He rode along,
   He let them still attend Him,
    And smiled to hear their song.

2. And since the LORD retaineth
    His love for children still,
   Though now on high He reigneth,
    To do GOD's holy will,
   We'll flock around His banner
    Who sits upon the throne,
   And cry aloud "Hosanna"
    To GOD's belovèd SON!

3. And should we fail proclaiming
    The great Redeemer's praise,
   The stones, our silence shaming,
    Might their Hosannas raise:
   But shall we only render
    The tribute of our words?
   No; while our hearts are tender,
    May they, too, be the LORD's!

888
Hugh Stowell

Fides 11.11.11.11

Marchel Davis

JESUS is our Shepherd, for the
 sheep He bled;
Every lamb is sprinkled with the
 blood He shed:
Then on each He setteth His own
 secret sign—
'They that have My SPIRIT, these,'
 saith He, 'are Mine.'

JESUS is our Shepherd, well we know
 His voice,
How its gentlest whisper makes our
 heart rejoice!
Even when He chideth, tender is His
 tone;
None but He shall guide us, we are
 His alone.

JESUS is our Shepherd, wiping every
 tear;
Folded in His bosom, what have we
 to fear?
Only let us follow whither He doth
 lead—
To the thirsty desert, or the dewy
 mead.

JESUS is our Shepherd, with His
 goodness now,
And His tender mercy, He doth us
 endow;
Let us sing His praises with a gladsome heart,
Till in heaven we meet Him, nevermore to part!

889 Huddleston P.M.

Arthur Berridge

For last verse, use lines 3 and 4 only.

NO room in the inn for the Saviour was found,
  Who from childhood was treated with scorn;
No place but the manger where cattle were brought,
  When in Bethlehem JESUS was born.

No home but the mountain of Olives was His,
  Though the bird of the air had its nest;
No love but the FATHER'S, whose bosom He left,
  Could give Him refreshment and rest.

No comforters came, when for comfort He looked,
  No pity, when pity He sought;
For sin He was wounded and smitten of GOD,
  And sinners did set Him at nought!

But heaven was opened to give Him the praise
  Denied Him by man on the earth;
And heavenly hosts broke forth in their songs
  Of wonder and joy at His birth.

And angels, who ministered oft to
    His need,
  Were sent to His help from the
    throne,
  When, weary and weak in the bitter-
    est hour,
  His people had left Him alone!

But neither the manger, the cross,
    nor the shame
  Are now by this Blessèd One known;
  Gethsemane's sorrows for ever are
    past,
  And the fruit of them all is His own.

And now that He dwells in the man-
    sions of bliss,
  He has room for each trusting one
    there,
  And His sorrows remembered will
    heighten the joy
  Which all will eternally share.

890   Samaria 8.7.8.5.D and Chorus

Words over

LITTLE thought Samaria's daughter,
On that ne'er-forgotten day
When the tender Shepherd sought her,
As a sheep astray,
That from sin He longed to win her,
Knowing more than she could tell
Of the wretchedness within her,
Sitting at the well:

Hear, oh, hear the wondrous story,
Let the winds and waters tell—
'Tis the CHRIST, the King of glory,
Sitting at the well!

By that well, with pitcher staying,
Listened she to words of truth,
While each thought was backward straying
O'er her wasted youth;
Hastening homeward with desire,
All His wondrous speech to tell,
Asked she, 'Is not the Messiah
Sitting at the well?'—

Now her thirsty soul has found Him,
Thrills with joy her throbbing breast;
Living waters all abounding
Give her spirit rest;
And she hastes to tell the story—
Oh, the rapture, none can tell!
She had found the King of glory,
Sitting at the well—

Living waters still are flowing
Full and free for all mankind,
Blessings sweet on all bestowing;
All a welcome find:
All the world may come and prove Him;
Every doubt will He dispel,
As she found who learnt to love Him,
Sitting at the well—

Hear, oh, hear the wondrous story,
Let the winds and waters tell—
'Tis the CHRIST, the King of glory,
Sitting at the well!

891   Mount Calvary L.M.D. and Chorus

A. Midlane   G.F Knowles

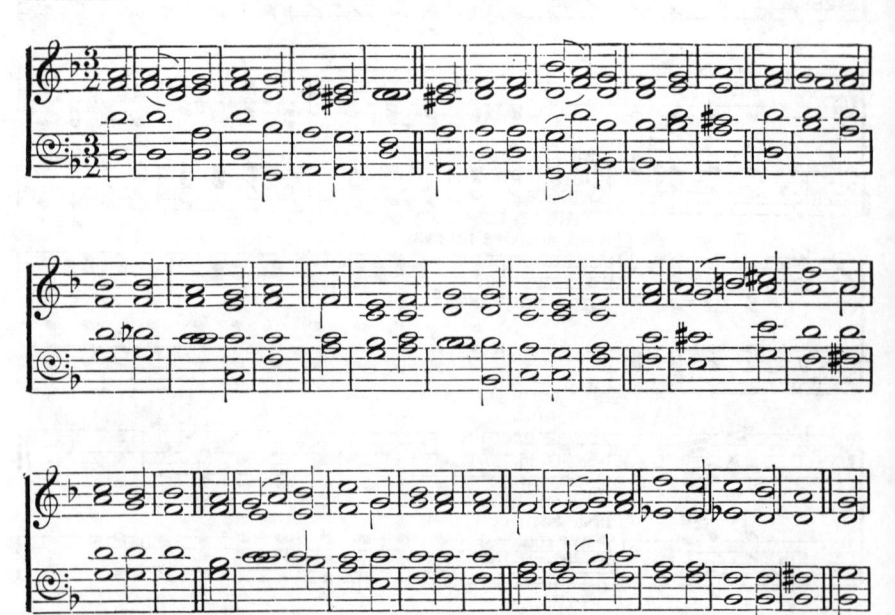

BETWEEN two thieves the Saviour
  died
While hanging on Mount Calvary,
And cruel soldiers pierced His side,
  And shed His blood on Calvary;
The chief priests mocked the Saviour
  too,
  And gave Him gall on Calvary;
All this He bore to save those who
  Thus treated Him on Calvary:

O Calvary! Mount Calvary!
The Saviour died on Calvary!
He died to save me from my sins,
Nailed to the cross on Calvary!

But though He suffered, groaned and
  died,
  And was entombed near Calvary,
Though GOD from Him His face did
  hide
  While on the cross on Calvary,
He soon arose in glorious might,
  And soared above Mount Calvary,
And now appears in glory bright,
  The Conqueror from Calvary!—

And, though now seated on the
  throne,
  He still remembers Calvary—
The cross, the nails, the spear, the
  groan,
  The dying, on Mount Calvary!
That children might be saved from
  wrath,
  CHRIST shed His blood on Calvary;
And blest are they who have true
  faith
  In Him who died on Calvary!—

892 St. Hugh C.M.
Dorothy A. Thrupp (Fingal 791) E.J. Hopkins

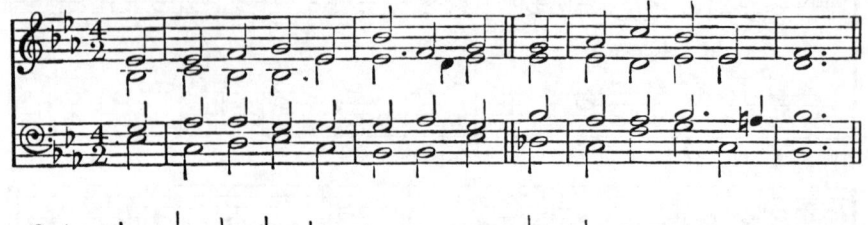

1. A WIDOWED mother lost her son;
   She had no son beside;
   He was her loved, her only one,
   And he fell sick and died.

2. And many a friend shed many a tear,
   But none had power to save;
   They placed the body on the bier,
   To bear it to the grave.

3. When, lo! a company appears,
   A band by JESUS led;
   JESUS can dry the mourner's tears—
   JESUS can raise the dead!

4. He touched the bier—the mourner's eyes
   Are fixed upon the LORD;
   "Young man, I say to thee, Arise!
   Is His almighty word.

5. He rises up—he speaks—he lives!
   No tear need now be shed;
   CHRIST to the widowed mother gives
   The son she mourned as dead.

6. And we need life, *eternal life*,
   Which CHRIST alone can give;
   Soon helpless we, in deadly strife,
   Might cease on earth to live.

893 Carlisle S.M.
(Narenza 678) C. Lockhart

"Pleasures for evermore!"
  Can this their portion be,
Who merit, if they had their due,
  Eternal misery?

"Pleasures for evermore!"
  With no more sin or pain;
And in the presence of the LORD
  For ever to remain!

"Pleasures for evermore,"
  While seeing Him they love;
Because He cleansed them by His blood,
  They sing His praise above.

894 Huddleston P.M.
Arthur Berridge

Words over

THE Saviour Jesus has gone to
    prepare
  Such a beautiful home in the sky;
    And He says He will come,
    And take to that home
  Every sinner that's born from on
    high.

How sweetly their voices shall praise
    Him there
  For the blessings His hand has
    bestowed!
    They shall shine there bright
    In their robes of white,
  For they all have been washed in
    His blood.

And crowns they shall wear of the
    purest gold,
  And a wonderful song they shall
    sing;
    And each shall cast down
    His glittering crown
  At the feet of the Heavenly King.

And happy amid that bright, joyous
    throng,
  Shall many a little one sing,
    How happy for me
    Among them to be,
  With the Giver of every good thing!

895 St. Magnus C.M.
(Crediton 388)

J. Clarke

THERE is a blessèd land above,
    A city pure and bright,
  Where all who know the Saviour's
    love
  Shall walk with Him in white.

His blood has freed them from their
    sin,
    And made them clean and fair;
  And His own hand shall lead them in,
    To dwell for ever there.

How blessèd is the song they sing,
    Heaven's sweet, eternal theme—
  Salvation to the glorious King,
    Who did their souls redeem!

'Twas He redeemed them from the
    earth,
    From sin, and woe, and shame;
  He made them His by heavenly birth,
    And there they praise His name!

896 Newtown P.M.
Anne Shepherd

1. AROUND the throne of God in heaven
Thousands of children stand,
Children whose sins are all forgiven,
A holy, happy band,
  Singing, Glory, glory, glory!

2. In flowing robes of spotless white,
See everyone arrayed,
Dwelling in everlasting light,
'Mid joys that never fade—

3. What brought them to that world above,
That heaven so bright and fair,
Where all is peace and joy and love,
How came those children there?—

4. Because the Saviour shed His blood,
To wash away their sin;
Now cleansed in that most precious flood,
Behold them white and clean!—

5. On earth they sought the Saviour's grace,
On earth they loved His name;
So now they see His blessèd face,
And stand before the Lamb—

897 Adelboden C.M.D

Swiss Melody

1 THE rain had poured unceasingly
    For many a night and day,
And all who lived upon the earth
    The flood had swept away.

2 But calmly in an ark upborne,
    Amid that death-strewn sea,
The GOD of grace had safely kept
    A little company.

3 And Noah, though around him spread
    One dismal, watery waste,
Knew that his GOD would keep them still,
    Till danger all was past.

4 Another flood is coming soon,
    Of fiery wrath and woe,
On all whose hearts have here refused
    The GOD of grace to know.

5 But JESUS is the living Ark,
    Where all who will may come,
And find in Him a hiding-place,
    A safe, a happy home.

6 Oh, happy they who enter now!
    Their sins are all forgiven,
And safe with JESUS they shall be
    When wrath is poured from heaven.

898   Jewels P.M.

W.O. Cushing   G.F. Root

WHEN He cometh, when He cometh
To make up His jewels,
All His jewels, precious jewels,
His loved and His own:

   Like the stars of the morning,
   His bright crown adorning,
   They shall shine in their beauty,
   Bright gems for His crown!

He will gather, He will gather
  The gems for His kingdom;
All the pure ones, all the bright ones,
  His loved and His own—

Little children, little children
  Who love their Redeemer,
Are the jewels, precious jewels,
  His loved and His own—

SUPPLEMENT
TUNES ONLY

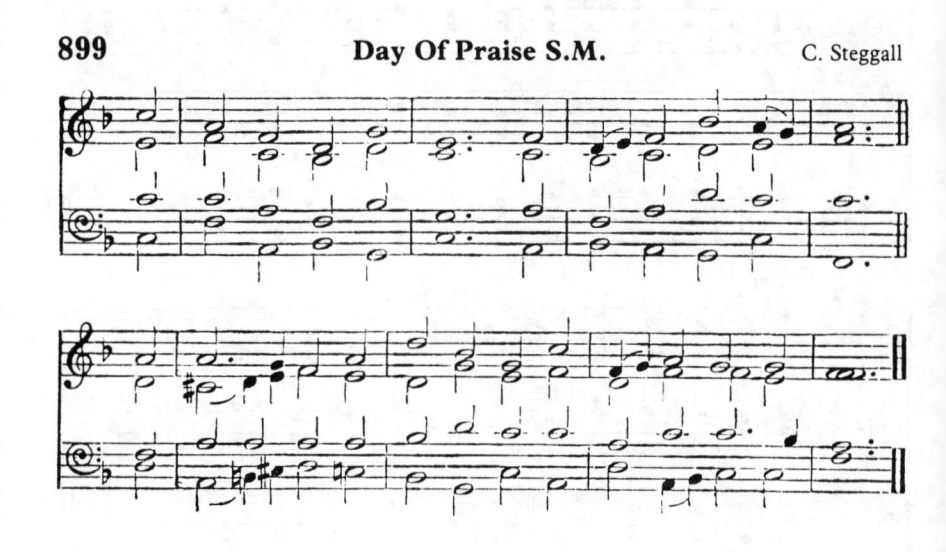

899 Day Of Praise S.M. C. Steggall

900 Diademata S.M.D G.J. Elvey

901   Deliverance S.M. and Chorus   Thos. Willey

902 Attercliffe C.M.
W. Mather

903 Miles Lane C.M.
W. Shrubsole

904 Blissful Hope C.M. and Chorus

CHORUS

905   **Land of Rest C.M.D.**   Robert S. Newman

906   **Gratitude L.M.**

907   **Wilton L.M.**   S. Stanley

908   Saved By Grace L.M. and Chorus   Geo. C. Stebbins

909   Hanover 5.5.5.5.6.5.6.5   Wm. Croft
(or 10.10.11.11)

910 Norfolk Park 6.5.6.5.D — H. Coward

911 St. John 6.6.6.6.8.8 — W.H. Havergal

912 Angeli 6.6.8.4

913 Fairford 7.6.7.6.D Schubert

914 My Song Shall Be Of Jesus 7.6.7.6.D W.H. Doane

915   **Wolvercote 7.6.7.6.D**   W.H. Ferguson

916 Thanksgiving 7.7.7.6 Douglas Russell

917 Maidstone 7.7.7.7.7.7 W.B. Gilbert

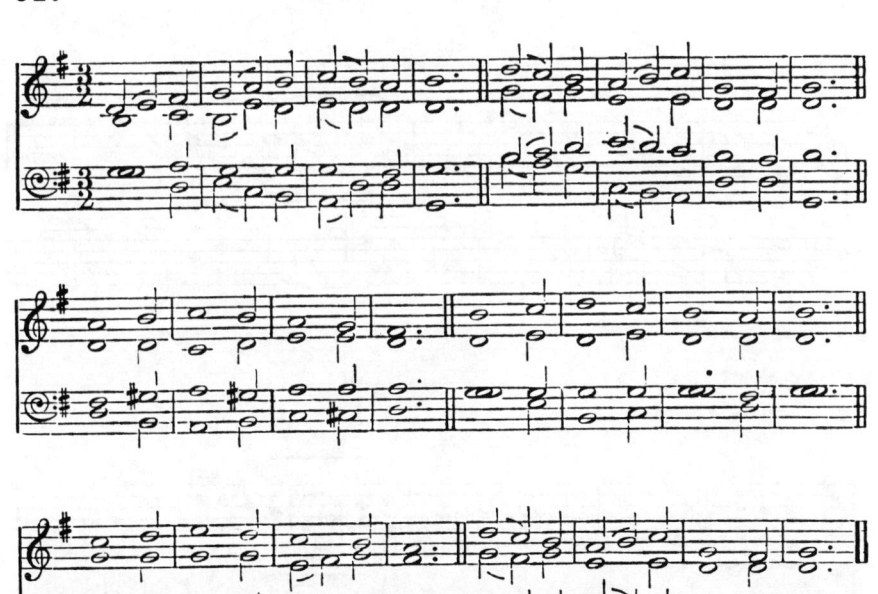

Easter Hymn 7.7.7.7.D

Lyra Davidica 1708

919   Hollingside 7.7.7.7.D   J.B. Dykes

920   **The Pleading Voice 8.5.8.5.D**   Clara H. Scott

921   **Mariners 8.7.8.7**   Sicilian Melody

922   **St. Raphael 8.7.8.7.4.7**   E.J. Hopkins

923   **Crown Him 8.7.8.7.D**   Geo. C. Stebbins (arr.)

924   **Amicus Divinus 8.7.8.7.D**   Geo. C. Stebbins

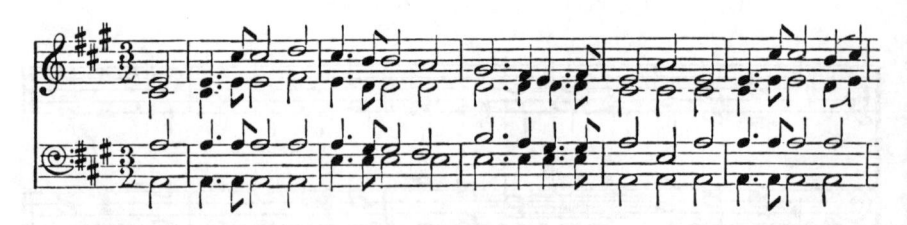

925   **Faben 8.7.8.7.D**   J.H. Willcox

926   **Sweetest Name 8.7.8.7.D**   W.B. Bradbury

927   **Delhi 8.8.8**   E.F. Rimbault

928   **Silverstone 8.8.8.6**   T.M. Mudie

929   David 8.8.8.8   From Handel

930   Stella 8.8.8.8.8.8   Hemy's Easy Tunes

931 Unde Et Memores 10.10.10.10.10.10   Wm. H. Monk

932 Belfield 11.8.11.8   E.W. Bullinger

933   Montreal 11.10.11.10   E.W. Bullinger

934   **O Perfect Love 11.10.11.10**   J. Barnby

935   **Datchet 11.11.11.11**   G.J. Elvey

936   **Dilexi 11.11.11.11**   J. Ellis

937 Precious Blood Of Jesus 8.5.8.3 and Chorus   J. Mountain

938 Repose P.M.

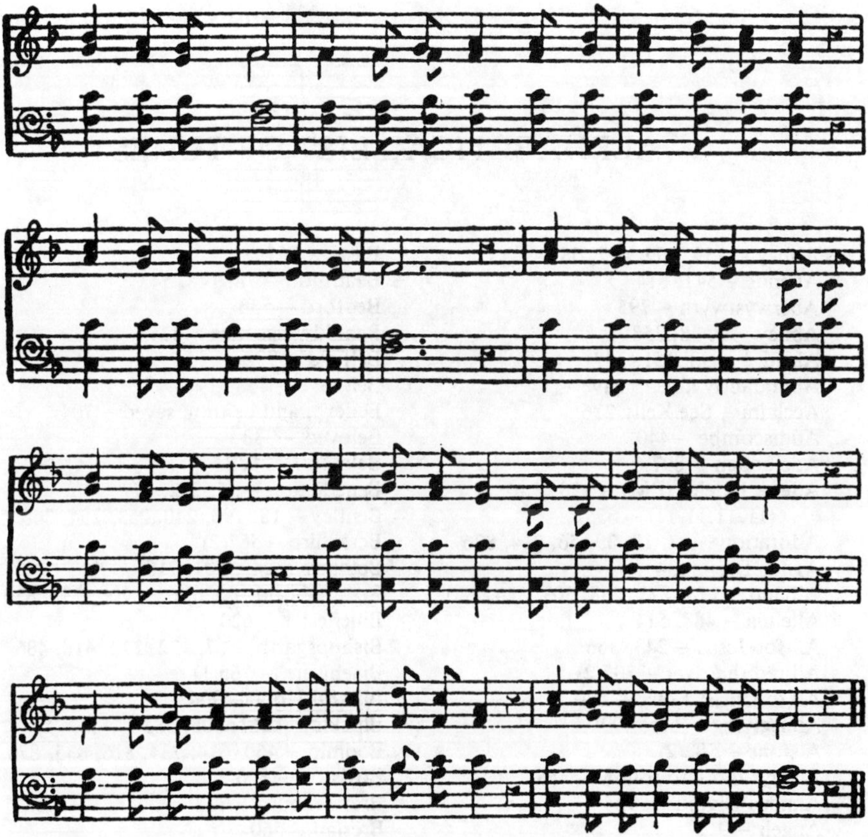

ALPHABETICAL LIST OF TUNES

Abbey – 259, 409, 457, 581
Abends – 571, 814
Aberwystwyth – 795
Abney – 2, 38, 258
Abridge – 98, 151, 307
Abundantly able to save – 749
Acclaim – See Kelly 216
Addiscombe – 440
Adelboden – 897
Adeste Fideles (PM) – 150
 (11.11.11.11) – 655
Adoration – 12, 19, 39, 56, 214, 876
Agnus Dei – 134
Albano – 118, 273, 468, 503, 524, 880
Alleluia – 488, 514
All for Jesus – 243, 366
All red the river – 702(2)
All to Christ I owe – 820
Almsgiving – 111, 499
Alstone – 582(2)
Always more to follow – 858
Amicus Divinus – 924
Angeli – 912
Angels' Story – 236
Angelus – 114, 565
Antwerp – 353, 490, 507, 584
Ar hyd y nos – 373, 681
Arizona – 834
Artavia – 598
Ashley – 542
At the Cross – 806
At the Cross there's room – 760
Attercliffe – 902
Auber – 647
Augustine – 3, 107, 119, 788
Aurelia – 171
Austria – 89
Azmon – 264, 367, 413, 504, 590

Ballerma – 339, 415, 697
Ballina – 531
Banquet – 110
Barton – 392, 574

Basle – 265
Beatitudo – 78, 144, 543
Bedford – 556
Behold what love – 424
Belfield – 932
Belgrave – 458
Believe, and be thou saved – 704
Beloved – 338
Belmont – 26, 33
Benediction – 15, 832, 877
Bentley – 18, 190, 240, 253, 294, 348
Berkshire – 567(2)
Bethany – 242, 501, 710
Better World – 626, 651, 706, 732, 850
Binchester – 620
Bishopsgarth – 67, 172, 372, 418, 486
Blaenwern – 766(1)
Blissful Hope – 904
Blockley – 261, 508, 585
Bodmin – 460, 614, 734, 816, 835, 870
Boylston – 800
Brandenburg – 222
Breslau – 560
Bristol – 227, 336, 354, 463, 839
Broomsgrove – 417, 485, 683
Bryn Cal faria – 285, 314
Buckland – 159, 446, 483, 580, 712
Bullinger – 96, 108
Byzantium – 355, 819

Caer Salem – 576(2)
Cairnbrook – 767
Call them in – 758
Call the weary home – 657
Calon Lan – 86, 128, 402
Cambridge – 252
Canada – 280, 365
Carlisle – 297, 320, 893
Castle Rising – 525, 605, 629
Celeste – 42, 399, 427, 538, 848
Chalvey – 686
Choose ye today – 717
Chorus Angelorum – 343

Christ arose – 726
Christchurch – 81
Christ is coming – 753
Church Triumphant – 586
Claremont – 47, 262, 724
Clarendon Street – 228, 419
Come believing – 757
'Come', is the Lord's invitation – 699
Come, thou weary – 674
Come unto Me (Dykes) (Vox Jesu) (7.6.7.6.D) – 519, 670
Come unto Me (Hasty) (10.10.10.6 and Chorus) – 859
Come unto Me (Stebbins) (10.10.10.10 and Chorus) – 738
Contemplation – 370(2)
Converse – 459
Corinth – 536
Credo – 349, 547, 559, 609
Crediton – 388
Cross of Jesus (Sankey) – 94
Cross of Jesus (Stainer) – 142, 266, 322
Crown Him – 923
Crüger – 83, 204, 577
Cwm Rhondda – 200, 405, 727

Dalehurst – 345, 370(1), 513
Darwall's 148th – 246, 789
Datchet – 935
David – 929
Dawn – 245
Day of Praise – 899
Day of Rest – 166, 272
Deep Harmony – 224
Deerhurst – 48, 65, 469, 709
Delhi – 927
Deliverance – 901
Dennis – 113, 182, 313, 719
Diadem – 206
Diademata – 900
Dilexi – 936
Dismissal – 505, 769
Dix – 700(1)
Doane – 165
Dominica – 496(2)
Dominus Regit Me – 801
Doncaster – 279
Dublin – 30, 70, 103, 173, 237, 277
Duke Street – 552, 843, 871
Dundee – 310(2)

Eagley – 329(2)

Easter Hymn – 918
Eden – 52, 54, 235
Egypt – 408
Ellacombe – 91, 437, 624, 878
Ellers – 690
Ellingham – 480
Ems – 535
Endemia – 594
Ephraim – 874
Evan – 154, 178, 191, 291, 474, 731
Evensong (Southgate) (8.4.8.4.8.8.8.4.) – 140, 327
Evensong (Summers) (8.7.8.7.7.7) – 619, 809, 875
Even thee – 653
Eventide – 287
Ever, my heart, keep clinging – 813
Ewing – 90, 439, 588
Excelling – 87, 127, 510

Faben – 925
Fading away – 745
Fairford – 913
Farewell Hymn (Bright Home of our Saviour!) – 241
Farrant – 50, 133, 157, 453
Festus – 220, 332, 361
Fides (Goshen Davis) – 888
Fingal – 131, 267, 389, 595, 650, 705, 791
Finlandia – 209
Firmament – 541
Forgiveness – 845
Fountain (C.M. and Chorus) – 441, 530, 684; (C.M.D. and Chorus) – 812
Fulda – 550
Fully persuaded – 787

Glasgow – 390, 473
Glorious home – 675
God is love – 493
Goodwin – 167
Gopsal – 10
Goshen (7.7.8.7.D) – 66, 79
Goshen (Davis) (Fides) (6.5.6.5 and Chorus) – 426
Gounod – 213
Grace Divine – 642
Gräfenberg – 358, 472, 534
Gratitude – 906

Hanover – 909

Happy morn – 707
Harewood – 540
Hark! Hark! Hark! – 750
Harts – 97
Hasten – 430
Have you any room for Jesus? – 766(2)
Have you been to Jesus? – 698
Hear and obey – 676
Hear God's blessed invitation – 754
Heathlands – 304
Helmsley – 201
Hereford – 359, 881
Hereford New – 1, 521
Herein is love – 730
His saving Name – 633
Hold Thou my hand – 82
Hollingside – 919
Holly – 570(2)
Homeland – 435
Homeward – 420
Houghton – 404
Ho! ye thirsty, Jesus calls you – 685
Huddersfield – 101, 180, 383, 393, 599, 810, 869
Huddleston – 889, 894
Hull – 59, 148, 517
Hursley – 260
Hyfrydol – 49

I am the Way – 831
Ibstone – 434(2)
Ich halte treulich still – 822
I looked to Jesus – 828
I love to tell the story – 662
In Memoriam (Maker) (8.8.8.4) – 363(2)
In Memoriam (Stainer) (8.6.7.6.7.6.7.6) – 885
Innsbruck – 566
Invitation – 682
Irish – 310(1)
Ishmael – 604, 770
It cleanseth from all sin – 808
It is finished – 696
It passeth knowledge – 239

Jazer – 13, 102, 284, 606
Jesus! I am resting – 179
Jesus is calling – 751
Jesus is waiting – 716
Jesus of Nazareth passeth by – 711(1)
Jewels – 898
Job – 582(1)
Joy! Joy! Joy! – 637

Just as I am (Barnby) – 289, 677
Just as I am (Bradbury) (8.8.8.6) – 793
 (LM) – 808

Kelly – 216
Kelso – 139, 771
Kensington New – 740
Kilmarnock – 369, 379
Kingsfold – 703

Ladywell – 545
Lancashire – 479, 646
Land of Rest – 905
Latimer – 401(2)
Laudate Dominum (Parry) – 325, 461
Laus Deo – 498
Leadeth – 414
Leoni – 247, 337, 589
Let the Saviour in – 733
Lewisham – 523, 725
Limpsfield – 692
Lion of Judah – 863
Llangloffan – 335
Llanllyfni – 573
Llef – 306, 783
Lloyd – 8, 158, 211, 299, 364
Look and live (Bliss) (7.6.7.3.D and Chorus) – 701
Look and live (Ogden) (PM) – 746
Look and thou shalt live – 702
Look away to Jesus – 838
Look to Me and be ye saved – 826
Look unto Me – 672
Lord, Thou art worthy – 842
Lost one wandering on – 761
Love Divine – 41, 121, 233, 511, 601, 837
Love's invitation – 720
Lucerne – 529
Lucius – 592, 841
Luther's Chant – 51, 69, 219, 454
Luther's Hymn (8.7.8.7.8.8.7) – 75; (8.7.8.8.7) – 591
Lymington – 16, 174, 189, 263, 286, 412, 537, 887
Lyngham – 824
Lynton – 60, 385, 840

Mackinley – 40, 248
Maidstone – 917
Main – 855
Mainzer – 23, 76, 218, 416, 578
Malvern – 866

Manna – 407
Mannheim – 29, 512
Manoah – 104, 238
Man of sorrows – 99
Marching – 391
Mariners – 921
Martyrdom – 68
Maryport – 347
Maryton – 61, 156, 442
Melcombe – 568(1)
Melita – 351, 381
Melling – 410(1)
Mercy's portal – 722
Mercy is boundless – 743
Meribah – 153, 244, 268, 290, 452, 470, 477
Mighty love – 833
Miles Lane – 903
Millennium – 634
Missionary – 205, 288, 492, 796
Moment by Moment – 630, 774
Moncton – 682(2)
Monkland – 57, 462, 575
Montgomery (11.11.11.11) – 326, 406; (PM) – 187
Montreal – 933
Morcambe – 135, 275
Morgenlied – 436
Morning Hymn – 567(1)
Morning Light – 487
Morningside – 357
Moscow – 62, 867
Mothers of Salem – 884
Mount Calvary (Chapman) (7.7.7.7) – 7
Mount Calvary (Knowles) (LMD and Chorus) – 891
Munich – 25, 93, 106, 129, 561, 737
My Redeemer – 847
My song shall be of Jesus – 914

Narenza – 295, 678
Nativity – 229, 323, 396
Nearer Home – 432
Nelson – 20, 85
Newcastle – 254
Newington – 563
Newton Ferns – 411, 557
Newtown – 896
Nicaea – 271
Nicomachus – 526, 583
None but Christ can satisfy – 756
Norfolk Park – 910
Not far from the Kingdom – 776

Nothing between – 183
Nothing but the Blood of Jesus – 803
Nothing to pay – 659, 661
Nottingham – 221
Not yet decided – 782, 784
Nyland – 185, 438, 572, 829

Oh, be saved – 718
Oh, come and linger not – 715
Oh, happy day! – 836
O Perfect Love – 934
Oh, precious words! – 627
Old Hundredth – 522, 533
Olivet – 680
Ombersley – 28, 138, 445
One half has not been told – 853
One there is who loves thee – 660
Only a step to Jesus – 775
Only trust Him – 663, 666
Ottawa – 569, 723
Overstrand – 382

Palmyra – 72, 729
Paradise No. 2 – 429
Pass me not – 387
Passion Chorale – 115, 558, 673
Pater Meus – 184
Pater Omnium – 44, 177, 257
Patience – 873
Pax Tecum – 342
Peace! Blessed Peace! – 763, 864
Peace, peace is mine – 865
Peel Castle – 579
Pembroke – 53, 112, 231, 449, 631
Penlan – 80, 199, 305, 316, 518, 587, 764
Petherton – 600
Petition – 311
Pilgrims – 747
Pisgah – 141
Plainfield – 494
Praise Him! Praise Him! – 849
Praise my soul – 155, 516
Precious Blood of Jesus (Burke) (PM) – 804
Precious Blood of Jesus (Mountain) (8.5.8.3 and Chorus) – 937
Purleigh – 481

Raynolds – 509
Redeemed by blood – 736
Redemption – 73, 632, 713, 735
Redemption Ground – 610, 618
Redhead No. 47 – 100

Redhead No. 76 – 794
Regent Square – 195, 202, 333, 544, 643
Rejoice and be glad – 687
Remember Me (Abney) – 2, 38, 258
Repose – 938
Requiem – 88, 856
Resolution – 395
Rest (Maker) (8.6.8.8.6) – 802
Rest (Moule) (C.M.) – 4, 693
Rest (Stainer) (8.8.8.8.8.8) – 282
Rex Regum – 607
Rhodes – 6, 230, 298, 356, 444, 447, 476, 821, 872
Rhuddlan – 147, 234, 308, 421, 527, 596, 622
Richmond – 186, 318, 422
Rimington – 37, 203, 456, 532
Rousseau – 752
Rutherford – 137, 546, 645

St. Agnes (Durham) (C.M.) – 21, 27
St. Agnes (Langran) (6.4.6.4.D) – 742; (10.10.10.10) – 132
St. Aiden – 193
St. Alphege – 109, 207, 386, 502, 564
St. Ann – 451
St. Bees – 352
St. Bernard – 5, 122, 163, 249, 301, 368, 448, 562
St. Beuno – 433, 555, 818
St. Botolph – 377
St. Catherine – 43, 84, 350, 548
St. Cecilia – 371, 434(1)
St. Chrysostom – 711(2)
St. Columba – 188
St. Cuthbert – 755, 780
St. Denio – 175, 317, 400, 668
St. Ethelwald – 380, 397, 679
St. Flavian – 32, 319, 464, 648
St. Fulbert – 120, 126, 161, 329
St. George – 145, 496(1)
St. Gertrude – 649
St. Hugh – 892
St. James – 31, 46, 95
St. John (Calkin) – 9, 58, 664
St. John (Havergal) – 911
St. John's, Hoxton – 125, 215
St. Luke – 330, 748
St. Magnus – 105, 169, 475, 895
St. Matthew – 116, 269, 374, 398, 667, 797
St. Matthias – 324, 549, 608
St. Michael – 309, 790

St. Oswald – 152
St. Peter – 24
St. Raphael – 922
St. Saviour – 296, 303, 341, 360
St. Stephen – 64, 212
St. Theodulph – 491(2)
Safe in the arms of Jesus – 805, 817
Saffron Walden – 283, 346, 671
Sagina – 197
Salvation – 654
Samaria – 890
Samson – 568(2)
Samuel – 334, 450
Sandys – 431, 879
Saved by grace – 908
Saviour, keep me near the Cross – 854
Sawley – 36, 482, 807
Saxby – 593, 597
Scatter seeds of kindness – 484
Seeking for me – 815
Sharon – 22, 77, 162, 708
Sheltered Dale – 274, 362
Silchester – 11, 226, 331, 425, 500
Silverstone – 928
Since I have been redeemed – 846
So near to the Kingdom! – 777
Sound His Praise – 860
Southgate (Evensong) – 140, 327
Southport (Davies) (S.M.) – 312, 378, 617
Southport (Lomas) (8.8.8.4) – 363(1)
Southwell – 376, 478
Sovereignty – 786
Spanish Hymn – 515
Speed away – 638
Spohr – 17
Stella – 930
Stephanos – 658
Stockton – 644
Stracathro – 278, 554
Stroudwater – 375, 471
Stuttgart – 130, 143, 217
Suffer them to come – 886
Sunnyside – 883
Supremacy – 74
Surrey Chapel – 868
Sussex – 194, 210, 302, 691
Swabia – 615
Sweetest Name – 926

Tallis' Canon – 45, 570(1)
Te Laudant Omnia – 623
Tell me the old, old story – 602

Tetelestai – 694
Thanksgiving – 916
The Giver of rest – 688
The Good Shepherd – 467
The Gospel of Thy grace – 641
The half was never told – 851
The harvest is passing – 639, 773
The hem of His garment – 689
The Light of the World – 652
The love that gave Jesus to die – 857
The Master's call – 741
The ninety and nine – 636
Theodora – 384
The pleading voice – 920
The quiet hour – 792
The Saviour's call – 656
The Solid Rock – 811
There are moments – See scatter seeds of kindness 484
There is a fountain (Fountain) – (CM and Chorus) – 441, 530, 684; (CMD and Chorus) – 812
There is a love – 861
There is a life for a look – 659, 661
There is pardon for you – 739
There's a light – 192
There's a refuge in God – 765
There's One who has loved thee – 665
Thornbury – 276
Through the Name of Jesus – 744
Tichfield – 603
'Tis the Blood – 799
Tiverton – 63, 170
To all eternity the same – 611
To God be the glory – 862
Too late, too late – 785(1)
Tours – 423, 844
Tranquillity (Jesus! I am resting) – 179
Trentham – 198, 798
Trewen – 315
Triumph – 14, 506, 576, 669
Troyte's Chant – 124
Trumpet call – 640
Truro – 428, 625
Tuam – 225

Unde et Memores – 931
Under His wing – 328
Unity – 281
University – 466
University College – 149, 168, 293, 394, 403, 827

Veni Domine (4.6.8.8.4) – 255, 300
(10.8.8.4) – 176
Verbum Pacis – 528
'Verily, verily' – 852
Vienna – 410(2)
Vox Dilecti – 612
Vox Jesu (Come unto Me–Dykes) – 519, 670

Warrington – 443
Warwick – 340
Weber – 35, 164, 465
Weeping will not save thee – 714
Wells – 123, 256
We sing of a Saviour's love – 882
Westminster – 160, 208, 270, 551, 830
What shall the harvest be? – 520
When the harvest is past – 772
Where will you spend eternity? – 781
Whitburn – 34, 55, 92, 250, 292, 497
Who is He? – 613
Whosoever will – 628
Why do you wait? – 768
Why not tonight? – 779
Will you be there? – 863
Williams – 759, 825
Wilton – 907
Wiltshire – 136, 146, 223
Wimborne – 196, 621
Winchester New – 71, 232, 455, 823
Windsor – 785(2)
Wolvercote – 915
Wonderful love – 778
Wonderful words of life – 721
Wondrous Love – 635
Woodlands – 539
Woolwich – 251
Work, for the night is coming – 489
Worship – 344
Would you taste of joy? – 695

Yarmouth – 401
Ye must be born again – 616
Yet there is room (Courtney) – 762
Yet there is room (Sankey) – 763, 864
Yorkshire – 181

Zenana – 495
Zoan – 321, 491(1), 553
Zurich – 117, 728

METRICAL INDEX

(A few tunes are shown under more than one metre where by custom they are so used.)

SM
Augustine — 3, 107, 119, 788
Boylston — 800
Cambridge — 252
Canada — 280, 365
Carlisle — 297, 320, 893
Day of Praise — 899
Dennis — 113, 182, 313, 719
Dominica — 496(2)
Doncaster — 279
Huddersfield — 101, 180, 383, 393, 599, 810, 869
Narenza — 295, 678
Rhodes — 6, 230, 298, 356, 444, 447, 476, 821, 872
St. Beuno — 433, 555, 818
St. Ethelwald — 380, 397, 679
St. George — 145, 496(1)
St. Michael — 309, 790
Sandys — 431, 879
Silchester — 11, 226, 331, 425, 500
Southport (Davies) — 312, 378, 617
Swabia — 615
Trentham — 198, 798
Tuam — 225
Woolwich — 251
Zurich — 117, 728

SM and Chorus
Believe, and be thou saved — 704
Chalvey — 686(1)
Deliverance — 901
Egypt — 408
Ishmael — 604, 770
Mercy's Portal — 722

SMD
Diademata — 900
Ich halte treulich still — 822
Llanllyfni — 573
Moncton — 686(2)
Nearer Home — 432

CM
Abbey — 259, 409, 457, 581
Abney — 2, 38, 258
Abridge — 98, 151, 307
Albano — 118, 273, 468, 503, 524, 880
Attercliffe — 902
Azmon — 264, 367, 413, 504, 590
Ballerma — 339, 415, 697
Beatitudo — 78, 144, 543
Bedford — 556
Belgrave — 458
Belmont — 26, 33
Binchester — 620
Bristol — 227, 336, 354, 463, 839
Byzantium — 355, 819
Chorus Angelorum — 343
Claremont — 47, 262, 724
Contemplation — 370(2)
Crediton — 388
Dalehurst — 345, 370(1), 513
Diadem — 206
Dublin — 30, 70, 103, 173, 237, 277
Dundee — 310(2)
Eagley — 329(2)
Evan — 154, 178, 191, 291, 474, 731
Farrant — 50, 133, 157, 453
Fingal — 131, 267, 389, 595, 650, 705, 791
Glasgow — 390, 473
Gräfenberg — 358, 472, 534
Irish — 310(1)
Jazer — 13, 102, 284, 606
Kilmarnock — 369, 379
Lloyd — 8, 158, 211, 299, 364
Lucius — 592, 841
Lyngham — 824
Lynton — 60, 385, 840
Manoah — 104, 238
Martyrdom — 68
Miles Lane — 908
Nativity — 229, 323, 396
Oh, happy day! — 836

Rest – 4, 693
Richmond – 186, 318, 422
St. Agnes (Durham) – 21, 27
St. Ann – 451
St. Bernard – 5, 122, 163, 249, 301, 368, 448, 562
St. Botolph – 377
St. Flavian – 32, 319, 464, 648
St. Fulbert – 120, 126, 161, 329(1)
St. Hugh – 892
St. James – 31, 46, 95
St. Magnus – 105, 169, 475, 895
St. Peter – 24
St. Saviour – 296, 303, 341, 360
St. Stephen – 64, 212
Sawley – 36, 482, 807
Southwell – 376, 478
Stracathro – 278, 554
Stroudwater – 375, 471
Tiverton – 63, 170
Too late, too late – 785(1)
University – 466
Warwick – 340
Westminster – 160, 208, 270, 551, 830
Wiltshire – 136, 146, 223
Windsor – 785(2)

CM and Chorus
At the Cross – 806
Behold what love – 424
Blissful Hope – 904
Castle Rising – 605
Ellacombe – 624, 878
Fountain – 441, 530, 684
His saving Name – 633
I am the Way – 831
Kingsfold – 703
Love's Invitation – 720
None but Christ can satisfy – 756
Oh, Precious Words! – 627
One half has not been told – 853
Only trust Him – 663, 666
Paradise No. 2 – 429
Redeemed by Blood – 736
Rex Regum – 607
Since I have been redeemed – 846
The half was never told – 851
'Tis the Blood – 799
Vox Dilecti – 612
Wondrous Love – 635

CMD
Adelboden – 897

Castle Rising – 525, 605, 629
Dawn – 245
Ellacombe – 91, 437, 624, 878
Ladywell – 545
Land of Rest – 905
St. Matthew – 116, 269, 374, 398, 667, 797
The Saviour's Call – 656

CMD and Chorus
There is a fountain (Fountain) – 812

LM
Abends – 571, 814
Alstone – 582(2)
Angelus – 114, 565
Antwerp – 353, 490, 507, 584
Arizona – 834
Berkshire – 567(2)
Blockley – 261, 508, 585
Bodmin – 460, 614, 734, 816, 835, 870
Breslau – 560
Church Triumphant – 586
Deep Harmony – 224
Duke Street – 552, 843, 871
Eden – 52, 54, 235
Festus – 220, 332, 361
Forgiveness – 845
Fulda – 550
Gratitude – 906
Hereford – 359, 881
Holly – 570(2)
Hursley – 260
It cleanseth from all sin (Just as I am–Bradbury) – 808
Job – 582(1)
Llef – 306, 783
Luther's Chant – 51, 69, 219, 454
Mackinlay – 40
Mainzer – 23, 76, 218, 416, 578
Maryton – 61, 156, 442
Melcombe – 568(1)
Morning Hymn – 567(1)
Nicomachus – 526, 583
Old Hundredth – 522, 533
Ombersley – 28, 138, 445
Rimington – 37, 203, 456, 532
Samson – 568(2)
Saxby – 593, 597
Tallis' Canon – 45, 570(1)
Truro – 428, 625
Warrington – 443
Whitburn – 34, 55, 92, 250, 292, 497

Williams – 759, 825
Wilton – 907
Winchester New – 71, 232, 455, 823

LM and Chorus
Credo – 609
Leadeth – 414
Melita – 381
Oh, come and linger not – 715
Redemption Ground – 610, 618
St. Matthias – 608
Saved by grace – 908
The Solid Rock – 811
Where will you spend eternity? – 781
Why not tonight? – 779
LMD Mackinlay – 40, 248

LMD
Mackinlay – 40, 248

LMD and Chorus
Mount Calvary (Knowles) – 891

4.6.8.8.4
Patience – 873
Veni Domine – 255, 300

5.5.5.5.6.5.6.5
Hanover – 909
Houghton – 404
Laudate Dominum (Parry) – 325, 461

6.4.6.4.D
St. Agnes (Langran) – 742

6.4.6.4.6.6.6.4
Broomsgrove – 417, 485, 683
Worship – 344

6.5.6.4 and Chorus
Christ arose – 726

6.5.6.5
The quiet hour – 792

6.5.6.5 and Chorus
Goshen (Davis) (Fides) – 426
Norfolk Park – 910
Sunnyside – 883

6.6.4.6.6.6.4
Malvern – 866
Moscow – 62, 867

Olivet – 680

6.6.6.6
Ibstone – 434(2)
St. Cecilia – 371, 434(1)

6.6.6.6 and Chorus
Darwall's 148th – 789
Spanish Hymn – 515

6.6.6.6.4
Homeward – 420

6.6.6.6.8.8
Adoration – 12, 19, 39, 56, 214, 876
Christchurch – 81
Darwall's 148th – 246, 789
Gopsal – 10
Harewood – 540
St. John (Calkin) – 9, 58, 664
St. John (Havergal) – 911
Samuel – 334, 450

6.6.8.4
Angeli – 912
St. John's, Hoxton – 125, 215
Verbum Pacis – 528

6.6.8.4.D
Leoni – 247, 337, 589

6.6.8.6.8.8
Nelson – 20, 85
Pisgah – 141

6.10.10.6
Hereford New – 1, 521
Millennium – 634

7.6.7.3.D and Chorus
Look and live (Bliss) – 701

7.6.7.5.D
Work for the night is coming – 489

7.6.7.6
Barton – 392, 574
St. Alphege – 109, 207, 386, 502, 564

7.6.7.6.D
Angels' Story – 236
Aurelia – 171
Bentley – 18, 190, 240, 253, 294, 348

Come unto Me (Dykes) – 519, 670
Cross of Jesus (Sankey) – 94
Crüger – 83, 204, 577
Day of Rest – 166, 272
Doane – 165
Ewing – 90, 439, 588
Fairford – 913
Goodwin – 167
Lancashire – 479, 646
Llangloffan – 335
Lymington – 16, 174, 189, 263, 286, 412, 537, 887
Missionary – 205, 288, 492, 796
Morning Light – 487
Munich – 25, 93, 106, 129, 561, 737
My song shall be of Jesus – 914
Nyland – 185, 438, 572, 829
Passion Chorale – 115, 558, 673
Penlan – 80, 199, 305, 316, 518, 587, 764
Petition – 311
Rutherford – 137, 546, 645
St. Theodulph – 491(2)
Salvation – 654
Thornbury – 276
Tours – 423, 844
Vox Jesu (Come unto Me–Dykes) – 519, 670
Wolvercote – 915
Zoan – 321, 491(1), 553

7.6.7.6.D and Chorus
Always more to follow – 858
I love to tell the story – 662
Only a step to Jesus – 775
Plainfield – 494
Safe in the Arms of Jesus – 805, 817
Tell me the old, old story – 602

7.6.7.6.7.7.7.6
Limpsfield – 692

7.6.7.6.8.6.7.6
Ellacombe – 437

7.7.7.6
Redhead No. 47 – 100
Thanksgiving – 916
Troyte's Chant – 124

7.7.7.7
Brandenburg – 222
Buckland – 159, 446, 483, 580, 712
Ellingham – 480

Ephraim – 874
Harts – 97
Look to Me and be ye saved – 826
Melling – 410(1)
Monkland – 57, 462, 575
Mount Calvary (Chapman) – 7
Newington – 563
Nottingham – 221
St. Bees – 352
Theodora – 384
University College – 149, 168, 293, 394, 403, 827
Vienna – 410(2)
Weber – 35, 164, 465

7.7.7.7 and Chorus
Saviour, keep me near the Cross – 854
Te Laudant Omnia – 623
Tichfield – 603

7.7.7.7.7.7
All red the river – 700(2)
Dix – 700(1)
Heathlands – 304
Maidstone – 917
Redhead No. 76 – 794
Wells – 123, 256

7.7.7.7.D
Aberystwyth – 795
Easter Hymn – 918
Hollingside – 919

7.7.7.8
Man of sorrows – 99

7.7.8.7.D
Bishopsgarth – 67, 172
Goshen – 66, 79

7.8.7.8 and Chorus
Nothing but the Blood of Jesus – 803

8.3.8.3.8.8.8.3
Auber – 647
Better World – 626, 651, 706, 732, 850

8.4.8.4.8.8.8.4
Ar hyd y nos – 373, 681
Herein is Love – 730
Main – 855
Southgate (Evensong) – 140, 327

8.5.8.3
Bullinger – 96, 108
Cairnbrook – 767
Come thou weary – 674
Stephanos – 658

8.5.8.3 and Chorus
Precious Blood of Jesus (Mountain) – 937

8.5.8.5
Pass me not – 387

8.5.8.5.D
Pater Meus – 184
The Pleading Voice – 920

8.6.7.6.7.6.7.6
In Memoriam (Stainer) – 885

8.6.8.4
St. Cuthbert – 755, 780

8.6.8.6.6.6 and Chorus
Wonderful Words of Life – 721

8.6.8.6.8.6
Sheltered Dale – 274, 362
Spohr – 17

8.6.8.6.8.8
Ever, my heart, keep clinging – 813
Palmyra – 72, 729
Supremacy – 74

8.6.8.8.6
Newcastle – 254
Rest – 802

8.7.8.4
Lost one wandering on (Filey) – 761

8.7.8.5.D
Tranquillity (Jesus! I am resting) – 179

8.7.8.5.D and Chorus
Samaria – 890

8.7.8.7
All for Jesus – 243, 366
Cross of Jesus (Stainer) – 142, 266, 322
Laus Deo – 498
Love Divine – 41, 121, 233, 511, 601, 837
Lucerne – 529
Marching – 391
Mariners – 921
Newton Ferns – 411, 557
St. Oswald – 152
Sharon – 22, 77, 162, 708
Stuttgart – 130, 143, 217
Sussex – 194, 210, 302, 691
Wimborne – 196, 621

8.7.8.7 (Iambic)
Dominus regit me – 801
St. Columba – 188

8.7.8.7 and Chorus
Blaenwern – 766(1)
Christ is coming – 753
'Come', is the Lord's invitation – 699
Grace Divine – 642
Have you any room for Jesus? – 766(2)
I looked to Jesus – 828
It is finished – 696
My Redeemer – 847

8.7.8.7.4
God is love – 493

8.7.8.7.4.7
St. Raphael – 922

8.7.8.7.7.7
Evensong (Summers) – 619, 809, 875
Gounod – 213
Ottawa – 569, 723
Requiem – 88, 856

8.7.8.7.8.7
Benediction – 15, 832, 877
Bryn Calfaria – 285, 314
Caer Salem – 576(2)
Corinth – 536
Cwm Rhondda – 200, 405, 727
Dismissal – 505, 769
Helmsley – 201
Kensington New – 740
Lewisham – 523, 725
Mannheim – 29, 512
Praise my soul – 155, 516
Regent Square – 195, 202, 333, 544, 643

Rhuddlan – 147, 234, 308, 421, 527, 596, 622
Rousseau – 752
The good Shepherd – 467
Triumph – 14, 506, 576, 669

8.7.8.7.D
Alleluia – 488, 514
Amicus Divinus – 924
Austria – 89
Banquet – 110
Bethany – 242, 501, 710
Bishopsgarth – 372, 418
Call them in – 758
Calon Lan – 86, 128, 402
Come believing – 757
Converse – 459
Crown Him – 923
Deerhurst – 48, 65, 469, 709
Excelling – 87, 127, 510
Faben – 925
Hyfrydol – 49
Sweetest Name – 926
There are moments – 959
There's a Light – 192

8.7.8.7.D and Chorus
Morgenlied – 436
Scatter seeds of kindness – 484
Would you taste of joy? – 695

8.7.8.7.8.8.7
Luther's Hymn – 75

8.7.8.8.7
Luther's Hymn – 591

8.8.6.8.8.6
Hull – 59, 148, 517
Innsbruck – 566
Meribah – 153, 244, 268, 290, 452, 470, 477
Pembroke – 53, 112, 231, 449, 631
Purleigh – 481

8.8.6 8.8.8.6
Happy morn – 707

8.8.8
Delhi – 927
St. Aidan – 193

8.8.8.4
Almsgiving – 111, 499
In Memoriam (Maker) – 363(2)
Southport (Lomas) – 363(1)

8.8.8.5
Kelly (or Acclaim) – 216

8.8.8.6
Agnus Dei – 134
Just as I am (Barnby) – 289, 677
Just as I am (Bradbury) – 793
Saffron Walden – 283, 346, 671
Silverstone – 928

8.8.8.8
Celeste – 42, 427, 538, 848
David – 929

8.8.8.8 and Chorus
Under His Wing – 328

8.8.8.8.8.8
Basle – 265
Credo – 349, 547, 559, 609
Melita – 351
Pater Omnium – 44, 177, 257
Rest – 282
St. Catherine – 43, 84, 350, 548
St. Chrysostom – 711(2)
St. Matthias – 324, 549, 608
Sagina – 197
Sovereignty – 786
Stella – 930

8.8.8.8.D
Firmament – 541
Trewen – 315

8.9.9.9
Celeste – 399

9.8.9.8.D
Redemption – 73, 632, 735

9.9.9
Homeland – 435

10.6.10.6 and Chorus
The hem of His garment – 689

10.8.8.4
Veni Domine – 176

10.8.10.8.D and Chorus
Addiscombe – 440

10.8.11.8 and Chorus
The Master's call – 741

10.10
Pax Tecum – 342

10.10.4.6
Yet there is room (Courtney) – 762

10.10 and Chorus
Peace! Blessed Peace! – 763, 864
Yet there is room (Sankey) – 763, 864

10.10.10.6
Artavia – 598

10.10.10.6 and Chorus
Come unto Me (Hasty) – 859
'Verily, verily' – 852
Suffer them to come – 886

10.10.10.10
Ellers – 690
Eventide – 287
Morcambe – 135, 275
Peel Castle – 579
St. Agnes (Langran) – 132
Woodlands – 539

10.10.10.10 and Chorus
Come unto Me (Stebbins) – 738
Look unto Me – 672

10.10.10.10.4
It passeth knowledge – 239

10.10.10.10.10.10
Unde et Memores – 931
Yorkshire – 181

10.10.11.11
Hanover – 909
Houghton – 404
Laudate Dominum (Parry) – 325, 461

11.8.11.8
Belfield – 932
Beloved – 338

11.9.11.9 and Chorus
Through the Name of Jesus – 744

11.10.11.10
Finlandia – 209
Hold Thou my hand – 82
Montreal – 933
O Perfect Love – 934
Peace, peace is mine – 865
Raynolds – 509

11.10.11.10 and Chorus
Lord, Thou art worthy – 842
Pilgrims – 747

11.11 and Chorus
Rejoice and be glad – 687

11.11.11.11
Abundantly able to save – 749
Adeste Fideles – 655
Clarendon Street – 228, 419
Datchet – 935
Dilexi – 936
Fides (Goshen, Davis) – 888
Lion of Judah – 863
Look away to Jesus – 838
Maryport – 347
Montgomery – 326, 406
St. Denio – 175, 317, 400, 668
St. Luke – 330, 748
There's a refuge in God – 765
There's One Who has Loved Thee – 665
Will you be there? – 863

11.11.11.11 and Chorus
Fading away – 745
Farewell Hymn (Bright Home of our Saviour!) – 241
Mighty Love – 833
St. Gertrude – 649
So near to the Kingdom! – 777
To God be the glory – 860, 862

12.11.12.11
Surrey Chapel – 868

12.11.12.11 and Chorus
The harvest is passing – 639, 773

12.12.12.10
Nicaea – 271

12.12.12.12 and Chorus
Speed away – 638

PM
Adeste Fideles – 150
All to Christ I owe – 820
Ashley – 542
At the Cross there's room – 760
Ballina – 531
Bishopsgarth – 486
Call the weary home – 657
Choose ye today – 717
Ems – 535
Endemia – 594
Even thee – 653
Fully persuaded – 787
Glorious home – 675
Hark! Hark! Hark! – 750
Hasten – 430
Have you been to Jesus? – 698
Hear and obey – 676
Hear God's blessed invitation – 754
Ho! Ye thirsty, Jesus calls you – 685
Huddleston – 889, 894
Invitation – 682
Jesus is calling! – 751
Jesus is waiting – 716
Jesus of Nazareth passeth by – 711(1)
Jewels – 898
Joy! Joy! Joy! – 637
Kelso – 139, 771
Latimer – 401(2)
Let the Saviour in – 733
Look, and live (Ogden) – 746
Look, and thou shalt live – 702
Manna – 407
Mercy is boundless – 743
Moment by moment – 630, 774
Montgomery – 187
Morningside – 357
Mothers of Salem – 884
Newtown – 896
Not far from the Kingdom – 776
Nothing between – 183
Not yet decided – 782, 784
Oh, be saved! – 718
One there is who loves thee – 660
Overstrand – 382
Petherton – 600
Praise Him! Praise Him! – 849
Precious Blood of Jesus (Burke) – 804
Redemption – 713
Repose – 938
Resolution – 395
Seeking for me – 815
Sound His praise – 860, 862
Stockton – 644
Tetelestai – 694
The Giver of Rest – 688
The Gospel of Thy grace – 641
The Light of the World – 652
The love that gave Jesus to die – 857
The ninety and nine – 636
There is a love – 861
There is a life for a look – 659, 661
There is pardon for you – 739
To all eternity the same – 611
Trumpet call – 640
Unity – 281
Veni Domine – 300
Weeping will not save thee – 714
We sing of a Saviour's love – 882
What shall the harvest be? – 520
When the harvest is past – 772
Who is He? – 613
Whosoever will – 628
Why do you wait? – 768
Wonderful love – 778
Yarmouth – 401
Ye must be born again – 616
Zenana – 495

INDEX OF HYMNS
(First lines)

A blessing for you—will you take it?	717
A broken and a contrite heart	258
A child of Adam's sinful race	470
A cry, as of pain, again and again	495
A debtor to mercy alone	315
A fulness resides in Jesus, our Head	461
"A little while" of mingled joy	509
"A little while" our Lord shall	177
A mind at "perfect peace"	341
A perfect path of purest grace	161
A Rock that stands for ever	321
A ruler once came to Jesus by night	616
†A widowed mother lost her son	892
"Abba, Father!" now we call Thee	87
"Abba, Father!" we approach	86
Abide with me—fast falls the even-	287
According to Thy gracious word	122
Afar off from God, in the broad	655
Alas! and did my Saviour bleed?	2
All, all beyond is bright	434
All blessing, honour, glory, power	541
All hail the power of Jesu's name!	206
All praise and thanks, Lord Jesus	546
All scenes alike engaging prove	526
All that we were—our sins, our guilt	5
All the path the saints are treading	162
"All things are ready," come; oh	678
"All things are ready," come; the	679
All times are times for praising	590
Almost persuaded now to believe	784
Am I a soldier of the cross	396
Amen! one lasting, long Amen!	522
Amidst us our Belovèd stands	114
And will the Judge descend?	770
Another year is dawning!	574
Are you weary and sad	659
Are your souls the Saviour seeking?	681
Arise! ye warriors of the cross	486
†Around the throne of God in heaven	896
Around this grave, Lord Jesus	553
Around Thy table, holy Lord	105
Art thou weary? Art thou languid?	658
As, gathered to Thy precious name	103
As sinners saved, we love to sing	850
As sinners saved we praise and sing	220
Author of our salvation	18
Awake, and sing the song	226
Awake, awake, O sleeper!	673
Awake, my soul, and with the sun	567
Awake, my soul, awake and raise	823
Awake, my soul, in joyful lays	218
Be present at our table, Lord	586
Bear forth the banner!	490
Before the throne of God above	332
Before Thy mercy-seat, O Lord	475
Behold! a spotless Victim dies	4
Behold a Stranger at the door	734
Behold, behold the Lamb of God	651
Behold, how good and pleasant	294
Behold, my soul, the Saviour	93
Behold the amazing sight	3
Behold the empty tomb	728
Behold the Lamb for sinners slain!	707
Behold the Lamb of God	704
Behold the Lamb! 'tis He who bore	705
Behold the Lamb with glory crowned	151
Behold the manner of God's love	706
Behold the sin-atoning Lamb	759
Behold the throne of grace!	444
Behold Thy servants keeping	558
Behold, what love, what boundless	424
†Between two thieves the Saviour	891
Bless thou the Lord, my soul, and	578
Blessèd be God, our God	1
Blessèd feast! Most gracious token	121
Bounteous Source of every good	580
Brethren, let us join to bless	57
Bride of the Lamb, there is for thee	211
"Buried" in the grave of Jesus	557
By Christ redeemed, in Christ	111
By faith in a glorified Christ	863
By Thee, O Christ, redeemed	589
By Thee, O God, invited	16
By threefold title I am Thine	254
Call the weary home	657
Call them in—the poor, the	758

Can heavenly friendships pass away	591
Cease, O thou wandering soul	719
Children of the heavenly king	410
Christ a full salvation bringeth	649
Christ ever lives!	300
Christ has done the mighty work	623
Christ is coming! Let creation	200
Christ is coming, quickly coming	753
Christ's grave is vacant now	298
Come, all who love the Lord	425
Come, anxious one, and lowly kneel	720
Come, every soul by sin opprest	666
"Come," is the Lord's invitation	699
Come, let us all unite to sing	732
Come, let us join our cheerful songs	229
Come, let us of our blessèd hope	178
"Come, let us reason," saith the	663
Come, let us sing the matchless	231
Come, let us sing the song of songs	69
Come, saints, your grateful voices	223
†Come, sing once again the sweet	882
Come, Thou Fount of every blessing	217
Come, thou weary! Jesus calls thee	674
Come to the Saviour now!	682
"Come unto Me!" An echo, soft	738
"Come unto Me!" In tend'rest tone	755
"Come unto Me, ye weary"	670
Come, weary, anxious, laden soul	671
Come, ye sinners, poor and wretched	669
Come, ye that know the Saviour's	227
Compared with Christ, in all beside	264
Crowns of glory ever bright	827
Done is the work that saves	10
Ere Thy word our hearts engage	480
Eternal praise, our God, shall	244
Eternal Word, Eternal Son!	74
Ever, Lord, our souls to Thee	462
Faint not, Christian, though	403
Fairer than all of earth-born	547
Father, how great is Thy delight	208
Father, I know that all my life	362
Father, I praise Thy name	145
Father, let Thy heavenly grace	563
Father of mercies! in Thy word	482
Father, Thy children all are blest	360
Father, Thy name our souls would	144
Father, to seek Thy face	450
Father, we commend our spirits	210
Father, we, Thy children, bless	402

Father, whate'er of earthly bliss	368
Fill Thou my life, O Lord my God	269
"For ever with the Lord!"	432
For the bread and for the wine	124
For Zion's sake I will not rest	504
Forgiveness! 'twas a joyful sound	845
Forsaken once e'en of Thy God	45
Forth from the Father's loving	262
From all that dwell below the skies	532
From Egypt lately come	408
From every stormy wind that blows	442
From far we see the glorious day	193
From Greenland's icy mountains	492
Fully persuaded—Lord, I believe	787
Gathered, Lord, around Thy	108
Glory be to God the Father	536
Glory, glory, everlasting	15
Glory, honour, praise and power	542
Glory to God on high! Let	866
Glory to God on high! Peace	867
Glory to Thee, my God, this night	570
Glory unto Jesus be!	159
Go, labour on—spend, and be spent	497
God be with you till we meet again!	531
God in mercy sent His Son	603
"God is light"—the Cross proclaims	601
"God is love; by Him upholden	576
"God is love!" His word has said it	493
God loved the world of sinners lost	635
God moves in a mysterious way	310
God of all grace, Thou only wise!	358
God of our salvation, hear us	512
God sent His only Son to die	730
God speaks from heaven—in *love*	697
God tells me how I may be saved	729
God's almighty arms are round me	373
God's grace has found the wondrous	605
God's love is *everlasting* love	611
Grace is the sweetest sound	810
Grace, our highest thought transcend-	642
Grace! 'tis a charming sound	331
Gracious Lord, my heart is fixèd	234
Gracious Shepherd! loving Saviour!	467
Grant, Lord, the faith that overcomes	375
Great Captain of salvation	588
Great God of wonders! all Thy ways	786
Great the joy when Christians meet!	293
Guide us, O Thou great Jehovah!	405
Hail to the Lord's Anointed	204
Happy they who trust in	314

Hard after Thee I follow	392
Hark! Hark! Hark!	750
Hark! Hark! the voice of Christ	747
Hark, how the gospel trumpet	625
Hark! my soul; it is the Lord	352
Hark, sinner, while God from on	773
Hark! ten thousand voices crying	152
Hark! the voice of Jesus calling	752
Hark! the voice of Jesus crying	488
Hark! the voice of love and mercy	622
Hark! 'tis the watchman's cry	485
Hast Thou not finished all, O God	724
Hasten, O sinner, to be wise	783
Have I an object, Lord, below	257
Have ye counted the cost	395
Have you any room for Jesus	766
Have you been to Jesus for His	698
Have you on the Lord believed?	858
He dies! He dies! the lowly Man	209
He leadeth me, O blessèd thought!	414
He lives, the great Redeemer lives!	456
He sitteth o'er the waterfloods	374
He who once was dead, now liveth!	727
Head of the Church triumphant!	172
Head of the new Creation	205
Hear God's blessèd invitation	754
Hear now the gospel sound	683
Hear, O sinner! mercy hails you	740
Heavenly Father! by Thy Spirit	391
Heavenly Father! in Thy wisdom	142
Heavenly Father! joy and gladness	143
Heirs of salvation, chosen of God!	407
Henceforward, till the Lord shall	517
Here, Lord, we come Thyself to meet	116
Here, Lord, we own the truth	555
Here, O my Lord, I see Thee face to	132
Himself He could not save!	664
His be the Victor's name	297
Hither come, behold, and wonder!	708
Ho! ye that thirst, approach the	684
Ho! ye thirsty, Jesus calls you	685
Holy Father, through Thy grace	465
Holy Father, we address Thee	88
Holy Father, we would praise Thee	89
"Holy, Holy, Holy Lord!"	35
Holy Lamb, who Thee receive	384
Holy Saviour! we adore Thee	155
Hope of our hearts—O Lord, appear	191
How blessed is the tie that binds	530
How condescending and how kind	606
How firm a foundation, ye saints of	326
How gentle God's commands	313

How good is the God we adore	538
How great, our Father, was Thy love	146
How long, O Lord, our Saviour	185
How many sheep are straying	494
How pleasant is the sound of praise!	37
How precious were those parting	343
How solemn are the words	617
How sweet and sacred is the place	118
How sweet is the story of God's	860
How sweet the cheering words	722
How sweet the gospel trumpet	624
How sweet the name of Jesus, In	25
How sweet the name of Jesus sounds	24
How vast, how full, how free	604
How wondrous a Saviour is God's	668
I am a stranger here	420
"I am the Way," the Saviour said	831
I am waiting for the dawning	192
I bless the Christ of God	818
I cannot tell what may befall	552
I fain would give Thee deepest	154
I have a home above	280
I have a song I love to sing	846
I hear the Saviour say	820
I hear the words of love	790
I heard the voice of Jesus say	797
I lay my sins on Jesus	796
I left it all with Jesus long ago	382
I looked to Jesus in my sin	828
I love to tell the story	662
I once was a stranger to grace and	330
I once was bound by Satan's chains	812
I praise Thy name, O Jesus, Lord	307
I rest in Christ, the Son of God	284
I saw the cross of Jesus	829
I've a message from the Lord	746
I've found a Friend, oh such a Friend!	372
I was a wandering sheep	822
I will sing of my Redeemer	847
If human kindness meets return	104
†If I come to Jesus	883
If I could find the *oldest* heart	644
If the way seem but to darken	366
In God I have found a retreat	328
†In heathen lands they bow	879
In heavenly love abiding	316
In holy contemplation	305
In holy ties together bound	566
In love we part, as brethren	518
In nought of goodness dare I trust	799
In songs of praise, our God, to Thee	91

In Thee, O Lord, believing	335
In Thine own presence, Lord	62
In Thy name, O Lord, assembling	29
"It is finished!" sinners hear it	725
"It is finished!" what a gospel!	696
It is the blood, Christ's precious	620
It passeth knowledge, that dear love	239
Jehovah is our strength	246
Jerusalem the golden	439
Jesus, and shall it ever be	261
Jesus, before Thy face we fall	454
Jesus Christ is passing by	712
Jesus! how much Thy name unfolds	27
Jesus! I rest in Thee	20
Jesus! immutably the same	291
Jesus, in His heavenly temple	77
Jesus! in Thee our eyes behold	78
Jesus! in Thy blest name	447
Jesus! in whom all glories meet	76
†Jesus is our Shepherd, for the	888
Jesus is tenderly calling thee home	751
"Jesus" is the name we treasure	837
Jesus is waiting, O sinner, for you!	716
Jesus, Lord, I trust Thee—name of	838
Jesus, Lord, Thy love to me	854
Jesus, Lord, we know Thee present	110
Jesus! Lover of my soul	795
Jesus, my Lord, 'tis sweet to rest	353
Jesus, my Saviour, to Bethlehem	851
Jesus never answered, "Nay"	700
Jesus! O name of power divine	323
Jesus! of Thee we ne'er would tire	390
Jesus our Lord, with what joy Thou	859
Jesus our Lord, with what joy we	842
Jesus, our Saviour and our Lord!	472
Jesus, our Saviour Thou, and Lord	473
Jesus shall reign where'er the sun	203
Jesus, spotless Lamb of God!	164
Jesus, the Father's only Son	267
Jesus, the Lord, our righteousness!	232
Jesus the Lord, when here below	711
Jesus! the sinner's Friend	798
Jesus! the very thought of Thee	21
Jesus, Thou joy of loving hearts!	138
Jesus, Thou source of true delight	474
Jesus, Thou true and living Vine	131
Jesus, Thy boundless love to me	351
Jesus, Thy dying love I own	51
Jesus! Thy name we love	344
Jesus! we remember Thee	100
Jesus! where'er Thy people meet	443
†Jesus, who lived above the sky	881
Jesus, whose blood was shed on earth	453
Join all the glorious names	19
Joy! Joy! Joy! there is joy in	637
Just as I am—without one plea	793
Just as Thou art—how wondrous	71
Just as thou art, without one trace	677
Just on the threshold! Oh, why not	774
"Kept by the power of God"	380
Lamb of God! our souls adore Thee	48
Lamb of God! Thou now art	49
Lead us, Saviour, by Thy power	242
Let all who know the joyful sound	631
Let earth and heaven agree	634
Let earthly themes now cease	6
Let the waves of blessing roll	874
Let us love, and sing, and wonder!	213
Let us rejoice in Christ the Lord	318
Let us sing of the love of the Lord	857
Let us, with a gladsome mind	575
Light of the World! shine on our	478
Like as the days of Noah were	650
Like sheep we went astray	821
†Little thought Samaria's daughter	890
Lo! He comes, with clouds descending	201
Look to Jesus, weary one	701
"Look to me, and be ye saved!"	826
Look to the Saviour on Calvary's tree	702
"Look unto Me, and be ye saved!"	703
"Look unto Me!"—the Saviour	672
Look, ye saints, the sight is glorious—	202
Lord, accept our feeble song	168
Lord and Saviour, we remember	96
Lord, dismiss us . . . Bid us all	506
Lord, dismiss us . . . Fill our hearts	505
Lord, e'en to death Thy love could go	50
Lord God, Thou didst in Eden	564
Lord, I desire to live as one	270
Lord, in Thy form and comeliness	156
Lord, in Thy holy presence	577
Lord Jesus, are we one with Thee?	70
Lord Jesus! at whose glorious feet	471
Lord Jesus Christ, in wondrous grace	250
Lord Jesus Christ, our Saviour Thou	68
Lord Jesus Christ, we seek Thy face	34
Lord Jesus, come, crowned with	176
Lord Jesus, Friend unfailing!	276
Lord Jesus, I love Thee, I know	228
Lord Jesus, in Thy name alone	28
Lord Jesus, in Thy name we	125

Lord Jesus, make Thyself to me	549	My song shall be of Jesus	844
Lord Jesus, meeting in Thy name	554	"My times are in Thy hand"	312
Lord Jesus, on Thy promise	479	My tongue shall spread the Saviour's	136
Lord Jesus, save!	873	My Well-beloved is holy	207
Lord Jesus, Thou who only art	282		
Lord Jesus, to tell of Thy love	848	New every morning is the love	568
Lord Jesus, we are waiting	386	No blood, no altar now	139
Lord Jesus, we would come apart	339	No bone of Thee was broken	115
Lord Jesus, when I think of Thee	376	"No condemnation!" O my soul	301
Lord, now we part in Thy blest	508	No future but glory, Lord Jesus	241
Lord of life and King of glory	233	No gospel like this feast	119
Lord of the harvest! God of love!	870	No lips like Thine, most blessèd Lord	273
Lord of the worlds above!	39	No more we seek a resting-place	595
Lord, speak to me, that I may speak	292	†No room in the inn for the	889
Lord, Thy ransomed Church is waking	501	No shadows yonder! all light and	435
Lord, we accept with grateful hearts	585	No terrors of the law we hear	614
Lord, we are Thine! our God Thou art	248	No theme on earth I love so well	808
Lord, we see the day approaching	194	None teacheth, Lord, like Thee	476
Lord, when we bend before Thy throne	464	Not all the blood of beasts	800
Lord, wherever two or three	446	Not far, not far from the Kingdom	776
Lost one! wandering on in sadness	761	Not to condemn the sons of men	618
Love's redeeming work is done	222	Not to ourselves we owe	11
Low in the grave He lay	726	Not what I am, O Lord, but what	275
		Not what these hands have done	788
"Man of sorrows!"	99	Not yet decided, not yet forgiven	782
Man's day is fast receding	190	Nothing between, Lord, nothing	183
Many sons to glory bringing	243	Nothing, either great or small	694
Master, we would no longer be	260	Now, in a song of grateful praise	219
May the grace of Christ our Saviour	511	Now may the gospel's conquering	871
May the love of God the Father	510	Now may the Spirit from above	36
May the power that brings salvation	877	Now the silent grave is keeping	596
May the shining of God's word	483		
'Mid the splendours of the glory	195	O blessèd God! how kind	334
'Midst the darkness, storm, and sorrow	184	O blessèd Jesus! who but Thou	238
Mourner, wheresoe'er thou art	760	O blessèd Lord, we praise Thee now	64
Much in sorrow, oft in woe	394	O blessèd Lord, what hast Thou done	63
My blessèd Saviour, Thou hast	389	O blessèd Saviour, is Thy love	170
My days are gliding swiftly by	418	O blessèd Saviour, Son of God	148
My Father, when I hear Thy voice	306	O Christ, our living Head, in Thee	278
My God and Father, I am Thine	249	O Christ, Thou heavenly lamb	383
My God, I am Thine	357	O Christ, Thou Son of God	573
My God, my Father, while I stray	363	O Christ, we praise Thee for Thy	539
My God, the spring of all my joys	355	O Christ, what burdens bowed Thy	17
My heart is fixed, O God	274	O come, Thou stricken Lamb of God	54
My heart, O Lord, rejoices	348	Oh, come to the Saviour, believe in	739
My hope is built on nothing less	811	Oh, do not let the word depart	779
My Saviour, I would own Thee	263	Oh, eyes that are weary, and hearts	347
My Saviour, Thou Thy love to me	350	O Father, all-creating	561
My Shepherd is the Lamb	337	Oh for a thousand tongues to sing	824
My Shepherd! Thou art, in the	338	Oh for the robes of whiteness	236
My Shepherd, who for sin atoned	336	Oh for the Spirit's breath	872
My Shepherd will supply my need	340	O friends and fellow-sinners, come	656

O God of glorious majesty	398
O God of matchless grace	141
O God, our help in ages past	451
O God, Thou now hast glorified	84
O God! we see Thee in the Lamb	359
O God, what cords of love are Thine	354
O God, who didst an equal mate	559
O God, whose wondrous name is Love	324
O gracious Shepherd, bind us	166
Oh, happy day that fixed my choice	836
Oh, happy day, when first we felt	835
O happy home! O happy home!	429
Oh, have you not heard of that	778
O Head, so full of bruises	94
O holy Saviour, Friend unseen!	289
Oh, how blessèd to be bidden	130
O Jesus Christ, most holy	519
O Jesus Christ, our Saviour	311
O Jesus, everlasting God!	53
O Jesus, gracious Saviour	288
O Jesus, Lord, 'tis joy to know	153
O Jesus, Lord, 'tis Thee alone	283
O Jesus, Lord, whose hands and feet	259
Oh, joy of the justified, joy of the free	833
Oh, joyful day, oh, glorious hour	59
O Lamb of God, still keep us	165
O Lord, amidst the gloom of night	303
O Lord, as we more fully learn	550
O Lord, by Thee invited	109
O Lord, how infinite Thy love!	126
O Lord! I would delight in Thee	277
O Lord, in nothing would I boast	830
O Lord of heaven, and earth, and sea	499
O Lord, Thy bounteous hand hath	583
O Lord, Thy love's unbounded	286
O Lord, 'tis joy to look above	158
O Lord, we adore Thee	150
O Lord, we know it matters nought	31
O Lord, we would abound in praise	463
O Lord, we would the path retrace	157
O Lord, what hast Thou wrought!	295
O Lord, when Thou didst man create	560
O Lord, while we confess the worth	556
O Lord, who now art seated	167
O Love divine, how sweet Thou art!	290
O Love divine, what hast Thou done	43
O Love, thou fathomless abyss	349
O my Saviour, crucified!	7
O patient, spotless One!	378
Oh, precious blood, oh, glorious death	807
O precious Saviour, deep Thy pain	173
Oh, precious words that Jesus said	627

O saving name! O name of power!	26
O Saviour, I have nought to plead	346
O Saviour! we adore Thee	174
O Saviour! we are Thine	252
O sinners, come to Jesus!	737
O spotless Lamb of God, in Thee	814
Oh, teach me what it meaneth—	645
Oh, teach us more of Thy blest ways	163
Oh, tell through the breadth of	632
Oh that the Lord's salvation	502
Oh, the love of Christ is boundless	710
Oh, they've reached the sunny shore	594
O Thou tender, gracious Shepherd	127
O *weary* soul, now seeking peace	715
Oh, what a glorious truth is this—	626
Oh, what a lonely path were ours	388
Oh, what a Saviour is Jesus the Lord!	630
Oh, what a Saviour—that He died	852
†Oh, what a welcome little children	886
Oh, what shall we feel in Thy presence	175
Oh, why not, say why not, God's	748
Oh, wonder surpassing! that Christ	639
Oh, wondrous hour, when, Jesus, Thou	52
Of all the gifts Thy love bestows	819
Oft we, alas! forget the love	92
On earth the song begins	56
On His Father's throne is seated	643
On that same night, Lord Jesus	129
On what has now been sown	876
One spirit with the Lord	279
One sweetly solemn thought	431
One there is above all others—oh	855
One there is, above all others, well	856
One there is who loves thee	660
One thing, my Father, only one	367
Once again the gospel message	757
Once more before we part	515
Once more, our God, with hallowed	30
Once Thy servants toiled in rowing	529
Only a step to Jesus!	775
Only one heart to give	251
Onward! upward! homeward!	426
Our Father, bless the bounteous	582
Our Father, "it is well"	365
Our Father, let our concord be	548
"Our Father!" oh, what gracious	361
Our Father sits on yonder throne	364
Our Father, Thou art Light and Love	296
Our Father! we adore and praise	481
Our Father, we would worship	83
Our God and Father, dost Thou try	369
Our God and Father, now behold	581

Our God, for children dear we plead	466
Our God, soon as Thy Son had died	32
Our God, Thou gavest Thine own Son	329
Our God, whose justice did awake	61
Our life is now no more a dream	415
Our rest is in heaven, our rest is not	406
Our souls are in God's mighty hand	441
Ours are peace and joy divine	281
Passing onward, quickly passing	769
Peace: blessèd peace! yes	864
Peace, peace is mine! 'tis peace of	865
Peace! perfect peace!—in this	342
Peace was *procured* by Christ	690
Peace! what a precious sound!	680
Peace with God—how great a treasure	691
†"Pleasures for evermore!"	893
Poor, weak, and worthless though I am	816
Poor, weary wanderer, wilt thou come	667
Praise be to Jesus, His mercy is free	743
Praise God, from whom all blessings	533
Praise Him! Praise Him! Jesus, our	849
Praise the Lord, who died to save us	14
Praise the Saviour, ye who know Him	216
Praise to the Word made flesh	540
Praise thy Saviour, O my soul!	97
Praise ye Jehovah! Praise the Lord	82
"Praise ye the Lord!" again, again	212
Precious, precious blood of Jesus	804
Press forward and fear not, though	400
Redeemed by blood of God's	736
Redemption! oh, wonderful	735
Refuse Him not, O man!	771
Rejoice and be glad! the Redeemer	687
Rejoice, rejoice, believers!	438
Rejoice, ye saints, rejoice and praise	381
Repeat the story o'er and o'er	851
Rest of the saints above	433
Revive Thy work, O Lord! Thy mighty	869
Revive Thy work, O Lord! Thy work	500
Revive us, Lord Jesus, give times	868
Rich and plenteous is the harvest	498
Rise, my soul, behold 'tis Jesus!	22
Rise, my soul, thy God directs thee	411
Rise, my soul, with joy and gladness	333
Rise up and hasten, my soul, haste	430
Rock of Ages, cleft for me!	794
Safe enrolled, the promise ever	302
Safe in the arms of Jesus	817
Salvation! oh, salvation!	654

Salvation! oh, the joyful sound!	731
Salvation to our God!	215
Salvation—what a precious word!	629
Saved through the blood of Jesus	805
Saviour, follow with Thy blessing	875
Saviour, loving Saviour	792
Saviour, Thou art waiting, waiting	179
Saviour, through the desert lead us!	421
Saviour, we worship Thee	101
Saviour, whene'er I think of Thee	268
Saviour, who Thy flock art feeding	469
See! Israel's gentle Shepherd stands	468
See mercy, mercy from on high	608
See the blessèd Saviour dying	709
See the Saviour! sinners slew Him	723
Shall the prey not be snatched from	713
She only touched the hem of His	689
Show me Thy wounds, exalted Lord!	55
Since now we live because Christ died	551
Since Thou, Lord Jesus, didst appear	562
"Sing aloud to God our strength"	304
Sing softly, for Jesus is passing this	745
Sing them over again to me	721
Sinner, is thy heart now troubled?	718
Sleep on, belovèd, sleep	598
So near to the kingdom; yet what	777
Soft the voice of mercy soundeth	809
Soldiers of Christ! arise	397
Son of God! exalted now	149
Son of God! with joy we praise	65
Soon and "for ever"—such promise	600
Soon shall our Master come	180
Soon, soon, our Lord, the living One	597
Soon will the Master come—soon	181
Sovereign grace o'er sin abounding	285
Sow in the morn thy seed	496
Sowing the seed by the dawn-light	520
Speed Thy servants, Saviour, speed	527
Spread the news! spread the news!	638
Stand up! stand up for Jesus!	487
Still on the homeward journey	572
Stricken, smitten and afflicted	621
Sun of my soul, Thou Saviour dear	571
Sweet are the seasons when we wait	460
Sweet feast of love divine!	117
Sweet is the work, O Lord Most High	579
Sweet is the work, our God and King	224
Sweet the moments, rich in blessing	41
Sweet the theme of Jesu's love!	221
Sweet was the hour, O Lord, to Thee	840
Sweeter, O Lord, than rest to Thee	841
Tell me the old, old story	602

Tell out, tell out glad tidings	646
The atoning work is done	9
"The battle is the Lord's!"	393
†The Bible tells us Jesus *came*	880
The blast of the trumpet, so loud	640
The blood of Christ has precious been	98
The blood of Christ, Thy spotless	802
The contrite heart is incense sweet	38
The countless multitude on high	23
The cross! the cross! the Christian's	401
The cross! the cross! the wondrous	806
The day of glory bearing	199
The Father gave His only Son	13
The gloomy night will soon be past	186
The glory shines before me!	437
The God of Abraham praise	247
The gospel of Thy grace my stubborn	641
The happy morn is come	58
The Head that once was crowned	169
The Lamb of God to slaughter led	46
The Lamb was slain! let us adore	44
The Lord Himself shall come	599
The Lord is risen; the Red Sea's	135
The Lord of glory! who is He?	75
The love of God is righteous love	610
"The Master is come, and calleth"	741
The night is far spent, the day is at	187
The night is wearing fast away	188
The night shall soon be over	189
The people of the Lord can say	593
The perfect righteousness of God	609
The Prince of Life, once slain for us	299
†The rain had poured unceasingly	897
The sands of time are sinking	137
The Saviour bears a lovely name	839
The Saviour comes! no outward	612
†The Saviour Jesus has gone to pre-	894
The Saviour lives, no more to die	843
The Saviour's blood on Calvary shed	813
The servants of the Lord go forth	525
The Son of God is come to save	925
The veil is rent—lo! Jesus stands	33
The wanderer no more will roam	134
The whole world was lost in the	652
There are moments quickly passing	484
There is a better world we know	647
†There is a blessèd land above	895
There is a fold where none can stray	245
There is a fountain filled with blood	791
There is a *love* our souls have only	861
There is a name I love to hear	345
There is a name—one only name	448
There is an eye that never sleeps	458
There is life in a look at the Crucified	661
†There's a Friend for little children	885
There's a refuge in God for the sin-	765
There's a Stranger at the door	733
There's a voice that is calling to thee	676
There's not a grief, however light	319
There's One who has loved thee	665
There were ninety and nine	636
"They wandered in the desert"	423
Thine ever—loved and chosen	253
Thine, Jesus, Thine!	255
This is not our place of resting	196
This is the feast of heavenly wine	120
This marriage union now complete	565
This world is a wilderness wide	399
Thou art gone up before us, Lord	385
Thou art Love, our God and Father	266
Thou art the everlasting Word	72
Thou God of power, and God of love!	449
Thou great Redeemer, precious Lamb	237
Thou hast stood here, Lord Jesus	587
Thou hidden love of God, whose	265
Thou life of my life, blessèd Saviour	73
Thou, O God, Thy love commendest	832
Thou Son of God! the woman's Seed	452
Though faint, yet pursuing, we go	317
Though troubles assail, and dangers	325
Thousands and thousands stand	214
Through Jesus one, we do not part	513
Through the dark path of sorrow	419
Through the day Thy love has kept	569
Through the love of God our Saviour	327
Through the name of Jesus mercy	744
Through Thy precious body broken	140
Through waves, through clouds and	309
Thy children, God of Love, unite	379
Thy gracious presence, O our God	422
Thy heart, O Lord, with love o'er-	377
Thy love to me, my Lord, I own	853
Thy love we own, Lord Jesus!	79
Thy name we bless, Lord Jesus!	66
Thy name we love, Lord Jesus!	67
Thy servants, Lord, are dear to Thee	524
Thy way, not mine, O Lord	371
Thy work, not mine, O Christ	789
"Till He come!" Oh, let the words	123
'Tis finished all: our souls to win	235
" 'Tis finished," cried the dying	693
'Tis heaven where Jesus is	225
'Tis "he that hath the Son hath life"	648
'Tis Jesu's precious blood alone	801
'Tis past, the dark and dreary night	133
'Tis softly breathed by heaven's air	780

'Tis sweet to think of those at rest	592	Well known, O Lord, this land to Thee	413
To Calvary, Lord, in spirit now	47	What a Friend we have in Jesus	459
To Christ the Lord let every tongue	8	What can the sinner do?	615
To-day God's mercy calls thee	764	What can wash away my stain?	803
To-day the Saviour calls	742	What grace, O Lord, and beauty shone	160
To dying sons of men	686	What raised the wondrous thought	198
To Father, Son, and Holy Ghost	534	What was it, O our God	12
To God be the glory! great things	862	What will it be to dwell above	197
To God, my thirsty soul	356	†When He cometh, when He cometh	898
To Him who is able to keep us	535	†When, His salvation bringing	887
To Him who saved us from the world	545	When I survey the wondrous cross	40
To Thee, O blessèd Saviour!	272	When Israel, by divine command	409
To those who love Thee, gracious Lord	477	†When mothers of Salem	884
To us our God His love commends	607	When the harvest is past and the	772
"Too late, too late!" how sad the	785	When this passing world is done	256
"Trust ye in the Lord for ever"	387	When two or three together meet	445
†'Twas God who gave the precious	878	When we reach our peaceful dwelling	436
'Twas Thy love, O God, that knew us	147	Where high the heavenly temple	455
		Where in this waste, unlovely world	370
Unto Him who loved us, gave us	544	Where will you be when earth is past	781
Unto the Lamb that once was	543	While golden moments swiftly glide	112
Unworthy our thanksgiving	80	While in sweet communion feeding	128
Uplift the gospel banner	491	While to several paths dividing	514
		Who are these that go with gladness	523
		Who is He in yonder stall	613
We are but strangers here	417	Whoever receiveth the Crucified One	749
We bless our God that we	507	"Whosoever heareth," shout	628
We bless our Saviour's name	113	Why did the paschal beast	297
We bless Thee, O our Father	90	Why do you wait, O lost one?	768
We come, our gracious Father	106	Why 'neath the load of your sins	688
We give eternal praise	81	Why those fears? Behold, 'tis Jesus	308
We go to meet Thee, Saviour	171	Wilt thou come, or wilt thou linger?	767
We go with the redeemed to taste	416	With Christ we died to sin	230
We have heard the joyful sound	692	With contrite spirits now we sing	102
We know there's a bright and a	675	With Jesus in our midst	107
We'll sing of the Shepherd that died	42	With joy we meditate the grace	457
We love to sing with one accord	60	With the sweet word of peace	528
We part to meet again	521	Within the Father's bosom	240
We praise Thee, blessèd God	85	Without a cloud between	182
We're a pilgrim band in a stranger	440	Without blood is no remission	619
We're not of the world that fadeth	404	Work, for the night is coming	489
We're pilgrims in the wilderness	412	Worthy, worthy, worthy, Thou	271
We sing of the realms of the blest	427	Would you taste of joy and gladness	695
We sing, our God and Father	537		
We sing the praise of Him who died	834	Yes, dear soul, a voice from heaven	653
We tell abroad a Saviour's love	633	Yes, for me my Saviour careth	322
We thank Thee, Lord, for this our	584	Yes, we part, but not for ever	516
We've no abiding city here	428	Yet one more call, belovèd one	756
We would remember, Lord, Thy cross	95	Yet there is room! Love, love	762
We would the debt of love repay	503	"Yet there is room!" The Lamb's	763
Weeping will not save thee	714	Your harps, ye trembling saints	320

†Hymns marked thus are for children